NORMALITY AND THE LIFE CYCLE

NORMALITY AND THE LIFE CYCLE

A Critical Integration

EDITED BY

DANIEL OFFER AND MELVIN SABSHIN

Basic Books, Inc., Publishers   New York

Library of Congress Cataloging in Publication Data

Main entry under title:

Normality and the life cycle.

   Includes references and index.
   1. Developmental psychology.   2.   Mental health.
I.   Offer, Daniel.   II.   Sabshin, Melvin.   [DNLM:
1.   Mental health.   2.   Life change events.   3.   Social
adjustment.   4.   Adaptation, psychological.   5.   Behavior.
6.   Human development.   WM 105 N842]
BF713.N67   1984   155   83–45376
ISBN 0–465–05148–0

CONTENTS

CONTRIBUTORS   vii

PREFACE   ix

ACKNOWLEDGMENTS   xv

PART I

THE LIFE CYCLE

1. Infancy: Perspectives on Normality   3
    Robert N. Emde and James F. Sorce

2. Middle Childhood: Normality as
    Integration and Interaction   30
    Bennett L. Leventhal and Kenneth Dawson

3. Adolescence: Empirical Perspectives   76
    Daniel Offer and Melvin Sabshin

4. Young Adulthood: Stages of Maturity   108
    Robert L. Arnstein

5. Middle Adulthood: Settling into the
    World—Person, Time, and Context   145
    Bertram J. Cohler and Andrew M. Boxer

6. Late Adulthood: Love, Work, and
    the Normal Transitions   204
    Nancy Datan and Jeanne Thomas

7. Aging: Biopsychosocial Perspectives   230
    Nancy A. Newton, Lawrence W. Lazarus, and Jack Weinberg

PART II

THEORETICAL AND METHODOLOGICAL PERSPECTIVES

8. Psychoanalytic Perspectives on Normality   289
    Robert Michels

9. Developmental Fusion of Intuition and Reason:
    A Metabiological Ontogeny   302
    Arnold J. Mandell and Jonas Salk

10. An Epidemiologic View of Mental Illness,
    Mental Health, and Normality   315
    Gerald L. Klerman and Myrna M. Weissman

11. Normality from a Health Systems Perspective   345
    Boris M. Astrachan and Gary L. Tischler

PART III

TOWARD AN INTEGRATIVE APPROACH TO
NORMALITY AND THE LIFE CYCLE

12. Culture, Values, and Normality   364
    Daniel Offer and Melvin Sabshin

13. Patterns of Normal Development   393
    Daniel Offer and Melvin Sabshin

14. Implications and New Directions   426
    Daniel Offer and Melvin Sabshin

NAME INDEX   441

SUBJECT INDEX   451

CONTRIBUTORS

ROBERT L. ARNSTEIN, M.D. Chief Psychiatrist, Yale University Health Services; Clinical Professor of Psychiatry, Yale University School of Medicine.

BORIS M. ASTRACHAN, M.D. Professor of Psychiatry, Yale University; Director, Connecticut Mental Hospital Center.

ANDREW M. BOXER, M.A. Laboratory for the Study of Adolescence, Department of Psychiatry, Michael Reese Hospital and Medical Center; Committee on Human Development, University of Chicago.

BERTRAM J. COHLER, Ph.D. William Rainey Harper Professor of Social Science in the College; Professor, Departments of Behavioral Science (Human Development), Education, and Psychiatry, University of Chicago.

NANCY DATAN, Ph.D. Professor of Psychology, West Virginia University.

KENNETH DAWSON, M.D. Senior Child Fellow, Department of Psychiatry, University of Chicago.

ROBERT N. EMDE, M.D. Professor of Psychiatry, University of Colorado School of Medicine.

GERALD L. KLERMAN, M.D. George Harrington Professor of Psychiatry, Harvard Medical School; Director of Research, Psychiatry Service, Massachusetts General Hospital.

LAWRENCE W. LAZARUS, M.D. Director, Geropsychiatric Program, Illinois State Psychiatric Institute; Assistant Professor, Department of Psychiatry, Rush Medical College.

BENNETT L. LEVENTHAL, M.D. Assistant Professor, Departments of Psychiatry and Pediatrics; Director, Child Psychiatry, University of Chicago.

ARNOLD J. MANDELL, M.D. Professor of Psychiatry, University of California at San Diego.

ROBERT MICHELS, M.D. Chairman and Professor, Department of Psychiatry, Cornell University Medical College; Psychiatrist-in-Chief, New York Hospital.

NANCY A. NEWTON, Ph.D. Psychologist, Older Adult Program, Institute of Psychiatry, Northwestern Memorial Hospital; Former Research and Training Consultant, Geropsychiatric Program, Illinois State Psychiatric Institute.

DANIEL OFFER, M.D. Chairman, Department of Psychiatry, Michael Reese Hospital and Medical Center; Professor of Psychiatry, University of Chicago.

MELVIN SABSHIN, M.D. Medical Director, American Psychiatric Association.

JONAS SALK, M.D. Founding Director and Resident Fellow, Salk Institute for Biological Studies.

JAMES F. SORCE, Ph.D. Bell Laboratories.

JEANNE THOMAS, Ph.D. Behavioral Science Division, University of Wisconsin, Parkside.

GARY L. TISCHLER, M.D. Professor of Psychiatry, Yale University School of Medicine; Director, Yale Psychiatric Institute.

JACK WEINBERG, M.D. Former Director, Illinois Mental Health Institutes; Former Professor of Psychiatry, Rush Medical College and Abraham Lincoln School of Medicine, University of Illinois.

MYRNA M. WEISSMAN, Ph.D. Professor of Psychiatry and Epidemiology, Yale University School of Medicine; Director of Depression Research Unit, Connecticut Mental Health Center.

PREFACE

Normality and/or mental health* have been controversial subjects since the beginning of psychiatry and psychology. The interpretation of how these forms should be defined, however, has much greater implications for mental health policies today than at any other time in history. We have been deeply involved with this problem for many years and, in fact, anticipated many of the current developments. This book was begun at the time of the publication of the Presidential Commission Report on Mental Health (1978). To us, the Presidential Report confirmed the necessity of clarifying what is meant by normality throughout the life cycle. As we complete this volume in 1983, current policy debates reinforce our beliefs that much work needs to be done in conceptualization and investigation of normal behavior.

In addition to updating our own ideas concerning normality and mental health, this volume will take into account the considerable amount of new empirical data, clinical observation, theoretical conceptualization, and general understanding of normal human behavior. Indeed, we believe that the question "What is normal behavior really like?" is so important that the field itself deserves an integrative name. Thus we have coined a term, *normatology,* to heighten awareness and interest in the subject (see chapter 14 for details). This book is a contribution toward this effort.

The purpose of this book is to document what we know about normality, or mental health, throughout the life cycle. In contrast to Jahoda's (1958) and, more recently, Coan's (1977) concepts of positive mental health, we believe that the behavioral and social sciences are not yet at the point of development wherein the known can be separated from the valued (see chapter 12). Smith (1969) has been an eloquent critic of the perspective of Jahoda and others. He brings to light the obstacle that every worker in the field of normality and mental health had difficulty in overcoming: namely, the intermingling of one's own values in the concepts one views as mentally healthy or normal. We also want to try to better comprehend why, under seemingly similar circumstances, one person copes successfully with his or her internal and external psychological

*The terms normality and mental health are used interchangeably throughout this book.

events and another person is unable to cope. Before we can answer this question, we need to know all we can about psychopathology and its psychodynamic, biological, and sociocultural roots. We also need to better understand the complexities of normal behavior and psychology.

Our book is divided into three parts. The first part, "The Life Cycle," is divided into seven chapters. Each chapter is written by one or more serious investigators who have spent most of their professional lives studying individuals who fit within the age constraints of the chapter. The stages of life covered by the first seven chapters are as follows: chapter 1, first year of life; chapter 2, ages 1 to 14; chapter 3, ages 14 to 18; chapter 4, ages 18 to 25; chapter 5, ages 25 to 45; chapter 6, ages 45 to 65; and chapter 7, age 65 and over.

The chapters present what is currently known about an individual's normal behavior, his or her psychosocial functioning, and his or her development. We have intentionally chosen investigators whose backgrounds differ considerably (e.g., sociologists, neuroscientists, biologists) in order to highlight overriding similarities and important differences in conceptualizing both about normality and about development.

The second part of the book gives theoretical and methodological perspectives on normal development and mental health from four different points of view: (1) psychoanalysis; (2) biological sciences; (3) epidemiology; and (4) the health system.

Scholars from these four areas present the underlying concepts that are useful in examining the life cycle from their vantage point. They also either critically examine the data presented in the first part of the book or present an original overview of normality from their own, specialized standpoint. Indeed, the importance of this section for the implications for mental health policies is explicitly discussed in chapter 11.

The third part represents the editors' attempt at integrating the previous approaches to normality. It is a theoretical discussion of the underlying principles that contributes to our understanding of mental health and normal development. It deals with issues, such as the potential conflict between empiricism and values, in interpreting data.

In the final chapter, "Implications and New Directions," we discuss the implications of the findings presented herein for future behavioral and social science research concerning normality and mental health. We also discuss the implications of the definition of mental health in the formulation of public policy in all the mental health fields.

We believe that this book represents the first attempt to link normality with the full range of the life cycle. How unique is this approach? We are, of course, aware of the fact that Freda Rebelsky and Lynn Dorman have edited a very fine series of nine volumes entitled *Life-Span Human Devel-*

*opment** that present a thorough survey of developmental psychology. As they say in the Foreword to the series, the books were written for students and instructors in life-span developmental psychology courses. Lidz's (1980) article in the third edition of the *Comprehensive Textbook of Psychiatry*, "The Life Cycle," is a theoretical article based on psychoanalytic concepts and assumptions. While Lidz uses many Eriksonian ideas to buttress his discussion, he presents almost no empirical data to support his ideas. On the whole, his is a psychopathological view of the life cycle. Wolman and associates (1982) have edited a volume entitled *Human Development* that also surveys, in detail, developmental psychology. In contrast, the editors of this volume are psychiatrists and psychoanalysts. Our bias has clearly manifested itself in our selection of contributors and chapter topics. It is of great interest (and unfortunately true) that there is not enough overlap between our volume and the series just described.

We sincerely hope that one result of the increased interest in *normatology* will be better and more effective cross-disciplinary communication. In a recent article, however, Elkind (1982) has urged clinicians (particularly in the field of child psychiatry) to abandon any pretext of being researchers. Rather he states that "developmental psychology [should] be seen as a science of child psychiatry" and furthermore, "rather than expect child psychiatrists to do research, practice, administer, and teach, it seems reasonable to relegate the research to those trained and committed to this line of endeavor." It seems to us that if we followed Elkind's advice, the all-too-wide gulf between developmental psychology and clinical psychiatry will widen to the point where there would be no communication at all between the disciplines. In our opinion the same individual has to integrate the disciplines. Only then will the two fields not be isolated and will the knowledge gained in one be useful to the other.

In the entire field of *normatology* there are two dramatically opposed positions: (1) hard-line methodologists who emphasize an almost atheoretical approach and whose measurements seem to miss the forest for the concentration on the trees; and (2) introspective clinicians and those who have profound doubts about the scientific study of human beings. These are the clinical investigators who favor the case study method. They base their theories on their own experience and intuition. We believe that both positions tend to weaken considerations of normality in the full sense. In the ultimate sense this book is an attempt to bridge this gulf between these two visions of man- and womankind.

The first edition of our book, *Normality: Theoretical and Clinical Concepts of Mental Health*, was published by Basic Books in 1966. The second

---

*Baltes, Reese, and Nesselroade 1977; Kalish 1975; Michel and Moore 1978; Munroe and Munroe 1975; Peters and Willis 1978; Sherrod, Veitz, and Friedman 1978; and Troll 1975.

edition came out in 1974. In these books we have defined what we have previously called *the four perspectives of normality* (Offer and Sabshin 1974). The perspectives encompass all definitions found in the vast literature surveyed. While there is obviously some overlap among perspectives, they are different and they can help investigators organize their data. Such organization is necessary, because the essential set of data obtained by investigators is only too often tied to their own orientation and belief system. This is discussed in some detail in chapter 12.

The first perspective, *normality as health,* includes the traditional medical-psychiatric approach, which equates normality with health and views health as an almost universal phenomenon. Many investigators have assumed behavior to be within normal limits when no manifest pathology is present. They focused on defining pathology, leaving undefined the large residue as "normal" or "healthy." Placed on a scale, normality would be the major portion of a continuum and abnormality would be the small remainder. This definition of normality seems to correlate with the activity of the model of the doctor who attempts to free patients from grossly observable symptoms. To this physician, the lack of unfavorable symptoms indicates health. Health in this context refers to a *reasonable* rather than an *optimal* state of functioning. The psychiatrist subscribing to such an approach is interested in the prevention of disease; for him or her, prevention implies the treatment of the symptoms that overtly interfere with the patient's adequate functioning. This perspective is also appealing to policy makers who wish to restrict the reimbursement of psychiatric care to people with severe mental illness.

The second perspective, *normality as utopia,* which is most widely held by psychoanalysts, conceives of normality as that harmonious and optimal blending of the diverse elements of the mental apparatus that culminates in optimal functioning, or "self-actualization." Such definitions emerge clearly, although most often implicitly, when psychoanalysts grapple with the complex problem of discussing their criteria of a successful treatment.

Dating from Freud's conception of normality as an ideal fiction, the normality as utopia view has almost become the trademark of the psychoanalyst. This is an area where Freudian and neo-Freudian analysts, in their tendency to equate the normal person with the ideal one, speak in similar terms. Definitions of the ideal person differ considerably, but almost all psychoanalysts, either explicitly or implicitly, conceive of normality in terms of ideal functionings. To a significant extent, this perspective poses complex policy problems and leads, in part, to the perception that the mental health field is a bottomless pit.

The third perspective, *normality as average,* is commonly employed in normative studies of behavior. This approach is based on the mathematical principle of the bell-shaped curve and its applicability to physical, psychological, and sociological data. This perspective, based as it is on the application of the "normal" bell-shaped curve to human data, contrasts sharply with the two perspectives just described. Those perspectives visualize normality and abnormality primarily as a straight-line continuum, and differ as to where the line should be drawn. However, the normality as average perspective conceives of the middle range as normal and both extremes as deviant. The normative statistical approach is used to find a way to describe each individual in terms of general assessment and total scores; interindividual variability is explained only within the context of the total group. This perspective is extremely disturbing to those who believe that it takes the poetry out of the mental health field. It also makes the concept of normality potentially equivalent to mediocrity and dullness.

The fourth perspective, *normality as transactional systems*, stresses that normal behavior is the end result of interacting systems that change over time. In contrast to proponents of the other three perspectives, those who advocate this position insist that normality be viewed from a standpoint of temporal progression. Many of these investigators, although believing that temporal changes are essential to any complete definition of normality, may adopt a limited definition as a working hypothesis. Such a definition would then fall under the rubric of one of the three other perspectives. Other investigators, whose concepts of normality can be classified logically under one of the other three perspectives, often may add a qualifying clause to the effect that their definitions of normality and health are amenable to evolutionary changes. As time passes, the content of statistical averages, the range of health, and the composition of ideal values may all be changed. This perspective has conceptual appeal, but its complexity frightens many people who then feel compelled to revert to one of the other three perspectives.

To a certain extent, each perspective complements the others, so that together they represent the behavioral and social sciences' approach to normality—a total field of *normatology*. There is a need to examine concepts of normality and definitions of normal behavior through time and across cultures, for these concepts change, and understanding how they change will broaden our knowledge of the meaning of the various concepts and definitions. This book attempts to fill that need.

DANIEL OFFER
MELVIN SABSHIN
Chicago and Washington
January 1984

REFERENCES

Baltes, P. B.; Reese, H. W.; and Nesselroade, J. R. 1977. *Life-Span Developmental Psychology: Introduction to Research Methods*, in *Life-Span Human Development Series*, ed. F. Rebelsky and L. Dorman. Monterey, Calif.: Brooks/Cole.

Coan, R. W. 1977. *Hero, Artist, Sage or Saint*. New York: Columbia University Press.

Elkind, D. 1982. "Piagetian Psychology and the Practice of Child Psychiatry." *Journal of the American Academy of Child Psychiatry* 21:435–45.

Jahoda, M. 1958. *Current Concepts of Positive Mental Health*. New York: Basic Books.

Kalish, R. A. 1975. *Late Adulthood: Perspectives on Human Development*, in *Life-Span Human Development Series*, ed. F. Rebelsky and L. Dorman. Monterey, Calif.: Brooks/Cole.

Lidz, T. 1980. "The Life Cycle." In *The Comprehensive Textbook of Psychiatry*, vol. 3, ed. H. I. Kaplan, A. M. Freedman, and B. J. Sadock, pp. 114–34. Baltimore, Md.: Williams & Wilkins.

Michel, G. F., and Moore, C. L. 1978. *Biological Perspectives in Developmental Psychology*, in *Life-Span Human Development Series*, ed. F. Rebelsky and L. Dorman. Monterey, Calif.: Brooks/Cole.

Munroe, R. L., and Munroe, R. H. 1975. *Cross-Cultural Human Development*, in *Life-Span Human Development Series*, ed. F. Rebelsky and L. Dorman. Monterey, Calif.: Brooks/Cole.

Offer, D., and Sabshin, M. 1966, 1974. *Normality: Theoretical and Clinical Concepts of Mental Health*. New York: Basic Books.

Peters, D. L., and Willis, S. L. 1978. *Early Childhood*, in *Life-Span Human Development Series*, ed. F. Rebelsky and L. Dorman. Monterey, Calif.: Brooks/Cole.

President's Commission on Mental Health, 1978. Report to the President. Washington, D.C.: U.S. Government Printing Office.

Sherrod, K.; Vietz, P.; and Friedman, S. 1978. *Infancy*, in *Life-Span Human Development Series*, ed. F. Rebelsky and L. Dorman. Monterey, Calif.: Brooks/Cole.

Smith, M. B. 1969. *Social Psychology and Human Values*. Chicago: Aldine.

Troll, L. E. 1975. *Early and Middle Adulthood: The Best Is Yet to Be, Maybe*, in *Life-Span Human Development Series*, ed. F. Rebelsky and L. Dorman. Monterey, Calif.: Brooks/Cole.

Wolman, B. B., et al., eds. 1982. *Handbook of Developmental Psychology*. Englewood Cliffs, N.J.: Prentice-Hall.

ACKNOWLEDGMENTS

Our interests in the theoretical and empirical concepts of normality and mental health began over twenty years ago, when one of us (Daniel Offer) was a psychiatric resident and the other (Melvin Sabshin) was Director of Psychiatric Residency Training at Michael Reese Hospital in Chicago.

The idea for this volume came from a friend, Seymour Weingarten, who, in 1979, encouraged us to work on a new edition of *Normality*. Many colleagues have helped us in thinking through some of the issues discussed in this book. They have given generously of their time and effort. They include Dr. P. Barglow, Dr. D. X. Freedman, Dr. R. R. Grinker, Sr., Dr. Ken Howard, Dr. Richard Markin, Dr. Eric Ostrov, Dr. Steven Sharfstein, Dr. Charles Strozier, and the late Judith Offer. The psychiatric residents and fellows at Michael Reese Hospital have also been most helpful in their discussions of the concepts.

We were also fortunate in having excellent secretarial and administrative help from Faye Meaderds, Merry Russell, Marie Allison, LaVerne Evans, Xing Jung, and Carol Davis.

This study was supported, in part, by the Adolescent Research Fund: In Memory of Judith Offer, of the Department of Psychiatry, Michael Reese Hospital and Medical Center.

DANIEL OFFER
MELVIN SABSHIN
Chicago and Washington
January 1984

PART I

THE LIFE CYCLE

1

Robert N. Emde
and James F. Sorce

Infancy: Perspectives
on Normality

An enormous amount of recent research and clinical attention has been focused on infancy. Significant findings have been considerable, but psychologists and health-care professionals still encounter vast areas of uncertainty. Central to many of these areas is one penetrating issue—that of normality. Normality is almost always considered in infancy work, yet assumptions about it are major, worrying about it continues, and views about its appropriate criteria differ. In our own work, we have found that the "four perspectives on normality" offer opportunities for clarification. This chapter sets forth our thinking about these perspectives and reviews concepts of normality in terms of both traditional ways of evaluating infants and more recent trends.

Work on this chapter was supported by NIMH Project Grant #2 RO1 MH 22803 and by Research Scientist Award #5 KO2 MH 36808 to Dr. Emde.

Thanks are also due Drs. Arnold Sameroff and Lulu Lubchenco, who contributed their perspectives and knowledge through personal communications.

Infancy and the Four Perspectives of Normality

As Offer and Sabshin (1974) emphasize, the four perspectives are not prioritized or ordered in any necessary way. We begin with the utopian perspective because it frames our discussion about infancy.

NORMALITY AS UTOPIA (WHAT ARE THE GOALS OF DEVELOPMENT?)

The usefulness of discussing the perspective designated as normality as utopia is that it reveals what we value. It also reveals our hidden assumptions, some of which we can acknowledge as helpful and others not. For infancy, there are two striking features about this perspective. First, its ideals are adult oriented; second, it is goal oriented rather than oriented toward current functioning.

Adult Ideals and Infancy. For those of us who are older, infancy represents a special time of life when our utopian values seem to prevail. Infancy tends to be where our hopes lie, where there are promises and beginnings, and where there are few disappointments and few failures. In many ways, infancy is a time of life we treasure most because of this, and perhaps also because we are built by evolution to find the baby physically appealing and a desirable object for caring, cuddling, and loving (Emde 1980; Lorenz 1943). Considering this, it should not be surprising to learn that in infancy research and in clinical work the values of the adult world have an intensified influence. This influence has resulted in several problematic tendencies that lead to a distortion of our understanding.

At the beginning of what might be considered the modern era of infancy research, Spitz and Wolf (1946) drew attention to dangers inherent in a tendency toward "adultomorphism." In this, the adult sees the typical infant, who cannot speak, as nonetheless reflecting adult experience; assumptions are made about complex mental functions such as fantasy formation and other abilities that are imputed to the infant in the absence of confirmatory evidence. As such, this tendency may represent a form of wish fulfillment on our part—a tendency to idealize the normal infant in terms of what we imagine we once had and lost, whether it be the blissful breast, mother, a life with fewer frustrations, or an oceanic self-experience.

Related to adultomorphism is another tendency of adults we have somewhat awkwardly labeled "theoreticomorphism"—the tendency of researchers to idealize infants in terms of their own theories (Emde and Robinson 1979). Here adult wish fulfillment is abstract rather than personal and is based on the desire for theoretical consistency. Recent examples of this tendency have taken the form of seeing the infant as primarily "competent" in one sphere or another. Overall, this tendency results in our idealizing the infant with a skewed emphasis on our particular theoretical interest, whether it be seeing the infant as sensory surface (perceptual theories), as thinker (cognitive theories), as learner (learning theories), as social and psychosexual being (psychoanalytic theories) (see review of infancy research according to these topics in Kessen, Haith, and Salapatek 1970).

Adult values influence our idealization of infancy in another rather negative way. As Kagan, Kearsley, and Zelazo (1978) have highlighted, we tend to see the infant as a diminished, imperfect, or opposite version of what we value as ideal in adults. Thus, since we idealize abstract symbolic intelligence in adults, we see the infant as naive, presymbolic, and concrete. In the social domain we therefore see a progression from the infant as egocentric and selfish to the ideal adult who is altruistic and has an enlightened self-interest. In the sexual domain our progression goes from infantile impulses that are uncontrolled and unbridled to adult impulses that are modulated and sublimated.

Still, it would be wrong to reject these adult views out of hand. While all idealizations can be seen as problematic to the extent that they assume much and distort reality, they also can be seen as containing truths both in terms of values and in terms of exaggerating certain elements of reality. The assumptions of adults are not necessarily bad. Adultomorphism can be useful for a new mother who is faced with a newborn's nonspecific expressions and responses. She expects her baby to be sad when left alone; she assumes the child is frustrated and angry when the infant has been crying unattended for a period. We would consider these assumptions, although based on adult expectations of how a baby would feel, as empathic and as useful guides for caregiving. Similarly, "theoreticomorphisms," although risky, can lead to useful hypotheses, new findings, and new theory. Kagan and associates (1978) are particularly critical of the negative idealization tendency since it directly operates against the infant's being seen in terms of current functioning (what is) and states the case in terms of what the child is expected to become. But even here there is an important truth. The infant moves from states of undifferentiation toward differentiation and development is, quite naturally, goal oriented.

Goals of Development.   The second striking feature of the utopian perspective is that it is goal oriented, both in terms of biology and in terms of social ideals.

Modern biology (Bertalanffy 1968; Waddington 1940) has directed the attention of infancy researchers to the fact that our genetic heritage prescribes developmental pathways that are crucial for adaptation. Corollaries of this goal-oriented view include the facts that: (1) biologically important developmental pathways tend to be buffered against stress; (2) there are multiple developmental pathways on the way to achieving developmental goals; and (3) there are self-righting tendencies in development after early hurts or deficits.* What is the ideal or utopia for adaptation? Few, if any, would believe this to be an appropriate scientific question. But we must be aware that since there is not total agreement about the nature or number of best pathways for such developmental goals, there is plenty of room for the influence of ideals. Certainly a variety of utopian ideals influence views about the "best match" between our biology and differing environments (see the section on normality as a transactional system, p. 9).

It is important for researchers and clinicians, when considering normality in infancy, to make known their guiding orientations about goals of development. Not only is there variation among individuals but there are secular trends in which goals are emphasized. Reigel (1976) and Sameroff and Harris (1980) have discussed these broad trends in terms of the role of ideology in the dialectic of development. Because of social change, they point out, normality becomes redefined. Today we value social cooperation and democratic-social ideals more than authoritarian ones. Therefore, our psychology of development is active oriented, organizational, and participatory (whether we look at learning, cognitive, or psychoanalytic theory). It is not passive oriented, drive reduction oriented, mechanistic, or authoritarian as it has been. Today egalitarianism is valued as opposed to the social Darwinism of earlier times; therefore, our psychology of development acknowledges sexual differences and strengths and encourages exploring a variety of sex roles and options in the parenting environment. Finally, today's research and clinical practice is likely to welcome biological models that point to multiple pathways in development. There will be vigorous exploration of "compensatory factors" in the development of physically and mentally handicapped infants who now, as a matter of public policy, are going to be "mainstreamed" and treated as "normal" in as many respects as possible.

NORMALITY AS AVERAGE (WHAT IS EXPECTABLE IN RELATION TO OTHERS?)

As is true for other times of life, the normality as average perspective is central for infancy. Most developmental tests, such as the Bayley test, use "normative age standards." These are average, statistical age groupings for mapping how an individual performs in relation to others and for

*See Bell and Harper (1977); McCall (1979); Sameroff and Chandler (1975); and Scarr and Salapetek (1970).

estimating the extent of normality or deviation. Specific issues of assessment will be considered later, but for now several general features about the use of averages in infancy seem important to review.

First, "averages" are used to typify what is normal about developmental or growth functions in general—that is, for the onset of developmental milestones such as smiling, crawling, or grasping, or for the onset of cognitive functions such as object permanence. But statistical averages are apt to be misleading when thinking of individuals. Infant development occurs rapidly and is uneven in rate. As a consequence, the group average for some developmental functions will vary greatly at certain ages and less so at others; it also is worth remembering that an individual's rate of change will in no way be typified according to a group average (McCall, Eichorn, Hogarty 1977).

Second, averages are used to typify differences in the behavior of subgroups of infants. Thus males are characterized by some as more active, vigorous, and "aggressive" while females are more responsive to touch (Maccoby and Jacklin 1980). But we must beware of the tendency to convert statements about group differences (differences that are small and based on large numbers of subjects studied) into assumptions about what is average or normal. What is most prominent, in fact, is the range of variability within each sex and the overlap of distributions of functions. Further, such statements tell us nothing about an individual: many normal females are more active than many normal males. We should not interpret normality for subgroups of infants without knowing about distributions of relevant functions.

Third, there are important secular trends. As a result of social changes, our subjective (as well as our statistical) standards of average change over time, and these guide our behavior accordingly, as theories of social and cognitive psychology will emphasize. For infancy, the increase in full-time working mothers, the increased participation of fathers in infant caregiving, the diminished birthrate, the decline of the extended family, and the increased divorce rate all have led to a shift in views of what is expectable in the infant's family environment. Changes in the American birthing scene over the past decade have been momentous. Expectations have shifted from birth being a necessary surgical ordeal (involving mother, nurse, and doctor) to the event being a major opportunity for "family development." Expectations are that fathers, mothers (and sometimes siblings) will enthusiastically and actively participate in the labor, childbirth, and postpartum experience. Soon after birth, infants are expected to be socially interactive and awake; a decade ago their social behaviors were not appreciated and they were expected to be sleepy, a fact we now understand as due to the effects of sedation given to mothers during labor (Brazelton 1961; Emde and Robinson 1979; Klaus and Kennell 1976).

Fourth, the context of immediate experience also bears on what is expectable. Consider the following common but different situations. A mother from a large family with many children sees her persistently fussy two-month-old as typically irritable; she has seen this kind of behavior before and knows that with patience her infant will "grow out of it." Another mother, with a first child and from a small family, sees the same behavior as a major problem; considerably upset, she consults her pediatrician. Her infant is considered "colicky" and intervention takes place with the prescription of medication and a follow-up visit. In another example of contrasts, two Down's syndrome infants were born into different neighborhoods. In one case the infant was born into a neighborhood where another Down's infant had been born only a month earlier; the parents had frequent opportunities for comparisons and for group activities with handicapped infants. In the other case, the Down's infant was born into a family that had no neighbors with handicapped children. In this family, much more of the infant's behavior was seen as deviant and strange, as the family had few guides for what was "average" under the circumstances. Finally, the importance of context can be dramatized by imagining the attitudes of two families about the "normality" of a stuffy nose in their young infants. Neighbors of one family have recently experienced the tragedy of sudden infant death syndrome. No such event has occurred for the other family.

NORMALITY AS HEALTH (WHAT IS A REASONABLE STATE OF ABSENCE OF DISCOMFORT OR DISABILITY? THE CONCEPT OF RISK.)

In infancy the normality as health perspective has been dominated by the pediatric concept of risk. Here the question is less one of assessing the current state of discomfort or disability and more that of determining if there are features that make it likely that the infant is in danger of major illness or death either in infancy or later. For example, the newborn who is "small for date," especially if premature, is at higher risk for infant mortality and for developing later problems (i.e., cerebral palsy). The risk concept is important because it can lead to increased vigilance and early intervention when vital functions show compromise. Since risk will be discussed in the next section, only a few general points will be made here. First, although risk is sometimes based on individual factors (such as an idiosyncratic pattern of behavioral or physiological disturbance), it is usually defined by population variables. That is, compared with a relevant base population, the infant is seen from a statistical point of view to be born earlier than normal or to be lighter than normal. For this reason the concept of risk involves the normality as average perspective as well as the normality as health perspective.

Second, the concept of risk has now been applied to psychiatry. In the psychiatric application, the risk concept has primarily been used in terms of a reference population. Thus, because of known statistical outcomes for certain populations, infants born to teenage mothers or to parents from impoverished environments are known to be at increased risk for later psychosocial disorders. But there are individual factors as well. Infants who have physical disabilities, who are developmentally retarded, and who are regarded as persistently irritable are also at increased risk (Rutter 1980; Thomas and Chess 1980).

Our third general point is that normality as health is not synonymous with continuity over development. In fact, the low-risk infant may be less predictable than the high-risk counterpart. This makes good biological sense if we think of a range and a variability in behavior as being adaptive, given the variability encountered in human environments.

NORMALITY AS A TRANSACTIONAL SYSTEM (WHAT IS EXPECTABLE IN THE MIDST OF CHANGE?)

As Offer and Sabshin (1974) describe, this perspective involves interacting systems over time; it is a process view of normality that deals with change rather than with cross-sections of behavior. In infancy not only is change rapid but, as already noted, the wide individual variability in behavior and in its rate of change makes for low predictability. Investigators involved in longitudinal studies have been disappointed to find few behavioral continuities from infancy to early childhood. As a result, attention has increasingly been directed toward "discontinuities," or times of qualitative transition in behavior (Emde, Gaensbauer, and Harmon 1976; McCall, 1979).

It is now recognized that there is a need for new dynamic developmental models to represent this situation. These models must address the question: What is expectable in the midst of change? They must deal with self-regulation in the midst of new integrative transformations. They must encompass the changing relations between infant and environment and represent the fact that infant and parent negotiate successive new levels of organization that cannot be predicted in any linear fashion from the behavior of one or the other.

A transactional perspective makes it impossible to view the infant alone in thinking about normality. We must look at infant and parent, for each defines the other' normality. In this, there will necessarily be issues of matching of behaviors, of adult developmental changes and of life event changes—all of which must be taken into account. Further, we

must be wary of mislabeling as abnormal what may be transitional processes of adaptation to new and stressful situations. This view has been
emphasized in family therapy where it has been pointed out that an
individual's upset and perturbation may be mislabeled as pathological.
Minuchin (1974) recommends that families be understood first as a social
system in transformation; those who enter treatment are considered "average families in transitional situations, suffering the pains of accommodation to new circumstances" (p. 60).

The normality as transaction perspective seems more difficult to describe and quantify than the normality as average or normality as low
risk for death or illness perspective. Still, it is the only perspective that
directly attempts to view change within complex shifting systems. The
rest of this chapter therefore reflects an undeniable fact: researchers and
clinicians of infancy have found it increasingly necessary to adopt this
perspective.

Historical Traditions in Evaluating Infants

THE DIFFERENTIAL PSYCHOLOGY—IQ TRADITION

The historical roots of our present-day view of normality in human
infancy are strongly embedded in the mental testing movement that
flourished in the late 1800s and early 1900s (Brooks and Weinraub 1976).
The aim of this movement was to measure the abilities and skills that
were assumed to reflect an individual's level of intellectual functioning.
The initial motivation for developing tests of mental abilities grew out of
the practical social need for improving the education of school-age children. In France, Binet was commissioned to develop an objective test that
would measure individual differences in children's abilities to perform
school-appropriate tasks; the hope was to identify those who were mentally deficient and in need of special training. Binet's success in developing a useful test of complex mental functioning (including judgment,
comprehension, and reasoning) led, after a series of revisions (Binet and
Simon 1905, 1908; Kuhlmann 1911), to the Stanford-Binet Scale (Terman
1916), which became the test of choice for educators in both France and
the United States. An individual's IQ, originally stated in terms of age
level, soon became stated in relation to age-adjusted norms; thus the
normality as average perspective became quantified.

The beginnings of interest in *infants* can be traced to England during
the late 1800s. At that time Charles Darwin's theory of evolution was
providing a theoretical rationale for studying the developing infant (Dar-

win 1859, [1872] 1965). No longer was it sufficient to identify normal functioning in adults; rather, one needed to understand the origins of adult behaviors. Initially "baby biographers" accepted the challenge of Darwin's theory by observing the onset of normal behaviors in infancy and describing their developmental course (Darwin 1877; Preyer 1882). Although these first accounts were notoriously distorted by parental and theoretical biases, taken together they did suggest that infant behaviors normally unfolded in orderly sequences, although the rates of development differed among individuals (Goodenough 1949).

This growing interest in infants, combined with the popularity of the mental testing movement, created the need for a standardized test of infant behaviors. Thus the 1930s saw the publication of a number of scales designed to catalog the developing behavioral repertoire of normal infants. Perhaps the most influential attempts to collect comprehensive norms of infant behavioral development were Arnold Gesell's Developmental Schedules (Gesell and Amatruda 1941; Gesell et al. 1940), Charlotte Buhler's Baby Tests (1930), Mary Shirley's longitudinal studies (Shirley 1933), and Nancy Bayley's California First Year Mental Scale (1933). Taken together, the major contribution of these scales was that through extensive observations of infants in varying contexts, both cross-sectionally and longitudinally, age norms for a wide variety of infant behaviors were established. The behaviors of greatest interest were those that were assumed to be intimately related to intellectual functioning. In face, two important assumptions about the nature of intelligence seemed to characterize these early infant tests. First was the belief that intelligence is truly a *general* trait having strong hereditary underpinnings, although somewhat modifiable by environmental factors. Second, and related to the first, was the belief that this general trait is relatively *stable* throughout an individual's developmental life span. Given this concept of intelligence, a major problem eventually surfaced with each of these standardized tests, namely their poor predictive validity. Study after study documented this problem. Not only was it true that poor predictability accompanied longer intertest intervals, but the younger the child, the poorer the predictability. In fact, infant tests administered before the age of eighteen months had practically no relationship to any later assessment of mental functioning, while predictive validity remained poor until children reached six to seven years of age.

The dismal failure of early infant tests to predict later functioning led some to place the blame on serious inadequacies in the tests themselves. The conviction that an individual's underlying intellectual trait is truly stable remained, but weaknesses in test construction (such as small sample size, lack of standardization, lack of adequate administration instruc-

tions, subjective scoring criteria, lack of statistical evaluation of reliability) prevented researchers from detecting what was thought to be an
underlying consistency. From this viewpoint, the solution to the "diagnostic problem" was to improve these early tests. Thus the Cattell Infant Intelligence Scale (1940), the Northwestern Intelligence Test (Gilliand 1949, 1951), and the Griffiths' Scale (1954) were developed with
greater attention toward adequate test construction. The Bayley Scales
of Infant Development (Bayley 1969) utilized a large collaborative sample of infants providing the best-yet available basis for normative evaluations in the United States. Still, predictive validities remained disap-
pointingly low.

Ultimately the inability to predict subsequent mental functioning could
no longer be dismissed as an artifact of a poor testing instrument. Researchers of the differential psychology tradition have been forced to
reassess their assumptions about the nature of intelligence. As early as
1970, Bayley suggested, based on an analysis of her testing data, that
there was no general factor of intelligence during the first three years of
life, but rather several sets or groups of mental functions that changed
dramatically throughout development. These separate clusters of mental
functions first organize according to one structure and then later reorganize to from a qualitatively different mental structure. The types of abilities
and the level of functioning that characterize one mental structure are not
necessarily related to the kinds of mental abilities and level of functioning that will occur after a dramatic reorganization of these functions.
Given such a view, two important changes in infant testing need to be
made. First, a single overall score is no longer an adequate indicator of
underlying intelligence; what is now needed is a technique for indentify-
ing separate mental abilities. Second, rather than looking for continuity
and stability in mental development, one should be looking for a particular organization among separate abilities at point A, followed by a dramatically different reorganization of the abilities at point B.

Today's infant testing has not yet taken up Bayley's suggestion even
though it has since been echoed by others. Indeed, the Bayley test itself
(with single normative scores for mental age and motor age) is in such
widespread use that it has the status of a "marker variable" among infancy researchers (Bell and Hertz 1976), and it seems to be the most
accepted test among health-care professionals who go beyond a simple
pediatric screening device. Nonetheless, it would appear that the mental
testing movement is contributing to a shift in paradigms with respect to
understanding normal development in infancy. Our discussion of recent
trends will carry this further.

THE PEDIATRIC-NEUROLOGIC TRADITION*

The view that standardized infant tests could serve as valuable diagnostic tools for evaluating an infant's current level of functioning was influential during the 1960s, as a desire for accurate medical diagnosis pushed the field of infant testing to develop assessments for even the first weeks after birth. From the outset, the major aim of the pediatrician was to identify those infants who were at varying degrees of "risk" for illness. The concept of risk implied a combination of two normality perspectives, that of health and that of statistical average. Normal, low-risk infants are not only healthy in current terms but have a low probability of future illness based on the absence of specific prenatal or perinatal factors that are known to be statistically associated with subsequent infant illness.

For very young infants, the diagnosis of risk for disease generally focuses on the infant's physical maturity, central nervous system functioning, and sensory functioning. Of all of these areas, perhaps the one most frequently emphasized is the condition of the nervous system, wherein damage, either prenatally or perinatally, can lead to motor disorders (e.g., cerebral palsy), mental disorders (retardation), and behavioral disorders. Pioneers in addressing this problem were Thomas and Saint-Anne Dargassies (Thomas, Chesni, and Saint-Anne Dargassies 1960; Saint-Anne Dargassies 1977), who attempted to map out the maturational stages of the normally developing nervous system as it evolved from a fetus, through the birth process, into the normal neonate. Their strategy was to identify basic neurological features that characterize the normal infant at various gestational ages, where "normal" was defined in terms of those features most frequently found in a large population of infants.

Once basic knowledge of neurological organization as a function of gestational age had been established, the next step was to obtain reliable information about abnormal neurological functioning. Pioneering work in this area was carried out by Prechtl and his colleagues. Prechtl and Beintema (1964) developed a neurological examination in order to diagnose abnormal nervous system functioning as soon as possible following birth. They emphasized that early assessment would be valuable since damage to the central nervous system (CNS) due to injury and other birth complications often results in symptoms that are present soon after birth but then disappear. While some neonates recover completely from early symptoms, others have problems that reappear in infancy or childhood in the form of cerebral palsy, mental retardation, or learning disabilities. Thus in studying neurological abnormalities present at birth one

*Personal communications from Lulu Lubchenco, M.D., contributed much to our summary of this tradition.

should assess the extent to which subsequent development might also be abnormal. Since it is impractical to administer a time-consuming examination to every neonate, the following strategy came about: only those infants evaluated as being "high-risk" at birth would be recommended for a complete neurological examination. High-risk infants are defined as those (1) who show symptoms of having suffered brain damage (e.g., poor muscle tone, abnormal posture, abnormal spontaneous movement, marked asymmetries, neonatal seizures) or (2) whose medical history involved conditions statistically associated with damage to the nervous system (premature birth, birth trauma, mothers with diabetes or toxemia) (Prechtl 1977).

Another major contribution of Prechtl to the pediatric-neurological tradition was his documentation of the importance of organismic "state." Following Wolff (1959), he noted that the intensity of a particular neurological function, and often its very presence or absence, was dependent on the neonate's behavioral state—quiet sleep, rapid-eye-movement sleep, quiet wakefulness, active wakefulness, or crying. Therefore, the results of a neurological examination are only valid when the behavioral state during the administration of each test item is known, where the optimum behavioral state for each item is the one in which a medium intensity response is consistently found (Prechtl 1977; Prechtl and Beintema 1964). From an operational standpoint, state can be defined rather simply as a pattern of behavioral and/or physiological variables that repeat themselves in an individual over time (see Hutt, Lenard, and Prechtl 1969). The usefulness of the state concept for understanding the patterns of activity and of reactivity in the normal newborn has since received extensive confirmation for behavioral (Wolff 1966) and psychophysiological measures (Anders, Emde, and Parmelee 1971).

Lubchenco has also contributed to the assessment of normality and risk. Over the course of more than two decades, she attempted to identify those newborns at risk for mortality or morbidity, becoming convinced that a major cause of such neonatal problems is abnormal intrauterine growth (see Lubchenco [1976] for a summary). According to her, the best index of whether an individual infant has experienced normal versus abnormal patterns of intrauterine growth involves a combined score involving birthweight and gestational age. For example, in one study carried out at the University of Colorado Medical Center from 1966 to 1968, birthweight and gestational age together contributed 75 percent of the predictive value to morbidity or mortality during the neonatal period. When the five-minute Apgar score (presumably reflective of problems arising during the birth process) was also taken into account, the predictive value increased still further. Figure 1.1, well known in pediatric cir-

FIGURE 1.1
Classification of Newborns by Birth Weight and Gestational Age

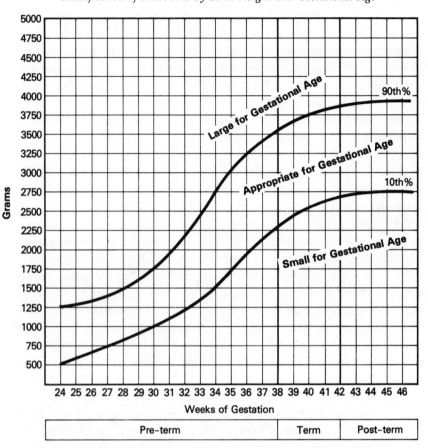

GA-BW distribution: GA to be estimated from first day of LMP and classified by completed weeks:
37 weeks + 0 days = 37 weeks
37 weeks + 6 days = 37 weeks
GA: subdivided along abscissa into three categories:
a. Preterm (Pr) = All infants less than 38 weeks GA, i.e., 37 weeks + 6 days or less.
b. Term (T) = All infants between 38th and 42nd weeks GA.
c. Postterm (Po) = All infants of 42 or more weeks GA.
BW: Within *each* GA group, three subgroups of infants are defined by BW:
     a. LGA = Infants above 90th percentile.
     b. AGA = Infants between 90th and 10th percentile.
     c. SGA = Infants below 10th percentile.
Thus, nine groups of newborn infants are defined and coded as follows:
Pr-LGA Born before 38th week, BW above 90th percentile.
Pr-AGA Born before 38th week, BW between 10th and 90th percentile.
Pr-SGA Born before 38th week, BW below 10th percentile.
T-LGA Born between 38th and 42nd weeks, BW above 90th percentile.
T-AGA Born between 38th and 42nd weeks, BW between 10th and 90th percentile.
T-SGA Born between 38th and 42nd weeks, BW below 10th percentile.
Po-LGA Born at or after 42nd week, BW above 90th percentile.
Po-AGA Born at or after 42nd week, BW between 10th and 90th percentiles.
Po-SGA Born at or after 42nd week, BW below 10th percentile.

NOTE: Reprinted by permission of the author and the publisher, from F. C. Battaglia and L. O. Lubchenco, "A Practical Classification of Newborn Infants by Weight and Gestational Age." *Journal of Pediatrics* 71 (1967): 161.

cles, illustrates the relative concepts of normality and risk in relation to birthweight and gestational age.

This application for the pediatric risk concept has had a fundamental influence on research regarding normality. Those now studying developmental processes—whether from pediatric, psychological, or psychiatric disciplines—make use of criteria for ensuring normality by means of appropriate birth weight, gestational age, and Apgar scores. In this way infants are selected who are "normal," that is, who are at low risk for pediatric morbidity.

Still, pediatricians involved in risk research have been troubled by an additional fact: although knowing a neonate's birthweight-by-gestational-age classification enables predictions about the general case, the ability to predict illness for an individual newborn is a much more difficult task. The major problem stems from the fact that newborns, in comparison with older infants and children, have a limited ability to react to stress or illness: their major reaction involves a "turning-off" or "shutting down" regardless of the particular nature of their illness. The current challenge in risk research is to differentiate between those "high-risk" babies who will probably be normal without any further intervention from those neonates who, if left without appropriate medical intervention, will experience more serious illnesses and handicaps. A current hope is that diagnosis will benefit from use of the Brazelton Neonatal Behavioral Assessment scale (1973). Behavioral assessment may provide additional information about an infant's individual patterns of adapting to the environment, as well as noting how an infant can have an effect on the caregiving environment. Lubchenco (pers. com. 1980) gives an interesting example of its use. In a study of polycythemic infants, the Brazelton Scale was given at eight hours after birth. The assessment dramatized the fact that those infants who were truly sick could not get into an alert state. Nurses reported great difficulty in attempts to awaken them, yet once aroused they usually began immediate crying. In either state, asleep or crying, feeding was a difficult task. In contrast, those polycythemic infants who were less seriously ill did not exhibit this behavioral state cycle and were less difficult to feed.

Finally, it is important to note that a basic assumption of the pediatric-neurologic tradition has been that complications during pregnancy or birth cause CNS damage that becomes related to subsequent disturbances of attention, cognition, learning, and motoric abilities. Thus standardized neurological examinations were viewed as a way of assessing the extent of CNS damage for prediction of which infants would suffer from subsequent problems. However, empirical studies failed to substantiate relationships between prenatal and perinatal trauma and later developmental outcome.* Putting it another way, just as mental tests in infancy failed to predict to later development, neurological tests of newborns were unable to differentiate, in any general way, between normality and subsequent pathology. There are a number of possible explanations for this lack of prediction. First, it may be due to methodological problems in relating early neurological abnormalities to subsequent psychological dysfunction. Some abnormal responses appearing during a newborn examination may be temporary symptoms that do not reflect permanent brain damage. Thus the number of "false positives" included in a high-risk neonatal sample could dampen significant relationships. In addition, subsequent psychological abnormalities are typically defined by gross measures, such as IQ, which also add "noise" to the statistical analysis. However, it is also possible that the problem occasioned by a lack of prediction is again reflective of an inappropriate developmental model. As we indicated for the differential psychology-IQ tradition, a shift appears to be in progress; rather than the linear cause-effect model of perinatal factors directly causing permanent psychological dysfunction, a transactional model is being suggested (Sameroff and Chandler 1975). This model takes account of the fact that some infants appear to be remarkably resilient to insults and adaptable to a wide variety of environments. Thus to improve prediction of long-term consequences, one needs to know about the nature of the infant's interactions with his or her environment, both social and medical. With respect to the social environment, study after study has shown the overriding importance of socioeconomic status (SES). While high SES appears to minimize the deleterious effects of perinatal complication, low SES increases the risk that these complications will have poor developmental outcomes. With respect to the medical environment, a variety of medical intervention strategies have been developed that prevent illnesses from causing permanent handicaps or deaths and can even enable infants to function relatively normally, as long as early diagnosis and treatment take place. Of course, to the extent that this occurs prediction may decline, since it is possible for even severe cases to have outcomes that look generally normal.

THE PSYCHIATRIC-PSYCHOANALYTIC TRADITION

The psychiatric and psychoanalytic tradition of normality has carried with it a pervasive concern for *individuality*. For theoreticians and researchers this concern has given a special focus to infancy, where the roots of individual variablity are presumably to be found, in terms of both differential inborn factors and differential experience. Thus Freud,

*See Broman, Nichols, and Kennedy (1975); Corah et al. (1965); Graham et al. (1962); and Werner, Bierman, and French (1971).

in formulating psychoanalytic theory, not only wrote of stage-related general processes of development in infancy ([1905] 1953) but, like Darwin before him and Piaget after him, made observations of particular infants in his own family. These observations drew his attention to the individual nature of experience involved in early dream formation ([1900] 1953) and in early mastery through play ([1920] 1955). With the accumulation of clinical experience and theory, the differential importance of early experience became increasingly emphasized. This was especially so as Freud enumerated his anxiety series for normal development ([1926] 1959) and gave salience to variations in overall stimulation and in maternal separation as factors for personality formation. Interestingly, it was just these two dimensions of early experience—amount of stimulation and maternal separation—that were explored later in infant observations and clinical studies of Spitz (1945, 1946), Levy (1937), Anna Freud and Burlingham (1944), Bowlby (1969, 1973, 1981), and Mahler (1968). Indeed, studies on these dimensions led not only to a description of the normal but to a demarcation from the normal of a large number of infant pathological syndromes that are considered important today (these include syndromes of deprivation, neglect, abuse, anaclitic depression, and "insecurity of attachment").

It is not surprising that this tradition, emphasizing the importance of early experience for personality formation, was one that led to major programmatic research as mental health research flourished in the decades following World War II. Longitudinal studies of normal development were undertaken with a rationale of discovering early patterns of individual differences in experience and tracing these from infancy through childhood and beyond.* Academic departments of psychiatry, supported by the National Institute of Mental Health, established programs of infancy research that initially shared a special interest in individual differences.† These programs, as they gained increasing methodological sophistication, attended to the complexity of behavioral development in terms of motivational, psychophysiological, and social factors. Still, individual differences, although specifiable at any infant age, were not found stable in any simple sense. Partly this seemed to be appreciated as complexity not yielding to analysis from still inadequate methods, but even more it seemed to be appreciated as a reflection of the

---

*See Benjamin (1959); Block (1971); Escalona and Heider (1959); and Kagan and Moss (1962).

†For example, at Harvard University, Wolff (1966); at Boston University, Sander (1969) and Stechler and Carpenter (1967); at Albert Einstein, Bridger and Birns (1963) and Escalona (1968); at the University of Illinois, Greenberg (1964); at Stanford University, Korner (1964); at the University of Michigan, Fraiberg (1968); at the University of Colorado, Emde, Gaensbauer, and Harmon (1976).

nature of early development itself. As was the case for the differential psychology and pediatric-neurologic traditions, this has suggested a change in models. Normal development is not strictly linear, and attention is now directed to understanding qualitative reorganizations as well as continuities in developmental processes.

The concept of temperament has come to occupy an important place in more recent categorizations of what is normal in infancy. As a result of their original New York Longitudinal Study, Thomas, Chess, and their coworkers (1977) designated nine categories of behavioral style for infants. These included activity level, rhythmicity, approach-withdrawal, adaptability, sensory threshold, intensity of reaction, quality of mood, distractibility, and attention span persistence. Although based on parental perceptions rather than direct infant observations, these categories of "temperament" have shown themselves to be quite useful in subsequent longitudinal studies of this group and of others, and a practical categorization scheme based on the work has been applied to pediatric settings (Carey 1972). Further, categories similar to these have been found useful in a variey of direct observational studies by behavioral geneticists (see Buss and Plomin 1975; Goldsmith and Campos 1982; Wilson 1978). To what extent these categories truly reflect infant temperament is still debatable. Nonetheless it is undeniable that the New York Longitudinal Study categories capture behavioral constellations that seem to be meaningful for clinicians and researchers and may typify some relatively enduring features in the infant-parent system. They also serve to empahsize the individuality of infants within a normal range of functioning. However, the conditions under which such patterns of functioning might remain stable over time and the conditions under which particular patterns might represent a risk for subsequent childrearing difficulties are still a matter for research (Bates 1980; Thomas and Chess 1980).

Finally, mention must be made of a more recent development in the psychiatric tradition, namely the infant mental health movement. Arising partly out of social concerns for enhancing the early environment of infants in disadvantaged populations and partly out of concerns for handicapped infants, this movement gathered momentum from specific psychiatric problems. These included infant syndromes of neglect, deprivation, abuse, and depression, and problems of prevention and helping families to "get a good start." In spite of the fact that this movement already has a journal (*Infant Mental Health Journal* which began publication in 1980), a national newsletter (*Zero to Three*, Bulletin of the National Center for Clinical Infant Programs, which published its first volume in 1980), and a world congress (the First World Congress of Infant Psychiatry was held in Portugal in 1980), it is difficult to say if it will offer a changing view of normality. It is clear that what has been called "infant psychiatry" (Howells 1979) contains perspectives from many disciplines and includes a concern for parents as well as infants, but it now has little in the way of a unifying conceptual orientation.

More Recent Trends

More recent trends have reflected an increasing concern with developmental processes and the normality as transaction perspective. Because they are multidisciplinary and appear to challenge traditional ways of evaluating infants, we believe two such trends are worthy of special note.

COGNITIVE PSYCHOLOGY AND ASSESSING NORMALITY IN HANDICAPPED INFANTS*

In spite of our review of changing trends, it remains true that infant tests such as the Bayley Scales were put together in the tradition of differential psychology. As we have discussed, this tradition originally had two aspects: (1) a belief in the idea that there was a general capacity of intelligence that could be characterized in the infant and that would remain the same at all ages, and (2) a commitment to the strategy of normative testing, wherein performance is evaluated against "averages of others of the same age." The fact that infant tests do not predict intelligence as measured at later ages has now been documented by many.[†] But, as we discussed, the tests are still quite useful in assessing current functioning in a standard manner. One can see how an infant is performing in relation to others, and, with repeated testing, one can document gross changes in performance.

Cognitive psychology, arising from the tradition established by Jean Piaget (1950), approaches matters from another direction. Testing is conducted to understand the processes involved in problem solving rather than to match standard outcomes of performance. "Intelligence," or adaptation, is thought of not as a general capacity but as a series of functions that build on early functions. Scaling of test results is *ordinal*, based on where an individual is functioning in a developmental series of a particular domain, rather than normative, based on a comparison with others. This tradition is theoretical rather than statistical; it is based on

---

*This section owes much to personal communications from Dr. Arnold Sameroff.

[†]For example, see Bayley (1970); McCall, Eichorn, and Hogarty (1977); and the reviews of Honzik (1976) and Lewis (1976).

Piaget's epigenetic model and designed so that items follow in a necessary sequence. The designers of the Uzgiris-Hunt Scales (1975) and other infant scales in this tradition (Cosati-Lazine 1968; Escalona and Corman, unpublished) have been interested in evaluating what a child knows rather than where the child stands in relation to others; the scales are thus said to be criterion-based rather than normative-based.

Such an approach has a special relevance to the assessment of current functioning in handicapped infants. Why should we be concerned with handicapped infants in a treatise on normality? There are two reasons. For one, society properly insists that we find a way to assess normal functioning in the handicapped since "mainstreaming" of such individuals has now become official policy. For another, assessing adaptive functioning in those with sensorimotor deficits may highlight issues of assessment in those without such deficits.

In assessing infants with cerebral palsy, with major sensory deficits such as blindness or deafness, and with deficits related to mental retardation, one must plan for limitation of disability and for remediation. One must be able to evaluate strengths and weaknesses in the ways an individual infant processes information, solves problems, and explores the world. The problems associated with tests derived from the differential psychology tradition soon become apparent. Not only does it lack meaning to evaluate one or two general capacities of performance (the Bayley test has two general scores) in the face of sensorimotor deficits that might make it impossible to perform standard test items, but it also lacks meaning to compare a handicapped infant's performance against averages of others of the same age. Those who have worked with the handicapped have documented how even infants with major handicaps can use alternative modes for reaching common developmental goals. Two dramatic examples of this are provided by the sequence leading to object permanence. Decarie (1969), in working with thalidomide infants (tragically born without arms and legs), found that these infants could use substitute channels for typical eye-hand coordinations such as between shoulders, chin, and eyes, or between toes and eyes. Fraiberg (1977), in her work with congenitally blind infants, showed how the developmental sequence leading to object permanence could take place using auditory modality substitutes for visual schemata in sensorimotor coordinations. Obviously a cognitive approach, which is flexible and criterion-based, could capture these adaptive transformations; a normative-based approach could not.

As Sameroff has emphasized (pers. com. 1979), what is needed is the development of broad assessment procedures for use with infants who are handicapped. These should be scales that would allow the indepen-

dent evaluation of cognitive items and the perceptual and motor performance capacities that are required to pass these items. In effect, such assessment procedures would combine features of what we have called the
cognitive-ecology approach and the differential-normative approach by
finding age norms for sequential functions. We consider it likely that the
near future will see a variety of alternative scales of intellectual functioning for children with deficits in specific perceptual or motor areas. The
assessment of normality, thought of as adaptive functioning under conditions of handicap, is likely to undergo a significant advance.

SOCIAL ECOLOGY

Increasingly, infancy researchers have come to grips with the complexities of development. This stems in part from an appreciation of unpredictability and the range of variability involved in adaptive change. It
also stems from an appreciation of the fact that there are qualitative
transformations in development, times of rather wondrous synthetic activity, which challenge us because they are nonlinear and so poorly understood. Further, it stems from advances in research technology: we
now have a variety of multivariate and time series computerized approaches for handling complex data. But perhaps most of all, it stems
from an interest in understanding social relationships as they develop.
The recognition that such social relationships must be understood not in
isolation but in a variety of ecological settings has led to the trend we
designate as social ecology. Just as it is true that the behavior of an infant
may have as much to do with the past history of the caregiving relationship as it does with the past history of either infant or caregiver, so it is
also true that the caregiving relationship will be different in major ways
in different family environments.

This is an application of the transactional perspective in its strictest
sense. A restatement of this application may be helpful. Early social behavior, when viewed over time, is not interactional in the sense our statistics and methods had previously assumed. Factors are not summative.
Instead, both the infant and the caregiving environment are changing
over time, and these changes are interdependent; they mutually influence one another (Sameroff and Chandler 1975). Such changing levels of
mutual influence are not easy to characterize. Nonetheless, there is some
hope that continuities in the regulation of social relationships may
emerge where continuities in individual development have not.

One example of this trend occurs in the recent thinking about temperament. Thomas and Chess (1980) talk about continuity as consistency in
individual-environment interaction. They bring their notion of "the
goodness of fit" to bear on this. There must be a goodness of fit between

(1) the capacities and (2) the characteristics of the individual, and between (1) the opportunities and (2) the demands of the environment. It seems to us that the first items refer to what is *possible* and the second, to *what is*. Furthermore, it seems likely that future clinician-researchers will characterize "what is" in terms of its *variability* as well as what is usual or average.

Another important example of this trend occurs in thinking about "ecological transitions" in infant development. As conceptualized by Bronfenbrenner (1977), ecological transitions come about because of the fact that society and environment settings are changing and because individuals are developing. When such transitions occur, reciprocal influences among individuals, families, and ecological settings are characteristic. "Normality" must encompass this view.

Conclusion

In conclusion, we return to the normality as utopia perspective. This perspective is on a different level of abstraction from Offer and Sabshin's other three perspectives of normality. The other perspectives are self-evident and clearly useful. This one is not. In fact, it contains a paradox: normality is unreachable if it is an ideal, and to adhere to this perspective would be to maintain that no one is, or could be, normal. (Indeed, the word utopia in its etymology, literally means "no place.") Thus this view of normality begs for clarification. It should evoke the following questions: What are the ideals we have in mind? Which ideals are useful and which are too far removed and illusory?

In our introduction we mentioned the heightened intensity with which we idealize infancy. We discussed several unacknowledged ideals stemming from our adult-based view. In concluding, we add still another entry to our catalog of unacknowledged ideals—that of predictability. The development of the ideally normal infant is supposed to be predictable. This ideal has been presented in each of the three disciplinary traditions we have reviewed. When brought into the light of day, predictability is perhaps the most surprising distortion of all, but in this we are victims of our idealized scientific methods. We would like to see development as linear and simple. Holding up "Ockham's razor" for science, we strive for parsimony in our explanations and we often assume that once something is analyzed into its simplest components, it is then wholly understood. Further, as clinicians, when we have constructed retrospective biogra-

phies with our patients, it has seemed easy to trace the "red thread backward" to relatively simple developmental antecedents of current difficulties. But the last two decades of research have found that looking forward
is another matter. The story of newborn behavioral assessment offers a
poignant research "case history."

The Brazelton Neonatal Behavioral Assessment Scale (NBAS), following earlier assessment scales of Graham, Matarazzo, and Caldwell (1956)
and of Rosenblith (1975), has done much to document the complexity
and organization of the newborn's normal behavior. In addition to showing the newborn's repertoire of coordinated activities, it documents the
newborn's ability to orient to a variety of stimuli, to regulate behavioral
state in response to stress, and to engage affective interchanges from
caregivers. The excitement of being able to show what the newborn
could do spread from pediatrics and psychology into psychiatry, nursing,
and childbirth education. But one hope for the NBAS was not sustained.
It did not turn out to be a developmental predictor. Initially, the multidisciplinary group of investigators who collaborated in developing the scale
hoped that a clinical concern for individual differences (an important
incentive for developing the scale) would be rewarded by predictive validation. It was hoped that stable individual differences would be found in
"temperament" patterns, if not patterns of risk for developmental deviance. However, in one clinical setting after another, careful studies revealed that the stability of individual differences (i.e., predictability) was
only moderate or poor during the newborn period and was worse beyond
it (see the collection of reports in the monograph edited by Sameroff
1978a). Disappointment was marked as teams of investigators tried to
find explanations for this in terms of differences in the training of exam-
iners, in methods of carrying out examinations, and in techniques of data
analysis. None of these factors accounted for poor stability. At length, it
was realized that the struggles with stability and prediction yielded another important lesson, one about the need for dynamic developmental
models. Horowitz, Sullivan, and Linn (1978) and Sameroff (1978b)
pointed out that "test-retest unreliability" should be considered data instead of error and that the struggles to establish stability indicated how
hard it is to encompass the development of a dynamic system with standard statistical techniques.

Two biological principles, adaptively important for development and
therefore preprogrammed in our species, seemed apparent. Both of these
principles operate against the expectation of stable individual differences
in behavior. The first principle is that of variability of behavior. An individual newborn with variability and a range of behavior would have

more opportunities for matching or synchronizing such behaviors with any given environment. The second principle is that of reorganization of behavior. Adaptive changes appear in infant behavioral organization due not only to interaction with specific caregivers but also to maturational shifts in organization after the newborn period; stability across periods of reorganization would not be expected. In other words, it appears that just as positive aspects of the NBAS document the newborn's organized complexity in current functioning, its negative aspects (i.e., its poor stability over time) document the dynamic complexity of development itself (Emde 1978).

As the NBAS example illustrates, multidisciplinary views allow us to avoid errors from our own angles of perspective. In this spirit, we offer two final examples of views that need to be taken into account in thinking about normality in infants. The first has to do with society in general and the second with parents in particular.

The views of society are related to a current debate about whether we should have a subfield designated as infant psychiatry. Although there are infant psychiatric syndromes, and it is possible to designate them in the current American Psychiatric Association–sponsored diagnostic scheme (DSM-III 1980), there are unanswered questions about predictability and there are concerns about the untoward social effects of psychiatric labeling. But germane to our topic is a professional dissatisfaction: we tend to overdiagnose illness and underdiagnose health. Critics have voiced the opinion that statistically we have ended up calling far too many people "ill"—thus encroaching on what is expectable or average in life and what is, in effect, adaptation to environmental change. The public has reacted vigorously against the latter tendency, particularly in Europe where it is often viewed as an inappropriate assumption by those seeking to gain "power" through medical diagnosis. Diagnostic trends, including thresholds for "abnormality," are partly influenced by the availability of services, by economic conditions, and by political reality. It is a larger aspect of a transactional view to realize that when economic conditions are more stringent or when a conservative attitude predominates, there is often a tendency to consider more as normal and less as abnormal.

Appropriately, we end with a view from parents. For mothers and fathers, individuality is more important than normality. Expectations deriving from what is normal according to any of the four perspectives can be misleading and can interfere with a caregiver's getting to know his or her particular baby who, in many respects, is like no other baby in the world. Perhaps there is some irony in our realizing that for parents, it is respect for individuality that is natural and "normal," not concern for what is normal in general. We must not forget that it is in appreciating individuality that wonderment occurs. From this, love develops.

REFERENCES

Anders, T.; Emde, R.; and Parmelee, A., eds. 1971. *A Manual of Standardized Terminology, Techniques and Criteria for Scoring States of Sleep and Wakefulness in Newborn Infants.* Los Angeles: UCLA Brain Information Service, NINDS Neurological Information Network.

Bates, J. E. 1980. "The Concept of Difficult Temperament." *Merrill-Palmer Quarterly:* 299–319.

Bayley, N. 1933. *The California First-Year Mental Scale.* Berkeley, Calif.: University of California Press.

————. 1969. *Bayley Scales of Infant Development.* New York: The Psychological Corporation.

————. 1970. "Development of Mental Abilities." In *Carmichael's Manual of Child Psychology,* ed. P. H. Mussen, vol. 1, pp. 1163–1209. New York: John Wiley & Sons.

Bell, R. Q., and Harper, L. V. 1977. *Child Effects on Adults.* Hillsdale, N.J.: Lawrence Erlbaum Associates.

Bell, R. Q., and Hertz, T. W. 1976. "Toward More Comparability and Generalizability of Developmental Research." *Child Development* 47:6–13.

Benjamin, J. D. 1959. "Prediction and Psychopathological Theory." In *Dynamic Psychopathology in Childhood,* ed. L. Jessner and E. Pavenstedt, pp. 6–77. New York: Grune & Stratton.

Bertalanffy, L. von. 1968. *Organismic Psychology Theory.* Barre, Mass.: Clark University Press with Barre Publishers.

Binet, A., and Simon T. 1905. "Methodes nouvelles pour le diagnostic du niveau intellectual des anormaux." *L'Année Psychologique* 11:191.

————. 1908. "Le développement de l'intelligence chez les enfants." *L'Année Psychologique* 14:1.

Block, J. 1971. *Lives Through Time.* Berkeley, Calif.: Bancroft Books.

Bowlby, J. 1969. *Attachment and Loss, vol. 1: Attachment.* New York: Basic Books.

————. 1973. *Attachment and Loss, vol. 2: Separation: Anxiety and Anger.* New York: Basic Books.

————. 1981. *Attachment and Loss, vol. 3: Loss: Sadness and Depression.* New York: Basic Books.

Brazelton, T. B. 1961. "Psychophysiologic Reaction in the Neonate. II. The Effects of Maternal Medication on the Neonate and His Behavior." *Journal of Pediatrics* 58:513–18.

————. 1973. *Neonatal Behavioral Assessment Scale.* London: Heinemann Medical Books.

Bridger, W. H., and Birns, B. 1963. "Neonate's Behavioral and Autonomic Responses to Stress During Soothing." *Recent Advances in Biological Psychiatry* 5:1–6.

Broman, S. H.; Nichols, P. L.; and Kennedy, W. A. 1975. *Preschool I.Q.: Prenatal and Early Developmental Correlates.* New York: John Wiley & Sons.

Bronfenbrenner, U. 1977. "Toward an Experimental Ecology of Human Development." *American Psychologist,* July, 513–31.

Brooks, J., and Weinraub, M. 1976. "A History of Infant Intelligence Testing." In *Origins of Intelligence,* ed. M. Lewis, pp. 19–58. New York: Plenum.

Buhler, C. 1930. *The First Year of Life.* New York: John Day.

Buss, A. H., and Plomin, R. A. 1975. *A Temperament Theory of Personality Development.* New York: John Wiley & Sons.

Carey, W. B. 1972. "Clinical Applications of Infant Temperament." *Journal of Pediatrics* 81:823–26.

Cattell, P. 1940. *The Measurement of Intelligence of Infants and Young Children.* New York: The Psychological Corporation.

Corah, N. L., et al. 1965. "Effects of Perinatal Anoxia After Seven Years." *Psychological Monographs,* vol. 79, no. 596.

Cosati, I., and Lezine, I. 1968. *Les étapes de l'intelligence sensori-motrice.* Paris: Les éditions du centre de psychologie appliquée.

Darwin, C. 1859. *The Origin of Species.* London: John Murray.

―――. 1877. "A Biological Sketch of an Infant." *Mind* 2:285–94.

―――. [1872] 1965. *The Expression of the Emotions in Man and Animals.* Chicago: University of Chicago Press.

Decarie, T. 1969. "A Study of the Mental and Emotional Development of the Thalidomide Child." In *Determinants of Infant Behavior,* ed. B. Foss, vol. 4, pp. 167–87. London: Methuen.

Diagnostic and Statistical Manual of Mental Disorders (DSM-III), 3rd ed. 1980. Washington, D.C.: American Psychiatric Association.

Emde, R. N. 1978. "Commentary." In "Organization and Stability of Newborn Behavior: A Commentary on the Brazelton Neonatal Behavior Assessment Scale," ed. A. J. Sameroff, pp. 135–38, *Monographs of the Society for Research in Child Development,* vol. 43, nos. 5–6.

―――. 1980. "Emotional Availability: A Reciprocal Reward System for Infants and Parents with Implications for Prevention of Psychosocial Disorders." In *Parent-Infant Relationship,* ed. R. M. Taylor, pp. 87–115. New York: Grune & Stratton.

Emde, R. N., and Robinson, J. 1979. "The First Two Months: Recent Research in Developmental Psychobiology and the Changing View of the Newborn." In *American Handbook of Child Psychiatry,* ed. J. Noshpitz and J. D. Call, vol. 1, pp. 72–105. New York: Basic Books.

Emde, R. N.; Gaensbauer, T. J.; and Harmon, R. J. 1976. "Emotional Expression in Infancy; A Biobehavioral Study." *Psychological Issues* vol. 10, no. 37.

Escalona, S. K. 1968. *The Roots of Individuality.* Chicago: Aldine.

Escalona, S. K., and Corman, H. "Albert Einstein Scales of Sensorimotor Development." Unpublished.

Escalona, S. K., and Heider, G. M. 1959. *Prediction and Outcome.* Menninger Clinic Monograph Series, No. 14. London: Imago.

Fraiberg, S. 1968. "Parallel and Divergent Patterns in Blind and Sighted Patients." *Psychoanalytic Study of the Child* 23:264–300.

―――. 1977. *Insights from the Blind: Developmental Studies of Blind Children.* Basic Books: New York.

Freud, A., and Burlingham, D. 1944. *Infants Without Families; The Case for and Against Residential Nurseries.* New York: International Universities Press.

Freud, S. [1900] 1953. "The Interpretation of Dreams." In *The Standard Edition of the Complete Psychological Works of Sigmund Freud* (hereafter *Standard Edition*), ed. J. Strachey vols. 4–5. London: Hogarth Press.

―――. [1905] 1953. "Three Essays on the Theory of Sexuality." In *Standard Edition,* ed. J. Strachey and A. Freud, vol. 7, pp. 125–245. London: Hogarth Press.

―――. [1920] 1955. "Beyond the Pleasure Principle." In *Standard Edition,* ed. J. Strachey, vol. 18, pp. 3–64. London: Hogarth Press.

―――. [1926] 1959. "Inhibitions, Symptoms, and Anxiety." In *Standard Edition,* vol. 20. London: Hogarth Press.

Gesell, A., and Amatruda, C. 1941. *Developmental Diagnosis.* New York: Paul B. Hoeber.

Gesell, A., et al. 1940. *The First Five Years of Life.* New York: Harper.

Gilliand, A. R. 1949. *The Northwestern Intelligence Tests: Examiner's Manual, Test A: Test for Infants 4–12 Weeks Old.* Boston: Houghton Mifflin.

―――. 1951. *The Northwestern Intelligence Tests: Examiner's Manual, Test B: Test for Infants 13–36 Weeks Old.* Boston: Houghton Mifflin.

Goldsmith, H., and Campos, J. 1982. "Toward a Theory of Infant Temperament." In *The Development of Attachment and Affiliative Systems,* ed. R. N. Emde and R. J. Harmon, pp. 161–93. New York: Plenum.

Goodenough, F. L. 1949. *Mental Testing.* New York: Rinehart.

Graham, F. K.; Matarazzo, R. G.; and Caldwell, B. M. 1956. "Behavioral Differences Between Normal and Traumatized Newborns: II. Standardization, Reliability and Validity." *Psychological Monographs,* vol. 70, no. 428.

Graham, F. K., et al. 1962. "Development Three Years After Perinatal Anoxia and Other Potentially Damaging Newborn Experiences." *Psychological Monographs,* vol. 76, no. 522.

Greenberg, M., and Morris, N. 1974. "Engrossment: The Newborn's impact upon the Father." *American Journal of Orthopsychiatry* 44(4):520–31.

Greenberg, N. H. 1964. "Origins of Head-Rolling (Spasmus Nutans) During Early Infancy." *Psychosomatic Medicine* 26, no. 2:162–71.

Griffiths, R. 1954. *The Abilities of Babies.* London: University of London Press.

Honzik, M. P. 1976. "Value and Limitations of Infant Tests: An Overview." In *Origins of Intelligence,* ed. M. Lewis, pp. 59–95. New York: Plenum.

Horowitz, F. D.; Sullivan, J. W.; and Linn, P. 1978. "Stability and Instability in the Newborn Infant: The Quest for Elusive Threads." In "Organization and Stability of Newborn Behavior: A Commentary on the Brazelton Neonatal Behavior Assessment Scale," ed. A. J. Sameroff, pp. 29–45, *Monographs of the Society for Research in Child Development,* vol. 43, nos. 5–6.

Howells, J. G. 1979. *Modern Perspectives in the Psychiatry of Infancy.* New York: Brunner/ Mazel.

Hutt, S. J.; Lenard, H. G.; and Prechtl, H. 1969. "Psychophysiological Studies in Newborn Infants." In *Advances in Child Development and Behavior,* ed. L. P. Lipsitt and H. W. Reese, vol. 4, pp. 127–72. New York: Academic Press.

Kagan, J., and Moss, H. A. 1962. *Birth to Maturity.* New York: John Wiley & Sons.

Kagan, J.; Kearsley, R. B.; and Zelazo, P. R., eds. 1978. *Infancy: Its Place in Human Development.* Cambridge, Mass.: Harvard University Press.

Kessen, W.; Haith, M. M.; and Salapatek, P. H. 1970. "Human Infancy: A Bibliography and Guide." In *Carmichael's Manual of Child Psychology,* 3rd ed., P. Mussen, vol. 1, pp. 287–445. New York: John Wiley & Sons.

Klaus, M. H., and Kennell, J. H. 1976. *Maternal Infant Bonding.* St. Louis: C. V. Mosby.

Korner, A. F. 1964. "Some Hypotheses Regarding the Significance of Individual Differences at Birth for Later Development." *Psychoanalytic Study of the Child* 19:58–72.

Kuhlmann, F. 1911. "Binet and Simon's System for Measuring the Intelligence of Children." *Journal of Psycho-asthenics* 15:76.

Levy, D. 1937 "Primary Affect Hunger." *American Journal of Psychiatry* 94:643–52.

Lewis, M. 1976. "What Do We Mean When We Say 'Infant Intelligence Scores'? A Sociopolitical Question." In *Origins of Intelligence,* ed. M. Lewis, pp. 1–18. New York: Plenum.

Lorenz, K. Z. 1943. "Die angregorenen Formen Möglicher Erfahrung." *Zeitschrift für Tierpsychologie* 5:235–409.

Lubchenco, L. 1976. *The High Risk Infant.* Philadelphia: W. B. Saunders.

McCall, R. B. 1979. "The Development of Intellectual Functioning in Infancy and the Prediction of Later I.Q." In *Handbook of Infant Development,* ed. J. D. Osofsky, pp. 707–41. New York: John Wiley & Sons.

McCall, R. B.; Eichorn, D. H.; and Hogarty, P. S. 1977. "Transitions in Early Mental Development." *Monographs of the Society for Research in Child Development* 42:1–108.

Maccoby, E. E., and Jacklin, C. N. 1980. "Sex Differences in Aggression: A Rejoinder and Reprise." *Child Development* 51:964–80.

Mahler, M. 1968. *On Human Symbiosis and the Vicissitudes of Individuation, vol. 1, Infantile Psychosis.* New York: International Universities Press.

Minuchin, S. 1974. *Families and Family Therapy.* Cambridge, Mass.: Harvard University Press.

Offer, D., and Sabshin, M. 1974. *Normality: Theoretical and Clinical Concepts of Mental Health.* New York: Basic Books.

Piaget, J. 1950. *Psychology of Intelligence.* London: Routledge & Kegan Paul.

Prechtl, H. F. R. 1977. *The Neurological Examination of the Full-term Infant,* 2nd ed. Clinics in Developmental Medicine No. 63. London: Spastics Society and Heinemann.

Prechtl, H. F. R., and Beintema, D. 1964. *The Neurological Examination of the Full-term Newborn Infant.* Little Club Clinics in Developmental Medicine, No. 12. London: Spastics Society and Heinemann.

Preyer, W. 1882. *The Mind of the Child.* New York: D. Appleton & Co.

Riegel, K. 1976. "The Dialectics of Human Development." *American Psychologist* 31:689–700.

Rosenblith, J. F. 1975. "Prognostic Value of Neonatal Behavioral Tests." In *Exceptional Infant, vol. 3: Assessment and Intervention,* ed. B. Z. Friedlander, G. M. Sterritt, and G. E. Kirk, pp. 157–72. New York: Brunner/Mazel.

Rutter, M., ed. 1980. *Scientific Foundations of Developmental Psychiatry.* London: Heinemann.

Saint-Anne Dargassies, S. 1977. *Neurological Development in the Full-term and Premature Neonate.* New York: Excerpta Medica.

Sameroff, A. J. 1978a. "Organization and Stability of Newborn Behavior: A Commentary on the Brazelton Neonatal Behavior Assessment Scale." *Monographs of the Society for Research in Child Development,* vol. 43, nos. 5–6.

———. 1978b. "Summary and Conclusions: The Future of Newborn Assessment." In "Organization and Stability of Newborn Behavior: A Commentary on the Brazelton Neonatal Behavior Assessment Scale," ed. A. J. Sameroff, pp. 102–17, *Monographs of the Society for Research in Child Development,* vol. 43, nos. 5–6.

Sameroff, A. J., and Chandler, M. 1975. "Reproductive Risk and the Continuum of Caretaking Casualty." In *Review of Child Development Research,* ed. F. D. Horowitz, vol. 4, pp. 187–244. Chicago: University of Chicago Press.

Sameroff, A. J., and Harris, A. E. 1980. "Dialectical Approaches to Early Thought and Language." In *Psychological Development from Infancy,* ed. M. H. Bornstein and W. Kessen, pp. 339–72. Hillsdale, N.J.: Lawrence Erlbaum Associates.

Sander, L. W. 1969. "The Longitudinal Course of Early Mother-Child Interaction: Cross Case Comparison in a Sample of Mother-Infant Pains." In *Determinants of Infant Behavior,* ed. B. M. Foss, vol. 4, pp. 189–227. London: Methuen.

Scarr, S., and Salapatek, P. 1970. "Patterns of Fear Development During Infancy." *Merrill-Palmer Quarterly* 16:53–90.

Shirley, M. 1933. *The First Two Years.* Minneapolis: University of Minnesota Press.

Spitz, R. 1945. "Hospitalism: An Inquiry into the Genesis of Psychiatric Conditions in Early Childhood." *Psychoanalytic Study of the Child* 1:53–74.

———. 1946. "Anaclitic Depression: An Inquiry into the Genesis of Psychiatric Conditions in Early Childhood, II," *Psychoanalytic Study of the Child* 2:313–42.

Spitz, R., and Wolf, K. M. 1946. "The Smiling Response: A Contribution to the Ontogenesis of Social Relations." *Genetic Psychology Monographs* 34:57–125.

Stechler, G., and Carpenter, G. 1967. "A Viewpoint on Early Affective Development." In *The Exceptional Infant,* ed. J. Hellmuth, vol. 1, pp. 163–89. Seattle: Special Care Publications.

Terman, L. M. 1916. *The Measurement of Intelligence.* Boston: Houghton Mifflin.

Thomas A. and Chess S. 1977. *Temperament and Development.* New York: Brunner/Mazel.

———. 1980. *The Dynamics of Psychological Development,* pp. 1–287. New York: Brunner/Mazel.

Thomas, A.; Chesni, Y.; and Saint-Anne Dargassies, S. 1960. *The Neurological Examination of the Infant.* Little Club Clinics in Developmental Medicine, no. 1. London: Spastics Society and Heinemann.

Uzgiris, I. C., and Hunt, J. McV. 1975. *Assessment in Infancy.* Urbana, Ill.: University of Illinois Press.

Waddington, C. 1940. *Organizers and Genes.* Cambridge: Cambridge University Press.

Werner, E. E.; Bierman, J. M.; and French, F. E. 1971. *The Children of Kauai: A Longitudinal Study from the Prenatal Period up to Age 10.* Honolulu: University of Hawaii Press.

Wilson, R. 1978. Presentation to the Louisville Conference on Temperament, Louisville, Kentucky.

Wolff, P. 1959. "Observations on Newborn Infants." *Psychosomatic Medicine* 21:110–18.

———. 1966. "The Causes, Controls and Organization of Behavior in the Neonate." *Psychological Issues,* no. 17. New York: International Universities Press.

2

Bennett L. Leventhal
and Kenneth Dawson

Middle Childhood: Normality as Integration and Interaction

Introduction

In describing the period of childhood—equivalent, in the United States, to the years between three and twelve—it is particularly important to consider "normality" and the empirical data that define it. For the first time in the life span, during childhood what is "normal" or "abnormal" can be poignantly and consciously crucial to the growing individual, as well as to the adults around him or her. The child is self-aware and self-conscious. To differ significantly from the norm (in any direction) can be a psychological burden to the child—if only because the very fact of the difference entails social consequences and sometimes damaging self-labeling. To be exceptional in childhood may mean to be unacceptable. What is the norm (or, at least, perceived as such) looms large in the lives of children and parents.

From among the various aspects of the concept of normality (Offer and Sabshin 1974), some are readily suited to the subject of this chapter. The

The authors wish to thank Zanvel E. Klein, Ph.D., Theresa Pestrak, M.A., and Mrs. LaJune Whitney for their valuable assistance in the preparation of this chapter.

relatively recent conceptualization of normal childhood as a transactional *system* (see, e.g., Sameroff 1975) has had extraordinary impact on developmental psychology. Although by no means the final word on the subject, the idea of childhood as a system has opened for study the constant interplay of parent and youngster—for instance, their accommodation to one another and the "goodness of fit." The pitfall of "nature vs. nurture," previously a serious hazard in thinking about how human organisms grow, was hard to avoid until the systems approach was elaborated and penetrated scientific consciousness.

We are fortunate, as well, in now having considerable hard data from both cross-sectional and longitudinal studies on normal development in children. It has become traditional, perhaps, to bemoan the fact that the studies vary in quality and in scope, that they almost always are uncoordinated with one another and rarely replicated, and that they too frequently depend on instruments of questionable reliability and validity. Nonetheless, it remains the case that we can talk now with unparalleled assurance of "average" values along many important dimensions of growth in children. In that sense of "normal," we undoubtedly know much more today than we did in the past about what to expect in children and what is (or should usually be) "good enough." Much of what will be discussed in this chapter is drawn from a number of large-scale studies of children, some of which have a history of three generations of both subjects and investigators.

Normality as *health* or as an utopian ideal for which one is constantly groping is probably of relatively less interest to students of childhood. We have already conceded, by implication, that to the child or parent, the *meaning* of some recognizable deviation cannot be dismissed; certainly, all of us carry around notions of "health" and "illness" that have a powerful affective charge and influence over behavior. For the more aloof scientific observer, nonetheless, "health" in childhood is a rather clumsy notion—particularly in the psychological domain. One hesitates to use it when characterizing an individual because it is altogether likely that one psychological function (e.g., intelligence) can be well developed at the same time that an equally significant function (e.g., social skills) lags well behind the average. What is more, any one psychological attribute is hard to trace over time in a rapidly developing individual. To the extent that it can be traced, an attribute often undergoes remarkable swings in its "maturity" relative to other functions (see Wenar 1982). One is understandably reluctant to speak of good and ill health when the characteristic in question is so volatile.

Clinicians know not only how unstable over time are some of the characteristics of children, but also that they are subject to particular settings. Thus the Isle of Wight studies (Rutter et al. 1970), which investigated a large cohort of children and, among other things, looked at where the youngsters were showing problems, found that some children did well at home but poorly in school; for others, exactly the opposite was true. For children with psychological difficulties, in other words, it was relatively *unusual* for the problems to be ubiquitous. This fact has been noted in connection with evaluating the efficacy of therapeutic interventions with children. Behavioral approaches, for example, are often (unjustly) criticized or praised on the basis of symptom relief that does not generalize across settings (see Wahler 1969).

Findings such as these raise the potentially devastating objection that it makes no sense altogether to speak of "normal" or "abnormal" behavior in children without specifying (at least) where the behavior or psychological characteristic manifests itself. The reply that the data transcend setting because they were gathered randomly is probably not true, in the first place, and, if true, likely to obscure—not just neutralize—the contributions of setting to the appearance and maintenance of the individual's psychological function. Indeed, this objection makes its claim because of the very force of the idea we have endorsed—that normality is a transactional system.

It should be noted, as well, that "normality" is not a standard that is reached by majority decision. As we have already suggested, it is very much in the eyes of the beholder. The Isle of Wight studies showed clearly, for instance, that families varied markedly as to what (in some "absolute" sense) tipped the child's behavior over the threshold into abnormality (Rutter et al. 1970). Some families seemed unbelievably tolerant of a child's acting out; others were impressively thin-skinned and worried about behavior that most families would probably hardly have noticed. In this regard, how and why different individuals/families learn, adopt, and abandon standards of judgment are interesting questions but not relevant to our current endeavor. *That* they do, however, is very much to the point. The clinician sees the judgment of normality itself as clinically meaningful and, therefore, of importance. It is of keen interest to the clinician why and when a particular incident or behavior "tips the balance" and brings the child into the limelight of parental worry or the "pink slip" of pedagogic concern.

On the matter of "normal" childhood, the clinical enterprise has clearly benefited simply from viewing the young patient from the perspective of normal growth (see A. Freud 1981). There has been, in fact, a confluence of interest in this regard. Psychologists sometimes find themselves studying psychopathological conditions in children so as to better understand the more usual course of development, while psychotherapists are by now familiar faces and serious investigators in the arenas of normal childhood—the hospital nursery, the home, the preschool, and the day care center. It is hard to know which of the disciplines—developmental psychology or clinical psychology and psychiatry—has stepped farthest into the traditional domain of the other. At this point, the borders are blurred.

The outlook of the clinician (as well as his or her experience) is singularly advantageous to pursuing the subject of normality in childhood. Although this chapter will, in general, stay clear of clinical material and discussions, it is nonetheless informed by the authors' experience in looking at the "whole child" (a tired phrase but one still worth retaining). Perhaps no endeavor more than the medical/psychiatric forces one to take seriously the task of integrating conflicting models of behavior, layers of explanation, and strategies of intervention and influence. What is an absolute necessity in psychiatric practice is of equal interest in understanding the forces behind and the nature of normality in childhood in general.

Childhood development is the sum of a group of functions, ultimately grounded in molecular and biological forces, whose phenotypes are shaped by the individual's previous experiences, the current milieu, and the pressures of interplay at any point in time with other developmental functions struggling for expression. In the following pages, we have chosen to discuss (from among the virtually limitless number of variables) a representative cluster of aspects of normal development in childhood.

We start with "biological" development; under this heading are included neurological and physical growth and unfolding. Biology is the substrate of all development. At the next level are the developmental functions that most immediately represent the integration of "simpler" biological growth and maturation. These elemental functions include motoric behavior and cognitive, moral, affective, and language development. The mélange of achievements in these areas determines, to an important extent, the nature of development at the next higher level—that of social, interpersonal behavior (broadly conceived) and the quality and nature of internal, subjective experiences.

This chapter is not intended to be comprehensive, but rather to be a model for a conceptual approach to normality in childhood. From among the possible alternatives, a limited number of topics have been selected for two interrelated reasons. They have, first of all, attracted the attention of researchers (there are good data on these variables, in other words). Second, although they are not the only areas of importance, no survey of children in general (or even of a specific child) could ignore any of these variables. They are of proven importance to parents, teachers, clinicians, and children themselves.

How we go from the substrate to the apparent, outer layer—from the simple to the complex, the unitary to the multiple, the objective to the subjective—is a perennial problem. We shall mention examples where the integrations seem particularly apt or easily attempted. We leave to the end of the chapter a review of what has been discussed and the more problematic venture of putting it all together.

Biological Development

Biological functions are the foundation of human existence. The complex biochemical and physiologic processes make higher level integrated activities possible. These biological forces are neither static nor isolated from the development process. "Normal" biological development has schedules that impact on higher levels of function and are themselves affected by experience and environment. The biological characteristics of the individual child (or adult), the strengths or weaknesses, are the primary determinants of the individual's adaptive capacity and hence his or her ability to function. The "goodness of fit" between the individual's biology and ecology may be the most critical aspect of normality.

Biological measures are plentiful, and biological measures of "normal" development are increasingly available. This remarkable quantity of data, however, may reflect nothing more significant than the ease of measurement, rather than have general significance to the functioning individual. The direct social and behavioral impact of most biological measures remains unclear.

GENERAL SOMATIC DEVELOPMENT

A child's general physical appearance is often the initial and most obvious basis for the development of environmental responses to him or her. Physical attractiveness and overt manifestations of gender affect the full spectrum of interactions between individuals. For the child emerging into the social world outside the family, responses to physical appearance may have substantial impact on other aspects of development.

There are normative values for *somatic* physical development. These are primarily derived from either longitudinal studies or from cross-sectional samples of large numbers of children. The tabulations yield statistical definitions of height and weight, for example. These so-called norms tell us little about how certain physical attributes came to be and what their impact will be on the lives of the children. As any school-teacher can verify, there are significant interindividual variations in physical growth. Exogenous factors such as nutrition, physical activity, illness, and socioeconomic status may affect an individual's physical development. However, genetic endowment is the most important determinant of growth. Parental size and gender are powerful predictors of the future size of the child.

Unlike the prenatal period, infancy, and adolescence—which normally are characterized by fast growth and differentiation of organ systems—childhood is a time of regular but limited growth. Although the velocity of general somatic growth is quite rapid from birth to age two, it declines substantially between three and five years, settling into a pattern of limited growth. Almost 50 percent of adult somatic growth is achieved by most children at ages three to five (Tanner 1962). Most body measurements—such as trunk height, the majority of skeletal and muscular dimensions—and internal organs—such as liver, spleen, and kidney—follow this general growth pattern.

Most growth occurs by increases in cell number and cell size, but different systems grow differently. Additional growth and organization is accomplished by increase in cell size (Brasel and Gruen 1978; Wolff 1984). In skeletal muscle, the increase in cell number continues only through adolescence, whereas in the liver and heart the proliferation continues into adulthood. The predominant type of growth (increased numbers or increased size) is a factor in determining vulnerability to environmental stresses. Rapidly dividing cells are more sensitive to toxins and other stressors. Hence "normal" somatic adaptability may be determined by the particular phase of growth an organ system is experiencing.

There are significant exceptions to the general pattern of somatic growth. For example, lymphoid tissues continue to grow rapidly throughout childhood, attaining almost twice the adult volume by the beginning of puberty. This developmental characteristic enhances the child's capacity to resist infections and the sequelae of the bumps and bruises of active childhood exploration.

The relatively large proportion of protective, subcutaneous fat of infancy peaks at about one year and then declines. Even though adipose cells increase in number until about age six, the percent of body fat declines after the first year of life, accounting for the substantial difference in appearance in the toddler and the leaner, trimmer, school-age child. In late childhood, this pattern once again changes, allowing for increased fat accumulation in physiologic anticipation of puberty. Girls normatively have more fat, and a gender gap becomes more evident as adolescence approaches. This difference in growth and distribution leads to the radical divergence in physical appearance that signals the end of childhood.

Gender differences are notable but their overall significance is unclear. For example, girls reach 50 percent of their adult height slightly sooner than do boys, but they start puberty and stop growing earlier. This may account for the "normative" difference in somatic growth potential between the sexes.

General physiologic function reaches nearly adult levels during childhood. Cardiac rates decline from 100 beats per minute (bpm) at age two to 80 bpm by late childhood. Kidney and bone marrow functions stabilize by five or six years. Basal metabolic rates decline throughout childhood despite the child's increasing activity (Sinclair 1969). At the same time, pulmonary capacity increases throughout childhood, allowing for increased oxygen/carbon dioxide exchange necessitated by this activity.

In sum, the general somatic growth of the child expands during childhood but in a relatively slow fashion. While the differences between age three and ten are noticeable, one year's growth in childhood does not make as substantial a difference as a comparable time period in infancy or adolescence.

Few studies have related somatic growth to psychological development. There is some evidence that larger, taller, and earlier maturing children score higher on tests of intellectual development, are more assertive, and have more self-confidence than smaller, shorter, later maturing children (Jones 1965). Both clinical experience and some harder data (see, for example, Brackbill and Nevill 1981; Faust 1960; Weatherly 1964) attest to the fact that there can be a certain amount of psychological cost associated in childhood with being noticeably tall or short or slim or heavy. Children at the extremes of the distribution of the physical growth curve seem to show up disproportionately in psychiatric facilities. It is not known whether a cause-and-effect relationship exists between advanced physical maturation and improved psychological and intellectual functioning or whether both are a result of other (perhaps common) factors governing positive adaptation.

NEUROBIOLOGICAL DEVELOPMENT

Neurobiological development encompasses a broad number of developmental lines that account for interactions between the child and his or her environment. Neurobiological studies are tantalizing because they provide quantitative measures of the substances that give life to the personality and psyche.

Developmental neurobiology is a relatively new discipline. Certainly, detailed studies of the child's developing nervous system have just begun. Meaningful descriptive data are not abundant.

Neuroanatomic studies have the longest history. The neonate's brain is 25 percent of adult weight. Brain weight increases rapidly from birth to 70 percent of adult weight at two years, 90 percent at five years, and 95 percent by ten years of age (Tanner 1978). For behavior, total brain weight *per se*, is of only limited significance. Instead, maturational patterns of specific areas are more likely to have functional implications. Regional patterns of myelinization are an indication of regional patterns of brain maturation.

Investigators have observed the the brain can be divided into three zones that mature at different rates (Trevarthen 1974; Yakovlev and Lecours 1967.) The median zone, which includes the thalamus and hypothalamus, begins myelinization just before birth and continues past age ten into puberty. These areas govern and process visceral activity and hormonal functions. In the paramedian zone, including the limbic cortex and basal ganglia, myelinization begins just after birth but is completed before age ten. This area controls expressive vocalization and extrapyramidal motor functions such as postural and automatic movements. Finally, the supralimbic zone of the cerebral cortex also begins myelinization soon after birth, but supralimbic development continues well into the fourth decade. This observation suggests that normal neurobiological development continues until later into life and that cortical development has the longest interval of change. The implications of this are unclear. This prolonged development may indicate increased potential for flexibility and adaptation. But it may also involve greater vulnerability to developmental interferences and later psychopathology.

The variability in the maturation of different neurological systems (Yakovlev and Lecours 1967) seems to be coordinated with the sequence and pattern of developing abilities and skills in the normal child. The myelinization of the optic nerves and visual association areas at three to four months of age, for instance, corresponds to the onset of a specific visually based social awareness in the neonate in the presence of the social smile response. Similarly, motor and sensory nerve roots myelinate by the sixth month and basic cortical connections are in place at twelve months to allow for locomotion.

Unfortunately, as higher level integrated functions develop, some specific anatomic maturational correlates become more difficult to identify. Auditory function appears to mature by age four along with the cerebellar peduncles. This latter area is also involved in control of the balance and fine-motor skills that are so essential for the relatively sophisticated play and other activities of the preschool and early school-age child.

The development of more extensive neural networks seems temporally related to increasing cognitive and more complex social functions. The myelinization of long association and commisural fiber tracts is not completed until late childhood. These systems participate in the transfer of information between the cerebral hemispheres and are, therefore, important for facilitating utilization of right and left brain functions. Other tracts responsible for integrated functions do not myelinate until adolescence or later. For example, the reticular formation, which regulates arousal levels and attentional ability, does not mature until adolescence. Similarly, callosal fibers and some cortical association areas do not fully mature until adulthood.

Finally, neuroanatomic studies indicate that cortical maturation follows discrete patterns. Studies of cerebral cortex maturation by Conel and Rabinowicz (1979) complement the investigations of Yakovlev and Lecours. Instead of neuronal myelination, however, they measured parameters including cerebral cortex thickness, neuronal density, and histological evolution. They too found evidence of regional and systemic patterns of maturation. Each cerebral lobe, each area of each lobe, and each layer of each area had discrete developmental rates. Depending on the cortical area, there was also a degree of individual variation. The primary visual area and the motor center of speech seemed to develop at about the same rate in everyone. However, other areas, such as the receptive and conductive speech centers, showed marked variation from one person to another.

Other findings reported by Rabinowicz were that all layers reach a similar state of maturation for the first time between fifteen months and two years of age. At age six there is a decrease in total thickness and an increase in the number of nerve cells in most areas. As development progresses, this process of cerebral remodeling is followed by increased thickness and decreased cell density. In most areas, by the time the individual is between eight and ten years of age, cortical thickness begins to approach that of the adult.

The neuroanatomic development shows substantial changes in childhood. Though the changes are not as dramatic as those seen in infancy, they seem to set the anatomic base for the increasingly complex functions of adolescence and beyond.

NEUROPHYSIOLOGY

Neurophysiologic assessment is methodologically problematic. Although a number of peripheral measures have been developed, the electroencephalogram (EEG) remains the best-studied direct central measure of neurophysiologic functioning. While fundamentally measuring superficial cortical function, the EEG still allows for a glimpse at central electrophysiologic maturation. Newer techniques such as evoked brainstem potential and Brain Electrical Activity Mapping (BEAM) (Duffy, Burchfiel, and Lombroso 1979) allow for more direct, sensitive appreciation of developmental processes.

Studies of EEGs of normal children reveal maturational changes with age, most of which can be documented during sleep. As with neuroanatomical findings, there is individual variation without known pathology. In newborns, the average duration of sleep is sixteen hours, of which 50 percent is REM (Roffwarg, Musio, and Dement 1966). Sleep at birth is also characterized by rapid onset of REM sleep. The latency of the onset of REM increases during infancy and is about three to four hours in the four-and-one-half to seven-year-old age group. REM latency decreases as children mature further. By midadolescence, it is at the adult level (fifty to seventy minutes). There are also other shifts in the organization of sleep during childhood. At about age three months, there is a change from disorganized infantile sleep patterns to the beginning of more mature forms (Metcalf and Jordan 1972). By age two, children average thirteen hours of sleep, 25 percent of which is REM. This decreases to eleven hours by age four and to about ten hours by age eight. As the child gets older, the percent of REM time remains about the same while the duration of sleep decreases.

The significance of REM sleep is unclear. It has been associated with dreaming, but the role and importance of dreaming lacks substantial empirical study, particularly in children. Electrical evidence of "pre-dreaming" reportedly begins at about twelve months, and children frequently recount the first dream experience by eighteen to twenty-four months (Metcalf 1979). It is unknown whether this reflects psychological growth, increased language development, or some other phenomenon.

Other changes in sleep architecture occur with maturation. Several EEG changes take place at age five to six months. K complexes are clearly distinguishable, well-formed sleep spindles appear unmistakably, and drowsy hypersynchrony is first seen. The latter continues to be seen normally until about age six (Metcalf 1979). There is some controversy about sleep spindle activity during the second year. Metcalf and Jordan (1972) have reported an increase in sleep spindle activity during this time, but Tanguay and associates (1975), for example, found a decrease at age one that persisted until age five.

The second half of the first year marks the first appearance of high-voltage delta waves, indicating Stage 3–4 sleep (Anders 1981). By age three in normal children, most of the structural organization of sleep states has been completed. By age five, the diurnal sleep-wake cycle is achieved and the afternoon nap can be missed (Anders, Carskadon, and Dement 1980).

Other aspects of the EEG have been investigated. Waking rhythms have been of some interest. However, like sleep records, there is sufficient "normal" variation to make it difficult to arrive at conclusions other than the fact that EEG patterns and responses vary with age and thus represent a developmental process that requires further study.

NEUROENDOCRINOLOGY

Childhood neuroendocrine function is of particular interest. The psychoanalytic concept of latency in a physiologic and psychologic sense would suggest a relative inactivity of sex hormones in this age range. On the other hand, the clearer separation of male and female behavior in childhood has to be accounted for.

Neuroendocrine studies indicate that the hypothalamic-pituitary-gonadotropin-gonadal system operates in infancy but is suppressed during childhood to a low level of activity (Grumbach 1978). This system regulates reproductive function. Adrenal mechanisms, a second system involved in the secretion of the androgens, becomes activated at about age eight in both girls and boys. The activation of this system and its role in puberty are now well understood, although "adrenarche" does *not* seem to be necessary for normal puberty to occur (Reiter and Grumbach 1982).

Centrally, the arcuate nucleus of the medial basal-hypothalamus appears to be the control center for gonadotropin-releasing hormone stimulation, although other parts of the brain such as the limbic system also have some influence. According to Reiter and Grumbach (1982), the arcuate pulse generator is highly functional after twelve days of age. Gonadotropins are released episodically with transient increases in testosterone in males until age six months and estradiol in females until the child is a year old. This activity declines until puberty.

Animal studies suggest that male or female mechanisms, such as phasic output of luteinizing hormone in adult females, develop due to the presence or absence of particular sex hormones in infancy. The development of male or female sexual behavior also seems to depend, at least to some extent, on hormonal influences (MacKinnon 1979). With age, the hypothalamic-pituitary-gonadotropin-gonadal system becomes extremely sensitive to negative feedback of gonadotropins; maximum sensitivity is reached at ages two to four, with intrinsic central nervous system inhibition of gonadotropin-releasing hormone greatest at about age four. This low level of gonadotropins and sex-hormone release continues until the late prepubertal period.

Sex hormones are not the sole product of the neuroendocrine system. Except for the growth hormone effect on stature, the activity of the other hormones in childhood is not unique to that stage of development. However, the sex hormones and perhaps the other neuroendocrine products may have indirect efforts on developing children. For example, the relatively brief exposure to sex hormones during gestation and infancy may (and most likely does) set the stage for the sex-associated differences in behavior that are noted in childhood and later. In particular, hemispheric lateralization differences between males and females (discussed in the following section) may be functionally related to this early hormonal exposure.

Therefore, there does not appear to be a major direct role for neuroendocrine systems in childhood. In sum, further research will most likely reveal a plateau of secondary phenomena. Although the notion of latency as a period of quiescence of "sexual" development may be supported in the broadest physiologic sense, both psychological and physiological processes continue and do not demonstrate anything more than a period of relative inactivity.

NEUROPSYCHOLOGY

Neuropsychological studies of children are a relatively new phenomenon. Previously, the discipline now called "neuropsychology" had been primarily interested in pathological states and not in normals. Recent studies have focused on the highest levels of human psychobiological functioning in the cerebral hemispheres. Particular attention has been directed at hemispheric specialization and interhemispheric communication, i.e., these studies considered where specialized functions reside in the brain and how these functions are implemented in coordination with other neural functioning. Among the many studies there have been attempts to identify where and how language and motor functions evolve, what are the sex differences in hemispheric development, and whether differential hemispheric function correlates with the behavioral differences between the sexes (see Maccoby and Jacklin, 1974, for an overview).

In most cases, one of the two cerebral hemispheres appears to have dominance. This generally correlates with handedness, thus leading to the usual case in which right-handed individuals demonstrate left-hemispheric dominance and left-handed individuals demonstrate right-hemispheric dominance. Dominance is not an absolute term, however. Indeed, there are varying degrees of dominance. For example, the left-hemispheric dominance of right-handers is generally greater than right-hemispheric dominance of left-handers. Additionally, certain cerebral functions appear to be relegated primarily to either the dominant or nondominant hemisphere. For most right-handed people, the dominant left hemisphere is largely responsible for analytical and logical cognitive functions such as language and mathematics. Conversely, the nondominant right hemisphere is more responsible for holistic or Gestalt perception and affective responses that would be manifested in such areas as art and music. Despite the apparent hemispheric specialization, the hemispheres collaborate in producing whole responses of the individual (Galin 1974). The extent of collaboration and relative dominance of the collaborating cerebral partners make for percepts and responses that differ from person to person.

The development of hemispheric specialization is not well understood. Some investigators now feel that each individual's pattern of cerebral organization is "preprogrammed" in infancy (Caplan and Kinsbourne 1981). There is evidence, for example, of asymmetric anatomical development of speech areas in infants (Wada, Clarke, and Hamm 1975; Witelson and Pallie 1973) and for the existence of lateralization even at birth (Eimas et al. 1971; Siqueland and Lipsitt 1966). Certainly both speech output and language decoding appear to be fully lateralized by age three (White and Kinsbourne 1980).

Lenneberg (1967) has argued that the development of hemispheric specialization is the result of experience. A somewhat less extreme position is that hemispheric specialization is preprogrammed but that individual preferences are developed by experience with a particular mode of problem solving. However, the child's preferred cognitive mode is not necessarily consistent with the "preprogrammed" hemispheric specialization. For example, at times a left-dominant child might prefer to use a right-dominant style of approach to a particular school task such as reading. As a result, the child might not become as good a reader as a child who is right dominant but assumes a left-dominant approach to reading.

Interestingly, there appear to be significant differences between boys and girls in terms of left and right hemisphere development. For girls, the left hemisphere matures earlier than it does in boys (Taylor 1969). This may be the result of generally earlier physical maturity in girls, but it is more likely due to a sexual dimorphism in the neural organization underlying cognition (Waber 1976; Witelson 1976).

Generally, girls are developmentally more advanced relative to boys in regard to cortical functions such as onset of speech, expressive language, speech articulation, and lateralization of speech perception. All of these activities are primarily associated with left-hemisphere specialization. Not only are girls more advanced than boys in speech, but they maintain this advantage throughout childhood (Garai and Scheinfeld 1968). Girls also demonstrate greater verbal fluency than do boys (Gaddes and Crockett 1975).

It has been reported that as early as age six boys perform in a manner consistent with right-hemisphere specialization (Witelson 1976). By eleven years of age, males generally perform better on functions with right hemispheric specialization such as spatial visualization and part-whole relationships (Wolff and Hurwitz 1976).

Caplan and Kinsbourne (1981) determined that girls surpass boys in their degree of verbal proficiency but that the difference between the sexes declined with increasing age. Regardless of age, greater preference for verbal strategies (not sheer verbal ability) was associated with better reading skills in children of both sexes.

Despite the apparent superiority of girls in verbal skills, their reading ability, as a group, is not superior to that of boys. The reasons for this remain unclear, but it has been suggested that cultural factors may influence some girls not to choose verbal strategies and therefore not to maximize their potential in reading (Maccoby and Jacklin 1974).

Hemispheric control and coordination of motor function also demonstrate significant sex differences. Because speech is such an integral part of language, it has been suggested that the lateralization of language and motor function may have a functional relationship. Indeed, hemispheric lateralization of language function may really be derivative of (or at least related to) specialization for fine-motor control (MacNeilage 1980).

Regarding motor development, girls, at least at earlier ages, seem to have the advantage. Until age eight, girls are superior to boys in a variety of both fine and gross motor skills. On tests of these skills (such as pegboards and rapidly repeated movements) girls continue to function better into their adolescence. Girls six to ten years of age are also consistently more accurate in keeping beat with a metronome (Wolff and Hurwitz 1976), which further illustrates these subtle differences between the genders in motor behavior.

Hand and sex differences decrease rapidly after age twelve, admittedly, but only for relatively easy tasks. On more difficult tasks, right-handed adult women continue to demonstrate better fine-motor control than do men. This implies that after age five the sex differences and right-left asymmetries of skilled motor performance are developmentally stable throughout life. However, there is also evidence that functions which involve hemispheric coordination may undergo transformation well into adulthood, an observation consistent with the evidence for myelinization of commissural tracts late in life (Wolff 1984).

NEUROTRANSMITTERS

The ultimate responsibility for the interneuronal transmission of information lies in the neurotransmitter systems. There are a number of known and putative neurotransmitters but studies of their relationship to specific functions or the process of development are limited. There are only very few studies of neurotransmitters in childhood. Some studies have suggested that at least some neurotransmitter systems do not mature until middle childhood or adolescence (e.g., Albright et al. 1983; Leckman et al. 1980). There appear to be some secondary indicators of developmental variability of neurotransmitter metabolism. (For example, monoamine oxidase activity decreases with age [Robinson el al. 1977].) However, there is little information available about the ontogeny of other neurotransmitters such as serotonin and norepinephrine or of opiates such as endorphins or enkephalins (Cohen and Young 1977).

Neurotransmitter correlates of childhood function remain to be clarified. The many unanswered questions about the role of neurotransmitters in learning, memory, and social function are the subject of considerable interest, but "normal" data are not yet available.

Simple measurement of neurobiological systems cannot account for the broad variations in adaptive human functioning. The complex interactions between social experiences and biology is interesting but not yet well studied in children.

Deprivation syndromes provide an interesting model for this problem. Separating the effects of social deprivation from its frequently concomitant experience, malnutrition, is a difficult task. The issue of malnutrition also raises the question of what constitutes nutrition adequate to support "normal development." On both of these issues there is considerable controversy. Malnutrition in human infants may lead to reduced head circumference and brain weight, which can be correlated, in turn, with a decrease in the number and size of brain cells (Balazs, Lewis, and Patel 1979). Similarly, animal studies indicate that malnutrition can affect myelinization, arborization of neuronal processes, and levels of neurotransmitters (McKhann, Coyle, and Benjamins 1973).

Rutter (1980) has noted that intellectual defects in children malnourished in infancy are not completely overcome by improved social and economic conditions. However, a recent study that attempted to control for social factors found that intellectual defects due to malnutrition in infancy can be completely overcome if the child is raised in supportive home and school environments (Beardslee et al. 1982). Whatever the individual roles of social and nutritional deprivation, it is clear that both severely limit the possibility of normal childhood.

The possible ameliorative effects of stimulating environments are related to the larger question of the effects of experience on nervous system development. Most data in this area come from animal studies. There is evidence to suggest that experiential factors *can* stimulate growth of neuronal processes, the formation of connections between neurons, and changes in synaptic function (Greenough 1975; Kandel 1979). Equally important is the question of whether experience (or lack of experience) during development is irreversible. Are there critical periods in development when relatively specific environmental events are essential to normal maturation? In animals, there do appear to be critical periods. For example, kittens deprived of visual stimuli never seem completely to overcome visual defects, even with later experience in normal light. This is thought to be due to lack of development of the visual processing area of the brain (Greenough 1975; Meyersburg and Post 1979).

The issue of critical periods in humans remains controversial. The human behavioral apparatus is much more resilient than was once thought (Kagan 1976; Wolff 1970), a state of affairs that tends to weigh against the notion of critical periods. Evidence to the contrary is, nonetheless, not lacking. There appears to be a time in infancy, for instance, when the absence of development of normal selective attachments prevents fully normal social development. Deprivation in infancy also leads to enduring linguistic and intellectual impairment (Rutter 1980). People who do not learn to read in childhood may never be able to read well. Gender identity, as well, appears to be irreversibly established by age two and one-half (Lewis 1982). It is known that the visual system in human infants is very sensitive to deprivation. Infants with monocular cataracts do not develop normal binocular vision if this defect is not corrected before age four months. Children with abnormal binocular interaction (strabismus) suffer permanent visual impairment if this condition is not treated before age five (Newell 1982).

That social interaction and experience play a key role in neurobiological development is almost certain. The specifics of this role, however, remain unclear, particularly for the developmental age of childhood. In any case, it is still essential that childhood be considered a period of development exquisitely sensitive to a wide spectrum of stimuli, social and otherwise. From a biological framework, childhood should not be considered a latent or quiet period of development but rather one during which the development of higher level, integrated functions is proceeding.

What are integrated functions? For the purposes of this chapter, integrated functions are those that require complex interactions between two or more fundamental components of the developing individual. It is a principle of development that the level and degree of these interactions progress with age in the developing individual. What follows is a brief examination of a few of these integrated functions.

Motor Development

Early research on the development of motor behavior in children concentrated on describing which motor abilities the "average" child acquires at certain ages. One of the best-known examples of this work is the series published by Arnold Gesell and his colleagues at Yale (e.g., Ames et al. 1979)—accounts based on cross-sectional studies of the expectable behaviors of children, including their motor behavior at different ages. They also devised instruments for developmental assessment that allow the clinician to rate an individual's progress in the acquisition and mastery of a variety of skills (e.g., Knobloch and Pasmanick 1974) and compare this progress to what the investigators had found to be "normal."

Several observers of the development of motor behavior in children have concluded that essential gross motor abilities develop during the first five years of life and then stabilize at the end of the fifth year (e.g., Hughes and Riley 1981). (There is evidence that perceptual abilities also coalesce at about this age [Powell and Gaines 1982].)

Motor behavior provides one of the clearest examples of the vicissitudes of normal developmental progress. For example, the eighteen-month-old can walk well and can even run but can't really kick a ball. The two-year-old can kick a ball but can't walk with a smooth gait. The three-year-old walks better but seems to become clumsier by three and one-half. The four-year-old is generally better coordinated and may even be able to roller skate. The five-year-old can skip and has well-developed manual abilities. The six-year-old is at first more clumsy than the five-year-old, but then stabilizes. From ages six to twelve, motor abilities generally seem to increase with age in nearly linear fashion.

During the period from birth to age six, some sex differences in motor behavior emerge. Boys, for instance, use their whole bodies in throwing, while girls have more limited movement. Girls seem more capable than boys of accurate movement in tasks such as hopping and skipping. And, although boys are stronger than girls and are better at throwing, running, and feats of strength, girls are more accomplished in tasks involving rhythmic and accurate locomotor activities (Cratty 1970).

Motor activity can be examined from a variety of perspectives. For example, motor development in children can be divided into four phases (Gallahue 1982). The *reflexive movement* phase extends from prenatal life to age one. Movement in this phase is involuntary and subcortically controlled. The *rudimentary movement* phase extends from birth to age two, overlapping the reflexive movement phase. Here movement is voluntary, beginning with inhibition of reflexes, but is maturationally determined. The *fundamental movement* phase begins at age two and lasts until age seven. This is a time of exploration and experimentation. Movement during this phase is not just maturationally determined but also depends on learning. The *sports-related movement* phase begins at age seven and lasts until age fourteen and up. During this phase the child applies his or her movement abilities to recreational, competitive, and expressive activities rather than—as before—learning movement for its own sake.

Other researchers have attempted to analyze those basic motor abilities in children that are involved in overall motor development. Rarick (1980) identified six basic components of motor behavior in children that have been experimentally validated across age, sex, and intellectual ability. They are: (1) strength/power/body size; (2) gross limb-eye coordination; (3) fine visual-motor coordination; (4) fat or dead weight; (5) balance; and (6) leg power and coordination. Seven similar factors were identified by Hughes and Riley (1981) and used to design a test of motor development. Their factors are: static balance, eyes open; static balance, eyes closed; elementary ball handling; leg strength and balance; object control; aiming; and dynamic balance. Examination of the child from these various perspectives provides for adequate description of normal motor activity.

Regardless of which perspective or perspectives are utilized, it is still difficult to know how children acquire motor skills. Most investigators feel that in addition to maturational factors, learning and perceptual abilities are important. Some form of intersensory or cross-modal linkage between the visual and kinesthetic modalities also seems to be required (Hulme et al. 1982). There is also some apparent connection between motoric and cognitive development. Children seem to learn motor tasks with more facility as their ability to process information increases, which usually is a function of age (Barclay and Newell 1980). Mentally retarded children are often behind in motor development too. Although children who are normal intellectually may also be motorically delayed, a significant percentage of these youngsters catch up on motor development with time (Lundberg 1979). There is no evidence, however, that intensive motor training leads to accelerated intellectual development (American Academy of Pediatrics 1982; Rarick 1980).

Unquestionably, childhood is a period of intense motor activity. This activity is essential to the development of independent function away from the family. It is also critical for the evolution of the complex social interactions such as sports and other play that are so much a part of the life of childhood. Progressively higher levels of motor function also allow developing children to explore and experiment with the world about them. This interaction between motor function and cognitive development is perhaps one of the more characteristic aspects of normal childhood.

Cognitive Development

Studies of cognitive development are attempts to examine how individuals come to know. Most investigators indicate that cognitive development follows an epigenetic model in that successive stages are built on the previous level of function. Jean Piaget's work forms one of the theoretical and empirical bases for this area of development. His work has been repeatedly examined by a number of empirical investigators and continues to be a productive approach to cognitive development in children.

Piaget theorized that, ontogenetically, there is a progression of intellectual development in childhood from knowledge derived from physical actions upon objects to that derived from cognitive actions upon ideas. Accordingly, four factors are important for cognitive development: maturation, experience of the physical environment, actions of the social environment, and equilibration or self-regulation. Piaget (1970) felt that self-regulation is the fundamental factor necessary for coordination of the other three.

Piaget divides cognitive development into four periods. (The following chronological age differentiations are only guidelines.) The first, from birth to age two, is called the sensorimotor period. During this period the infant's manifestations of intelligence appear in sensory perceptions and motor activities but he or she has no capacity for logical reasoning or responding to more than what is present at the moment. Object permanence is attained at about nine to twelve months; that is, only then does the infant begin to remember objects that are out of sight. Between twelve and eighteen months, a "Copernican revolution" occurs as the child goes from a kind of solipsism to the awareness that objects exist independent of his or her awareness of them (Piaget 1970; Pulaski 1980).

During the preoperational period, from ages two to seven, the child learns to deal with the world symbolically and develops prelogical reasoning. The bulk of language development occurs during this period (language is the major vehicle for the manipulation of symbols and ideas). Children come to believe that everything has a reason and a purpose which they can (or must) immediately divine. They have a sense of magical omnipotence and a self-centeredness that leads them to expect that everyone also thinks exactly as they do. The child tends to see inanimate objects as being alive, to view natural phenomena as having been created by human beings, and to consider everything that can be represented by a noun as tangible and real.

Piaget divided this preoperational period into two stages: the preconceptual stage (ages two to four) and the prelogical or intuitive stage (four to seven). During the former, children demonstrate imitation and memory in drawings, dreams, language, and make-believe play. This is the time, as well, when the first attempts at conceptualization appear. During the intuitive stage, prelogical reasoning appears but it is based on perceptual appearances and lacks the stable, reversible character of operational thinking. As an example, Piaget described his daughter who at age six and one-half had trouble understanding why two birds of different species but the same black color did not behave the same way (Pulaski 1980).

The third period, from ages seven to twelve years, is the period of concrete operations. That it should begin at seven corresponds with the traditional view that seven is the age of reason (Pulaski 1980; Shapiro and Perry 1976) and also the time when certain crucial perceptual abilities develop (Piaget 1970; Powell and Gaines 1982; White 1965). During this period, the child comes to demonstrate the ability to form logical groups of concrete objects, to reason logically, to organize thoughts into coherent, total structures, and to arrange them in hierarchic or sequential relationships.

The child can now also think logically about things he or she had experienced and manipulate them symbolically, as in arithmetic operations. The classic Piagetian example is the feat of conservation—the ability to understand that certain attributes of an object are preserved even though that object is transformed in appearance. Prior to age seven, for instance, a child thinks that sugar dissolved in water simply ceases to exist (after all, "I can't see it"). By age seven or eight, the child considers the dissolved sugar to have preserved its substance—but in small, invisible grains that have neither weight nor volume. By age nine or ten, each grain of sugar is thought to have weight and the sum of the weight is considered equivalent to the weight before dissolution. By age eleven to twelve, even volume is considered to have been maintained (Piaget 1970).

The fourth period, arising from age twelve to adulthood, is that of formal operations. During this period the child becomes able to reason logically about abstract propositions and other things or properties never directly experienced. Formal operations are distinct from concrete operations in that the former use the hypotheticodeductive method while thinking in the formal mode is propositional and reflective (Wright 1966).

Piaget, his colleagues, and other developmental researchers have experimentally validated many of his ideas about the sequence of cognitive development in children. Piagetian theory has, however, been challenged on a number of grounds. The age limits of the various periods suggested by Piaget, based on his studies of Swiss children, may be rather specific to that group and, at any rate, far from universal. A more telling objection (one with clinical implications) is that children in the preoperational period—despite their egocentricity—seem able to respond to each other emotionally (Pulaski 1980). They also seem to remember their mother's faces quite early in life even though object permanence is not attained until later. Very young children, in fact, probably have differential abilities to remember animate as opposed to inanimate objects (Bell 1970; Silverman 1980).

Piagetian theory has also been criticized for ignoring individual differences other than those concerned with rates and levels of development. Neo-Piagetians have included individual affective factors, cognitive style, and memory abilities in their discussions of cognitive development, but some have felt that even this approach is too narrow. They have called for the consideration of other factors such as cultural differences, the role of language representation or coding, differences in information concepts, and the effects of exposure to the media.

Other cogent criticisms of Piaget's theory include the observation that he relies too heavily on verbal self-reports of children, thereby ignoring the fact that at least until age seven there is often little correspondence between what a child says and what he or she understands (as indicated by nonverbal behavior) (Wright 1966). Furthermore, one might question the Piagetian idea of a smooth developmental progression from sensorimotor intelligence to abstract intelligence. Intelligence test scores in infants under eighteen months do not predict scores in children after age four or five except in cases of very low intelligence (Bayley 1966). It is possible that intelligence tests in later childhood simply do not adequately measure sensorimotor intelligence or that there is a dichotomy between cognitive and motor development as children grow older. It also appears that cognitive factors required for successful execution of motor tasks are different from those associated with academic achievement (Rarick 1980). Thus, rather than being a cumulative, epigenetic process throughout childhood, cognitive development may progress because of different, simultaneously interacting factors.

One would, at any rate, not be at all surprised to learn that cognitive development in childhood is a complex phenomenon whose intricacies cannot be encompassed by any theory currently available. The best theory of cognitive development would account both for characteristics which appear to be common to all children, as well as individual and group differences (Fowler 1980). We are nowhere near such a state of affairs. At this stage of our science, Piaget's stands alongside a small number of other approaches to the study of human learning as interesting and heuristically valuable first efforts. For the student of human behavior, the area of cognitive development in childhood is a major arena for theory and research. Although empirical data are increasingly available, we are fated, however, to jury-rigging concepts for some time both within this domain and between the entire field of cognition and the equally important areas of language, personality, and social development.

Language Development

Language as defined by Cooper, Moodley, and Reynell (1978) is the "ability to understand and use symbols, particularly verbal symbols, in thinking and as a form of communication" (p. 8). Developmentally, the ability to talk seems less important than the ability to understand language and to use it in thought. Research on childhood language has concentrated on the milestones of language function in infancy and early childhood (McCarthy 1954), on characterizing the phonology, syntax, and semantics of speech in the young, and on the mechanisms of language acquisition (Braine 1971; Carroll 1971; McNeill 1970). Although much progress has been made, there remain difficulties in identifying the significance of particular language behaviors and in handling diverse and contradictory theories (Ferguson and Garnica 1975; Lewis 1982).

Fundamentally, language development appears to be the result of biological, maturational factors that interact with the environment (Lenneberg 1967). Even with no language stimulation, as in a household with congenitally deaf parents, children will start babbling (Lenneberg, Rebelsky, and Nichols 1965), but the development of speech appears to depend on regular exposure to speaking people.

Babbling, which may last up to age fifteen months (Lecours 1975), seems neither the beginning of true language nor even a "bridge" to language in any sense (McNeill 1970), although it may allow for exercise of the speech apparatus and serve social functions for the child. Echolalia may appear by four to seven months. This seems to be the beginning of learning the motor patterns of speech production and mastering the phonemic stock of a child's linguistic community. Echolalia, a dominant linguistic activity through the second year of life, may last normally until ages thirty to thirty-six months (Lecours 1975).

According to Cooper, Moodley, and Reynell (1978), early language development can be seen as a process of coming to understand and use symbols that are increasingly arbitrary. For example, the child first acquires the understanding of a symbol such as "quack-quack," which has more of a "perceptual" similarity to the object it denotes, and only later moves to using the word "duck," a more arbitrary symbol. Cooper and associates characterize the period from eight to twelve months as the stage of the development of prelanguage. During this time the child develops object permanence and a situational understanding of words that have meaning only as a part of a familiar sequence of events.

The age of the first word is variable. Most investigators agree that by about twelve months of age children speak more than one word. There may be a period where babbling decreases markedly before true speech begins. By about eighteen months, the child's vocabulary is usually growing and may be as large as twenty words. Some children will have already learned to name simple objects and pictures and to respond to questions. By twenty-four to thirty-six months, there is a steady increase in the number of named items and objects pointed to on verbal request. This is also a time of first phrases, sentences, pronouns, and prepositions (McCarthy 1954).

The period from twelve to twenty-six months, when symbolic understanding is achieved, overlaps with the development of verbal comprehension (Cooper, Moodley, and Reynell 1978). During this time object recognition develops. For example, the child knows how to *use* a cup appropriately. As verbal comprehension is mastered, the child begins to appreciate the meaning contained in a pattern of verbal symbols and to move from just a situational understanding of phrases to independent understanding of words. By twenty-six months of age, the child can relate two named objects (as in the instruction "Put the brush in the box"). By the age three or four, the child can follow more complex directions, including the use of abstractions, prepositions, and negatives.

The expressive language stage follows the same sequence as verbal comprehension, but three to six months later. Children's auditory discrimination of spoken language and verbal comprehension develops prior to the successful use of verbal expression. By age two, most children can produce words other than simple object naming. Many use three-(or more) word sentences. Vocabulary may be up to 200 words. Appropriate use of pronouns comes at about two and one-half. Children's speech at this stage has been called "telegraphese" because of the absence of articles and auxiliary verbs (Moskowitz 1978; Schlesinger 1975). Most children have acquired nearly complete syntax and are reasonably fluent in everyday conversation by age four or five, although language skill development continues for many years after this (K. E. Nelson 1977).

By age three and one-half, language has assumed a directive function for practical activities. Children at this age "talk themselves through" situations. By age four or five, this function begins to be internalized and to become unconscious. Language also becomes important in concept formation as the ability develops to label a concept with a sign. Cooper, Moodley, and Reynell (1978) call this process the development of the "intellectual use of language" because the directive function of language has become internalized as verbal thinking. The process continues to perfect itself well into school age or later.

After age five, the length of sentences increases. A child of age six and one-half uses sentences that average five words in length and seven-word sentences by early elementary school. The mean number of words per sentence in written composition is 10 at age eight, 11 at ages nine and ten, 11.5 at age eleven, 13 at age twelve, and 14.5 at age thirteen (McCarthy, 1954). The ability to distinguish between words that sound alike also sharpens considerably with age—from about 65 percent at age three to 92 percent at age eight. Pronunciation of consonant sounds follows a similar progression. On the average, boys are about one year behind girls in these abilities. After age eight, there are little data on either auditory discrimination of word sounds or pronunciation (Carroll 1971).

A child's vocabulary, about 1500 words at age five, increases to about 3000 words by the end of the first grade. Beyond age five, children refine their syntactic and conversational abilities. At around age ten, for example, they master the connotative distinction in English between two sentences like the following: "The monkey tells the dog to jump off" and "The monkey promises the dog to jump off" (K. E. Nelson 1977). Before this age, the child would assume that in both sentences it was the dog that was to do the jumping.

There is a gradual and progressive increase from the primary grades through adolescence in a child's ability to use language effectively in conversation as well as by defined criteria such as average length of utterance or communication units, relative absence of unintelligible or grammatically confused speech, and overall grammatical complexity (Carroll 1971). By age twelve, children no longer need to rely on adult coaching, prompting, and encouragement in conversation. By this age, as well, they have reasonable ability to understand and produce figurative expressions such as similes and metaphors (K. E. Nelson 1977).

Memory seems to be particularly relevant in language development after age five, as it becomes increasingly important to be able to systematically organize, store, and retrieve semantic information. Semantic retrieval is much slower at age seven than it is in adulthood (K. E. Nelson 1977). Some reading and writing competence is attained by age seven, but handwriting competence in languages such as English and French is not attained until several years later. Indeed, semantic competence is probably not achieved until the middle of the second decade or later (Lecours 1975).

Sources of individual differences in language development in children without sensory handicaps or medical/psychiatric illnesses include quality of language exposure, individual language style, innate abilities, sex, and socioeconomic status. The primary factor in language development—aside from native ability—is the quality of language to which the child is exposed (Carroll 1971). Other things being equal, the richer the language exposure the faster and better the individual develops language within the boundaries of his or her innate capacities. Examples of language exposure include "caretaker speech" and "recasting" in adult-toddler communication (Moskowitz 1978; K. E. Nelson 1977).

Girls talk earlier and are more advanced on various measures of language skill during childhood than are boys, who, in fact, are more prone to language disorders such as dyslexia. Low socioeconomic status is associated with lower verbal intelligence, which may, in turn, be associated with delayed language development (Carroll 1971).

Language may have an *interpersonal* function, expressing an interpersonal bond; an *instrumental* function, getting a desired object or action; or a *referential* function, exchanging information for its own sake (K. E. Nelson 1977). In beginning to use language, different children emphasize one of these functions over the others and go on to develop primarily either an "expressive" style, emphasizing the interpersonal and instrumental functions, or a "referential" style of language.

The Berkeley Growth Study indicates that, as early as age one, certain speech behaviors are indicative of later language development, especially in females (Bayley 1968). A British study showed a high correlation between speech development at age two and one-half, reading ability at age eight, and written composition skills at age ten (Sampson 1962, 1964). Whatever the reasons for the early start in the successful use of speech, it apparently has important implications for the acquisition of other language-related skills later in life.

The relative lack of research in language development after about age eight seems to be, in part, a problem in knowing what to examine. There is some evidence that language development from middle childhood through adulthood is a regular, almost linear process, although much is still not understood about it.

Speech and language development appears to be a focal point of child development. Language skills, perhaps, represent the ultimate integrative process in that cognitive and motor skills are so essential for production of language while social interaction is in a cause-and-effect relationship with it.

Moral Development

As one directly approaches the most complex of human functions, social interaction, it becomes evident that there is some need for rules by which to govern it. Certainly, biological and ecological limits are critical; however, an "internal" set of rules develops as well. Defined by a variety of terms, this moral development is another key to the socialization of the child.

At about age seven or eight, children evince increased interest in "the rules of the game." Prior to this they seem to be unconcerned about rules and have the attitude that everyone can win simultaneously. By age ten to twelve, nearly every child in a community agrees on what constitute the rules of a game such as marbles and is concerned with playing by these rules (Piaget 1965).

Piaget's work on the development of moral cognition has led to the conceptualization of two successive stages. *Heteronomous* morality, the earlier stage (from about age seven to ten), is characterized by a feeling of obligation to comply with rules derived from higher authority. There is a tendency to perceive right and wrong in terms of the results of behavior rather than intent and there is a belief in imminent justice. *Reciprocity*, the later stage (beginning at about age ten to twelve) incorporates the view that rules are derived from reciprocal social agreements. This both implies and reflects a newfound recognition of diversity of opinion about right and wrong and the ability to see things from the other person's point of view. The two stages of moral development enunciated by Piaget coincide nicely with the stages of concrete operations and formal operations, respectively, and were thought to be the result of an interaction between cognitive development and social experience. According to

Hoffman (1970), experimental evidence supports the presence and sequence of Piaget's stages in Western middle-class society, but not in lower socioeconomic groups or other societies such as American Indian communities.

On the basis of Piaget's ideas, Kohlberg (see Colby et al. 1983) developed his own hierarchy of moral cognition in childhood and added further stages in adulthood. He divided the development of moral cognition into levels and stages within levels.

The first level, corresponding to the entire period before reciprocity, Kohlberg termed "Preconventional Morality." In this level, stage 1 is heteronomous morality, characterized by avoidance of punishment and respect for the sheer superior power of authorities. An individual in this stage continues to maintain an egocentric point of view. Stage 2, that of individualism, instrumental purpose, and exchange, features rather concrete ideas about fairness and reciprocity, namely that of "You scratch my back, I'll scratch yours" (Bereiter 1978). A child during this stage is aware that everyone has his own interests to pursue and that these often conflict; what is "right" is therefore seen as only relative.

The second level of moral development is called "Conventional Morality." The first stage of this level, stage 3, is defined by mutual interpersonal expectations and by interpersonal conformity. One lives, therefore, by the Golden Rule. The child during this stage needs to be a good person in his or her own eyes and in the eyes of others. Stage 4, that of social system and conscience, is a "law-and-order" orientation. During this time, children take the point of view of the system and consider individual relations in terms of their place within it. They have the ability to take the perspective of others who have legitimate interests.

Kohlberg's third level, "Postconventional Morality," is rarely seen except in adulthood. In the first stage of this level, stage 5, the dominant theme is that of social contract or utility and individual rights. During this later stage of development, individuals have a feeling of having voluntarily entered into a social contract and uphold a belief in "the greatest good for the greatest number." Stage 6 that of, universal ethical principles, is characterized by a belief that particular laws or social agreements are valid because they rest on self-chosen ethical principles.

Kohlberg and his colleagues (Colby el al. 1983) have shown that most ten-year-olds were at stage 1, stage 2, or in between; only a small number were between stage 2 and 3. (Their longitudinal study began at age ten so they did not have data on younger children.) Most early adolescents, ages thirteen to fourteen, were between stages 2 and 3. Kohlberg also found that children advanced sequentially through the stages and that one determinant of advancement is exposure to moral learning at a higher stage.

Experimental evidence for Kohlberg's hierarchy has been uneven. Like Piaget's two-stage conceptualization, Kohlberg's hierarchy appears to apply most consistently to middle-class persons in Western society (Hoffman 1970; Saltzstein 1983). Kohlberg's longitudinal study is composed entirely of male subjects, a fact that Gilligan (1982) and others have cited as extremely problematic. Gilligan has postulated that the moral cognition of females is different from that of males in that girls are oriented toward care and response.

The significance of any theory of the development of moral cognition, it could be argued, rests in a strongly positive relationship between the capacity for moral cognition and moral behavior. (Admittedly, other factors influence moral behavior—for example, environmental supports and personal preference [Fischer 1983; Saltzstein 1983].) Studies of the relationship between stage of moral cognitive development and delinquent or criminal behavior have, however, yielded inconsistent results (Blasi 1980; Hains and Miller 1980; Wonderly and Kupfersmid 1980). It is apparent that good actions are controlled by more than cognitive apperceptions of the nature of morality.

According to psychoanalytic theory, morality is related to the development of the ego ideal and of the superego. The ego ideal arises out of coming to terms with the "lost narcissism" of early childhood (Coles 1981). The superego arises out of the necessity of obedience to parents and the desire to please them. There is general agreement among psychoanalytic theorists that the basic processes of conscience formation are accomplished by age five or six, although the development of the superego continues for many years after this (Hoffman 1970). Regrettably, there is little in the way of empirical data to support this conclusion.

Important both to the cognitive and psychoanalytic theories of moral development is the capacity for empathy. However, there has been little research on this aspect of development. It appears that both infants (Murphy 1980) and preschool children (Murphy 1937) show evidence of empathic responses to others. The relationship between constructs like empathy, egocentrism, and decentering—crossing "school" lines—remains to be elucidated.

Psychosocial and Psychosexual Development

The development of personality during early and middle childhood is a question of the highest (or, to speak horizontally and not vertically, the broadest) of integrative functions. Entering into personality during the

years between three and twelve are all the elements of growth and maturation which have already been alluded to in previous sections—human
biological underpinnings as well as motor skills, language, cognition, and
values. It should be obvious, however, that what is meant by "personality" transcends these constituents and that even the definition of the term
is subject to disagreement. The following discussion emphasizes those
enduring characteristics of the child's functioning that reveal themselves
most sharply in his or her interaction with other people as a social being.
The particular areas of interest—chosen, once again, because of their
clinical import and their apparently crucial role at this stage of the child's
life—are those of peer relations and the nature of play. Before proceeding
to a discussion of these topics, however, some homage must be paid to a
traditional, influential, and clinically quite pervasive theory of child personality and social development—psychoanalysis. (For those interested
in a highly readable and up-to-date presentation of psychoanalytic thinking on development during the years of childhood, volume 2 of *The
Course of Life* [Greenspan and Pollock 1980] is highly recommended.)

Early and middle childhood can be seen as a period of socialization
(Peters and Willis 1978). With the development of ambulation, language,
and sphincter control, the child is increasingly capable of social
interaction.

According to psychoanalytic theory, the time when sphincter control is
developed—about age two to three—is the "anal" period of psychosexual
development. Issues related to sphincter control may be expressed by the
child symbolically in other behaviors with distinctly interpersonal ramifications (Lewis 1982). Erikson (1959) designated the conflict during this
period as that of "autonomy vs. shame and doubt" because matters of
individual will were central in development and were engaging the
child's interests and energy.

Freud and other psychoanalytic theorists attempted to describe personality development in childhood by positing the existence of sexual and
aggressive drives in search of objects. Erikson's integration of social and
cultural factors with psychoanalytic ideas is an interesting and often fascinating application of the psychosexual model to the realm of the
psychosocial.

The corrective of Erikson serves only to highlight Sigmund Freud's
relative neglect of interest in the impact of peers on the growing child.
Freud restricted most of his serious model-building to the figures within
the nuclear family. The other children conjured up by Freud were one's
siblings, not one's friends or schoolmates.

During the "oedipal period" (from about age three to six), children
manifest clearly "sexual" behavior and interest for the first time. They

notice differences between the male and female anatomy and are frankly curious about pregnancy and childbirth. They may wish to displace the parent of the same sex and marry the parent of the opposite sex, but at the same time worry about being punished for these wishes. Erikson saw the psychosexual conflict during this phase of childhood as that of "initiative vs guilt."

Socially, the oedipal period is the time when most children start school and are exposed extensively to making a go of it with both teachers and fellow students. Furthermore, as Piaget has pointed out, there is a significant shift from parallel play seen at age two to the cooperative play and sharing seen at age five and older (Peters and Willis 1978). How a child develops socially at this stage is, no doubt, also influenced by cognitive factors, temperament, parent-child attachment, other familial factors such as parents and the influences of siblings, affect, capacity for empathy, socioeconomic status, school environment, and stress (Parke and Asher 1983).

The period from about age six to puberty was termed "latency" by Freud because he thought the sexual drives were repressed due to castration anxiety, as well as biological factors (Furman 1980). It is now generally agreed that sexual behavior may be seen in latency-age children but that it is not as overt as it is during the oedipal period or adolescence (Reese 1966). There appears to be a preference during this period for friends of the same sex. Harry Stack Sullivan has presented a much more detailed discussion of the importance of friends and "chums" to the growth of the person (Sullivan 1953). According to Erikson, the critical conflict throughout this time is that of "industry vs. inferiority." The latency child works. If he or she doesn't, the child gets into personal and social trouble.

Some authors divide latency into two or more phases. Bornstein (1951), for instance, described "early" latency (five-and-one-half to eight years of age) as characterized by a strict and harsh superego, a pull toward regression as a means of defending against sexual impulses, and the use of defense mechanisms like reaction formation, denial, and identification with the aggressor (e.g., boys become like their fathers rather than rivals with them). "Late" latency, lasting from age eight to ten, typically shows less of the effects of a strict superego and demanding sexual impulses. The child turns more to school and the peer group and is able to sublimate impulses through play and schoolwork (Kramer and Rudolph 1980).

Psychoanalytic theory deserves more than just faint praise. It is easier to characterize and quantify external behaviors than to describe in public and replicable terms what experience means to a particular child or what motivates a youngster's social behavior. The method of psychoanalysis, together with the discoveries it has made or suggested, is an invaluable and unique entrée into the world of the child. Nonetheless, when transferred into the arena of developmental psychology, psychoanalysis as a body of facts seems wanting. Much of the psychoanalytic corpus on personality development is based on treatment cases or on rather global observations of individual children, families, and groups. An important innovation in recent years has been the burgeoning interest in more empirically grounded research into child development conducted or heavily influenced by psychoanalysts (e.g., Brody and Axelrad 1978; Mahler, Pine, and Bergman 1975; Murphy and Moriarty 1976). The fruits of these studies are awaited eagerly. As it stands, the "factual" developmental assumptions of classical psychoanalysis, insofar as they are testable at all, have had only limited verification (see, e.g., Fisher and Greenberg 1977).

Another important question raised by many about psychoanalytic theories of personality development is how much they really do represent the "natural" unfolding of the biologically determined and universal maturational sequence Freud had predicated (Shapiro and Perry 1976). The use and usefulness of metapsychological constructs such as ego, id, and superego have also been questioned vigorously even by stalwarts of psychoanalysis like Schafer (1976) and Leites (1971). Research designs are particularly difficult to formulate and implement in psychoanalytic inquiries, moreover, because of the nature of the questions being asked and the nagging sense that the usual methods and canons of empirical investigations are hopelessly beside the point. For areas of life like meaning and subjectivity that so strongly lay a claim to our interest, we may need a whole new philosophy of science, not just more careful collection of usable data.

Peer Relationships

By the time of early childhood, the child is launched more vigorously by his or her family into the social world of adults and peers. The years between toddlerhood and adolescence—the subject of this chapter—are of the utmost significance in helping the child eventually to become a group member, an intimate with an age or generation mate, and a parent/nurturer/teacher for someone younger. Peers come to play increasingly important roles for the growing child as he or she is able to bring them into his or her psychological world, learn to deal with them singly and in groups, and to choose and be chosen by a few for especially close relationships.

Wenar (1982) has distinguished between what he calls mere "sociability," a general interest in others of one's own age, and "friendships," which denotes a more intense level of involvement and with a select number of individuals. The trajectory of social involvement with peers moves, then, from the generalized sociability of early childhood to the establishment of firmer friendships in the years of latency. By preadolescence, the typical child in our culture—at least the girl—has also had years of experience in a "gang," or clique or group, a forerunner of the powerful peer groups of the teenage years.

FUNCTIONS OF PEER RELATIONS

In his review of children's peer relations, Asher (1978) described a number of the functions which peers provide the growing child. Among them are play, emotional security, the setting of norms, instruction (often in the form of modeling), and life adjustment (apparently, the quality of peer relationships in childhood is predictive of the level of mental health and adjustment later in life). There is a separate section of this chapter for the subject of play. In the following pages, we pursue Asher's outline for the other four functions of childhood peer relations.

Emotional Security.   In a strange situation, the presence of even an unfamiliar peer is a source of relative comfort to a nursery school child. As measured by the amount of exploratory movement around the room and the display of positive affect, Schwarz (1972) found that four-year-olds are most at their ease when in the company of a child whom they already know and least comfortable when alone. Having a child in the room from another class, however, was better than being alone. One is reminded of the early work of Butler (1954) who showed that rhesus monkeys will work simply to provide themselves the opportunity to watch other monkeys at play. Primates are social beings.

Interestingly, the work of Ispa (1977) has shown that the presence of a familiar adult eliminates the differences for the child between having a familiar or unfamiliar peer for company. Nonetheless, the child is still more comfortable in the company of a familiar child than a familiar adult.

According to Barker and Wright (1955), by the time of school age, about 50 percent of a child's social interactions are with other children. At age two, the proportion is only about 10 percent. It is noteworthy, however, that children tend to produce more "sociable" as well as more *aggressive* acts against their own age peers than against children either older or younger. That too may reflect a certain sense of security in the relationship with compeers.

Setting of Norms. Middle childhood is apparently the period of life when adherence to the perceived norms of the group is at its most rigid. The literature suggests, furthermore, that there is some cultural variability here. Black children may peak on this dimension earlier in middle childhood than do their white counterparts (Minuchin 1977).

One gets the sense that norm setting in this phase of life has been relatively underemphasized in the literature, although it is not hard to show the presence of normative activity, particularly when groups of children are set to competing with one another and common goals are highlighted (Sherif et al. 1961). Even well before the school years, children operate along well-defined roles, rules, and pro-social standards— particularly in regards to gender-appropriate activities and associations. Adolescents are more readily identified than are younger children as likely to be under the sway of popular opinion and the mores of the group. Perhaps we have been distracted, first of all, by thinking that the impact of norm-setting is visible only in deviance from adult norms; adolescents, with their greater opportunity for action and their developed ability to think and talk about what they do, have grabbed the headlines here. In fact, norms among children are most frequently in the direction *endorsed* by the adult and parental world. It is also possible, *however*, that research on middle childhood as a whole is rapidly being made obsolete as, in both directions, the forms and usages of adolescence spread themselves into other stages of the life cycle.

Instruction. Either explicitly or through the medium of modeling, peers have an enormous influence upon one another. One need only think about how one first learned the rules of a popular game like baseball to realize that the tradition of instruction is incorporated in several parallel streams. Without minimizing the role of the adult teacher, one can still recognize that from time immemorial children have been telling and showing one another how to get along in the world. Sometimes the nature of the teaching conforms to the facts of living, other times it does not. Myths about human sexuality, for example, have survived in what one suspects is an ancient, child-to-child oral tradition not greatly influenced by adult knowledge or teaching.

Given the importance of peers as sources of security and in setting standards of behavior and value, it is not at all surprising that peers can effectively teach. Csapo (1972), for example, showed that emotionally disturbed children who were disruptive in the classroom could learn more adaptive comportment when seated next to exemplars of more appropriate behavior. (In this setting, the instructions were for the children to model themselves deliberately after their peers.)

Life Adjustment. Ineffective peer relations in childhood predict to adult psychiatric disorder and must be considered an important adaptational failure. According to Robins (1966), for example, some 70 percent of adult antisocial disorders have their apparent roots in childhood forms of the same general type of activity. Indeed, there is an unusually direct relationship over time between childhood antisocial behavior and adult psychopathy, probably because the early adjustment failures tend to be self-perpetuating and reinforcing (see Sroufe and Rutter, 1984). It must nonetheless be recalled that " . . . most antisocial children do *not* become antisocial adults" (Robins 1978, p. 611). In only half or fewer cases, do even highly antisocial children become highly antisocial adults. There is some contradiction in the literature as to whether the link between the quality of early peer relations and later criminal behavior is seen in lower socioeconomic groups as well as middle and upper classes.

It is of the essence to be clear just what one means by "poor" or "ineffective" peer relations in childhood as a predictor of later outcome. There are differences between problems of social isolation and withdrawal—which may be associated with later schizoid or borderline conditions—aggressive and antisocial activities, and simple refusal to accept and endorse adult norms. Although any kind of serious and extended problem with peers may place a child at risk, the specific nature of the difficulty may be a crucial shaping variable.

THE DEVELOPMENT OF SKILLS

Among others, Rubin (1980) has made major contributions to our understanding of the skills developed by children in learning how to initiate relationships with peers and to maintain them over time. He has described four general areas of interest: (1) how the child gains entry into group activities; (2) the capacity to convey to one's peers a sense of approval and support; (3) how to manage conflicts; and (4) the exercise of sensitivity and tact in peer relationships.

The description by Corsaro (1979) of the steps taken by a child to make herself welcome when she comes upon two children already busily at play reminds one forcefully of a Peace Corps community development worker wooing the natives. Nonverbal entry—"hanging around" the area of interaction—is followed by actively encircling the scene (walking around), producing and engaging in similar behavior (in parallel play), and, finally, a reference to affiliation ("We're friends, right?"). With younger children, a more direct approach ("Can I play?") is apt to be rebuffed when a boy or girl tries to join an activity already proceeding among other children. Older children, however, do make successful use of the more direct strategem.

It is the child who pays attention to others, praises them, shows open affection to them, and accedes to their requests who is usually endorsed as the more popular (Hartup, Glazer, and Charlesworth 1967). This does not mean that the child is sycophantic or intrusive. To the contrary. In maintaining friendships, pacing and a light touch are crucial.

This sense of what is appropriate and the ability to be flexible in applying some of the "rules" of good friendship are vital to peer relationships and show themselves in many ways. How one rebounds from rejection, for example, is important since, as has already been pointed out, relationships among school-age children are certainly not free of arguments and difficulties. To be too easily discouraged by rejection is to make it likely that one will remain self-righteously isolated. For this reason, as well, managing conflicts or avoiding them diplomatically is also a feature of a well-adjusted and socially successful child.

Just how one learns social skills—how to initiate social contacts and how to keep them going—is not well understood. Some data suggest that the child provided with relatively few opportunities for social contacts with peers is at a disadvantage in this regard (Rubin 1980). Apparently, in getting on with people one learns—at least in part—by doing.

Among preschoolers, "best friend" relationships can change over the course of several weeks (Marshall and McCandless 1957); as children grow older, friendships are stable for much longer periods and tend to involve interaction, amusement, and fun, as well as problem solving.

As Hartrup (1980) has summarized, there is a decided gender difference in the nature of the social networks of children. The friendship networks of boys tend to be more "extensive," i.e., involving larger numbers of individuals with each of whom the relationship is not necessarily very deep. Girls, on the other hand, are characterized by "intensive" friendship systems; fewer people are involved and the demands made upon each are relatively greater.

Among ten- and eleven-year-olds, dyadic friendships tend to be more exclusive—for girls more so than boys—and more persistently exclusive over the course of time. For example, a girl newcomer entering a school in the middle of the year would probably have a harder time making close friends with female peers than would her male counterpart with male peers (Eder and Hallinan 1978).

The clinician's interest in the friendship patterns of children derives from the fact that peers are the witnesses and sponsors of psychological growth. Developmentalists have known this for a long time. The sadness and loneliness of the unpopular child should remind us that youngsters have always known about the importance of friendships. The examination of these social networks probably should have even greater standing now that we have come to realize the extent to which the quality of relationships with peers in childhood influences the course of future development.

Play

In describing the nature and function of children's play, authors almost invariably sound stodgy and ridiculously academic. It is quite as if they were at pains to explain how a joke "works"—not a very rewarding effort. Insofar as the listener is concerned, either he or she has no sense of humor in the first place (the task is then hopeless) or lacks the necessary knowledge to appreciate the funny side of the story (a crash course won't help much). The other possibilities, of course, are that the teller hasn't much facility as a raconteur or that the story just isn't amusing. Children's play *is* serious business, but one needn't get morbid about it. Whatever the function of play for cognitive and social development, role rehearsal, catharsis, affective communication, and the spending of "surplus" energy—the theories of play abound—it is, after all, a source of profound pleasure for children, one which occupies a good deal of their life.

Occasionally, our view of children's play gets obscured by tradition. Many texts still refer the reader, for example, to Parten's findings (1932) that, until about the age of three-and-a-half, nursery school children do not play cooperatively with one another. In fact, as Rosenblatt (1980) has pointed out, a number of recent studies agree unequivocally that cooperative play occurs as early as eighteen to twenty months of age (see, for instance, Rubenstein and Howes [1976]). Clearly, one must keep replicating studies—particularly classic studies—to avoid the possibly severe limitations of cohort effects.

Fein (1978) has called our attention to a second source of obfuscation in appreciating the play of children—our unwillingness at times to see things for which our perfectly reasonable theories cannot, at the moment, account. Piaget and a number of other developmental theorists have emphasized, for example, the preschool child's egocentricity and his or her utter difficulty in taking the perspectives of others or transcending his or her own self-interests.

Yet the development of sociodramatic play during this period challenges this characterization. Play is a form of commonplace behavior that, if it happens at all, presupposes skills that children are supposed to lack. More important, it presupposes an orientation to others, an eagerness to exchange perspectives, and some notion, however vague, that persons are invariant and conserved, whereas the roles and perspectives that they adapt change and shift (Fein 1978, p. 82).

One is reminded forcefully of the debate among clinicians as to whether there could be such an entity as depression in childhood, given an adherence to classical psychoanalytic theory. Phenomena have a way of ignoring theories, and vice versa.

In this section, our major concern is to illustrate some of the psychosocial aspects and implications of play. (It should be clear, nonetheless, that play is engaged circularly with the development of language, of thought, and of fine and gross motor skills.) Although play is not necessarily always in the physical presence of others, it is almost always socially tinged. The "others" are there, sometimes in only vague fantasy form, sometimes more elaboratedly and consciously.

For our purposes, then, it is best to emphasize the latter two of the four stages and types of play described by Smilansky (1968): (1) functional play—that involving only simple, repetitious muscle movements (think of the play typical of infants); (2) constructive play—objects are manipulated to make things (toddler play); (3) dramatic play—taking on and exchanging "theatrical" roles with other children around certain initially simple, then much more complicated themes or stories (appears as early as three years of age, peaks at about age five, and then disappears rather suddenly from the repertoire of children [Fein 1978]); and (4) games with rules. In the following discussion, we have followed the lead of Fein (1978) and Rosenblatt (1980).

SOCIODRAMATIC PLAY

Paley (1979, 1981), in her descriptions of the dramatized "stories" of young children which she uses in teaching them, has presented us with a treasury of these selections. She seems deliberately to have eschewed linking her work to that of developmental psychologists, but Paley is by no means naive about how and why children grow cognitively and socially. In her transcriptions of the story-plays, one sees, for example, how play and *the* play demand some implicit knowledge and mastery of the rules of social interaction, e.g., shared signals for entry and exit ("Let's pretend that. . ." or "I'm not playing anymore"), simple turn-taking, and longer, complex chains of action and dialogue (see Garvey 1974).

The number of simultaneous participants in play grows in typical fashion over the course of childhood. At age three, children play in dyads or in the groups of three. By age five, up to five children play together at a time and the interactions, besides being longer, are more stable. With entry into primary school, there is a continuing growth in the size of the group within which the individual child plays.

It may well be that the increasing comfort with the stimulation of larger numbers and the greater ability to handle the complexities of the social situation are important in determining the kinds of activities in which children can engage. Dramatic play may cease to flourish in latency in part because the numbers of potential playmates make for very unwieldy theater. One recalls that one reason, at least, that toddlers tend not to play with other children very well or for very long is that they are so unpredictable (for one another) that interactions tend soon to end in squabbles, disagreements, and physical strife (see Bronson 1975). Toddlers, moreover, have no rules for reconciling. How many can play a certain kind of game and how well they can play it help to determine the nature of the activity to be selected and its popularity. In the same vein, it is not at all surprising that the quality of sociodramatic play varies with socioeconomic class and privilege (Smilansky 1968). One suspects that the mastery of social rules, particularly as they are reflected in the niceties of speech, is a determining factor. The deleterious effects of poverty in children are often seen most readily in speech and language (Bernstein 1972).

In middle childhood, the fantasy play of girls is more likely to involve objects and to be relatively physically sedate. Boys, on the other hand, seem to prefer the rough-and-tumble (Smith 1977). What is operative is, it seems, a distinguishing characteristic which has both biological and sociocultural roots. Boys, in general, have a higher level of activity than girls do. Boys tend to be "externalizers" and girls tend to be "internalizers" (see Achenbach 1982; Al-Issa 1982). The differences in the style of play (the aggressiveness, who chases and who is chased, the frequency of mock fighting) also appear in non-human primates who have not had the opportunity to be socialized by other monkeys and to learn "appropriate" sex-role behaviors (see Harlow and Mears 1979).

According to Minuchin (1977), summarizing work by Sutton-Smith (1972), there has been a shift over time in this country such that the games of boys and the games of girls are much more similar today than ever before. Once again, we are reminded that we must keep looking for what is there, rather than for what we expect to find. Whatever is part of a biological substrate is quite malleable. Girls nowadays may be encouraged or permitted to be more physically active. It remains the case, however, that girls' play and games tend to be less "complex" than those of boys in terms of role differentiation, player interdependence, size of playgroup, explicitness of goals, number of rules, and the emphasis on individual play rather than team formation (Lever 1978). Girls, in other words, still have socialization experiences in an important area of their lives that may put them at a relative disadvantage for assuming later roles of leadership in complex, structured organizations.

GAMES WITH RULES

We have alluded in other parts of this chapter to the growing importance of rules in middle and late childhood. The interest in rules has echoes in cognitive and moral development, of course, as well as in a temporary, age-appropriate style of "defense"—that of obsessiveness, isolation of affect, intellectualization, and rigidity (Chess and Thomas 1976).

The activities favored by children at this stage of their lives are board and card games, as well as formal and informal "team" sports. With age, the individual participant tends to have at least the opportunity for more and more complex thinking, internal rehearsal, and "risk," plus the exercise of skills and planning. Whatever else the function of play in larger groups, it prepares the child for sustained cooperation with others, emphasizes aspects of social organization and leadership congruent with those of adult society, and breeds dedication to the group and the ideas it embodies.

Summary and Conclusions

Normal childhood—no more complex a phenomenon than any other level of development, but no less so—cannot be viewed from just a single perspective. We have discussed this aspect of human ontogenesis first from a micro-substrate view, then tried to relate these substrates to "higher" levels of functioning. It is these "higher" levels of functioning that constitute the uniqueness of the human child.

Although biologic substrates constitute the final common pathway of organismic function, it is the quality of the integrated functions that is the ultimate measure of normal childhood. The integration of the variety of functions is a difficult task for the child, even with excellent support and guidance from the environment.

Investigators have found it difficult to conceptualize this period of development. Data are available, but they are sparse and often grounded in empirical investigations that are limited in scope. Although the consideration of childhood as a period of latency has made childhood less attractive to researchers, that is not the whole story. A major stumbling block is the sheer intricacy of the child's work of consolidating and integrating the widely disparate skills with which he or she has been endowed and has developed. Attempts have been made to integrate neurobiological data with these higher level functions (Heilbrun 1979; Meyersburg and Post 1979). These attempts are interesting but pose more questions than they answer.

There is a clear need for developing an empirical base for concepts of normality in childhood. Absent that base, should it be assumed that we cannot conceive of a normal child? We think not. Instead, a working model must evolve. The model cannot be undimensional. For clinical purposes, "goodness of fit" constitutes the critical issue in determining normal development in childhood. The concern for the adaptive capacity of a child is a key to the concept of normal development.

The child's normal adaptation is not, in fact, unlike a key operating a lock. The child can be represented as the key with characteristic bumps and grooves that allow it to fit a given lock or make the match impossible. The lock itself represents a receptive or unreceptive environment. Not only must the key fit the channel of the lock, but it must match the tumblers. There is some degree of tolerance in the lock. If the child's characteristics meet the environment's characteristics within an acceptable range of tolerance, then there is adequate fit. The better the fit, the easier the lock turns and the better the child moves through childhood.

This analogy can be carried a step farther, and it is this additional step that is the critical aspect of normality. How do the child and his or her environment change and adapt to each other? Like the key that can be reground and the lock's tumblers that can be reworked, modifications can be made so that the child and environment are in synchrony with one another and permit the epigenetic process to continue. This ability to change and adapt is the measure of "goodness of fit" and, hence, of normality. When the fit is not good enough, the developmental processes of childhood are disrupted.

Is "goodness of fit" an adequate definition of normality in childhood? Probably not, but the empirical base for a more precise definition simply does not exist. Most children use the period of childhood as a time of active adaptation, integration, and consolidation. Middle childhood is neither passive nor "latent." Although we need to know more, we already know this: middle childhood is yet another period of life during which the doors to a happy and successful adolescence and adulthood are being unlocked.

REFERENCES

Achenbach, T. M. 1982. *Developmental Psychopathology,* 2nd ed., New York: John Wiley & Sons.

Al-Issa, I. 1982. "Gender and Child Psychopathology." In *Gender and Psychopathology,* ed. I. Al-Issa, pp. 53–81. New York: Academic Press.

Albright, L. A., et al. 1983. "CSF Polyamines in Childhood." *Archives of Neurology* 40:237–40.

American Academy of Pediatrics. 1982. Policy Statement. "The Doman-Delacato Treatment of Neurologically Handicapped Children." *Pediatrics* 70(5):810–12.

Ames, L. B., et al. 1979. *The Gesell Institute's Child from One to Six.* New York: Harper & Row.

Anders, T. F. 1981. "The Development of Sleep Patterns and Sleep Disturbances from Infancy Through Adolescence." *Advances in Behavioral Pediatrics* 2:171–90.

Anders, T. F.; Carskadon, M. A.; and Dement, W. C. 1980. "Sleep and Sleepiness in Children and Adolescents." *Pediatric Clinics of North America* 27(1):29–43.

Anthony, E. J. 1956. "The Significance of Jean Piaget for Child Psychiatry." *British Journal of Medical Psychology* 29:20–34.

Asher, S. R. 1978. "Children's Peer Relations." In *Social and Personality Development,* ed. M. E. Lamb, pp. 91–113. New York: Holt, Rinehart and Winston.

Balazs, R.; Lewis, P. D.; and Patel, A. J. 1979. *Nutritional Deficiences and Brain Development.* In *Human Growth,* ed. F. Falkner and J. M. Tanner, vol. 3, pp. 180–224. New York: Plenum Press.

Barclay, C. R., and Newell, K. M. 1980. "Children's Processing of Information in Motor Skills Acquisition." *Journal of Experimental Child Psychology* 30:98–108.

Barker, R., and Wright, H. 1955. *Midwest and its Children: The Psychological Ecology of an American Town.* New York: Harper and Row.

Bayley, N. 1966. "Part III: Mental Measurement." In *Human Development,* ed. F. Falkner, pp. 397–407. Philadelphia: W. B. Saunders.

————. 1968. "Behavioral Correlates of Mental Growth: Birth to Thirty-six Years." *American Psychologist* 23:1–17.

Beardslee, W. R., et al. 1982. "The Effects of Infantile Malnutrition on Behavioral Development: A Follow-up Study." *American Journal of Clinical Nutrition* 35:1437–41.

Bell, S. M. 1970. "The Development of the Concept of Object as Related to Infant-Mother Attachment." *Child Development* 41:291–311.

Bereiter, C. 1978. "The Morality of Moral Education." *The Hastings Center Report* 8(2):20–25.

Bernstein, B. 1972. "A Socio-linguistic Approach to Socialization." In *Directions in Sociolinguistics,* ed. J. J. Gumperz and D. Hymes, pp. 67–93. New York: Holt, Rinehart and Winston.

Blasi, A. 1980. "Bridging Moral Cognition and Moral Action: A Critical Review of the Literature." *Psychological Bulletin* 88(1):1–45.

Bornstein, B. 1951. "On Latency." *Psychoanalytic Study of the Child* 6:279–85.

Brackbill, Y., and Nevill, D. D. 1981. "Parental Expectations of Achievement as Affected by Children's Height." *Merrill-Palmer Quarterly* 27:429–41.

Braine, M. S. D. 1971. "The Acquisition of Language in Infancy and Childhood." In *The Learning of Language,* ed. C. E. Reed, pp. 2–95. New York: Appleton-Century-Crofts.

Brasel, J., and Gruen, R. K. 1978. "Cellular Growth: Brain, Liver, Muscle and Lung." In *Human Growth,* ed. F. Falkner and J. M. Tanner, vol. 2, pp. 3–19. New York: Plenum Press.

Brody, S., and Axelrad, S. 1978. *Mothers, Fathers, and Children: Explorations in the Formation of Character in the First Seven Years.* New York: International Universities Press.

Bronson, W. C. 1975. In *Friendship and Peer Relations,* ed. M. Lewis and L. A. Rosenbloom, pp. 131–52. New York: John Wiley & Sons.

Brook, C. G. D. 1978. "Cellular Growth: Adipose Tissue." In *Human Growth,* ed. F. Falkner and J. M. Tanner, vol. 2, pp. 21–33. New York: Plenum Press.

Butler, R. A. 1954. "Incentive Conditions Which Influence Visual Exploration." *Journal of Experimental Psychology* 48:19–23.

Caplan, B., and Kinsbourne, M. 1981. "Cerebral Lateralization, Preferred Cognitive Mode, and Reading Ability in Normal Children." *Brain and Language* 14:349–70.

Carroll, J. B. 1971. "The Development of Native Language Skills Beyond the Early Years." In *The Learning of Language,* ed. C. E. Reed, pp. 97–156. New York: Appleton-Century-Crofts.

Chess, S. and Thomas, A. 1976. "Defense Mechanisms in Middle Childhood." *Canadian Journal of Psychiatry* 21:519–25.

Cohen, D. J., and Young, G. J. 1977. "Neurochemistry and Child Psychiatry." *Journal of the American Academy of Child Psychiatry* 16(3):353–411.

Colby, A., et al. 1983. "A Longitudinal Study of Moral Judgment." *Monographs of the Society for Research in Child Development* 48:1–96.

Coles, R. 1981. "Psychoanalysis and Moral Development." *American Journal of Psychoanalysis* 41(2):101–13.

Cooper, J.; Moodley, M.; and Reynell, J. 1978. *Helping Language Development.* New York: St. Martin's Press.

Corsaro, W. A. 1979. " 'We're friends, right?' Children's Use of Access Rituals in a Nursery School." *Language in Society* 8:315–36.

Cratty, B. J. 1970. *Perceptual and Motor Development in Infants and Children.* New York: Macmillan.

Csapo, M. 1972. "Peer Models Reverse the 'one bad apple spoils the barrel' Theory." *Teaching Exceptional Children* 5:20–24.

Duffy, F. H.; Burchfiel, J. H.; and Lombroso, C. T. 1979. "Brain Electrical Activity Mapping (BEAM): A Method for Extending the Clinical Utility of EEG and Evoked Potential Data." *Annals of Neurology* 5:309–32.

Eder, D. and Hallinan, M. T. 1978. "Sex Differences in Children's Friendships." *American Sociological Review* 43:237–49.

Eichorn, D. H. 1970. "Physiological Development." In *Carmichael's Manual of Child Psychology,* 3rd ed., ed. P. H. Mussen, pp. 157–283. New York: John Wiley & Sons.

Eimas, P. D. et al. 1971. "Speech Perception in Infants." *Science* 171:303–6.

Falkner, F., and Tanner, J. M. 1978, 1979. *Human Growth* (3 vol.). New York: Plenum Press.

Faust, M. S. 1960. "Developmental Maturity as a Measure of Prestige of Adolescent Girls." *Child Development* 31:173–84.

Fein, G. G. 1978. "Play Revisited." In *Social and Personality Development;* ed. M. E. Lanb, pp. 70–90. New York: Holt, Rinehart and Winston.

Ferguson, C. A., and Garnica, O. K. 1975. "Theories of Phonological Development." In *Foundatons of Language Development: A Multidisciplinary Approach,* ed. E. H. Lenneberg and E. Lenneberg, vol. 1, pp. 153–80. New York: Academic Press.

Fischer, J. W. 1983. "Illuminating the Process of Moral Development." *Monographs of the Society for Research in Child Development* 48:97–107.

Fisher, S., and Greenberg, R. P. 1977. *The Scientific Credibility of Freud's Theories and Therapy.* New York: Basic Books.

Fowler, W. 1980. "Cognitive Differentiation and Developmental Learning." *Advances in Child Development and Behavior* 15:163–206.

Freud, A. 1981. "Psychopathology Seen Against the Background of Normal Development." In *The Writings of Anna Freud, Vol. 8. Psychoanalytic Psychology of Normal Development, 1970–1980,* pp. 82–95. New York: International Universities Press.

Furman, E. 1980. "Early Latency—Normal and Pathological Aspects." In *The Course of Life: Psychoanalytic Contributions Toward Understanding Personality Development, vol. 2: Latency, Adolescence and Youth,* ed. S. I. Greenspan and G. H. Pollock, pp. 1–32. Washington, D.C.: U.S. Government Printing Office.

Gaddes, W. H., and Crockett, D. J. 1975. "The Spreen-Benton Aphasia Tests, Normative Data as a Measure of Normal Language Development." *Brain and Language* 2(3):257–80.

Galin, D., and Ornstein, R. 1974. "Individual Differences in Cognitive Style: I. Reflective Eye Movements." *Neuropsychologia* 12:367–76.

Gallahue, D. L. 1982. *Understanding Motor Development in Children.* New York: John Wiley & Sons.

Garai, J., and Scheinfeld, A. 1968. "Sex Differences in Mental and Behavioral Traits." *Genetic Psychology Monographs* 77:169–299.

Garvey, C. 1974. "Some Properties of Social Play." *Merrill-Palmer Quarterly* 20:163–71.

Gilligan, C. 1982. "New Maps of Development: New Visions of Maturity." *American Journal of Orthopsychiatry* 52(2):199–212.

Greenough, W. T. 1975. "Experiential Modification of the Developing Brain." *American Scientist* 63:37–46.

Greenspan, S. I., and Pollock, G. H., eds. 1980. *The Course of Life: Psychoanalytic Contributions Toward Understanding Personality Development*, vol. 2: *Latency, Adolescence and Youth.* Washington, D.C.: U.S. Government Printing Office.

Grumbach, M. M. 1978. "The Central Nervous System and the Onset of Puberty." In *Human Growth*, ed. F. Falkner and J. M. Tanner, vol. 2, pp. 215–38. New York: Plenum Press.

Hains, A. A., and Miller, D. J. 1980. "Moral and Cognitive Development in Delinquent and Nondelinquent Children and Adolescents." *Journal of Genetic Psychology* 137:21–35.

Harlow, H. F., and Mears, C. 1979. *The Human Model: Primate Perspectives.* Washington, D.C.: Winston.

Hartup, W. W. 1980. "Peer Relations and Family Relations: Two Social Worlds." In *Scientific Foundations of Developmental Psychiatry*, ed. M. Rutter, pp. 280–92. London: Heinemann.

Hartup, W. W.; Glazer, J. A.; and Charlesworth, R. 1967. "Peer Reinforcement and Sociometric Status." *Child Development* 38:1017–24.

Heilbrunn, G. 1979. "Biological Correlates of Psychoanalytic Concepts." *Journal of the American Psychoanalytic Association* 27(3):597–626.

Hoffman, M. L. 1970. "Moral Development." In *Carmichael's Manual of Child Psychology*, 3rd ed., ed. P. H. Mussen, pp. 261–359. New York: John Wiley & Sons.

Hughes, J. E., and Riley, A. 1981. "Basic Gross Motor Assessment: Tool for Use with Children Having Minor Motor Dysfunction." *Physical Therapy* 61(4):222–30.

Hulme, C., et al. 1982. "Visual Kinaesthetic and Cross-modal Judgments of Length by Normal and Clumsy Children." *Developmental Medicine and Child Neurology* 24:461–71.

Ispa, J. 1978. "Familiar and Unfamiliar Peers as 'Havens of Security' for Soviet Nursery Children." Paper presented at the Meeting of the Society for Research in Child Development, New Orleans, March, 1977. Cited in S. R. Asher, "Children's Peer Relations," in *Social and Personality Development*, ed. M. E. Lamb, p. 94. New York: Holt, Rinehart and Winston.

Jones, M. C. 1965. "Psychological Correlates of Somatic Development." *Child Development* 36:899–911.

Kagan, J. 1976. "Emergent Themes in Human Development." *American Scientist* 64:186–96.

Kandel, E. R. 1979. "Psychotherapy and the Single Synapse." *New England Journal of Medicine* 8:1028–37.

Klausmeier, H. J., and Allen, P. S. 1978. *Cognitive Development of Children and Youth.* New York: Academic Press.

Klausmeier, H. J., et al. 1979. *Cognitive Learning and Development: Information Processing and Piagetian Perspectives.* Cambridge, Mass.: Ballinger.

Knobloch, H., and Pasamanick, B. 1974. *Gesell and Amatruda's Developmental Diagnosis*, 3rd ed. New York: Harper & Row.

Kramer, S., and Rudolph, J. 1980. "The Latency Stage." In *The Course of Life: Psychoanalytic Contributions Toward Understanding Personality Development*, vol. 2: *Latency, Adolescence and Youth*, ed. S. I. Greenspan and G. H. Pollock, pp. 109–19. Washington, D.C.: U.S. Government Printing Office.

Leckman, J. F., et al. 1980. "CSF Monoamine Metabolites in Child and Adult Psychiatric Patients." *Archives of General Psychiatry* 37:677–81.

Lecours, A. R. 1975. "Myelogenetic Correlates of the Development of Speech and Language." In *Foundations of Language Development, A Multidisciplinary Approach*, E. H. Lenneberg, and E. Lenneberg, vol. 1, pp. 121–35. New York: Academic Press.

Leites, N. 1971. *The New Ego.* New York: Science House.

Lenneberg, E. H. 1967. *Biological Foundations of Language.* New York: John Wiley & Sons.

Lenneberg, E. H.; Rebelsky, F. G.; and Nichols, I. A. 1965. "The Vocalizations of Infants Born to Deaf and Hearing Parents." *Human Development* 8:23–37.

Lever, J. 1978. "Sex Differences in the Complexity of Children's Play and Games." *American Sociological Review* 43:471–83.

Lewis, M. 1982. "Language Development." In *Clinical Aspects of Child Development*, 2nd ed., ed. M. Lewis, pp. 51–60. Philadelphia: Lea & Febiger.

Lundberg, A. 1979. "Dissociated Motor Development." *Neuropadiatrie* 10(2):161–82.

McCarthy, D. 1954. "Language Development in Children." In *Manual of Child Psychology*, 2nd ed., ed. L. Carmichael, pp. 492–630. New York: John Wiley and Sons.

Maccoby, E. E., and Jacklin, C. N. 1974. *The Psychology of Sex Differences*. Stanford, Calif.: Stanford University Press.

McKhann, G. M.; Coyle, P. K.; and Benjamins, J. A. 1973. "Nutrition and Brain Development." *Research Publications Association for Research in Nervous and Mental Disease* 51:10–22.

MacKinnon, P. C. B. 1979. "Sexual Differentiation of the Brain." In *Human Growth*, ed. F. Falkner and J. M. Tanner, vol. 3, pp. 183–221. New York: Plenum Press.

MacLean, P. D. 1982. "Evolutionary Brain Roots of Family, Play, and the Isolation Call." The Adolf Meyer Lecture, 135th Annual Meeting of the American Psychiatric Association, May 18, Toronto.

MacNeilage, P. F. 1980. "Speech Production." *Language and Speech* 23:3–23.

McNeill, D. 1970. "The Development of Language." In *Carmichael's Manual of Child Psychology*, 3rd ed., ed. P. H. Mussen, pp. 1061–1161. New York: John Wiley & Sons.

Mahler, M. S.; Pine, F.; and Bergman, A. 1975. *The Psychological Birth of the Human Infant: Symbiosis and Individuation*. New York: Basic Books.

Marshall, H. R., and McCandless, B. R. 1957. "A Study of Prediction of Social Behavior of Preschool Children." *Child Development* 28:149–59.

Martin, S. D. B. 1971. "The Acquisition of Language in Infant and Child." In *The Learning of Language*, ed. C. E. Reed, pp. 2–95. New York: Appleton-Century-Crofts.

Metcalf, D. R. 1979. "Organizers of the Psyche and EEG Development: Birth Through Adolescence." In *Basic Handbook of Child Psychiatry*, ed. J. D. Noshpitz, vol. 1, pp. 63–71. New York: Basic Books.

Metcalf, D. R., and Jordan, K. 1972. "EEG Ontogenesis in Normal Children." In *Drugs, Development, and Cerebral Function*, ed. W. L. Smith, pp. 125–44. Springfield, Ill.: Charles C. Thomas.

Meyersburg, H. A., and Post, R. M. 1979. "An Holistic Developmental View of Neural and Psychological Processes." *British Journal of Psychiatry* 135:139–55.

Minuchin, P. P. 1977. *The Middle Years of Childhood*. Monterey, CA.: Brooks/Cole.

Moskowitz, B. A. 1978. "The Acquisition of Language." *Scientific American* 239(5):92–109.

Murphy, L. B. 1937. *Social Behavior and Child Personality*. New York: Columbia University Press.

————. 1980. "Psychoanalytic Views of Infancy." In *The Course of Life: Psychoanalytic Contributions Toward Understanding Personality Development, vol 1: Infancy and Early Childhood*, ed. S. I. Greenspan and G. H. Pollack, pp. 313–63. Washington, D.C.: U.S. Government Printing Office.

Murphy, L. B., and Moriarty, A. E. 1976. *Vulnerability, Coping, and Growth*. New Haven: Yale University Press.

Nelson, K. 1977. "First Steps in Language Acquisition." *Journal of the American Academy of Child Psychiatry* 16(4):563–83.

Nelson, K. E. 1977. "Aspects of Language Acquisition and Use from Ages 2–20." *Journal of the American Academy of Child Psychiatry* 16(4):584–607.

Newell, F. W. 1982. *Ophthamology: Principles and Concepts*, 5th ed. St. Louis: C. V. Mosby.

Offer, D., and Sabshin, M. 1974. *Normality: Theoretical and Clinical Concepts of Mental Health*, rev. ed. New York: Basic Books.

Paley, V. G. 1979. *White Teacher*. Cambridge, Mass.: Harvard University Press.

————. 1981. *Wally's Stories*. Cambridge, Mass.: Harvard University Press.

Parke, R. D., and Asher, S. R. 1983. "Social and Personality Development." *Annual Review of Psychology* 34:465–509.

Parten, M. B. 1932. "Social Play Among School Children." *Journal of Abnormal and Social Psychology* 28:136–47.

Peters, D. L., and Willis, S. L. 1978. *Early Childhood*. Monterey, Calif.: Brooks/Cole.

Piaget, J. 1965. *The Moral Judgment of the Child*. New York: Free Press.

————. 1970. "Piaget's Theory." In *Carmichael's Manual of Child Psychology*, 3rd ed., ed. P. H. Mussen, pp. 703–32. New York: John Wiley & Sons.

Powell, G. J., and Gaines, R. 1982. "Original Communications." *Journal of the National Medical Association* 74(2):115–23.

Pulaski, M.A.S. 1980. *Understanding Piaget.* New York: Harper & Row.

Rabinowicz, T. 1979. "The Differentiate Maturation of the Human Cerebral Cortex." In *Human Growth: Neurobiology and Nutrition,* ed. F. Falkner, and J. M. Tanner, vol. 3, pp. 97–123. New York: Plenum Press.

Rakic, P., and Yakovlev, P. I. 1968. "Development of the Corpus Callosum and Cavum Septi in Man." *Journal of Comparative Neurology* 32(1):45–72.

Rarick, G. L., 1980. "Motor Development: Cognitive-Motor Relationships in Growing Years." *Research Quarterly for Exercise and Sport* 51(1):174–92.

Reese, H. W. 1966. "Attitudes Toward the Opposite Sex in Late Childhood." *Merrill-Palmer Quarterly* 12:157–63.

Reiter, E. O., and Grumbach, M. M. 1982. "Neuroendocrine Control Mechanisms and the Onset of Puberty." *Annual Review of Physiology* 44:595–613.

Robins, L. N. 1966. *Deviant Children Grown Up.* Baltimore, Md.: Williams & Wilkins.

————. 1978. "Sturdy Childhood Predictors of Adult Antisocial Behavior: Replications from Longitudinal Studies." *Psychological Medicine* 8:611–22.

Robinson, D. S., et al. 1977. "Monoamine Metabolism in Human Brain." *Archives of General Psychiatry* 34:89–92.

Roffwarg, H. P.; Muzio, J. N.; and Dement, W. C. 1966. "Ontogenetic Development of the Human Sleep-Dream Cycle." *Science* 152:604–19.

Rosenblatt, D. B. 1980. "Play." In *Scientific Foundations of Developmental Psychiatry,* ed. M. Rutter, pp. 292–305. London: Heinemann.

Rubenstein, J., and Howes, C. 1976. "The Effects of Peers on Toddler Interaction with Mother and Toys." *Child Development* 47:597–605.

Rubin, Z. 1980. *Children's Friendships.* Cambridge, Mass.: Harvard University Press.

Rutter, M. 1980. "The Long-term Effects of Early Experience." *Developmental Medicine and Child Neurology* 22:800–815.

Rutter, M.; Tizard, J.; and Whitmore, K., eds. 1970. *Education, Health, and Behaviour.* London: Longmans.

Salamy, A. 1978. "Commisural Transmission: Maturational Changes in Humans." *Science* 200:1409–11.

Saltzstein, H. D. 1983. "Critical Issues in Kohlberg's Theory of Moral Reasoning." *Monographs of the Society for Research in Child Development* 48:108–19.

Sameroff, A., and Chandler, M. 1975. "Reproductive Risk and the Continuum of Caretaking Casualty." In *Review of Child Development Research,* vol. 4, ed. F. D. Horowitz, pp. 187–244. Chicago: University of Chicago Press.

Sampson, O. C., 1962. "Reading Skill at Eight Years in Relation to Speech and Other Factors." *British Journal of Educational Psychology* 32:12–17.

————. 1964. "Written Composition at Ten Years as an Aspect of Linguistic Development: A Longitudinal Study Continued." *British Journal of Educational Psychology* 34:143–50.

Schafer, R. 1976. *A New Language for Psychoanalysis.* New Haven, Conn.: Yale University Press.

Schlesinger, I. M. 1975. "Grammatical Development—The First Steps." In *Foundations of Language Development, A Multidisciplinary Approach,* ed. E. H. Lenneberg and E. Lenneberg, vol. 1, pp. 203–22. New York: Academic Press.

Schwarz, J. C. 1972. "Effects of Peer Familiarity on the Behavior of Preschoolers in a Novel Situation." *Journal of Personality and Social Psychology* 24:276–84.

Shapiro, T., and Perry, R. 1976. "Latency Revisited: The Age 7 Plus or Minus 1." *Psychoanalytic Study of the Child* 31:79–105.

Sherif, M., et al. 1961. *Intergroup Conflict and Cooperation: The Robbers Cave Experiment.* Norman, Okla.: University of Oklahoma Press.

Silverman, M. A., 1980. "The First Year After Birth." In *The Course of Life: Psychoanalytic Contributions Toward Understanding Personality Development. vol. 1: Infancy and Early Childhood,* S. I. Greenspan, and G. H. Pollock, pp. 147–76. Washington, D.C.: U.S. Dept. of Health and Human Services.

Sinclair, D. 1969. *Human Growth After Birth.* New York: Oxford University Press.

Siqueland, E. R., and Lipsitt, L. P. 1966. "Conditioned Head-turning in Human Newborns." *Journal of Experimental Child Psychology* 3:356–76.

Smilansky, S. 1968. *The Effects of Sociodramatic Play on Disadvantaged Preschool Children.* New York: John Wiley & Sons.

Smith, P. K. 1977. "Social and Fantasy Play in Young Children." In *Biology of Play*, ed. B. Tizard and D. Harvey, pp. 123–45. London: Heinemann.

Sroufe, L. A., and Rutter, M. 1984. "The Domain of Developmental Psychopathology." *Child Development*, 55:17–29.

Sullivan, H. S. 1953. *The Interpersonal Theory of Psychiatry*. New York: W. W. Norton.

Sutton-Smith, B. 1972. *The Folkgames of Children*. Austin, Tex.: University of Texas Press.

Tanguay, P. E., et al, 1975. "Evolution of Sleep Spindles in Childhood." *Electroencephalography and Clinical Neurophysiology* 38:175–81.

Tanner, J. M. 1962. *Growth at Adolescence*, 2nd ed. Springfield, Ill.: Charles C. Thomas.

————. 1978. *Foetus Into Man*. Cambridge, Mass.: Harvard University Press.

Taylor, D. C. 1969. "Differential Rates of Cerebral Maturation Between Sexes and Between Hemispheres." *The Lancet*, July 19, pp. 140–42.

Trevarthen, C. 1974. "Cerebral Embryology and the Split Brain." In *Hemispheric Disconnection and Cerebral Function*, ed. M. Kinsbourne and L. W. Smith, pp. 208–36. Springfield, Ill.: Charles C Thomas.

Waber, D. P. 1976. "Sex Differences in Cognition: A Function of Maturation Rate?" *Science* 192:572–73.

Wada, J. A.; Clarke, R.; and Hamm, A. 1975. "Cerebral Hemispheric Asymmetry in Humans." *Archives of Neurology* 32:239–46.

Wahler, R. G. 1969. "Setting Generality: Some Specific and General Effects of Child Behavior Therapy." *Journal of Applied Behavior Analysis* 2:239–46.

Weatherly, D. 1964. "Self-Perceived Rate of Physical Maturation and Personality in Late Adolescence." *Child Development* 35:1197–1210.

Wenar, C. 1982. *Psychopathology from Infancy Through Adolescence*. New York: Random House.

White, N., and Kinsbourne, M. 1980. "Does Speech Output Control Lateralize over Time? Evidence from Verbal-manual Time-sharing Tasks." *Brain and Language* 10:215–23.

White, S. H. 1965. "Evidence for a Hierarchical Arrangement of Learning Processes." *Advances in Child Development and Behavior* 2:187–220.

Witelson, S. F. 1974. "Hemispheric Specialization for Linguistic and Nonlinguistic Tactual Perception Using a Dichotomous Stimulation Technique." *Cortex* 10(1):3–17.

————. 1976. "Sex and the Single Hemisphere: Specialization of the Right Hemisphere for Spatial Processing." *Science* 30:425–27.

Witelson, S. F., and Pallie, W. 1973. "Left Hemisphere Specialization for Language in the Newborn: Neuroanatomical Evidence of Asymmetry." *Brain* 96:641–46.

Wolff, P. H. 1970. "Critical Periods in Human Cognitive Development." *Hospital Practice* 5(11):77–87.

————. 1984. "On the Origins of Individuality: A Developmental-Neuropsychological Approach." *The Roots of Individuality and Psychopathology*. In press.

Wolff, P. H., and Hurwitz, I. 1976. "Sex Differences in Finger Tapping: A Developmental Study." *Neuropsychologia* 14:35–41.

Wonderly, D. M., and Kupfersmid, J. H. 1980. "Promoting Postconventional Morality: The Adequacy of Kohlberg's Aim." *Adolescence* 15(59):609–31.

Wright, J. C. 1966. "Cognitive Development." In *Human Development*, ed. F. Falkner, pp. 367–96. Philadelphia: W. B. Saunders.

Yakovlev, P. I., and Lecours, A. R. 1967. "The Myelogenetic Cycles of Regional Maturation of the Brain." In *Regional Development of the Brain in Early Life*, ed. A. Minkowski, pp. 3–70. Oxford: Blackwell Scientific.

3   Daniel Offer
                    and Melvin Sabshin

Adolescence: Empirical Perspectives

Introduction

From the standpoint of many adults, including a surprisingly large number of mental health professionals, adolescence must be a tumultuous development period (see, e.g., Erikson 1959; A. Freud 1946, 1958; Blos 1962; Rabichow and Sklansky 1980). For these individuals, if an adolescent does not go through a serious and prolonged identity crisis, something is or will be very much disturbed about his or her psychological development.

Being critical of this perspective, the editors of this volume have assumed responsibility for this particular chapter. We have several assumptions and objectives in mind. First, the value system of the entire volume emphasizes the necessity for empirical data in formualting a theory of psychological phases of development. Ultimately, theoretical formulation will be a vital part of better understanding the life span and its substages. Theories exclusively or even primarily based on disturbed patients or deviant individuals may be greatly misleading. For example, the battle between those who theorize about the universality of psychopathology during male and female menopause and empiricists who question this formulation because data to support it is lacking recapitulates debates about adolescent development. Second, we do not discount the possibility of a high incidence and prevalence of psychopathology in adolescents.

To deny serious problems out of a theoretical bias is, of course, no more scientific than to assume universal psychopathology in this age group. Third, we recognize that the resolution of these conceptual dilemmas will be extremely complicated, arduous, and lengthy. Descriptions of those with relatively benign courses during their adolescence will be questioned by many who may claim that the identity crisis in these teenagers is either submerged and hence even more insidious or that the smooth sailing represents cases of "arrested development," namely, of individuals who are overly attached to their parents. Fourth, we include data on biological and cognitive development as well as psychosocial development. We have attempted to show the relationship between these systems as we believe that the ultimate integration of these multiple developmental pathways is essential for a better understanding of adolescence and indeed of the entire life cycle. Fifth, we emphasize an overall empirical approach in order to gain further insight into the biopsychosocial aspects of the life cycle as a whole.

We recognize that our own empirical value systems have also produced biases. Hulbert's (1981) review in the *New Republic* of one of the editor's books (Offer, Ostrov, and Howard 1981a) clearly demonstrates how controversial our empirical approach is for those who traditionally believe that "Stürm und Drang" best typifies adolescent feelings and behavior. Indeed, Hulbert states that one can gain more insight from studies of suffering youth than from a normative approach. Nevertheless, in this chapter we hope to stimulate an interlocking series of studies that will lead to more and more specific theory formulation. We also hope to encourage prospective and retrospective investigations of the long-term impact of variations in adolescent coping with developmental stresses.

Definition of Normal Adolescence

The span of years devoted to adolescent development will vary in different cultures and with different definitions. The term adolescence no longer is equivalent to pubescence as it had been used in Western cultures until the beginning of the twentieth century. The onset of puberty, through phenomena such as menarche, is a biological event with many psychosocial consequences. It can no longer be equated with adolescence. To begin with, menarche in girls is a relatively late pubertal event, although in many Western girls it actually precedes adolescence. In addition, adolescence, the process of growing from childhood to adulthood, was in the past of relatively short duration. Up to the twentieth century, by the time most boys and girls reached the age of sixteen they were to all practical purposes adults. They were biologically mature, socially capable, working, and relatively stable individuals. We do not know whether they were also mentally healthy young adults. Suffice it to say here that the definitions of the end of adolescence have always been deeply influenced by the culture in which the adolescents grew up.

In the last eighty years, within Western cultures, middle-class adolescence has become a progressively longer stage (Kett 1977). The concept of reasonable independence as the criterion of the end of adolescence has been translated into financial independence and/or marriage. If this criterion is accepted, a high school student who upon graduation begins to work and marries at nineteen experiences a shorter period of parental dependence and hence adolescence than the individual who continues his or her education, attending college and graduate school, and is supported by parents until the age of twenty-six, marrying at twenty-eight. This person will tend to have a much longer adolescence.

In this chapter we will concentrate on the high school years (ages fourteen to eighteen). We discuss the reactions of adolescents to their changing body, to their emotional needs, and to their peer relations. We also discuss the relationships between parents and teenagers as well as the reactions of the culture at large to adolescents. Some discussion also focuses on the psychological development as it differentially affects male and female adolescents, adolescents in different cultures, and two different groups of adolescents studied eighteen years apart.

In our general discussion of the high school adolescent, we will discuss the typical, average teenager. Two overriding concepts will aid us. First, we will discuss adolescents free from disturbing physical, psychological, and social signs and symptoms. We will not discuss those adolescents with gross deviancy or overt symptomatology. We are interested in the ordinary, average, or modal teenager. While this teenager may be less "interesting," he or she also has less psychopathology. Hence we will use the normality as healthy perspective to aid us in our definition of what constitutes normal adolescence. Second, we shall use the normality as average perspective in order to describe the adolescent's functioning cross-sectionally (Offer and Sabshin 1974).

Many investigators assume that adolescents are in emotional turmoil most of the time. Once one has accepted this point of view, it is difficult to conceptualize a balanced, stable adolescent. It is also difficult to conceive of an ideal adolescent. Indeed, the normality as utopia perspective produces contradictions for those who postulate subsequent utility of adolescent turmoil. We will discuss the normality as transactional systems in chapter 14 since this perspective focuses on change over time, and is most applicable to the life cycle as a whole.

The majority of studies on normal adolescents in the United States have been on the middle-class adolescent. In this country, most adolescents are conspicuously grouped by their presence in a school setting. Most fourteen- to eighteen-year-olds are in high school, and the vast majority belong to the middle class. The term teenager is often used to refer to the high school–age adolescent. Individual variances, as well as the specification of developmental tasks, have to take place within the school system as well as in their home and family, the community they live in, and their biological givens. The majority of studies on adolescents included studies of volunteers, surveys, and clinically oriented investigations of specially selected normal adolescents. In the past there were virtually no studies on normal, lower-class adolescents. Recently the recognition of the limitations inherent in confining studies to the middle-class population has led to increased clinical studies of normal working-class adolescents (see, e.g., Lewis and Looney 1983). The findings are surprisingly similar to those studies that will be described.

Not all high school–age teenagers attend high school. Approximately 20 percent have gross symptoms (Offer, Ostrov, and Howard 1984). A significant number of adolescents also do not attend regular high school. They are either at home or in hospitals, treatment centers, special schools, training schools or work. Our studies do not include these adolescents.

Studies of normal adolescents present special challenges since the ordinary language of psychopathology might not adequately describe the nuances of normal adolescent development. New concepts might have to be used that better describe the normal adolescent. It is our thesis that adolescence should be understood as a transitional stage conceptually similar to other transitional stages, such as menopause or retirement. The transitional process allows the adolescent to gradually adjust to growth and development. It avoids potential crisis and allows for gradual growth to take place. Each cycle in life will bring new challenges and opportunities, but the changes will be incorporated into the basic personality structure. At the end of high school, the majority of the normal, middle-class, American adolescents enter a new phase—young adulthood. This slower transition is not necessarily the same in other social, ethnic, or cultural groupings.

During the past two decades one of us (D. Offer) has empirically studied the developmental psychology of normal adolescents (Offer and Offer 1975; Offer, Ostrov, and Howard 1981a). The study included different cohorts of normal suburban, urban, and rural white, middle-class, male and female adolescents in ninety different samples. The first study began in 1962 and the last one in 1981. Hence we have test data on 20,000 adolescents covering a span of nineteen years. A smaller number of normal adolescents were studied in depth using projective psychological testing of the adolescents and clinical interviews with them and their parents. These studies were done in Chicago suburbs during the same period. The findings of the larger survey study correlated positively with that of the smaller in-depth study.

The main empirical biological and cognitive data are summarized in the next sections. Later we report on our findings on psychosocial development and on adolescent self-image.

Biological Development

Current research clearly indicates that puberty is not a sudden new development but part of a gradual process that begins at conception. However, for the vast majority of adolescents puberty has been completed long before adolescence has terminated. In the studies quoted in this section, the normality as average perspective of biological measurements is used. Hence we will be talking about what occurs in most adolescents. We make no attempt to be comprehensive and to include the various biological difficulties and/or diseases that confront adolescents. We are cognizant, of course, of the variability that exists among normal adolescents as they grow up. However, we will cover only the major biological markers, such as physical development including secondary sex characteristics and endocrine levels. We will not delve into the complex interrelationship during puberty itself between the biological and the psychosocial since in the absence of correlative empirical studies, it is based mostly on speculative theoretical concepts that are beyond the scope of this chapter. (See Petersen and Taylor 1980 for an excellent discussion of these concepts.)

PHYSICAL DEVELOPMENT

The most comprehensive study of physical development has been conducted in England (Tanner 1962, 1972). The changes in physical characteristics, which are the most obvious of the biological changes in the male and female adolescent, occur over a period of what Tanner has called the five pubertal stages. As table 3.1 indicates, for males only, the stages consist of genital development; for females only, they consist of breast

TABLE 3.1
Pubertal Stages

| | Characteristic | | |
Stage	Genital Development[a]	Pubic-Hair Development[a,b]	Breast Development[b]
1	Testes, scrotum, and penis are about the same size and shape as in early childhood.	The vellus over the pubes is not further developed than over the abdominal wall, i.e., no pubic hair.	There is elevation of the papilla only.
2	Scrotum and testes are slightly enlarged. The skin of the scrotum is reddened and changed in texture. There is little or no enlargement of the penis at this stage.	There is sparse growth of long, slightly pigmented, tawny hair, straight or slightly curled, chiefly at the base of the penis or along the lubia.	Breast bud stage. There is elevation of the breast and the papilla as a small mound. Arcolar diameter is enlarged over that of stage 1.
3	Penis is slightly enlarged, at first mainly in length. Testes and scrotum are further enlarged than in stage 2.	The hair is considerably darker, coarser, and more curled. It spreads sparsely over the function of the pubes.	Breast and areola are both enlarged and elevated more than in stage 2 but with no separation of their contours.
4	Penis is further enlarged, with growth in breadth and development of glans. Testes and scrotum are further enlarged than in stage 3; scrotum skin is darker than in earlier stages.	Hair is now adult in type, but the area covered is still considerably smaller than in the adult. There is no spread to the medial surface of the thighs.	The arcola and papilla form a secondary mound projecting above the contour of the breast.
5	Genitalia are adult in size and shape.	The hair is adult in quantity and type with distribution of the horizontal (or classically "feminine") pattern. Spread is to the medial surface of the thighs but not up the linea alba or elsewhere above the base of the inverse triangle.	Mature stage. The papilla only projects with the arcola recessed to the general contour of the breast.

[a] For boys.
[b] For girls.

NOTE: Reprinted, by permission of the publisher, from A. C. Petersen and B. Taylor, "The Biological Approach to Adolescence: Biological Change and Psychological Adaptation," in *Handbook of Adolescent Psychology*, ed. J. Adelson, p. 127. New York: John Wiley & Sons, 1980.

development; and for both males and females they consist of pubic hair development.

Of all the measurements during puberty and adolescence, height is less influenced by environmental and/or psychosocial factors than any other biological variable. For boys, growth in height is completed on the average by age sixteen; 90 percent of the boys complete their growth by the age seventeen and one-half. Some boys do not begin their adolescent growth spurt until as late as sixteen. Skeletal maturation, indicated by closure of the bone epiphyses, is completed by age seventeen on the average. Growth in strength continues through this period from sixteen to nineteen for males.

Penis growth generally ends at age fifteen, although with some boys growth may continue until about sixteen and one-half. The testis usually has completed its growth by age sixteen, though in some individuals growth may not be complete until age eighteen. Pubic hair development is generally completed in the male by age sixteen; again, some boys do not achieve the adult distribution of pubic hair until age eighteen. Axillary hair develops about two years later than pubic hair; for both males and females, the greatest amount of axillary hair is not achieved until the third decade of life. Facial hair shows growth similar to axillary hair in terms of the ages at which adult distribution is attained. Hair on the chest is frequently the last secondary sex characteristic to be attained in males, and in some males an adult distribution may not be developed until the late twenties. In general, however, most sixteen-year-olds look like fully grown men in terms of secondary sex and other physical characteristics. The change in the voice pitch usually occurs relatively late in the adolescent male.

It seems that the biological apparatus has to function smoothly before the individual can mature psychosocially. Since middle-class adolescence takes longer, a fact that has become more widespread in the past fifty years, the individual's biological apparatus matures earlier than his or her psychosocial characteristics. It is as if the biological characteristics have to be in place for a while for the psychosocial characteristics to blossom. Or, by way of contrast, if this "critical time" is not present and individuals behave as if they are mature psychosocially when they are not, the results will not be good. The different individual systems will not work together, and the adolescents will find themselves in continuous stress.

Genital development is parallel to physical development and proceeds earlier than psychosocial development. The male genital development is depicted in figure 3.1.

The time of the first ejaculation of seminal fluid has often been de-

FIGURE 3.1
Schematic Sequence of Events at Puberty
An average girl (upper) and boy (lower) are represented. The range of ages within which each event charted may begin and end is given by the figures placed directly below its start and finish.

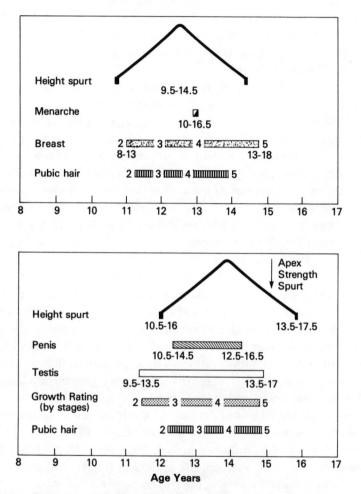

NOTE: Reprinted, by permission of the publisher, from J. M. Tanner, "Sequence and Tempo in Somatic Changes in Puberty," in *Control of the Onset of Puberty,* ed. M. M. Grumbach, G. D. Grave, and F. E. Mayer, p. 448. New York: John Wiley & Sons, 1974.

scribed as the male's analog to menarche. It usually occurs one year after the beginning of penis growth (Petersen and Taylor 1980). Very little research has been done on the factors influencing the first ejaculation. As has been suggested by Tanner (1969), the timing of the first ejaculation may be due to cultural factors that are associated with the reporting of the events. No systematic work has been done to date to describe this phenomenon, and specifically to ascertain whether live sperms are present during the first ejaculation. The prostate greatly increases in size at the time of penile growth.

Girls, in general, develop earlier than boys (Marshall and Tanner 1969). By age sixteen almost all girls appear to be adult females physically. While in the United States the average age of girls at menarche is in normal adolescents twelve and one-half, it may occur as late as sixteen and one-half. Menarche generally occurs shortly after the peak growth in height. The uterus undergoes a growth spurt between the ages of ten and seventeen, but it continues to grow after that time. Although adolescent girls theoretically have the capacity to bear children once they have gone through puberty, a recent study has shown that at least 55 percent of the girls' menstrual cycles were anovulatory in the first two postmenarcheal years (Apter and Vihko 1977).

In general, male and female genital and breast development differs only by about six months; pubic hair development is about two years later for males than for females (Petersen and Taylor 1980). The sex differences in mature height, achieved during or just prior to the period from sixteen to nineteen years, are thought to be due to the sex difference in the timing of maturation rather than a qualitative difference in the adolescent growth spurt. The factors influencing growth in adolescence are not yet completely understood, but the hypothesis that adult males are taller than adult females because of the influence of testosterone in adolescence has been largely discarded (Rosenfield 1971, 1974). Estrogen has also been found to influence growth (Rosenfield 1974). It is interesting that after years of research, the biological factors that contribute to growth, and specifically height, are still so poorly understood.

Other physical variables change markedly during adolescence. Blood hemoglobin and the number of red blood cells increase more significantly in male than in female adolescents (Young 1971). The male adolescent has therefore a greater capacity for carrying oxygen in the blood, which results in greater abilities to sustain physical exercise. This fact should be tied in to the facts that male muscles develop more extensively than those of females, while the percentage of fatty tissues in females is greater than in males. Obviously this results in increased physical strength of adolescent males. How much of this difference in muscular strength and capacity to endure physical strain is due to cultural influences and how much is due to basic, inherited, biological differences between males and females remains to be studied.

An interesting corollary to this question is seen in the world of sports. The increased physical strength of adolescent males occurs later than the growth spurt for adolescent females. Is it possible that the phenomenon of female adolescent stars in sports, such as tennis and gymnastics, relates to their earlier physical development? Adolescent males are not able to compete successfully in these sports with more mature men, for it takes males longer to achieve their physical potential than it does females. Hence a thirteen-year-old male tennis player has never competed successfully with young-adult male tennis players. It seems to us that this phenomenon is dictated by biological markers that are different in the two sexes. There is no question but that the hormonal balance is essential for developing certain typologies of body types. It has recently been suggested that female athletes have a harder time getting pregnant because of shifts in their endocrine system. It is possible to speculate, therefore, that the difference in body type between males and females is, at least in part, due to biological factors. It is questionable whether the physical strength of the two sexes would be identical even under equal cultural opportunities.

To be fully understood, the development of hormonal systems of adolescents has to be traced back to the earlier stages. At puberty the luteinizing hormone (LH) and the follicle-stimulating hormone (FSH) increase in fluid discharge in females. Studies of sex hormones in adolescent boys and girls show that the two important sex hormones (estrogen and testosterone) operate differently. Testosterone is present almost only in the male. Estradiol, the more potent the estrogens, is the one responsible for the differentiation of the female sex. It is important to stress that endocrinological studies of puberty are in a stage of flux. The hormones are an essential part of development, but their secretion, level, and function are part of an open biopsychosocial system, of which they are part. The hormones influence the system are are, in turn, influenced by it. Hormonal development does not stop at puberty. Rather, hormonal secretion increases and peaks after adolescence, around the age of twenty. No current research is available to explain what makes the endocrine levels stabilize in young adulthood after they have peaked. We also do not know what starts the decline in endocrine levels shortly after young adulthood. Careful longitudinal research on hormonal development throughout the life cycle is sorely missing.

Cognitive Development

FORMAL OPERATIONAL THOUGHT

The work of Piaget (1948, 1950, 1952, 1972) has had a profound impact on our understanding of the development of cognition in adolescents. With the help of Inhelder (1958), Piaget was able to give even more systematic attention to the development of logical thought in adolescence. Piaget claimed that formal operations, the logical thought characteristic of adolescence, begin at about ages eleven to twelve and is fully developed by ages sixteen to seventeen. If this is the case, formal thought would usually be fully developed in adolescence proper.

Formal thought involves reasoning based on verbal propositions. An individual with formal thought capabilities can make hypothetical deductions and entertain the idea of relativity. Particularly when new to the growing adolescent, formal thought may be creative although at times bizarre or grandiose since these thoughts still lack a strong grounding in reality and experience.

The direction of the thought processes changes with formal thought. There is a reversal of direction between reality and possibility; instead of deriving a rudimentary type of theory from the empirical data as is done in concrete inferences, formal thought begins with a theoretical synthesis of what is possible and then proceeds to what is empirically real (Inhelder and Piaget 1958).

With formal operations, the adolescent can combine propositions and isolate variables in order to test hypotheses. Furthermore, the operations can be performed using symbols rather than the concrete objects or events characteristic of earlier stages. Piaget has grouped these propositional operations under two systems, a combinatorial system and a transformational system, each with four possibilities. These two systems, cross-classified, form the basis of the total formal operational system that includes sixteen (four times four) propositional operations.

According to Piaget, most adolescents achieve the formal operations stage—hence it is a normal part of adolescent development.* In that sense, Piaget's concepts of cognition would fit our normality as average perspective. Piaget links the capacity for formal operations to the maturation of the brain at puberty. Does the failure of many adolescents, and even adults, to demonstrate formal operations imply that their brains are immature? A more likely explanation is that brain maturation is a neces-

---

*As will be pointed out later, although most normal adolescents achieve the formal operation stage, many adolescents lose the ability to function at the formal thought level in adulthood.

sary but not sufficient condition for formal operations. What is needed, once the brain is mature, is practice and experience with these functions. Indeed, training studies (e.g., Siegler, Liebert, and Liebert 1973) demonstrate that adolescents can be taught formal operations when they have not already acquired them, though Piaget (1972) questions whether such training produces real competence or mere performance capability.

In Piaget's work, the emphasis is on the adolescent as an active explorer and as a synthesizer of his or her own ways of conceptualizing reality. Awareness of self begins when the infant starts to differentiate among preverbal schema for ways of effecting various results in the physical world. Specifically, self, body, internal world, and external world become distinguished as requiring different kinds of sensorimotor schema for the attainment of various consequences (Piaget 1968).

Another facet of Piaget's theory involves cognitive readiness to form and differentiate concepts. Thus implicit in the ordinary use of the word self is the quality of continuity over time. Correspondingly, the development of object permanence—a development achieved by the child through active experimentation with objects—is a precondition of the formation of a concept of self. Other processes, such as the imitation and internalization of the behavior of others, that greatly facilitate the formation of a self also require a certain amount of cognitive readiness prior to being initiated. In Piaget's theory the imitation of others begins early in childhood as a way of mastering and perpetuating what are preverbally experienced as external and interesting phenomena. Imitation requires the functional capacity to assimilate sounds and movements made by others into schema involving the child's own production of those events. Thus the imitation of a wink involves the complex association of visual and kinesthetic cues and the child's reproduction of them. With differentiation from others, object permanence, and a growing ability to imitate, the self is perceived as more similar to, but still separate from, others.

With time, the child becomes increasingly able to take on the role of others, a process facilitated by exposure to differences of opinion, the need to communicate with strangers, and experience with the contradictory wills of others. Concomitant with this increasing ability to take the point of view of other people is the process of "decentering," which involves decreasing egocentrism and increasing objectivity about the self. With adolescence comes the development of the abilities to induce rules and to manipulate the laws of logic; at this time adolescents can strive for self-consistency and also try out new ideas about themselves. They can entertain the possibility of rejecting others' views about themselves. The possible connection among this trying out of new selves, the rejection of old ways of thinking, and feelings of loneliness in adolescence has been commented on by Kohlberg and Gilligan (1971). Ostrov and Offer (1980) have said:

> No one ever becomes so self-sufficient as to stop needing the ongoing approval and recognition of others. From the beginning of life the ability to survive has flowed from other people. Without the ability to attract others' attention and benevolent ministrations, none of us could have survived. As adults, people's need for people can be under stood in cognitive terms. . . . The less tangible the reality, the more influential are the opinions of others (though for many people, opinions of others are much more important than their own self-evaluation). Self-perceptions are eminently a social reality, the convergence of a multiplicity of other people's evaluation of behaviors and appearances. While there is a complex interaction between people's manipulations of others' evaluations of themselves and people's incorporations of others' evaluations, it is apparent that without such feedback people may begin to lose their sense of self and even their sense of reality. The threat of not knowing one's own self must blend subtly for most, if not all, people with the threat of annihilation felt by the utterly helpless infant.
>
> The normal person may gain distance from needs of other people's esteem by increasing competence and internalization of approval-giving functions, but no person can eliminate entirely the need for other people. Therefore, everyone is susceptible to loneliness. The degree, frequency, and quality of a person's loneliness will be a function of what developmental tasks the person is coping with, his degree of emotional health, and the society in which he lives. This is as true among adolescents as among people at every other stage in life. (P. 44)

Piaget has built his research on in-depth observation on a limited number of children and adolescents. Because Piaget (like Freud before him) was primarily concerned with an in-depth understanding of the few children and adolescents he studied, it was left to others to determine how applicable his findings were to the population at large. When one studies a select sample (in Piaget's case he originally studied his own children), one needs to leave room for others expanding on one's research. Research on a broader sample ipso-facto will bring in new findings and new questions. Piaget never concerned himself with samples, statistical techniques, and levels of significance. He believed that he studied truth as he saw it, and left it to others to discover the details. In addition, he believed in the overriding importance of innate biological forces that naturally unfold in each individual. He undervalued the strength and significance of environmental and cultural influences.

Piaget's scientific philosophy is best described in his conversations with Bringuier (1980). In these conversations, Piaget prides himself in being a formalist (a Platonist). In addition, he clearly describes his epistemological point of view. He is an idealist who searches for knowledge as a theoretical abstract. Hence we can only approximate these ideals in our development. Careful analysis indicates that Piaget, like Freud, fits our normality as utopia perspective. The work of Dulit (1972), for example, shows conclusively that the majority of adolescents have not achieved formal operations as defined by Piaget. Dulit studied three groups of adolescents: age fourteen, ages sixteen to seventeen, and a group of gifted sixteen- to seventeen-year olds; in addition, he studied a group of average adults. He found that only about 10 percent of the younger group and 35 percent of the adult group had attained formal operations. About 60 percent of the gifted group functioned at the fully formal level; only about 25 to 33 percent of the adults could successfully perform the experiments measuring formal operations. In all groups, males were two to four times as likely to function at the formal level than were boys. Hobbs (1973), Elkind (1961, 1962), Tomlinson-Keasey (1972), and Graves (1972) report similar results though the percentages of individuals attaining formal operations appear to be dependent on the particular experiments performed, some being more difficult than others. Indeed, Bynum, Thomas, and Weitz (1972) found evidence for only eight of the sixteen propositional operations in formal thought. Furthermore, as Elkind (1975) points out, unlike earlier stages of cognitive functioning, formal operations are not necessary for most adult roles in our society; their importance must therefore be kept in perspective. Psychological functioning, like other skills, has to be continuously experienced in order to be continuously mastered. Formal operations, or the ability to think in the abstract, has to be continuously practiced in order to be retained. Individuals whose jobs do not require abstract thinking and whose private lives are simple and concrete will lose the ability to function at the formal thought level, despite the fact that they may have achieved it during their high school years. There might also be gradual decline over time in the ability to function at the formal thought level even later in life. In addition, a passing comment concerning cognitive development may be in order here. The extensive psychological research on cognition has involved mostly cross-section of the normal, that is, nonpatient, adolescent population. Our information on cognition in psychiatrically disturbed patients is not as extensive as for nonpatients. Much more research is necessary before we can document the various cognitive styles and forms in all adolescents. For example, some recent research on juvenile delinquents shows that one cannot easily differentiate them from normal adolescents. In addition, contrary to previous belief, the juvenile delinquents we studied were more field independent than our normal controls (Offer, Marohn, and Ostrov 1979). In other words, delinquency can reflect stable adaptive styles that are independent from internal psychological stresses and tensions.

Empirical Studies of Adolescent Self-image and Psychosocial Development

In this section we focus on studies of the self because it is a central psychological issue crucial to normal adolescent development. While we could have focused on other relevant issues, such as identity, we believe that our data demonstrate the major psychosocial aspects of the adolescent period.

Adolescence is a critical period with respect to psychological development of the self. An increased ability to think logically and abstractly ensures a more coherent and well-articulated view of self, while richer social experience and greater knowledge ensure a more complex social construction of the adolescent's own reality. At the same time, adolescence is a stage in life rich in a variety of issues, such as emerging sexuality, separation from family, the quest to form a new nuclear family, increased motility, and striving for vocational identity and autonomy. Components of the self will emerge most clearly in this developmental stage, as self-feelings are tested in the crucible of dramatic physiological, psychological, and social changes. It seemed reasonable to us to gather information about adolescents directly from adolescents. They are as competent as other observers to provide such data (Offer and Offer 1975).

In order to gather information, one of us (D. Offer) constructed, in 1962, the Offer Self-Image Questionnaire for Adolescents (OSIQ). The OSIQ is a self-descriptive personality test whose goal it is to assess the adjustment of teenage boys and girls between the ages of thirteen and nineteen. It measures the teenagers' feelings about their own psychological world in eleven content areas, or scales. The scales are: (1) Impulse Control; (2) Mood; (3) Body Image; (4) Social Relations; (5) Morals; (6) Sexual Attitudes and Behavior; (7) Family Relations; (8) Mastery of the External World; (9) Vocational and Educational Goals; (10) Psychopathology; and (11) Superior Adjustment (Coping).

The eleven scales are made up of 130 individual items, with ten to twenty items in each scale. The scales are combined to cover five major psychosocial areas of adolescence: (1) The Psychological World (scales 1, 2, 3); (2) The Social World (scales 4, 5, 9); (3) The Sexual Self (scale 6); (4) The Family (scale 7); and (5) The Ability to Cope (scales 8, 10, 11).

Since 1962 the questionnaire has been used in over one hundred different samples and has been administered to over 20,000 teenagers. The populations included males and females; younger and older teenagers;

normal, delinquent, psychiatrically distrubed, and physically ill adolescents; urban, suburban, and rural adolescents in the United States as well as in Canada, Australia, Israel, and Ireland. The samples cover the entire range of the middle class; only a limited number of lower-class subjects have been tested. The cross-cultural data were all collected in the 1970s. We have normative data from the 1960s, 1970s, and 1980–81.

Our particular operational approach rests on two major assumptions. First, it is necessary to evaluate the adolescents' functioning in multiple areas since they can master one aspect of their world while failing to adjust in another. Second, adolescents' psychological sensitivity is sufficiently acute to allow us to utilize their self-descriptions as a basis for reliable selection of subgroups. Empirical work with the questionnaire has validated these assumptions.

In general, our goal has been to study a group of adolescents not previously studied by psychiatric researchers: the mentally healthy, or normal, adolescent. We collected the data directly from adolescents, with the aim of discovering what their world was like and how they perceived it.

The focus of this section is to summarize the results of a recent study utilizing the OSIQ (Offer, Ostrov, and Howard 1981a). As the findings correlated well with data collected from other sources, we will not detail the large number of studies available. The results have been previously compared to other survey studies (Douvan and Adelson 1966; Rosenberg 1979) to clinical studies of normal adolescents (Block 1971; Offer and Offer 1975); to family studies (Lewis et al. 1976); and to a recent study of adolescent self-image by Dusek and Flaherty (1981).

THE PSYCHOLOGICAL WORLD

Surprising as it might be to many theoreticians, the vast majority of normal adolescents studied stated that they are happy, strong, and self-confident. The adolescents do not feel inferior to others, including their peers, and they do not feel that others treat them adversely.

The normal adolescents also report themselves to be relaxed under usual circumstances. They believe that they can control themselves in ordinary life situations, and they have confidence that when presented with novel situations, they will find themselves prepared. Normal adolescents generally believe that they have control over their lives.

In another area, that of body image, the data indicate that normal adolescents feel proud of their physical development and that the vast majority of them believe that they are strong and healthy. This should not be surprising since a feeling of physical health usually goes hand in hand with positive psychological feelings. Boys present a much more positive body image than do girls. Even though most girls are proud of their body, a significant number (43 percent) often feel ugly, unattractive, and ashamed of their body. Adolescent girls are also more depressed,* lonely, and vulnerable to being hurt than boys. On the other hand, girls are more sensitive to their own feelings as well as to the feelings of others.

In comparing adolescents from the early 1960s to those of the late 1970s and early 1980s, we find that the current generation of normal teenagers is somewhat less secure about their body image and their self-esteem. (See chapter 12, where the implications of cultural differences are discussed in detail.) They stated that they have more overt behavioral problems. The current (1979 and 1980) generation of adolescents are more worried about their future and less hopeful about their ability to function as adults than are the adolescents from the early 1960s. These worries translate into personal concerns about psychological issues. Hence their relatively lower self-esteem, which we found is a function of insecurity about their economic and vocational future. It is important to note that we found no significant differences in self-esteem between the American teenagers and those of similar groups studied in Israel, Ireland, Australia, and Canada.

THE SOCIAL WORLD

The highest endorsed item, "A job well done gives me pleasure," shows the work ethic in its purest form. Ninety-six percent of our adolescent subjects say they agreed with this item. Both boys and girls are unreservedly work oriented. They say they will be proud of their future professions and that they will like their work. The majority of the adolescents sampled seem to believe there will be a job waiting for them, ready to be taken when they are ready to take it. The notion of a career is part of their everyday world. Similarly, they also state that they do not wish to be supported by someone else; their ethics clearly tell them that they are better off working than being supported for the rest of their lives.

Normal adolescents enjoy the company of others, and good feelings result from having group social experiences. They can learn a lot from others, they say, and they like to help their friends. They regard social relations as a process of give and take, and they report being able to exchange feelings with others. They state that they value social relationships from both the pragmatic and hedonistic points of view, and they do

---

* Depression is used here in its colloquial meaning to connote sadness. Behaviorally it manifested itself in mild episodes of short (one to two days) duration and without the psychomotor retardation so characteristic of classical depression. There were no psychosomatic symptoms to speak of. It is, therefore, quite different from the psychiatric diagnosis of depression.

not have any difficulties making friends. They also stated that they do not consciously exploit others. However, boys affirm more strongly than girls that they would not stop at anything if they were "done wrong." This finding tempers the benign image the adolescents have presented so far. It suggests that a majority of adolescents believe that if they are hurt, they would lash back without necessarily attempting to understand the circumstances that provoked that hurt.

As a group, these adolescents see themselves as making friends easily. They believe that they will be as likely to be successful socially and vocationally in the future as they are now.

The adolescent girls sampled have significantly stronger moral attitudes and beliefs than the adolescent boys. The girls generally act out in antisocial ways considerably less than do the boys. The girls also have more positive attitudes toward schoolwork and future vocations. The adolescent girls also affirm social values (e.g., friendships) more than do the boys. In general, the boys seem somewhat more autonomous and less other-oriented than the girls.

Adolescents in the early 1960s had more positive social self-images than those in the late 1970s and early 1980s. Adolescents in past generations were less lonely and valued friendships somewhat more than do current adolescents. We believe that the increase in loneliness observed among adolescents is related to the overall decrease in self-esteem and the increase in worries they have concerning their future. The future is not as secure, and hence the adolescents are more concerned about their own individual future, job security, and so on. This situation cannot help but leave individuals with the feeling that it is everyone for himself. From a cross-cultural perspective, nevertheless, American adolescents had a slightly higher positive social self-image than did adolescents from Israel, Ireland, Australia, and Canada.

THE SEXUAL SELF

In general, the findings show that normal adolescents are not afraid of their sexuality. Seven out of ten adolescents state that they like the recent changes in their body. Both boys and girls strongly reject the statement that their bodies are poorly developed, and both sexes indicate that they had a relatively smooth transition to emerging sexuality. Nine out of ten subjects say "no" to the statement "The opposite sex finds me a bore." A majority of subjects state that having a friend of the opposite sex is important to them. Adolescent boys appear to be more open about their sexuality than are the girls. They think about sex more often, say that dirty jokes are fun at times, and deny that it is hard for a teenager to know how to handle sex in a right way. Adolescent boys also more often report that they attend sexy shows. Of course, this fact may be culturally determined.

Among normal adolescents, sexuality did not show significant differences across the five cultures studied or across time. There are no good, reliable, valid studies of sexual behavior among normal adolescents. Generalizations from deviant populations cannot fill the empirical void with which we are confronted. For example, in our study of juvenile delinquents, we found that 85 percent of the male and female delinquents (average age 15.6) had an active sexual life (Offer, Marohn, and Ostrov 1979). The Sorensen report (1973) similarly shows dramatic increases in sexual activity among high school students. Yet it is important to remember that Sorensen had a 30 percent response rate on his questionnaire, an unacceptable return rate. We simply do not have adequate data on the sexual experience of the majority of normal, middle-class adolescents. Based on our earlier studies (Offer and Offer 1975) as well as more current data (Offer, Ostrov, and Howard 1981a, normal, middle-class teenagers have not experienced a "sexual revolution." They are conservative in their sexual behavior and move slowly in the direction of sexuality. We found that there were no significant changes in attitudes toward sexuality among adolescents from 1962 to 1982. However, we did note one important change. In the past adolescents felt comfortable with their sexual feelings and attitudes. In the current generation, a significant percentage of adolescents believe that they should be more active sexually. When teenagers are not as active sexually as they feel they ought to be, they feel insecure or inferior. This feeling is further strengthened when parents communicate to their adolescent children their feelings that young people today are more active sexually (Offer, Ostrov, and Howard 1982). We found that American parents of today's teenagers believe that their children are more attractive to the opposite sex and more active sexually than the adolescents themselves feel they are (Offer, Ostrov, and Howard 1982). We have not observed this particular phenomenon in the other cultures we studied. Adolescents in the other countries described themselves as relatively conservative in their attitudes toward sexuality.

THE FAMILY

Contrary to many generation-gap hypotheses, our results indicate a general feeling of mutual satisfaction between parents and teenagers. By and large, parents are viewed as being patient and optimistic toward their adolescent children. They are seen as people. Contrary to prevailing mythology, the normal adolescents we studied do not perceive any major problems between themselves and their parents. They believe that their parents are satisfied with them, and they feel close to and do not seem to harbor significant negative feelings toward their parents. Moreover, these feelings seem to extend through time. Not only do these teenagers have positive feelings toward their parents in the present, but they feel that these good feelings have been true in the past. The parents, in turn, also have positive feelings about their adolescent children. In addition, they expect that these positive feelings will persist into the future. The adolescents also viewed their parents as sharing good relationships with each other. Seven out of ten adolescents believe that they have a say in family decisions. This also illustrates the fact that normal adolescents do have a sense of autonomy within the harmonious family (see, e.g., Lewis et al. 1976). A significant minority maintains that their parents are right even when they are strict, so they are able to see beyond their immediate needs. This fact illustrates that these adolescents believe that irrespective of their own feelings, the parents do things for the good of the child.

No significant differences were found between males and females or between the generations regarding the family. From a cross-cultural perspective, adolescents in Israel, Ireland, Canada, and Australia have even more positive feelings toward their families than do American teenagers. The difference may be due to a higher rate of divorce in the United States as compared to the other countries. Although two-thirds of the adolescents still grow up within a two-parent family system, a significant minority grow up within a one-parent family. Such a breakdown of the nuclear family would tend to raise an adolescent's doubts concerning the importance of family for him or her. It might also increase the adolescent's dependence on the peer social system at the expense of positive feelings toward his or her own family.

In a recent study of middle-class families in four Midwestern suburbs, we found that parents of normal adolescents can accurately predict the self-image of their adolescent children (Offer, Ostrov, and Howard 1982). This is in marked contrast to most mental health professionals, who seem unable to do so (Offer, Ostrov, and Howard, 1981*b*).

THE ABILITY TO COPE

In general, the normal adolescents studied are comfortable in their social world and adjust well to it. Once again, in contrast to prevailing mythology, they are hopeful about their future and believe that they can actively participate in activities that will lead to their success. They seem to have the skills and confidence necessary to carry this hope through to fruition. They are optimistic and enjoy challenges; they try to learn in advance about novel situations. They believe that they are just as able to perform as their peers are. The adolescents exhibit the willingness to do whatever work is necessary to achieve their goals. They like to put things in order. Moreover, even if they fail, they believe that they can learn from experience.

The normal adolescents state that they do not experience the gross symptoms listed in the psychopathology scale. On the whole, the adolescents see themselves as being without major problems. This does not mean, however, that everyone in the normal samples said he or she did not have problems. A significant minority did not feel very secure about their coping abilities. The data indicate that about one out of five normal adolescents feels empty emotionally and finds life full of problems without apparent solutions in sight. A similar number of adolescents state that they are confused most of the time and that they hear strange noises.* In other words, although most subjects report that they are doers and get pleasure from putting things in order, some are uncertain about what is going on around them and what their capacity to affect the world is. Still, the decisiveness of the vast majority of our subjects comes through strongly in our data.

Young adolescent girls (thirteen to fifteen years) have more psychiatric symptoms and are not able to cope with problems that come their way as well as either older girls (sixteen to eighteen years) or young or old adolescent boys. A small number of them experience more depression, anxiety, shame, and confusion. In other words, they are more prone to developing diagnosable psychiatric syndromes such as depression or phobia. When compared to the older adolescent boys, older adolescent girls also exhibit more psychiatric symptoms, but the findings are not as significant as for the young adolescent girls.

There are no significant differences between adolescents in the 1960s and 1970s, although more adolescents from the earlier period believed that the world was an exciting place to live in than adolescents in the later period.

The cross-cultural sample consisted of male and female high school students (ages fourteen to eighteen years) who were defined by the respective countries as middle class. They were comparable to the American samples in that their parents were mostly skilled workers, businessmen, or professionals. The Irish, Canadian, and Australian samples were studied in English, while the Israeli sample was studied in Hebrew. The cross-cultural samples were compared directly to the American samples. In studying the four other cultures for whom we had comparable data, we found that the Israeli adolescents seemed to cope better with their external world than the Canadian and the American adolescents. The

---

*We do not interpret these as hallucinatory phenomena.

Israelis enjoyed solving difficult problems more and were more action oriented. The Irish and the Australian adolescents did not cope as well with their world as the American, Canadian, or Israeli adolescents.

These findings clearly demonstrate how the majority of normal adolescents experience and cope with their major life events. The similarities between different samples of normal adolescents outweigh their differences. For example, noteworthy differences occur in normal high school students from fourteen to eighteen years. Stability is a considerably more important event than change (see also Dusek and Flaherty 1981). Gender differences are considerably more in evidence. In general, it has been our finding that adolescent girls find the high school years more taxing psychologically. Hence they have more signs and symptoms, have more problems with their affect than boys, and do not cope as well with their life. On the other hand, boys have relatively lower moral standards and value their family and interpersonal relationships less. We believe that adolescent girls have a harder time coping with their aggression than adolescent boys. Perhaps one of the reasons for this is that sports are not as readily available to them as to the boys. Girls, more often than not, turn the aggression inside and hence they appear more introspective and value interpersonal relationships more than their male peers (see also Hill 1981; Offer 1969).

Historical Perspective: A Brief Note

Kett (1977) has shown how the life of the adolescent has changed during the past two centuries. His monograph is a general account of growing up in different historical periods in the United States. Few studies have stressed the influence of the historical era in which adolescents live on their personality development. The pioneering studies of Nesselroade and Baltes (1974) have shown that the time frame in which a study is conducted must be taken into account. In this context, we compared the adolescents we studied in 1962 to those we studied in 1980. We found, similar to Campbell's (1981) study on adults, that the early-1960s teenagers were functioning somewhat better, felt somewhat better, and on the whole were more satisfied with their life. Whether this is a beginning of a downward trend or is a wavelike phenomenon, we do not know. It is, however, important to watch further developments in this area. We found few changes in sexual attitudes among middle-class adolescents between the 1960s and late 1970s group. In general, there is little evidence to suggest an emergence of a "sexual revolution" in the high school years. The dramatic change in sexual attitudes and behavior that has been noticed has been after high school.

In order to have a fuller understanding of adolescent behavior, we should have better data on how culture influences personality development during adolescence. We possess very little data on this most interesting aspect of personality development. Our limited study found more differences cross-culturally, but we could not separate cause and effect. We do not know how much the "American style" of research methodology is acceptable and/or relevant to adolescents in different cultures. Research methodologies in different cultures, as well as the more general impact of the culture on personality, are discussed in greater detail in chapter 14.

In a previous study Offer and Offer (1975) described three developmental growth patterns: (1) continuous growth; (2) surgent growth; and (3) tumultuous growth. Normal adolescent males follow one pattern from childhood to adulthood. The adolescents in the first group were favored by circumstances. Their genetic and environmental backgrounds were excellent. They had a strong ego, were able to cope well with internal and external stimuli, and had mastered previous developmental stages without serious setbacks. They accepted general cultural and societal norms and felt comfortable within this context. The adolescents in the second group were different only in that their genetic and environmental backgrounds were not as free of problems and traumas as the continuous-growth group. Both groups were free of adolescent turmoil. Together they comprised approximately 80 percent of the normal sample. The third group consisted of the remaining 20 percent. These subjects came from less favorable backgrounds than did groups 1 and 2. The familial background was not as stable, there was history of mental illness in the family, the parents had marital conflicts, and the families also had more economic difficulties. The adolescents' moods were not as stable and they were prone to depression (this term is used in the colloquial sense). In general, these boys displayed what we have described as adolescent turmoil.

The adolescents with turmoil had significantly more psychiatric difficulties than teenagers in the other two growth groups. They had more psychiatric symptomatology and received significantly more psychotherapy (see also Masterson 1967). The followup studies of Offer and Offer (1975) show that the adolescents with turmoil did not do as well as those with relatively less problems. In addition, Masterson and Costello (1980) demonstrated that adolescents with severe emotional turmoil do well only with the aid of long-term intensive psychotherapy. They do not just grow out of it.

Discussion

The turmoil theory of adolescent development proposes that adolescents normally undergo significant disruption in their personality organization. This disruption, in turn, leads to fluctuation in moods, changeable and unpredictable behavior, confusion in thought, and rebellion against one's parents. Adolescents are viewed as needing to go through this period of turmoil in order to successfully separate from their parents and develop their own identity, learn how to relate well to male and female peers, and have a stable personality. If they do not go through turmoil during the adolescent years, they cannot, by definition, grow into mentally healthy, mature adults. The theory was first described by Hall (1904), who saw Stürm und Drang as characterizing the universal developmental psychology of adolescents. Hall stated that it was typical for adolescents to oscillate between the extremes of psychological functioning. Later Anna Freud (1946) expanded considerably on Hall's work. Her writings have become a foundation of psychoanalytic concepts on the subject.

Anna Freud's work emphasizes the changes that take place during adolescence and how totally disruptive these changes are for the individual. The biological changes that occur during puberty are endowed with tremendous powers resulting in the creation of chaos in the adolescent's psyche. Freud (1946) compares the effect of puberty on the adolescent to the beginning phase of an acute psychotic reaction. In other words, the weakening of the ego together with increased strength of the instinctual forces makes it almost impossible for the adolescent to function in a balanced and harmonious way: "The relation established between the forces of the ego and the id is destroyed, the painfully achieved psychic balance is upset, with the result that the inner conflicts between the two institutions blaze afresh" (p. 158).

Adolescents remind Anna Freud of the patients described by Helene Deutsch as being "as if" because they do not have the capacity to have truly consistent and stable interpersonal relationships. Freud (1946) says:

The struggle between the two antagonists, the ego and the id, has scarcely ended [in latency] . . . before the terms of agreement are radically altered by the reinforcement of one of the combatants. The physiological process which marks the attainment of physical sexual maturity is accompanied by a stimulation of the instinctual process, which is carried over into the psychic sphere in the form of an influx of libido. . . . The naughtiness of the latency period turns into the criminal behavior of adolescence. (Pp. 158–59)

Though surely the number of delinquents is small and their behavior does not characterize the majority of adolescents, according to Freud adolescents cannot "win." They are either controlled by their impulses and become a delinquent, or they are overrepressed and symptomatic, that is, depressed, phobic. In either case, adolescents cannot function well. According to Freud (1958), "To be normal during the adolescent period is by itself abnormal" (p. 275).

More recent psychoanalytic researchers have put forward similar views. In 1967 Peter Blos, a major contributor to the psychoanalytic literature on adolescence, wrote, "adolescence is the only period in human life during which ego regression and drive regression constitute an obligatory component of normal development" (p. 172). In 1962 he had written that profound reorganization of the emotional life occurs during early adolescence and adolescence proper, accompanied by well-recognized stages of chaos.

To Blos, adolescence is characterized by "excessive motility," "overwhelming" affect, and a "keen" self-awareness. It is characterized, in short, by a turmoil that only "abates with a gradual strengthening of controlling, inhibiting, guiding, and evaluative principles which render desires, actions, thoughts and values egosyntonic and reality-oriented." That Blos's views are not atypical of psychoanalytic thinking is shown by reference to similar statements in Deutsch (1967), Geleerd (1961), Jacobson (1961), Josselyn (1952, 1967), Laufer (1966), Pearson (1958), and Rabichow and Sklansky (1980). As further examples of the pervasive influence of the turmoil theory of adolescents, the interested reader might also study Ackerman (1958), Coleman (1961), Eissler (1958), Erikson (1959), and Fountain (1961). Even in as recent a publication as the third edition of the *Diagnostic and Statistical Manual of Mental Health* (1980), adolescent turmoil is seen as part of normal development: "Normal conflicts associated with maturing, such as 'adolescent turmoil,' are usually not associated with severe distress and impairment in occupational or social functioning" (p. 66). This is particularly striking, since the authors of the DSM-III pride themselves on sticking closely to observable behavioral patterns. In this instance, they swayed far away from empirical observation.

In essence, the teenagers we have surveyed portrayed themselves in ways that bear little resemblance to the stressed, stormy, and rebellious youths described originally by G. Stanley Hall (1904), Anna Freud (1946), and by later psychoanalytic theorists. As far as we know, almost every researcher* who has studied a representative sample of normal teenagers has come to the conclusion that by and large good coping and a smooth transition into adulthood are much more typical than the opposite. Among middle-class high school students, 80 percent can, in general, be described as normal, free of symptoms, and without turmoil.

There is no question but that extremely stressed teenagers who are in the midst of severe adolescent turmoil do exist. By their own self-report, 20 percent were among our group of "normal" adolescents. They attest to feeling empty emotionally, being confused most of the time, or hearing strange noises. These figures indicate that turmoil and maladaptation are a real and important part of many teenagers' lives. But while this figure is high—perhaps disturbingly so—it is useful to remember that these adolescents are far outnumbered by those making a relatively smooth transition to adulthood. Adolescents in turmoil consisted of an important subgroup. However, the often-cited attitudes that such adolescents are only going through a stage, or that he or she will outgrow this turmoil, may harm the teenagers. Disturbed youngsters are done no service when their mood swings are inaccurately seen as predictable, their negative affect as typical, and their extreme rebellion as understandably normal. It is a disservice to the deviant and disturbed adolescents who are in need of psychiatric care and are denied this help by mental health professionals who blithely assert that adolescents are just "going through a stage."

Every stage of life brings new challenges and opportunities. As adolescents enter young adulthood, their successes or failures during that stage are incorporated into their basic personality structure. Adolescence is probably no more transitional than the "midlife crises," "menopausal crises," "retirement crises," and so on that adults are thought to go through. Relatively few current workers have suggested that we call these adult stages transitional. Why do many theorists consider only adolescence transitional, especially when doing so tends to impart possible pejorative connotations and also serves to minimize the stable characteristic of adolescence?

A possible explanation of this tendency is that classical psychoanalytic theory (Freudian) basically has explained development in terms of the resolution of past conflicts. According to this theory, the adolescent has to rework the conflicts that were repressed during latency and then re-

---

*See Block 1971; Douvan and Adelson 1966; Elkin and Westley 1955; Gesell, Ilg, and Ames 1956; Grinker, Grinker, and Timberlake 1962; Hsu 1961; Masterson 1967; Offer 1969; Offer and Offer 1975; Offer, Ostrov, and Howard 1981a; Rutter et al. 1976; and Vaillant 1977.

emerge. This is, in part, why psychoanalyst Blos (1962) called adolescence the second individuation stage. According to him, adolescents reexperience their past conflicts and have a chance to resolve them. This resolution can be reached through a major crisis in behavior with serious repercussions in affect, cognition, and other internal states. The underlying theoretical premise is that the present is predetermined by what took place in the past. For example, if an adolescent is unable to develop meaningful and gratifying interpersonal relationships, then he or she most probably had poor relationships with his or her parents during the formation years. Lonely, isolated, depressed adolescents may need to recreate and understand their personal past and re-resolve it before they can resolve their current psychiatric difficulties. As correct as this clinical point of view may be for many psychiatric patients, it may not be applicable to most normal adolescents.

Events in each person's past, we agree, have a differential impact on present functioning and feelings. What is less clear is whether it is always necessary to recreate the past before developmental advancement can take place. In normal as contrasted to neurotic development, it is less likely that early relationships emerge intensely and continuously disrupt the present functioning of the individual. In the case of normals, conflicts and tasks specific to each developmental stage are coped with slowly, allowing for stability of personality configuration. Social and cultural structures also help the individual to maintain emotional equilibrium. Normal adolescents generally are hopeful, positive, and future oriented. Their positive experiences reinforce each other. When they do look back onto their own growth and development, they gain confidence from conflicts solved, traumas resolved without undue harm, and stress coped with successfully. Hence the past has less traumatic significance to normal adolescents. They do not find themselves continuously trying to recreate the past in order to better understand how to cope with it.

A variety of developmental theories exist that pertain to the psychological characteristics of adolescence.* Differences in tone among these theories should not obscure important theoretical differences among the various systems. For example, Piaget (1968) wrote about the adolescent as a philosopher who ponders his place in the world and struggles with his attempts to make sense of life. In contrast, psychoanalysts (Deutsch 1967; Erikson 1959; A. Freud 1946) describe adolescents as if they were ascetic, introspective, idealistic persons who challenge the "truths" of their elders.

Our data support none of these interpretations. We believe, instead,

*See, for example, Blos 1962; Conger 1975; Newman and Newman 1979; Stone and Church 1979; and Weiner 1970.

that each theory explains aspects of the psychology of certain adolescents, but that none is powerful enough to explain the psychology of adolescence in general.

One problem with current theories is that they tend to consist of expectations that adults have of adolescents, not the experience of adolescents themselves. As we have seen, data collected directly from normal adolescents are often significantly different from what many adults assume teenagers feel about themselves. Adolescence, as we have noted, is the world's most perfect projective device for adults. Adults' own fears and urges may interfere with their ability to correctly perceive what teenagers are really like. Leftover unfulfilled dreams and fantasies are easily projected onto adolescents and may also interfere with adults' understanding. Many adults hold on to the hope that their adolescent children will achieve what they have not been able to. Others fear that their children will surpass them. The vigor, strength, beauty, and sexual attractiveness of the growing adolescent may also threaten the adult. From a different perspective, to adults the growing young represent the adults' own inevitable demise. In addition, adults may need to put some distance between themselves and their young offspring to help prevent their acting upon their own, mostly unconscious, sexual impulses. Freud speculated in *Totem and Taboo* (1913) that the conflict between the generations is a continuous one, although it represents itself in a variety of forms. As correct as that statement may be for some adolescents, we wonder whether the conflict is as continuous and as dramatic as it is often portrayed.

Conclusion

We have presented data about normal adolescent development from different perspectives: the biological, the cognitive, and the psychosocial. Although the perspectives stress different aspects of the adolescent, it is important to keep in mind that in reality these different aspects function together.

The biological and cognitive data stress that by age sixteen most adolescents function as adults. It is reasonable, therefore, to assume that relatively normal adolescents at age sixteen and older should be able to communicate their feelings and thoughts about themselves in a more valid fashion than has been recognized by many mental health professionals. The identity crisis as described by Erikson (1956) is not bound to biological and cognitive data. As such it is a purer psychosocial phenom-

enon tied to a particular culture. As the society changes, so will the adolescent's search for identity. The cognitive and biological variables are
not static. Rather they change internally and are also affected by their
interaction with psychosocial variables. As the latter changes, so will the
cognitive and biological variables. An excellent example is seen in the
game of chess. In order to be a great chess player—a "grand master"—
one needs to possess particular temporal-spatial cognitive abilities. Most
grand masters begin to show their ability at adolescence. Until recently
there were no great female adolescent chess players. It seemed that females just did not possess this "innate" ability. Recently, with increased
experience, motivation, and opportunity, female adolescents have become much better chess players. Although top male chess players are still
considerably better than females, for the first time ever there are a number of female adult grand masters. This phenomenon has begun to take
place only since 1970.

Some more general questions concerning adolescent development
have to be considered more broadly. The life-cycle research endeavors
should help us in determining whether adolescence as a stage is indeed
more tumultuous for a larger number of individuals than any other transitional stage.What are the crucial childhood variables which predict
functioning during adolescence? Similarly, what factors during adolescence hold the key to correct predictions later in adulthood? The etiology
of both mental health and mental illness is multifactorial and multidimensional. No one factor, or even group of factors, can be singled out
in isolation as causing one or the other. The factors are part of the biopsychosocial system which continuously interact with one another. The factors' relationship change as their value (in weight) changes. Furthermore,
no two generations, or cultures, can reasonably be expected to be identical with one another. Thus it is imperative that we compare the adjustment of different groups of adolescents within the time dimension as well
as the social, psychological, and biological one.

REFERENCES

Ackerman, N. W. 1958. *The Psychodynamics of Family Life*. New York: Basic Books.
Apter, D., and Vihko, R. 1977. "Serum Pregnenolone, Progesterone, 17-Hydroxyproges-
terone, Testosterone, and 5-Dehydrotestosterone During Female Puberty." *Journal of Clini-
cal Endocrinology and Metabolism* 45:1039–48.
Block, J. 1971. *Lives Through Time*. Berkeley, Calif.: Bancroft Books.
Blos, P. 1962. *On Adolescence*. New York: Free Press.

————. 1967. "The Second Individuation Process of Adolescence." *Psychoanalytic Study of the Child* 22:162–85.

Bringuier, J.-C. 1980. *Conversations with Jean Piaget*. Chicago: University of Chicago Press.

Bynum, T. W.; Thomas, J. A.; and Weitz, L. J. 1972. "Truth Functional Logic in Formal Operational Thinking: Inhelder and Piaget's Evidence." *Developmental Psychology* 7:129–32.

Campbell, A. 1981. *The Sense of Well-Being in America: Recent Patterns and Trends*. New York: McGraw-Hill.

Coleman, J. S., 1961. *The Adolescent Society*. New York: Free Press.

Conger, J. J., ed. 1975. *Contemporary Issues in Adolescent Development*. New York: Harper & Row.

Deutsch, H. 1967. *Selected Problems of Adolescence*. New York: International Universities Press.

Diagnostic and Statistical Manual of Mental Disorders (DSM-III), 3rd ed. 1980. Washington, D.C.: American Psychiatric Association.

Douvan, E., and Adelson, J. 1966. *The Adolescent Experience*. New York: John Wiley & Sons.

Dulit, E. 1972. "Adolescent Thinking à la Piaget: The Formal Stage." *Journal of Youth and Adolescence* 4:281–301.

Dusek, J. B., and Flaherty, J. F. 1981. "The Development of the Self-Concept During the Adolescent Years." *Monographs of the Society for Research in Child Development* 46:191.

Eissler, K. R. 1958. "Notes of Problems of Technique in the Psychoanalytic Treatment of Adolescents." *Psychoanalytic Study of the Child* 13:223–54.

Elkin, F., and Westley, W. A. 1955. "The Myth of Adolescent Culture." *American Sociological Review* 23:680–83.

Elkind, D. 1961. "Quantity Conceptions in Junior and Senior High School Students." *Child Development* 32:551–60.

————. 1962. "Quantity Conceptions in College Students." *Journal of Social Psychology* 57:459–65.

————. 1975. "Recent Research on Cognitive Development in Adolescence." In *Adolescence in the Life Cycle*, ed. S. E. Dragastin and G. H. Elder, Jr., pp. 49–61. New York: Halsted Press.

Erikson, E. H. 1956. "The Problem of Ego Identity." *Journal of the American Psychoanalytic Association* 4:56–121.

————. 1959. "Identity and the Life Cycle." *Psychological Issues* 1:1–171.

Fountain, G. 1961. "Adolescent into Adult: An Inquiry." *Journal of the American Psychoanalytic Association* 9:417–33.

Freud, A. 1946. *The Ego and the Mechanism of Defense*. New York: International Universities Press.

————. 1958. "Adolescence." *Psychoanalytic Study of the Child* 16:225–78.

Freud, S. [1913] 1955. "Totem and Taboo." In *The Standard Edition of the Complete Psychological Works of Sigmund Freud*, ed. James L. Strachey, vol. 13, pp. 1–164. London: Hogarth Press.

Geleerd, E. R. 1961. "Some Aspects of Ego Vicissitudes in Adolescence." *Journal of the American Psychoanalytic Association* 9:394–405.

Gesell, A.; Ilg, F.; and Ames, L. 1956. *Youth: The Years from Ten to Sixteen*. New York: Harper & Row.

Graves, A. J. 1972. "Attainment of Mass, Weight and Volume in Minimally Educated Adults." *Developmental Psychology* 7:223.

Grinker, R. R., Sr.; Grinker, R. R., Jr.; and Timberlake, J. 1962. "A Study of 'Mentally Healthy' Young Males (Homoclites)." *Archives of General Psychiatry* 6:405.

Hall, G. S. 1904. *Adolescence: Its Psychology and Its Relation to Physiology, Anthropology, Sociology, Sex, Crime, Religion and Education*. New York: Appleton.

Hill, J. P. 1981. "School Structure, Informal Peer Networks and Social Development in Adolescence." Paper delivered at the Department of Psychiatry, Michael Reese Hospital and Medical Center, January 22, Chicago, Ill.

Hobbs, E. D. 1973. "Adolescent's Concepts of Physical Quantity." *Developmental Psychology* 9:431.

Hsu, F. L. K. 1961. "Culture Patterns and Adolescent Behavior." *International Journal of Social Psychiatry* 7:33–53.

Hulbert, A. 1981. "The Awkward Age." *The New Republic*, Oct. 28, 36–39.

Inhelder, B., and Piaget, J. 1958. *The Growth of Logical Thinking from Childhood to Adolescence*. New York: Basic Books.

Jacobson, E. 1961. "Adolescent Moods and the Remodeling of Psychic Structures in Adolescence." *Psychoanalytic Study of the Child* 16:164–84.

Josselyn, I. M. 1952. *The Adolescent and His World*. New York: Family Services Association of America.

————. 1967. "The Adolescent Today." *Smith College Studies in Social Work* 38:1–15.

Kett, J. F. 1977. *Rites of Passage: Adolescence in America, 1790 to the Present*. New York: Basic Books.

Kohlberg, L., and Gilligan, C. 1971. "The Adolescent as Philosopher." *Daedalus* 100:1051–86.

Laufer, M. 1966. "Object Loss and Mourning During Adolescence." *Psychoanalytic Study of the Child* 21:269–94.

Lewis, J. M., et al. 1976. *No Single Thread: Psychological Health in Family Systems*. New York: Free Press.

Lewis, J. M., and Looney, J. 1983. *The Long Struggle*. New York: Brunner/Mazel.

Marshall, W. A., and Tanner, J. M. 1969. "Variations in the Pattern of Pubertal Changes in Girls." *Archives of Disease in Childhood* 44:291–303.

Masterson, J. F., Jr. 1967. *The Psychiatric Dilemma of Adolescence*. Boston: Little, Brown.

Masterson, J. F., Jr., and Costello, J. 1980. *From Borderline Adolescent to Functioning Adult: The Test of Time*. New York: Brunner/Mazel.

Nesselroade, J. R., and Baltes, P. B. 1974. "Adolescent Personality Development and Historical Change: 1970–1972." *Monographs of the Society for Research in Child Development* 39:1–79.

Newman, B. M., and Newman, P. R. 1979. *An Introduction to the Psychology of Adolescence*. Homewood, Ill.: The Dorsey Press.

Offer, D. 1969. *The Psychological World of the Teenager: A Study of Normal Adolescent Boys*. New York: Basic Books.

Offer, D., and Offer, J. B. 1975. *From Teenage to Young Manhood: A Psychological Study*. New York: Basic Books.

Offer, D., and Sabshin, M. 1974. *Normality: Theoretical and Clinical Concepts of Mental Health*. New York: Basic Books.

Offer, D.; Marohn, R. C.; and Ostrov, E. 1979. *The Psychological World of Juvenile Delinquents*. New York: Basic Books.

Offer, D..; Ostrov, E.; and Howard, K. I. 1981a. *The Adolescent: A Psychological Self-Portrait*. New York: Basic Books.

————. 1981b. "The Mental Health Professional's Concept of the Normal Adolescent." *Archives of General Psychiatry* 38:149–52.

————. 1982. "Family Perceptions of Adolescent Self-Image." *Journal of Youth & Adolescence* 11:4, 281–91.

————. 1984. *Patterns of Adolescent Self-Image*. San Francisco: Jossey-Bass.

Ostrov, E., and Offer, D. 1980. "Loneliness and the Adolescent." In *The Anatomy of Loneliness*, ed. J. Hartog, J. R. Audys, and Y. A. Cohen, pp. 170–86. New York: International Universities Press.

Pearson, G. H. J. 1958. *Adolescence and the Conflict of Generations, An Introduction to Some of the Psychoanalytic Contributions to the Understanding of Adolescence*. New York: W. W. Norton.

Petersen, A. L., and Taylor, B. 1980. "Puberty, Biological Change and Psychological Adaptation." In *Handbook of Adolescent Psychology*, ed. J. Adelson, pp. 117–59. New York: John Wiley & Sons.

Piaget, J. 1948. *The Moral Judgment of the Child*, trans. M. Gabain. Glencoe, Ill.: The Free Press.

————. 1950. *The Psychology of Intelligence*, trans. M. Piercy and D. E. Berlyne. New York: Harcourt, Brace.

————. 1952. *The Language and Thought of the Child*. London: Routledge and Kegan Paul.

————. 1968. *Six Psychological Studies*. New York: Vintage Books.

————. 1972. "Intellectual Evolution from Adolescence to Adulthood." *Human Development* 15:1–12.

Rabichow, H. G., and Sklansky, M. A. 1980. *Effective Counseling of Adolescents*. Chicago: Follett.

Rosenberg, M. 1979. *Conceiving the Self*. New York: Basic Books.

Rosenfield, R. L. 1971. "Plasma Testosterone Binding Globulin and Indexes of the Concentration of Unbound Plasma Androgens in Normal and Hirsute Subjects." *Journal of Clinical Endocrinology and Metabolism* 32:717–28.

————. 1974. Discussion. In *Control of the Onset of Puberty*, ed. M. M. Grumbach, G. D. Grave, and F. E. Mayer, p. 360. New York: John Wiley & Sons.

Rutter, M., et al. "Adolescent Turmoil: Fact or Fiction." *Journal of Child Psychology and Psychiatry* 17:35–56.

Siegler, R. S.; Liebert, D. E.; and Liebert, R. M. 1973. "Inhelder and Piaget's Pendulum Problem: Teaching Preadolescents to Act as Scientists." *Developmental Psychology* 9:97–101.

Sorensen, R. C. 1973. *Adolescent Sexuality in Contemporary America*. New York: World.

Stone, L. J., and Church, J. 1979. *Childhood and Adolescence: A Psychology of the Growing Person*, 4th ed. New York: Random House.

Tanner, J. M. 1962. *Growth at Adolescence*. Springfield, Ill.: Charles C Thomas.

————. 1972. "Sequence, Tempo, and Individual Variation in Growth and Development of Boys and Girls Aged Twelve to Sixteen." In *Twelve to Sixteen: Early Adolescence*, ed. J. Kagan and R. Coles, pp. 1–24. New York: W. W. Norton.

Tomlinson-Keasey, C. 1972. "Formal Operations in Females from Eleven to Fifty-four Years of Age." *Developmental Psychology* 6:364.

Vaillant, G. E. 1977. *Adaptation to Life*. Boston: Little, Brown.

Weiner, I. B. 1970. *Psychological Disturbance in Adolescence*. New York: Wiley-Interscience.

Young, H. B. 1971. "The Physiology of Adolescence." In *Modern Perspectives in Adolescent Psychiatry*, ed. J. G. Howells, pp. 3–23. New York: Brunner/Mazel.

Young Adulthood:
Stages of Maturity

General Definitions

A discussion of young adulthood in a volume devoted to normality and the life cycle involves definitions of three terms: young adulthood, normality, and life cycle.

YOUNG ADULTHOOD

In their communications to contributors, Offer and Sabshin defined young adulthood as that period "from high school to the mid-twenties, when one has achieved intimacy. Issues such as identity have been reasonably resolved." The periods bounding young adulthood were adolescence, described as the period "through high school, dealing with changing in one's body and separating from one's parents" and middle adulthood, covering "intimacy, courtship, marriage, childbearing" and "the years from twenty-five to forty-five." Thus their definition implies a chronological age (seventeen or eighteen to twenty-five), accomplishment on certain intellectual or educational tasks (having finished high school), the attainment of certain psychological capacities (intimacy, identity), and, by inference, the expectation that other life events will not have occurred (marriage, childbearing).

A review of the literature reveals that there seems to be no real agreement on the definition of adulthood or on its span and subdivisions. Modell, Furstenberg, and Hershberg (1976) comment that "it is an open question whether individuals in any given society hold a common notion of adulthood" (p. 9). Adjectives such as "early," "middle", and "late" are applied differentially without precise agreement on the age periods that they designate. Furthermore, although there is more agreement on the general age at which the period begins than on its close, even the beginning is confused by the fact that some use "late adolescence" to describe the period from seventeen to twenty-two, while some use "youth," some use "postadolescence," and others feel that these ages signify young adulthood. Offer and Offer (1975) illustrate the confusion by stating, "late adolescence, or young adulthood as we have labeled the post-high school years" (p. 172) and "adolescence does not necessarily end at 22 . . ." (p. 173). Kimmel (1974), alluding to gender differences, cites the Neugarten, Moore, and Lowe study in which middle-aged respondents described a "young man" as eighteen to twenty-two and a "young woman" as eighteen to twenty-five. Reversing the difference, the shorter *Oxford English Dictionary* defines adolescence as the period between fourteen to twenty-five for males and twelve to twenty-one for females. Levinson and associates (1978) define childhood and adolescence as from zero to twenty-two years and early adulthood as from seventeen to forty-five, introducing the concept of a transitional period, the years between seventeen to twenty-two, as the "early adult transition," a period of overlap between stages. Thus, depending on how restrictively one views the terms, one can prolong adolescence to twenty-five or begin adulthood at seventeen.

The end of young adulthood has an even broader age span. Offer and Sabshin suggest twenty-five; Guntrip and Marshall (1973) cite thirty; Levinson and coworkers (1978) define the "middle adult transition" as forty to forty-five. Sometimes a term such as youth implies a definition by behavior. The age range of "youth" is usually not specified, but the term frequently describes a period when individuals have many adult capabilities but have not assumed adult responsibilities—in other words, a time when some social definitions of adulthood do not yet apply. Parsons (1949) states: "by contrast with the emphasis on responsibility in the [adult male] role, the orientation of the youth culture is more or less specifically irresponsible" (p. 272). Jung (1971), however, states that youth "extends roughly from the years just after puberty to middle life, which itself begins between the thirty-fifth and fortieth year" (p. 8).

NORMALITY

Offer and Sabshin (1974) have designated four definitions of normality: as health, as utopia, as average, and as transactional systems.

For the purpose of this discussion, normality as health can be equated to normality as *mental* health. This, in turn, leads to questions of the definition of mental health, a complex subject about which much has been written. To cite just three authors: Hartmann (1964) speaks of the concept in terms of ego development and adaptation; Erikson (1950) speaks in terms of crises that need to be favorably resolved; while White (1975) refers to five growth trends covering the stabilizing of ego identity, the freeing of personal relationships, the deepening of interests, the humanizing of values, and the expansion of caring.

Normality as utopia is even more difficult to describe, although in an attempt to develop a comprehensive psychology, psychoanalysts (Sachs 1977) tend to mix normality as health with normality as utopia. Furthermore, normality as utopia may require a social context (Lacy and Hendricks 1980; Wallerstein 1975) even though some theorists have attempted to describe normative psychological functioning and dissociate this ideal from the environment. However, even within a given society, socioeconomic differences may make certain personality traits more desirable in some social classes (Havighurst 1971). Thus the lower-class male may need to be aggressive to survive, whereas the upper-middle-class male may use aggression constructively but may be less dependent on aggressiveness for survival. Therefore aggressiveness as a trait may not be "utopian."

Normality as average seems less related to psychological functioning, although the concept can be used to differentiate usual psychological states from abnormal ones and sometimes to provide ranges of "normal." Thus averages can be applied to biological norms, such as size, and to such mattters as intelligence, although as Offer and Sabshin (1974) point out that if one applies the bell-shaped curve principle, both extremes will be "deviant." Geniuses, however, tend to be considered "rare" rather than "deviant," and, similarly, one is more likely to consider the very tall individual unusual and the dwarf abnormal. It is only when there is distortion in "normal" proportions—for example, in acromegaly—that the tall individual becomes "abnormal." This, of course, illustrates how values can intrude on expressions of the concept of normality even when considering normality as average.

Normality as transactional systems introduces the concept of time. Unlike the first three definitions, it is impossible to describe this perspective in static terms. This concept is closely allied to the life-cycle concept, which by implication involves a movement through time with change an expectable part of the system. Modell, Furstenberg, and Hershberg (1976) quote Katz as saying that there are a variety of accomplishments necessary to reach full adult status, and one does not accomplish all simultaneously. According to Symonds and Jensen (1961): "Becoming an adult requires making an adjustment with respect to three important areas—

education, vocation, marriage" (p. 202). Many of the psychological functions that one hopes the full-fledged adult will achieve do not necessarily proceed at the same rate for everyone or even at the same pace within a given individual. Thus the achievement of intimacy, an Erikson (1950) criterion, may proceed slowly in a given individual, whereas the commitment to an occupation may occur early and not shift.

These approaches to normality are useful points of reference, but, inevitably, many of the views espoused by both theorists and empirical investigators implicitly combine more than one. Thus sociologists often measure normality by averages although they often discuss by implication normality as utopia (at least for a given society) and normality as transactional systems in the sense of the capacity to negotiate certain life events within a social context. Psychoanalysts, psychiatrists, and psychologists are concerned with normality as health, but this often becomes equivalent to normality as utopia, and they frequently discuss these ideas in transactional terms of adaptation or mental capacities. They much less often discuss normality as average although the more phenomenologically oriented may establish "norms" based on the presence or absence of certain characteristics.

LIFE CYCLE

The life cycle concept in simplest terms encapsulates the idea that all individuals go through a series of periods or stages during life with each period having characteristic patterns. This is quite apparent in biological terms, but psychoanalysts beginning with Freud have been intrigued with the concept of a psychological life cycle, and much of the early psychoanalytic research involved the delineation of "psychosexual stages" of development during childhood. In many instances the psychological theory was based on the ontogenetic concept and the development that is observable in biological terms. The division into developmental periods was somewhat arbitraty but found to be useful. Often these were simply listed in popular terms as childhood, adolescence, adulthood, and old age. The earlier psychoanalysts were concerned primarily with the first two periods, but Jung (1971) talked about the stages of life, and the development of ego psychology allowed the extension of the developmental model into adulthood. This led Erikson (1980) to put forth his epigenetic concept and to delineate eight psychological stages from infancy to old age (1950).

The interest of psychiatrists, psychoanalysts, and psychologists in the period of adulthood is relatively recent (Katchadourian 1978). After a long period when the major focus of concern with individual psychological development was on the periods of childhood and adolescence, there is now growing investigation of later development.* Actually, the idea that later development occurs is rather new, because up until recently there was, at least implicitly, the notion that "development," in the sense that it had been used to describe psychological events in childhood and adolescence, stopped when one reached adulthood. On the other hand, sociologists and anthropologists have been interested for some time in the social context of adult societies, and they have described in detail transitional rites and social roles (see, e.g., Mead 1928, among many others).

Specific Definitions

ADULTHOOD

Adulthood is a state often referred to, usually with the implication that a relatively clear concept is being communicated. Probably the word does communicate a general concept, but when one attempts precise definition, the concept becomes quite elusive. *Webster's Dictionary* defines adult as "fully developed (as in size, strength, or intellectual capacity): fully mature: grown-up." It defines the adjective "mature" as "having attained the normal peak of growth and development." Thus the definitions imply an ongoing, somewhat inevitable process, but no comment on the endpoint is made. The definition of "mature," moreover, introduces the concept of normality without making any attempt to define it.

MATURITY

When a fruit becomes mature, we say that it is ripe. If the process continues, the fruit becomes overripe or rotten. Fruit and humans differ, but the comparison underlines the idea of growth, a peak period, then decay. Furthermore, the process of maturing often has an implied standard against which it is measured. One talks about premature and postmature births to indicate deviation from the expectable duration of gestation. In human growth and development, however, there is no agreement on the endpoint of "ripeness," and the standard against which maturity is measured is both multiplex and rather variable. The human is composed of a series of abilities and biological systems that reach peaks at different times (Timiras 1978). The general concept of adulthood seems to encompass all the peaks—but rather loosely. Although adulthood and maturity are not synonymous, in determining them one can use a stan-

*See Colarusso and Nemiroff (1979); Gould (1972); Levinson et al. (1978); and Vaillant and Milofsky (1980).

dard of physical or biological development, of intellectual development, of psychological or emotional development, of what might be called sociocultural development, or some combination of all four measured against age.

Furthermore, there is evidence that there are gender differences in the maturing process,* but whether these are primarily the result of biological differences or result from sociocultural differences in rearing and in social expectations is not clear (Whitbourne and Waterman 1979). In more recent times the women's movement has served to narrow the distinction in social role expectations of males and females in U.S. society, but the movement is still too new for researchers to be able to state definitely how it will affect the maturing process for women in the longer term (Abrahams, Feldman, and Nash 1978). Furthermore, these changes may be restricted to the more educated and higher socioeconomic segment of the society (Lowenthal, Thurnher, and Chiriboga 1975).

It is immediately apparent that the four standards used to measure maturity are composed of different characteristics. Physical or biological growth has a forward thrust of its own, if nutrition is adequate and illness does not supervene.† In general, an individual grows in height and weight during childhood, reaches puberty—at which time various secondary sexual characteristics appear—and continues to grow during adolescence as well as to develop reproductive capacity. Eisenberg (1980) describes the biological termination of adolescence as the closing of the osseous epiphyses and the completion of sexual maturation. Although there are individuals who fail to develop as expected, the majority do, and it is not too difficult to designate a rough period in an individual's twenties when a biophysiological "peak" is reached (Marshall 1973). One could use as an endpoint the age at which growth in height stops, weight reaches a relatively stable state, and various physiological measures (strength, speed, cardiac output, respiratory capacity) are at a maximum (Timiras 1978).‡

Intellectual development in its later stages depends in large measure on educational efforts. Thus although an individual who leaves school in early adolescence will almost certainly develop better judgment, a greater fund of knowledge, and, perhaps, more complex ways of thinking as a

---

*See Blos (1980); Gilligan (1982); Nawas (1971); and Ritvo (1976).

†This is not quite accurate, because Spitz (1945) has shown that emotional nurturance as well as food is necessary for average growth and development in infants.

‡As is so often the case in the complex organism that is a human being, peaks in specific physical abilities, such as athletic skills, may occur earlier or later than the expectable overall peak. For example, female swimmers often peak in their teens and football quarterbacks, in their thirties. In these instances the requisite skills may be particularly related to adolescent body types or depend on experience and emotional stability as much as on physical strength or speed.

result of experience and inevitable exposure to new sources of information, major intellectual development will usually not occur without the challenges and discipline of formal education. Because the interest in and opportunity for continuing educational effort vary in different societies and in different social groups within a society, the peak of intellectual development is difficult to ascertain (Arlin 1975). It can be measured by various tests (Baltes and Labouvie 1973), although certain mental abilities may not have easily defined zeniths, and such capacities as judgment may be almost impossible to measure.

The psychological or emotional standard is the most complex, partly because it is the least tangible. Thus one's theoretical framework may determine the definition of adulthood. There have been two main streams of investigation. One has emerged from the psychoanalytic tradition, using information from child observation and adult and child psychoanalysis. Freud started with the reconstruction of psychosexual development in childhood, and a series of analysts have extended the developmental story to include adolescence (Aarons 1970; Blos 1962; A. Freud 1958). The individual reaches adulthood by completing the psychological tasks of adolescence, a process that psychoanalysts have attempted to explicate in terms of the unconscious and by postulating theoretical constructs of mental structure, such as ego, ego ideal, and self. Other investigators, using very different techniques (such as questionnaires and personality scales) have tended to focus on overt behavior. These two sets of data frequently seem unrelated although they purport to describe the same process.

The sociocultural standard is the most variable and will differ from one society to another and in different groups even within one society. Anthropological studies demonstrate that admission to adult status is signified by different customs or ages and may be defined by social role, religious participation, biologic capacity, or simple chronologic age. Even in Western society, which displays some consistency in attitudes toward maturing, there are variations at least partially determined by educational systems. Because there is a tendency to make one sociocultural measure the ability to fulfill certain roles—that is, to be relatively self-supporting and to take responsibility for a work or family role appropriate to the society—graduation from student status is usually implied. The sociocultural standard is also difficult to characterize because it may be composed of some relatively specific criteria that may not be present in a given individual who still must be considered an adult. Thus societies have laws that govern when certain behavior, such as driving a car, drinking, voting, or military service, is permitted, but an individual may be adult without ever engaging in any of these behaviors. Other sociocultural criteria, such as working, being self-supporting, marriage, and childrearing, are much more open to circumstances and value judgments and may be subject to fairly rapid change in the modern world. Marriage, for example, is no longer considered as essential a step in the attainment of adulthood as it once was. Not long ago, in certain social groups it was not thought inappropriate for an unmarried daughter to live at home, help with the household tasks, and not have a paid job. Even in so short a time as thirty years, Parsons's (1949) description of the adult role for the urban woman as "the woman's fundamental status is that of her husband's wife, the mother of his children . . ." (p. 274) seems quite outdated or, at best, incomplete.

INTERACTION OF STANDARDS OF MATURITY

There are significant and important interactions among the standards of maturity. For example, if a society demands, or allows for the development of, highly technical achievement, there may be a sanctioned state in which the individual reaches one criterion of adulthood, such as intimacy, while postponing others, such as self-support, in the interests of furthering intellectual development through education. Prelinger (1974), has suggested that the whole period of adolescence is a modern invention resulting from the stretching out of education for more than a small segment of the population and from the consequent postponement of some social role behavior, such as family formation and expectations for self-support. Similarly Blos (1979) says "puberty is an act of nature and adolescence is an act of man" (p. 405) and B. Hamburg is quoted as saying that as a result of complex educational demands "achievement of full social maturity has tended to be increasingly delayed" (Hamburg, Coelho, and Adams 1974, p. 417). Broad sociocultural changes are involved, notably the industrial revolution with its emphasis on technical skill and knowledge, the decline of farming, and in certain countries, at least, the enactment of child labor laws that prevented a child from immediately entering the industrial workforce.

Similarly, an individual may have reached adult status by all external criteria set by a society and remain psychologically unable to fill the expected role. The same may be true for the interaction between the biological and the psychological. It is not so uncommon for an individual to be characterized as having the emotions of a child in an adult body, and while this statement may be somewhat flippant, it may accurately describe a real situation: for example, an individual may be biologically capable of producing a child but not psychologically ready to take responsibility for its rearing.

There may be even more complex interactions between the sociocultural and the psychological. The overall attitudes of a society toward individual achievement, family, social class, and occupation will have a considerable influence in determining the adult psychological qualities needed and, consequently, may influence the psychological tasks that must be completed in order to reach adulthood (Murphey et al. 1963). In a society that favors individualism, allows free choice in marriage, encourages upward social mobility, and has no arbitrary restrictions on choice of occupation, a considerable degree of psychological autonomy tends to be viewed as necessary for coping successfully. If the society is socially stratified, arranged marriage is traditional, occupation is determined by family heritage, and few choices exist for the individual in any sphere, the same degree of psychological autonomy may not be essential.

Opinions differ whether the concept of normality requires a context or social group against which to judge the individual (Wallerstein 1975), but the problem becomes greater when one attempts to relate normality to a given life period, the definition of which itself is subject to different approaches. If one defines the period by age alone, it is possible to consider individuals in that age period and describe a range of normality. But for most observers of the young-adult period, age is not a very valid method of definition, and there has been a tendency to view the expectability of certain events, both external and internal, as determining or defining the period. However, these events may vary considerably within a general societal context depending on the subgroups observed. Thus the individual who goes no further than high school will be on a different timetable from the individual who goes on to college and graduate school. There may even be differences between individuals who go no further than college and those who enter certain graduate programs (King 1980). Do the same standards apply to each?

Kilpatrick (1974) feels that the society needs "an equivalent of the primitive rite of passage. As it stands now no one really knows the criteria for adulthood in this country. Is it the drivers' license? the high school diploma? the vote? the army? marriage? child raising? the achievement of economic independence?" (p. 411). Jordan (1978) gives an interesting account of adulthood in the United States from the historical viewpoint, stressing the different ages at which different adult actions were permitted. He quotes Blackstone's summary of the differing ages at which males and females may be considered mature. He points out that there are even differences between states in, for example, age of marriage without parental consent. Goldstein (1978) discusses the concept of the "adult" as it has been elucidated in secular law.

Contributing, however, to the difficulties in establishing sociocultural standards of normality and maturity is the social change occurring in U.S.

society. Keniston (1963) discusses aspects of social change in the contemporary era in contrast with past periods and emphasizes the technological changes that power this change and create strain. He comments on the impact of this change on identity and on the youth culture, and notes that one byproduct of the change is the impossibility of having parental exemplars because the world in which the parents grew up was inevitably different from the world the children will inhabit, and, therefore, the necessary capacities and adaptations will differ. He states: "Parents can no longer hope to be literal models for their children; institutions cannot hope to persist without change in rite, practice, and custom" (p. 186). However, he asserts that it is essential to maintain some values and principles to provide continuity amid rapid change.

These considerations lead to the conclusion that there is a close sociocultural connection between adult status and social role that involves expectations that society has of individuals as well as expectations that individuals have of themselves. The social role aspect, however, must have a concurrent psychological aspect, and there are certain individuals who do not fulfill any of the social roles but who seem to have reached an adult psychological state. How one defines this state and describes the transition from adolescence into it are difficult problems, but ones that must be addressed in any discussion of normality and young adulthood.

Theoretical Views of Adulthood

The theoretical literature on adulthood is both diverse and fragmentary and, thus, is quite difficult to review in any depth or in an orderly fashion. Truly comprehensive coverage is beyond the scope of this chapter; the subject can include the entire psychoanalytic literature related to mental functioning, the developmental psychology literature, as well as cross-cultural studies and many different types of personality studies. As one might anticipate, it divides into several rough categories, which can be loosely described as focusing on the psychological, the sociological, and what might be described as the biological, or discussions of physical growth and intellectual development. Divisions, in part, follow social science disciplines, but even within each social science discipline there tends to be several subcategories. These may be determined by the methodology of the research study (e.g., cross-sectional vs. longitudinal or clinical interview vs. questionnaire) but more often by the theoretical approach of the investigator. Furthermore, there are many "crossovers"

in which there is a combining of sociocultural and psychological considerations. For example, separation from the family of origin, a frequently
mentioned criterion of adulthood, has both a social, or external, aspect
and a psychological, or internal, aspect. Only selected examples will be
cited, and examples from the more sociocultural approach will be addressed first.

SOCIOCULTURAL VIEW

Neugarten (1971) has written perceptively about the young-adult period from the sociopsychological viewpoint. She points out that developmental theories are frequently based on biological models of growth.
These models work reasonably well when considering childhood but less
well in adulthood. As the individual life history becomes longer, the
differences between individuals become greater because of the accumulation of differing experiences. She states: "Adults use major life events as
the markers of time; they evaluate themselves in relation to a socially-
defined time, age norms, and age expectations of self and others. Thus a
social clock must be superimposed over the biological clock in the study
of lives" (1971, p. 85). According to Sternschein (1973), Neugarten feels
that each age status has "recognized rights, duties, and obligations; and
each with a succession of turning points and a timetable for the ordering
of life events" (p. 640). Neugarten states unequivocally that although the
norms vary somewhat among groups, for any given group "norms and
actual occurrences are closely related" (1969, p. 124) and "the age norms
operate as a system of social controls" (1969, p. 124). She also points out
(1971) that in a period such as young adulthood when events, such as
marriage and parenthood, may occur, age can be misleading because
these events will have an inevitable effect on personality. Consequently,
cohort study results that include some individuals who have experienced
these events and some who have not should not really be considered in
the aggregate.

An example of the approach based on "marker" events is found in
Modell, Furstenberg, and Hershberg's 1976 study of social change and
transition to adulthood in historical perspective. They describe five transitions: "exit from school; entrance to the work-force; departure from the
family of origin; marriage; and the establishment of household" (p. 9).
Using statistical methods, they then analyze the ages at which these
events take place in 1880 and in 1970. Perhaps somewhat surprisingly,
their results indicate that there is less difference between 1880 and 1970
than one might expect. There has been a shift to a later age in leaving
school and a greater spread in the age range of this event; there are more
women in the workforce; but the age spread for the latter three events

has narrowed. They conclude that "growing up, as a process, has become briefer, more normful, bounded, and consequential—and thereby more demanding on the individual participants" (p. 30).

PSYCHOLOGICAL VIEW

There are various ways of approaching the problem of measuring psychological development. One is to describe the developmental tasks of adolescence and assert that, if these are accomplished, the adult psychological state has been reached. A second is to provide a description of the adult state in psychological terms. Although these seem like straightforward approaches, a review of the literature reveals that there is wide variation in descriptions of both. An exhaustive treatment is beyond the scope of this discussion, but some consideration of current major theories is appropriate.

The psychological literature is replete with terms that in themselves are in need of definition, a task also beyond the scope of this chapter. However, a few terms that recur in relation to development can be traced to certain major theorists. "Identity" and "ego identity" are two concepts popularized by Erikson (1950, 1956). The term "intimacy" in a special context owes its frequent reference to Erikson's sixth stage of the life cycle. Focus on "ego development" and "adaptation" probably derive their prominence from the work of Anna Freud (1937) and Hartmann (1958), "self" from Kohut (1971), and separation-individuation as applied to adolescence from Blos (1967). All these terms are frequently cited as relevant to the transition to adulthood and, consequently, to the concept of normality in the young adult.*

In 1945 and 1946 Erikson introduced the concept of identity as a result of his observations of two Indian tribes, and he initially seemed to stress social identity—how the Indian child learns the identity that he or she is to have as an adult member of the tribe or community. He recognized, however, the dual nature of the identity concept; it has both an internal and an external component. In an expansion of his observations and thinking, he explicated (1950) eight stages of the life cycle and described a primary crisis (or turning point) for each, leading to one of two outcomes—success or failure in resolving the crisis. Erikson constructed a diagram with his eight age stages on the vertical axis and his eight conflicts on the horizontal axis, creating sixty-four boxes. Although he does not assign specific ages for his stages, the adolescent crisis outcomes initially were defined as "identity vs. identity diffusion" and the late

*Schafer (1973) writes persuasively about the difficulties with these terms and about their imprecise and overlapping use. Similarly, Abend (1974) makes a heroic attempt to sort them into some order.

adolescent or young adult crisis outcomes as "intimacy vs. isolation." Although these were the "ascendant" crises for the age periods described, Erikson's format is considerably more complex because each of the axes has lesser crises in all the other age periods. Technically, then, all sixty-four boxes can be filled in, although Erikson outlines only the general schema. In his most recent diagram (1978) he adds the word "fidelity" to the adolescent crisis and "love" to that of young adulthood.

Erikson unquestionably has been one of the most influential theorists, and there seems to be remarkable acceptance of his fifth and sixth life-cycle stages—identity versus identity diffusion, (identity confusion, in his latest version) and intimacy versus isolation—even though the precise nature of these crises is open to interpretation. His conceptualizations have formed the basis of a number of studies, using several different investigational methods, and his terms appear in the writings of many succeeding researchers. Marcia (1966) developed the Identity Status Scale based on a quadripartite interpretation of the Erikson concepts of moratorium and crisis. He developed scales for foreclosed identity, moratorium, achievement, and identity diffusion. A whole series of studies have been performed using this instrument and attempting to measure identity status (Bourne, 1978a,b; Marcia, 1976; Meilman 1979). A related series of studies was conducted by Orlofsky (1976) based on Erikson's stage of intimacy versus isolation, and other investigators have interrelated the intimacy measure with identity status (Marcia 1980). Recently Vaillant and Milofsky (1980) conducted an empirical study of Erikson's life stages on a sample of men.

There has been a general acceptance of the importance of an established identity in the determination of maturity. This again is unquestionably Erikson's influence, but there has been considerable range in the definition of identity. In attempting a synthesis of cognitive and ego psychology, Adams (1977) describes a personal identity and a social identity. He comments that Erikson integrates the two into ego identity. Adams describes social identity as "the social configuration that arises from one's self-perception and others' perception of the individual's position in social space" (p. 151) and personal identity as "a fusion or summation of membership roles, past and present identifications, and personal character all of which are united by a cognitive network structure and are summarized by the person into self-definitions which answer the 'Who am I question'" (p. 151). He further describes personal identity as "internal psychological structure that consists of self-images, values, attitudes, and thoughts" (p. 151). In reviewing the state of research on ego identity, Bourne (1978b) says that identity formation involves "intrapsychic structuralization, acquisition of social and vocational skills, internalization of societal norms prescriptive of 'adult' behavior" (p. 387). He feels that psychoanalysts provide "the most comprehensive theoretical framework for understanding the intrapsychic development processes that contribute to the young person's consolidation of an identity" (p. 387). He cites two theories primarily: the separation-individuation concept of Blos and Kohut's internalization of self-regulatory functions.

Two psychoanalytic theorists who are known primarily for work on the adolescent period, Anna Freud and Blos, address the psychic events that lead to the adult psychological state. In her elaboration of the concept of "developmental lines," Freud (1963) states: "From the infant's complete emotional dependence to the adult's comparative self-reliance and mature sex and object relationships [there is] a graduated developmental line which provides the indispensable basis for any assessment of emotional maturity or immaturity, normality or abnormality" (p. 246). She describes several such lines involving id, including libidinal phases and aggressive drives, and ego, including apparatuses, functions, and defenses. According to Freud, "notions of average normality . . . expect a fairly close correspondence between growth on the individual lines" (p. 262); disequilibrium between lines is only pathogenic if the imbalance is excessive; and "moderate disharmony does no more than produce the many variations of normality with which we have to count" (p. 264). Although there is some implication that there is an internal force that powers the developmental process, Freud does not ignore the influence of the environment, both family and culture, determining how the process will evolve.

Blos has been one of the most prolific writers on the adolescent period, and he has addressed two problems that relate to young adulthood. The first involves the psychological events of adolescence, and the second is the question of when and how adolescence ends. Actually much of Blos's theory is drawn from psychoanalytic work with individuals he terms late adolescents. However, since they are often in college and at least eighteen, many would place them in the young-adult group.

In regard to the psychological events of adolescence, Blos focuses primarily on the "second individuation process," a term he adapts from Mahler, Pine, and Bergman's (1975) initial separation-individuation phase of childhood. He describes this process in adolescence as "the shedding of family dependencies, the loosening of infantile object ties in order to become a member of society at large or, simply, of the adult world" (1979, p. 142). He goes on to say that "The disengagement from internalized objects—love and hate objects—opens the way in adolescence to the finding of external and extrafamilial love and hate objects" (p. 143). The violence of the break with parents is directly proportional to the difficulty of disengagement that may be manifested by geographical separation and the espousal of oppositional values. Blos feels that the latter may be necessary for the adolescent to maintain a sense of psychological integrity. For Blos, that individuation implies that the individual takes increasing responsibility for "what he does and what he is" rather than attributing the responsibility to parents or other adults. Although he postulates a "developmental momentum of growth and maturation," Blos feels that the disengagement from internal objects can only be achieved by "ego and drive regression" in the service of development. This regression will reanimate "the infantile emotional involvements and . . . the concomitant ego positions (fantasies, coping patterns, defensive organization) . . ." (1979, p. 169) allowing for disengagement from internal objects.

In discussing the end of adolescence, and by implication the beginning of adulthood, Blos refers to character formation and four developmental preconditions that must be resolved in some fashion. He defines character as "the outcome of psychic restructuring" and "the manifest sign of a completed, although not necessarily complete, passage through adolescence" (1979, p. 172). Or again "Character formation reflects the structural accommodations that have brought the adolescent process to a close" (p. 188). The four preconditions are the second individuation process, residual trauma, ego continuity, and sexual identity. The first has already been described. Residual trauma involves mastery of childhood traumas. Ego continuity has to do with establishing a historical life perspective that has an integrating effect. The attainment of sexual identity is crucial because, Blos feels, if sexual ambiguity prevails, maturational processes will be defeated all along the line. He relates the latter to deidealization and the formation of the ego ideal, which he feels is an important adolescent task. He refers to this entire process as personality consolidation and sums up its importance by saying:

> The process of internalization and automatization in character formation establish and stabilize the psychic internal milieu, thus enabling man to shape his environment, singly and collectively, by impressing on it those conditions that correspond most favorably with the inviolability and integrity of his personality. (1979, p. 191)

Thus Blos defines entry into adulthood as dependent on this consolidation of personality, but he makes clear that while this must occur in normal development, its occurrence is no guarantee of "normality." In a long discussion of the epigenesis of adult neurosis, he states that adult neurosis cannot develop unless the consolidation closing adolescence has occurred.

Psychoanalysts have developed elaborate theories of development through adolescence, but until very recently they have been much less concerned with adult development. Colarusso and Nemiroff (1979) have reviewed the current state of psychoanalytic theory on the subject and find it often contradictory as well as incomplete. They present seven hypotheses, which, summarized, view adult development as (1) not differing from that in the child, (2) an ongoing dynamic process, (3) focusing on "continuing 'evolution' of existing psychic structure," (4) with "the fundamental developmental issues of childhood" remaining in altered form, (5) "influenced by the 'adult' past as well as the childhood past," (6) deeply influenced by physical change. (7) A final hypothesis states that "a central, phase-specific theme of adult development is the normative crisis precipitated by the recognition and acceptance of the finiteness of time and the inevitability of personal death" (p. 68). Although their discussion largely considers psychological development in orthodox psychoanalytic terms, they also stress the importance of physiological changes and cite studies that indicate the adult is not either structurally stable or subject only to physiological regression.

The theorist who has offered probably the most profound discussion of issues related to development and normality is Heinz Hartmann. Perhaps because of the greater complexity of his theoretical approaches, his commentary, while highly influential among psychoanalysts, has never achieved the widespread popular exposure that Erikson's "crises" or even Blos's separation-individuation concept in adolescence have received. Hartmann's concept of adaptation (1958) is frequently applied, and he is given credit for initiating the focus on ego psychology that has occurred in the last forty years, but the many facets of his thinking in regard to "normal psychology" and "mental health," terms that he considered very seriously, have not been as widely embraced as those of other psychological theorists.

Hartmann immediately recognizes that the "term 'ego' is often used in a highly ambiguous way, even among analysts" (1964, p. 114). It is not synonymous with "personality" or "self," but is defined by functions, and he says that "ego" is used "where, for the purpose of developmental studies, a differential consideration of various ego functions would be indicated" (p. 107). He describes a series of ego functions including organizing and controlling functions, motility, perception, reality testing, action and thinking, the promotion of independence from the immediate impact of stimuli by defenses, character, and the synthetic function. He then discusses the operation of the ego in dealing with the other mental structures (id and superego) and the external environment. He states: "Thus, adaptation is primarily a reciprocal relationship between the organism and its environment" (1958, p. 24). Adaptation is only capable of definition in relation to something else: "Thus an unhampered 'capacity for achievement and enjoyment,' simply considered in isolation, has nothing decisive to tell us concerning the capacity for adapting oneself to reality" (1964, p. 15). In considering adaptation and mental health, he elucidates the concept of "preparedness for *average expectable* environmental situations and for *average expectable* internal conflicts" (1958, p. 55).

Through the concept of adaptation Hartmann in many ways integrates aspects of internal, psychological forces with external, social pressures. Adaptation, however, is not simply a matter of compliance with external demands. "Acceptance of reality demands beyond a certain individual threshold may lead to conflicts with the instinctual drives and consequently, given certain conditions, to the development of phenomena that will interfere with successful adaptation" (1964, p. 61). He also talks of "ego interests," under which rubric he subsumes wishes for social status, wealth, professional success, comfort, and influence, all of which he characterizes as "useful." According to Hartmann, "it is often maintained that the freedom of the individual to subordinate other tendencies to what is useful for him makes the difference between healthy and neurotic behavior. Actually this is too small a basis on which to build a definition of health" (p. 66). Hartmann believes that all three systems must be integrated. He also discusses value judgments in the concept of health and relates normality to health although there are overtones of normality as utopia.

Another major theoretical approach is that of Kohut (1971), who has developed a theory of the development of self based on psychoanalyses of individuals with narcissistic personality disorders. While he rarely addresses issues of normality, aspects that relate to normal psychological development can be inferred. Kohut feels that primary narcissism or the grandiose self of early childhood must be transformed into mature self-esteem and the archaic idealized parental imagoes transformed into mature values. If this is accomplished, the individual then has achieved a cohesive personality. In a commentary on Kohut's work, Wolf cites the "transformation from preadolescent idealized parental imagoes to the post-adolescent idealized ethics and values" (1980, p. 48). He also comments that "in our society . . . our adolescents are given the time, space, resources, and freedom to transform and consolidate their selves more nearly in harmony with the ambitions and goals of their nuclear self as it emerged in early childhood" (p. 49). Kohut delineates two of the qualities related to maturity as "humor" and "wisdom." He relates humor to maintaining "a sense of proportion, which can be expressed through humor" (1971, p. 324), and again cites "a balanced mixture of ideals and humor" (p. 325). He describes wisdom as "a cognitive and emotional position the attainment of which might be considered one of the peaks of human development, not only, narrowly, in the analysis of the narcissistic personality disorders but in the growth and fulfillment of the human personality altogether" (p. 326). He recognizes, however, that the wisdom may be limited and partial.

TASKS OF ADOLESCENCE AND YOUNG ADULTHOOD

A number of authors have commented on the tasks of adolescence that, by inference, must be completed prior to reaching adulthood. However, since definitions of the period of adolescence, late adolescence, and early adulthood overlap, it is difficult often to separate tasks of one period from another, and no attempt will be made to do so. The most frequently mentioned task is that of separation from parents.[*] Offer and Offer (1975) state it most simply: "The establishment of a self separate from the parents is one of the major tasks of young adulthood. The adolescent must disengage himself from parental domination" (p. 167). A second major task is described variously as ego synthesis (Blotcky and Looney 1980) or identity formation (Erikson 1968), and many authors cite some related concept.[†] A third major task is the development of a capacity for intimacy.[‡] Closely related is the concept of achievement of genital primacy[§] and the establishment of a sexual identity (Blos 1979). Stabilization of character structure is listed as a major task by Blotcky and Looney (1980), Bryt (1979), and Wittenberg (1968) and the development of a time perspective by Bühler (1968), Neugarten (1969), and Wittenberg (1968). A final major task involves commitment to a set of life goals that encompasses vocation and work role. This task is mentioned by Bryt (1979), Bühler (1968), Erikson (1968), Guntrip (1973), Heynemann (1976), Kimmel (1974), Lidz (1968), and Neugarten (1966). The task is sometimes described in relation to autonomy.[‖]

DIFFERENCES IN MALE AND FEMALE DEVELOPMENT

Although the major theoretical discussions of adolescent and young-adult development are often couched in neuter terms, it does not require

[*] See Blos (1979); Blotcky and Looney (1980); Fry and Rostow (1942); Goethals and Klos (1976); Guntrip (1973); Kimmel (1974); Levinson et al. (1978); Lidz (1968); Murphy et al. (1963); and Neugarten (1969).

[†] See Kimmel (1974); Levinson et al. (1978); Neugarten (1979); Rutter (1980); Schafer (1973); Spiegel (cited in Marcus 1973); and Wittenberg (1968).

[‡] See Blotcky and Looney (1980); Bryt (1979); Erikson (1968); Fischer (1981); Kimmel (1974); Lidz (1968); Neugarten (1969); Sullivan (1953); and Wittenberg (1968).

[§] See Bryt (1979); Erikson (1968); Lidz (1968); Marcus (1973); and Sullivan (1953).

[‖] See Bryt (1979); Levinson et al. (1978); Medley (1980); Murphey et al. (1963); and Spiegel (quoted in Marcus 1973).

great perceptive powers to discover that, not uncharacteristically, they are usually based on the male (Adelson and Doehrman 1980). Yet in psychoanalytic work on earlier phases of development there is the clear recognition that male and female psychological development is not identical. Furthermore, even the most superficial consideration of the adolescent period leads to the obvious conclusion that biological events in the postpubertal period inevitably establish differences between males and females, and one would expect these to create parallel psychological differences.

In recent years, partly as a result of the women's movement, which has focused more attention on features specific to women, there has been increasing interest in, and acknowledgment of, these differences. In considering the adolescent female's separation-individuation process, Blos (1980), states that the process in females relates to the preoedipal ties to the mother whereas the male adolescent focuses on oedipal issues. In a critique of Freud's theories of female psychology, Schafer (1974) makes a similar point in noting Freud's emphasis on the oedipal phase while neglecting preoedipal events in the girl's development. He relates this to Freud's teleological view of development that was predicated on organization for the purpose of propagating the species or what he calls Freud's "evolutionary value system." Ritvo (1976) gives a detailed account of the steps necessary for the adolescent girl to reach womanhood. Weissman and Barglow (1980) discuss female development in the context of newer studies relating to neuroendocrine, central nervous system, and cognitive development. They question whether some of the explanations based on psychological phenomena really result from biological factors.

Jenks (1981) quotes Chodorow as stating that during the young-adult age period, females will have difficulties with separation and males with relationships because femininity is defined by attachment and masculinity by separation. In a small study she contrasts female development in this age period with Levinson's findings on male development and states that the women needed to establish "an early adult life structure that allows women to integrate and consolidate affiliative and achievement needs" (p. 51). Gilligan (1982) and Miller (1976) raise serious questions about the standards used to measure development, which they feel are almost always based on the male and focus on independence. They suggest that standards of connection and interdependence are more applicable to females and, if applied, would result in a different estimate of female development.

As has already been noted, gender differences are presumably influenced in part by anatomical differences, which are likely to have differing psychological impact. It is not clear, however, to what degree "anatomy

is destiny" (a phrase ascribed to Freud) and to what extent purely biological differences are subordinated to sociocultural forces (Group for the
Advancement of Psychiatry 1975). Ticho (1976) discusses the process of
achieving female autonomy for the young-adult woman as it has been
influenced by social change. There is considerable evidence to suggest
that sociocultural influences are extremely important in the developmental process, and changes in social role expectations create wide changes in
developmental experience. Thus if the primary role of the adult woman is
seen as propagator of the species, a different set of traits and capacities is
encouraged than if this role is incidental or ancillary. Consequently, how
one looks at female development is affected (Schafer 1974). This is readily
demonstrated in any cross-cultural study, such as Erlich's (1978) of Polish women students.

Concepts of Mental Health

The concept of mental health, which is often confused with normality,
has been considered by a series of investigators who stress either internal
psychic operations or external behavioral observations. Cox (1970)
quotes Bond on the subject:

> The individual earns classification as normal when he is a "going concern,"
> accepts the limitations and the possibilities of reality, carries on a life work
> appropriate to his natural gifts and training, and maintains harmonious rela-
> tionships. Essential to this conceptualization is the expectation that, in achiev-
> ing this level of performance, the individual experiences a degree of inner
> tranquility and fulfillment sufficient to make the gestures of living worth the
> effort they require. (P. 15)

Offer and Sabshin (1974) quote Jones, Klein, and Glover as each providing slightly different definitions of mental health covering the same
general areas of functioning, and Hartmann (1964), Tartakoff (1966), and
Menninger (cited in Rees 1951) are others who have provided definitions.
Krapf (1961) states that "the behavior of the mentally healthy person is
always characterized by the qualities of *reasonableness* and *balance*" (p.
441) and speaks of "an equilibrium of the psyche with reason and ego
predominating" (p. 444). Jahoda (1958) provides an especially comprehensive discussion and includes the concept of environmental mastery,
which involves: "(1) the ability to love; (2) adequacy in love, work, and
play; (3) adequacy in interpersonal relations . . ." (p. 53), among other
abilities. C. W. Heath (1954) states that " 'normal' is defined as the *bal-*

anced, harmonious blending of functions that produce good integration. Many kinds of such integrations are reflected in widely divergent types of personality and behavior" (p. 3).

According to Anna Freud (1981):

> To have reached the stage of genital sexuality, on the one hand, and to be able to work effectively, on the other hand, used to be quoted as the hallmark of adult normality in the early era of psychoanalysis. Since then, many other demands have been added to those requirements. Normal adults are also expected to hold their own with regard to self-esteem and emotional balance . . .; to be in rational control of their own body and its functions and to safeguard its well-being; to discharge emotion through mental pathways . . . ; to reduce panic in the face of dangers to mere signal anxiety, which initiates effective defense; to have outgrown a purely egocentric view of the world . . . ; to see themselves on a par with others and to react to their peers on a basis of equality; to be able to enjoy pleasure but to behave and function according to the reality principle, taking full cognizance of the importance of cause and effect. (P. 130)

One of the most difficult aspects of the problem is the consistent use of the term ego as the psychological entity most related to mental health and "normal" functioning in the young adult. As has already been suggested, there is considerable overlap and disagreement about the definition of ego (Hauser and Daffner 1980) and its relation to other concepts that have some similarity, such as self, identity, I, and Allport's (1955) suggested term, proprium. Lichtenstein (1977) discusses the distinction at some length, as does Abend (1974). Loewald (1980) points out that the term ego is used in two different ways: as one of the three substructures of the mental apparatus (ego, superego, id), and as a term for the totality of mind or personality, which Hartmann calls self. In the narrowest sense ego is an organizing agency. Hartmann (1964) actually states that the term ego is frequently used when ego functions would be more accurate, and according to Blanck and Blanck (1979), "the ego is better defined, not simply by its functions, but by its function*ing* as an organizer. From this it follows that ego qua ego *is* organizing process" (p. 18).

Loevinger (1976) has described states of ego development: presocial state, symbiotic, implusive, self-protective, conformist, conscientious-conformist, conscientious, individualistic, autonomous, and integrated. The four facets of this single coherent process are impulse control and character development, interpersonal style, conscious preoccupations, and cognitive style. Loevinger feels that "some, but not all ego functions will develop as an organic unity" (p. 5), but there is no average age for each state. Adams (1977) quotes Ausubel and Sullivan as stating that the "ego constitutes the conceptual essence of a person's notion of himself as a functioning individual endowed with certain attributes related to role and status," (p. 152) and then continues: "It is our belief that ego identity can best be conceptualized as a cognitive growth and structural differentiation process that evolves with cognitive stage development and ego maturation" (p. 153). Jacobs, Pugatch, and Spilken (1968) define ego strength and relate healthy ego functioning to flexible, adaptive coping mechanisms. Vaillant (1977) describes ego development as reflecting "unfolding patterns of mastering and making sense of our own experience." In reviewing Piaget and Kohlberg, he states that developmental psychologists have been increasingly persuaded that moral development and ego development appear to be a single process. Hartmann (1964), Kimmel (1974), Blos (1979), Anna Freud (1963), and Allport (1955) discuss various aspects of ego maturation, but it is not always easy to understand how the process occurs. Ritvo (1976), Ticho (1976), Gilligan (1982), and Miller (1976) illustrate the point that maturation and the criteria for mental health differ for women. Miller implies that in the future, the criteria for men may be closer to those for women rather than vice versa.

Several investigators and theoreticians discuss particular aspects of ego functioning. The most relevant for this discussion is the concept of coping mechanisms and defenses. Kroeber (1963) constructs a complex scheme in which he elaborates ten ego mechanisms and divides each into a defense mechanism and a coping mechanism. For example, he lists the ego mechanism of "sensitivity" and designates the defense aspect as "projection" and the coping aspect as "empathy." He then devises an equation to describe mental health: "Mental Health $= f\left(\frac{\text{sum } C}{\text{sum } D}, E, Dr\right)$, where C represents the sum of ratings of coping mechanisms; D, the sum of ratings of defense mechanisms; E, the total of general ego mechanisms . . . ; and Dr, an estimate of drive" (p. 197). Haan (1969) develops a tripartite model of ego functioning that involves coping mechanisms, defense mechanisms, and ego failures. From these she evolves six triads, which describe ego processes. She states that effectiveness based on these processes is an important measure of ego functioning. Silber and associates (1961); Jacobs, Pugatch, and Spilken (1968); Hamburg, Coelho, and Adams (1974); and Vaillant (1977) are other investigators who stress the ego's coping functions.

Empirical Research on Young Adulthood

What then is the research base for these theoretical statements and conclusions? As has already been suggested, the two main streams are the psychoanalytic, largely clinical in origin, and what may be called the "psychological," investigations based largely on nonpatient populations that are studied by a variety of measures. Psychoanalytic theorists usually derive their data from extremely small samples drawn from individuals who are in treatment, that is, patients. While these patients may be functioning at high levels and even may be in psychoanalytic treatment largely for nonmedical reasons such as training, the standard of the normal is often deduced from observations about the abnormal and depends on the reconstruction of past psychological events. "Psychological" studies are often difficult to compare or integrate because the approaches vary rather widely. Some are longitudinal (see Livson and Peskin 1980), some cross-sectional, and at least one reconstructional. Some depend primarily on a series of interviews, some primarily use personality scales of one sort or another, and some use projective tests rather extensively. Many combine two or more of these procedures. In this methodology conclusions are based on derived indices (e.g., personality scales); interpreted materials (e.g., Rorschach); self-report (e.g., interviews or questionnaires); and objective data (e.g., jobs, marital status, etc.). Although several of the investigators are actually psychoanalysts or, at any rate, seem well acquainted with psychoanalytic theory, their conclusions inevitably are based on different kinds of data.

Several longitudinal studies have started with a group of subjects that are selected either randomly or for their "normality." Some of these studies have attempted to describe a specific change, such as the movement from high school to college (Offer and Offer 1975; Silber et al. 1961), while others have been longer-term studies starting from childhood and proceeding to adulthood (e.g., Oakland Growth Study and Berkeley Guidance Study [MacFarlane 1964], Fels Institute Study [Kagan and Moss 1962]). A few, such as the Grant Study (C. Heath 1945), the Student Council Studies (Cox 1970), and the Adviser Study (R. Heath 1979), have begun with college students and followed them for varying lengths of time. Still others have been retrospective (Levinson 1978) or cross-sectional studies (Gould 1972). There have also been studies of the development of specific aspects of personality or psychological functioning, such as Piaget's (1977) on cognitive development, Kohlberg and Kramer's (1969) on moral development, Sarrel and Sarrel's (1979) on sexual development, and Loevinger's (1976) on ego development.

Of the longitudinal studies, Offer and Offer (1975) followed a group from high school through their fourth post–high school year. They were careful to define normality as "average" in their selection, eliminating "outstanding" subjects as well as individuals who had required psychotherapy or who were in difficulty for delinquent behavior. The group chosen were all males in their first year of high school. Data collected derived from interviews and identity scales (using the Hess, Henry, Sims instruments), as well as Rorschachs. As the study progressed the focus was on normality as "health," and the investigators found a considerable stability. They described three groups that demonstrated different passages through adolescence—the continuous-growth group, the surgent-growth group, and the tumultuous-growth group. While all groups were within the range of normal, the authors stressed that only the latter group showed evidence of the kind of turmoil that is often described as characteristic of all adolescents.

Silber and coworkers (1961) followed fifteen high school seniors through their first year of college, and described various attributes and coping strategies that they used or that characterized them. These were divided into: (1) general personality attributes: reaching out for new experience, tendency toward activity, and pleasure in mastery; (2) developing a self-image adequate to the new situation: by referring to analogous past experience, by referring to continuity with present self-image, by advance learning about the new situations, by role rehearsal as college students and adults, by group identification, by lowering level of aspirations, and by selectively perceiving encouraging elements in the new situation; and (3) maintaining distress within manageable limits: support from shared experiences, usefulness of worry, present activity in anticipating future concerns, and fantasy rehearsal of future behavior. The investigators judged the competence of coping by the effectiveness of accomplishing the task and the cost to the individual of this effectiveness.

In a study of change during college, Katz and associates (1968) followed two groups who entered University of California, Berkeley, and Stanford in 1961 by questionnaire, interview, and psychometric methods. Although the subjects were not consciously very concerned about change, the study indicated that change occurred. They learned

> to make certain decisions without seeking permission from parents . . . to regulate their own time and handle their own money . . . they move toward closer relationships and toward the assumption of the marital role. . . . they express their own impulses more freely, and are more able to pursue their own desires. . . . they lessen previous constrictive and restrictive controls over their own impulses, and adopt more tolerant and permissive attitudes toward the behavior of others. (P. 5)

Katz and associates state that these changes "may be considered part of normal maturation" and that "Such maturation may be heavily influenced by the social setting and social expectations" (p. 6).

Vaillant (1977) conducted a long-range follow-up study on 95 men of the original 268 subjects chosen as subjects in the Grant Study (C. Heath

1945), a study started at Harvard in the late 1930s. The initial conception was to choose "normal" young college men, a quality that was based on judgment of self-reliance, academic success, and what Vaillant calls a stoic quality. These men were followed periodically by various methods over a thirty-five year period and then interviewed by Vaillant. Although the endpoint of his study goes far beyond young adulthood by anyone's definition, his ideas about the qualities involved in adaptation are relevant. He concluded that mental health exists and can be discussed operationally in terms that are, at least in part, free from moral and cultural bases. He also feels that human development continues through human life and that lives change and have discontinuities. Thus it was not always easy to predict at ages twenty to twenty-two how the individual would fare later, although the "best outcome" individuals tended to be well integrated and practical in late adolescence (e.g., in college) and the "worst outcomes," asocial. Vaillant couches most of his theoretical findings in relation to "mechanisms of defense" of which he lists eighteen in hierarchal order ranging from psychotic defenses through immature and neurotic to mature defenses. He lists five mature defenses: sublimation, altruism, suppression, anticipation, and humor. It is his contention that the "best outcome" individuals shifted in adulthood to more mature defenses or modes of adaptation, and that the "profile" of a given individual's use of mature mechanisms correlates closely with "health" and "maturity." He relates this developmental concept to the stage-development concepts of Piaget (1977), Loevinger (1976), and Kohlberg and Kramer (1969). Vaillant also relies heavily on Freud's definition of health as the ability to work and to love (Erikson 1980), and he redefines health as "the joyful expression of sex and anger" and amplifies this to show "how healthy coping mechanisms harness sex and aggression in the service of working and loving . . ." (p. 53).

Vaillant's study gives a rather different picture than that of R. Heath (1979), who interviewed sixty-four men twenty-five years after graduation from Princeton. Heath had a more restricted purpose in mind—to determine the impact of their years at Princeton. Half the group had been research subjects in an "advisee" project of Roy Heath's while they were in college, and the other half were loosely matched "controls"—classroom students of his who were not in the advisee project. Although the interview samples give much evidence of adult development, there seems generally to be more continuity between college and follow-up impressions than in Vaillant's work. This, however, may be an artifact of the method, in which the interviewer was a constant, and the style of the report, which draws fewer conceptual conclusions. Both studies stress the importance of relationships in college and later life as the outstanding hallmark of psychological health, and there seems to be a relatively high correlation between the general ability to establish friendships and the capacity to maintain an intimate relationship, for example, in marriage.

Cox (1970) describes the Student Council studies, which followed sixty-three "well-endowed, well-educated, and effectively functioning" students (p. 1), all chosen as subjects because they were elected members of their college student council. The subjects were interviewed and given psychological tests, and their families were interviewed. The follow-up study was conducted roughly ten years later at which time most had achieved "effective activity" and "emotional stability." A mental health scale was developed that was based on areas of functioning: further education, work, marriage, parenthood, management of money, and relation to parents. Cox states that the mental health values were based on heterosexuality and family orientation, "adaptations that promote survival." She also speaks of age-appropriate functioning: "The thirty-year-old will have accepted a sex-appropriate role in a heterosexual society" (p. 21).

Block (1971) did a follow-up study of two subject groups that were connected with the Institute of Human Development in Berkeley. One group, the Berkeley Guidance study, was started in 1929 with a cohort of infants twenty-one months old, and the second group, the Oakland Growth Study, was started in 1932 with a group of fifth graders. When the follow-up study was done the first group was approximately thirty years of age and the second, thirty-seven. Block describes the difficulties of using data that had already been collected and then describes the follow-up studies, which involved intensive interviews, a personality inventory, and two projective tests, As a result of this study, Block divided the male group into five types that he labeled ego resilients, belated adjusters, vulnerable overcontrollers, anomic extroverts, and unsettled undercontrollers. He divided the female group into six types: female prototypes, cognitive copers, hyper-feminine repressives, dominating narcissists, vulnerable undercontrollers, and lonely independents. Block relates these different types to Loevinger's ego developmental stages, stating that some of the groups were still operating at the opportunistic, conformist, or conscientious stage. From Block's viewpoint, only one of the groups had really reached the autonomous stage, and two others were approaching it.

In a cross-sectional study of clinic outpatients, Gould (1972) developed seven homogeneous age groups from sixteen to sixty years. He constructed a questionnaire describing issues highlighted by each age group. The questionnaire was then administered to 524 nonpatients. As a result he found two distinct age periods in the young adult range: eighteen to twenty-two and twenty-two to twenty-eight. In the former the individuals were in the process of taking steps to implement separation from parents. He states: "Their own autonomy is felt to be established, but in jeopardy" (p. 525). In the latter, however, the subjects felt established, autonomous, and separate from the family; they were engaged in the work of being adults.

In a reconstructional study Levinson and coworkers (1978) studied forty men between the ages of thirty-five and forty-five. The subjects were chosen on the basis of four carefully selected occupations: biologists, executives, hourly workers, and novelists. There were ten of each, and from interview material and limited projective testing, retrospective accounts of each subject's development were obtained. From this information, somewhat to the surprise of the investigators, consistent patterns of life-cycle periods emerged, which were labeled childhood and adolescence, early adulthood, middle adulthood, and late adulthood. One of the most significant findings led to the concept of the existence of five-year periods of transition between each of the major periods. Within the major period a "life structure" was built; for the period of "entering the adult world," the life structure provided "a workable link between the valued self and the adult society" (p. 57).

Kagan and Moss (1962) did a follow-up evaluation of seventy-one of the original eighty-nine individuals in the Fels Research Institute study. The subjects entered the study group at birth, and their ages at follow-up were between twenty and twenty-nine. A major finding was that sex-typed characteristics that were culturally supported, that is, aggressiveness for males and passive-dependency for females, continued from childhood to adulthood. They state: "A behavior will show long-term stability if that behavior is congruent with the cultural definition of the sex role of the individual" (p. 129).

In a follow-up in connection with the Berkeley Guidance Study performed when the subjects were approximately thirty, MacFarlane (1964) found less overall consistency. Many of the most mature adults had trouble in childhood and adolescence, and many of the most successful in childhood and adolescence failed to achieve their predicted potential. She felt that "parenthood turns out to be a very important period for consolidating identity and for expanding maturity" (p. 123).

Symonds and Jensen's (1961) findings were consonant with those of Kagan and Moss. In a thirteen-year follow-up study of twenty-eight out of an original forty subjects, evenly divided between males and females, performed when the subjects were twenty-six to thirty-one, there was considerable persistence of personality characteristics, particularly those revealed by fantasy story response. There was some increase in depression as a "natural result" of the disillusionment with adolescent fantasy and expectation.

Discussion

Where does all this leave the subject of normality and the young adult? Several points are immediately apparent.

First, aspects of context and setting create differences and must be specified. No simple overarching definition is possible. For our society, however, adulthood may be said to begin in the age range of seventeen to nineteen years. This corresponds to the time at which most individuals finish compulsory schooling. Paths then divide: some go on to college, while others take jobs, enter the military, and/or assume more household responsibility. The latter group is assuming the social roles expected of men and women in adult society. While those who go on to college will not be assuming these roles for some time, their school situation makes them responsible for themselves in many ways, so it is not inappropriate to say that they have entered the adult period.

The "social role" aspect, however, does influence individuals and how others view them. Such factors as marriage, parenthood, economic independence, and job responsibility press an individual toward an adult position, and a person who fills these roles will be viewed by society as adult, whereas the individual who has not may be less automatically assumed to have attained adult status—even if the psychological maturation, however one measures it, of the two individuals is roughly similar. Although there may be chicken-and-egg arguments, for example, in regard to such actions as marriage or parenthood, there seems little question that entering those states tends to evoke greater psychological maturation unless the original action is one of escape, as Wittenberg (1968) states it may be, or irresponsibility. Thus there is an interactive effect between such social actions and the resultant states (see MacFarlane 1964) that inevitably affects the individual's psychic functioning and presses in the direction of maturation.

Second, in addition to the social role aspect there is the psychological aspect, which involves completing the tasks of adolescence and tackling the tasks of young adulthood. Depending on one's theoretical background, this aspect is conceptualized in various ways, but most investigators agree that it involves some sort of separation from the family and some "integration" of the personality into a reasonably coherent functioning entity. This coherent entity is variously called ego, self, I, proprium, person, or inner identity. Psychoanalysts (such as Blos, Kohut, and Schafer) believe that the process is primarily unconscious and involves separation from the internal parental representatives persisting from early childhood. Schafer (1973) states: "Genuine emancipation seems to be built on revision, modulation, and selective acceptance as well as rejection, flexible mastery, and complex substitutions and other changes of aims, representations, and patterns of behavior" (p. 45). The process that is observed is the conscious manifestation of the internal process, and it may appear quite at odds with the underlying process or may appear—superficially—to be quite successful—that is, the young adult may be geographically separate and financially independent, but still psychologically very attached.

Third, in a prior publication this author (Arnstein 1980) designated conscious choice as an important element in the young-adult period, which is often a period of experimentation. Some of this choice may be the result of the psychological maturation process, but much of it is related, as Neugarten suggests, to the social clock phenomenon. Choices include occupational, marital, friendship, religious, and moral ones. Although the qualities required by such choices—capacity for commitment and intimacy, accepted sexual orientation, and self-esteem—may be essential to the success of the choice in terms of the individual's attainment of satisfaction and fulfillment, there again undoubtedly is a reciprocal effect between the experimentation (making a series of choices) and the development of these capacities.

All the longitudinal research evidence suggests that one of the most important capacities to develop before the young-adult period commences or in it is a capacity for friendship.* The psychological aspects of friendships, while not studied nearly as thoroughly as overtly sexualized relationships, probably require a degree of emotional control, basic trust, and self-definition that are important hallmarks of maturity. Although friendships made at earlier periods may endure, friendships made during this period probably have a better chance of lasting because they occur between individuals who are more "formed" and whose "form" is closer to that personality which will characterize the adult individual. Clinical experience suggests that those individuals who describe an absence of friendships during the young-adult period are more likely to display difficulties that appear to relate to maturation.

Finally, the young-adult period is one in which an important achieve-

*See Adelson and Doehrman (1980); R. Heath (1979); Katz et al. (1968); Vaillant (1977); and Wallerstein (1975).

ment is the formation of a satisfactory "philosophy of life," or Weltan-schaung, a term used by Wittenberg (1968) and Hartmann (1960). The achievement of this Weltanschaung does not mean that aspects of it may not change with life experience, but it does imply a kind of self-consciousness about one's life that seems to be a desirable developmental step. Neugarten (1969) comments that young adulthood is the first pe-riod in which the individual becomes conscious of the life cycle. Kohlberg and Kramer (1969) would probably discuss Weltanschaung in terms of a person's reaching his or her highest state of moral development, from which a mature attitude or stance toward life can be inferred. Expressed in other words, an adaptive value system is accepted. Smith (1963) speaks of "selective behavior—in which a person chooses, rejects, takes interest in, approves, disapproves—with respect to a physical, social, or ideal object" (p. 328).

This suggests that an essential accomplishment for the young adult is the development of a personally acceptable code of behavior which is potentially satisfying to the individual. Some would add the stipulation that the behavior must also be consonant with external reality, but others would demur. Although those "others" would probably agree that cer-tain behaviors are self-defeating and, therefore, not likely to lead to ful-fillment, they would cite situations in which behavior was self-defeating from some conventional societal standpoint but worth the external conse-quences in the individual's internal view. Thus some investigators stress the active aspect of ego functioning or behavior by which the individual may actually try to "change" reality. The relationship between "passive" adjustment and "active" manipulation is clearly a continuum because, if the behavior is too divergent from reality, it is likely to be viewed as fanaticism or psychosis.

Thus for most individuals the period of young adulthood from eigh-teen to twenty-five will be a period both of experimentation and choice. Since most people will have finished secondary school by this age, two somewhat divergent paths present themselves: either to go on to further education or to enter permanently the world of work.* The latter path probably allows for a narrower range of experimentation in that the availability of jobs may severely limit what is possible. After taking a job there can, however, be some experimentation and development in rela-tionships, in the establishment of a personal code of behavior, or even possibly in career choice. Although both males and females usually fol-low one of these two paths, there may be attitudinal differences between

---

*Although these alternatives are the most usual, a number of individuals who intend to obtain further schooling may well interrupt this process by taking a temporary job, by travel, or by "doing nothing" for a period.

the sexes. The male is likely to look on a job as prelude to a lifetime of employment, whereas the female may have this view but may also consider a job as an interim occupation until marriage and childrearing occurs.

The individual who goes on to college usually is encouraged to experiment in many ways. Although some enter college with clear career goals and pursue an undeviating course toward those goals, many are uncertain or change their interests as a result of college experience. Furthermore, since college students come from a mixture of backgrounds, there is considerable opportunity to talk with and relate to individuals with different experiences, ideas, and values. Thus while for college students the young-adult period may be one of considerable change and uncertainty, by its end most will usually have made some consolidation of choice in career direction. A more permanent relationship may be postponed because individuals are still in one form of training or another, but very often a relationship pattern is established that will eventually lead to a permanent relationship. Males and females who pursue higher education are probably more similar in their development than those who do not, although some women will experience college as a period of expansion without any intention of pursuing a career. Their preference is for marriage and childrearing, which may occur shortly after college. In recent years, however, more women anticipate combining marriage and career.

The psychological development that occurs during this period seems largely to do with establishing a modus vivendi that is reasonably satisfying and that looks forward to further development at later ages. In the United States, at least, some psychological separation from parents is usually involved as well as an ability to balance various internal needs with external reality, which includes the needs of others that impinge. This balancing includes the capacity to make choices, which in turn assumes the willingness to close off certain options, often the most difficult aspect of making the choice. As has been pointed out, adaptation to external reality does not only mean to be compliant but also subsumes the ability at times to modify that reality, so that when one speaks of balancing, one implies an active component of psychological functioning as well as a passive capacity to adjust.

Furthermore, the individual needs the ability to cope not only when in relative control of the environment but also when "things go wrong," as they inevitably will for most people to some degree and at some time. Hartmann (1958) speaks of the "average expectable environment," which is a useful concept when one is discussing "normality." Clearly there are situations of extreme stress that most people will not experience. Although one could define mental health and normality as the ability to survive every conceivable human condition, since most individuals will not be subjected to the most extreme stresses, they do not know how they would react under such circumstances. Therefore it makes more sense to talk of "the average expectable environment."

It is clear that the young-adult period is one that requires more study. The research that has been done has added measurably, but it also highlights the difficulties. It demonstrates, furthermore, that no discussion of normality in young adulthood can be complete without stressing the impact of values on such a topic. This point must be stressed, because throughout both theoretical discussions and formal research studies, results are constantly affected by the value standards applied. Sometimes the bias is overt, as in Cox (1970), but often it is covert. In general, the values implicit are of a heterosexually oriented society, in which family formation and childrearing are expected; upward social mobility is, if not expected, considered desirable; geographical mobility is common; and a degree of psychological independence is considered advantageous. Education follows a common pathway, and, at least until recently, educational progress was expected to occur at relatively standard ages. This makes it unclear how to view individuals who reach the age commonly referred to as young adult who do not conform to one or another of these values. Despite statements that "ours is a pluralistic society," there is unquestionably an undercurrent that regards such lack of conformity with suspicion. This supicion runs a gamut, depending on the particular topic, from mild to considerable. For example, some view a homosexual orientation as illness, some view it as immorality, and some, as developmental arrest. To regard it as a "normal" variant requires a shift in values; in regard to homosexuality, such a shift has occurred for some researchers, but by no means for all. Similarly, while most would view a conscious decision not to marry or, if married, not to have children more benignly than a homosexual life-style, such a choice would probably still be thought "unusual."

In the final analysis one must live with oneself as a person, and, while there is unquestionably a relatively wide range of psychological functioning that would come under the heading of "normal," no matter how defined, it would seem that the young-adult period is one in which the individual establishes a conscious foundation that will be built on throughout life. Although most psychoanalytic and psychological theorists feel that the deeper foundation of personality functioning is laid down in early childhood and adolescence, its more manifest and persisting form probably appears in young adulthood. This in a sense is what is referred to by the concept of integrating one's personality into a coherent whole.

At this point it would perhaps be reasonable to suggest the qualities that designate "normality" in the young adult, and it is tempting to try to do so. A review of the literature on the topic, however, should engender a degree of caution. Although it is impossible to document without personal knowledge of the individual investigators, there arises the uneasy feeling that each list tends to include those qualities that are especially valued by the investigator and perhaps even those qualities that he or she feels are, or wishes were, embodied in his or her own personality. If this is true, to create a new "summary" list, although possible, would probably say more about this author and his values than about the state of normality in the young adult. Therefore, such an effort can appropriately be eschewed.

It is perhaps sufficient to cite a subject in R. Heath's (1979) study who talks of the need to stop pretending to be something that you are not and "to face yourself in the mirror" (p. 289). This implies an acceptance of self, an attitude of self-respect, and presumably a kind of dignity in dealing with others. Although not all—or even perhaps many—people have achieved this by the end of the young-adult phase of the life cycle, if they are making progress toward this goal, they would be approaching a kind of normality as health, perhaps even as utopia, and by implication as transactional systems. They would unquestionably not be average because many individuals spend a lifetime without reaching such a psychological state, but they would be reassuringly human because the notion of self-acceptance carries with it the idea that many emotions, deficits, and mistakes of behavior can be tolerated, if not condoned, along with one's talents, accomplishments, and triumphs.

REFERENCES

Aarons, Z. A. 1970. "Normality and Abnormality in Adolescence: With a Digression on Prince Hal—'The Sowing of Wild Oats.'" *Psychoanalytic Study of the Child* 25:309–39.

Abend, S. M. 1974. "Problems of Identity: Theoretical and Clinical Applications." *Psychoanalytic Quarterly* 43:606–38.

Abrahams, B.; Feldman, S. S.; and Nash, S. C. 1978. "Sex Role Self-concept and Sex Role Attitudes: Enduring Personality Characteristics or Adaptations to Changing Life Situations?" *Developmental Psychology* 4:393–400.

Adams, G. R. 1977. "Personal Identity Formation: A Synthesis of Cognitive and Ego Psychology." *Adolescence* 12:151–65.

Adelson, J., and Doehrman, M. J. 1980. "The Psychodynamic Approach to Adolescence." In *Handbook of Adolescent Psychology*, ed. J. Adelson, pp. 99–116. New York: John Wiley & Sons.

Allport, G. W. 1955. *Becoming*. New Haven, Conn.: Yale University Press.

Arlin, P. K. 1975. "Cognitive Development in Adulthood: A Fifth Stage?" *Developmental Psychology* 11:602–6.

Arnstein, R. L. 1980. "The Student, the Family, the University, and Transition to Adulthood." In *Adolescent Psychiatry*, ed. S. C. Feinstein et al., vol. 8, pp. 160–72. Chicago: University of Chicago Press.

Baltes, P. B., and Labouvie, G. V. 1973. "Adult Development of Intellectual Performance: Description, Explanation, and Modification." In *The Psychology of Adult Development and Aging*, ed. C. Eisdorfer and M. P. Lawton, pp. 157–219. Washington, D.C.: American Psychological Association.

Blanck, G., and Blanck, R. 1970. *Ego Psychology II: Psychoanalytic Developmental Psychology*. New York: Columbia University Press.

Block, J. 1971. *Lives Through Time*. Berkeley, Calif.: Bancroft Books.

Blos, P. 1962. *On Adolescence: A Psychoanalytic Interpretation*. New York: Free Press.

―――. 1967. "The Second Individuation Process of Adolescence." *Psychoanalytic Study of the Child* 22:162–86.

―――. 1979. *The Adolescent Passage*. New York: International Universities Press.

―――. 1980. "Modifications in the Traditional Psychoanalytic Theory of Female Adolescent Development." In *Adolescent Psychiatry*, ed. S. C. Feinstein et al., vol. 8, pp. 8–24. Chicago: University of Chicago Press.

Blotcky, M., and Looney, J. C. 1980. "Normal Female and Male Adolescent Psychological Development: An Overview of Theory and Research." In *Adolescent Psychiatry*, ed. S. C. Feinstein et al., vol. 8, pp. 184–99. Chicago: University of Chicago Press.

Bourne, E. 1978. "The State of Research on Ego Identity: A Review and Appraisal." *Journal of Youth and Adolescence* 7:223–53, 371–93.

Bryt, A. 1979. "Developmental Tasks in Adolescence." In *Adolescent Psychiatry*, ed. S. C. Feinstein and P. L. Giovacchini, vol. 7, pp. 136–46. Chicago: University of Chicago Press.

Bühler, C. 1968. "The Course of Human Life as a Psychological Problem." *Human Development* 11:184–200.

Colarusso, C. A., and Nemiroff, R. A. 1970. "Some Observations and Hypotheses about the Psychoanalytic Theory of Adult Development." *International Journal of Psychoanalysis* 60:59–72.

Cox, R. D. 1970. *Youth into Maturity*. New York: Mental Health Materials Center.

Eisenberg, L. 1980. "The Relativity of Adolescence: Effects of Time, Place, and Persons." In *Adolescent Psychiatry*, ed. S. C., Feinstein et al., vol. 8, pp. 25–40. Chicago: University of Chicago Press.

Erikson, E. H. 1945. "Childhood and Tradition in Two American Indian Tribes." *Psychoanalytic Study of the Child* 1:319–50.

―――. 1946. "Ego Development and Historical Change." *Psychoanalytic Study of the Child* 2:359–96.

―――. 1950. *Childhood and Society*. New York: W. W. Norton.

―――. 1956. "The Problem of Ego Identity." *Journal of the American Psychoanalytic Association* 4:56–122.

―――. 1968. *Identity: Youth and Crisis*. New York: W. W. Norton.

―――. 1978. "Reflections on Dr. Borg's Life Cycle." In *Adulthood*, ed. E. H. Erikson, pp. 1–32. New York: W. W. Norton.

―――. 1980. *Identity and the Life Cycle*. New York: W. W. Norton

Erlich, I. 1978. "Polish Women Students—Attitudes Toward Career and Marriage." *Journal of the American College Health Association* 26:334–37.

Fischer, J. L. 1981. "Transition in Relationship Style from Adolescence to Young Adulthood." *Journal of Youth and Adolescence* 10:11–25.

Freud, A. 1937. *Ego and the Mechanisms of Defense*. London: Hogarth Press.

―――. 1958. "Adolescence." *Psychoanalytic Study of the Child* 13:255–78.

―――. 1963. "The Concept of Developmental Lines." *Psychoanalytic Study of the Child* 18:245–65.

―――. 1981. "The Concept of Developmental Lines: Their Diagnostic Significance." *Psychoanalytic Study of the Child* 36:129–36.

Fry, C. C., and Rostow, E. G. 1942. *Mental Health in College.* New York: Commonwealth Fund.

Gilligan, C. 1982. "New Maps of Development: New Visions of Maturity." *American Journal of Orthopsychiatry* 52:199–213.

Goethals, G. W., and Klos, S. 1976. *Experiencing Youth.* Boston: Little, Brown.

Goldstein, J. 1978. "On Being Adult and Being an Adult in Secular Law." In *Adulthood,* ed. E. H. Erikson, pp. 149–269. New York: W. W. Norton.

Gould, R. L. 1972. "The Phases of Adult Life: A Study in Developmental Psychology." *American Journal of Psychiatry* 129:521–32.

Group for the Advancement of Psychiatry. 1975. *The Educated Woman: Prospects and Problems.* New York: Group for the Advancement of Psychiatry.

Guntrip. H. A. 1973. "Young Adult: 18 to 30 Years—Personality." In *The Seven Ages of Man,* ed. R. R. Sears, and S. S. Feldman, pp. 69–73. Los Altos, Calif.: William Kaufman.

Haan, N. 1969. "A Tripartite Model of Ego Functioning Values and Clinical and Research Applications." *Journal of Nervous and Mental Disease* 148:14–31.

Hamburg, D. A.; Coelho, G. V.; and Adams, J. E. 1974. "Coping and Adaptation: Steps Toward a Synthesis of Biological and Social Perspectives." In *Coping and Adaptation,* ed. G. V. Coelho, D. A. Hamburg, and J. E. Adams, pp. 403–40. New York: Basic Books.

Hartmann, H. 1958. *Ego Psychology and the Problem of Adaptation.* New York: International Universities Press.

—————. 1960. *Psychoanalysis and Moral Values.* New York: International Universities Press.

—————. 1964. *Essays on Ego Psychology.* New York: International Universities Press.

Hauser, S. T., and Daffner, K. R. 1980. "Ego Functions and Development: Empirical Research and Clinical Relevance." *McLean Hospital Journal* 5:87–110.

Havighurst, R. J. 1971. "Social Class Perspectives on the Life Cycle." *Human Development* 14:110–24.

Heath, C. W. 1945. *What People Are.* Cambridge, Mass.: Harvard University Press.

Heath, R. 1979. *Princeton Retrospectives.* Princeton, N.J.: Class of 1954, Princeton University.

Heyneman, S. P. 1976. "Continuing Issues in Adolescence: A Summary of Current Transition to Adulthood Debates." *Journal of Youth and Adolescence* 5:309–25.

Jacobs, M. A.; Pugatch, D.; and Spilken, A. 1968. "Ego Strength and Ego Weakness. Comparison of Psychiatric Patients and Functioning Normals." *Journal of Nervous and Mental Disease* 147:297–308.

Jahoda, M. 1958. *Current Concepts of Positive Mental Health.* New York: Basic Books.

Jenks, J. A. 1981. "Adolescent to Woman: The Quest for Integration of Affiliation and Achievement." Master's thesis. Smith College School of Social Work.

Jordan, W. D. 1978. "Searching for Adulthood in America." In *Adulthood,* ed. E. H. Erikson, pp. 189–200. New York: W. W. Norton.

Jung, C. G. 1971. "The Stages of Life." In *The Portable Jung,* ed. J. Campbell, pp. 3–72. New York: Viking Press.

Kagan, J. and Moss, H. A. 1962. *Birth to Maturity.* New York: John Wiley & Sons.

Katchadourian, H. A. 1978. "Medical Perspectives on Adulthood." In *Adulthood,* ed. E. H. Erikson, pp. 33–60. New York: W. W. Norton.

Katz, J., et al. 1968. *No Time for Youth.* San Francisco: Jossey-Bass.

Keniston, K. 1963. "Social Change and Youth in America." In *Youth: Change and Challenge,* ed. E. H. Erikson, pp. 161–87. New York: Basic Books.

Kilpatrick, W. 1974. "Identity, Youth, and the Dissolution of Culture." *Adolescence* 9:407–13.

Kimmel, D. 1974. *Adulthood and Aging.* New York: John Wiley & Sons.

King, S. H. 1980. "The Effect of Graduate School on Identity Issues." *Journal of the American College Health Association* 29:151–54.

Kohlberg, L., and Kramer, R. 1969. "Continuities and Discontinuities in Childhood and Adult Moral Development." *Human Development* 12:93–120.

Kohut, H. 1971. *The Analysis of the Self.* New York: International Universities Press.

Krapf, E. E. 1961. "The Concepts of Normality and Mental Health in Psychoanalysis." *International Journal of Psycho-Analysis* 42:439–47.

Kroeber, T. C. 1963. "The Coping Functions of the Ego Mechanisms." In *The Study of Lives,* ed. R. W. White, pp. 178–99. New York: Atherton Press.

Lacy, W. B., and Hendricks, J. 1980. "Developmental Models of Adult Life: Myth or Reality." *International Journal of Aging and Human Development* 11:89–110.

Levinson, D. J., et al. 1978. *The Season's of a Man's Life.* New York: Knopf.

Lichtenstein, H. 1977. *The Dilemma of Human Identity.* New York: Jason Aronson.

Lidz, T. 1968. *The Person.* New York: Basic Books.

Livson, N., and Peskin, H. 1980. "Perspectives on Adolescence from Longitudinal Research." In *Handbook of Adolescent Psychology*, ed. J. Adelson, pp. 47–98. New York: John Wiley & Sons.

Loevinger, J. 1976. *Ego Development.* San Francisco: Jossey-Bass.

Loewald, H. W. 1980. *Papers on Psychoanalysis.* New Haven, Conn.: Yale University Press.

Lowenthal, M. F.; Thurnher, M.; and Chiriboga, D. 1975. *Four Stages of Life.* San Francisco: Jossey-Bass.

MacFarlane, J. W. 1964. "Perspectives on Personality Consistency and Change from the Guidance Study." *Vita Humana* 7:115–26.

Mahler, M. S.; Pine, F.; and Bergman, A. 1975. *The Psychological Birth of the Human Infant.* New York: Basic Books,

Marcia, J. E. 1966. "Development and Validation of Ego Identity Status." *Journal of Personality and Social Psychology* 3:551–58.

————. 1976. "Identity Six Years After: A Follow-up Study." *Journal of Youth and Adolescence* 5:145–61.

————. 1980. "Identity in Adolescence." In *Handbook of Adolescent Psychology*, ed. J. Adelson, pp. 159–87. New York: John Wiley & Sons.

Marcus, I. M. 1973. "The Experience of Separation-Individuation in Infancy and Its Reverberations Through the Course of Life: 2. Adolescence and Maturity. Panel Report." *Journal of the American Psychoanalytic Association* 21:155–68.

Marshall, W. A. 1973, "Young Adult: 18 to 30 Years—The Body." In *The Seven Ages of Man*, ed. R. R. Sears and S. S. Feldman, pp. 63–68. Los Altos, Calif.: William Kaufman.

Mead, M. 1928. *Coming of Age in Samoa.* New York: William Morrow.

Medley, M. L. 1980. "Life Satisfaction Across Four Stages of Adult Life." *International Journal of Aging and Human Development* 11:193–209.

Meilman, P. W. 1979. "Cross-Sectional Age Changes in Ego Identity Status During Adolescence." *Developmental Psychology* 15:230–31.

Miller, J. B. 1976. *Toward a New Psychology of Women.* Boston: Beacon Press.

Modell, J.; Furstenberg, F. F., Jr.; and Hershberg, T. 1976. "Social Change and Transitions to Adulthood in Historical Perspective." *Journal of Family History* 1:7–34.

Moss, H., and Kagan, J. 1964. "Report on Personality Consistency and Change from the Fels Longitudinal Study." *Vita Humana* 7:127–38.

Murphey, E. B., et al. 1963. "Development of Autonomy and Parent-Child Interaction in Late Adolescence." *American Journal of Orthopsychiatry* 33:643–53.

Nawas, M. M. 1976. "Change in Efficiency of Ego Functioning and Complexity from Adolescence to Young Adulthood." *Developmental Psychology* 4:412–16.

Neugarten, B. L. 1966. "Adult Personality: A Developmental View." *Human Development* 9:61–73.

————. 1969. "Continuities and Discontinuities of Psychological Issues in Adult Life." *Human Development* 12:121–30.

————. 1976. "Introduction to the Symposium: Models and Methods for the Study of the Life Cycle." *Human Development* 14:81–86.

Offer, D., and Offer, J. B. 1975. *From Teenage to Young Manhood: A Psychological Study.* New York: Basic Books.

Offer, D., and Sabshin, M. 1974. *Normality.* New York: Basic Books.

Orlofsky, J. L. 1976. "Intimacy Status: Relationship to Interpersonal Perception." *Journal of Youth and Adolescence* 5:73–89.

Parsons, T. 1949. "Age and Sex in the Social Structure of the United States." In *Personality in Nature, Society, and Culture*, ed. C. Kluckhohn and H. A. Murray, pp. 269–81. New York: Knopf.

Piaget, J. 1977. "The Stages of Intellectual Development in Childhood and Adolescence." In *The Essential Piaget*, ed. H. E. Gruber and J. J. Voneche, pp. 814–19. New York: Basic Books.

Prelinger, E. 1974. "Crises of Identity." In *The Identity Crises*, ed. M. D. Keys, pp. 25–46. New York: National Project Center for Film and the Humanities.

Rees, J. R. 1951. *The Health of the Mind.* New York: W. W. Norton.

Ritvo, S. 1976. "Adolescent to Woman." *Journal of the American Psychoanalytic Association* 24 supp.:127–39.

Rutter, M. 1980. *Changing Youth in a Changing Society.* Cambridge, Mass.: Harvard University Press.

Sachs, D. M. 1977. "Current Concepts of Normality. Panel Report." *Journal of the American Psychoanalytic Association* 25:679–93.

Sarrel, L. J., and Sarrel, P. M. 1979. *Sexual Unfolding.* Boston: Little, Brown.

Schafer, R. 1973. "Concepts of Self and Identity and the Experience of Separation-Individuation in Adolescence." *Psychoanalytic Quarterly* 42:42–60.

———. 1974. "Problems in Freud's Psychology of Women." *Journal of the American Psychoanalytic Association* 22:459–86.

Silber, E., et al. 1966. "Adaptive Behavior in Competent Adolescents: Coping with the Anticipation of College." *Archives of General Psychiatry* 5:354–65.

Smith, M. 1963. "Personal Values in the Study of Lives." In *The Study of Lives,* ed. R. W. White, pp. 324–47. New York: Atherton Press.

Spitz, R. A. 1945. "Hospitalism. An Inquiry into the Genesis of Psychiatric Conditions in Early Childhood." *Psychoanalytic Study of the Child* 1:53–74.

Sternschein, I. 1973. "The Experience of Separation-Individuation in Infancy and Its Reverberations Through the Course of Life: Maturity, Senescence, and Sociological Implications. Panel Report." *Journal of the American Psychoanalytic Association* 21:633–46.

Sullivan, H. S. 1953. *The Interpersonal Theory of Psychiatry.* New York: W. W. Norton.

Symonds, P. M., and Jensen, A. R. 1961. *From Adolescent to Adult.* New York: Columbia University Press.

Tartakoff, H. H. 1966. "The Normal Personality in Our Culture and the Nobel Prize Complex." In *Psychoanalysis—a General Psychology,* ed. R. M. Loewenstein et al., pp. 222–52. New York: International Universities Press.

Ticho, G. R. 1976. "Female Autonomy and Young Adult Women." *Journal of the American Psychoanalytic Association* 24 supp.:139–57.

Timiras, P. S. 1978. "Biological Perspectives on Aging." *American Scientist* 66:605–14.

Vaillant, G. E. 1977. *Adaptation to Life.* Boston: Little, Brown.

Vaillant, G. E., and Milofsky, E. 1980. "Natural History of Male Psychological Health: IX. Empirical Evidence for Erikson's Model of the Life Cycle." *American Journal of Psychiatry* 137:1348–60.

Wallerstein, R. S. 1975. *Psychotherapy and Psychoanalysis: Theory, Practice, Research.* New York: International Universities Press.

Weissman, S., and Barglow, P. 1980. "Recent Contributions to the Theory of Female Adolescent Psychological Development." In *Adolescent Psychiatry,* ed. S. C. Feinstein, et al., pp. 214–30. Chicago: University of Chicago Press.

Whitbourne, S. K., and Waterman, A. S. 1979. "Psychosocial Development During the Adult Years: Age and Cohort Comparisons." *Developmental Psychology* 15:373–78.

White, R. W. 1975. *Lives in Progress,* 3rd ed. New York: Holt, Rinehart.

Wittenberg, R. 1968. *Postadolescence.* New York: Grune and Stratton.

Wolf, E. S. 1980. "Tomorrow's Self: Heinz Kohut's Contribution to Adolescent Psychiatry." In *Adolescent Psychiatry,* ed. S. C. Feinstein, et al., vol. 8, pp. 41–50. Chicago: University of Chicago Press.

5

Bertram J. Cohler
and Andrew M. Boxer

Middle Adulthood: Settling into the World– Person, Time, and Context

Introduction

The course of personality development during the adult years, between the time of entrance into characteristic adult roles and the latter half of life, is of central importance both in the study of the life cycle and for the mental health professions. Realization of feelings of satisfaction within intimate relationships, reconciliation of conflicting needs within the family, particularly those between parents and their young children, and attainment of feelings of meaningfulness and satisfaction with regard to work and career advancement represent significant issues confronting adults as well as those in the mental health field who work with them.

Much of our current understanding of psychosocial development during the adult years has been derived either from reconstruction in clinical psychoanalysis or from systematic findings based on psychiatric research, including that regarding the major psychoses. While such findings provide important information about mental health during the adult years,

Earlier versions of this chapter have benefited from discussions with and comments from several colleagues. The authors would like to thank Drs. Offer and Sabshin, Florence Halprin, and Amy Shapiro for their incisive criticisms. Stephanie Kalfayan provided invaluable assistance with the organization of bibliographic materials.

they often fail to consider either the selective effects of adult memories of the past or the complex interplay between biological predispositions and both the course of personality development and characteristics of the social surround. Much research on psychosocial adaptation among both acute and chronic psychiatric patients has generally been focused on the unique characteristics associated with particular disturbances. Findings from these studies have often not been placed in the context of larger issues concerning personality development and adjustment across the adult years, although much of what has been learned about mental illness has relevance for the study of adult development and aging, just as findings from research on well adults has applications in understanding the course of psychiatric illness (Stein et al. 1978; Vaillant 1977).

A life-course perspective provides an understanding of issues of normality and psychopathology across the adult years that complements and extends those provided by psychoanalysis and psychiatry. This perspective views development in terms of individual differences, including those determined by temperament and unique life experiences, together with socially defined patterns of wishes and intents, including those that are historically determined. Particular patterns of adjustment and disturbance are understood in terms of transactions between person and social system over time, a view consistent with Grinker's (1967) emphasis on a systems approach in psychiatry, as well as with Offer and Sabshin's (1976) description of normality as a transactional system changing over time. Where this approach departs from earlier formulations is in the recognition that *continuity of actions across the life course cannot be assumed* and that the determinants of personality development across the adult years remain as a problem to be investigated. For example, a first psychiatric hospitalization in young adulthood cannot simply be understood in a linear manner by looking backward to predisposing, antecedent factors and conditions related to this adverse life event.

This chapter is an effort to apply this life-course approach to the study of the adult years, during which time persons assume those cardinal roles of spouse, parent, and worker that are synonomous with adulthood in our society. Discussion of the relationship between person and social role provides increased understanding of the interpersonal world of adulthood, as well as of the consequences of particular life events and social roles for continued adjustment.

Normality and Life-Course Social Science

Understanding of particular life stages or phases in the context of the life course represents an enduring perspective in the study of lives (Baltes 1979). However, over the past twenty years, as results from pioneering longitudinal studies have been reported in the literature,* earlier assumptions of development across the life course as necessarily linear and continuous have had to be qualified. Particularly in the area of personality development, it has become clear that earlier experiences are not necessarily related to later outcomes.[†] The life-course perspective on development has led to renewed appreciation of the importance of such factors as socially shared definitions of the course of life, historical forces, and both expected and accidental life events as determinants of individual personality development.

The significance of this social-psychological perspective has become particularly important as a result of recent, detailed studies of personality development across the second half of life.[‡] While earlier longitudinal research had focused primarily upon childhood as the central determinant of adult actions and intents, findings from longitudinal studies have suggested that no one phase of the life cycle may be identified as "primary" for later outcomes (Baltes, Reese, and Lipsitt 1980) and that significant personality development continues across the second half of life.[§]

OPERATIONAL DEFINITION OF NORMALITY

From the perspective of life-course social science, issues of mental health and adaptation must be understood in the context of the life cycle as a whole, including continued performance of expected roles as well as resolution of stress associated both with expected life events characteristically related to particular segments of the life course and also eruptive and unusually adverse life events. A life-course perspective complements and extends the transactional systems perspective on normality formulated by Offer and Sabshin (1974). From a life-course perspective, normality may be operationally defined as the subjectively experienced

* See, for example, Block with Haan (1971); Elder (1974); Jones, et al. (1971); Kagan and Moss (1962); Maas and Kuypers (1974); and Vaillant and McArthur (1972).
 [†] See Clarke and Clarke (1976); Cohler (1981a,b); Gergen (1977, 1980); and Riegel (1977).
 [‡] See, for example, Eichorn et al. (1981); Fiske (1980b); Levinson (1977); Vaillant (1977); and Vaillant and Milofsky (1980).
 [§] See Maas and Kuypers (1974); Munnichs (1966); Neugarten et al. (1964); Reichard, Livson, and Peterson (1962); and Thomae (1976).

sense of congruence between socially shared definitions of those roles or identities salient at successive points across the life course and the personal attainment of them.

This definition emphasizes the extent to which personal adjustment is a consequence of subjective understandings of socially defined actions and intents.* Enactment of roles understood as appropriate for a particular, socially defined age leads to an increased sense of social participation. To the extent that these roles are enacted in an expected manner, and at approximately that point in the life course which is believed to be "on time"—that is, socially sanctioned—increased feelings of positive morale are realized.† To the extent that enactment of a valued role is "off-time," feelings of lack of congruence and lowered morale result (Bacon 1974; Seltzer 1976). This definition emphasizes a subjective state, that of positive morale or life satisfaction, rather than behavioral evidence of psychological impairment, such as particular diagnostic categories, explicit symptom patterns, or psychiatric ratings, as the defining criterion for normality. While acknowledging the importance of findings based on measures of impairment in community studies, such as those of Midtown Manhattan (Srole et al. [1962] 1977) or other community surveys (Kaplan 1971; Lowenthal et al. 1967; Schwab et al. 1979), the present discussion is concerned with more than the absence of symptoms. Rather the focus is on factors associated with a positive state (Jahoda 1958) understood as subjective feelings of happiness or well-being (Bradburn 1969; Bradburn and Caplovitz 1965).

This chapter explores this view of normality as applied to two decades of life, the thirties and forties, which represent middle adulthood. It is during these two decades that most men and women have married and have "settled down" to the task of raising children, and when a series of job changes and promotions lead men, in particular, to the peak of their careers. Important issues across these two decades include increasing acceptance and enactment of the role of mentor or teacher of the next generation, both within the family and at work (Levinson 1977), reconciliation of conflicting expectations between the demands of family and of work, and of being expected simultaneously to care for young children and, often, aging parents as well. Experiences within the family and at work lead both to unique sources of satisfaction and also to a variety of feelings of (role) strain, conflict, and overload for the generation "in the

---

* It is not intended that this definition supply ethical criteria for judging the moral worth of individuals' behavior within a society or of a society itself.

† See McCall and Simmons (1980); Neugarten (1970); Neugarten and Hagestad (1976); Neugarten, Moore, and Lowe, (1965); and Stryker (1980).

middle," feelings that are unique to these two decades of life (Hagestad 1981; Neugarten 1979*b*).*

DIMENSIONS OF TIME

Social and Chronological Age. Considered as a biological index, age in years provides little important information about experiences across the life course. Wide variations in life experiences among persons of roughly the same age, together with the impact of both cohort and social status on definition of the life cycle, further affect subjective understandings of the life course.[†] The rapid social change characteristic of contemporary society has had an impact on these subjective definitions of age; although there are fewer traditional timetables and synchronized age-related roles than in previous decades, there are both a greater number of role transitions and delineated life periods than in the past (Chudacoff 1980; Modell, Furstenberg, and Herschberg 1976; Neugarten and Hagestad 1976). The delineation of such periods of the life course as adolescence, midlife, and very old age are unique to contemporary society (Demos and Boocock 1978; Demos and Demos 1969).

Only when considered in terms of a shared understanding of the life course, defined in a particular manner by persons of a particular generation and cohort, does age become a meaningful marker of the life course.[‡] This normative perspective has been understood in social science as a "symbolic interactionist" approach, because of the emphasis on definition of the self and the social world in terms of learned or internalized elements of the social surround that define both personhood and social relations. The symbolic representation of the social world fosters particular actions and thus organizes behavior appropriate to the particular setting.

As Stryker (1980) has emphasized, the symbolic interactionist framework provides a definition both of the means and ends of human actions and intents. The ways in which persons define and understand these

---

*In line with our definition of normality, middle age has been characterized as a state of mind more than a fixed number of years (Neugarten and Datan 1974). While chronological age may be a parsimonious way of organizing research data on the life cycle, chronological definitions of middle age defy precise specification. As will be explicated, depending on such things as social class, sex, and ethnic group, the markers of middle age have been found to vary. We have focused on the middle adult years as those during which individuals create highly complex and demanding role portfolios when compared to other points in the life cycle.

[†] See Elder (1975); Elder and Rockwell (1978); Neugarten and Hagestad (1976); Neugarten and Moore (1968); Riley (1976); and Rossi (1980*b*).

[‡] See Bengtson, Kasschau, and Ragan (1977); Clausen (1972); Elder (1975); Elder and Rockwell (1978); Hogan (1978); Neugarten and Datan (1973); Neugarten and Hagestad (1976); Ragan and Wales (1980); and Riley (1978).

actions and intents are always determined by a social template for experience, based on the totality of such experiences across the life course. The
social construction of reality (Berger and Luckman 1966) complements
the more traditional focus in psychiatric and psychological research on
understanding the actions and intents of particular persons, for this template provides the elements of personality that are further modified with
subsequent experience.*

The importance of this symbolic interactionist perspective may be seen
in the understandings persons have of the meaning of particular ages. As
Neugarten and Hagestad (1976) and Rossi (1980b) have shown, subjective understanding of the meaning of present age is a consequence of
shared understandings of the significance of that age. Individuals create
for themselves a set of anticipations; they carry with them a set of social
clocks by which they measure themselves with regard to major life
events (Neugarten 1970) across the life course. Persons psychologically
prepare, rehearse, and come to expect a series of life events, making
subjective assessments of the extent to which they are "on-time" or "on-
course" in terms of expected life events. For example, it is now generally
expected in our society that men and women will marry by their mid to
late twenties. If a first marriage should not occur until the forties, the
marital partners themselves, as well as their significant others, would
perceive the marriage as "off-course" in terms of expected timing of life
events. More important, the forty-year-old who expected to marry at
twenty and still finds him- or herself single is likely to feel "off course,"
with accompanying feelings of alienation and regret. If widowhood
comes too early—that is, for a twenty-five- or thirty-year old—such an
unexpected event is experienced as a particularly stressful life crisis (Lopata 1979).

Feelings of self-esteem are tied to shared perceptions of being more or
less "on-time" or "off-time" across the life course. Realization that an
event is taking place at a time other than when it is expected leads to
feelings of being "off-time" and, often, lowered morale (Seltzer 1976).
Particularly important as a determinant of morale is the impact of the
timing of life events in terms of the social support system available (Atch-

---

* Symbolic interactionist approaches should be differentiated from those characteristic of
ethnomethodology and social phenomenology. Ethnomethodology is concerned primarily
with the origins of those cardinal ideas used to construct lives and lacks any particular time
perspective. The important perspective is the other, understood as a social construction and
learned through reciprocal interaction. Social phenomenology is concerned with the manner in which persons form those definitions of reality that are accepted by the symbolic
interactionists as the basis of social life (Gubrium and Buckholdt 1977). Social phenomeno-
logists, following Husserl, start with the self rather than the other and attempt to understand the self in terms of the other (for a review of the concept of "construction" in ethnomethodology, see Frank 1979).

ley 1975; Elder and Rockwell 1978; Troll 1975). A woman widowed in her sixties or seventies is "on-time" for this event. She is able both to look to friends of her own age, who are also likely to be experiencing widowhood, as role colleagues sharing a common event and to learn from them the manner of negotiating this new role. A woman in her thirties does not have such a group of role colleagues available to help her; the fact that she is "off-time" for this event further increases her sense of distress; not only is she more isolated from possible sources of help, but, in addition, she senses that her loss is not expected in terms of anticipated life-cycle events.

SUBJECTIVE PERCEPTIONS OF TIME

The adult's sense of time is related to a number of both inner and outer contingencies. While it is during middle age that a major reorientation of the self occurs,* such a reorientation is contingent on the major social structures in which one is involved: work, family, and the preoccupations that result from such involvements—productivity, generativity, love and care for others, and the meaning one derives from all major life involvements.

Through the passage of time across the life course, persons maintain a sense of self-coherence by drawing on the past, present, and future, in differing ways, depending on their position in the life cycle.[†] The subjective sense of time has been shown to vary with chronological age in a number of gross dimensions: an increase in the value of time with increased age (Wallach and Green 1968); the ways in which the past, present, and future are differentially valued (Bortner and Hultsch 1972; Boxer and Cohler 1980); and the relativity of time itself—that is, one year out of twenty will seem longer than one out of eighty (Janet 1877; cf. Neugarten and Hagestad 1976).

While it has been demonstrated that there are age-related and generational differences in the perception and meaning of time across the life course,[‡] such perceptions have also been found to vary by social class (Neugarten and Moore, 1968; Neugarten, Moore, and Lowe 1965) and sex (Neugarten and Petersen 1957), as well as by culture (Smith 1961; see also Bloch 1977). For example, the perception of middle age itself has been found to vary by social class: blue-collar workers tend to define

*See Bühler and Massarik (1968); Cohler 1981a); Erikson (1963); Fiske (1980a); Jung (1933); Levinson (1977); Lowenthal et al. (1975); Neugarten (1967); Neugarten et al. (1964); and Vaillant (1977).

[†]See Back and Gergen (1963); Butler (1963); Falk (1970); Frank (1948); Lens and Gailly (1980); Lieberman and Falk (1971); Revere (1971); and Revere and Tobin (1980–81).

[‡]See, for example, Bortner and Hultsch (1972); Cottle (1976); Cottle and Klineberg (1974); Gorman and Wessman (1977); Kastenbaum (1966); Neugarten (1967); Rakowski (1979); Revere (1971); and Verstraeten (1980).

middle age in terms of weakening and decline; upper middle class respondents describe middle age as beginning at a chronologically later
age, as a period of great productivity—a peak in life—a time when one
has come into one's own, especially with regard to competency and personal power (Neugarten and Petersen 1957).

ADAPTATION, DEFENSE, AND COPING IN ADULTHOOD

The impact of particular life events on adult functioning is determined
both by the timing of these events in terms of the life course as a whole
and also by characteristic patterns of coping both with unexpected or
eruptive events and also with normative or expected ones (Brim and Ryff
1980; Pearlin 1975). Influenced by earlier psychoanalytic formulations
stressing metapsychological concepts such as libido, the first discussions
of adaptation in adulthood emphasized particular modes of defense
against the emergence of repressed and unacceptable infantile mental
conflicts.* However, as A. Freud ([1937] 1946) has cautioned, defenses
should not be viewed as necessarily invariant in their expression; evidence of maturity is characterized by the flexible use of a number of
defenses rather than by overdetermined reliance on particular defenses.
Subsequent studies of conflict and defense (Miller and Swanson 1960;
Swanson 1961) have supported A. Freud's earlier critique of assumptions
of invariant (genetic) ordering of defenses.

Following Freud's ([1923] 1961) reformulation of his metapsychology
to include increased consideration of ego processes (an effort foreshad-
owed as early as 1895 in his "Project for a Scientific Psychology"), together with such later advances as Hartmann's ([1939] 1958) consideration of the relative autonomy of ego processes and White's (1963)
consideration of independent ego energies leading to the concept of ef-
fectance motivation, there has been a shift in the study of defenses to
include both the concepts of defense and coping in terms of inner conflict
and life events. Additional support has been provided for consideration
of the importance of coping techniques in adaptation as a result both of
developmental studies of young children,† and also the development of
taxonomies for studying defense and coping in adulthood (Haan 1972,
1977; Kroeber 1963). In delineating the structure of coping in adulthood,
Haan's (1977) discussion supports Offer and Sabshin's (1974) observation that much of our present understanding of defense and adaptation

---

*See Abraham ([1921] 1960, [1924] 1960); Freud ([1899] 1965, [1905] 1953, [1937] 1964);
Reich ([1933] 1949); and Rickman (1928).

†See Benjamin (1961); Escalona (1968); Korner (1971); Murphy (1962); Murphy and
Moriarty (1976); and Wolff (1966).

has been derived from a portrayal of normality as a goal never actually attained.

The significance of the shift from a consideration solely of an invariant hierarchy of defenses, in response to conflict, to recognition of the significance of styles of defending and coping with life events, particularly those that are adverse or hazardous, has been shown in studies of the impact of stressful life events on large numbers of persons within community settings (Kaplan 1971), as well as in studies of particular adverse life events such as premature births, which are generally not anticipated (Kaplan and Mason 1960). In addition, careful psychometric studies over the past decade have led to important advances in the measurement of life events and to the study of their impact on persons experiencing these events.* This approach has generated findings quite different from those that might have been expected. For example, both Cohen and Lazarus (1973) and Sarason (1977) report that among persons requiring surgery, coping mechanisms characterized by avoidance or denial (of the seriousness of the situation) were more closely associated with positive postsurgical outcomes than those characterized by vigilance and active efforts at mastery. Less often, discussions of life events and coping have been additionally informed by a life-course perspective (Shanan 1976). For example, Haan (1977) has considered stability of particular coping techniques from adolescence to mid-adulthood, while Bray and Howard (1980) have studied the extent to which patterns of coping at midlife can be predicted from those observed earlier in young adulthood. Findings from such studies suggest that the impact of normative and eruptive life events cannot be understood apart from the changing subjective interpretations of these events associated with their expected timing across the course of life (Rossi 1980*b*).

HISTORICAL EVENTS AND THE LIFE COURSE

The definition of life events as more or less stressful, and as requiring a particular mode of coping in the service of adaptation, does not exist independent of the shared understandings of these events at any one point in time or during particular historical epochs. Partially as a result of the findings of longitudinal studies that have pointed to the impact of historical processes on changing understandings of life events, there has been increased study of the historical context itself as an important determinant of life patterns and personality (Elder 1974, 1979; Riegel 1977).

*See Brim and Ryff (1980); Dohrenwend and Dohrenwend (1974); Holmes and Rahe (1967); Horowitz and Wilner (1980); Lazarus (1974, 1980); Paykel, Prusoff, and Uhlenhuth (1971); Pearlin (1980); and Pearlin and Schooler (1978).

The significance of this larger historical context has long been recognized by European scholars (Mannheim [1928] 1952) as an important defining characteristic of modal personality (Inkeles and Levinson 1954), but has only recently been applied within American social science.*

Shared historical experiences lead to a similar template for understanding life events. For example, Elder (1974, 1979), studying successive cohorts of persons who were children before and during the Great Depression, reports that the Depression had particular impact upon these persons now in midlife. Those middle-aged persons who, as children, experienced moderate privation (defined by a loss of more than a third of pre-depression parental family income) were classified by Elder as having had economically deprived childhoods. When this cohort of middle-aged persons from middle-income backgrounds suffering privation is contrasted with age-mates from the Depression who did not suffer such economic losses, interesting findings emerge. As contrasted with their less deprived age-mates, those persons who suffered economic privation in childhood seem as adults to be somewhat more stable and hard-working and to have enjoyed greater financial success, but also to be more cautious about their careers, plagued by continuing fears of financial reversal. They also tend to be more indulgent toward their children, apparently making restitution for their own childhood privation.

In a more recent reanalysis of these findings, Elder (1979) selected groups of middle-aged persons who experienced economic privation either as young children or as adolescents, using two cohorts from the Berkeley Studies born ten years apart. Adverse impact of such privation seems to occur largely among the boys who were younger when hardship struck, with these boys showing greater loss of self-esteem attendant upon hardship. As middle-aged men, those who were youngsters at the time of hardship report greater feelings of inadequacy and are both more self-contained and bothered than men of comparable age who were older at the time of the original childhood hardship. Among women in the two cohorts, such striking differences fail to appear; middle-aged women who were younger when experiencing hardship do not appear to differ in present adjustment from those who were older. Indeed, women younger at the time of encountering hardship seem even more competent than those who were older.†

---

*See Bengtson and Cutler (1976); Cain (1967); Demos and Boocock (1978); Elder (1974, 1975, 1979); Riley, Johnson, and Foner (1972); and Schaie (1973).

†In one of the cohorts (Berkeley) that Elder (1979) analyzed, economic loss differentially affected relations within the family based on the quality of the pre-Depression marital bond. In cases where there was marital harmony, economic loss enhanced relations of fathers with their sons and daughters. Without marital harmony and with fathers being unable to provide sufficient economic support, girls were able to become closer to mothers, while boys lost emotional support both of mothers and, particularly of fathers. The boys and girls in this cohort were young children during the Depression.

Elder (1979) explains this sex difference in terms of the implications for appropriate childhood sex-role identification. Boys in deprived families, particularly boys younger at the time of economic misfortune, tended to view this economic privation as a consequence of their father's failure to achieve in the world. Elder infers that these boys believed that such paternal misfortune presaged their own future difficulties. However, girls were able to draw close to their mothers at such times and to seek comfort from them. Mothers appeared more able to provide comfort for their daughters than fathers were for their sons, since failure in life led the fathers to withdraw from the family and to experience lowered self-esteem.

FAMILY LIFE CYCLE AND INDIVIDUAL LIFE COURSE

The historical approach is of significance both when studying individual lives and when studying the family itself. Current demographic changes in family formation add up to what will be the changing texture of middle age. While across the last half century a majority of the critical life-cycle events in the family have shown little variation among women, the lower the level of education attained, the earlier a woman is likely to begin her family (Spanier and Glick 1980). However, the last decade brought a slight upswing in the age of first marriage, and the timing of the family formation process itself has been undergoing considerable changes. From 1930 to 1944 U.S. marriage tended to lead to relatively small families formed over longer durations. From 1945 to 1964 marriages experienced rapid childbearing within a shorter period of time. From 1965 to 1974 marriages tended to form families quickly but had far fewer births in total; more births occurred within a given period of time, although cumulative births were drastically lower (Tsui and Bogue 1978).

At the same time, while the empty nest and grandparenthood have tended to come earlier across the last few decades, with widowhood coming later for women and lasting longer (Neugarten and Brown-Rezanka 1978), this pattern may be reversed in the coming decades. With age at first marriage increasingly postponed, family formation will come later and result in middle-aged parents who still have young children in the household. In addition, it has been estimated that 40 percent of first marriages for women twenty-five to thirty-five will end in divorce, so that there will be a higher proportion of divorced women who will reach midlife in the 1980s (Glick 1980; Neugarten and Brown-Rezanka 1978). While for men the period of economic dependency has lengthened at one end, with a greater period of time spent in education preparing for a career, some are opting for earlier retirement (Neugarten and Datan 1973). Employment patterns for women are changing as well, with a greater number of women in the labor force than previously, particularly after the years that their children have reached school age (Giele 1982; Hoffman and Nye 1974; and Kanter 1977b).

The timing of family formation, changing economic needs within the family, and the timing and course of occupational careers of both men and women are all affected by each other. For example, Oppenheimer (1974) has reported on a study of working-class men in their forties and fifties born during the 1930s. His findings show that median family incomes were lowest at precisely those points at which family economic needs were most pressing. Oppenheimer termed this pressure a "life-cycle squeeze," which places additional pressure on the wife and mother to seek outside employment, further affecting the quality of marital interaction and the relationship between parents and children, as parents struggle to realize the standard of living to which their families aspired (Oppenheimer 1977). Earlier studies have documented similar tensions among middle-aged, middle-class parents and their offspring (Billig and Adams 1957).

Across the decade of the eighties, a dominant portion of the United States population will be between the ages of thirty and fifty, as members of the baby boom (1947–1957) realize midlife. With gains achieved in life expectancy throughout the twentieth century, the middle years have become an increasingly significant phase of the life course, and one that occupies an ever greater period of time. Such demographic changes indicate that middle adulthood is likely to be different in several respects across the next decades than has been characteristic in the past and that these changes are likely to affect individual and family life in significant ways.

CYCLES AND TASKS IN THE FAMILY AND INDIVIDUAL LIFE COURSE

Characterization of timing across the life course in terms of expected or normative events assumes the existence of a number of transitions, including both entrance into new roles and exits from old roles, successively, from childhood to old age. Accompanying each such role shift, as well as changes in the definition of existing roles, is a task or issue that must be resolved (Havighurst 1953). Central to this concept of *developmental task* is the assumption of an epigenetic or stepwise process in which the failure to resolve earlier tasks has implications for the capacity to resolve later ones. This concept has been represented in traditional psychoanalytic formulations by Freud's *Three Essays* ([1905] 1953), Abraham's ([1924], 1960) essay on stages of the libido, and, most recently, Erikson's classic statement, *Childhood and Society* (1963).

Little systematic evidence has been provided in support of the intrinsic stage or stepwise ordering of phases or stages of the life cycle, beyond the obvious tasks, such as parenthood, which result from expectable role transitions. Discussions by Kagan (1980), Gergen (1980), Neugarten (1979a), Cohler (1981a,b), and others suggest that the life cycle may not be so neatly ordered as has often been portrayed. Much of what is presumed to be orderly psychological development may be better understood as the result of random events, taking place without any predetermined order. It has also been suggested, primarily by psychoanalytic theorists, that particular developmental challenges can be better understood as crises or conflicts between self and others than as tasks or issues to be resolved (Bibring 1959; Erikson 1963; Rapaport 1963). As Rossi (1968) has noted in her discussion of parenthood, the use of the term crisis prejudges the question. Any particular issue or task becomes a crisis to the extent that problems are encountered in achieving a successful resolution. A sense of crisis is but one outcome suggested by the series of role-associated developmental tasks negotiated (in socially shared ways at appropriate ages) across the life course (Rossi 1980b).

More recently the concept of developmental task has been extended from person to family, from initial courtship to death of the surviving spouse (Duvall and Hill 1948; Hill and Hanson 1960; Hill and Rodgers 1964). As originally formulated, this concept of family life cycle did not sufficiently differentiate between chronological age of parent and offspring (Hudson and Murphy 1980), nor did it take into account the impact of particular historical factors in shifting definitions of phases in the family life cycle. It also failed to consider differences in perceptions of the family life cycle for men and for women, with socially defined age as the single most important organizer of adult lives for men and age of children as the single most important organizer of women's conceptions of their place in the life course (Spanier, Sauer, and Larzelere 1979). Furthermore, this approach did not separate the impact of marriage from child-rearing as factors important in the definition of phases in the family life cycle (Nock 1979). More recent formulations (Hill and Mattessich 1979) have incorporated these observations: stages in the family life cycle are now understood in terms of the impact of particular role transitions, both on individual family members and also on the family as a psychosocial unit (Burgess 1926). These stages are viewed in terms of the impact of social and historical changes on the individual's perceptions of his or her place in the life course. Changes in the role portfolios of particular family members have an impact on the family unit as a whole. Individual and family careers both must be understood in the context of changing perceptions of the salience of particular events as significant in the definition of age across cohorts.

Work, Career, and Family Across the Middle Years

PARENTHOOD AND SEX ROLES

Spanier, Sauer, and Larzelere's (1979) observation concerning the quite different developmental organizers used by men and women across the middle years is of critical importance in understanding normality through middle adulthood. It is during the decades of the thirties and the forties that men and women are likely to draw on different personal resources in experiencing their lives as more or less satisfying and "on time," in terms of presently shared definitions of the life course. This difference in understanding the middle years, based on adult sex roles, is largely determined by the fact of parenthood itself (Gutmann 1975, 1977). Prior to parenthood, career success at work and the capacity to maintain satisfying adult relationships represent important issues in the lives of both men and women. However, with the advent of parenthood, a new developmental task becomes salient for both sexes.

This formulation of the impact of parenthood on definitions of adult roles is consistent with findings from a number of studies of parental attitudes and of perceptions of the parental role. These studies show that even within couples sharing a nontraditional orientation toward the division of labor on the basis of sex roles, the advent of parenthood calls forth a more traditional definition of their roles.* Mothers view their own roles much more as those of homemaker and primary caretaker for children and view their husband's role principally as that of provider. Both mothers of young children and their husbands presume that their husbands would not be readily available to help with children during these first years after the advent of parenthood, a time when the husband and father is particularly concerned with his own career development. As a result of the parents' own particularly traditional definitions of their family roles across these middle years, their children begin to rehearse these same roles for themselves, preparing for their own future parenthood. Girls learn the expressive and kin-keeping role within the family (Firth, Hubert, and Forge 1970; Komarovsky 1962) at the same time that boys learn increasing self-reliance. This transmission of stereotyped sex-role socialization across generations (Parsons and Bales 1955), inspired by the parental imperative, has led Chodorow (1978) to portray the successive socialization of girls in the roles of their mothers as the "reproduction of mothering," a critique shared by Bernard (1975) and Gilligan (1979) re-

*Belsky (1981); Cowan, et al. (1978); Hoffman (1978); Hoffman and Mannis (1978); Lamb (1978); and Shereshefsky et al. (1973).

garding the extent to which women in contemporary urban society have adopted this expressive or instrumental orientation.

For both men and women, it is during the middle years that continuing concern for community and society is most salient. Feelings of responsibility for child care extend beyond the family, to other social institutions, such as the school (including the PTA) and a variety of voluntary associations within the community, including union representation at work and civic betterment. Within the family itself, both men and women have become the generation "in the middle," responsible simultaneously for the care of dependent children and, increasingly, dependent parents. At the same time that parents provide for the care of their children, this concern with generativity extends to the community itself (Erikson 1963). Particularly among men who will have worked their entire adult life, the middle years often mark the zenith of career success. There is an expectable shift from having a career sponsored by a mentor, to becoming the mentor for younger colleagues (Levinson 1977; Levinson et al. 1978), suggesting that for men worklife may increasingly present issues similar to parenthood.

During these same middle years, the wife and mother may enter the work force for the first time since marriage or reenter the work world with increased commitment, as children grow to young adulthood and no longer require care on such a continuing basis. The wife's career trajectory may cross that of her husband during these middle years, with the wife experiencing increasing career success and opportunities at the same time that her husband begins to confront the limits of his hopes and aspirations (Rapoport et al. 1977). Such differing experiences may effect not only the marital relationship, but also that of each parent with his or her children. Issues of marriage, parenthood, and work must be viewed as interrelated in understanding the satisfaction that men and women achieve in their lives during these middle years (Lowenstein 1980).

WOMEN IN THE MIDDLE YEARS: ISSUES OF FAMILY AND WORK

For adult women, parenthood continues as the cardinal role through the middle years. Reviewing findings from a number of cross-national studies, Veevers (1979) reports that 85 percent of all married women become parents, characteristically in the mid-twenties. In the United States, more than 90 percent of ever-married women aged thirty to forty-five have at least one child, with two children still the "norm" (U.S. Bureau of Commerce 1977). Equally striking, less than three percent of younger women plan to remain voluntarily childless; successive National Opinion Research Center (NORC) national surveys show that no more than 8 percent of adults consider it desirable *not* to have children. The few studies that have been reported concerning voluntary childlessness (Bram, 1974, 1978; Veevers 1973, 1979) suggest that the decision among otherwise fecund couples not to have children is elected primarily by highly educated, upper-middle-class couples, where each spouse has professional employment and where motherhood would interfere in the wife's career and the couple's dual income. Such couples appear to have an unusually companionate marriage in which offspring are perceived as a disadvantage and where there is particularly great emphasis upon self-actualization.

Characteristically, the decision to remain childless by couples who presumably could have children is one that is understood as inherently "deviant." Society could not continue to exist across more than one generation if couples did not continue to have children and, as a consequence, to perpetuate society itself (Parsons 1951; Radcliffe-Brown 1952). It is certainly not surprising that the decision to remain childless is one that is disapproved of; the reports of Bram (1978), Veevers (1979), and Lowenstein (1980) document the extent to which voluntarily childless couples feel disapproved of by family, neighbors, friends, and coworkers. Understood in terms of the present discussion, these voluntarily childless couples are "off-time" for an event that has critical social consequences.

PARENTHOOD AND MORALE

Psychosocial issues related to the assumption of the roles of spouse and parent have been discussed in chapter 4. Of particular relevance for this discussion is the systematic variation reported by different investigators regarding the impact of parenthood on feelings of personal and marital satisfaction reported by mothers through the middle years. Reviewing studies of marital satisfaction reported by couples across the years of active parenting, Campbell, Converse, and Rodgers (1976), Rollins and Galligan (1978), Schram (1979), and Gove and Peterson (1980) have described a flat "U shaped" curve: feelings of both personal and marital satisfaction appear to be high during first years after marriage, decreasing rapidly with the birth of the first child, remaining low across the years when there are children at home, and increasing once again as young-adult offspring begin their own lives apart from their parents (Andrews and Withey 1976; Houseknecht 1979; Humphrey 1975). Other studies have documented the extent to which women experience role strain and overload together with lowered morale as a result of the transition to parenthood, problems that characteristically increase with the births of subsequent children.*

*See Dyer (1963); LeMasters (1957); Meyerowitz and Feldman (1966); Rossi (1968); Russell (1974); and Yalom et al. (1968).

Across the years of active parenting, the feelings of role strain and overload among women, who must meet the multiple and conflicting demands of homemaker, wife, and mother, contribute to feelings of depression that appear to be characteristic of the lives of adult women through the middle years in contemporary urban society.* While Fischer and associates (1979) and Srole and Fischer (1980), reporting on changes in adjustment among women in their restudy of Midtown Manhattan, claim that these changes represent the effect of changes over the past two decades in definition of women's roles, Klerman and Weissman (1980) have questioned the extent to which this restudy does show such changes, since quite different methods for reporting psychological states were used than in the original study reported by Srole and his colleagues in 1962 (1977) and these different reporting methods would have led to an underreporting of depressive symptoms in the restudy. Indeed, studies by Weissman and her associates (1978, 1979) of an industrial northeastern community have shown that as many as 24 percent of the women were markedly depressed at the time of the survey.

Review of findings from studies of sex roles and lowered morale all appear to point in a single direction, that of the impact on women as homemaker, mother, and "kin-keeper" for both own and husband's family bearing the accumulated role and stressful life events of the entire extended family.[†] Recent feminist critiques of the "motherhood mandate" (Russo 1979) have further added to the problems encountered by these women as wives and mothers; efforts at showing options that really do not exist, particularly within the working-class subculture, do not assist these women in obtaining increased feelings of life satisfaction. Ironically, an unintended effect of the women's movement, particularly within the working-class subculture, may be an increase in feelings of role strain and lowered morale as expectations continue to clash with the reality of daily life.

MOTHERHOOD AND WORK

As all children finally become of school age, the lives of women are dramatically altered. It is not surprising that the percentage of mothers in the work force nearly doubles after there are no children of preschool age in the family (Hoffman and Nye 1947). At the same time, it should be noted that if a child should be out of school for some time, it is the wife

---

*See Bart (1971); Bart and Grossman (1976); Brown and Harris (1978); Cohler et al. (1974); Gove (1972); Gove and Tudor (1973); Klerman and Weissman (1980); Pearlin (1975); Pearlin and Johnson (1977); Radloff (1975 1980); Ripley (1977); and Weissman and Klerman (1977).

[†]See Bardwick and Douvan (1971); Chodorow (1978); Cohler and Grunebaum (1981); Firth, Hubert, and Forge (1970).

and mother who is generally expected to remain home and provide child-care.* It is still generally the case that the woman's career or work is regarded as "discretionary" and supplemental to an extent not true for her husband, particularly during the years when there are children still living at home (Gove and Peterson 1980; Lopata and Norr 1980; Sweet 1973).

In general, work appears to be much less important as a factor shaping self-esteem among women than among men through the middle years. Bernard (1975) has noted that many of the discussions of the significance of work in women's lives overlook the importance of the nature of the work itself. Among middle-class women, work may be used as a means of filling otherwise empty time while children are in school, rather than as a satisfying activity in its own right, while among working-class women work has not been experienced as a career with its own intrinsic rewards. Rather it is an exchange of labor for pay in order to supplement the income of the husband and father. Particularly among working-class families, if the wife's pay or status at work is likely to exceed that of the husband, serious family conflicts may develop. Consistent with Bernard's observations, Blood and Wolfe (1960) have reported that employed middle-class wives had the highest morale of any group of either husbands or wives, while Nye (1960) reports that employment is generally more satisfying for middle-class than for working-class women.[†]

There have been notable cohort differences in the involvement of women in the work force, with fewer women working during the years just after World War II, the era of the growth of the suburbs, than within previous cohorts of women. Those women who became mothers just after the war lived in an era of prosperity unique in American history and, for the first time, had the genuine option of not having to work in order to help support the family (Cohler and Grunebaum 1981). In addition, since homes were often more distant from the workplace than earlier, there was much less possibility of working part time. With an "all-or-none" choice between working and remaining at home, women with young children decided to remain at home, following an adult life course that included at least part-time work later in the family life cycle, and that has, in the intervening years, come to seem "typical" (Modell, Furstenberg, and Hershberg 1976; Uhlenberg 1974).

Since 1960, particularly among middle-class women, there has been increased interest in entering (or reentering) the labor force, leading to

---

*See Bernard (1974); Hoffman (1978); Rapoport et al. (1977); and Yankelovich, Skelly, and White (1977).
    [†]See Birnbaum (1971); Brown and Harris (1978); Gover (1963); and Nathanson (1980).

the development of the "dual career" family (Rapoport and Rapoport 1976). Much of this interest has been sparked by a reevaluation of the definition of the woman's role so characteristic for the previous generation (Van Dusen and Sheldon 1976). It is less clear that this has been the case among working-class women (Sawhill 1974). While careful survey data are lacking, findings from the *Better Homes and Gardens* study (Social Research Inc. 1972) together with reports from interview studies (Cohler and Grunebaum 1981; Rubin 1976) suggest that the women's movement may have had relatively little impact among traditionally conservative working-class women socialized from earliest childhood to a more conformist and dependent mode of interpersonal relations appropriate for a workplace in which there are many bosses and little control over decision making (Kohn 1969; Komarovsky 1962). There can be little doubt that the rampant inflation of the past decade has meant that, among both middle-class and working-class families, issues of women's work may be much less discretionary and supplemental than across preceding generations.

WOMEN AND MARRIAGE THROUGH THE MIDDLE YEARS

While there is some evidence that both middle-class and working-class women prefer part-time to full-time work during the years of active parenting, the critical factor in determining the impact of work on morale among women is the extent to which husband and wife agree upon the wife's decision to work or remain at home (Gove and Peterson 1980; Orden and Bradburn 1969). Within both middle- and working-class families, the strain encountered in husband's workplace appears to have a particularly negative impact on the wife's morale (Burke, Weir, and DuWors 1980; Siassi, Crocetti, and Spiro 1974).

Erikson (1963) emphasizes the importance for both men and women of the capacity for intimacy in adulthood as an important determinant of positive morale. Intimacy includes both the capacity for sharing feelings, including wishes and fears, and also the capacity for achieving a mutually satisfying regulation of sexuality. On the basis of the literature on mate selection (Murstein 1976; Winch 1958, 1967; Winch, Ktsanes, and Ktsanes 1955) it has become clear that persons marry others who share their own values and who are perceived as similar in interests and worldview, rather than those whose views are reciprocal (Gottman 1979). At the same time, it is apparent that the decision to marry is based, to a large extent, on socially determined factors beyond the particular personality of either marital partner or qualities of their relationships. Cultural expectations, such as prohibitions on particular interreligious or interethnic marriages, the nature of the couple's social network, and position in the life course all influence the decision to marry (Bott 1971; Cohler and Grunebaum 1981; Ryder, Kafka and Olson 1971).

Since the classic studies of Terman and Oden (1959), Burgess and Wallin (1953), Blood and Wolfe (1960), and Pineo (1961), there has been considerable systematic investigation of factors associated with material satisfaction. When dimensions such as power and influence (Blood and Wolfe 1960), communication, and shared feelings (Cutler and Dyer 1965) are examined, the extent to which the couple can achieve consensus within the marriage appears to be critical in such diverse aspects of adult life as work patterns and sexuality (Gottman 1979; Rausch et al. 1974; Waring et al. 1980). The extent of agreement and the process by which agreement is achieved is as important as the specific outcome of decisions made by husband and wife.

Little is known about the role of sexual expression in determining marital satisfaction; most research on sexuality and marriage has been concerned with issues of frequency and mode of sexual expression (Laws 1980; Wilson 1975). Bernard (1964) has suggested that concern with sexual satisfaction may be greater among husbands than among wives, although Wilson's (1975) report suggests that, overall, wives are less satisfied than husbands with sexual expression within the marriage. Women tend to see sexuality as a part of overall intimacy to a greater extent than men, who seem more likely to differentiate between sexual satisfaction and other aspects of relationships.

Only one study (Clark and Wallin 1973) has directly considered the relationship between sexual expression and overall marital expression. Wives reporting a more positive sexual adjustment also reported higher overall marital satisfaction. However, consistent with Ehrmann's (1964) review, the nature of previous sexual experiences may be more important than marital satisfaction in predicting present sexual satisfaction. With the exception of Laws's (1980) review, there has been little attempt to understand sexual expression and marital satisfaction in life-course terms. Laws notes, for example, that sexual interest appears to diminish somewhat among men after midlife, while it appears to increase somewhat for women. Clearly shared understandings of meaning and significance of sexual expression, changing with age and across cohorts, are important in the experience of sexuality and marriage among men and women throughout adulthood.

The overall quality of the marriage, as evaluated both by husband and wife, appears to more closely approximate the husband's perceptions of the marriage than those of the wife (Bernard 1972, 1975; Troll 1975; Veroff and Feld 1970). Further, as Campbell, Converse, and Rodgers

(1976) show, across the years of marriage men report greater satisfaction with their marriage than is characteristic for their wives.

Such findings have led Bernard (1975) to suggest that the husband rather than the wife is the principal beneficiary of marriage in contemporary society. Finally, it should be noted that, with the exception of reports by Pearlin and Lieberman (1979) and Rossi (1980a), as well as those of Campbell, Converse, and Rodgers (1976) mentioned earlier, factors such as the timing of shifting role responsibilities across adulthood are seldom included in studies of life satisfaction and adult adjustment.

WOMEN AND THE MIDLIFE TRANSITION

Mothers and Adolescent Offspring. As children become adolescent and begin to establish their own lives outside the family, fathers, in particular, appear to worry more about their offspring than earlier (Yankelovich, Skelly, and White 1977), but both parents, particularly mothers, find themselves increasingly with free time. As Bernard (1975) has observed, the "tipping point" has arrived at which it is unquestionably correct in contemporary society for the wife and mother to seek increased commitment to activities outside the home, including paid work. At the same time, this change within the family may lead to new interpersonal issues for the marriage itself.

While parenthood lasts across the entire time from first pregnancy to oldest age (Benedek 1973), the phase of active parenting generally comes to an end when children reach mid to late adolescence, highlighting, once again, the quality of the marital relationship. Where serious problems in the achievement of intimacy have existed over the course of many year, these problems now become increasingly apparent. In addition, the struggles of adolescent offspring to seek appropriate expression of reawakened sexual wishes may lead to increased problems on the part of parents in modulating their own sexual tensions (Cohler 1977; Giovacchini 1970).

In general, parents report increased satisfaction derived from having adolescent children in contrast to younger children (Boxer et al. 1984). In their decade review Spanier and Lewis (1980) quote Rollins and Galligan's (1978) observation that "caring for young children puts a crunch on the time, energy, and economic resources of parents and results in a decrease in the marital satisfaction of parents" (p. 83). Rossi (1980a) notes the importance of considering marital satisfaction and involvement in parenting within particular cohorts. At least within the present cohort, less well educated women appear to enjoy caring for younger children to a greater extent than older children, while among better educated women, parenting adolescents results in greater satisfaction than caring for younger children, presumably because adolescent children can communicate better with their parents and, as a result of experiences during the high school and college years, increasingly share common interests.

The apparent challenge to authority posed by at least some adolescent offspring remains a source of conflict for their parents. Blos (1967), Lidz (1977), and others have pointed to the importance of the adolescent "rebellion" against the parent as a part of the process of separation from the family and individuation expected among adults in our society. Such rebellion may be more a function of the quite different interests or "developmental stakes" of family members (Bengtson and Kuypers 1971), with the younger generation concerned primarily with the creation of a meaningful life plan and their parents involved in justification or validation of the manner in which they have led their lives and managed the stewardship of the larger social order. Selective continuity across generations appears to be more significant than social change in both attitudes and values.* Both parents and young-adult offspring attempt to minimize the extent of the "generation gap" that exists within *their* family (Bengtson and Cutler 1976). Even when there is not exact correspondence between the values of the two generations, offspring may express the same themes as those of their parents (Jennings and Nemi 1968; Kandel and Lesser 1972). For example, in studies of campus radicals during the 1960s, those students who were most activist on the "new left" had parents who had been activist on the "old left" a generation earlier.†

With the advent of young adulthood, offspring leave home to begin their own lives, part of an interdependent family unit yet living independently. It is important to note that much more extensive contact is maintained across generations in contemporary urban society than has been appreciated by social critics. A number of studies have shown that adults maintain frequent personal and telephone contact with their parents, and that such contact is characteristic of relations within the family of adulthood in our society.‡ Particularly among mothers and their young-adult daughters, continuing socialization of the next generation to the roles of kin-keeper and caretaker ensures that mothers and daughters will have continuing contact (Chodorow 1978; Rossi 1968).

Motherhood and the "Empty Nest." As young adults negotiate interdependent relations with their parents, marrying, creating their own house-

---

*See Adelson (1970); Campbell (1969); Douvan and Adelson (1966); Thomas (1971); and Yankelovich (1972).

†See Angres (1974); Bild (1974); Flacks (1971); Troll, Neugarten, and Kraines (1969); see also Nassi (1981).

‡See Adams (1968); Cohler and Grunebaum (1981); Hill et al. (1970); Litwak (1960a,b); Shanas (1961, 1973, 1979); Sussman (1954); Sussman and Burchinal (1962); and Young and Geertz (1961).

holds, and having their own children, they begin to develop the more stereotyped sex-role orientation that is a function of the parental imperative (Gutmann 1975, 1977) at the same time their parents are moving away from such stereotyped sex roles. It is at this time that men become less explicitly concerned with issues of career and income and that women, free to become more deeply involved in work, begin to realize the opportunity for increased career success.

In other respects, at least within current cohorts, many of the issues first posed by that stage of family life when offspring become adolescent are accentuated with the transition to the "empty nest." While formerly it had been believed that the transition to the empty nest represented a source of lowered morale, findings reported by a number of researchers* indicate that the departure of young-adult offspring from the home has little negative impact on the morale of either parent. Several of these studies report increased satisfaction from the marriage and decreased parental role strain. Increased satisfaction with children and, generally, an increased sense of morale appear to accompany this transition to the empty nest. In a recent study of three-generation families, it was noted that failure for a young-adult child to *leave home* at the expected or anticipated time increased strain and conflict among parents and their young-adult children (Wilen 1979).

Psychological Changes Among Women at Midlife. Discussion of midlife as a unique developmental task in the life course has been recognized in both the scholarly and popular literature (Rubin 1979) as unique to our age. Perhaps the earliest systematic formulation of midlife as a developmental task or psychological phenomenon was based on observations by Jung (1933), who described the increased introversion associated with the transition to midlife. Erikson has described a similar transition in the life course, understood as a struggle between the need to care for others and the need to care for self (generativity versus stagnation), while Lasch (1978) and, particularly, Kernberg (1980) note the increased preoccupation with self, or narcissistic orientation, that accompanies middle age. Perhaps the most detailed discussion of this transition to midlife has been given by Neugarten and associates (Neugarten 1973; Neugarten and Datan 1973; Neugarten et al. 1964), who note that as a consequence of this changing perception of place within the life cycle, there is, some time during the years from the mid-forties to the mid-fifties, a growing realization that there may be less time left to be lived than has been lived already. However, as Tizard and Guntrip (1959) have noted, such real-

---

*See Axelson (1960); Blood and Wolfe (1960); Campbell, Converse, ard Rodgers (1976); Deutscher (1964); Glenn (1975); Lowenthal (1975); Lowenthal, Fiske, and Chiriboga (1972); Menaghan (1978); Mullan (1980); Radloff (1980); Rubin (1979); and Stinnet, Collins, and Montgomery (1970).

ization may also give greater depth of meaning and value both to present life and also to future expectations.

With the transition to midlife, persons appear to stop looking forward, considering goals to be achieved, and begin to look backward, reviewing the past rather than preparing for the future. This leads to increased preoccupation with inner life, termed interiority (Neugarten 1973). This process of reminiscence is a consequence of the increasing awareness of the finitude of life (Munnichs 1966) and of preparing for the reality of death (Jaques 1965, 1981); death becomes personalized in new ways (Rothstein 1967).* Such reminiscence is selective: the past is used in mid-life primarily as a means of solving problems (Revere 1971; Revere and Tobin 1980–81). Sometime later, with the transition to old age, there is a shift to the use of the past primarily in order to complete the life review (Butler 1963) and to prepare for imminent death.

Most systematic research to date on the midlife crisis has been reported among men (Levinson 1977; Levinson et al. 1978; Vaillant 1978). Where research has been carried out concerning women at midlife, findings have been concerned principally with the climacterium, and the impact of menopause on self-esteem. As McKinlay, Jeffreys, and Thompson (1974) observe, timing of menopause occurs with wide variation across the second half of adulthood; a number of symptoms of supposed aging are attributed to the menopause that are, in fact, independent of this transition point in the woman's reproductive cycle. Notman (1979), reviewing the contributions of earlier psychoanalytic formulations to the study of women at midlife (Benedek 1959; Deutsch 1945) notes the defensive posture of these earlier investigators regarding women's social roles, in which women appeared to make little contribution to either family or community outside of that associated with reproduction. Most research has not shown the menopause to be the biosocial crisis earlier described by Deutsch and Benedek. It is ironic, as Neugarten and Datan (1973), Fiske (1980b), and Rossi (1980b) all noted, that so much of the research on women at midlife has concerned issues of bodily change when, in fact, men rather than women seem most clearly preoccupied with such changes across the second half of life. For women, aging appears to be defined primarily in terms of role losses, such as that associated with widowhood, perhaps the single most significant life event for women across the second half of life, while, for men, changes in physical appearance and stamina appear to be a significant marker of aging.

*Marshall (1978) has reviewed other evidence and concluded that the frequency of thoughts about death does not increase with age, although the circumstances in which people think about death may vary by life stage. In addition, we would caution that frequency should not be equated with saliency. As Marshall noted, when faced with illness, middle-aged and older individuals may think about the possibility of death.

Men in the Middle Years: Issues of Work and Family

THE WORLD OF WORK

Particularly for men in our society, self-definitions and evaluations are tied to the world of work. Through the roles of worker and *provider* self-assessments are made with regard to how well one is succeeding as husband and father. Work has a major impact on life-style, values, habits, and interpersonal relations for a large portion of the life cycle.* The evolution of work in modern society has been discussed by many scholars, among whom Hannah Arendt (1958) and Max Weber ([1904–5] 1958) detailed the ways in which work has become an end in itself. Our consumer society is a society of workers; this has come about through the emancipation of laboring activity itself, which clearly preceded the political emancipation of laborers (Arendt 1958). Who men are and what they do are for the sake of "making a living." Currently, occupational choice and mobility are strongly related to factors of selective continuity within the family. Many of the determinants of occupational choice begin in childhood. The myriad of influences that are strongly related to family background include available role models that may affect patterns of motivation and personality styles (Aldous, Osmond, and Hicks 1979; Veroff and Feld 1970).

In their extensive review of the literature, Aldous, Osmond, and Hicks concluded that students are allocated to educational programs that roughly index their family background and to a destined occupation that reflects this background. Early in the course of life, a father's income affects a son's occupational outcome by the resources that are available to be invested in education and training. Men in higher- and middle-level occupations are better able to transmit educational and occupational values, since they have the personal resources with which to encourage father-son identification (Aldous, Osmond, and Hicks 1979), even though work commitments may prevent their full participation in the family. It is at the peak of one's career, or when one is "topping out," that the strongest relationship may be discerned in the continuity of work patterns through men's lives.

In middle age social competence in role performance is often at a plateau (Havighurst 1957). When family background effects are strongest on a son's income, in the middle years, the occupational achievement of this son is very critical for his own children, particularly for males. The life-cycle squeeze, discussed earlier, may make it difficult for a man's earn-

*See Erikson (1963); Henry (1971); Kohn (1980); Veroff and Feld (1970); see also Kanter (1977).

ings to meet family needs and the rising costs of education (Oppenheimer 1974; Wilensky 1963). Aldous, Osmond, and Hicks discuss the ways in which the number and ages of a man's children would mediate the magnitude and severity of this economic squeeze. Oppenheimer's analysis made clear that only for men with higher status occupations do median earnings tend to peak in congruence with family needs. In addition, as Rossi (1980b) has underscored, in the 1950s many couples had children one after another, with little space between them. In a society that is now coming to require at least four years of postsecondary schooling for entry into skilled occupations, these parents have many added financial burdens placed upon them as their children reach late adolescence and they themselves are well into their middle years.

Perhaps owing to the centrality and rigidity of work commitments required of them, males commonly perceive cues in the work situation as markers of their "progress" and the onset of middle age. Particularly for younger workers, self-assessment is tied to subjective evaluation of competence in the workplace (Kornhauser 1965). Life line and career line are perceived as closely related (Neugarten 1967). While these cues and their timing may vary from occupation to occupation and across social class, men compare themselves to their peers as a means of self-assessment (Gould 1974). In complex organizations and hierarchies it is, indeed, difficult for success to mean anything other than vertical movement and mobility (Kanter 1977). These mobility patterns appear to reach their peak in middle age.*

For example, in Levinson and coworkers' sample of middle-class men, the twenties and thirties were a time for *building* one's career. However, in Rubin's (1976) study of blue-collar workers, the occupational movement was horizontal rather than vertical but men were, nonetheless, seeking not only better wages and working conditions but increased meaning and fulfillment. In Clausen's analysis of a group of the Berkeley subjects (1976), men who changed jobs between the ages of thirty and forty were more likely to do so because of dissatisfactions; those who changed jobs after age forty did so because of opportunities for advancement. During middle age it was those who had moved from working class to middle class who were much less likely to aspire to further advancement. In Lowenthal's (1975) California Transitions Study, for working-class men in midlife work-related stresses played a critical role in their adaptation. Preoccupations seemed to stem from the lack of occupational advancement and worries about retirement income. Similar to Elder's findings (1974; Elder and Rockwell 1978), men who had experienced the vicissi-

*Clausen (1976); Coleman and Neugarten (1971); Jaffe (1971); Levinson et al. (1978); and Warner and Abegglen (1955).

tudes of the Depression were fearful and cautious about their current income status and the prevailing economic conditions.

In a longitudinal study of AT&T managers, Bray, Campbell, and Grant (1974) found that over a period of eight years, many men now in their mid-thirties had found that the reality of their occupational status did not match up with their "rosy" expectations. While over the eight years the mental abilities of these men had developed and their administrative skills had remained largely stable, no differential changes were discerned between those who were rated as more successful or who had advanced up the ranks as expected and those who did not. While occupational involvements increased for those who had been most successful, those who were rated less successful showed increased familial and marital involvement (Rychlak 1974). While causal implications are not entirely clear, over the course of the years these men became more realistic about their careers. Those who had left the company did not differ, generally, from those who had remained, although they did differ from those rated in the top 10 percent of the group in terms of management ability. Thus terminators included many who were capable, but few who were quite outstanding. Other studies (e.g., Kohen 1975) also have shown that men who are forced to seek another job are not any less likely to succeed at upward mobility than those who leave voluntarily.

The increasing degrees of specialization of knowledge required for work today has particularly important consequences for the course of men's careers. Sarason (1977) has discussed the many problems that arise, particularly for highly educated men, as a result of the "one life— one career imperative." Professional training is now a mini-career in itself, and the payoffs are often less compelling. It is easier to divorce one's spouse than to change careers. Those with high aspirations are required to pursue a lengthy course of education with a concomitant set of values that may lead to feelings of frustration and disillusionment, particularly for people in the middle years.

Rice's (1980) study of a group of highly gifted academicians highlights the ways in which the meaning of work is derived from a larger social context, while differentially affecting older and younger men. The older, middle-aged men in this study, when reflecting on their aspirations as young men, felt they had succeeded in meeting their dreams but questioned the meaning of their work in the context of common, economic, and political conditions that had affected their lives and the institutions in which they had been working. More generally, the meaning of work has changed considerably for postwar, atomic-age generations, thus affecting old and young at differential points in their occupational careers.[*]

[*]Rice (1980); Sarason (1977); Soddy and Kidson (1967); and Sofer (1970).

Kohn and his associates (Kohn 1969, 1980; Kohn and Schooler 1978) have examined the elements of occupations to discern the determinants of job satisfaction. By investigating the structural complexity of a variety of occupations, they have determined that the substantive complexity of work is not only related to job satisfaction and occupational commitment, but also to a number of psychological functions, such as valuation of self-direction, self-esteem, and intellectual flexibility. Through longitudinal analyses, the relationship between substantive complexity of a job and intellectual flexibility was found to be a reciprocal one. Cognitive processes in adulthood were subject to environmental influences and also showed a remarkable degree of flexibility. The intrinsic meaning of work and psychological impact of a job resulted not just from status, income, or social supports but from meaningful challenges that the work itself had contained. The most important challenge was that of mastering complex tasks (see also Csikszentmihalyi 1975). More critical than social status in determining the experience of work is responsibility and judgment that a job requires. Working-class occupations often demand conformity to an external standard of performance and the need to follow directives in a specified manner; professional middle-class occupations most often necessitate reliance on an internal standard of excellence and decision making that is based on individual judgment rather than external authority.

Bray and Howard's (1980) analysis of life satisfactions of middle-aged managers found that career satisfaction was a bridge between career success and life satisfactions. While success in one's career was related to satisfaction with it and general life satisfaction, career success and life satisfaction were not significantly related to each other. Bray and Howard concluded that career success did not necessarily lead to happiness but only to satisfactions in the career domain. The most successful at work were not likely to be the most successful in marriage or family life. Others have suggested that men highest and lowest in occupational success are those with the least marital satisfaction (Aldous, Osmond, and Hicks 1979).

Career change at midlife has gained increasing attention. Recent reports by Krantz (1977) and Osherson (1980) have examined the ways in which highly successful men have entered states of crisis or dissatisfaction and have made radical changes in career and life style. This often entailed a great deal of uncertainty and risk-taking and major life changes across several domains. The issue of second careers is likely to attract more interest as retirement age lengthens and life expectancy increases. However, currently a major midcareer change may necessitate a role transition without benefit of socially patterned supports to ease adjustment (Fogarty 1975; Mortimer and Simmons 1978). Job change itself at midlife may be more frequent than previously thought. Most adult men change occupations at least once. In a longitudinal study of a large, representative sample of men ages forty-five to fifty-nine, Kohen (1975) found that increased job satisfaction was strongest for men who remained in the same company over a five-year period. However, economic gains were high for those who changed employers as well as for those who had remained in the same companies. Many men were willing to give up a certain degree of job satisfaction in exchange for gains in earnings. Over the course of the five years of this study, one in four men had changed occupations. Since beginning work after completing schooling, three out of four respondents had made occupational changes.

MEN, FAMILY, AND FATHERHOOD

The psychological impact of marriage and fatherhood may vary by their timing, the coordination of social roles available to men, and the availability of social support. Hogan (1978), for example, examined the impact of military service on the life course of men born during the 1920s. The manpower needs necessitated by war had a major impact on the lives of these men, particularly with regard to the timing of their military service. Consequently many of these men married prior to completing school and beginning work, thus altering the average expectable course of events in their lives. Comparing this cohort with men born after 1937, the latter group was much more successful in reaching adulthood in a normatively prescribed manner, even though college attendance was more common among the younger group. Since there is now a trend for later age at marriage, the younger men were more easily able to postpone marriage than the older men. The older men who had experienced a deviant ordering of life events experienced much higher rates of marital disruption compared to the younger men.

The timing of fatherhood may also be critical in the ways in which men adjust to their roles as parents. Nydegger (1973) found that men who were late fathers had greater ease and were more effective in that role than those who were early fathers. Early fathers may be burdened by many role strains, because parenthood has occurred at a time when career building demands much investment of time and energy.

Men's involvement in the world of work as well as their feelings of success and satisfaction with it differentially affect marital and family relations. Men in middle-level occupations with no severe time constraints placed upon them are apparently those who are able to take the most active participatory role in their families, with concomitant levels of marital satisfaction higher than other groups (Aldous, Osmond, and

Hicks 1979). In a reanalysis of data from the survey on the quality of American life (Campbell, Converse, and Rodgers 1976), Simpson and England (1980) found that wives' evaluations of their marriages were higher with increasing socioeconomic status, regardless of whether that status was based on their own or their husbands' resources. However, husbands' perceptions of marital solidarity were not affected by either their own or their wives' socioeconomic status. But men's participation in household work may be one area quite affected by income. Model (1981) found that the greater the earning differential between husbands and wives, the less were husbands likely to participate in household chores. When husbands do help with housework, they may help with only those tasks that are pleasant and more enjoyable, leaving their wives to handle those that are least satisfying (Rapoport et al. 1977). Normative role expectations appear to be particularly salient in midlife (Thurnher 1976).

While in middle age men may come to measure their actual achievements against their aspirations and dreams, a recent study (Harry 1976) using cross-sectional data analyzed men's happiness patterns in relation to stage in the family life cycle. Possibly due to the rigidity of their work commitments, men tended to change their definitions of happiness across the life course, rather than their behavior. Happiness was defined differently at different points in the life cycle. During the time of parenting young children men tended to define their happiness in relation to family life. During earlier and later stages the men looked beyond the family for sources of satisfaction. The author concluded that because of the strains of the family life cycle, men's principal adaptations are attitudinal. Overall happiness did increase with age. Medley (1980) found a similar pattern; unlike the women in his sample, for men life satisfaction was found to be related to age and stage in a monotonic fashion. While middle-aged men are often at the peak of their careers and role performance, leisure activities for those who have sufficient time and money commonly include work in organizations, home embellishment, and spectator sports (Gordon, Gaitz, and Scott 1976).

Thurnher (1976) found that middle-aged men's positive feelings toward their wives were associated with overall life satisfaction but did not seem to influence day-to-day moods. Those men who were likely to feel dissatisfaction with their marriages were men who felt that family responsibilities and pressures hindered the attainment of personal goals. Unlike the case of women, men's feelings and perceptions of spouse and children were closely intertwined.

Middle-aged men tend to report greater sexual interest and activity than women, with a gradual, although not inevitable, decline with age

(Pfeiffer, Verwoerdt, and Davis 1972). Married women tend to attribute the cessation of sexual relations to their husbands; in congruence with this perception, men tend to attribute decreased sexual relations to themselves (Pfeiffer, Verwoerdt, and Davis 1972). It is often the men's loss of capacity or interest that determines middle-aged women's decreasing sexual activity (Kinsey et al. 1953).

While there have been discussions of the male climacteric (e.g., Henker 1981), this should not be regarded as an equivalent to the female menopause. The direction and magnitude of changing hormone levels and their relationship to sexual activity is unclear, although there are no dramatic, normative changes in the hormone levels of middle-aged men (Corby and Solnick 1980; Everitt and Huang 1980).* Further research is needed to examine the ways in which psychological preoccupations interface with gradual, age-related physiological changes and the important mediating factors in men's sexual desires and functioning (Colarusso and Nemiroff 1981; Masters and Johnson 1966).

Current conceptions of the father's role in the family delineate a set of activities that are largely supportive and supplementary to those of a mother. Fathers are an important support, but not the main ingredient, in family life (Rapoport et al. 1977) Fathers are viewed as models for their sons and as providers. A likely exception may be the case of single fathers (Rosenthal and Keshet 1981), although when compared with single mothers, they are clearly in the minority (Weiss 1979). In addition, single fathers may be more likely to bring in additional help and support in raising children; they may feel less guilty than mothers in sustaining their work commitments at the same time that they are expected to be provider and nurturer (Rosenthal and Keshet 1981; Weiss 1979).

During the past decade fatherhood has gained increasing attention (Cath, Gurwitt, and Ross 1982; Lamb 1981; Price-Bonham 1976). Often this literature focuses on the ways in which fathers affect their children's development. Observational studies have only recently begun to focus on the important ways in which father-child interaction may facilitate child development (Lamb 1976, 1978; Pedersen 1980). The history of child development is replete with family studies in which reports of father-child relations were obtained only from mothers or the children themselves. Previous conceptions of fathers have been largely based on the

---

*There are numerous methodological difficulties that must be examined when comparing various hormonal studies, such as the measurement of the hormones themselves; the use of various types of radioimmunoassays or bioassays; the times of day the data are collected; the role of other mediating mechanisms such as sexual activity level (and possible influence of certain types of pheromones); and the problem of inference with regard to the direction of effects, which can be reciprocal as well as linear.

reports of others rather than on observations or reports from fathers. Recent observational studies demonstrate the responsivity of fathers to their infants in highly specific and structured situations.

While father absence or paternal deprivation may be a critical variable in the development of children's sex-role identities and personalities,* (Biller 1976), the ways in which offspring affect fathers' development is a less documented area in need of investigation. Ross (1979, 1984) has examined the images of fathering portrayed in Freud's early writings. Father was a tyrant-disciplinarian and model of aggressivity, which was a threat to both sons and daughters. This father was the antecedent super-ego. At the same time, the fathers in Freud's case histories were quite generative and nurturant figures. Ross (1984) points out that the oedipal father portrayed in classic psychoanalytic theory was "dethroned" in the 1950s and 1960s by the preoedipal mother of ego psychology.

Benedek's discussions of parenting (1959, 1973), and fatherhood (1970) in particular, focused attention on the motivational sources of fatherhood, particularly on fathers' identifications with their own fathers and their children. There can be no doubt that fathers change and grow as a consequence of parenting their developing children. Indeed, children do shape paternal identity (Ross 1984). While clinical reports have informed our understanding of the ways in which children affect their fathers, whether it be through the consolidation of issues of generativity in the role of provider or through the recapitulation of their own inner conflicts via those of their children, the research evidence for these changes are not yet entirely systematic or apparent.

MIDLIFE TRANSITION

While few would argue that men do not have the potential to provide nurturant relations, their capacity to do so appears to be highly limited in the context of our current conceptions of the male role. In this regard, Levinson and associates (1978) have discussed the mentor relationship as a mixture of friend and father. A good mentor acts as a guide for a younger man, ushering him into the adult world. He acts as a teacher, sponsor, and friend. Yet, at the same time, it was noted that the mentor relationship was rarely smooth and frequently ended painfully (Levinson et al. 1978). Feelings of exploitation, envy, and competition often emerged to override the positive aspects of these relationships. In Levinson's study of men, friendships, in general, were often absent.

---

*It is important to bear in mind that father absence does not describe the ecological setting of a family but only what is missing from this setting. There are numerous kinds of family compositions, in which the father is absent, each of which may carry a different psychological impact (see Kellam, Ensminger, and Turner 1977).

Recent discussions of the male role* have examined the limitations in adaptation that may result as a consequence of rigid adherence to the traditional male sex role. Some have characterized this as the "inexpressive male" syndrome (Balswick and Peek 1971).

The rather dramatic differences between men's and women's friendship patterns has a historical precedent. While male bonding may have a functional determinant in human evolution (Tiger 1969), women have typically developed close and intimate relationships with other women, a mode of relationship stressed particularly in the nineteenth century (Faderman 1981; Smith-Rosenberg 1975). Lewis (1978) has pointed out that while males tend to report more same-sex friendships than women, most of these are not close, intimate, or characterized by self-disclosure. A number of studies have demonstrated that through the life course, American males have often not engaged in close male friendships, at least not without some anxieties and guilt, and that self-disclosure as a dimension of intimacy is quite low between males.[†] Middle-aged people, in general, may feel a heightened sense of obligation to sustain their various social relations (Shulman 1975). However, there may be important differences between men and women in working-class and middle-class families. Among working-class men there may be more homosocial relations, with greater degrees of sex segregation. However, Hess (1979) has suggested that for middle-class men, the proposition of "all eggs in one basket" is likely to be operating. These men may look at their marriage and to their wives for all of their interpersonal needs and for sources of support.

In a recent study of three-generation families, Snow (1980) found that middle-aged men perceive a greater extent of emotional bondedness across family members than did middle-aged women, although the women reported more frequent contact with family members than did their husbands. Not confronted with the strains associated with the everyday relations in the family, men may be less likely to express negative feelings about these relationships than women.

Erikson's (1980b) recent discussion of the Freud-Jung correspondence highlights the rather dramatic and explicit illustration of the satisfactions and pitfalls associated with middle-aged men's relationships with one another, as issues of intimacy and generativity were played out between these two gifted scholars. Freud was fifty when this correspondence with Jung (who was in his early thirties) began. In this correspondence we are able to glean the ways in which work and love were woven into the lives

---

*See Harrison (1978a); Pleck (1981); Pleck and Brannon (1978); and Pleck and Sawyer (1974).

[†]See Hess (1979); Jourard (1971); Komarovsky (1974, 1976); Olstad (1975); Pleck (1975); and Powers and Bultena (1976).

of these men. In describing one dimension of this relationship, Erikson (1980b) notes that generativity here was

> self-generation, the care given more or less consciously and more or less verbosely (for only creative people have their own words for such things) to one's own continued identity renewal, tied as it now is to a net of commitments. The mutual support of such further development is the main psychosocial function of friendship. It permits a reciprocal narcissistic monitoring which allocates to each partner the self-love necessary for creative activity and yet also, by intimate critique, keeps it within necessary limits. How the attending mutual indulgences—here in a gradually professionalized form—is apt to threaten friendship itself, we will observe in both correspondences. (P. 48)

That the relationship ended in what Erikson calls "vindictive rejectivity" attests to the difficulties of maintaining it.

The constraints that operate in preventing men from achieving intimate nonconflictual relationships with other men have been discussed by Lewis (1978). These include feelings of competition, homophobia (fears of being or appearing homosexual) (see Morin and Garfinkle 1978), socially conditioned aversion to vulnerability and openness, and a lack of role models by which to model expressive behavior.

That the conception of the traditional male role may prove "hazardous" to men's well-being is documented in the sex differentials in mortality (Harrison 1978b). Men's greater vulnerability to heart disease may result from socialization into aggressive, competitive role behaviors that take their toll on middle-aged men. Among the middle aged, alcoholism and suicide are markedly more prevalent among men than women (Boyd and Weissman 1981). The majority of middle-aged male suicides occur in those over the age of forty. Men who are depressed or alcoholic are at high risk for suicide, although these syndromes are probably historically conditioned (Boyd and Weissman 1981; Wenz 1980).

Anticipation of the empty nest, with the last child about to leave home, is rarely experienced as a crisis for men (Fiske 1980a,b). Men are more likely to be concerned with issues of retirement related to their future financial status and survival. With a lessening of the parental imperative, middle-aged men may shift from active to more receptive and passive modes of mastery (Gutmann 1975, 1977). There is less of a need to maintain the repressions set up by the requirements of parenthood. Previously suppressed communalistic and narcissistic needs surface once again. The demands to be a primary economic provider to one's children are less pressing, and affiliative aspects of personality can now gain expression. In Fiske's sample (1980b) such a shift from active to passive mastery was also noted in a group of men facing retirement and followed-up five years later.

Changing sex roles may alter these patterns (see, e.g., Zepelin 1980–81). Ironically, while many younger men may discuss egalitarian ideas of their roles, in her sample of young-adult men Komarovsky (1976) found that few could actually conceive of themselves as sharing equally (or their jobs permitting them to do so) in the responsibility and care of their children. Alternatives to traditional patterns of childrearing (assuming primary responsibility for child care) seemed, to the young men, to be a kind of role reversal, and were not acceptable to most.

While there may be a high degree of stability in men's temperament over time (Costa, McCrae, and Arenberg 1980), many changes occur at midlife. These changes may frequently cause many difficulties for middle-aged men; thus it is no surprise that entrance into (i.e., awareness of) middle age may be linked with considerable stress (Rosenberg and Farrell 1976). Formerly devalued and unmasculine aspects of the self may be embraced in midlife, as middle-aged men begin to discover changing patterns of emotional relatedness (Peskin and Livson 1981), as well as a reawakening of the sensual and aesthetic (Gutmann 1976, 1980) aspects of their personalities. Prosen, Martin, and Prosen (1972) found that middle-aged men tend to revise their memories of their mothers in the direction of increased idealization; they also perceive the greatest extent of emotional bondedness with their mothers, compared to other relationships in their families (Snow 1980). In a recent cross-sectional study (Feldman, Biringen, and Nash 1981), compassion increased in an almost linear fashion for men from young adulthood to grandfatherhood. In this study, the largest sex differences in expressivity occurred, in the predicted direction, during active parenting.

Gutmann (1976, 1980) has discussed the problems of coping with the psychological changes of midlife. The middle-aged man may externalize the unfolding of his passivity with the abuse of alcohol or psychosomatic illness, or he may try to recreate his previous world through a younger "adoring" woman. Since changes occurring in the middle-aged woman are toward more autonomous, aggressive modes of mastery and expression, such changes may heighten the middle-aged man's needs to locate his "unfolding passivity" away from a wife who doesn't respond to her husband's succorant needs (Gutmann 1976).

Levinson and associates (1978) have discussed the individuation tasks of middle age as the integration of polarities between young and old, masculine and feminine, and attachment and separation. In Vaillant and Milofsky's (1980) recent reconceptualization of adult life, for men, career consolidation is necessary in order to master the capacity for intimacy. Such consolidation may require the internalization of mentors and the transformation of self-preoccupations. Thus one can become the mentor for another, part of one's generativity, and become one of the "keepers of meaning," passing on one's values and ideals to younger generations.

Brim's (1976) summary of the many determinants of the midlife crisis for men includes: changing hormones; the measurement of one's aspirations against actual achievements; the restructuring of "dreams"; issues of generativity; awareness of the finitude of life; changing relationships within the family; and status and role changes in the interpersonal world. We wish to emphasize that the extent to which middle age may be experienced as a crisis is not only a function of the timing and sequencing of these changes, but also of their personal and social meaning. The world of work, as we have examined and detailed its current importance in men's lives, is the central context in which middle age takes on its primary significance.

The Place of the Stable Years in the Course of Life

During the past decade there has been increased understanding of the nature of personality change across the second half of life, largely as a result of reports from a number of longitudinal studies in which subjects themselves had reached middle or late life. While recognizing the value of longitudinal research in understanding the place of adulthood in the life course, a number of problems of method should be noted that limit generalizability of particular findings. A first problem concerns emphasis on demonstration of continuity rather than change over time. Much longitudinal research has assumed that development proceeds in a linear manner, with future attainments or changes directly associated with those of past years. Recently this assumption has been called into question. Gergen (1980), Kagan (1980), and Cohler (1981b) all have noted the limitations associated with linear assumptions regarding the course of development. Gergen (1977) has suggested that the course of development is essentially unpredictable, subject to chance. A major task across the course of life is to make "sense" of such chance events, weaving these events into a narrative that provides meaning and coherence. From this perspective the most interesting question in longitudinal research is that of the factors influencing the maintenance of an internally consistent account of the course of life at different points in life (Cohler 1981b).

A second major issue in longitudinal research concerns the impact of cohort and history on a particular group of persons studied over time. Beginning with Mannheim's ([1928] 1952) discussion of the problem of generations and including the important contributions of Ryder (1965), Cain (1967), and Riley (1976), the concept of generation has played an important role in studying changes over time in values and ideology. However, as Elder (1974, 1975, 1979) has shown, the significance of particular historical circumstances is of critical importance in the very definitions that persons have of their own life.

From the perspective of method, as Schaie (1965) and Nesselroade and Baltes (1974) have shown, such factors as year of birth, age of measurement, and present age, when applied to longitudinal studies, all are confounded in ways that defy investigation: it is essential that longitudinal research include measurements of persons at a particular age in cohorts obtained at different times. A major problem to date has been the definition of the cohort to be studied in longitudinal research. While two groups of persons born as little as one year apart may suffice as separate cohorts according to critics of longitudinal research, the definition of cohort to be used in a particular study depends, in large part, on the questions addressed by the research.

Cohort represents only one of a number of factors limiting generalizability possible in longitudinal research or, indeed, any research in the behavioral and social sciences. The assumption has frequently been made that the findings from social science investigation are replicable in the same manner as those from the natural sciences. In fact, groups are seldom comparable across studies, with differences in social status, age or cohort, and ethnicity frequently overlooked in replications. While recognizing such problems of replication, it is possible to make at least some tentative conclusions about the role of the middle years in the life course on the basis of findings from longitudinal studies. These findings come from essentially three studies, those of the Fels Institute in Ohio (Kagan and Moss 1962), the Institute of Human Development at Berkeley (Jones 1967; Jones et al. 1971), and the Harvard Grant study (Vaillant 1977). In general, these studies have been concerned with predictions forward from childhood or adolescence to adulthood, although more recent reports from the Berkeley studies have also concerned findings from the adult years forward to middle and late adulthood (Eichorn et al. 1981).

The now-classic report from the Fels study, *Birth to Maturity* (Kagan and Moss 1962) represents the first contemporary report on personality development from childhood to adulthood employing both longitudinal design and complex methods of data analysis. Using ratings of home visits and laboratory observations across several points in early and middle childhood, together with detailed assessment of personality in adulthood, correlations were obtained between childhood and adulthood measures for several personality traits, including aggression, dependency, achievement, and appropriate sex-role identification. While statistically significant, these correlations between child and adult measures accounted for little shared variance. The highest correlations over time were reported for the variables of aggression and achievement among men; within each sex, childhood ratings of dependency and passivity were significantly correlated with relevant sex-role defined characteristics in adulthood: men rated in childhood as more passive appeared as adults to be less competitive, while girls rated as more dependent during childhood maintained a more dependent relationship with their own parental family during adulthood. Findings from a subsequent multivariate analysis (Ryder 1967) suggested that childhood achievement orientation among men is related to adult competitiveness, while childhood adventurousness is related to adult ease in social relationships and increased sexual activity.

The Fels report has been criticized as maximizing chance relationships and as reflecting largely cultural definitions of personality rather than genuine aspects of continuity or change in such attributes over time. A major problem of method also confronted the Fels investigators, since childhood and adult measurements were made with quite different sources of data. Similar problems are presented by the studies reported from the Institute of Human Development of the University of California at Berkeley, where three separate longitudinal studies begun in the Bay Area in the mid-to-late 1920s have been merged into a single, continuing, multigenerational study. Data from such disparate sources as home observations and psychometric evaluations, and ranging across the life cycle, from birth through middle age, have been rendered equivalent across studies using the Q-sort technique, a ninety-item forced-choice rating technique developed by Block (1958).

It would be impossible in the space of a single chapter to review all relevant findings from this continuing research effort. Selected findings have been summarized by Eichorn (1973) and in a monograph edited by Jones and others (1971). Perhaps the most impressive such predictive effort from the Berkeley research has been reported by Elder (1974, 1975, 1979), already discussed in this chapter. While Elder's primary interest has been in the relationship between aspects of childhood socialization and adult adjustment, Haan and Day (1974), Peskin (1972), Livson and Peskin (1980), and Peskin and Livson (1981) have been concerned with the association between adolescent personality development and adjustment during the stable adult years.

Two themes characterize findings reporting adult correlates of childhood characteristics in the Berkeley studies: (1) the impact of shared understandings of personal expression across the life course, and (2) the significance of temperamental factors, including mood and tempo. It is not surprising to learn that culturally defined attributes of behaviors such as sex-role definitions are so important in organizing adult personality, since internalization of the situation is a major determinant of personal expression, as recognized by "symbolic interactionist" perspectives in social science developed by Cooley, Mead, Thomas and others (Cooley 1902; Janowitz 1966; Strauss 1964). Nor is it surprising to observe the powerful impact of temperament, understood as a constitutionally based determinant of individual tempo, which sets limits on personal expression (Thomas and Chess 1977; Thomas et al. 1963). The question is whether, after accounting for the impact of norms and temperament, any additional effect of experience can be observed. However, focus on the issue of stability and continuity over time has been so central to the Berkeley study that change over time has been less explicitly discussed.

The impact of sex-role expectation is seen most clearly in findings using the Q-sort technique in a study of personality development from childhood to adulthood (Block with Haan, 1971), documenting the extent to which men and women shifted over the years in the direction of increasingly sex-role defined constructons of personality, similar to Gutmann's (1975) discussion of the parental imperative. From the high school years to adulthood, men became increasingly responsible and independent, while women became more stereotypically feminine. Block and Haan also show significant correlations between adolescent and adult attributes, particularly in the areas of cognitive functioning and temperament. Similar findings regarding the importance of temperament in adolescence and adulthood have been reported by Peskin (1972), who shows that boys who are most placid during the preadolescent era are most irritable during adolescence but also most well adjusted in adulthood. Girls rated as most independent, controlled, and confident during the preadolescent years, and also the least controlled and mature during the adolescent decade, are most well adjusted as women at mid-adulthood. Finally, Peskin reports that inclusion of *both* preadolescent and adolescent characteristics predict more effectively to adulthood than either decade by itself.

Continuing study of these men and women in subsequent reports by N. Livson and Peskin (1980) and Peskin and N. Livson (1981) show that subtle variation in these temperamental factors marks the course of development across the stable years of mid-adulthood. Associations between adolescent and adult ratings are lower at age thirty than at age forty, suggesting that characteristics of adolescence have a "sleeper" effect, showing a greater salience at some points in the adult years than at other points, a finding also noted by F. Livson (1981) in her study of women at midlife. F. Livson also notes that correlations between adolescent characteristics and adult adjustment are lower for women than for men, but concurs with the observation of N. Livson and Peskin that adults appear to draw on adolescent experiences for assistance to a greater extent when they are in their forties than in their thirties.

Haan and Day (1974) have also reported on the impact of temperamental factors from childhood to adulthood, noting the same "sleeper" effect in the impact of earlier states on adult adjustment reported by N. and F. Livson and by Peskin. Haan and Day report that such temperamental factors as impulsivity, or tempo of talking, show particular stability over time, together with mood and morale. However, at least some changes in personal expression over time can be best understood in terms of prevailing shared understandings of characteristic personal expression expected at particular points in the life cycle. Philosophic interests and concern with giving to others, rather than receiving from them, seem particularly age related, in the manner described by Erikson (1963, 1980a), while other aspects of personality less clearly understood as related to social age, such as seriousness, appear to have little continuity over time.

Investigators using the Berkeley data have been concerned not only with the possible association between childhood characteristics and aspects of adult adjustment, but also with the forward association of aspects of the stable adult years with adjustment to aging. The most complete set of findings has been reported by Maas and Kuypers (1974) and Eichorn and associates (1981).

Consistent with findings reported by Haan and Day (1974) in their study of the association between Q-sort ratings of adolescence and adulthood, Mussen and his colleagues also find temperamental and cognitive factors most stable from middle to later adulthood, together with feelings of positive morale. The findings reported by Maas and Kuypers are complex and include assessment at ages thirty and seventy, both of personality and life style, among parents of the subjects in one of the Berkeley studies. Women were observed to show greater stability than men across the forty years of the study, with those women *least* well adjusted in late life showing the greatest personality stability over time. On the other hand, men showed greater stability than women in life style; once again, it was among those men most dissatisfied with their lives at age thirty that continuity (in lack of life satisfaction) was observed, continuing to age seventy. Discontinuity, and the capacity for change, perhaps as a consequence of changing socially shared definitions of person and setting, seem to be most closely associated with continuing positive adjustment into old age.

With the exception of Elder's more recent use of the data from the Berkeley studies, much of the concern of investigators using these data has been with the demonstration of continuity and stability over time from childhood to mid-adulthood, and from mid-adulthood to old age. Where discontinuity appears, problems are encountered in the interpretation of findings, including Maas and Kuypers's report that stability in personal expression and life style may be associated from mid to late adulthood with less favorable adjustment. A similar concern with demonstration of continuity rather than change over time appears in the reports by Vaillant, who followed to middle age a cohort of former Harvard college students, graduates during the early 1940s.

Drawing on the model for personality development formalized by Erikson (1963, 1980*a*), Vaillant has coded interviews of these men during their college years concerning their childhood experiences, together with interviews obtained during the college years from the men's parents, and has related ratings of earlier adjustment to midlife evaluation of personality and adjustment. In a series of papers (Vaillant 1974*a,b*, 1975, 1976, 1978, 1979; Vaillant and McArthur 1972), and a monograph (1977), and in contrast to many other longitudinal reports, Vaillant has implicitly relied upon a life-course model, assuming that adjustment at particular phases of the life cycle is a function of the experience of present life circumstances in terms of socially shared definitions. His reports of the lives of these unusually talented and successful men suggest that periods of stress and role strain are inevitable, and that successful adjustment at one phase of the life cycle, such as adolescence, is not necessarily associated with successful adjustment at another. However, these men do report that the period of their lives from twenty-one to thirty-five was the least happy, while that from about age thirty-five to the present (roughly age fifty) was the most satisfying.

In contrast to men rated as having had better childhoods, those men blindly rated as having had the "worst" childhood (stressful life events, conflict with parents, unusual difficulties negotiating expectable socialization tasks, rated from parent interviews during the college years) showed greater psychiatric impairment, less involvement with parental family, less satisfying interpersonal relationships in adulthood, and greater reliance upon drugs and alcohol. Men with the worst childhoods were also reported as showing too little emotion in their present life and an unusual degree of calm in their present adjustment. Finally, they were less likely to be willing to take vacations than men with more adequate childhoods. While the men with less adequate childhood environments were far more likely than men with better childhoods to be regarded as poorly adjusted in adulthood, there was little association between childhood environment and rated maturity of defenses in adulthood, based on a rating of defense mechanisms on a scale of maturity of defenses showing high interrater reliability.

In more recent work, Vaillant and Milofsky (1980) have extended these earlier findings to a second study of men at midlife, drawn from a group of working-class men previously studied by Glueck and Glueck (1950). Ratings were made of childhood environment, though they were not coded in precisely the same way as in the Harvard group; while significantly related to adult adjustment, relatively little shared variance was explained by childhood characteristics within this working-class group, although lower morale earlier in adulthood was associated with less successful adjustment at midlife.

Overall, the impact of the past on present adjustment across the stable years of adulthood is less striking, on the basis of three quite different kinds of studies of adulthood, than would be expected on the basis of currently accepted propositions in psychiatry and psychoanalysis. To a greater extent than has often been realized, adult lives appear to be shaped by socially shared definitions of the course of life, particularly as a result of the continuing comparison of one's own place in the life course with that which is expectable.

Conclusion

This chapter has considered issues of normality and mental health from a perspective which assumes that persons continually evaluate their own status and role attainments in terms of socially shared understandings of the life course. Current life-cycle position is contrasted with that which is expectable for persons of the same sex, cohort, and social status; increased congruity between expected and achieved roles and identities in the course of life leads to increased feelings of morale or life satisfaction, which is the essence of normality or positive adjustment. To the extent that persons experience themselves as "off-time" with regard to their place in the course of life, they feel increased tension and incongruity between expectable and current achievements. In addition, as a result of being off-time for expectable life events, relevant role colleagues, experiencing similar events, may not be present to serve as a source of support in dealing with shared difficulties, leading to increased feelings of personal distress and isolation.

The period of settling into the expectable adult roles of worker, spouse, and parent, extending to the midlife transition, results in the creation of a role portfolio more complete and complex than at any other point in the life course. Both the transition into these adult roles and the inevitable feelings of conflict, strain, and overload among roles lead to unique sources of distress that must be resolved to facilitate continued positive morale.

Impairment in adjustment, such as is manifested in psychiatric symptoms, is understood as a response to the inability to maintain a continuing sense of congruence between expectations and attainments. Aspects of biology codetermine this sense of congruence across the adult years. Not just in the major mental disorders, but also in the appearance of physical disorders such as diabetes or the cardiovascular disorders, genetic predispositions interact with characteristics of life context to shape vulnerability and resilience. Unpredictable, adverse life events happening "off-time" and preventing both anticipatory socialization and also support from role colleagues experiencing similar events may serve as a trigger for the appearance of either increased vulnerability or resilience, as in Elder's (1974, 1975, 1979) description of responses to economic privation in the Great Depression. Much remains to be learned about the relative impact of biology, personal experience, and social context as factors associated with the maintenance of personal congruence over time.

This chapter has reviewed available evidence regarding the process of acquiring characteristic adult roles, together with factors associated with a more or less successful enactment of them, among both men and women and across social strata. This perspective on normality during the middle adult years has direct implications for practice as well as for continued research. Within psychiatry, selection factors determining who seeks treatment, together with reports of adjustment across the adult years based largely on psychiatric patients suffering from the major mental disorders, have led to an understanding of the course of life across the adult years that is necessarily limited.

Consideration of difficulties in adjustment leading to the expression of psychiatric symptoms, together with the need for intervention based on a life-course perspective, provides a dimension that supplements traditional psychiatric research. This life-course perspective places the patient in a social context that imposes particular limitations and that provides particular opportunities for development. For example, to the extent that a patient is "off-time" in terms of expectable role attainments in adulthood, problems in realizing a satisfactory adjustment become increasingly difficult. For the adult already limited in possible life satisfaction as a consequence of recurrent psychotic episodes, delay in the realization of appropriate adult roles, which so often accompanies this impairment, further compounds the impact of the disturbance on personality and adjustment.

This perspective on normality during middle-adulthood, based on assumptions of life-course social science, should not be viewed as inconsistent with more traditional psychological perspectives emphasizing wishes and intents. The manner in which persons understand and act upon their present circumstances is a consequence of currently experienced aspects of the total situation, so well expressed in Kurt Lewin's ([1946] 1964) concept of the "life-space." This chapter has focused on social circumstances contributing to the present experience of self and social context; aspects of the social surround are internalized and evaluated in terms of presently realized attainments. We have delineated those social attainments that are important in adult lives from young adulthood through middle age. Clearly, the same life-course perspective can be extended to the study of the life cycle as a whole, with the character of present adjustment always understood in terms of shared understandings of the course of life.

REFERENCES

Abraham, K. [1921] 1960. "Contribution to a Discussion on Tic." In *Selected Papers*, ed. K. Abraham, pp. 323–25. New York: Basic Books.
————. [1924] 1960. "A Short Study of the Development of the Libido, Viewed in the Light of the Mental Disorders." In *Selected Papers*, ed. K. Abraham, pp. 418–502. New York: Basic Books.
Adams, B. 1968. *Kinship in an Urban Setting*. Chicago: Markham Publishing Co.
Adelson, J. 1970. "What Generation Gap?" *New York Times Magazine*, 18 January.
Aldous, J.; Osmond, M.; and Hicks, M. W. 1979. "Men's Work and Men's Families." In *Contemporary Theories about the Family*, ed. W. R. Burr et al., vol. 1, pp. 227–56. New York: Free Press.
Andrews, F., and Withey, S. 1976. *Social Indicators of Well-Being: Americans' Perceptions of Life Quality*. New York: Plenum.
Angres, S. 1974. "Intergenerational Relations and Value Consensus Between Young Adults and Their Parents." Ph.D. diss., University of Chicago.
Arendt, H. 1958. *The Human Condition*. Chicago: University of Chicago Press.
Atchley, R. 1975. "Dimensions of Widowhood in Later Life." *Gerontologist* 15:176–78.
Axelson, L. 1960. "Personal Adjustments in the Postparental Period." *Marriage and Family Living* 22:66–70.
Back, K., and Gergen, K. 1963. "Apocalyptic and Serial Time Orientations and the Structure of Opinions." *Public Opinion Quarterly* 27:427–42.
Bacon, L. 1974. "Early Motherhood, Accelerated Role Transition, and Social Pathologies." *Social Forces* 52:333–41.
Balswick, J., and Peek, C. 1971. "The Inexpressive Male: A Tragedy of American Society." *Family Coordinator* 20:363–68.

Baltes, P. 1979. "Life-span Developmental Psychology: Some Converging Observations on History and Theory." In *Life-Span Development and Behavior*, ed. P. Baltes and O. G. Brim, vol. 2, pp. 256–81. New York: Academic Press.

Baltes, P.; Reese, H.; and Lipsitt, L. 1980. "Life-span Developmental Psychology." *Annual Review of Psychology* 31:65–110.

Bardwick, J., and Douvan, E. 1971. "Ambivalence: The Socialization of Women." In *Women in a Sexist Society*, ed. V. Gornick and B. Moran, pp. 147–59. New York: Basic Books.

Bart, P. 1971. "Depression in Middle-aged Women." In *Woman in Sexist Society*, ed. V. Gornick and B. K. Moran, pp. 163–86. New York: Basic Books.

Bart, P., and Grossman, M. 1976. "Menopause." *Women and Health* 1:3–11.

Belsky, J. 1981. "Early Human Experience: A Family Perspective." *Developmental Psychology* 17:3–23.

Benedek, T. 1959. "Parenthood as Developmental Phase: A Contribution to the Libido Theory." *Journal of the American Psychoanalytic Association* 7:389–417.

———. 1970. "Fatherhood and Providing." In *Parenthood: Its Psychology and Psychopathology*, ed. E. J. Anthony and T. Benedek, pp. 167–83. Boston: Little, Brown.

———. 1973. "Discussion: Parenthood as a Developmental Phase." In *Psychoanalytic Investigations: Selected Papers*, by T. Benedek, pp. 401–7. Chicago: Quadrangle Press.

Benjamin, J. 1961. "The Innate and the Experiential in Development." In *Lectures in Experimental Psychiatry*, ed. H. W. Brosin, pp. 19–42. Pittsburgh: University of Pittsburgh Press.

Bengtson, V., and Cutler, N. 1976. "Generations and Intergenerational Relations: Perspectives on Age Groups and Social Change." In *Handbook of Aging and the Social Sciences*, ed. R. Binstock and E. Shanas, pp. 130–88. New York: Van Nostrand.

Bengtson, V., and Kuypers, J. 1971. "Generational Differences and the Developmental Stake." *Aging and Human Development* 2:249–60.

Bengtson, V.; Kasschau, P.; and Ragan, P. 1977. "The Impact of Social Structure on Aging Individuals." In *Handbook of the Psychology of Aging*, ed. J. Birren and K. W. Schaie, pp. 327–53. New York: Van Nostrand.

Berger, P., and Luckman, T. 1966. *The Social Construction of Reality: A Treatise on the Sociology of Knowledge*. New York: Doubleday.

Bernard, J. 1964. "The Adjustments of Married Mates." In *Handbook of Marriage and the Family*, ed. H. Christensen, pp. 675–740. Chicago: Rand McNally.

———. 1972. *The Future of the Family*. New York: World.

———. 1974. *The Future of Motherhood*. New York: Dial Press.

———. 1975. *Women, Wives and Mothers: Values and Options*. Chicago: Aldine Press.

Bibring, G. 1959. "Some Considerations of the Psychological Process in Pregnancy." *Psychoanalytic Study of the Child* 14:113–21.

Bild, B. 1974. "Young Adult-Parent Relationships and Consensus." Ph.D. diss. University of Chicago.

Biller, H. B. 1976. "The Father and Personality Development: Paternal Deprivation and Sex-role Development." In *The Role of the Father in Child Development*, ed. M. E. Lamb, pp. 89–156. New York: John Wiley & Sons.

Billig, O., and Adams, R. W. 1957. "Emotional Conflicts of the Middle-aged Man." *Geriatrics* 12:535–41.

Birnbaum, J. 1971. "Life-Patterns, Personality Style, and Self-esteem in Gifted Family Oriented and Career Committed Women." Ph.D. diss. University of Michigan.

Bloch, M. 1977. "The Past and Present in the Present." *Man* (n.s.) 12:278–92.

Block, J. 1958. *The Q-Sort Method in Personality Assessment and Psychiatric Research*. Springfield, Ill.: Charles C Thomas.

Block, J., with Haan, N. 1971. *Lives through Time*. Berkeley, Calif.: Bancroft Books.

Blood, R., and Wolfe, D. 1960. *Husbands and Wives: The Dynamics of Married Living*. New York: Free Press.

Blos, P. 1967. "The Second Individuation Process of Adolescence." *Psychoanalytic Study of the Child* 22:162–86.

Bortner, R., and Hultsch, D. 1972. "Personal Time Perspective in Adulthood." *Developmental Psychology* 7:98–103.

Bott, E. 1971. *Family and Social Network*, 2nd ed. London: Tavistock.

Boxer, A. M., and Cohler, B. J. 1980. "Personal Time Orientations and Intergenerational

Conflicts in Three-generation Families." Paper presented at the Annual Meetings of the Gerontological Society of America, San Diego, Calif., November.

Boxer, A., et al. 1984. "Parents' Perceptions of Young Adolescents." In *Parenthood: A Psychodynamic Perspective*, ed. R. Cohen, B. J. Cohler, and S. Weissman. New York: Guilford Press.

Boyd, J. H., and Weissman, M. M. 1981. "The Epidemiology of Psychiatric Disorders of Middle Age: Depression, Alcoholism and Suicide." In *Modern Perspectives in the Psychiatry of Middle Age*, ed. J. G. Howells, pp. 201–22. New York: Brunner/Mazel.

Bradburn, N. 1969. *The Structure of Psychological Well-Being*. Chicago: Aldine Press.

Bradburn, N., and Caplovitz, D. 1965. *Reports on Happiness*. Chicago: Aldine Press.

Bram, S. 1974. "To Have or Have Not: A Social-Psychological Study of Voluntary Childless Couples, Parents, and To-be Parents." Ph.D. diss., University of Michigan.

―――――. 1978. "Through the Looking Glass: Voluntary Childlessness as a Mirror of Contemporary Changes in the Meaning of Parenthood." In *The First Child and Family Formation*, ed. W. B. Miller and L. Newman, pp. 368–91. Chapel Hill, N.C.: Carolina Population Center and University of North Carolina.

Bray, D., and Howard, A. 1980. "Career Success and Life Satisfactions of Middle-aged Managers." In *Competence and Coping During Adulthood*, ed. L. Bond and J. Rosen, pp. 258–87. Hanover, N.H.: University Press of New England.

Bray, D. M.; Campbell, R. J.; and Grant, D. L. 1974. *Formative Years in Business: A Long-Term AT&T Study of Managerial Lives*. New York: John Wiley & Sons.

Brim, O. G., Jr. 1976. "Theories of the Male Mid-life Crisis." *Counseling Psychologist* 6:2–9.

Brim, O. G., Jr., and Ryff, C. 1980. "On the Properties of Life Events." In *Life-Span Development and Behavior*, ed. P. Baltes and O. G. Brim, Jr., vol. 3, pp. 368–88. New York: Academic Press.

Brown, G., and Harris, T. 1978. *Social Origins of Depression: A Study of Psychiatric Disorder in Women*. New York: Free Press.

Bühler, C., and Massarik, F., eds. 1968. *The Course of Human Life*. New York: Springer.

Burgess, E. 1926. "The Family as a Unity of Interacting Personalities." *Family* 7:3–9.

Burgess, E., and Wallin, P. 1953. *Engagement and Marriage*. New York: Lippincott.

Burke, R.; Weir, T.; and DuWors, R. 1980. "Work Demands on Administrators and Spouse Well-Being." *Human Relations* 33:253–78.

Butler, R. 1963. "The Life-Review: An Interpretation of Reminiscence in the Aged." *Psychiatry* 26:65–76.

Cain, L. 1964. "Life Course and Social Structure." In *Handbook of Modern Sociology*, ed. R. E. L. Farris, pp. 272–309. Chicago: Rand McNally.

―――――. 1967. "Age Status and Generational Phenomena: The New Old People in Contemporary America." *Gerontologist* 7:83–92.

Campbell, A.; Converse, P.; and Rodgers, W. 1976. *The Quality of American Life: Perceptions, Evaluations, and Satisfactions*. New York: Russell Sage.

Campbell, E. 1969. "Adolescent Socialization." In *Handbook of Socialization Theory and Research*, ed. D. Goslin, pp. 821–60. Chicago: Rand McNally.

Cath, S. H.; Gurwitt, A. R.; and Ross, J. M. 1982. *Father and Child: Developmental and Clinical Perspectives*. Boston: Little, Brown.

Chodorow, N. 1978. *The Reproduction of Mothering: Psychoanalysis and the Sociology of Gender*. Berkeley, Calif.: University of California Press.

Chudacoff, H. P. 1980. "The Life Course of Women: Age and Age Consciousness, 1865–1915." *Journal of Family History* 5:274–92.

Clark, A., and Wallin, P. 1973. "Women's Sexual Responsiveness and the Duration and Quality of Their Marriages." *American Journal of Sociology* 7:80–98.

Clarke, A., and Clarke, A. 1976. *Early Experience: Myth and Evidence*. New York: Free Press.

Clausen, J. A. 1972. "The Life-course of Individuals." In *Aging and Society: A Sociology of Age Stratification*, ed. M. Riley, M. Johnson, and A. F. Toner, vol. 3, pp. 457–514. New York: Russell Sage.

―――――. 1976. "Glimpses into the Social World of Middle Age." *International Journal of Aging and Human Development* 7:99–106.

Cohen, F., and Lazarus, R. 1973. "Active Coping Processes, Coping Dispositions, and Recovery from Surgery." *Psychosomatic Medicine* 35:375–89.

Cohler, B. J. 1977. "The Significance of the Therapist's Feelings in the Treatment of

Anorexia Nervosa." In *Adolescent Psychiatry*, ed. S. Feinstein and P. Giovacchini, vol. 5, pp. 352–84. Chicago: University of Chicago Press.

———. 1981a. "Adult Developmental Psychology and Reconstruction in Psychoanalysis." In *The Course of Life: Psychoanalytic Contributions Toward Understanding Personality Development. Vol. III: Adulthood and the Aging Process*, ed. S. I. Greenspan and G. H. Pollock, pp. 149–99. Washington, D.C.: U.S. Government Printing Office, DHHS Publication No. (ADM)81-1000.

———. 1981b. "Personal Narrative and Life-course." In *Life-Span Development and Behavior*, ed. P. Baltes and O. G. Brim, Jr., vol. 4, pp. 206–43. New York: Academic Press.

Cohler, B. J., and Grunebaum, H. 1981. *Mothers, Grandmothers, and Daughters: Personality and Child-Care in Three Generation Families*. New York: John Wiley & Sons.

Cohler, B., et al. 1974. "Social Role Performance and Psychopathology among Recently Hospitalized and Non-hospitalized Mothers, II: Correlates with Life-stress and Self-reported Psychopathology." *Journal of Nervous and Mental Disease* 159:81–90.

Colarusso, C. A., and Nemiroff, R. A. 1981. *Adult Development*. New York: Plenum.

Coleman, R., and Neugarten, B. L. 1971. *Social Status in the City*. San Francisco: Jossey-Bass.

Cooley, C. H. 1902. *Human Nature and the Social Order*. New York: Scribner.

Corby, N., and Solnick, R. L. 1980. "Psychosocial and Physiological Influences on Sexuality in the Older Adult." In *Handbook of Mental Health and Aging*, ed. J. E. Birren and R. B. Sloan, pp. 893–921. Englewood Cliffs, N.J.: Prentice-Hall.

Costa, P.; McCrae, R.; and Arenberg, D. 1980. "Enduring Dispositions in Adult Males." *Journal of Personality and Social Psychology* 38:792–800.

Cottle, T. 1976. *Perceiving Time: A Psychological Investigation*. New York: Wiley-Interscience.

Cottle, T., and Klineberg, S. 1974. *The Present of Things Future*. New York: Free Press-Macmillan.

Cowan, C. P., et al. 1978. "Becoming a Family: The Impact of a First Child's Birth on the Couple's Relationship." In *The First Child and Family Formation*, ed. W. Miller and L. Newman, pp. 296–324. Chapel Hill, N.C.: Carolina Population Center and University of North Carolina.

Csikszentmihalyi, M. 1975. *Beyond Boredom and Anxiety*. San Francisco: Jossey-Bass.

Cutler, B., and Dyer, W. 1965. "Initial Adjustment Processes in Young Married Couples." *Social Forces* 44:195–201.

Demos, J., and Boocock, S., eds. 1978. *Turning Points: Historical and Sociological Essays on the Family*. Chicago: University of Chicago Press.

Demos, J., and Demos, V. 1969. "Adolescence in Historical Perspective." *Journal of Marriage and the Family* 31:632–38.

Deutsch, H. 1945. *The Psychology of Women*. New York: Grune & Stratton.

Deutscher, I. 1964. "The Quality of Post-parental Life: Definitions of the Situation." *Journal of Marriage and the Family* 26:52–59.

Dohrenwend, B., and Dohrenwend, B. 1974. *Stressful Life-Events: Their Nature and Effects*. New York: John Wiley & Sons.

Douvan, E., and Adelson, J. 1966. *The Adolescent Experience*. New York: John Wiley & Sons.

Duvall, E. and Hill, R. 1948. *Report of the Committee on the Dynamics of Family Interaction*. Washington, D.C.: National Conference on Family Life.

Dyer, E. 1963. "Parenthood as Crisis: A Restudy." *Journal of Marriage and Family Living* 25:196–201.

Ehrmann, W. 1964. "Marital and Nonmarital Sexual Behavior." In *Handbook of Marriage and the Family*, ed. H. Christensen, pp. 585–622. Chicago: Rand McNally.

Eichorn, D. 1973. "The Berkeley Longitudinal Studies: Continuities and Correlates of Behavior." *Canadian Journal of Behavioral Sciences* 5:297–320.

———, et al., eds. 1981. *Present and Past in Middle Life*. New York: Academic Press.

Elder, G. 1974. *Children of the Great Depression*. Chicago: University of Chicago Press.

———. 1975. "Age Differentiation and the Life Course." *Annual Review of Sociology* 1:165–90.

———. 1979. "Historical Change in Life Patterns and Personality." In *Life-Span Development and Behavior*, ed. P. Baltes and O. G. Brim, Jr., vol. 2, pp. 118–61. New York: Academic Press.

Elder, G., and Rockwell, R. 1978. "Economic Depression and Postwar Opportunity: A

Study of Life-patterns and Health." In *Research in Community and Mental Health*, ed. R. Simmons, pp. 249–304. Greenwich, Conn.: JAI Press.

Erikson, E. H. 1963. *Childhood and Society*, rev. ed. New York: W. W. Norton.

—————. 1980a. "Elements of a Psychoanalytic Theory of Psychosocial Development." In *The Course of Life: Psychoanalytic Contributions toward Understanding Personality Development. Vol. I: Infancy and Early Childhood*, ed. S. Greenspan and G. Pollock, pp. 11–61. Washington, D.C.: U.S. Government Printing Office, DHHS Publication No. (ADM)80-786.

—————. 1980b. "Themes of Adulthood in the Freud-Jung Correspondence." In *Themes of Work and Love in Adulthood*, ed. J. Smelser and E. H. Erikson, pp. 43–74. Cambridge, Mass.: Harvard University Press.

Escalona, S. 1968. *The Roots of Individuality*. Chicago: Aldine Press.

Everitt, A. V., and Huang, C. Y. 1980. "The Hypothalamus, Neuroendocrine, and Autonomic Nervous Systems in Aging." In *Handbook of Mental Health and Aging*, ed. J. E. Birren and R. B. Sloan, pp. 100–133. Englewood Cliffs, N.J.: Prentice-Hall.

Faderman, L. 1981. *Surpassing the Love of Men: Romantic Friendship and Love between Women from the Renaissance to the Present*. New York: William Morrow.

Falk, J. 1970. "The Organization of Remembered Life Experience of Older People: Its Relation to Anticipated Stress, to Subsequent Adaptation and to Old Age." Ph.D diss., University of Chicago.

Feldman, S.; Biringen, Z.; and Nash, S. 1981. "Fluctuations of Sex-related Attritions as a Function of Stage of Family Life Cycle." *Developmental Psychology* 17:24–35.

Firth, R.; Hubert, J.; and Forge, A. 1970. *Families and Their Relatives: Kinship in a Middle Class Sector of London*. New York: Humanities Press.

Fischer, S., et al. 1979. "Long-range Influences on Adult Mental Health: The Midtown Manhattan Study, 1954–1974." In *Research in Community and Mental Health*, ed. R. Simmons, pp. 305–33. Greenwich, Conn.: JAI Press.

Fiske, M. 1980a. "Changing Hierarchies of Commitment in Adulthood." In *Themes of Work and Love in Adulthood*, ed. N. Smelser and E. Erikson, pp. 238–64. Cambridge, Mass.: Harvard University Press.

—————. 1980b. "Tasks and Crises of the Second Half of Life: The Interrelationship of Commitment, Coping, and Adaptation." In *Handbook of Mental Health and Aging*, ed. J. Birren and R. B. Sloan, pp. 337–73. Englewood Cliffs, N.J.: Prentice-Hall.

Flacks, R. 1971. *Youth and Social Change*. Chicago: Markham Publishing Co.

Fogarty, M. P. 1975. *Forty to Sixty: How We Waste the Middle Age*. London: Center for Studies in Social Policy by The Bedford Press.

Frank, A. W. 1979. "Reality Construction in Interaction." *Annual Review of Sociology* 5:167–91.

Frank, L. E. 1948. "Time Perspectives." In *Society as the Patient*, ed. L. E. Frank, pp. 339–58. New Brunswick, N.J.: Rutgers University Press.

Freud, A. [1937] 1946. *The Ego and the Mechanisms of Defense*. New York: International Universities Press.

Freud, S. [1899] 1962. "Screen Memories." In *The Standard Edition of the Complete Psychological Works of Sigmund Freud* (hereafter *Standard Edition*), ed. J. Strachey, vol. 3, pp. 299–322. London: Hogarth Press.

—————. [1905] 1953. "Three Essays on the Theory of Sexuality." (1905). In *Standard Edition*, ed. J. Strachey, vol. 7, pp. 130–243. London: Hogarth Press.

—————. [1923] 1961. "The Ego and the Id." In *Standard Edition*, ed. J. Strachey, vol. 19, pp. 3–68. London: Hogarth Press.

—————. [1937] 1964. "Constructions in Analysis." In *Standard Edition*, ed. J. Strachey, vol. 23, pp. 255–70. London: Hogarth Press.

Giele, J. Z., 1982. "Women, Work and Family Roles." In *Women in the Middle Years*, ed. J. Z. Giele, pp. 115–50. New York: John Wiley & Sons.

Gergen, K. 1977. "Stability, Change, and Chance in Understanding Human Development." In *Life-Span Developmental Psychology: Dialectical Perspectives on Experimental Research*, ed. N. Datan and H. Reese, pp. 135–58. New York: Academic Press.

—————. 1980. "The Emerging Crisis in Life-span Developmental Theory." In *Life-Span Development and Behavior*, ed. P. Baltes and O. G. Brim, Jr., vol. 3, pp. 31–63. New York: Academic Press.

Gilligan, C. 1979. "Woman's Place in Man's Life Cycle." *Harvard Educational Review* 49:431–46.

Giovacchini, P. 1970. "Effects of Adaptive and Disruptive Aspects of Early Object Relationships upon Later Parental Functioning." In *Parenthood: Its Psychology and Psychopathology*, ed. E. Anthony and T. Benedek, pp. 527–37. Boston: Little, Brown.

Glenn, N. 1975. "The Contribution of Marriage to the Psychological Well-being of Males and Females." *Journal of Marriage and the Family* 37:594–600.

Glick, P. 1980. "Remarriage: Some Recent Changes and Variations." *Journal of Family Issues* 4:455–78.

Glueck, S., and Glueck, E. 1950. *Unravelling Juvenile Delinquency*. New York: The Commonwealth Fund.

Gordon, C.; Gaitz, C. M.; and Scott, J. 1976. "Leisure and Lives: Personal Expressivity Across the Life Span." In *Handbook of Aging and the Social Sciences*, ed. R. Binstock and E. Shanas, pp. 310–41. New York: Van Nostrand Reinhold.

Gorman, B., and Wessman, A. 1977. *The Personal Experience of Time*. New York: Plenum.

Gottman, J. 1979. *Marital Interaction: Experimental Investigations*. New York: Academic Press.

Gould, R. 1972. "The Phases of Adult Life: A Study in Developmental Psychology." *American Journal of Psychiatry* 129:521–31.

Gould, R. E. 1974. "Measuring Masculinity by the Size of a Paycheck." In *Men and Masculinity*, ed. J. Pleck and J. Sawyer, pp. 96–100. Englewood Cliffs, N.J.: Prentice-Hall.

Gove, W. 1972. "The Relationship between Sex Roles, Marital Status, and Mental Illness." *Social Forces* 51:34–44.

Gove, W., and Peterson, C. 1980. "An Update of the Literature on Personal and Marital Satisfaction: The Effect of Children and the Employment of Wives." *Marriage and Family Review* 3:63–96.

Gove, W., and Tudor, J. 1973. "Adult Sex Roles and Mental Illness." *American Journal of Sociology* 78:812–35.

Gover, D. 1963. "Socio-economic Differential in the Relationship between Marital Adjustment and Wife's Employment Status." *Marriage and Family Living* 25:452–558.

Grinker, R. 1967. "Normality Viewed as a System." *Archives of General Psychiatry* 17:320–24.

Gubrium, J. F., and Buckholdt, D. R. 1977. *Toward Maturity: The Social Processing of Human Development*. San Francisco: Jossey-Bass.

Gutmann, D. 1975. "Parenthood: A Key to the Comparative Study of the Life Cycle." In *Life-Span Developmental Psychology: Normative Life Crises*, ed. N. Datan and L. Ginsberg, pp. 167–84. New York: Academic Press.

———. 1976. "Individual Adaptation in the Middle Years: Developmental Issues in the Masculine Mid-life Crisis." *Journal of Geriatric Psychiatry* 9:41–59.

———. 1977. "The Cross-cultural Perspective: Notes toward a Comparative Psychology of Aging." In *Handbook of the Psychology of Aging*, ed. J. Birren and K. W. Schaie, pp. 302–26. New York: Van Nostrand, Reinhold.

———. 1980. "The Post-parental Years: Clinical Problems and Developmental Possibilities." In *Mid-Life: Developmental and Clinical Issues*, ed. W. Norman and T. Scaramella, pp. 38–52. New York: Brunner/Mazel.

Haan, N. 1972. "Personality Development from Adolescence to Adulthood in the Oakland Growth and Guidance Studies." *Seminars in Psychiatry* 4:399–414.

———. 1977. *Coping and Defending: Processes of Self-Environment Organization*. New York: Academic Press.

Haan, N., and Day, D. 1974. "Longitudinal Study of Change and Sameness in Personality Development: Adolescence to Later Adulthood." *International Journal of Aging and Human Development* 5:11–39.

Hagestad, G. O. 1981. "Problems and Promises in the Social Psychology of Intergenerational Relations." In *Stability and Change in the Family*, ed. R. Fogel et al., pp. 11–46. New York: Academic Press.

Harrison, J. B. 1978a. "Men's Roles and Men's Lives." *Signs: Journal of Women in Culture and Society* 4:324–37.

———. 1978b. "Warning: The Male Sex Role May Be Dangerous to Your Health." *Journal of Social Issues* 34:65–86.

Harry, J. 1976. "Evolving Sources of Happiness for Men Over the Life Cycle: A Structural Analysis." *Journal of Marriage and the Family* 38:289–96.

Hartmann, H. [1939] 1958. *Ego Psychology and the Problem of Adaptation,* trans. D. Rapaport. New York: International Universities Press.

Havighurst, R. 1953. *Human Development and Education.* New York: Longmans-Green.

————. 1957. "The Social Competence of Middle-aged People." *Genetic Psychology Monographs* 56:296–348.

Hayes, M. P., and Stinnett, N. 1971. "Life Satisfaction of Middle-aged Husbands and Wives." *Journal of Home Economics* 63:669–94.

Henker, F. O., III. 1981. "Male Climacteric." In *Modern Perspectives in the Psychiatry of Middle Age,* ed. J. G. Howells, pp. 304–12. New York: Brunner/Mazel.

Henry, W. E. 1971. "The Role of Work in Structuring the Life Cycle." *Human Development* 14:125–31.

Hess, B. B. 1979. "Sex Roles, Friendship, and the Life Course." *Research on Aging* 1:494–515.

Hill, R., and Hansen, D. 1960. "The Identification of Conceptual Frameworks Used in Family Study." *Marriage and Family Living* 12:299–311.

Hill, R., and Mattessich, P. 1979. "Family Development Theory and Life-span Development." In *Life-Span Development and Behavior,* ed. P. Baltes and O. G. Brim, Jr., vol. 2, pp. 161–204. New York: Academic Press.

Hill, R., and Rodgers, R. 1964. "The Developmental Approach." In *Handbook of Marriage and the Family,* ed. H. T. Christensen, pp. 171–214. Chicago: Rand McNally.

Hill, R., et al. 1970. *Family Development in Three Generations.* Cambridge, Mass.: Schenkman Publishing Co.

Hoffman, L. 1978. "Effects of the First Child on the Woman's Role." In *The First Child and Family Formation,* ed. W. Miller and L. Newman, pp. 340–67. Chapel Hill, N.C.: Carolina Population Center and University of North Carolina.

Hoffman, L., and Manis, J. 1978. "Influences of Children on Marital Interaction and Parental Satisfactions and Dissatisfactions." In *Child Influences on Marital and Family Interaction,* ed. R. Lerner and G. Spanier, pp. 165–214. New York: Academic Press.

Hoffman, L., and Nye, F. 1974. *Working Mothers.* San Francisco: Jossey-Bass.

Hogan, D. 1978. "The Variable Order of Events in the Life Course." *American Sociological Review* 43:573–86.

Holmes, T., and Rahe, R. 1967. "The Social Readjustment Rating Scale." *Journal of Psychosomatic Research* 11:213–18.

Horowitz, M., and Wilner, N. 1980. "Life-events, Stress, and Coping." In *Aging in the 1980s; Psychological Issues,* ed. L. Poon, pp. 363–74. Washington, D.C.: American Psychological Association.

Houseknecht, S. 1979. "Childlessness and Marital Adjustment." *Journal of Marriage and the Family* 41:259–65.

Hudson, W., and Murphy, W. 1980. "The Non-linear Relationship Between Marital Satisfaction and Stages of the Family Life Cycle: An Artifact of Type I Errors." *Journal of Marriage and the Family* 42:263–67.

Humphrey, M. 1975. "The Effect of Children on the Marriage Relationship." *British Journal of Medical Psychology* 48:273–79.

Inkeles, A., and Levinson, S. 1954. "National Character: The Study of Modal Personality and Sociocultural Systems." In *Handbook of Social Psychology,* ed. G. Lindzey, pp. 977–1020. Cambridge, Mass.: Addison-Wesley.

Jaffe, A. J. 1971. "The Middle Years." *Industrial Gerontology,* September (special issue).

Jahoda, M. 1958. *Current Concepts of Positive Mental Health.* New York: Basic Books.

Janet, P. 1877. "Une illusion d'optique interne (The illusion of the inner image)." *Revue Philosophie* 1:497–502.

Janowitz, M., ed. 1966. *W. I. Thomas on Social Organization and Social Personality.* Chicago: University of Chicago Press.

Jaques, E. 1965. "Death and the Mid-life Crisis." *International Journal of Psycho-analysis* 46:502–14.

————. 1981. "The Midlife Crisis." In *The Course of Life: Psychoanalytic Contributions toward Understanding Personality Development. Vol. III: Adulthood and the Aging Process,* ed. S. I. Greenspan and G. H. Pollock, pp. 1–23. Washington, D.C.: U.S. Government Printing Office, DHHS Publication No. (ADM) 81-1000.

Jennings, M., and Niemi, R. G. 1968. "The Transmission of Political Values from Parent to Child." *American Political Science Review* 62:169–84.

Jones, M. C. 1967. "A Report on Three Growth Studies at the University of California." *The Gerontologist* 7:49–54.

Jones, M. C., et al., eds. 1971. *The Course of Human Development: Selected Papers from the Longitudinal Studies.* Waltham, Mass.: Xerox Publishing Corp.

Jourard, S. M. 1971. *The Transparent Self.* New York: Litton.

Jung, C. G. 1933. *Modern Man in Search of a Soul.* New York: Harcourt, Brace & World.

Kagan, J. 1980. "Perspectives on Continuity." In *Constancy and Change in Human Development,* ed. O. G. Brim, Jr., and J. Kagan, pp. 26–74. Cambridge, Mass.: Harvard University Press.

Kagan, J., and Moss, H. 1962. *Birth to Maturity.* New York: John Wiley & Sons.

Kandel, D., and Lesser, G. 1972. *Youth in Two Worlds.* San Francisco: Jossey-Bass.

Kanter, R. M. 1977a. *Men and Women of the Corporation.* New York: Basic Books.

———. 1977b. *Work and Family in the United States: A Critical Review and Agenda for Research and Policy.* New York: Russell Sage Foundation.

Kaplan, B. H. 1971. *Psychiatric Disorder and the Urban Environment.* New York: Behavioral Publications.

Kaplan, D., and Mason, E. 1960. "Maternal Reactions to Premature Birth Viewed as an Acute Emotional Disorder." *American Journal of Orthopsychiatry* 30:539–52.

Kastenbaum, R. 1966. "On the Meaning of Time in Later Life." *Journal of Genetic Psychology* 109:9–25.

Kellam, S. G.; Ersminger, M. A.; and Turner, R. J. 1977. "Family Structure and Mental Health of Children." *Archives of General Psychiatry* 34:1012–22.

Kernberg, O. 1980. *Internal World and External Reality: Object Relations Theory Applied.* New York: Jason Aronson.

Kinsey, A. C., et al. 1953. *Sexual Behavior in the Human Female.* Philadelphia: W. B. Saunders.

Klerman, G., and Weissman, M. 1980. "Depressions among Women: Their Nature and Causes." In *The Mental Health of Women.*, ed. M. Guttentag, S. Salasin, and D. Belle, pp. 57–92. New York: Academic Press.

Kohen, A. I. 1975. "Occupational Mobility among Middle-aged Men." In U.S. Department of Labor, Manpower R & D Monograph 15, *The Pre-Retirement Years, Vol. 4: A Longitudinal Study of Labor Market Experience of Men.* Washington, D.C.: U.S. Government Printing Office, DHEW Publication No. 029-00237-1.

Kohn, M. 1969. *Class and Conformity: A Study in Values.* Homewood, Ill.: Dorsey Press.

———. 1980. "Job Complexity and Adult Personality." In *Themes of Work and Love in Adulthood,* ed. N. J. Smelser and E. H. Erikson, pp. 193–210. Cambridge, Mass.: Harvard University Press.

Kohn, M., and Schooler, C. 1978. "The Reciprocal Effects of the Substantive Complexity of Work and Intellectual Flexibility: A Longitudinal Assessment." *American Journal of Sociology* 84:24–52.

Komarovsky, M. 1962. *Blue Collar Marriage.* New York: Random House.

———. 1974. "Patterns of Self-disclosure among Male Undergraduates." *Journal of Marriage and the Family* 36:677–86.

———. 1976. *Dilemmas of Masculinity: A Study of College Youth.* New York: W. W. Norton.

Korner, A. 1971. "Individual Differences at Birth: Implications for Early Experience, and Later Development." *American Journal of Orthopsychiatry* 41:608–19.

Kornhauser, A. 1965. *Mental Health of the Industrial Worker: A Detroit Study.* New York: John Wiley & Sons.

Krantz, D. L. 1977. "The Santa Fe Experience." In *Work, Aging, and Social Change: Professionals and the One Life-One Career Imperative,* ed. S. B. Sarason, pp. 165–88. New York: Free Press.

Kroeber, T. 1963. "The Coping Functions of the Ego Mechanisms." In *The Study of Lives,* ed. R. White, pp. 178–99. New York: Atherton.

Lamb, M. E. 1976. "The Role of the Father: An Overview." In *The Role of the Father in Child Development,* ed, M. E. Lamb, pp 1–63. (2nd ed., 1981). New York: John Wiley & Sons.

———. 1978. "Influence of the Child on Marital Quality and Family Interaction During the Prenatal, Perinatal, and Infancy Periods." In *Child Influences on Marital and Family Interaction: A Life-Span Perspective,* ed. R. Lerner and G. Spanier, pp. 137–64. New York: Academic Press.

Lasch, C. 1978. *The Culture of Narcissism.* New York: W. W. Norton.

Laws, J. L. 1980. "Female Sexuality Through the Life-span." In *Life-Span Development and Behavior,* ed. P. Baltes and O. G. Brim, Jr., vol. 3, pp. 207–52. New York: Academic Press.

Lazarus, R. 1974. "Psychological Stress and Coping in Adaptation and Illness." *International Journal of Psychiatry in Medicine* 5:321–33.

————. 1980. "The Stress and Coping Paradigm." In *Competence and Coping during Adulthood,* ed. L. Bond and J. Rosen, pp. 28–74. Hanover, N.H.: University Press of New England.

LeMasters, E. E. 1957. "Parenthood as Crisis." *Marriage and Family Living* 19:352–55.

Lens W., and Gailly, A. 1980. "Extension of Future Time Perspective in Motivational Goals of Different Age Groups." *International Journal of Behavioral Development* 3:1–17.

Levinson, D. 1977. "The Mid-life Transition: A Period in Adult Psychosocial Development." *Psychiatry* 40:99–112.

Levinson, D., et al. 1978. *The Seasons of a Man's Life.* New York: Knopf.

Lewin, K. [1946] 1964. "Behavior and Development as a Function of the Total Situation." In *Field Theory in Social Science,* ed. K. Lewin, pp. 238–304. New York: Harper Torchbooks.

Lewis, R. A. 1978. "Emotional Intimacy Among Men." *Journal of Social Issues* 34:108–21.

Lidz, T. 1977. *The Person,* rev. ed. New York: Basic Books.

Lieberman, M., and Falk, J. 1971. "The Remembered Past as a Source of Data for Research on the Life-cycle." *Human Development* 14:132–41.

Litwak, E. 1960a. "Occupational Mobility and Extended Family Cohesion." *American Sociological Review* 25:9–21.

————. 1960b. "Geographical Mobility and Extended Family Cohesion." *American Sociological Review* 26:258–71.

Livson, F. 1981. "Paths to Psychological Health in the Middle Years: Sex Differences." In *Present and Past in Middle Life,* ed. D. Eichorn et al., pp. 195–222. New York: Academic Press.

Livson, N., and Peskin, H. 1980. "Perspectives on Adolescence from Longitudinal Research." In *Handbook of Adolescent Psychology,* ed. J. Adelson, pp. 47–98. New York: John Wiley & Sons.

Lopata, H. 1979. *Women as Widows: Support Systems.* New York: Elsevier-North Holland.

Lopata, H., and Norr, K. 1980. "Changing Commitments of American Women to Work and Family Roles." *Social Security Bulletin* 43:3–14.

Lowenstein, S. F. 1980. "Toward Choice and Differentiation in the Midlife Crises of Women." In *The Evolving Female: Women in a Psychosocial Context,* ed. C. L. Heckerman, pp. 158–88. New York: Human Sciences Press.

Lowenthal, M. F. 1975. "Psychosocial Variations Across the Adult Life Course: Frontiers for Research and Policy." *Gerontologist* 15:6–12.

Lowenthal, M. F.; Fiske, M.; and Chiriboga, D. 1972. "Transition to the Empty Nest: Crisis, Challenge, or Relief?" *Archives of General Psychiatry* 26:8–14.

Lowenthal, M. F., et al. 1967. *Aging and Mental Disorder in San Francisco.* San Francisco: Jossey-Bass.

Lowenthal, M. F., et al. 1975. *Four Stages of Life: A Comparative Study of Women and Men Facing Transitions.* San Francisco: Jossey-Bass.

Maas, H., and Kuypers, J. 1974. *From Thirty to Seventy.* San Francisco: Jossey-Bass.

McCall, G., and Simmons, J. 1980. *Identities and Interactions: An Examination of Human Associations in Everyday Life,* rev. ed. New York: Free Press.

McKinlay, S.; Jeffreys, M.; and Thompson, B. 1974. "Investigation of the Age at Menopause." *British Journal of Preventive and Social Medicine* 28:16–17.

Mannheim, K. [1928] 1952. "The Problem of Generations." In *Essays on the Sociology of Knowledge,* by K. Manneheim, trans. P. Kecskemeti, pp 276–322. New York: Oxford University Press.

Marshall, V. W. 1978. "The Myth of the Mid-life Crisis." Paper presented at the Seventh Annual Scientific and Educational Meeting, Canadian Association on Gerontology, Edmonton, Alberta, October.

Masters, W. H., and Johnson, V. E. 1966. *Human Sexual Response.* Boston: Little, Brown.

Medley, M. 1980. "Life Satisfaction Across Four Stages of Adult Life." *International Journal of Aging and Human Development* 11:193–208.

Menaghan, E. 1978. "The Effect of Family Transitions on Marital Experience." Ph.D. diss., University of Chicago.

Meyerowitz, J., and Feldman, H. 1966. "Transition to Parenthood." *Psychiatric Research Reports* 20:78–84.

Miller, D., and Swanson, G. 1960. *Inner Conflict and Defense.* New York: Dryden-Holt.

Model, S. 1981. "Housework by Husbands: Determinants and Implications." *Journal of Family Issues* 2:225–37.

Modell, J.; Furstenberg, F.; and Hershberg, T. 1976. "Social Change and Transitions to Adulthood in Historical Perspective." *Journal of Family History* 1:7–32.

Morin, S. F. and Garfinkle, E. M. 1978. "Male Homophobia." *Journal of Social Issues* 34:29–47.

Mortimer, J. T., and Simmons, R. G. 1978. "Adult Socialization." *Annual Review of Sociology* 4:421–54.

Mullan, J. 1980. "Parental Distress and Happiness in Marriage: The Transition to the 'Empty Nest.' " Ph.D. diss., University of Chicago.

Munnichs, J. 1966. *Old Age and Finitude: A Contribution to Psychogerontology.* Basel: Karger.

Murphy, L. B. 1962. *The Widening World of Childhood: Pathways toward Mastery.* New York: Basic Books.

Murphy, L. B., and Moriarty, A. E. 1976. *Vulnerability, Coping, & Growth: From Infancy to Adolescence.* New Haven: Yale University Press.

Murstein, B. 1976. *Who Will Marry Whom: Theories and Research in Marital Choice.* New York: Springer.

Mussen, P., et al. 1980. "Continuity and Change in Women's Characteristics over Four Decades." *International Journal of Behavioral Development* 3:333–47.

Nassi, A. J. 1981. "Survivors of the Sixties: Comparative Psychosocial and Political Development of Former Berkeley Student Activists." *American Psychologist* 36:753–61.

Nathanson, C. 1980. "Social Roles and Health Status Among Women: The Significance of Employment." *Social Science and Medicine* 14A:463–71.

Nesselroade, J., and Baltes, P. 1974. "Adolescent Personality Development and Historical Change: 1970–1972." *Monographs of the Society for Research in Child Development,* vol. 39, no. 154.

Neugarten, B. L. 1967. "The Awareness of Middle Age." In *Middle Age,* ed. R. Owen. London: British Broadcasting Co. (Reprinted in *Middle Age and Aging,* ed. B. L. Neugarten, pp. 93–98. Chicago: University of Chicago Press, 1968.)

————. 1970. "Dynamics of Transition of Middle Age to Old Age: Adaptation and the Life Cycle." *Journal of Geriatric Psychiatry* 41:71–87.

————. 1973. "Personality Change in Late Life: A Developmental Perspective." In *The Psychology of Adult Development and Aging,* ed. C. Eisdorfer and M. P. Lawton, pp. 311–38. Washington, D.C.: American Psychological Association.

————. 1979a. "Time, Age, and the Life-cycle." *American Journal of Psychiatry* 136:887–94.

————. 1979b. "The Middle Generations." In *Aging Parents,* ed. P. Ragan, pp. 258–66. Los Angeles: University of Southern California Press.

Neugarten, B. L., and Brown-Rezanka, L. 1978. "Midlife Women in the 1980s." In *Women in Midlife: Security and Fulfillment, Part I.* Select Committee on Aging and Subcommittee on Retirement Income and Employment. U.S. House of Representatives, 95th Congress, 2nd session, Comm. Pub. No. 95-170.

Neugarten, B. L., and Datan, N. 1973. "Sociological Perspectives on the Life Cycle." In *Life-Span Developmental Psychology: Personality and Socialization,* ed. P. Baltes and K. W. Schaie, pp. 53–69. New York: Academic Press.

————. 1974. "The Middle Years." In *The American Handbook of Psychiatry,* rev. ed., ed. S. Arieti, vol. 5, pp. 592–608. New York: Basic Books.

Neugarten, B. L., and Hagestad, G. O. 1976. "Age and the Life Course." In *Handbook of Aging and the Social Sciences,* ed. R. H. Binstock and E. Shanas, pp. 35–55. New York: Van Nostrand Reinhold.

Neugarten, B. L., and Moore, J. 1968. "The Changing Age Status System." In *Middle Age and Aging,* ed. B. Neugarten, pp. 5–21. Chicago: University of Chicago Press.

Neugarten, B. L., and Peterson, W. 1957. "A Study of the American Age-grade System." *Proceedings of the Fourth Congress of the International Association of Gerontology* 3:497–502.

Neugarten, B. L.; Moore, J.; and Lowe, J. 1965. "Age Norms, Age Constraints, and Adult Socialization." *American Journal of Sociology* 70:710–17.

Neugarten, B. L., et al. 1964. *Personality in Middle and Late Life.* New York: Atherton Press.

Nock, S. 1979. "The Family Life-cycle: Empirical or Conceptual Tool?" *Journal of Marriage and the Family* 41:15–26.

Notman, M. 1979. "Midlife Concerns of Women: Implications of the Menopause." *American Journal of Psychiatry* 136:1270–74.

Nydegger, C. N. 1973. "Late and Early Fathers." Paper presented at the Annual Meetings of the Gerontological Society, Miami Beach, Fla., November.

Nye, F. I. 1961. "Maternal Employment and Marital Interaction: Some Contingent Conditions." *Social Forces* 40:113–19.

Offer, D., and Sabshin, M. 1974. *Normality: Theoretical and Clinical Concepts of Mental Health,* 2nd ed. New York: Basic Books.

————. 1976. "Normality." In *Comprehensive Textbook of Psychiatry/III,* ed. H. I. Kaplan, A. M. Freedman, and B. J. Sadock, vol. 1, pp. 608–13. Baltimore: Williams & Wilkins.

Olstad, K. 1975. "Brave New Men: A Basis for Discussion." In *Sex: Male/Gender: Masculine,* ed. J. Petras, pp. 160–78. Port Washington, N.Y.: Alfred Publishing Corp.

Oppenheimer, V. 1974. "The Life-Cycle Squeeze: The Interaction of Men's Occupational and Family Life-Cycles." *Demography* 11:227–45.

————. 1977. "The Sociology of Women's Economic Role in the Family." *American Sociological Review* 42:387–405.

Orden, S. R., and Bradburn, N. 1969. "Working Wives and Marriage Happiness." *American Journal of Sociology* 74:392–407.

Osherson, S. D. 1980. *Holding on or Letting Go: Men and Career Change at Midlife.* New York: Free Press.

Parsons, T. 1951. *The Social System.* New York: Free Press.

Parsons, T., and Bales, R. F. 1955. *Family: Socialization and Interaction Process.* Glencoe, Ill.: Free Press.

Paykel, E.; Prusoff, B.; and Uhlenhuth, E. 1971. "Scaling of Life Events." *Archives of General Psychiatry* 25:340–47.

Pearlin, L. 1975. "Sex-roles and Depression." In *Life-Span Developmental Psychology: Normative Life Crises,* ed. N. Datan and L. Ginsburg, pp. 191–207. New York: Academic Press.

————. 1980. "Life Strains and Psychological Distress Among Adults." In *Themes of Work and Love in Adulthood,* ed. N. Smelser and E. Erikson, pp. 174–92. Cambridge, Mass.: Harvard University Press.

Pearlin, L., and Johnson, J. 1977. "Marital Status, Life-strains, and Depression." *American Sociological Review* 42:704–15.

Pearlin, L., and Lieberman, M. 1979. "Social Sources of Emotional Distress." In *Research in Community and Mental Health,* ed. R. Simmons, pp. 217–48. Greenwich, Conn.: JAI Press.

Pearlin, L., and Schooler, C. 1978. "The Structure of Coping." *Journal of Health and Social Behavior* 19:2–21.

Pederson, F. A. 1980. "Research Issues Related to Fathers and Infants." In *The Father-Infant Relationship: Observational Studies in the Family Setting,* ed. F. A. Pedersen, pp. 1–20. New York: Praeger.

Peskin, H. 1972. "Multiple Prediction of Adult Psychological Health from Preadolescent and Adolescent Behavior." *Journal of Consulting and Clinical Psychology* 38:155–60.

Peskin, H., and Livson, N. 1981. "Uses of the Past in Adult Psychological Health." In *Present and Past in Middle Life,* ed. D. H. Eichorn et al., pp. 153–81. New York: Academic Press.

Pfeiffer, E.; Verwoerdt, A.; and Davis, G. C. 1972. "Sexual Behavior in Middle Life." *American Journal of Psychiatry* 128:82–87.

Pineo, P. 1961. "Disenchantment in the Later Years of Marriage." *Marriage and Family Living* 23:3–11.

Pleck, J. 1975. "Male-Male Friendship: Is Brotherhood Possible?" In *Old Family/New Family: Interpersonal Relationships,* ed. N. Glazer-Malbin, pp. 229–44. New York: Van Nostrand Reinhold.

————. 1981. *The Myth of Masculinity.* Cambridge, Mass.: M.I.T. Press.

Pleck, J., and Brannon, R. 1978. "Male Roles and the Male Experience: Introduction." *Journal of Social Issues* 34:1–4.

Pleck, J., and Sawyer, J. 1974. *Men and Masculinity.* Englewood Cliffs, N.J.: Prentice-Hall.

Pohlman, E. 1969. *The Psychology of Birth Planning.* Cambridge, Mass.: Schenkman Publishing Co..

Powers, E. A., and Bultena, G. L. 1976. "Sex Differences in Intimate Friendships in Old Age." *Journal of Marriage and the Family* 38:739–47.

Price-Bonham, S. 1976. "Bibliography of Literature Related to Roles of Fathers." *The Family Coordinator* 25:489–512.

Prosen, H.; Martin, R.; and Prosen, M. 1972. "The Remembered Mother and the Fantasized Mother: A Crisis of Middle Age." *Archives of General Psychiatry* 27:791–94.

Radcliffe-Brown, A. E. 1952. *Structure and Function in Primitive Society.* New York: Free Press.

Radloff, L. S. 1975. "Sex Differences in Depression: The Effects of Occupation and Marital Status." *Sex Roles* 1:249–65.

————. 1980. "Risk Factors for Depression: What Do We Learn from Them?" In *The Mental Health of Women*, ed. M. Guttentag, S. Salasin, and D. Belle, pp. 93–110. New York: Academic Press.

Ragan, P., and Wales, J. 1980. "Age Stratification and the Life Course." In *Handbook of Mental Health and Aging*, ed. J. Birren and R. B. Sloane, pp. 377–99. Englewood Cliffs, N.J.: Prentice-Hall.

Rakowski, W. 1979. "Future Time Perspective in Later Adulthood: Review and Research Directions." *Experimental Aging Research* 5:43–88.

Rapoport, R. 1963. "Normal Crises, Family Structure, and Mental Health." *Family Process* 2:68–80.

Rapoport, R., and Rapoport, R. 1976. *Dual Career Families Reexamined.* New York: Harper & Row.

Rapoport, R., et al. 1977. *Fathers, Mothers and Society.* New York: Basic Books.

Raush, H., et al. 1974. *Communication, Conflict and Marriage.* San Francisco: Jossey-Bass.

Reich, W. [1933] 1949. *Character Analysis.* New York: Farrar, Straus & Cudahy/Noonday Press.

Reichard, S.; Livson, F.; and Peterson, P. 1962. *Aging and Personality.* New York: John Wiley & Sons.

Revere, V. 1971. "The Remembered Past: Its Reconstruction at Different Life Stages." Ph.D. diss., University of Chicago.

Revere, V., and Tobin, S. 1980–81. "Myth and Reality: The Older Person's Relationship to His Past." *International Journal of Aging and Human Development* 12:15–26.

Rice, R. E. 1980. "Dreams and Actualities: Danforth Fellows at Mid-career." *American Association for Higher Education Bulletin* 32:3.

Rickman, J. 1928. "Psychoanalysis of the Psychoses." *International Journal of Psycho-Analysis, Supplement No. 2.* London: British Psychoanalytic Society & Bailliere, Tindall.

Riegel, K. 1977. "The Dialectics of Time." In *Life-Span Developmental Psychology: Dialectical Perspectives on Experimental Research*, ed. N. Datan and L. Ginsberg, pp. 3–45. New York: Academic Press.

Riley, M. 1976. "Age Strata in Social Systems." In *Handbook of Aging and the Social Sciences*, ed. R. Binstock and E. Shanas, pp. 186–217. New York: Van Nostrand Reinhold.

————. 1978. "Aging, Social Change and the Power of Ideas." *Daedalus Journal of the American Academy of Arts and Sciences* 107:39–52.

Riley, M.; Johnson, M.; and Foner, A. 1972. *Aging and Society, Vol. III: A Sociology of Age Stratification.* New York: Russell Sage.

Ripley, H. 1977. "Depression and Life-span Epidemiology." In *Depression: Clinical, Biological, and Psychological Perspectives*, ed. G. Usdin, pp. 1–27. New York: Brunner/Mazel.

Rollins, B., and Feldman, H. 1970. "Marital Satisfaction over the Family Life Cycle." *Journal of Marriage and the Family* 32:20–28.

Rollins, B., and Galligan, R. 1978. "The Developing Child and Marital Satisfaction of Parents." In *Child Influences on Marital and Family Interaction: A Life-Span Perspective*, ed. R. Lerner and B. Spanier, pp. 71–102. New York: Academic Press.

Rosenberg, S. D., and Farrell, M. P. 1976. "Identity and Crisis in Middle-aged Men." *International Journal of Aging and Human Development* 7:153–70.

Rosenthal, K. M., and Keshet, H. F. 1981. *Fathers without Partners: A Study of Fathers and the Family after Marital Separation.* Totowa, N.J: Rowman & Littlefield.

Ross, J. M. 1979. "Fathering: A Review of Some Psychoanalytic Contributions on Paternity." *International Journal of Psycho-Analysis* 60:317–27.

Ross, J. M. 1984. "Fathers in Development: An Overview of Recent Contributions." In *Parenthood: A Psychodynamic Perspective,* ed. R. Cohen, B. Cohler, and S. Weissmann. New York: Guilford Press.

Rossi, A. 1968. "Transition to Parenthood." *Journal of Marriage and the Family* 30:26–39.

―――. 1980a. "Aging and Parenthood in the Middle Years." In *Life-Span Development and Behavior,* ed. P. Baltes and O. G. Brim, Jr., vol. 3, pp. 137–205. New York: Academic Press.

―――. 1980b. "Life-span Theories and Women's Lives." *Signs: Journal of Women in Culture and Society* 6:4–32.

Rothstein, S. 1967. "Aging Awareness and Personalization of Death." Ph.D. diss., University of Chicago.

Russell, C. 1974. "Transition to Parenthood: Problems and Gratifications." *Journal of Marriage and the Family* 36:294–303.

Russo, N. 1979. "Overview: Sex Roles, Fertility, and the Motherhood Mandate." *Psychology of Women Quarterly* 41:7–15.

Rubin, L. 1976. *Worlds of Pain: Life in the Working-class Family.* New York: Basic Books.

―――. 1979. *Women of a Certain Age: The Midlife Search for Self.* New York: Basic Books.

Rychlak, J. F. 1974. "Life Themes: Enlargers and Enfolders." In *Formative Years in Business: A Long-Term AT&T Study of Managerial Lives,* ed. D. W. Bray et al., pp. 82–128. New York: John Wiley & Sons.

Ryder, N. 1965. "The Cohort as a Concept in the Study of Social Change." *American Sociological Review* 30:843–61.

Ryder, R. 1967. "Birth to Maturity Revisited: A Canonical Reanalysis." *Journal of Personality and Social Psychology* 1:168–72.

Ryder, R.; Kafka, J.; and Olson, D. 1976. "Separating and Joining Influences in Courtship and Early Marriage." *American Journal of Orthopsychiatry* 41:450–64.

Sarason, S. B. 1977. *Work, Aging, and Social Change: Professionals and the One Life-One Career Imperative.* New York: Free Press.

Sawhill, I. 1974. "A Perspective on Women and Work in America." In *Work and the Quality of Life: Resource Papers for Work in America,* ed. J. O'Toole, pp. 98–105. Cambridge, Mass.: MIT Press.

Schaie, K. W. 1965. "A General Model for the Study of Developmental Problems." *Psychological Bulletin* 64:94–107.

―――. 1973. "Methodological Problems in Descriptive Developmental Research on Adulthood and Aging." In *Life-Span Developmental Psychology: Methodological Issues,* ed. J. Nesselroade and H. Reese, pp. 253–80. New York: Academic Press.

Schram, R. 1979. "Marital Satisfaction over the Family Life-cycle: A Critique and Proposal." *Journal of Marriage and the Family* 41:7–12.

Schwab, J., et al. 1979. *Social Order and Mental Health: The Florida Health Study.* New York: Brunner/Mazel.

Seltzer, M. 1976. "Suggestions for the Examination of Time-Disordered Relationships." In *Time, Roles, and Self in Old Age,* ed. J. Gubrium, pp. 111–25. New York: Human Sciences Press.

Shanan, J. 1976. "Levels and Patterns of Social Engagement and Disengagement from Adolescence to Middle Adulthood." In *The Developing Individual in a Changing World, Vol. II: Social and Environmental Issues,* ed. K. Riegel and J. A. Meacham, pp. 601–10. Chicago: Aldine.

Shanas, E. 1961. "Living Arrangements of Older People in the United States." *Gerontologist* 1:27–29.

―――. 1973. "Family-kin Networks and Aging in Cross-cultural Perspective." *Journal of Marriage and the Family* 35:505–11.

―――. 1979. "Social Myth as Hypothesis: The Case of the Family Relations of Old People." *Gerontologist* 19:3–9.

Shereshefsky, P., et al. 1973. *Psychological Aspects of a First Pregnancy and Post-Natal Adaptation.* New York: Raven Press.

Shulman, N. 1975. "Life Cycle Variations in Patterns of Close Relationships." *Journal of Marriage and the Family* 37:813–21.

Siassi, G.; Crocetti, G.; and Spiro, H. 1974. "Loneliness and Dissatisfaction in a Blue-collar Population." *Archives of General Psychiatry* 30:261–65.

Simpson, I. H., and England, P. 1980. "Conjugal Work Roles and Marital Solidarity." *Journal of Family Issues* 2:180–204.

Smith, R. J. 1961. "Cultural Differences in the Life Cycle and the Concept of Time." In *Aging and Leisure,* ed. R. W. Kleemeier, pp. 83–111. New York: Oxford University Press.

Smith-Rosenberg, C. 1975. "The Female World of Love and Ritual: Relations Between Women in Nineteenth-century America." *Signs: Journal of Women in Culture and Society* 1:1–29.

Snow, R. B. 1980. "Middle-aged Persons' Perceptions of Their Intergenerational Relations." Ph.D. diss., University of Chicago.

Social Research, Inc. 1972. *Changing Perception of Good in Modern Life: A Study of Trends in the Thinking of American Homemakers.* Chicago: Social Research, Inc.

Soddy, K., with Kidson, M. C. 1967. *Men in Middle Life.* London: Tavistock.

Sofer, C. 1970. *Men in Mid-Career: A Study of British Managers and Technical Specialists.* Cambridge: Cambridge University Press.

Spanier, G., and Glick, P. 1980. "The Life Cycle of American Families: An Expanded Analysis." *Journal of Family History* 5:97–111.

Spanier, G., and Lewis, R. 1980. "Marital Quality: A Review of the Seventies." *Journal of Marriage and the Family* 42:805–39.

Spanier, G.; Sauer, W.; and Larzelere, R. 1979. "An Empirical Evaluation of the Family Life Cycle." *Journal of Marriage and the Family* 41:27–38.

Srole, L., and Fischer, A. 1980. "The Midtown Manhattan Longitudinal Study vs. The Mental Paradise Lost Doctrine." *Archives of General Psychiatry* 37:209–21.

Srole, L., et al. [1962] 1977. *Mental Health in the Metropolis: The Midtown Manhattan Study,* rev. ed. New York: Harper Torchbooks.

Stein, S., et al. 1978. "Mid-adult Development and Psychopathology." *American Journal of Psychiatry* 135:676–81.

Stinett, N.; Collins, J.; and Montgomery, J. 1970. "Marital Need Satisfaction of Older Husbands and Wives." *Journal of Marriage and the Family* 32:428–34.

Strauss, A., ed. 1964. *George Herbert Mead: On Social Psychology.* Chicago: University of Chicago Press.

Stryker, S. 1980. *Symbolic Interactionism: A Social Structural Version.* Reading, Mass.: Benjamin/Cummings Publishing Co.

Sussman, M. 1954. "Family Continuity: Selective Factors Which Affect Relationships Between Families at Generational Levels." *Marriage and Family Living* 16: 112–20.

Sussman, M. and Burchinal, L. 1962. "Kin Family Network: Unheralded Structure in Current Conceptualizations of Family Functioning." *Marriage and Family Living* 24:231–40.

Swanson, G. 1961. "Determinants of the Individual's Defense Against Inner Conflict." In *Parental Attitudes and Child Behavior,* ed. J. Glidewell, pp. 5–41. Springfield, Ill.: Charles C Thomas.

Sweet, J. 1973. *Women in the Labor Force.* New York: Seminar Press.

Terman, L. 1938. *Psychological Factors in Marital Happiness.* New York: McGraw-Hill.

Terman, L. M., and Oden, M. H. 1959. *Genetic Studies of Genius: V. The Gifted Group at Mid-life.* Stanford, Calif.: Stanford University Press.

Thomae, H., ed. 1976. *Patterns of Aging: Findings from the Bonn Longitudinal Study of Aging. Contributions to Human Development,* Monograph no. 3. Basel: Karger.

Thomas, A., and Chess, S. 1977. *Temperament and Development.* New York: Brunner/Mazel.

Thomas, A., et al. 1963. *Behavioral Individuality in Early Childhood.* New York: New York University Press.

Thomas, L. E. 1971. "Family Correlates of Student Political Activism." *Developmental Psychology* 4:206–14.

Thurnher, M. 1976. "Midlife Marriage: Sex Differences in Evaluation and Perspectives." *International Journal of Aging and Human Development* 7:129–35.

Tiger, L. 1969. *Men in Groups.* New York: Random House.

Tizard, L., and Guntrip, H. 1959. *Middle Age.* London: George Allen & Unwin.

Troll, L. 1975. *Early and Middle Adulthood.* Monterey, Calif.: Brooks-Cole.

Troll, L.; Neugarten, B.; and Kraines, R. 1969. "Similarities in Values and Other Personality Characteristics in College Students and Their Parents." *Merrill-Palmer Quarterly of Behavior and Development* 15:323–27.

Tsui, A., and Bogue, D. 1978. "Declining World Fertility: Trends, Causes, and Implications." *Population Bulletin* 33:3–56.

Uhlenberg, P. 1974. "Cohort Variations in Family Life Cycle Experiences of U.S. Females." *Journal of Marriage and the Family* 36:284–92.

United States Bureau of Commerce. 1977. *Social Indicators, 1976.* Washington, D.C.: United States Government Printing Office.

Vaillant, G. 1974a. "Antecedents of Healthy Adult Male Adjustment." In *Life-History Research in Psychopathology*, ed. D. Ricks, A. Thomas, and M. Roff, vol. 3, pp. 230–42. Minneapolis: University of Minnesota Press.

———. 1974b. "Natural History of Male Psychological Health: II. Some Antecedents of Healthy Adult Adjustment." *Archives of General Psychiatry* 31:15–22.

———. 1975. "Natural History of Male Psychological Health: III. Empirical Dimensions of Mental Health." *Archives of General Psychiatry* 32:420–26.

———. 1976. "Natural History of Male Psychological Health: V. The Relation of Choice of Ego Mechanisms of Defense to Adult Adjustment." *Archives of General Psychiatry* 33:535–45.

———. 1977. *Adaptation to Life.* Boston: Little, Brown.

———. 1978. "Natural History of Male Psychological Health: VI. Correlates of Successful Marriage and Fatherhood." *American Journal of Psychiatry* 135:653–59.

———. 1979. "Natural History of Male Psychological Health: VIII. Effects of Mental Health on Physical Health." *New England Journal of Medicine* 301(23):1249–54.

Vaillant, G., and McArthur, C. 1972. "Natural History of Male Psychological Health: I. The Adult Life Cycle From 18–50." *Seminars in Psychiatry* 4(4): 415–27.

Vaillant, G., and Milofsky, E. 1980. "Natural History of Male Psychological Health: IX. Empirical Evidence for Erikson's Model of the Life Cycle." *American Journal of Psychiatry* 137:1348–59.

Van Dusen, R., and Sheldon, E. 1976. "The Changing Status of American Women: A Life Cycle Perspective." *American Psychologist* 31:106–16.

Veevers, J. 1973. "Voluntary Childlessness: A Neglected Area of Family Study." *The Family Coordinator* 22:199–205.

———. 1979. "Voluntary Childlessness: A Review of the Issues and Evidence." *Marriage and Family Review* 2:1–26.

Veroff, J., and Feld, S. 1970. *Marriage and Work in America.* New York: Van Nostrand Reinhold.

Verstraeten, D. 1980. "Level of Realism in Adolescent Future Time Perspective." *Human Development* 23:177–91.

Wallach, M. A., and Green, L. R. 1968. "On Age and the Subjective Speed of Time." In *Middle Age and Aging*, ed. B. L. Neugarten, pp. 481–85. Chicago: University of Chicago Press.

Waring, E., et al. 1980. "Concepts of Intimacy in the General Population." *Journal of Nervous and Mental Disorder* 168:471–74.

Warner, W. L., and Abegglen, J. C. 1955. *Occupational Mobility in American Business and Industry, 1928–1952.* Minneapolis: University of Minnesota Press.

Weber, M. [1904–1905] 1958. *The Protestant Ethic and the Spirit of Capitalism.* New York: Scribner's.

Weiss, R. S. 1979. *Going It Alone: The Family Life and Social Situation of the Single Parent.* New York: Basic Books.

Weissman, M., and Klerman, G. 1977. "Sex Differences and the Epidemiology of Depression." *Archives of General Psychiatry* 34:98–111.

Weissman, M., and Myers, J. 1978. "Rates and Risks of Depressive Symptoms in a United States Urban Community." *Acta Psychiatrica Scandinavia* 57:219–31.

Weissman, M.; Myers, J.; and Harding, P. 1979. "Psychiatric Disorders in a U.S. Urban Community: 1975–76." *American Journal of Psychiatry* 135:459–62.

Wenz, F. V. 1980. "Aging and Suicide: Maturation or Cohort Effect?" *International Journal of Aging and Human Development* 11:297–305.

White, R. 1963. *Ego and Reality in Psychoanalytic Theory.* New York: International Universities Press (Psychological Issues Monograph no. 11).

Wilen, J. 1979. "Changing Relationships Among Grandparents, Parents, and Their Young-Adult Children." Paper presented at the Annual Meetings of the Gerontological Society of America, Washington, D.C., November.

Wilensky, H. 1963. "The Moonlighter: A Product of Relative Deprivation." *Industrial Relations* 3:105–24.

Wilson, W. C. 1975. "The Distribution of Selected Sexual Attitudes and Behaviors Among the Adult Population of the United States." *Journal of Sex Research* 11:46–64.

Winch, R. 1958. *Mate Selection: A Study of Complementary Needs.* New York: Harper.

———. 1967. "Another Look at the Theory of Complementary Needs in Mate Selection." *Journal of Marriage and the Family* 29:756–62.

Winch, R.; Ktsanes, F.; and Ktsanes, V. 1955. "Empirical Elaboration of the Theory of Complementary Needs in Mate Selection." *Journal of Abnormal and Social Psychology* 51:508–14.

Wolff, P. 1966. *The Causes, Controls, and Organization of Behavior in the Neonate.* New York: International Universities Press (Psychological Issues Monograph no. 17).

Yalom, I., et al. 1968. "Post-partum 'Blues' Syndrome: A Description and Related Variables." *Archives of General Psychiatry* 18:16–27.

Yankelovich, D. 1972. *The Changing Values on Campus.* New York: Pocket Books.

Yankelovich, Skelly, and White, Inc. 1977. *Raising Children in a Changing Society: The General Mills American Family Report, 1976–1977.* Minneapolis, Minn.: General Mills.

Young, M., and Geertz, H. 1961. "Old Age in London and San Francisco: Some Families Compared." *British Journal of Sociology* 12:124–41.

Zepelin, H. 1980–81. "Age Differences in Dreams. I: Men's Dreams and Thematic Apperceptive Fantasy." *International Journal of Aging and Human Development* 12:171–86.

6

Nancy Datan
and Jeanne Thomas

Late Adulthood: Love, Work, and the Normal Transitions

When asked to describe the tasks of the healthy adult, Freud is said to have replied simply: "Love and work." In this chapter we shall explore the developmental transitions of late middle age, when the productive years of work and the reproductive family years are drawing to a close, as parents redefine their relationship to their grown children and workers prepare for a postretirement identity—in short, as love and work take on new meanings.

Our view of developmental transitions in adulthood is bounded in the first place by our disciplinary allegiance to the arena of developmental psychology—thus the reader will find only selected references to psychiatric literature, inclusions guided by a theorist's or researcher's visibility not in the field of psychiatry but in developmental psychology. While this is a natural limitation imposed by the finitude of any individual chapter and the limitations of its authors, it prompts a comment. It is a paradox in the sociology of knowledge and science that the frontiers of developmental psychology have often been advanced by the study of the nonnormative, beginning with Freud's suggestion that the disturbed individual offers us a highlighted picture of the normal conflicts of personality development, a truth that still holds today, when individual case histories become reflection, speculation, and finally theory and the broad-scale exploration which allows a phenomenon to be termed developmental.

A second bound on our approach is the selective view of biology, which is second nature to students of adult development and aging. While the developmental theorists of the life cycle search for regularities in adulthood comparable to the maturationally timed sequence of events seen in early development, the role of biology in adulthood is seen as ancillary by most: menopause and death are considered the only universal maturational events of a later life, and even the predictable biological decline in later adulthood shows such individual variation that developmental theory looks to the social context for predictable determinants of change.

We proceed from the premise that the normal developments of later life can be defined by two interrelated criteria: first, those that are typical of this period of the life span, and second, those with adaptive outcomes. While these criteria are often viewed separately, and it is certainly true that that which is statistically normative is not inevitably normal, the model of normality from which this chapter proceeds is that of an individual life course in a stable social context, where that which is typical is also adaptive.

The concept of age-grading emphasizes the developmental aspects of social roles. Neugarten and Datan (1973) describe the age-grade system as a social system shaping the life cycle: "Every society has a system of social expectations regarding age-appropriate behavior, and these expectations are internalized as the individual grows up and grows old, and as he moves from one age stratum to the next" (p. 59). Over the life course, the individual assumes a succession of socially defined age roles, encompassing a particular set of expectations concerning values and behaviors. Normative or typical occurrences of mid-adulthood are predicted by the age-grading system of a culture. Since these typical events are experienced as part of the social consensus concerning age-appropriate behavior, optimal adaptation is learned, in part, through anticipatory socialization, which in turn minimizes the stress of these developmental events. Thus the predictable and the adaptive are complementary facets of the normal transitions of later life.

The relationship between the typical and the optimal is suggested by Neugarten's (1970) claim that adults develop expectations of the usual times of occurrence for the life change of adulthood. When these shifts occur "on-time," they are generally not traumatic, since they can be anticipated and the adaptive response, perhaps, rehearsed. Lowenthal, Thurnher, and Chiriboga (1976) also indicate that important developmental events in adulthood are usually most stressful when they occur at unexpected times; changes conforming to internalized timetables tend to be mastered with greater ease.

Among the transitions that may be predictable and enhancing in later adulthood are changes in values and self-concept, adjustment to the empty-nest life-style, and preparation for retirement. These changes mirror three dimensions of the life course. The personality changes to be considered are intrapersonal occurrences, while adjustment to the post-parental stage marks a stage of the family life cycle, and preparation for retirement is an important process of occupational development.

A historical perspective will remind the reader of the limitations of this approach. While the notion of normal development as a set of predictable and adaptive changes may be of general applicability, the particular transitions considered in this chapter reflect a particular sociohistorical context. The influence of cultural and historical factors in shaping the course of development has been emphasized by Riegel (1977), who describes the interactions among four planes—the inner-biological, the individual-psychological, the cultural-sociological, and the outer-physical—as determinants of maturational events, and by Neugarten and Datan (1973), who have argued the importance of simultaneous consideration of life-time, social time, and historical time in the study of the life cycle.

The transitions to the empty nest and to retirement, here discussed as characteristic of normal transitions of adult growth, reflect this sociohistorical specificity. For example, the empty-nest phase has emerged only recently as a stage of the family life cycle. According to Hareven (1978), post-parental marriages were virtually nonexistent prior to the twentieth century. Later age at marriage, larger families, and lower life expectancy meant that most parents of earlier generations did not outlive the child-rearing period.

Preparation for retirement presents a similar example: voluntary termination of one's work role has been an option only for recent cohorts of workers. Donahue, Orbach, and Pollack (1960) point out that in earlier historical periods "the older person continued as a member of society in accordance with some function he was still able to perform or was allowed to perform . . . the aged person possessed no legally institutionalized *right* to continued support as a person *per se* unless he continued to perform some socially defined required function" (pp. 336–37). These authors identify several social and historical trends—including the development of an industrial technology, the changes in demographic structure, and the emergence of the nation-state—that have contributed to the institutionalization of retirement.

To sum up, the events by which we define normality in later adulthood in this chapter reflect the present social context. In other cultures and in other eras, other age-related changes may be typical and adaptive during this portion of the life span (Datan, Antonovsky, and Maoz 1981).

The Intrapersonal Dimension: Enlarging Visions and the Development of Generativity

A key concept in Erikson's psychosocial theory of the life cycle is the epigenetic principle, which is a paradigm of the growth process. His explanation of this principle is that "anything that grows has a ground plan, and that out of this ground plan the parts arise, each part having its time of special ascendency, until all parts have arisen to form a functioning whole" (1968, p. 93). The character of these stages is influenced by the interaction of somatic, ego, and societal processes, as well as by the outcome of earlier crises.

In the middle years of adulthood, the developmental crisis is that between generativity and stagnation. Erikson (1963) describes the central characterisitc of a favorable resolution of this issue as an active concern for the welfare of succeeding generations.

> Generativity, then, is primarily the concern in establishing and guiding the next generation, although there are individuals who, through misfortune or because of special or genuine gifts in other directions, do not apply this drive to their own offspring. And indeed, the concept of generativity is meant to include such more popular synonyms as *productivity* and *creativity*, which, however, cannot replace it. (P. 267)

Basic strengths reflected in the development of generativity are senses of productivity and of care. Successful resolution of this stage is facilitated by *all* social institutions, as all include provisions for the transmission of knowledge, skills, and roles from one generation to the next.

Havighurst (1972) suggests that among the developmental tasks of middle age is that of acquiring a sense of social and civic responsibility, a task he views as related to Erikson's construct of generativity. The scope of Havighurst's construct is more broadly social, however; this developmental task requires primary attention to opportunities for community service rather than to the welfare of offspring. According to Havighurst, the middle-aged are natural community leaders, rich in experience, influence, and energy. Frenkel-Brunswick (1968) feels that there is a shift in motivational emphasis in midlife, as primary concern moves from personal goals to more general idealistic objectives. Similarly, Kuhlen (1968) proposes that middle-aged men and women become increasingly occupied with service and affiliative needs rather than achievement needs; alternatively, desires for achievement may be gratified more through vicarious, rather than personal, accomplishments. Finally, Neugarten (1968) notes the emergence of a concern with the creation of social and biological heirs during middle age. Peck (1968) also asserts that ego transcendence—the desire to make an enduring contribution to offspring and community—is among the salient indices of growth in the middle and later years.

Levinson and associates (1978) have proposed that it is important for the middle-aged man to integrate tendencies toward authority and mutuality in interactions with younger adults. The goal, for the individual, is both to foster the development of offspring and younger colleagues and to offer them leadership and guidance. Although Levinson and coworkers describe maturational processes of men only, other aspects of individual differences are discussed. These authors indicate variations in patterns of midlife development, with particular attention to differences among occupational and social class groups.

Levinson and associates' work raises a second issue; according to these researchers, another goal of midlife development is the synthesis of masculine and feminine personality components. This observation is not an original one: earlier work has suggested that, in later periods of adult life, both men and women become more tolerant of cross-sex characteristics (Gutmann 1976; Neugarten and Gutmann 1964). For both sexes, this process may facilitate the development of generativity. Women, in becoming more assertive and instrumental as they age, may show greater interest and skill in making enduring contributions to their communities. Similarly, as men mature in directions of greater expressivity and affiliation, they may find satisfaction in enhancing the growth of children and occupational successors.

In sum, many theorists describe normal development in midlife in terms consistent with the idea of generativity. At this point, it is necessary to examine relevant data to determine the extent of empirical support for the description of generativity as an adaptive occurrence typical of middle age.

Neugarten (1968) interviewed one hundred middle-aged men and women concerning the central aspects of mid-adulthood. Her sample included university alumni, professional persons, and individuals selected from *American Men of Science* and *Who's Who in America*. These respondents agreed on several salient features of this stage, including a new sense of the finitude of their own lives and an awareness of their psychic distinction from both older and younger adults. Both of these realizations were related to a strong sense of responsibility for the younger generation and to the desire to create "social as well as biological heirs" (p. 95).

Levinson and coworkers made a similar attempt to characterize phases of adult life. The forty subjects in their study were all men between the ages of thirty-five and forty-five; respondents varied in their occupational, educational, and socioeconomic status backgrounds. As in Neugarten's (1968) study, these men were interviewed in order to obtain a detailed view of their perceptions of their past and present life styles and of important points of changes in their lives. Again, a prevailing theme was the emergence during midlife of a sense of personal mortality; coupled with a desire to make a lasting social contribution, this new sense of finitude prompted many men to act as mentors for younger adults. The authors describe the role of a mentor as one with parallels to the parental role, but one of greater complexity. According to Levinson and associates (1978), "a good mentor is an admixture of good father and good friend" (p. 333); in this case, the mentor serves as a model for younger persons as well as providing them with sponsorship and practical assistance.

Both Neugarten and Levinson and coworkers, then, found evidence congruent with the notion of generativity. Furthermore, there were similarities between the responses of two middle-aged cohorts in studies separated by a decade.

Haan and Day (1974) conducted a longitudinal study of personality change in adulthood. Their 136 subjects, participants in the Oakland Growth Study, or the Guidance Study, varied in intelligence, educational background, socioeconomic status, political attitudes, and marital status. Q-sort descriptive items were used to specify changes in character occurring between early adolescence (approximately age twelve) and later adulthood (approximately age fifty-one). Across this age range there was greater evidence of stability than of change in personality; some trends in the data, however, were consistent with the development of generativity in midlife. Haan and Day reported that, as subjects matured, they showed greater evidence of philosophical concerns and of social accountability and commitment, of productivity and dependability, and of being turned to for advice. Further, these changes were concurrent with decreases in maladaptation and defensiveness.

In an attempt to distinguish phases of adulthood, Gould (1972, 1978) examined data from cross-sectional samples of psychiatric outpatients and of white, middle-class nonpatients. Outpatients over the age of fifty expressed positive attitudes toward their families. In the nonpatient group, respondents in their forties revealed feelings of general stability and of marital satisfaction and of a strong interest in their children, friends, and social bonds outside the family. The responses of both groups are consistent with the development of generativity. Both groups indicated an increase in positive attitudes toward their children, although this difference appeared later for the outpatient subjects. These respondents, in addition, went through a process of life review.

Lowenthal and her associates (1976) conducted a major study of intra- and interpersonal transitions of adulthood. Consistent with the hypothesis of generativity, both middle-aged (mean age fifty) and preretirement (mean age sixty) men indicated greater concern with warm interpersonal relationships than did younger men. More important, the older men stressed the satisfactions of relationships with younger colleagues and of observing the growth and learning of younger occupational trainees. Middle-age women emphasized social service values, although many were unable to fulfill these goals due to their responsibilities as homemakers. Both men and women in the preretirement group endorsed humanitarian goals and purposes more frequently than did the younger adults; there were, however, sex differences in the means used to fulfill these aims. While both sexes appeared to transcend personal- and family-oriented goals, the older women were more often involved in religious pursuits than were younger women. The older men, in contrast, placed more stress on the creation of a social legacy than did women of any age group or younger men.

In sum, it appears that later adulthood is marked by broadened horizons, variously described as generativity, community responsibility, ego transcendence—concepts that converge around a single theme, an enlarged personal vision no longer focused upon the self and its achievements but upon the species and its well-being (Datan, in preparation). The developmental tasks of the early part of the life cycle, from which emerge the autonomous individual, are succeeded by the developmental tasks of later life, the tasks of the responsible individual (Datan 1980). As we shall see, the personality changes of later adulthood find their counterparts in the family and career life cycles.

Growing Pains: The Empty Nest and Other Family Transitions

The family is, historically and cross-culturally, a universal context of human development. In all cultures and in all eras, individuals are family members—inevitably members of a family of orientation and often members of a family of procreation. It is often true as well that one's family affiliation is a central factor in both self-definition and in social status and role ascription. Finally, consideration of family transitions is important because familial bonds are emotionally as well as socially significant.

The departure of young-adult offspring from the home has often been considered a normal event of middle age. This change is clearly a normative one: most adults are parents, and, as they reach middle age, their children, in turn, take on independent adult roles. Datan (1980) notes that children's departure from their parents home, viewed as an adaptive event, is an ancient cultural theme:

> Regret over departing children is not a theme in our folk inheritance. Indeed, quite the opposite is true: Children of all ages are turned out of the home. They are too hungry, too beautiful, too dangerous; if they threaten parental resources, they are sent away or killed . . . like the mid-life crisis of achievement, the empty nest of middle life is not a phenomenon of modernity but a theme echoing through Western culture for centuries. (P. 17)

This phase of family life has been viewed in several ways. Donahue, Orbach, and Pollack (1960) propose that the empty-nest period is analogous to the retirement process: women may "retire" from an occupational role early in adulthood, in order to assume full-time child rearing responsibilities; in mid-adulthood, with the diminishing of parental concerns, a second retirement occurs. Until the current generation of involved fathers sees their children leave home, it may be an overstatement to suggest that both parents retire from childrearing.

The departure of grown children redefines the parents' age: for example, Neugarten (1968) notes that women often define their age status with respect to family life-cycle transitions: even single women, in fact, think of the families that they may have had in assigning themselves to an age group. Likewise, Atchley (1976a) found that age norms may be ascribed on the basis of the age status of an individual's intimate associates, citing the example of parent's being defined as middle-aged upon their children's entry into young adulthood.

It may be useful to consider the empty-nest transition in terms of the ebb and flow in the composition of the family (McCollough 1980), giving attention to changes in the relationship of several generations. This perspective encompasses not only decremental family changes, as maturing children leave their parents' home and as aging grandparents die, but also incremental changes occurring upon young adult offspring's marriage and procreation.

Using this model, McCollough identifies issues that may confront middle-aged adults; as we shall see, these parallel Havighurst's (1972) description of developmental tasks of midlife. McCollough points out as a primary concern the transformation of the parental relationship, as children become more independent young adults. This transformation affects the parents' self-concepts, life styles, and even the marital relationship. Finally, the rapport between middle-aged men and women and their own parents is also likely to change, as the older generation encounters age-related decline in physical, financial, and/or social resources.

The relative salience of these issues may shift over the course of the post-childrearing periods. At the outset, the middle-aged parents may be most concerned with adjustment to children's increased autonomy, later with alterations in the marriage, and later still with adapting to the growing dependencies of their own aged parents (McCollough 1980; Troll, Miller, and Atchley 1979).

Researchers do not agree on the emotional quality of the postparental phase, which has also been described in various ways. Some feel that this transition is a necessarily difficult and critical one (Deutsch 1973), while others assert that these changes are welcomed, yielding freedom and autonomy (McCollough 1980). Neither position contradicts our view of the empty-nest transition as both normative and adaptive: although the phase may raise problematic issues, these issues may be favorably resolved. In an early investigation, Deutscher (1968) interviewed thirty-one middle-aged men and women in the postparental stage; most respondents had favorable views of this period of life. Many subjects emphasized their sense of increased freedom. The few subjects who held negative views of this period of adjustment associated their reaction with either the menopause or with their feeling that they had been unsuccessful in childrearing. Deutscher noted that women tended to have more extreme reactions to this phase, and he attributed this difference either to the greater saliency of family concerns for women or to the stronger social sanctions of emotional expressibility for men.

Lowenthal and Chiriboga (1972) examined sex differences in perception of the empty-nest period as compared to other major life transitions. These researchers were particularly interested in sex differences in perceptions within their sample of lower middle-class respondents. Overall, most viewed the coming changes favorably, and they expected that the satisfactions of parenting would continue after their youngest child left home. In fact, few considered this change to represent a major transformation of their lives. The women were, however, somewhat more negative in their evaluations than were the men; furthermore, men considered the adolescent years and the empty-nest period to be the most satisfying phases of the life cycle, while women tended to look back with nostalgia on the early years of marriage and parenthood.

Lowenthal, Thurnher, and Chiriboga (1976) investigated adjustment to postparental life and found similar sex differences. Women viewed the event as a major one, while men considered their approaching retirement more important. For some respondents the post parental stage was one of the best periods of their lives, due to decreased responsibilities and financial burdens and to increased potential for self-fulfillment. Others, however, evidenced less hope for the future than did subjects of any other age group: these middle-aged participants had apparently failed to formulate goals to succeed those of the childrearing years.

Some attention has also been given to changes in the relationship between middle-aged parents and their children at this time. Axelson (1960), on the basis of questionnaires administered to the parents of marriage license applicants, concluded that these changes were positive: both men and women in the postparental stage reported that they were less concerned with their children's welfare compared with parents whose children had not yet left home.

The men in Levinson and associates' (1978) study generally looked forward to the empty-nest period in the father-child relationship. For these men, this relationship became more flexible and more satisfying as new means of interaction—such as teaching, supporting, working, and playing—were incorporated. Some, however, reported feelings of envy and resentment at their children's new-found independence and potential, which coincided with a growing awareness of the finitude of their own lives; and others indicated an excessive, maladaptive concern with their children's success and welfare.

As we have seen, evidence is relatively sparse concerning the specific impact of the empty-next stage specifically upon parent-child relationships. Instead the individualistic bias that characterizes psychology (Sarason 1981) has led to research on the young adult's struggle for autonomy (cf. Gould 1978) or the impact of the empty-nest period upon the psychological well-being, the self-concept, and the goals of the middle-aged individual. In an attempt to define salient features and problems of this adjustment process, Spence and Lonner (1971) interviewed white, middle-class, urban women whose youngest child was graduating from high school. Among their findings was evidence that this transition prompted important changes in life styles and goals: it was necessary for these women to find new sources of involvement as an intensive concern with children's activities became less appropriate. The researchers noted that many of their participants were inadequately prepared for this change and that clinical intervention may be necessary in such cases. These respondents also indicated that this was a period of self-evaluation, and that their perceptions of their children's success in attaining adult status at an expected time was a central factor in the outcome of their self-assessment.

Lowenthal and Chiriboga (1972) found most of their respondents were hopeful and of high morale as they anticipated the departure of their children. As indicated earlier, these researchers were particularly interested in sex differences, and they indicated that the women in their sample were more extreme—both positively and negatively—in their evidences of morale and of hope.

Neugarten (1970) compared responses of middle- and working-class women whose families were intact, who were presently engaged in the adjustment to children's departure or whose children had left home. She used interview responses and objective and projective measures of anxiety, life satisfaction, and self-concept to examine the impact of the empty nest upon life satisfaction. Overall, she found that this period was not particularly stressful; in fact, the women whose children were no longer at home had higher ratings of life satisfaction than did the women in the two other groups.

In 1975 Glenn pooled data from six national surveys conducted between 1963 and 1973 assessing psychological well-being. Respondents of these surveys ranged in age from thirty-five to sixty-four and were categorized as parental couples (those whose children were still living at home) or postparental couples (those whose children had established their own households). Findings consistently indicated that the women in the postparental couples reported greater personal happiness than did the women in the parental couples; this difference was more marked for younger respondents. The pattern was less clear for men: differences in personal happiness between parental and postparental men were small in all surveys, and results indicated both increases and decreases in happiness. Glenn concluded that men's responses were less predictable than women's and that the transition to the empty nest was more often, though not inevitably, somewhat troublesome for fathers.

Lowenthal, Thurnher, and Chiriboga (1976) reported that middle-aged men and women went through a process of life review that seemed to be prompted by their children's growing autonomy. For women, this review was more exclusively tied to family concerns than for men, who also evaluated their occupational attainments. These men and women recognized the need for major reorientations of goals and means of goal achievement. The middle-aged women, especially, placed greater emphasis than did other age groups on attaining personal ease and contentment and, in anticipation of necessary changes, were often critical of their current characteristics. For many respondents these realizations were problematic: depression was not uncommon among these women and was often related to this restructuring process, as well as to unmet needs for husbands' support.

Finally, Harkins, (1978) examined psychological well-being in relation to this transition among a sample of white, upper middle-class women. This study was unique in comparing women who were and who were not launching children according to both an objective criterion (graduation of the youngest child from high school) as well as self-definitions of status regarding this period. On the basis of objective measures of psychological well-being, Harkins reported that empty-nest women did not differ from women whose children were still at home, but he noted that women *describing* themselves in the empty-nest period showed greater psychological well-being than did self-defined pre–empty-nest women.

The most useful predictor of a problematic transition was whether or not the timing of this event conformed to the individual's expectations, a result supporting the views of Neugarten and other investigators (Neugarten 1970; Neugarten and Datan 1973; Neugarten, Moore, and Lowe 1968). This may clarify the discrepancy between the results based on objective and subjective definitions of the empty-nest transition: women objectively defined as post–empty nest may have included those who did not feel that they had completed the transition. If these women considered themselves "off-time" for this event, the average well-being score for objectively defined post–empty-nest women might be accordingly lowered and, for this reason, might not differ from objectively defined pre–empty-nest women. Harkin's conclusion was that, in general, the effects of this adjustment were slight and that, unless the process occurred at an unexpected time, stress was likely to be minimal.

Discussion of the empty-nest transition would be incomplete without a brief indication of concurrent family adjustments. According to Havighurst (1972), a developmental task of middle age is the reestablishment of a relationship with the spouse as an individual. As children leave the home, parents must again learn to live together as a couple. Troll, Miller, and Atchley (1979) have outlined several possible outcomes of this process. The marriage may improve or, if both spouses strive to maintain intimate ties with children, the relationship may not change. In other instances, marital partners may begin to nurture one another instead of their children, or the relationship may dissolve.

Clinicians have identified specific problems of this process and noted treatment implications. Gutmann (1976; Gutmann, Grunes, and Griffin, 1980), for example, feels that the parental role imposes sex-stereotyped demands on both men and women; as this role ends, both are freed to engage in a wider range of behaviors. He also points out that clinical assistance may be necessary in adjustment to a spouse's increased androgyny as well as to one's own personality and behavioral changes (Gutmann 1980). Gould (1980) also emphasizes sex-role issues of midlife marriages: due to the sex-role expectations in traditional marriages, he feels that many middle-aged married women are trapped in unpromising situations. As children leave home, the traditional feminine role is eroded and many women lack the skills to take on new roles. Gould feels that it is important for therapists to acknowledge and deal with these sex-role issues. Finally, McCollough (1980) indicates that a central goal for marriage and for marital therapy is the achievement of intimacy between spouses as well as autonomy for both partners.

Despite clinicians' misgivings, research suggests that children's departure is more likely to enhance their parents' marriage than to threaten it. In interviews with middle-class, urban postparental couples, Deutscher (1969) found that most reported either no change or an increase in marital satisfaction following their children's departure from home. Further, of those couples reporting enhanced marital satisfaction, over half attributed the improvement to their children's absence, stating that there were fewer sources of conflict and more opportunities for direct interaction with the spouse. Lowenthal and Chiriboga (1972) found that men tended to have more favorable views both of their wives and of their marriages than did women; both, however, often indicated that they expected their relationship to be less conflicted when childrearing was no longer a source of concern. Axelson (1960) indicated that postparental couples reported greater satisfaction with their marriages and with the extent of their activity with their spouse than did pre-postparental couples. Similarly, Glenn (1975) found that national survey data indicated greater marital happiness for postparental individuals than for parents. And Lowenthal, Thurnher, and Chiriboga (1976) noted that their middle-aged respondents anticipated favorable changes in their marriages when their children left home; preretirement subjects confirmed an enhanced relationship with their spouses following their children's departure.

Relationships between middle-aged adults and their aging parents are more likely to be problematic than are marital relationships. Havighurst (1972) considers adjustment to increasing dependencies of aging parents to be one of the developmental tasks of midlife. The common research finding that both generations value mutual independence as well as close contact in their relationship (Troll, Miller, and Atchley, 1979) suggests that fulfilling this task may prove stressful. Clinicians have described potential problems in this process, such as difficulties in coping with bereavement and/or disabilities of the aged parent (McCollough 1980; Notman 1980; Zarit 1980). Zarit (1980) notes, further, that middle-aged children may encounter resistance from their parents if they attempt to assume responsibility for their parents' care. Parents may perceive their children's efforts as overprotectiveness, or they may view failure to provide such assistance as indicative of lack of concern. Either course of action may arouse resentment in elderly parents.

Research supports clinicians' warnings of strain in these inter-generational relationships. According to Lowenthal, Thurnher, and Chiriboga (1976), women in the two older groups of their study were troubled by increasing needs to assist their parents. Similar results appeared in another investigation of adult parent-child relationships (Robinson and Thurnher 1979), where parents' health status was identified as a key factor determining the affective quality of the relationship. Nearly half of their middle-aged subjects reported that the necessity to assume caregiving functions for their parents was stressful and confining at this point in their own lives: these respondents had anticipated greater freedom and opportunity for self-gratification as their parental responsibilities lessened. They were also keenly aware that the years that could be devoted to personal enjoyment were limited.

Some researchers suggest productive approaches to ameliorating these problems. Zarit (1980) emphasizes counseling middle-aged adults to limit the extent of assistance provided to parents and to meet parents' additional demands in a constructive and adaptive fashion. He also notes that group therapy may be a viable means of achieving these goals, and some data support this suggestion (Hausman 1979). In addition, Robinson and Thurnher (1979) indicate that it may be helpful to provide middle-aged adults with information on community support services for their parents. In a study of institutionalized aged persons and their children, Smith and Bengtson (1979) found that institutionalization, in relieving stress related to the elderly persons' needs for support, had enhanced family solidarity. These studies support a poignant folk saying: one mother can support ten sons, but ten sons cannot support one mother.

In sum, extended longevity has brought with it new transitions in the family life cycle. Parents outlive the childrearing period by several decades; at the same time, their own aging parents live to face possible dependency on their middle-aged children. With the "graying" of the American population, this trend is likely to become the norm and middle age is likely to become a period where one set of responsibilities is exchanged for another. Such a transformation in the family life cycle is likely to pose a challenge to cultural values of autonomy and independence—and perhaps lead eventually to a reemergence of the multigenerational extended family.

The Long Weekend: Transition to Retirement

Like the postparental period, retirement from work has evolved only recently as a phase of the occupational life cycle; however, this change is likely to be a primary one for the individual. Henry (1971) describes the pervasive influence of work upon the worker, arguing that work acts as a major agent of socialization: occupational training involves not only the development of a particular set of skills but also the indoctrination of values and attitudes and the provision of a context both for stability and for growth in these dimensions.

Given the central role of work in the social development of the individual, the termination of one's occupational role is a major transition in adult life. Because of the significance of this change, preparation for retirement—whether conscious or not—is an important process of midadulthood, and a number of writers have considered this preparatory process.

Although retirement is of personal relevance to all adults—even nonworking spouses are affected by a working spouse's retirement—the process does not have a single definition. Donohue, Orbach, and Pollack (1960) endorse a definition based on role theory, proposing that retirement be viewed as the shift from economic activity to economic inactivity, in accordance with social norms. Atchley (1976b) takes a broader view of retirement, asserting that this transition has phases encompassing much of the life cycle and impacts on noneconomic as well as economic issues. He argues that preparation for retirement should be a life-span process, beginning with enhanced awareness of the eventuality of the event and the consequent need for planning beginning in childhood and adolescence, even before the assumption of a work role. Later preparation should be more systematic and focused on specific concerns, such as financial and/or health issues.

Like Atchley, Fillenbaum (1971) endorses a long-term perspective of the retirement process, emphasizing the impact of early life events on this process:

> Retirement should not be viewed as an entirely separate stage of life, unconnected with what went before—it is not. Income in later years may be much

affected by pre-retirement income and specific job; health in old age may be related to health care when younger. Improvements made to life at an earlier age may well have a greater effect, and for a longer period of time, than advice given shortly before retirement. We need to view retirement as part of the *continuum* of life, and if we offer pre-retirement programs to younger persons, it is essential that retirement should be seen in this way. (P. 36)

Financial adjustment to retirement and provisions for this adaptation are of major concern. In fact, Atchley (1976*b*) notes that problems in adjusting to retirement are more often related to economic difficulties than to any other single factor, and he emphasizes the need for financial planning. Lowenthal, Thurnher, and Chiriboga (1976) found that concern over the adequacy of retirement income was an issue among respondents who were nearing this transition and that a number were planning retirement budgets. Other researchers have noted, however, that many workers, while aware of the importance of financial planning and eager to make such preparations, lack the necessary information and skills (Kasschau 1974; Morrison 1975). Formal preretirement programs often deal primarily with economic concerns, and although such an exclusive focus may not be appropriate, program participants are likely to welcome this assistance.

The retiring individual's relationships with family members are also likely to be affected, and the effects parallel the affect of the departure of children. Both positive and negative impacts of retirement upon marital satisfaction have been noted. Some workers desire nurturance as retirement approaches, and their spouses may serve as sources of emotional support (Donahue, Orbach, and Pollack, 1960; Lowenthal, Thurnher, and Chiriboga 1976). On the other hand, some couples anticipate increased conflict after retirement, as more time is spent together and, in some cases, spouses' interests have diverged (Lowenthal, Thurnher, and Chiriboga 1976).

Similarly, parent-child relationships may either benefit or suffer from the parents' retirement. Donahue, Orbach, and Pollack (1960) note that these relationships may be threatened if children fear increased dependency in their parents upon retirement. Atchley (1976*b*) points out that parents who had adjusted to the empty-nest transition through occupational involvement must confront this issue all over again upon retirement. On the other hand, Troll, Miller, and Atchley (1979) assert that, when health and finances are adequate, retired persons may enjoy increased contact and shared leisure pursuits with their children.

Havighurst (1972) notes that the cultivation of sources of adult leisure activities is a developmental task for middle age. Clearly, the shift from a work-oriented to a leisure-oriented life style is a central reorientation of this transition. Some authors have noted, however, that little preparation is typically made for this change. Donahue, Orbach, and Pollack (1960), on the basis of an early review of the retirement literature, conclude that few workers develop leisure skills prior to retirement. Miller (1968) argues that the adoption of a life style centered about leisure contradicts the dominant cultural values of productivity, goal direction, and industry. Atchley (1976b), however, suggests that some types of occupations—those demanding constant and effective use of interpersonal skills, for example—may actually serve as preparation for this aspect of the retirement transition.

It is apparent, then, that retirement is not a unidimensional change but one necessitating a variety of responses. Correspondingly, preparation for this period of adaptation must also be multifaceted. Atchley (1976b) has outlined several types of preadaptation for retirement, including conscious informal and conscious formal preparation. To date, research has concentrated upon formal planning—evaluation studies of preretirement counseling programs are typical. Most researchers agree, however, that these programs affect only a minority of workers. Informal preparation, though receiving less attention from investigators, is of broader impact.

Informal preparation may occur in several ways. A useful taxonomy categorizes these processes as intrapersonal, narrow-scope interpersonal, and broader scope interpersonal types of indoctrination. Intrapersonal preparatory adaptation includes changes in self-concept and values that ease the transition to retirement. Lowenthal, Thurnher, and Chiriboga's (1976) finding that respondents approaching retirement showed a relatively strong endorsement of values of personal ease and contentment suggests such a process. In addition, these investigators noted that respondents in their two older groups were engaged in a process of life review; however, men in this sample were more concerned than were the working women with evaluating their occupational attainments. Introspection and value changes such as these may be intrapersonal means of anticipatory adjustment.

Narrow-scope interpersonal preadaptation measures describe the acquisition of information about retirement other than through enrollment in a preretirement counseling program. Monk (1971), in an examination of the anticipation of retirement among administrative and professional men, interviewed employees between the ages of fifty and fifty-nine. These respondents—who were not likely to retire for ten to fifteen years—were keenly aware of the approaching event, and many had begun a search for information. They varied with respect to the degree of systematic search and even more with respect to information sources: colleagues, personnel workers, and private investment counselors were all cited as resource persons. However, the most frequently reported context of planning and discussion was within the family, and wives were often identified as primary partners in this type of preparation. These men found that reading on the subject of retirement was of little benefit.

Broader scope interpersonal means of informal retirement preparation occur through anticipatory socialization. However, according to Donahue, Orbach, and Pollack (1960), the lack of available role gradations for older workers renders this type of preparation unfeasible in most cases. Riley and associates (1969) assert that the retirement role lacks an adequate cultural definition and set of sanctions to structure such a socialization process. However, these authors also note that retirement is usually an expected transition and that sources of anticipatory socialization—such as increases in performance expectations and in competition from younger workers, and decreases in opportunities for advancement and for retraining—do exist.

Atchley (1976b) concurs: he specifies culturally defined privileges and obligations of the retiree—including, for example, the right to determine one's use of time and the expectation that general continuity of behavior will be maintained. He also identifies social symbols of approaching retirement, including the entry into a preretirement counseling program, the training of one's occupational successor, and retirement ceremonies. However, he considers these formalities inadequate rites of passage, since they typically emphasize separation from the occupational role but fail to give any ceremonial attention to the retiree's new opportunities and responsibilities. Rosow (1974) would concur, for he argues that the socialization to old age is socialization to a state of normlessness. If role-initiation aspects of retirement were incorporated into these rituals, Atchley feels, the events would be more positive and instructive ones.

More recently, informal preparation for retirement has been supplemented by more formal preretirement counseling programs. Charles (1971) noted that the earliest of these programs were offered in university settings soon after World War II; later these courses were offered through government and community agencies and through large business and industrial organizations. Recently interest in and implementation of such curricula have expanded. Kelleher and Quirk (1974) document these increases and also note the growing body of popular literature on this topic. However, it should be emphasized—as Atchley (1976b) does—that despite this surge of effort and of interest, relatively few workers are exposed to any formal preparation. Atchley (1976b) describes most programs as suited to the interests, needs, and skills of middle-status workers.

Formats of retirement preparation programs are varied. Courses centered about lecture/discussion sessions or individual counseling sessions with personnel workers are common (Kelleher and Quirk 1974), as are programs conforming to a group interaction model (Manion 1971). In some cases retired men and women have been incorporated into programs as resource persons (Donahue, Orbach, and Pollack 1960; Manion 1971). Evaluation indicates that these programs have favorable effects on workers' attitudes toward retirement, their planning for retirement, or both (Atchley 1976b Donahue, Orbach, and Pollack 1960; Kasschau 1974). Charles (1971), for example, studied the impact of a lecture-discussion series covering a variety of retirement issues and found generally positive effects upon workers' concerns, community involvement, and attitudes toward themselves and retirement.

Formal preretirement counseling programs affect relatively few workers, however; and demographic variables seem to govern participation. Atchley (1976b) found that most programs were planned for middle-income, literate employees of large corporations. In a survey of Duke University employees, Fillenbaum (1971) identified characteristics differentiating workers who desired these programs from those who did not. Employees of all ages in lower status occupations indicated that they would be likely to attend such a course; of the middle-status employees, it was primarily those over the age of forty-five who were interested in preretirement education programs; upper-status employees of all ages reported that they were not interested in this type of preparation.

Demographic variables also affect informal retirement planning. Although all of the respondents of Fillenbaum's survey endorsed retirement planning in principle, few had actually made plans; those workers who had were more highly educated and of higher occupational status than those who had not. Similarly, Kasschau (1974) reports that upper-status workers are most likely to engage in retirement planning, although their plans may be inadequate and unrealistic. Interestingly, middle-status workers, according to Kasschau, worry more about retirement than any other occupational group but are less likely to plan for the transition than are upper-status employees. Finally, in Lowenthal, Thurnher, and Chiriboga's (1976) cross-sectional study, workers in the preretirement group described as the most intellectual had made the most extensive retirement plans.

In a series of interviews with men employed by either an industrial corporation or by a public human services agency, Monk (1971) identified several rationalizations for avoiding retirement planning. One commonly cited reason was that financial preparations were futile, due to uncertain economic conditions. Other workers asserted that plans for changes in their life style were unnecessary, since they expected to remain active and involved in their professions after retirement. Still other men did not expect to live to retirement age; obviously such expectations eliminated any motivation for retirement planning. Monk interpreted these responses as indicative of denial and avoidance of the transition and related these defenses to "the lack of gratification and role incentives envisaged in the retirement stage" (p. 351).

The individual's transition to retirement, a legal status created by public policy, in turn requires a supportive public policy. Atchley (1976*b*) outlines several goals for policymakers: he feels that the expansion of community-based programs is essential in order to reach workers not offered such courses by their employers. He also notes that retirement preparation should be lifelong and thus could be incorporated into secondary, and even elementary, educational programs. If the suggestion of retirement planning as part of an elementary school curriculum seems somewhat startling upon first consideration, it is justified by the consistent finding that planning for retirement is the exception rather than the rule. But this merely broadens the question rather than answering it. In light of the fact that retirement is an expectable, legally mandated, age-graded transition, how is it possible to account for the relative infrequency of preretirement planning? This question is underscored by contrast with an age-graded transition occurring at the beginning of young adulthood, the complex of legal and political rights acquired at eighteen, for which the youth has been prepared through courses in American government, driver's education, and perhaps even on marriage and the family. While the transitions are by no means parallel—the education of youth is a cross-cultural universal, mandated by the long childhood and behavioral plasticity of humankind, while the transition to a postproductive period in the life cycle is a relatively recent phenomenon—we propose that historical considerations will account for only the lack of social institutions to ease the transition to retirement. In order to understand the reluctance of individuals to plan for a universal transition, we must turn to a speculative overview of the intrapsychic transitions of the life cycle.

The Intrapsychic Journey: Some Life-Cycle Speculations

In the brief theoretical excursion that follows, we will bring together life-cycle perspectives on the dynamic transformations in personality that occur in the three great relational modes: the erotic, the active, and the narcissistic, as Freud (1961) terms them; or, as Bakan (1966), Gutmann (1980), and others describe them, the communal, the agentic or aggressive, and the narcissistic. Put more simply, we shall describe life-cycle transformations in three dimensions of individual experience: attachments to others, activity, and the sense of self. As is obvious, we are using these concepts more loosely than many do, for the purpose of contrast among interacting processes over the life cycle rather than for precision of description of a single process at a particular stage (see, e.g., Kohut's [1977] treatment of narcissism).

We shall begin by considering each of the three relational modes separately, as it is transformed over the life cycle. Narcissism is first seen in infancy as primary infantile narcissism, reborn at adolescence as the adolescent's sense of omnipotentiality, reinvested in adulthood as one's child becomes the narcissistic extension of the self, and it finally reappears in old age in subdued form as the preoccupations of the life review. Active engagement with the world begins modestly with the dependent infant who can cry, suckle, and smile. Gradually the dependent infant is transformed by nurturant care into the autonomous adult who, in turn, assumes responsibility for others and finally, with advancing age and physical decline, once more becomes dependent. Erotic ties begin with the infantile, pregenital passions of the Oedipus complex, mature into the mutual genital love of adulthood and the ties of the parent to the child, and with old age undergo a regression to diffuse pregenital sensuality, together with the near-universal sexual deprivation consequent upon the death of a spouse.

Now let us turn this analysis around and consider the interaction of the three relational modes in each of the phases of the life cycle. In infancy, the self is the pre-Copernican center of the universe. Early in development, however, the primary narcissism characteristic of infants is subdued by the many inevitable failures of even the most nurturant world that teach the infant to recognize dependence on an adult caretaker and usher in the beginnings of the oedipal triangle. Yet at the same time that the developing infant is beginning to trust and depend on the caregiving parents, paradoxically, the first steps toward autonomy are also being taken. In brief, then: early in life primary narcissism is the natural state; slowly this yields to awareness of dependence on others, together with the almost imperceptible beginings of autonomous activity.

At the interface between adolescence and young adulthood, dramatic transformations have occurred in the three relational modes. The narcissism of infancy has become the omnipotentiality of adolescence, soon to be focused in young adulthood on the developmental task of finding a place in the very world that seemed once to revolve about the infant. The primitive object relations of the oedipal period have matured into a capacity for intimacy with a partner. Finally, the rudimentary steps toward autonomy have culminated in an adult now ready to begin the nurture of the next generation. To sum up: in young adulthood, narcissism seems to have given way to nurturance and thus been transformed into a narcissistic reinvestment in one's infant; dependency has been transformed into autonomy and then into responsibility for others; and the primal passions of the Oedipus complex have become the capacity for intimacy and the mutuality of adult genital love.

The transitions of middle age suggest sex-related differences reflecting the narcissistic insults of physical aging. Though Freud declared that love *and* work were the tasks of the healthy adult, an observer of contemporary society would find that somehow the tasks of love and work seem to have been bureaucratized: women love, men work. For women, physical aging threatens the capacity to love and be loved; for men, physical aging is a threat to the capacity to work (cf. Notman 1980), and the vast marketplace of American advertising—always a useful guide to the psychic underworld—exploits the sex-specific anxieties of each. Women learn from their mirrors that they won't be twenty-one forever, but that their husbands might be induced to love them a while longer if they choose the right moisturizer; the Angel of Death snatches men in the middle of the coffee break, while divine voices assure them that their prudent selection of insurance will maintain their productivity without interruption.

The narcissistic insults of physical aging highlight the middle-age changes in activity and in object relations. The family life cycle brings children to the omnipotentiality of adolescence just as their parents are confronting the finitude of middle and old age. Thus the narcissism once invested in the young child is threatened by the adolescent; the activity once expressed as responsibility for the children becomes superfluous as the children become responsible for themselves. At the same time, the middle-aged parents may see the mirror of their own eventual physical decline in their own aging parents; and the freedom that might have been anticipated as grown children leave home may increasingly become the exchange of one set of responsibilities for another.

In old age we see a resurgence of narcissism in the preoccupations of the life review. The autonomy of young adulthood and the responsibilities of middle age slowly become the dependency of old age, an unwelcome fall from power imposed by physical, social, and economic limitations. Gutmann (1980) has suggested that the genital eroticism of adulthood ebbs in later life, to become a diffuse pregenital sensuality, shadowed by the prospect of sexual deprivation through widowhood (Lopata 1980).

Taken separately, each of the three relational modes has a predictable life-cycle rhythm. As we have seen, however, in this tentative integrated overview, simultaneous consideration of the three relational modes across each of the phases of the life cycle suggests that there is no necessary synchrony at the intrapsychic level and that conflict, contradiction, and developmental ironies are the rule more often than not in the normal sequence of developmental tasks.

Conclusion: When Love and Work Are Done

We have proposed that normality is best seen as a synthesis of the normative and the adaptive. In so doing we presume a primitive logic to cultural evolution, which—we like to believe—is a process favoring the health of the individual as adaptive for the species (Datan, in preparation). Yet an evolutionary perspective has disquieting implications for the study of late middle age, when the tasks vital to the species—love of the next generation and productive work—are coming to an end. It is not surprising that our review of research on the transitions to the empty nest and to retirement provides no simple answers to the question "What does the normal adult do?" If, as Piaget has argued, behavior precedes cognition, we would like to propose that behavior and cognition precede the development of social institutions and social policies. That which is normal early in the life cycle has been enshrined in institutions ranging from public school to Dr. Spock. That which will come to be normal later in life as long life becomes the norm still awaits facilitative institutions reflecting the developmental tasks and the intrapsychic ironies of later life.

REFERENCES

Atchley, R. C. 1976a. "The Life-course, Age-grading, and Age-linked Demands for Decision Making." In *Life-span Developmental Psychology: Normative Life Crises*, ed. N. Datan and L. Ginsberg, pp. 261–78. New York: Academic Press.

———. 1976b. *The Sociology of Retirement*. Cambridge, Mass.: Schenkman Publishing Co.

Axelson, L. J. 1960. "Personal Adjustments in the Post-parental Period." *Marriage and Family Living* 22:66–70.

Bakan, D. 1966. *The Duality of Human Existence*. Boston: Beacon Press.

Brim, O. G., Jr. 1966. "Socialization through the Life-cycle." In *Socialization after Childhood: Two Essays,* ed. O. G. Brim, Jr., and S. Wheeler, pp. 1–50. New York: John Wiley & Sons.

Charles, D. C. 1971. "Effects of Participation in a Pre-retirement Program." *Gerontologist* 11:24–28.

Datan, N. 1980. "Midas and Other Mid-life Crises." In *Mid-life: Developmental and Clinical Issues,* ed. W. H. Norman and T. J. Scaramella, pp. 3–19. New York: Brunner/Mazel.

———. "Self and Species: Conflict and Transition in the Life Cycle of Women." In *Forbidden Fruits and Sorrow: Essays on Love, Work, and Adult Development,* by N. Datan, chap. 4. In preparation.

Datan, N.; Antonovsky, A.; and Maoz, B. 1981. *A Time to Reap: The Middle Age of Women in Five Israeli Sub-Cultures.* Baltimore: Johns Hopkins University Press.

Deutsch, H. 1973. *The Psychology of Women: A Psychoanalytic Interpretation. Volume 2: Motherhood.* New York: Bantam Books.

Deutscher, I. 1968. "The Quality of Post-parental Life." In *Middle Age and Aging: A Reader in Social Psychology,* ed. B. L. Neugarten, pp. 263–68. Chicago: University of Chicago Press.

———. 1969. "From Parental to Post-parental Life." *Sociological Symposium* 3:47–60.

Donahue, W.; Orbach, H. L.; and Pollack, O. 1960. "Retirement: The Emerging Social Pattern." In *Handbook of Social Gerontology: Societal Aspects of Aging,* ed. C. Tibbitts, pp. 330–406. Chicago: University of Chicago Press.

Erikson, E. H. 1963. *Childhood and Society.* New York: W. W. Norton.

———. 1968. *Identity: Youth and Crisis.* New York: W. W. Norton.

Fillenbaum, G. G. 1971. "Retirement Planning Programs: At What Age, and For Whom?" *Gerontologist* 11:33–36.

———. 1979. "The Longitudinal Retirement History Study: Methodological and Substantive Issues." *Gerontologist* 19:203–9.

Frenkel-Brunswick, E. 1968. "Adjustments and Reorientation in the Course of the Lifespan." In *Middle Age and Aging: A Reader in Social Psychology,* ed. B. L. Neugarten, pp. 77–84. Chicago: University of Chicago Press.

Freud, S. 1961. *Civilization and Its Discontents.* New York: W. W. Norton.

Glenn, N. D. 1975. "Psychological Well-being in the Post-parental Stage: Some Evidence from National Surveys." *Journal of Marriage and the Family* 37:105–10.

Gould, R. E. 1980. "Sexual Problems: Changes and Choices in Mid-life." In *Mid-life: Developmental and Clinical Issues,* ed. W. H. Norman and T. J. Scaramella, pp. 110–27. New York: Brunner/Mazel.

Gould, R. L. 1972. "The Phases of Adult Life: A Study in Developmental Psychology." *American Journal of Psychiatry* 127:521–31.

———. 1978. *Transformations: Growth and Change in Adult Life.* New York: Simon & Schuster.

Gutmann, D. L. 1976. "Parenthood: A Key to the Comparative Study of the Life-cycle." In *Life-span Developmental Psychology: Normative Life Crises,* ed. N. Datan and L. Ginsberg, pp. 167–89. New York: Academic Press.

———. 1980. "The Post-parental Years: Clinical Problems and Developmental Possibilities." In *Mid-life: Developmental and Clinical Issues,* ed. W. H. Norman and T. J. Scaramella, pp. 38–52. New York: Brunner/Mazel.

Gutmann, D.; Grunes, J.; and Griffin, B. 1980. "The Clinical Psychology of Later Life: Developmental Paradigms." In *Transitions of Aging,* ed. N. Datan and N. Lohmann, pp. 119–32. New York: Academic Press.

Haan, N., and Day, D. 1974. "A Longitudinal Study of Change and Sameness in Personality Development: Adolescence to Later Adulthood." *International Journal of Aging and Human Development* 5:11–39.

Harevan, T. K. 1978. "Family Time and Historical Time." In *The Family,* ed. A. S. Rossi, J. Kagan, and T. K. Harevan, pp. 57–70. New York: W. W. Norton.

Harkins, E. B. 1978. "Effects of Empty Nest Transition on Self-report of Psychological and Physical Well-being." *Journal of Marriage and the Family* 40:549–56.

Hausman, C. P. 1979. "Short-term Counseling Groups for People with Elderly Parents." *Gerontologist* 19:102–8.

Havighurst, R. J. 1972. *Developmental Tasks and Education.* New York: David McKay.

Henry, W. E. 1971. "The Role of Work in Structuring the Life-cycle." *Human Development* 14:125–31.

Kasschau, P. L. 1974. "Re-evaluating the Need for Retirement Preparation Programs." *Industrial Gerontology* 1:42–59.

Kelleher, C. H., and Quirk, D. A. 1974. "Preparation for Retirement: An Annotated Bibliography of the Literature, 1965–1974." *Industrial Gerontology* 1:49–73.

Kohut, H. 1977. *The Restoration of the Self*. New York: International Universities Press.

Kuhlen, R. G. 1968. "Developmental Changes in Motivation During the Adult Years." In *Middle Age and Aging: A Reader in Social Psychology*, ed. B. L. Neugarten, pp. 115–36. Chicago: University of Chicago Press.

Levinson, D. J., et al. 1978. *The Seasons of a Man's Life*. New York: Ballantine.

Lopata, H. Z. 1980. "The Widowed Family Member." In *Transitions of Aging*, ed. N. Datan and N. Lohmann, pp. 93–118. New York: Academic Press.

Lowenthal, M. F., and Chiriboga, D. 1972. "Transition to the Empty Nest." *Archives of General Psychiatry* 26:8–14.

Lowenthal, M. F.; Thurnher, M.; and Chiriboga, D. 1976. *Four Stages of Life*. San Francisco: Jossey-Bass.

McCollough, P. 1980. "Launching Children and Moving On." In *The Family Life Cycle: A Framework for Family Therapy*, ed. E. A. Carter and M. McGoldrich, pp. 171–96. New York: Gardner Press.

Manion, U. V. 1971. "Issues and Trends in Preretirement Education." *Industrial Gerontology* 1:28–36.

Miller, S. J. 1968. "The Social Dilemma of the Aging Leisure Participant." In *Middle Age and Aging: A Reader in Social Psychology*, ed. B. L. Neugarten, pp. 366–74. Chicago: University of Chicago Press.

Monk, A. 1971. "Factors in the Preparation for Retirement by Middle-aged Adults." *Gerontologist* 11:348–51.

Morrison, M. H. 1975. "The Myth of Employee Planning for Retirement." *Industrial Gerontology* 2:135–44.

Neugarten, B. L. 1968. "The Awareness of Middle Age." In *Middle Age and Aging: A Reader in Social Psychology*, ed. B. L. Neugarten, pp. 93–98. Chicago: University of Chicago Press.

———. 1970. "Dynamics of Transition from Middle Age to Old Age: Adaptation and the Life Cycle." *Journal of Geriatric Psychology* 4:71–100.

———. 1977. "Personality and Aging." In *Handbook of the Psychology of Aging*, ed. J. E. Birren and K. W. Schaie, pp. 626–49. New York: Van Nostrand Reinhold.

Neugarten, B. L., and Datan, N. 1973. "Sociological Perspectives on the Life Cycle." In *Life-span Developmental Psychology: Personality and Socialization*, ed. P. B. Baltes and K. W. Schaie, pp. 53–71. New York: Academic Press.

Neugarten, B. L., and Gutmann, D. L. 1964. "Age-sex Roles and Personality in Middle Age: A Thematic Appreception Study." In *Middle Age and Aging: A Reader in Social Psychology*, ed. B. L. Neugarten, pp. 58–71. Chicago: University of Chicago Press.

Neugarten, B. L.; Moore, J. W.; and Lowe, J. C. 1968. "Age Norms, Age Constraints, and Adult Socialization." In *Middle Age and Aging: A Reader in Social Psychology*, ed. B. L. Neugarten, pp. 22–28. Chicago: University of Chicago Press.

Notman, M. T. 1980. "Changing Roles for Women at Mid-life." In *Mid-life: Developmental and Clinical Issues*, ed. W. H. Norman and T. J. Scaramella, pp. 85–109. New York: Brunner/Mazel.

Peck, R. C. 1968. "Psychological Developments in the Second Half of Life." In *Middle Age and Aging: A Reader in Social Psychology*, ed. B. L. Neugarten, pp. 88–92. Chicago: University of Chicago Press.

Riegel, K. F. 1977. "The Dialectics of Time." In *Life-span Developmental Psychology: Dialectical Perspectives on Experimental Research*, ed. N. Datan and H. W. Reese, pp. 3–45. New York: Academic Press.

Riley, M. W., et al. 1969. "Socialization for the Middle and Later Years." In *Handbook of Socialization Theory and Research*, ed. D. A. Goslin, pp. 951–82. Chicago: Rand McNally.

Robinson, B., and Thurnher, M. 1979. "Taking Care of Aged Parents: A Family Cycle Transition." *Gerontologist* 19:586–93.

Rosow, I. 1974. *Socialization to Old Age*. Berkeley: University of California Press.

Sarason, S. B. 1977. *Work, Aging, and Social Change: Professionals and the One-Life, One-Career Imperative.* New York: Free Press.

———. 1981. *Psychology Misdirected.* New York: Free Press.

Smith, K. F., and Bengtson, V. L. 1979. "Positive Consequences of Institutionalization: Solidarity Between Elderly Parents and Their Middle-aged Children." *Gerontologist* 19:438–48.

Spence, D., and Lonner, T. 1971. "The 'Empty Nest': A Transition Within Motherhood." *Family Coordinator* 20:369–75.

Troll, L. E. 1979. "Women at Mid-life: Conditions for Transitions." *Generations* 4:7–9.

Troll, L. E.; Miller, S. J.; and Atchley, R. C. 1979. *Families in Later Life.* Belmont, Calif.: Wadsworth Publishing Co.

Wheeler, S. 1966. "The Structure of Formally Organized Socialization Settings." In *Socialization After Childhood: Two Essays,* ed. O. G. Brim, Jr., and S. Wheeler, pp. 51–116. New York: John Wiley & Sons.

Zarit, S. H. 1980. *Aging and Mental Disorders.* New York: Free Press.

7

Nancy A. Newton,
Lawrence W. Lazarus,
and Jack Weinberg

Aging: Biopsychosocial Perspectives

The stage of the life cycle considered old age represents the culmination of the life span. Coping mechanisms, life style, personality dynamics, values, and attitudes that have developed over a lifetime of experience are brought into play and modified once again to meet the challenges and developmental tasks of later life. This time of life also provides the opportunity for older adults to reevaluate and then to integrate their self-concepts in terms of accomplishments, failures, and other life experiences, with the potential for reaching a richer understanding of themselves and others.

Unfortunately, because of their need for health, social, and other services, Western society has tended to focus on the problems of the physically, cognitively, or psychologically impaired elderly. The needs of these individuals are great and the challenge to our society to provide adequate and humane care is serious. The physical, psychological, cognitive, and social losses that occur in late life can be devastating because they occur at a time when many older adults no longer have the financial resources, physical strength, energy, or effective social supports that enabled them to adjust to stress at a younger age.

The authors express appreciation to Anne Schneider, Ph.D., and Nancy Flowers, A.C.S.W., for their helpful suggestions and to Geri Byrd, Alice Ras, and Catharina Sabo for their assistance in preparing this chapter for publication.

The group of severely impaired elderly, however, constitute a minority of older people. In the United States only about 5 percent of people over age sixty-five are institutionalized (Shanas and Maddox 1976). Seventy-eight percent of the elderly are independent and live at home (U.S. Dept. of HEW, 1975). Although physical illness increases with age, a survey of men over age sixty-five found that only two in five reported restricted activity and one in four indicated an inability to carry on some major activity (Busse 1981).

Thus although the problems confronting this group of very impaired elderly are serious, our society's exclusive focus on this minority of older adults has led to a stereotypical and negatively biased view of late life. Western culture's discomfort with aging and its glorification of youth also contributes to negative stereotypes about the aging process. This chapter will therefore focus on the experiences of the vast majority of elderly people who do not experience incapacitating disability and who continue to have the resources to function independently. Even these "successful" elders can expect to experience physical, cognitive, and psychological changes as well as changes in their interaction with family and community. We will discuss and contrast these normal, healthy elderly with the minority who are seriously impaired. In addition, we will review the processes of adjustment and adaptation that occur in late life.

Problems in Defining Normal Aging

Attempts to define normal aging are complicated by the diversity within this age group, the changing nature of this period resulting from the dramatic increase in longevity, our limited knowledge of the biological underpinnings of the aging process, and the controversy regarding which empirical model is best suited for investigating late life. These issues will be discussed so as to provide a general framework for reviewing pertinent research regarding the major personality, social, cognitive, and biological changes occurring in people over age sixty-five.

DIVERSITY

There is more diversity among people over sixty-five than within any other age group. Subjects over age sixty-five demonstrate more within-group performance variability than any other age group on physiological, cognitive, and personality measures. One factor contributing to this intra-group diversity is the broad age range incorporated in this life period.

Neugarten (1974) captured this distinction in her classification of the "young-old" (age sixty-five to seventy-five) and the "old-old" (over age seventy-five). People in the age group sixty-five to seventy-five are more similar to those in the fifty-five to sixty-five age group with regard to health, socioeconomic status, and cognitive, personality, and developmental issues than they are to people over age seventy-five. In contrast, a significantly greater percentage of people over seventy-five live in long-term care facilities and experience debilitating physical illness. Only 2 percent of people between the ages of sixty-five and seventy-four are in long-term-care institutions compared to approximately 8 percent of adults seventy-five years of age and older (Busse 1981). Because of the greatly increased presence of physical illness in very late life, people over the age of seventy-five tend to be more vulnerable to stress and dependent on others to assume major roles in meeting their daily needs. As is true for most older people confronting major physical disability, the "old-old" may be more preoccupied with narcissistic issues and therefore concerned with physical needs and issues of survival.

Factors other than those related to chronological age are likely to contribute to the diversity within this developmental period. Each individual's many years of unique experience, his or her individual resolution of earlier life issues, and the values, attitudes, and personality characteristics that have developed through interaction with others all contribute to the development of a very individualized approach to life. As a result, some investigators have suggested that demarcating this age period into meaningful subgroups, using criteria such as life style or adjustment factors, would be more relevant than subdividing the elderly by chronological age and would provide a clearer framework for identifying common issues confronting the elderly. For example, Thomae (1980) suggests differentiating the elderly into such groups as elite aged (e.g., professionals who continue to be active in their work), normal aged, and institutionalized aged.

As in other stages of life, the experiences of men and women also tend to differ as they grow older. Women tend to maintain better physical health than men. Women also can expect to live longer. In 1979 sixty-five-year-old men could expect to live an additional 14.3 years compared to 18.7 years for sixty-five-year-old women (U.S. Bureau of the Census 1981). Because of these life expectancy differences, the ratio of men to women shifts dramatically in late life. There are 130 women to every 100 men in the age group sixty-five to seventy-four; after age seventy-five, there are 171 women to every 100 men (Busse 1981).

Men and women also tend to have different life-styles during late life. Only 14.7 percent of men live alone, compared to 40.9 percent of women. Only 38.0 percent of women continue to live with their spouse, compared to 75.5 percent of men (U.S. Bureau of the Census 1981). Finally, older women are more likely to be faced with poverty than are men. In 1979, 30.4 percent of women living alone compared to 25.3 percent of single men had incomes below the poverty line (U.S. Bureau of the Census 1981).

Reaction to stressful events in late life and the personality changes that occur may also be related to sex differences. For example, research suggests that men tend to be more disrupted than women by widowhood and that working women are more disrupted than men by retirement (Lowenthal and Chiriboga 1973).

AGING AS A LIFE STAGE IN TRANSITION

To a greater extent than any other period in the life span, the aging experience is in a rapid state of change. Twenty years from now, when the phenomenon of an extended life span is better understood and more familiar, and when the elderly constitute a larger proportion of the population and thus have a greater impact on our society's values and goals, the parameters and roles associated with late life are likely to be quite different from what they are today. Social phenomena such as retirement, social security, and segregated housing for the elderly are relatively new, and thus their influence on the nature of this life period continues to evolve. Only very recently could the average person conceive of his or her life span extending until age eighty or ninety, a change that places a new perspective on life for those who are now sixty or seventy.

IMPACT OF THE AGING PROCESS

Part of the complexity of defining normality in late life stems from the limitation of our knowledge about the biological underpinnings and parameters of the aging process. Birren and Renner (1977) suggested the following definition of aging: "Aging refers to the regular changes that occur in mature, genetically representative organisms living under representative environmental conditions as they advance in chronological age" (p. 4). As this definition indicates, age-related changes do not necessarily involve either decline or expansion. Because the etiology and thus the normal onset and progression of aging cannot be specified, researchers correlate "aging" changes with chronological age. However, in late life the correlation between chronological age and performance on psychological, physiological, cognitive, and social measures declines. Chronological age as a variable in and of itself does not generally account for a significant amount of variance on most measures of these variables administered across the life span.

Defining the impact of the aging process is made more complex because aging is not purely a biological phenomenon. As Botwinick (1981) suggests, there is social aging, behavioral aging, and biological aging. Weinberg's (1973) description of "agedness" illustrates the multidimensional nature of aging, reflecting personality as well as biological variables.

> Agedness is an assumed stance on the part of the organism that may or may not be due to organic dysfunction, but may be behavioristically characteristic of a unified complex of roles, assigned, ascribed and much too often acquired. It may be both character and pathology. It may be independent of any overt manifestations of organic disease and thus present itself as a mode of coping or adaptive behavior most economical to the character structure of the individual. Behavioristically speaking, one may manifest agedness quite early in one's life, though usually it is characteristic of the later periods of the life cycle. (P. 18)

CULTURAL ISSUES

Cross-cultural research investigating the parameters and dimensions of late-life experiences in varied agrarian and industrial societies, as well as research on subjects having different cultural backgrounds within Western society, indicates that cultural factors have a significant impact on the characteristics of late life and that any definition of late life "normality" is culturally based (Bengtson, Kasschau, and Ragan 1977). Cultural context is important in defining the specific social and family roles available to elderly people, in influencing the particular way in which the developmental tasks and issues of old age are expressed, and in setting standards for the "ideal" older adult. Several factors account for the pervasive influence that culture has on the characteristics of late life. Elderly people have lived within a particular culture a long time and thus have absorbed and become invested in its values and traditions. The elderly are therefore more concerned than people of other age groups about the continuation of their cultural heritage, possibly to ensure survival of their values, if not of themselves. In many cultures the elderly play an important role in the preservation of cultural traditions and values (Gutmann 1980a). In addition, because the "old-old" are physically more vulnerable than other age groups, they are more dependent on the cultural values and societal norms regarding old age to determine how they are treated and thus the quality of their lives.

METHODOLOGICAL ISSUES

Investigators who study normality in late life are confronted with a number of methodological and theoretical problems. Older adults are not an accessible population for study. They are not gathered in schools, universities, or workplaces. If they are congregated in one location, it is usually in institutions such as nursing homes; and research on this select segment of the elderly has led to negative and unfair overgeneralizations as to what "normal" older adults are like. In addition, as people reach old age, it becomes more difficult to isolate the effects of age itself from that of other variables, such as health problems and social role changes, which have major impact on any individual's functioning independent of age.

An additional problem is to define an appropriate empirical model for studying this period of life. The traditional assumption has been that the changes accompanying aging are quantitative in nature. Therefore, the same issues and measurable variables are viewed as equally important across the life span. Cross-sectional research designs that assume that differences between the performance of young and old subjects reflect the impact of age have been the model for studying these quantitative changes. Measures used in much of this research were generally developed for use with younger adults and thus are generally more relevant to their experience than to the experience of older people. Evidence that older subjects perform more poorly than younger subjects on many of these cognitive, physiological, and psychological measures has provided support for the belief that generalized decline occurs in late life. However, this research methodology not only places older subjects at a disadvantage, it also contaminates age and cohort variables without elucidating the unique aspects of late life.

An alternative model has grown out of the developmental framework for studying the life span. This model assumes that the changes that occur in each life stage, including late life, are qualitative rather than quantitative in nature. The belief is that old age is a stage of the life cycle in its own right, with unique gains and depletions (Gutmann 1980a). Therefore, the relevant issues, as well as the methods of investigating these issues, are presumed to change across the life span. This approach places less emphasis on age-group comparisons. Instead, direct observation and understanding of each life period is seen as the basis for the development of age-specific empirical measures and theories.

The following sections of this chapter address the personality, social, cognitive, and biological developments that shape the lives of "normal" people over age sixty-five. In general, we have focused on empirical studies of the vast majority of elderly people who have adjusted to the challenges of late life without incapacitating psychological problems and who continue to be able to live independently.

Personality in Normal Aging

As with many other areas of functioning, there is strong evidence from both cross-sectional and longitudinal research that many aspects of personality remain stable as one ages. Life satisfaction and morale remain consistent across the life span (Palmore 1970; Thomae 1976). Income, self-rated health, and, to a lesser extent, number of relationships and access to means of achieving goals show much stronger correlations to one's general outlook on life, as defined by morale and life satisfaction, than does age (Adams 1971; Neugarten 1977; Palmore and Kivett 1977). Old and young adults do not differ in adjustment although, as with life satisfaction, level of adjustment is influenced by health and attitude toward others (Thomae 1980).

The individual's perception of him- or herself as reflected in self-concept or self-image also appears to remain stable with age. Contrary to earlier beliefs, there is no evidence that the self-concept becomes negative with aging (Monge 1975; Trimakas and Nicolay 1974). In their interviews of eighty-seven middle-aged and elderly men, Reichard, Livson, and Petersen (1962) found that self-acceptance is likely to become greater with age. Although earlier research was equivocal, recent longitudinal studies demonstrate no general restriction of future time perspective in the elderly (Munnichs 1979; Thomae 1976). Personality characteristics that appear to accompany aging, such as increased cautiousness, increased introversion, decreased excitability and impulsiveness, and increased attention to practical needs are much less impressive than is the stability or similarity in personality traits as measured by objective measures across age groups (Botwinick 1981; Thomae 1980).

Personality style also appears to be consistent from middle age into late life. In addition, no one particular personality style is predictive of adjustment in late late, although for many older people adjustment is associated with continued activity and social involvement. Based on extensive interviews and personality assessment, several investigators have suggested typologies of personality style (Havighurst 1968; Reichard, Livson, and Petersen 1962). These investigators found that the individual's ability to integrate the emotional and rational aspects of his or her personality, to come to terms with role changes, and to establish a sense of continuity were as important as activity level in predicting adjustment. They also found that aging patterns were predictable during middle age and that personality constriction did not necessarily occur in late life.

The sense of continuity in one's own life is captured in Wilma Donahue's view of herself at seventy:

> I have more measure of feeling about aging when I see the people I was young with, at the university, and all of a sudden I see them in the version of old people. I may not have seen them for a long time, and then I see them after they've stepped over the threshold and are now looking old. I have never thought of them as older people and suddenly I see them as old and I gather a sense of their being different, and I have thought about this. To them, just like I am to myself, there is a consistent personality. I don't recognize that I was 20, 30, 40, 50, 60 and so forth. I just seem to be a consistent personality that's lived a whole life. I realize I look the same to them as they look to me. As far as my feeling is concerned, I don't have that sense. I have the same sense of being a whole person with spirit and interests that are consistent with my life. (Weinberg 1975, p. 2406)

Although personality style and personality traits as assessed by objective measures do not appear to change with age, there does appear to be a shift in focus of the aging adult's inner life. This is reflected in the elderly's view of themselves in relation to the environment, in their preoccupations and values, and, to some extent, in the type of internal coping mechanisms used. Both cross-sectional and longitudinal research indicates that in late life there is a movement away from preoccupation with the outer world and movement toward an inner-world orientation. It is as if the elderly create a new balance in their worldview, one in which the self has greater importance (Levinson 1978). With aging, there is greater preoccupation with inner life, decreased emotional cathexes toward environmental objects and persons, constriction in the ability to integrate complex impinging stimuli, and greater concern about satisfaction of one's own needs (Neugarten 1964). Elderly adults increasingly focus on health and bodily functions, inner affective experiences, and past life reminiscences.

Jung (1960) believed that this trend toward greater introversion begins as early as middle age and continues throughout late life. Cumming and Henry (1961) pointed to a similar phenomenon in their disengagement theory, but inaccurately predicted that this internal state would be reflected behaviorally in actual withdrawal from the social world.

One aspect of this increased focus on the self in late life is a reorganization of values. Ryff and Baltes (1976) found a transition in middle to old age from emphasis on instrumental values, such as ambition, to more concern about freedom and happiness. Aging is accompanied by less concern about achievement and the value of work. Increasing importance is placed on humanitarianism (Thomae 1980). Neugarten (1964) suggested that it also includes greater dedication to a core of personal values, with increase in superego qualities. There is a reestablishing of personal priorities in light of greater awareness of both decreasing energy and the finitude of life.

This reorganization of values also includes greater emphasis on meeting emotional needs and establishing and maintaining interpersonal affectional bonds. For example, in describing intergenerational relationships, adult children tend to emphasize the assistance-giving aspect of the relationship whereas their aging parents tend to emphasize the affectional components (Sussman 1976). Similarly, in his study of long-married couples, Roberts (1979–80) found that with increasing age more emphasis was placed on the quality of the relationship, with more attention given to the spouse's expressive affectional roles than to his or her instrumental functions.

Theorists who have viewed the aging process from a psychodynamic perspective have speculated on the meaning of this increased focus on inner life. Cath (1976) believes that there is a turning inward of libido in late life leading to accentuation of the enteroceptive apparatus. Thus messages of the body, including primitive needs and demands for gratification and somatic concerns, are more quickly perceived and responded to. As psychological energy becomes more limited, this increased narrowing of psychic focus to the self is adaptive in ensuring survival because available energy is channeled and directed toward meeting one's essential needs.

Weinberg (1975) believes that one way the elderly focus their energy and ego functions on essential needs is exemplified by the phenomenon of "exclusion of stimuli." Because aging curtails one's capacity to deal with a complex multitude of stimuli, superfluous details of everyday life are no longer attended to while attention is given to information that is most pertinent and psychologically relevant to the individual. "Exclusion of stimuli" is reflected the tendency of many older people who do not hear well to hear "what they should not hear" when issues pertaining to their well-being are discussed. Weinberg bases this mechanism on the psychoanalytic concept of subception and differentiates it from denial. In denial, the stimulus is perceived, cathected, and invested in before cathexis is withdrawn whereas in exclusion of stimuli "stimuli may be blocked at the point of entry, with a lowered threshold for only those stimuli relevant to one's narcissism, and by narcissism is meant survival value" (p. 2409).

Increased interiority is reflected not only in the focus of one's preoccupations but also in the individual's changing world and self views and coping strategies. Aging individuals become less oriented toward coping with stress by producing changes in the environment or in the stressful situation itself and more oriented toward accommodating themselves to the environment. As a result, adjustment is achieved through changed attitudes and self-perceptions as well as through modified views of the world.

This process was identified and examined in the Kansas City Studies of Adult Life. Neugarten and her colleagues (1964) used projective test data and interviews of 287 white urban men and women aged forty to seventy to study the personality changes that take place in the second half of life. They found that the majority of men aged forty to forty-nine assumed a stance of active mastery (Gutmann 1964). That is, these men viewed their environment as one that rewards boldness and risk taking and themselves as capable of meeting those opportunities. Their energies and attention were focused on interaction with the external world, and it was to that realm that they looked for justification, challenge, and stimulation.

In contrast, men in the older age groups tended to view the world as complex and dangerous and themselves as accommodating and conforming to outer world demands. As a result, men in the older age groups tended to maintain homeostasis via passive or magical mastery. Men taking a passive mastery stance withdrew from active engagement with the external world and disengaged themselves from feelings and excitement. Rather than achieving objectives through reshaping the environment, these men reshaped themselves to conform to external demands or their own superego strictures. Finally older men relying on magical mastery to achieve adjustment altered the world by perceptual fiat. That is, they seemed to operate on the principle that "wishing will make it so" (Gutmann 1964).

Evidence that people become more cautious and conservative as they age provides further support for the notion that they feel uncomfortable in attempting to change events by impacting on their environment. It is as if they become less trusting of their capacity to evaluate and make decisions about the world around them (Botwinick 1981).

From the perspective of cognitive personality theory, Thomae (1970) believes that cognitive revisions of the way one views the self and the self in the environmental context are essential to the individual's maintenance of a stable self-concept despite the multiple and varied narcissistic insults of late life. In order to maintain a balance between motivational needs and one's cognitions of the world and oneself, elderly adults, according to Thomae, use "cognitive restructuration." This process does not involve perceptual distortion. Instead beliefs, attitudes, and ways of thinking about stressful situations change so that meaning and relevance are given to failure and loss.

One important variable accompanying the shift from external to internal coping strategies may be the elderly person's feeling that he or she is powerless to change a given situation and thus, if adjustment is to occur, it must be achieved through alterations in attitudes. Carp (1975) provides an example of the effects of this sense of external impotency on the elderly's perceptions of situations. He interviewed elderly subjects regarding the adequacy of their current living situations before and after they were notified of transfer to better housing. Subjects who learned that they could move and thus no longer had to remain in inferior housing rated their current housing much more negatively than subjects who were not provided with the opportunity to move.

LATE LIFE FROM THE PERSPECTIVE OF SELF-PSYCHOLOGY

The psychology of the self, as theorized by psychoanalyst Heinz Kohut (1966, 1971, 1977) and others (Cath 1976; Meissner 1976) adds another dimension to our understanding of personality development across the life cycle that has special relevance to aging. The self may be defined as a developmental psychological structure responsible for maintenance of one's self-image, self-esteem, feelings and affects associated with bodily and psychological integrity, and relative need for others to idealize and to regulate self-esteem. Kohut believes that personality development across the course of life can be viewed not only from the more traditional perspective of the developmental progression from infantile autoeroticism to object love, but also from a second line of development that begins with the archaic nuclear self, progresses to the cohesive self, and finally attains, in varying degrees, higher forms of the self including potential transformation of the self across the second half of life. According to Kohut, during normal childhood development of the self sector of the personality, the child's tendency toward self-centeredness and grandiosity is responded to more or less empathically and appropriately by the parents who serve as selfobjects. The child experiences the attributes of the parenting objects as functions of the self or selfobjects. The parents' age-specific empathic and mirroring responses lead to the child's budding sense of confidence and sense of self, leading eventually and in varying degrees to feelings of cohesiveness and relative stability of self-esteem as well as to the capacity to use others in a sustaining and satisfying way during times of need.

In addition to the gradual transformation of grandiosity into self-integrated ambitions and goals, childhood idealizations of all-powerful and perfect parents (idealized parent imagoes) become modulated, internalized, and transformed into the ideal to which one aspires, as healthy admiration of others, and as one wishes to be associated with those one admires. During adulthood and the later phases of life, the self may be expressed through such developmental achievements as wisdom, creativity, humor, and an acceptance of life's finitude (see figure 7.1). Across adulthood, based on the more or less successful development of an integrated cohesive self, persons vary in their sense of cohesiveness and integration, from sustained feelings of vitality, spontaneity, and vigor, to feelings of enfeeblement, depletion, and, where functioning is seriously disrupted, a sense of inner fragmentation (Kohut and Wolfe 1978).

In the late 1970s Kohut made a slight but significant shift in conceptualizing the self, not in isolation but as a lifelong sequence of changing self-selfobject relationships. Psychopathology in general and self pathology in particular is therefore defined in terms not of this or that defect in the self but in terms of a disturbance of the self-selfobject relationship during a particular stage of life. Applying these concepts to the psychopathology of the elderly, Kohut (pers. com. 1980) suggests "focusing on the old and his environment as a unit rather than focusing only on the failures of the aged and on the defects of the self."

According to Meissner (1976), the basic problem of aging is that of narcissistic loss. Referring to Rochlin's (1965) discussion of the issue:

FIGURE 7.1
The Development of the Self

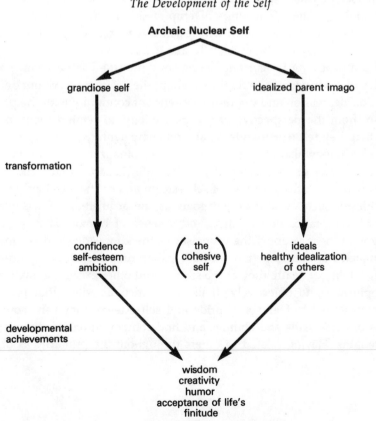

The greatest test of narcissism is aging or old age. All that has come to represent value and with which narcissism has long been associated is jeopardized
by growing old. The skills, mastery, and powers, all painfully acquired, which
provided gratifications as they functioned to effect adaptation wane in the last
phase of life. One's resources, energies, adaptability, and function, the intima-
cies of relationships upon which one depended, family and friends, are continually being depleted and lost. (Pp. 377–78)

The magnitude of an elderly person's reactions to a loss is dependent,
to some degree, on the amount of narcissistic and libidinal investment in
the lost function or object. For example, for aged persons whose intellectual achievements accounted for much of their pride and self-esteem,
reminders of their failing memory may provoke anger, rage, and depression. Kohut (1972) cites the example of the aging person who, because of
brain injury, is unable to solve simple problems. He becomes enraged
over the fact that "he is not in control of his own thought processes, of a
function which people consider to be most intimately their own, i.e., as a
part of the self" (p. 383).

Self psychology may provide a new way of understanding the personality's attempt to cope and to find restitution for the biopsychosocial
losses and stresses occurring in late life. Regression within the self sector
of the personality may serve adaptive functions by preserving one's self-
esteem and warding off feelings of emptiness and fragmentation. For
example, the retired industrialist whose self-esteem rested upon financial
successes may brag exhibitionistically about past accomplishments as a
way of compensating for current feelings of diminished self-esteem. The
tendency of older persons to reminisce about the past may serve not only
to stave off depression and to preserve a sense of continuity with the past
but also, from the perspective of self psychology, to remind them of a
time when they felt worthwhile, vital, and competent.

Self psychology also provides a useful conceptualization of normality
in the self sector of the personality in late life (Lazarus 1980). Elderly
persons with a healthy reservoir of self-esteem and confidence have usually achieved such developmental goals as the acquisition of wisdom,
creativity, acceptance of mortality, and a sense of humor. They enjoy
sharing with those younger than themselves the knowledge and wisdom
accumulated from life experiences. Rather than dreading and despairing
the inevitability of death, they approach this and other existential matters
philosophically and objectively. If illness restricts activities that previously contributed to feelings of pride and self-esteem, they can mourn
the loss of these skills and abilities and find compensation in remaining
ego strengths. Having related to others throughout life primarily as ob-

jects separate from the self rather than as selfobjects, they can mourn the loss of loved ones.

By realistically appraising current abilities and impairments, persons with a healthy, integrated self can gradually modify the cherished ideals and goals of their youth. In doing so, they are better protected from the depression that may ensue if they expected to perform as they once did. They can tolerate feeling angry and dejected when some physical illness, such as a stroke, prevents them from accomplishing their goals and ambitions. As Kohut and Wolf (1978) note: "If our self is firmly established, we shall neither be afraid of the dejection that may follow a failure nor of the expansive fantasies that may follow a success—reactions that would endanger those with a more precariously established self" (p. 415). Cath (1976) has noted that these individuals have the capacity to tolerate loss, to grieve, and to be depressed without losing basic self-respect or suffering irreparable damage to self-esteem.

LATE-LIFE DEVELOPMENTAL TASKS

A number of researchers have speculated about developmental tasks of late life. The most widely known are the theories of Erikson (1963). He identifies late-life tasks as involving issues of generativity versus stagnation and integrity versus despair. Generativity is the capacity to become invested in establishing and guiding the next generation. Achieving ego integrity involves emotional integration of life experiences and acceptance of life as it has been lived. This process involves the reconciliation of earlier goals and dreams to achievements actually accomplished, reevaluation and reconceptualization of earlier life experiences in light of later ones (a process McKee [1980–81] labels consummation), and the revision of one's sense of self in a way that is compatible with those experiences. Erikson (1963) believes that developing a sense of ego integrity allows one to "defend the dignity of his own life style against all physical and economic threats" (p. 268) and to face death without despair. This process represents growth and maturation in that it allows the elderly individual the opportunity to use a full lifetime's experience to come to terms with the self and the world. As Neugarten (1979) suggests, the process of having lived a long time with many and varied experiences is essential to developing a certain self-knowledge and worldly wisdom.

Although Erikson (1963) separates generativity and ego integrity into two separate tasks, Fiske (1980) believes that meeting these two tasks is an interrelated process so that commitment to one's own integrity and respect and support for future generations goes hand in hand. She also suggests that generativity and integrity are central issues throughout adulthood and that, as life experiences accumulate, maturation of these commitments is achieved.

Many theorists have agreed with Erikson that putting one's life into perspective is a major task of late life and suggest that reminiscence and self-reflection are key mechanisms for meeting this goal. Butler and Lewis (1977) believe that reminiscence occurs in all people in the final years of life and that it is characterized by the "progressive return to consciousness of past experiences and particularly the resurgence of un-resolved conflicts which can be looked at again and reintegrated" (p. 43). Memory for early life events becomes clearer and more vivid in late life, and there is increased ability to bring up material from the unconscious. Butler and Lewis suggest that "individuals realize that their own personal myth of invulnerability and immortality can no longer be maintained. All of this results in reassessment of life, which brings depression, accept-ance, or satisfaction" (p. 44). Reminiscence plays another important role in late life—it overcomes the split between old age and youth, leading to a sense of continuity with one's past life, according to Levinson (1978). Elderly adults must be able to accept the aging process, including changes in physiological, cognitive, and emotional functioning, while maintaining a consistent sense of what is the essential core of their being.

Late-Life Social Roles

One of the most marked and obvious features of the aging process is the change in social roles. In fact, it is one of these transitions—from the role of employee to that of retiree—that has led to age sixty-five as the tradi-tional boundary of old age in the United States. Within a brief time period, in the mid-sixties, the elderly are likely to be confronted with changed role positions in their relationships with their children, spouses, commu-nity, and society. Researchers have attempted to define: (1) the role of the aging adult in the family, the workplace, and society, and the expecta-tions that exist for how the elderly should function in these roles; and (2) how the aging adult adjusts to these role transitions. Despite former spec-ulations regarding the difficulties inherent in this period of rapid and major social role change (Rosow 1974), most elderly people do adapt and develop meaningful and satisfying life styles.

PARENTING

Despite prior beliefs about the disintegration of family ties and of the extended family in an increasingly mobile and industrialized society, empirical evidence shows that strong relationships exist between elderly parents and their children (Sussman and Burchinal 1962). This does not imply that there have been no changes in the nature and role demands of parent-child relationships over the last few decades. However, the evidence suggests that family relationships may have benefited, rather than suffered, from these changes.

The traditional view has been that intergenerational family ties were much stronger twenty-five to fifty years ago because the multigenerational family lived together, was dependent on mutual support for financial survival, and was tied together by common business or farming interests. This view has been challenged by Bengtson and Treas (1980) on several grounds. Only in very recent years have life spans increased to the point that there is an extended overlap in generations and thus the possibility of forming extended and lasting intergenerational family relationships. Second, living together was generally a result of economic necessity and the dependency of the aging parent on the adult child for financial support. Such forced closeness did not necessarily result in close affectional ties and, indeed, may have had a detrimental affect. The advent of social security in the 1930s decreased the financial dependency of the older generation, allowing family ties to grow and develop by choice rather than out of necessity. Bengtson, Olander, and Haddad (1976) also suggest that intergenerational cohort differences in values and attitudes—the "generation gap"—is largely a societal rather than a family phenomenon. Within families, the typical pattern continues to be that of shared belief and value systems.

The intergenerational family pattern that has developed within the last twenty-five years is one of "intimacy at a distance" (Sussman 1976). The great majority of elderly adults prefer to live in their own homes and to live independently, while maintaining frequent contact with their children (Bengtson and Treas 1980). A survey in 1962 found that 33 percent of older Americans live within a ten-minute drive of at least one child, and only 23 percent of older adults live more than thirty minutes away from one of their children (Bengtson and Treas 1980). Frequent family contact, whether it be through informal activities, ceremonial or family rituals, or exchange of help, is the typical family pattern (Bengtson and Treas 1980). For the elderly person whose social sphere narrows after retirement, these family contacts may serve increasingly important functions in enhancing self-esteem and providing social contact. Family ties that may have been tenuous and strained during the child's adolescent and early-adult years are likely to be strengthened and reestablished because of the aging parents' increased need for contact and help, which occurs concomitantly with the increasing maturity of their adult child.

Examining the dimensions of parent-adult child relationships, Bengtson and his colleagues (Bengtson and Treas 1980; Bengtson, Olander, and Haddad 1976) suggest three interrelated perspectives from which to view intergenerational ties: (1) associational solidarity is an objective measure of the frequency of contact between generations; (2) affectional solidarity is a subjective measure reflecting the quality of the relationship; and (3) consensual solidarity is the degree to which common values and beliefs are shared. Bengtson found that associational solidarity, although it may be strong even when generations are separated geographically, is increased by residential propinquity, by frequent communication, by a sense of filial responsibility, and by the number of female linkages. Females are particularly important, since daughters maintain more frequent contact with aging parents than do sons. The elderly adult's marital status is another important factor, since widows tend to be much more dependent on kin than married aged. These factors, as well as the extent of the elderly parent's dependency needs, determine the amount of help given by the middle-aged child to a parent.

Consensual solidarity is increased if the elderly parent was born in the United States, if the adult child has accepted changes in the parent's values that accompany retirement, and if the generations have shared educational, occupational, and peer-group experiences. Interviewing mothers over sixty and their adult daughters, Johnson and Bursk (1977) found that their relationship was rated more positively if the two shared similar values, viewed the relationship as being based on mutual trust and respect, and maintained realistic perceptions of each other.

An important aspect of the parent-adult child relationship is the role of the child as assistance-giver to the aging parent. All generations tend to see the family as the preferred source of help in a health or personal crisis (Hill et al. 1970; Sussman 1965). However, the elderly are most likely to be in need of family help. In addition to providing direct assistance, adult children can serve important mediating roles in the aging parent's relationship to a complex bureaucracy of health and social agencies. They can facilitate the aging parent's use of social agencies and also act as a buffer to protect the parent from an agency's overzealous intervention (Sussman 1976).

Whether families are able to negotiate the role reversal wherein the adult child serves as parent or principal caregiver to aging parents is dependent on the pattern and quality of earlier family ties as well as on the capacity of the adult child to achieve "filial maturity." Sussman (1976) defines filial maturity as the adult child's ability to take on the help-giving role in such a way that the aging parent experiences the adult child as dependable while not being made to feel as if he or she has become a burden.

While the responsibilities and duties of the adult child toward the aging parent can be clearly identified, it is less clear what the elderly parent has to contribute in exchange. In fact, some researchers have speculated that the vulnerable position and lowered self-esteem of the elderly is the result of their being in the position of only being able to take without having anything to give in return (Dowd 1975). Other investigators (Gutmann 1980a) believe the industrial revolution marked the onset of a diminished role for the elderly in the family, in contrast to the powerful position they held in patriarchal agrarian cultures when the oldest generation controlled the land and thus the wealth. However, research on family ties suggests that the elderly continue to play an important role within the family. In addition, Bengtson and Treas (1980) challenge the myth that the elderly are dependent recipients of intergenerational assistance. They cite several national surveys indicating that although two-thirds of the elderly respondents had received help from their families, over half had also given financial assistance to their adult children. In many families the older generation provides a backup parenting system to be called on in times of family crisis or even for baby-sitting or child care while parents work. The elderly adult also serves as maintainer and perpetuator of family and societal culture and traditions (Weinberg 1975). In an era of rapid shifts in cultural values, the place of elderly parents as living links to family and cultural heritage may be increasingly valued.

GRANDPARENTING

Not only are elderly people involved in ongoing relationships with their adult children, they are also likely to be grandparents. This is one of the few roles for the elderly in Western society that is associated with a positive stereotype. As Kahana and Kahana (1971) describe this image, grandparents are viewed as "good souls who are happy to give extra comfort, love, admiration, and time to the youngest generation and are revered for their good works by their grateful progeny" (p. 262). Some investigators have suggested that the role of grandparent is one avenue available to the elderly person for establishing a valued position within the family (Boyd 1969). Yet the limited research on grandparent-grandchild relationships indicates that the grandparenting role has somewhat less importance to both the elderly adult and the family. The elderly themselves usually identify grandparenting as a peripheral role in their own lives (Troll 1980; Wood and Robertson 1976). Neugarten and Weinstein

(1964) found that the majority of grandparents felt that this relationship had little impact on their self-concept.

Troll (1980) suggests that even though the term grandparent could imply ascriptive, normative, or ritualized behavior, actual grandparent-grandchild relationships within Western society are shaped by idiosyncratic and personality-determined behaviors. The lack of clear expectations and responsibilities allow grandparents to choose their own interactive style. In their study of 140 grandparents, Neugarten and Weinstein (1964) identified five styles of grandparent-grandchild interaction. The most frequent pattern was one in which clearly demarcated lines were maintained between parents and grandparents, with grandparents providing occasional gifts or services. A second pattern—the "fun seeker"—involved grandparent self-indulgence that emphasized pleasurable grandparent-grandchild interaction. Other styles of grandparent-grandchild interaction were less frequent, including the role of grandparent as surrogate parent, reservoir of family wisdom, or distant family figure.

Although personality variables appear to be important determinants influencing the style of grandparenting, the structure and impact of this role within the family system is largely out of the elderly adult's control. The adult parent plays a major part in setting the emotional tone as well as the actual boundaries of the grandparent-grandchild interaction (Robertson 1976). Two-thirds of the eighty-six young adults Robertson interviewed reported that their parents set the pace for the interactions with their grandparents by their attitudes, physical arrangements, and own relationships with the grandparents. Kahana and Kahana (1971) believe the adult parent's capacity to influence the quality and quantity of the grandparental interaction limits its meaningfulness for the elderly adult. They suggest that the greater the extent to which the older adult is a passive respondent to the expectations of others, rather than an active participant in shaping the meaning of grandparenting, the less involved will be the grandparent in the grandparenting role.

The age of the grandparent also influences the nature of his or her relationship to the grandchild. Neugarten and Weinstein (1964) found that younger grandparents demonstrated more diverse styles of relating to grandchildren. In addition, many younger grandparents established interactions with their grandchildren that focused on mutual enjoyment and fun-seeking whereas almost all older grandparents maintained more formal and distant relationships with their grandchildren. Life circumstances also influence grandparent-grandchild interactions. The increasing rate of divorce makes it difficult for many elderly people to maintain close ties with their grandchildren. Institutionalization also serves to disrupt the grandparent-grandchild relationship and thus the older person's ability to benefit from it (Kahana and Kahana 1971). Kahana and Kahana found that institutionalized grandparents had less spontaneous contact with their grandchildren; thus their descriptions of the relationship tended to be stereotyped and ritualized.

The development and changing needs of the grandchild also have a major influence on the type and extent of grandparent involvement. As children develop, their responses to grandparents change. Whereas young children respond to indulgent gift-giving, older children enjoy sharing activities with their grandparents (Kahana and Kahana 1970). Being a grandparent appears to be most satisfying when the child is young (Wood and Robertson 1976). However, by the time the adult reaches age sixty-five, his or her grandchildren are likely to be young adults themselves, or at least adolescents, and the relationship is likely to have changed. Just as adolescents are caught up in achieving independence from their parents, they are also involved in becoming more independent from their grandparents. In Robertson's (1976) study of college students, the students' strongest perception of the grandparent-grandchild relationship was of themselves as potential caretakers of the grandparent. There was little sense of what the grandparent contributed to the relationship—that is, there was no evidence that grandparents were viewed as role models, sources of financial support, or as potential mediators with their parents.

The significance of grandparenting for the elderly adult may lie in the role's symbolic and emotional implications as well as in the degree of intimate adult-child interaction or in the creation and development of this role as a valued one within the family system. Neugarten and Weinstein (1964) found that grandparents attribute the gratification in this role to a sense of biological renewal and continuity and emotional self-fulfillment. Benedek (1970), emphasizing the emotional content of grandparenting, believes that

grandparenthood is a new lease on life because grandparents—grandmothers more intensely than grandfathers—relive the memories of the early phase of their own parenthood in observing the growth and development of their grandchildren. Grandparenthood is, however, parenthood one step removed. Relieved from the immediate stresses of motherhood and the responsibilities of fatherhood, grandparents appear to enjoy their grandchildren more than they enjoyed their own children. Their instinctual wish to survive being gratified, they project the hope of the fulfillment of their narcissistic self-image to their grandchildren. Since they do not have the responsibility for raising the child toward that unconscious goal, their love is not as burdened by doubts and anxieties as it was when their own children were young. (P. 201)

MARITAL RELATIONSHIPS

The marital relationship is very important in the lives of many elderly people. In the midst of other losses and changes, this relationship may provide a familiar and comfortable pattern as well as a source of companionship and support (Butler and Lewis 1977). Married people constitute a large proportion of sociologically and psychologically healthy older individuals (Goldfarb 1968; Stinnett, Collins, and Montgomery 1970). In addition, the majority of middle-aged and older adults perceive their marital relationships as improving with age (Burr 1970; Rollins and Feldman 1970). It seems likely that over the life span, a marriage changes as the marital partners have different experiences, individually and together. Butler and Lewis (1977) believe that the three expectations found in older marriages are care during illness, household management, and emotional gratification. However, little is known about the life styles of long-married couples or about the important elements that affect a marriage lasting over fifty years.

Roberts (1979–80) interviewed fifty couples married an average of 55.5 years. This was a very select group of elderly subjects in that they all lived in their own homes, most rated their health as good or excellent, and almost all rated their personal happiness and marital adjustment very highly. The findings suggest that with increasing age, more emphasis is placed on the quality of the relationship, with more attention given to the spouse's expressive, affectional qualities than to his or her instrumental functions. Over half the subjects reported having been sexually active within the last five years. In addition, they described their marriage as companionship marriages, with little struggle for dominance. Roberts suggests that his results challenge traditional myths that life for older adults is primarily problem oriented, that older people are rigidly fixed in traditional roles, and that they do not value love and sex.

In 1978 it was estimated that at least 35,000 marriages a year involved at least one partner who was sixty-five or older (Rosenfeld 1978). Despite the frequency of late-life marriage, very little is known about couples who remarry or marry for the first time after age sixty-five. Cultural prejudices against late-life sexuality as well as economic barriers may discourage many older people from remarrying. For people who overcome these barriers, the limited data available indicates that remarriage is generally a positive step in which spouses experience mutual affection and pleasure (Rosenfeld 1978).

WIDOWHOOD

The great degree of individual variability in adjustment to the loss of a spouse makes generalizations difficult. Examination of most social and psychological variables reveals more differences within any group of widows and widowers than between groups of widows and married people (Atchley 1975). This large degree of variability reflects the influence not only of individual personality but also of varying sociocultural backgrounds and family structures. Based on her extensive study of widows of all ages, Lopata (1975) identifies the following four factors as influential in determining the degree and type of adjustment made by the widow: (1) the extent of dependence of the survivor on the now-deceased spouse; (2) the ways the couple enmeshed in the larger social system; (3) the resources and limitations available for establishing future life styles; and (4) the procedures by which the gap left by the deceased spouse is closed.

Lopata found that widowhood is less stressful and disruptive for older adults than for younger ones, perhaps because in old age, loss of a spouse is an age-appropriate expectation and because the older widow is more likely to have access to the support of similar-aged widows (Morgan 1976). Morale or life satisfaction of widows is less than that of elderly married people (Morgan 1976), and widowed people are more likely to identify themselves as old (Atchley 1975). It is difficult to evaluate whether this lower morale reflects the effects of widowhood per se or whether it is a result of the widow's increased susceptibility to financial problems and to the effects of diminished health. Financial problems are one of the primary concerns of widows, and income adequacy is an essential component in adjustment to widowhood (Atchley 1975; Lopata 1975). Some theorists have suggested that widowhood is more disruptive to men than to women (Lowenthal and Chiriboga 1973), perhaps because widowhood is a less age-appropriate expectation for men and because men, more than women, seem to experience increased dependency needs with aging (Gutmann 1964).

RETIREMENT

Retirement has been extensively studied, possibly because it is a clearly identifiable event that marks, for most people, the transition from middle to old age, and possibly because the role of the retired person is a fairly new one in our culture—one that has emerged over the last thirty years. It was traditionally assumed that retirement led to decline in physical well-being and mental health (Friedmann and Orbach 1974). It was believed that the abrupt disruption of work patterns and daily living habits and the accompanying need to develop and adjust to new patterns precipitated physiological and emotional collapse. However, there is no evidence of this (Friedmann and Orbach 1974; Sheppard 1976). In fact, retirement may even lead to improved health, as the physical and mental stress of work roles is alleviated (Friedmann and Orbach 1974). Earlier studies that found an increased death rate immediately following retirement seemed to reflect the fact that many people retire because they are in poor health, rather than because retirement itself leads to health problems.

The periods immediately preceding and following retirement are perceived by most people as times of increased stress (Dressler 1973; Friedmann and Orbach 1974; Reichard, Livson, and Petersen 1962). However, following a generally brief period of turmoil, most retirees find that there are gains which compensate for work-related losses and that problems associated with retirement are not as great as they may have expected (Reichard, Livson, and Petersen 1962; Streib and Schneider 1971). In addition, most workers anticipate retirement with positive feelings (Freidmann and Orbach 1974). Of all the variables related to successful adjustment, the most important appears to be attitude toward retirement (Friedmann and Orbach 1974; Sheppard 1976). This attitude reflects the worker's realistic appraisal of the financial and health situation he or she expects to face after retirement as much as it reflects social and psychological variables (Glamser 1976). Attitude toward retirement may also be affected by the type of work the future retiree does (i.e., both the nature of the specific job task and the skill level it requires) and whether the retirement is voluntary (Sheppard 1976). It does not seem to be affected by the subject's attitude toward his or her job prior to retirement (Glasmer 1976). Other important variables related to adjustment to retirement include the accuracy of the person's preconception of what retirement will be like and his or her postretirement income (Glamser 1976; Sheppard 1976).

Several theorists have suggested that retirement leads to a constriction of social and personal life style. Research, however, refutes this notion, indicating instead continuity in life style and social sphere before and after retirement. Friedmann and Orbach (1974) concluded, after reviewing the retirement literature, that

> it is now clear that whatever the complexities of the various relationships that can and do exist between retirement and social interaction of various types, there is no basis for the assumption that retirement causes or necessarily results in a constriction of life space and activity when the effects of health, SES, situational and cultural factors and lifetime patterns of adaptation are controlled. (P. 628)

Married couples also find little change in their relationship in terms of amount of time together, communication effectiveness, and emotional support after the immediate stress accompanying retirement has passed (Dressler 1973).

There is a large degree of individual variation in how the retiree replaces the role work played in his or her life, since people vary in the extent to which work played a significant role in their self-concept. Friedmann and Orbach (1974) suggest that in American society retirement is simply an exaggeration of the normal challenge of adjusting to leisure time that adults have been coping with for many years prior to retirement. Although retirement is a major adjustment, it is generally not unexpected. The long period of time the individual has to prepare psychologically for retirement may ameliorate its adverse effects.

For the elderly person who wishes to continue working, or for the worker who loses a job in the five to ten years before pensions and social security income are accessible, age-related discrimination encountered in the workplace can be significant and is well documented (Sheppard 1976). Once unemployed, older workers are more likely than younger ones to remain unemployed and to exhaust unemployment benefits. In addition, there is strong evidence that age is a factor in laying off workers aged fifty-five to sixty-four. The effects of loss of work on workers a bit younger than age sixty-five are likely to be much more psychologically devastating than is retirement at the age-appropriate time. Finally, people over sixty-five are generally viewed by prospective employers as poor workers and are thus discriminated against. This discrimination may be a result of unfounded stereotypes and prejudices against the elderly, as well-designed research demonstrates that the elderly are reliable, conscientious workers (Sheppard 1976).

SOCIETY

As adults age, they find themselves within a society that views them with discomfort. Within Western culture, treatment of the elderly is similar to that of other devalued minority groups. They are characterized by negative stereotypes and are subject to discrimination. When asked to describe the typical person over sixty-five, young adults, children, and even the elderly themselves generally respond with a fairly consistent and negative image. They perceive older adults as conservative, rigid, set in their ways, weak, dependent on others to meet their needs, passive, irritable, and stubborn (McTavish 1971; Thomae 1980). In addition, the elderly are viewed as lacking personal acceptability (Kidwell and Booth 1977). For example, adults tend to avoid and to maintain social distance even when the older adult is viewed in a positive light. Not only is it likely that age itself is somehow personally repulsive, but age is accompanied by characteristics, such as changed physical appearance and physical disability, that make younger adults tend to avoid the elderly

(Green 1981). Western society's discomfort with the issues of aging and dying contribute to these prejudicial attitudes.

How the elderly are affected by these prejudices is unclear. One effect may be to distance themselves from the stereotype. Although older people tend to describe the aged with the same stereotypes ascribed by younger people, the elderly also tend to avoid identifying themselves as old, thus excluding themselves from the stereotypes they have described (Rosow 1974). Such distancing mechanisms may actually serve to improve an older person's rating of his or her own situation and life satisfaction. Compared to the dismal stereotype of what the typical aged person is like, one's own problems may not appear so bad and one's strengths may seem quite good (Bultena and Powers 1976).

On the other hand, Kuypers and Bengtson (1973) suggest that society's negative views of the aged further increase older people's tendency to identify themselves as sick or inadequate. They label this process "social breakdown syndrome" (SBS). Kuypers and Bengtson believe that the elderly are vulnerable because age-related role losses and changes, loss of reference groups, and absence of age-appropriate norms increase their vulnerability to, and dependence on, societal labeling and stereotypes in forming their own self-perceptions. Because this societal labeling is negative, the person's feelings of uselessness and obsolescence are greater, thus contributing to increased vulnerability to psychological breakdown.

Gutmann (1980a) has been particularly interested in investigating what role the elderly played in earlier cultures and societies as well as in the United States. He points to the historically important role of the elderly in maintaining social order, in purveying the culture, and in providing spiritual leadership because of their assumed direct and special access to the gods. Gutmann hypothesizes that a major factor in the low position held by the elderly within modern society is that none of these functions áre highly valued because of Western civilization's preoccupation with industrialization and rapid change.

In addition, in earlier cultures and societies the elderly were likely to have held a great deal more material power over younger people than they do today, since they held the land and thus the source of wealth in the family. Their position of power has subsequently been eroded with the onset of industrialization and the accompanying direct access of the young to the means of obtaining wealth (Bengtson and Treas 1980; Gutmann 1980a). However, as the elderly continue to become an increasingly large segment of society with a more powerful political voice, they are likely to become reestablished as important shapers of the social fabric.

Adjustment in Late Life

Some of the most frequently asked questions in aging research pertain to the issue of adjustment to the aging process itself as well as to the crises and changes that tend to occur in late life. Interest in adaptation may have developed because the nature and extent of the environmental stresses and the narcissistic insults experienced after age sixty-five may be the clearest and most obvious unifying characteristic of this period. It is difficult to conceive of someone living to a very old age without confronting transitions in family, work, and societal roles, age-related changes in his or her body—in appearance, physical strength, health, cognitive abilities—and finally, the closeness of death. All these events are likely to disrupt the individual's usual pattern of behavior and threaten long-established values, beliefs, attitudes, and self-concepts.

Rosow (1974) hypothesized three important factors to be considered when looking at the impact of role transitions from one life stage to another: (1) the presence of socially sanctioned rites of passage, which publicly announce and symbolize the status change; (2) the social gains involved in the transition; and (3) the degree of role continuity across periods. He suggests that the transition to old age is difficult because it involves loss in social prestige rather than gain, it involves role discontinuity in many life areas, and it entails no clear rites of passage. In addition, Rosow suggests that this transition is quite different from earlier life-stage transitions because there is little pretransition preparation and because old age is a "normless" period in which expectations of older people's behavior are very vague.

That the role of the elderly in Western society is in a process of evolving and that expectations associated with this period are unclear is not surprising in light of the recent and marked increase in life span and the development of such influential factors as retirement. In addition, the elderly's role may be difficult to identify because Western culture's emphasis on instrumental production-oriented behaviors is out of sync with the shift in values that occurs for many older adults.

However, the literature indicates that Rosow's pessimism about the lack of preparation for the transition to old age and about adaptation itself is largely unfounded. The majority of elderly people adjust to retirement, widowhood, and changed parent-child relationships and appear to come to terms with the process of growing old. How the elderly individual accomplishes this adjustment and what characteristics differentiate

people who adjust from those who do not have long interested researchers. However, this area has been difficult to investigate because neither
the concept of stress nor of adaptation is easily defined—either theoretically or operationally.

STRESS

Operationally, stress has been defined in terms of the impact of single
life events, such as retirement or widowhood, or in terms of the life-
events approach of Holmes and Rahe (1967). These researchers assumed
that because disruption of homeostasis leads to stress, the degree of
change should provide an index of degree of stress. Therefore, their
schedule of recent events provides a measure of degree of change in life-
style and daily habits. However, the approach of correlating stress to the
occurrence of single or multiple events does not capture important aspects of the stress-adaptation phenomenon in late life.

First, the perception of the relative stressfulness of life events varies by
subject age (Sands and Parker 1979–80) as well as by sex and cultural
background (Eisdorfer and Wilkie 1977). For example, research indicates
that older subjects rate death-related events as requiring significantly less
adjustment than do younger subjects (Sands and Parker 1979–80). Widowhood is more stressful for younger adults (Lopata 1975); retirement
appears to be more stressful for women than for men (Lowenthal and
Chiriboga 1973). In their review of the literature using the Holmes and
Rahe stress model, Chiriboga and Cutler (1980) found that the events
included in the recent events inventories were frequently more relevant
to the experiences of younger than of older adults and that the degree of
disruption resulting from various life events declines with age. However,
when life-event scales incorporating age-relevant events are used, degree
of disruption may be found to be an important component in defining
stress across the life span, as Holmes and Rahe suggest. For example, in
his study of the adjustment of both sick and healthy elderly subjects to
either top- or poor-quality institutions, Lieberman (1975) found that the
best predictor of adjustment was simply the degree of change from previous living circumstances.

A second variable mediating the impact of a potentially stressful life
event is its timing in the life span. Through socialization, individuals
internalize normative expectations as to the age appropriateness of various life events such as retirement and widowhood. This system of social
age definitions provides "a frame of reference by which the experiences
of adult life are perceived as orderly and rhythmical" (Neugarten and
Datan 1973, p. 60). Neugarten has demonstrated that individuals are
very aware of age norms and age expectations, measuring and evaluating

their own life course in terms of them. In addition, life events that occur "on-time" in terms of these normative expectations are much more easily adjusted to than are unexpected, idiosyncratic events (Fiske 1980; Neugarten 1979). Events that occur developmentally on time "have been anticipated and rehearsed, the chief work completed, and the reconciliation accomplished without shattering the sense of continuity of the life cycle or the individual's coping strategies" (Neugarten 1979, p. 889). Fiske (1980) suggests that the difference in stressfulness of age-expectable and unexpectable events reflects the individual's tendency to attribute the cause of age-appropriate events to external forces beyond his or her own control and to blame him- or herself for idiosyncratic, unexpected occurrences, thus increasing the degree of stress associated with idiosyncratic events.

Third, single or multiple stressor models assume that the primary stress of old age is related to external factors, thereby ignoring the influence of internally mediated variables. Lowenthal and Chiriboga (1973) attempt to capture the importance of both types of stressors in their classification of first- and second-order stresses. First-order stress is viewed as resulting from environmental variables, whereas second-order stress reflects the impact of longstanding personality problems—for example, inability to form intimate relationships.

Stress is not only associated with external factors, such as social role changes, and internal variables, such as personality problems. In late life uncertainty about the future also provides a major source of uneasiness. Although fear of death appears to decline with age, there is increasing concern about illness and loss of physical and cognitive functioning. As Neugarten (1979) states, "Dependency and deterioration, not death itself, is the spector of old age" (pp. 890–91). Although the majority of elderly people continue to live independently, their ability to continue to do so is likely to be of increasing concern to both them and their families. Fears of dependency, poor health, and eventual nursing-home placement haunt many older adults.

Fourth, the impact of stress may not be the linear variable these models imply. Certain types and degrees of stress may facilitate personal growth and expansion whereas other degrees of stress may be disabling. Based on their study of stress and adaptation across the life span, Lowenthal and Chiriboga (1973) conclude that "presumptive social stress, whether recent or cumulative, positive or negative, may be associated with high morale, at least at some life stages. Conversely, some persons with little stress exposure may have low morale" (p. 229). They found that the presence of inner resources (e.g., capacity for mutuality, insight, and hope) mediates the relationship between stress and life satisfaction. Age was also important. Whereas teenagers demonstrating high life satisfaction had both many personal resources and high degrees of stress, elderly subjects who had few resources and little stress demonstrated the highest levels of morale for their age group. Attitude toward the event is also important in determining whether any level of stress is productive or disabling (Fiske 1980). Fiske developed a typology that attempts to divide stress into four categories according to the nature of the presumed stress (its frequency and severity) and the degree of the subject's preoccupation with it. Thus a subject's coping mechanisms are hypothesized to be quite different if he or she feels challenged when confronted by a stressful situation or if he or she is overwhelmed by that same situation.

ADAPTATION

Researchers and theorists have defined adaptation in a variety of ways: as a process of maintaining or regaining homeostasis; in terms of morale or life satisfaction; as the absence of physical or mental breakdown; and finally in terms of competence or personal growth. Just as there are multiple possible definitions, any one of these definitions can be assessed by any one of a number of measures that do not necessarily intercorrelate among themselves.

Just as what is stressful may be defined differently at different ages, what is considered adaptive behavior may likewise change with age. Fiske (1980) provides the example of the social isolate. During young adulthood this personality pattern may be very maladaptive, leading to both internal distress and social conflicts. However, the same pattern may be quite adaptive in old age. By that time the life-long social isolate may have learned to manage quite well alone and thus may be spared the stress accompanying loss of family and friends in late life. In contrast, Fiske believes that people who have frequently tried and failed to establish intimate relationships are very vulnerable in late life, particularly if they have blamed themselves for this failure.

Other factors affecting adjustment in late life are health status, level of cognitive functioning, financial resources, education, and the extent and type of coping mechanisms developed earlier in life (Fiske 1980; Lieberman 1975). If an individual reaches old age without having to confront major life crises, he or she will have failed to develop adequate coping mechanisms and thus will be ill-equipped to meet the demands of growing old. Similarly, personal coping styles developed earlier in life are likely to be carried over into old age.

Finally, an important variable mediating degree and type of adjustment is personality. For example, Havighurst (1968) found that personality was the pivotal dimension in describing an individual's pattern of aging and in predicting the relationship between level of activity and life satisfaction. Lieberman (1975) found that the capacity to maintain a coherent and consistent self-image was essential in adjustment of the elderly to changed living conditions.

Just as some investigators have studied adaptation to specific events or groups of events that accompany old age, others have taken aging as a whole and attempted to describe either patterns of adjustment to old age or variables that are predictive of adjustment to aging.

The two most widely known and debated models of adjustment to old age are the disengagement theory and the activity theory. The disengagement theory (Cumming and Henry 1961) proposes that during old age, society and the individual are involved in a process of disengaging, both psychologically and physically, from each other. This process, which can be observed in the withdrawal of the elderly from social, family, and community activities, was hypothesized to reflect processes going on within the elderly individual. Cumming and Henry believed that the elderly person's increasing preoccupation with internal processes is accompanied by an internal push to distance oneself from others. The task of old age was described as accepting and adjusting to this disengagement process.

When empirical evidence indicated that many well-adjusted older adults were active participants within their community (Havighurst 1968), the activity theory was proposed as an alternative model (Lemon, Bengtson, and Peterson 1972). It hypothesizes that the most well-adjusted elderly individuals are those who compensate for work and social losses by seeking and developing replacement social interaction. However, neither of these two theories can account comprehensively for the research findings. Although the majority of apparently happy elderly individuals are active, many socially isolated people also report high morale and high life satisfaction (Havighurst 1968; Reichard, Livson, and Petersen 1962). Similarly, it is not the amount of activity that an individual is involved in that seems to be the important variable, but rather the meaning and significance of that activity within the person's self-concept and value system. In summary, no one global theory will account for the many variables involved in adjustment to aging.

Lieberman (1975) developed a comprehensive model that attempts to describe and integrate the interracting variables which may be able to predict an individual's adjustment to stress. His predictive framework incorporates the individual's (1) resources (e.g., cognitive, energy potential, and biological); (2) current level of functioning (e.g., mental health, morale, social functioning, self-concept, and adequacy in accomplishing the tasks of late life); (3) social support network; (4) characteristics of the stressful event; (5) crisis management techniques (including personality traits and past performance in managing crisis); (6) degree of threat; (7) threat and loss management; and (8) amount of stress. Although his study found that only certain of these variables were correlated with adjustment, Lieberman's model provides a comprehensive picture of the interacting variables that may contribute to an individual's adaptation to stress. Development of a model that describes late-life adjustment is in the early stages as no empirically supported theoretical structure has been formulated which relates psychological and social variables and well-being and which accounts for a significant amount of the variance of adjustment (Lieberman 1978–79).

Survival and Longevity

Much of aging research focuses on the issues and tasks confronting the "young-old"—the age group sixty-five to seventy-five—who tend to continue to be in reasonably good health, to retain the capacity for active involvement in society, and to function in many other ways like younger people. However, with increasing age, much more of the individual's energies are focused on personal survival. In very late life, survival may be the major issue confronting the individual. Some investigators suggest that people who live best and longest are those who have made a personal commitment to self-protectiveness and who, through earlier life crises, have learned about personal survival (Fiske 1980; Loeb 1975). Age-related concentration of physical and psychological energy on immediate personal needs has considerable survival value in view of declining energy levels and increasing external and internal threats experienced by the elderly.

Factors correlated with long life vary from study to study, as subject selection criteria vary and as populations differing in culture, socioeconomic status, and cohort are investigated. Based on a comparison of long-lived and short-lived individuals in the Duke longitudinal study, Pfeiffer (1971) found that long-lived people were characterized by higher intelligence, sounder financial status, better-maintained health, and intact marriages. In contrast, in their longitudinal study of elderly Germans, Lehr and Schmitz-Scherzer (1976) found no differences between survivors and nonsurvivors based on health, family, job, and economic variables. Survivors were found to be more active and to have higher life satisfaction and a more positive outlook toward the future. Other studies have also found that activity level, involvement in social relationships, and high life satisfaction correlate with increased longevity (Britton and Britton 1972; Granick and Patterson 1971). These results indicate that a complex constellation of cultural, social, physiological, and psychological variables influence survival.

One consistent finding throughout research on longevity is that subjects who perform more poorly on cognitive tests die sooner.[*] When followed longitudinally, survivors and nonsurvivors differ both in initial levels of performance and in the degree of performance decline over time, with nonsurvivors showing the greatest decline (Botwinick 1977).

Several investigators have also pointed to a particular constellation of personality traits that may be associated with longevity. Neugarten (1979) labels this constellation the " 'adaptive paranoia' of old age." Combativeness may become a survival asset in late life. Lieberman (1975) found that elderly subjects who survived crises were "those who were aggressive, irritating, narcissistic and demanding" (p. 155). He believes that "a certain amount of magical thinking and perceiving oneself as the center of the universe with a pugnacious stance toward the world—even a highly suspicious one—seemed more likely to insure homeostasis in the face of a severe crisis" (pp. 155–56).

In contrast, a passive stance toward the environment may hasten mortality. For example, studying elderly Navajo Indians, Gutmann (1971) found that a passive stance contributed to the presence of chronic debilitating illness and thus was correlated with a higher rate of mortality. A passive stance in late life is also correlated with a higher incidence of depression, which, in the elderly, is frequently debilitating.

Cognitive Functioning in the Elderly

This section briefly reviews the literature on age-related changes in intelligence, memory, behavioral speed, and mental processing capacity. It also briefly discusses research on variables, such as health and personality; that moderate the relationship between age and cognition. Finally, although much of this section describes research comparing the performance of young and elderly subjects on structured learning and memory tasks, the last part presents an alternative model for viewing changes in cognitive functioning across the life span.

---

[*]See Botwinick (1977); Jarvik and Falek (1963); Lehr and Schmitz-Scherzer (1976); and Pfeiffer (1971).

INTELLIGENCE

Much of the research on cognitive functioning in the elderly has focused on the use of global measures of intelligence that incorporate assessment of verbal skills (knowledge of general information, arithmetic calculations, vocabulary, abstract verbal reasoning) and visuospatial skills. These measures were initially designed to predict school achievement in children and adolescents. The long-held belief that generalized decline in intellectual abilities begins in adulthood, possibly as early as age twenty to thirty, and continues progressively until old age and death was based on these measures (Wechsler 1958). However, by using cross-sectional age-group comparisons, this research does not distinguish between poor performance due to cohort differences in education and occupation and impairment due to age. Therefore, it overestimates the extent of decline in intellectual functioning. To correct for this overestimate of decline, longitudinal and cross-sequential research designs have been developed that control for cohort differences. As a result, more complex and less pessimistic patterns relating aging to changes in intelligence have emerged.

In his review of the literature, Botwinick (1977) found that there is only a 0.4 to 0.5 correlation between level of intelligence and age. This suggests that, at most, age accounts for approximately 20 percent of the variance in global intelligence measures. Until age seventy, chronological age accounts for less test performance variance than does subject cohort, education, health, occupation, and socioeconomic status (Willis and Baltes 1980).

Both cross-sectional and longitudinal research demonstrates that certain components of intelligence are more susceptible to the effects of aging than are others. Verbal skills, such as vocabulary, recall of general information, and awareness of social expectations and norms remain stable until very late in life. Performance on tasks that assess visuospatial skills, new learning, and response speed declines with age. Jarvik (1973) described this "classic" pattern of aging in her summary of a number of longitudinal studies:

> Despite differences in the composition of the samples with regard to age, intelligence, education, socioeconomic background, and other relevant variables, there appears to be at least one common threat leading toward a cohesive pattern of intellectual functioning in the later years of life. That thread seems to be a remarkable stability of verbal scores—whenever health has been preserved—accompanied by a relentlessly progressive decline in performance on speeded tasks. . . . And this pattern is evident under a wide variety of circumstances. (P. 65)

Botwinick (1977) concludes that this pattern of differential decline in visuospatial as opposed to verbal skills holds until age seventy to eighty, when generalized decline in all areas of intellectual functioning is more likely to be seen. This effect is independent of intelligence level. Research indicates that as high-and low-ability subjects age, they maintain their relative ability standing in comparison to their age-group peers and that subjects of all ability levels are equally subject to decline (Botwinick 1977).

MEMORY

The ability to recall information acquired naturally over the life span remains basically stable as people age (Fozard 1980). Elderly subjects remember common expressions, information concerning sports and movies, and names of well-known personalities as well as do younger subjects. Using a multiple-choice recognition task to assess recall of this type of information, Lachman and Lachman (1980) found that the store of total information increased with age and that the efficiency of retrieving this information remained constant across the life span. When required to remember newly presented information, however, elderly subjects demonstrate difficulty as compared to younger subjects. Extensive research has investigated the specific nature and degree of these deficits. Current models generally divide memory into the components of primary and secondary memory (Craik 1977). Primary memory (PM) is involved when the retained material is still being held consciously and is being rehearsed for encoding into secondary or long-term memory (SM). The capacity of PM appears to remain constant as people age. For example, immediate memory span, when assessed by immediate recall of information, such as a series of digits, does not decline with normal aging (Craik 1977). Decline is found, however, when elderly subjects are required to manipulate or reorganize information in PM, for example, when recalling a series of digits backward.

Greater age-correlated decrements are present in retrieval of recently learned information from secondary or long-term memory, particularly on free recall tasks that provide no cues to aid memory (Craik 1977). Evidence of greater age-related deficits on free recall than on recognition tasks led to the hypothesis that the age-related memory deficit involves a retrieval failure. This hypothesis suggests that by providing cues which aid retrieval of information from long-term memory, recognition tasks compensate for the retrieval problems and thus improve performance. However, there is also evidence that elderly subjects have less effective information-acquisition strategies (Craik 1977). They spontaneously use less complex and less rich organizational strategies in processing and encoding material (Craik 1977; Hartley, Harker and Walsh 1980). Therefore, they have a less elaborate SM network of coded and stored material to assist them in recalling information. When provided with assistance in using more complex learning strategies, age-related deficits in SM recall diminish but do not disappear.

MENTAL PROCESSING CAPACITY

A consistent finding across many experimental paradigms is that deficits increase as a task's complexity increases (Rabbitt 1977). Age-related performance differences are minimal on simple problem-solving, probability-matching, and immediate memory tasks. On these tasks, young and old subjects appear to use the same learning strategies. However, as a task's cognitive processing demands increase, older subjects perform more poorly, seemingly limited by their apparent inability to use sufficiently elaborate and flexible problem-solving approaches. It is not certain whether they are unable to devise appropriate strategies on these tasks or whether they continue to inappropriately apply simpler problem-solving techniques (Rabbitt 1977). Similar findings are present on divided attention tasks. When required to simultaneously attend to more than one task component, older subjects are severely handicapped as compared to younger adults (Hoyer and Plude 1980).

One explanation for these findings is that aging is associated with decreased processing resources (Craik and Simon 1980). Other investigators have suggested that with aging there is increased "perceptual noise" resulting in decreased ability to suppress internal and external irrelevant stimulation (Layton 1975). The decreased rate of mental processing in older subjects also may preclude the development of alternative, more complex, learning strategies (Cerella, Poon, and Williams 1980).

Although they do not spontaneously demonstrate complex problem-solving techniques, the elderly can make use of and thus benefit from training and task instructions that teach them more elaborate and effective strategies (Giambra and Arenberg 1980). Labouvie-Vief and Gonda (1976) found that elderly subjects performed more competently, even without specific instructions as to how to improve their performance, when they were given sufficient opportunity to become familiar with the laboratory task and to practice skills.

SPEED OF BEHAVIOR

One of the most consistent findings has been the increasing slowness that occurs in all areas of behavior with age. Performance differences between older and younger subjects are greatest on timed tasks and diminish when tasks are self-paced. Older subjects require more time to completely process a single perceptual event (Hoyer and Plude 1980), to scan and evaluate visually complex displays (Rabbitt 1977), to retrieve material from long- or short-term memory (Craik 1977), to learn newly presented information and solve problems (Rabbitt 1977), and to respond on simple and choice reaction time tasks (Mathey 1976). The components of general intelligence that show the greatest decline with age are ones that require speed as well as accuracy in response.

The pervasive loss of speed in cognitive behavior has led to the hypothesis that this loss is directly related to the neurobiological changes that occur with aging (Birren, Woods, and Williams 1980). A direct relationship to central nervous system (CNS) changes is also indicated by evidence that the greater involvement of CNS mediating processes in executing the behavior, the greater the age-correlated decrease in speed. For example, patellar reflex speed, in which there is little CNS input, appears to be unaffected by subject age (Clarkson 1978). Less slowing is seen on sensorimotor tasks than on tasks that involve mental processing (Birren, Woods, and Williams 1980). As the task's processing demands increase, the effects of age on response rate increase (Cerella, Poon, and Williams 1980). The greatest response time differences between young and old subjects are found, for example, on tasks that require simultaneous rehearsal and perception of different stimuli, attention to two or more components of a task, or manipulation rather than simple recall of information.

Birren, Woods, and Williams (1980) suggest that the underlying neurobiological change accounting for this loss of speed is either diffuse or occurs in key nuclei, such as the reticular system, which influence cortical, cerebellar, and brainstem functions simultaneously. Age-related changes such as reduction in synaptic density and neurotransmitters, reduction in the number of brain cells, and/or decrease in oxygenation of neural cells may be possible physical bases for decreased response speed.

The importance of mental processing speed in all areas of behavior has also led some investigators to suggest that this factor is central to any cognitive decline that occurs with aging (Birren, Woods, and Williams 1980). However, on certain types of self-paced tasks, elderly subjects (particularly those over seventy) are more inaccurate as well as slower than younger subjects. Thus although loss of speed is certainly of importance, it is unlikely to be the only factor in late-life cognitive decline.

CONFOUNDING VARIABLES

As a person ages, he or she is also likely to have increased health problems, to grow closer to death, and to experience personality changes—variables that independently influence cognitive functioning, thus confounding attempts to draw conclusions regarding the unique effects of aging.

Research indicates that much of the cognitive decline seen in older adults reflects the effects of poor health rather than aging. Even mild health problems can exert a detrimental influence. Birren and associates (1963) tested one group of elderly men who were free from any signs of disease and a second group who also would have been considered healthy by normal standards but who had minimal signs of illness. Only in the second group was there a correlation between physiological and cognitive measures, suggesting both that age itself is not a strong correlate of cognitive change and that even very minor health problems can lead to cognitive decline. Hulicka (1967) found that on three of four experimental memory tasks administered, age-related decrements were removed when subject health status was taken into account statistically. Finally, although it is demonstrated even by healthy elderly subjects, behavioral slowing with age is exacerbated in older adults with hypertension, coronary heart disease, and organic brain disease (Birren, Woods, and Williams 1980).

Closeness to death is another confounding variable in the relationship between age and cognitive change. There is a marked drop in cognitive functioning during the five to ten years just prior to death—"terminal drop" (Jarvik and Falek 1963; Riegel and Riegel 1972). Blum, Clark, and Jarvik (1973) found that whereas aging correlated with decline in visuospatial and perceptual skills, terminal drop was characterized by decline in verbal skills. Other researchers have supported the finding of decline just prior to death without pointing to any particular pattern of decline among cognitive functions (Hall et al. 1972; Reimanis and Green 1971).

Personality variables, such as level of motivation and cautiousness, also affect cognitive functioning. It has traditionally been assumed that elderly subjects perform poorly on laboratory tasks because they have little experience with such tasks, view them as meaningless, and thus lack sufficient motivation to perform well. However, the research of Eisdorfer and his colleagues, in which task performance and physiological indicators of autonomic nervous system arousal were measured simultaneously, suggests that elderly subjects experience debilitatingly high, rather than low, levels of motivation (Powell, Eisdorfer, and Bogdonoff 1964; Troyer et al. 1966). These investigators hypothesize that elderly subjects are so highly motivated that accompanying high levels of anxiety interfere with task performance.

Increased cautiousness is another personality characteristic that accompanies aging (Botwinick 1973), leading to the possibility that slower performance reflects a more cautious attitude in test taking. However, it is unlikely that the tendency to be more cautious accounts for the pervasive presence of behavioral slowing in both human and animal subjects or for its immunity to situational variables (Birren, Woods, and Williams 1980).

Data from the Bonn Longitudinal Study of Aging (BLSA) indicates that the relationship between other personality variables and performance on cognitive tasks is an area well worth further exploration. Reviewing the BLSA longitudinal data on psychomotor performance, Mathey (1976) found that performance on a choice reaction time task correlated with subjects' degree of activity, self-control, and level of adjustment. Subjective health ratings correlated more strongly with performance than did objective physiological measures.

QUALITATIVE VERSUS QUANTITATIVE COGNITIVE CHANGES

Much of the literature reviewed in this section views cognitive change in quantitative terms. This research assumes that although an individual's cognitive skills may improve or deteriorate with aging, the nature and usefulness of these skills remains constant across the life span. Some theorists argue that any cognitive changes occurring in adulthood are quantitative in nature (Flavell 1970). Others view changes in cognition across the life span as qualitative rather than quantitative. The qualitative framework emphasizes (1) the ecological validity of investigations of cognitive functioning in the elderly; (2) the heterogeneity, rather than the similarity, in cognitive functioning among elderly subjects; and (3) the reorganization of skills with aging, with refinement of some abilities compensating for the decline of others.

Investigations of quantitative cognitive changes have generally focused on age differences in the early acquisition phases of learning using test instruments and learning models developed for younger subjects. Thus these investigations are much more relevant to the cognitive experience of younger than older adults. Little is known, however, about the learning and problem-solving tasks that are required in later adult life, the relationship between these intellectual tasks and those of young adulthood, and the extent to which the knowledge and skills acquired as a young adult must be unlearned and replaced as one ages (Willis and Baltes 1980). Only after systematic investigation of these issues can the actual intellectual behavior of older adults and the ecology in which it occurs become the basis for the study of cognition and aging.

In support of this qualitative approach is evidence that aging adults are not passive victims of cognitive change. Instead they appear to actively reorganize skills and compensate for cognitive losses. When one hundred successful professional people were asked to describe changes in their ways of coping with the cognitive demands placed on them, they identified modifications in the way they both defined and approached problems. The limitations that accompany aging were also compensated for by increased willingness to take advice and by conservation of energy through limiting attention to essential task demands (Birren 1969).

The second focus of this framework is the heterogeneity of cognitive functioning in the elderly. Interindividual differences in cognitive functioning increase markedly with age, leading to more performance differences within a group of normal elderly subjects than between groups of elderly and younger adults. It is likely, therefore, that rather than a uniform, homogeneous pattern of aging, there are many different patterns with complex relationships to biological and personality variables. This evidence indicates the importance not only of longitudinal research that illuminates the multiple aging patterns, but of comparisons between identifiable groups of elderly subjects rather than between old and young subjects.

Finally, this framework focuses on the reorganization of skills with aging. Schaie (1977–78) presented a model that hypothesizes cognitive reorganization across the life span in reaction to life experiences. He believes that the "processes which have been documented for the acquisition of cognitive structures and functions in childhood and during the early adult phase may not be relevant to the maintenance and reorganization of structures required to meet the demands of later life" (pp. 130–31). Schaie postulates five sequentially occurring stages. Initially, in the acquisitive phase of childhood and adolescence, the cognitive task is to acquire knowledge and the emphasis is on learning purely for the sake of learning. The young adult enters the achieving phase when learning begins to be directed toward meeting the specific goals relevant to establishing an independent life style. During the executive and responsible stages of the adult years there is increasing emphasis on organizing, integrating, and interpreting information and applying this information to specific tasks and goals. Thus the issue in adulthood is how to best use knowledge that has already been acquired. These skills are not assessed by commonly used psychometric tests. Finally, in the "reintegrative stage," which occurs in old age, motivation and attitudinal variables increasingly temper cognitive processes. The complexity of adult cognitive structures has reached the overload stage, and the emphasis is on regaining simplicity and understanding "why should I know" rather than "what should I know" (adolescence) or "how should I use what I know" (adulthood).

This alternative framework necessitates the development of measures that are sensitive to the pertinent issues and life context of cognitive functioning in different age groups. It also draws attention to the potential meaning and importance of the significant differences in functioning within groups of elderly subjects and thus should enrich our understanding of aging.

CONCLUSION

As in many areas of aging research, investigations of cognitive functioning in the elderly are just beginning to illuminate the important issues and patterns. As elderly subjects begin to be viewed as a diverse group demonstrating multiple age-related patterns of cognitive change, researchers can explore which changes are primary to the aging process itself and which reflect the impact of other variables such as poor health, personality traits, and cohort effects. More questions are being asked regarding the specific cognitive components that are affected by age as well as the specific conditions that affect both cognitive functioning in late life and the degree of age-related change. Increasing attention is also being paid to the neurological basis for the changes that are consistently and strongly related to age, such as loss of speed. Finally, as researchers become sensitized to the value of exploring cognition from the perspective of older adults and their intellectual environment, new and important models become available for this research.

Biological Aspects of Normal Aging

This section reviews the problems and potentials of a biological perspective of aging including discussion of adaptive aspects of normative biological aging. Theories of biological aging will then be discussed, utilizing the central nervous system as a prototype of changes occurring in other organ systems during normal aging.

PROBLEMS

A strictly biomedical approach to aging has contributed to the portrayal of the normal aging process as a grim litany of physical and emotional ills (Butler and Lewis 1977). Physical decline and deterioration have been overemphasized. Biomedical researchers who use normal healthy adults as standards of normality may have a tendency to interpret normal biological changes of aging as indicative of decline and deterioration. Biomedical research has paid comparatively less attention to adaptive, homeostatic aspects of the generalized "slowing down" that occurs during aging. In addition, the potentials for the continued growth and development of elderly persons in the psychological and social realms, as discussed earlier in this chapter, have been the responsibility of social and behavioral scientists and are thus not considered as important variables by biomedical researchers.

Butler and Lewis (1977) believe the negative view of old age is a problem of Western civilization. Compared to Eastern culture and philosophy that places the individual self, his or her life and death within the process of the human experience, Western philosophy considers death and aging as outside of the self. Western civilization's high regard for individuality, control, and self-realization makes aging and death an outrage, an affront to man, rather than the logical and necessary process of old life making way for new. Negative societal attitudes toward aging have produced difficult problems for the elderly and for those preparing for old age.

Butler and Lewis (1977) further believe that until recently biomedical services have reflected society's denial and repression of aging. Research on normal development has concentrated primarily on childhood development and has seldom gone beyond the early-adult years. Many of the myths and misconceptions about aging prior to research beginning in the late 1950s arose partly because research concentrated on sick and institutionalized elderly, rather than normal elderly people living in the natural setting of their home and community. Studying only the impaired, institutionalized elderly and exposing medical and other health professional students only to this biased population encouraged health professionals to view the elderly as diseased and incapacitated. In actuality, as already mentioned, only 5 percent of those over age sixty-five in the United States reside in long-term care institutions.

Some of the myths about normal biological aging, since refuted, include the belief that cognitive and sexual impairment are normal concomitants of aging, that most older people are destined for institutionalization, and that the last phase of life is a period of only loss and depletion. Beginning in the 1950s investigators at Duke University (Palmore 1970) studied prospectively a group of healthy older people in the community. Some of their findings, which helped demythologize normal aging, included the following facts. (1) Decreased cerebral blood flow and oxygen consumption resulted from arteriosclerosis rather than inevitable concomitants of aging. Healthy elderly men (average age seventy-one) presented cerebral physiology and intellectual functioning that compared favorably with control subjects (average age twenty-one). Although there was slowing in speed and response to test items in the elderly subjects, this was correlated with environmental deprivation and depression, as well as physical decline. (2) Adaptation and survival were associated with the individual's self-view and sense of ongoing usefulness as well as health status. Individuals who were outgoing and who were interested in new activities and involvements were found to have the least disease and the longest survival.

Reviewing these longitudinal, prospective studies of normative aging, Butler and Lewis (1977) conclude that healthy elderly people tend to be optimistic, resourceful, and flexible. They attribute manifestations of mental illness to medical illness, personality factors, and sociocultural variables rather than to the normal aging process.

The view that aging is synonymous with disease and deterioration is challenged by other investigators (Birren and Renner 1977) who have demonstrated increasing variability in physiological functioning with increasing age. Chronological age has not been a reliable indicator of biological functioning.

POTENTIALS—AN ADAPTATIONAL MODEL

We propose a biological, adaptational model of normal aging that views the aging process as an orchestration of change in which there is an adaptive "slowing down" of interrelated biological systems. This model offers a distinct advantage over the traditional biomedical model of decline and deterioration because it takes into account the adaptive effect of change in one physiological parameter on other systems. For example, a decrease in an older person's muscle strength and ability to ambulate may be viewed on the one hand as indicative of decline, yet on the other hand this "slowing down" may be adaptive by protecting the older person from sudden exertion that could compromise the cardiovascular system. A mild degree of hypothyroidism in an older person with cardiovascular disease could have salutory effects on the heart. Rapid correction of such hypothyroidism may compromise cardiac functioning.

The increasing specialization in the medical field has fostered a tendency for specialists to focus on a particular subsystem of the complicated human being, sometimes without sufficient consideration of how treatment for one condition may aggravate another. For example, medication used to treat one disease may aggravate another organ system. Antihypertensive drugs can cause clinical depression, especially in those susceptible to depression, and neuroleptic drugs can aggravate Parkinson's disease, especially in older patients with diminished dopamine in the basal ganglia.

By considering the effects of medical interventions on other organ systems, by conceptualizing man as an interrelated biopsychosocial system, and by appreciating the adaptive aspects of normal as well as abnormal physiological changes with aging, health-care providers can be encouraged to take a multifactorial, comprehensive, biopsychosocial approach in the assessment and treatment of the elderly patient.

PHYSIOLOGICAL CHANGES THAT OCCUR WITH AGING

Although 86 percent of persons over age sixty-five in the United States have one or more chronic illnesses, Butler and Lewis (1977) believe that physical disease is not a necessary concomitant of aging. Many illnesses afflicting the elderly are treatable, possibly preventable, and probably retardable.

There is nevertheless a decrement in physiological functioning with increasing age, as demonstrated in figure 7.2. The average performance of thirty-year-old subjects on a number of physiological parameters is taken as 100 percent and the average decrement, as a percent of the performance of these thirty-year-old subjects, is projected linearly to age

FIGURE 7.2
Age Decrements in Physiological Functions in Males

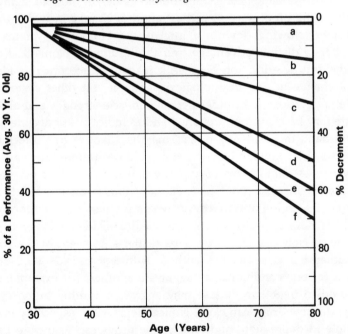

Mean values for 20- to 35-year-old subjects are taken as 100 percent. Decrements shown are schematic linear projections: (a) fasting blood glucose; (b) nerve conduction velocity and cellular enzymes; (c) resting cardiac index; (d) vital capacity and renal blood flow; (e) maximum breathing capacity, and (f) maximum work rate and maximum oxygen uptake.

NOTE: Reprinted, by permission of the publisher, from N. W. Shock, "Energy Metabolism, Calorie Intake and Physical Activity of the Aging," in *Nutrition in Old Age*, ed. L. A. Carlson (Uppsala: Almquist and Wiksell, 1972), 12.

eighty. It can be seen that variables associated with the maintenance of the internal environment of man under resting conditions show relatively little to no age trend (line a for fasting blood glucose). Nerve conduction velocity, which involves measurements in a simple organ system, shows an average decrement of approximately fifteen percent between ages thirty to eighty (line b). Vital lung capacity and renal blood flow (line d) in eighty-year-olds are only about one-half the average value of thirty-year-olds. Shock (1977) believes these performances (c through f) require the integrative activity of the cardiovascular, nervous, muscular, and respiratory systems and show the greatest decrements with age. Aging has a significant effect on the rate at which these variables are returned to resting levels after they have been displaced either experimentally or by responses to environmental factors. Rate of readjustment is substantially slower in the old than in the young.

This research demonstrating decremental changes in physiological functioning with age has several methodological flaws. These idealized norms are based on cross-sectional data that identify age differences rather than age changes. In addition, variations from these norms are common. Only with longitudinal prospective studies using repeated measurements of the same individual as he or she ages can one determine if these physiological decrements hold true in most individuals and in different subpopulations.

Biological Theories of Normal Aging

AGING AS THE BREAKDOWN OF REGULATORY MECHANISMS

Dilman (1971) suggests that the key process in aging is the gradual elevation of the threshold of sensitivity of the hypothalamic region of the brain to feedback suppression. In other words, as one ages one of the major regulator portions of the brain, the hypothalamus, becomes less responsive to feedback from other portions of the brain and body; this may account for the aging person's decreased adaptation to stress. Shock (1977) takes issue with this theory because there is no direct experimental evidence to show that when a specific quantitatively measured stimulus is applied to the hypothalamus, a diminished quantitatively measured response occurs.

Frolkis (1966, 1968) takes a multisystems view of aging as the sum total of unequal changes in regulatory processes at the molecular, cellular, and systems levels of the organism. With increasing age, the sensitivity of a series of effectors (heart, blood vessels, etc.) to the action of humoral factors increases, while their sensitivity to neural influences decreases. Frolkis supports his theory by citing many observations to show that, with increasing age, the minimal stimulus of a hormone (or drug) required to act upon an effector decreases; that is, in the aged animal, the effector's sensitivity to the chemical stimulus increases and the maximum possible response diminishes. Shock (1977) criticizes Frolkis's experimental conditions and designs and points to experiments that refute the latter's observations and conclusions (Roth 1975; Tuttle 1966). Additional contradiction of Frolkis's theory comes from the work of Gusseck (1972) and Adelman (1972), who have demonstrated that loss of binding sites in tissues from senescent animals may account for the reduction in responsiveness to various stimuli.

GENETIC THEORY OF AGING

The genetic theory postulates that a biological clock located in the DNA portion of the cell controls the aging process. Hayflick and Moorhead (1961) report that normal human fibroblasts, when cultured, underwent a finite number of population doublings and then died. Fibroblast cultures derived from embryo donors underwent significantly more population doublings than fibroblasts from older donors. Subsequent experiments demonstrated that cells could be removed from the culture, frozen for as long as twelve years, and, when returned to a cultured medium, would begin to divide. Regardless of the number of doublings reached by the population at the time the cells were preserved, the summated total number of doublings was fifty. It was later discovered that the given number of doublings, fifty, is the same for male or female cells. If true, then differences in life expectancy between men and women may not be attributable to intracellular differences but rather to differences in life style, environment, and other variables.

The genetic theory of aging is also supported by observations that descendants of long-lived families tend to live longer and by Darwinian principles regarding survival of the fittest.

IMMUNOLOGIC THEORY OF AGING

When a foreign substance is introduced into the body, the immune system responds in two ways. First, antibody molecules are produced that specifically bind the introduced substance. Second, cells are mobilized that specifically react with and destroy the invader. Walford (1969) and Burnet (1970), two advocates of the immunological theory of aging, believe that with the passage of time alterations and distortions occur within the immune system so that the system begins functioning in a self-destructive manner.

It is theorized that the progressive distortion of the immune system may contribute to a number of diseases in later life. For example, late-onset diabetes occurs in a mild form in almost half the population over age sixty-five and in a severe form in about 13 percent of people over age seventy-five. Adult-onset diabetes may be an autoimmune disease, representing an autoimmune reaction to insulin and to the cells that produce it. Another example is the characteristic loss of cortical neurons with aging; this may be associated with specific antibodies destructive to the brain as demonstrated in experiments in old mice (Nandy, Fritz, and Threatt 1975).

The Central Nervous System as Prototype of Normal Aging

A review of morphological, biochemical, and physiological changes occurring in the central nervous system with aging may exemplify changes occurring in other organ systems.

Organic mental disorders (the dementias) are not inevitable consequences of aging but rather are frequently caused by diagnosable medical illnesses that may be totally or partially reversible. Even patients with degenerative dementias, such as Alzheimer's disease and related disorders, are responsive to comprehensive, biopsychosocial treatment approaches (Lazarus 1978). Although severe organic mental disorders afflict more than 5 percent of elderly individuals in the United States and less severe forms of these disorders appear in an additional 10 percent, the vast majority of individuals over age sixty-five have no dysfunction of the central nervous system. There are, however, morphological, biochemical, and physiological CNS changes that may contribute to the elderly's increased vulnerability to psychiatric and neurological disturbances.

MORPHOLOGICAL CHANGES

There is a loss of central nervous system neurons associated with aging leading to a decline in the weight of the brain. In general, in humans by age ninety, the brain weighs about the same as the brain of a three-year-old child (Kaack, Ordy, and Trapp 1975).

Microscopically, senile plaques increase with advancing years, but these have not, in general, been significantly correlated with degree of psychopathology or intellectual impairment. As discussed earlier in this chapter, cognitive functioning is influenced not only by the brain's integrity but by multiple factors including previous education, emotional stability, personality traits, environmental stimulation, and so forth.

Changes associated with aging have been studied in different parts of the neurophil and the dendrites (Scheibel and Scheibel 1975) and the extracellular space (Bondareff and Narotzky 1972). Lipton and Nemeroff (1978) believe that morphological changes associated with aging contribute to the aging individual's decreased capacity to adapt to environmental changes and stress.

BIOCHEMICAL CHANGES

Neurochemical studies concerned with the aging process have concentrated on alterations in the functional activity of putative central nervous system neurotransmitters and related synthetic and degradative enzymes. These neurotransmitters are believed to be involved in interneuronal synaptic transmission and thereby influence mood states, cognitive functioning, and integrative functions. Studies in aging men and animals have revealed a reduction of catecholamine neurotransmitters such as norepinephrine (Samorajski 1975), a decrease in the functional capacity of cholinergic neurons (Timaras and Vernadakis 1972), and a reduction of enzymes responsible for the synthesis of other important neurotransmitters (McGeer et al. 1971). In addition, the enzyme MAO (monamine oxidase), responsible for the degradation of putative neurotransmitters, has been found by Robinson and associates (1972) to increase significantly with age, thereby reducing the amount of important monamine neurotransmitters such as norepinephrine. This process may increase the elderly's vulnerability to depression. Finch (1973) has postulated that CNS catecholamine systems may be the pacemakers of aging and that changes in monoamine neurotransmitter function may initiate neuroendocrine and peripheral endocrine changes that then affect changes in all body systems.

PHYSIOLOGICAL CHANGES

With increasing age, there is a gradual decrease in cerebral oxygen uptake by the brain and the sensitivity and responsiveness of organs and issues to sympathetic and parasympathetic nerve impulses tend to decline (Timaras and Vernadakis 1972). For example, when studying biochemical and physiological responses to CNS stimuli, McNamara and coworkers (1977) found catecholamine synthesis to be greater in young than in old animals after a single electroconvulsive treatment.

ADAPTIVE ASPECTS OF CNS CHANGES

These morphological, biochemical, and physiological concomitants to the aging process may predispose the elderly to emotional and neurological disorders. When examined in the light of their adaptive aspects, however, an alternative to the model of decline and deterioration emerges.

It can be said that there is a general "slowing down" of all organ systems during normative aging. If one organ system, such as the brain, were not to "slow down" in a corresponding fashion to other organ systems, a potentially dangerous imbalance could occur. For example, if signals from the brain were to entice a seventy-five-year-old to enter a marathon race but her body was not properly conditioned, the elderly runner would be vulnerable to injury.

The "selective inattention" noted by Weinberg (1975) may protect the aging individual from excessive input of sensory stimulation that could lead to anxiety and fatigue. Protection from excessive environmental stimulation may facilitate the elderly's tendency to reminisce and introspect, processes that serve adaptive purposes.

It is problematic to study normal biological aging from only a biological viewpoint since psychological and sociocultural variables interdigitate with biological factors. As Birren and Renner (1977) eloquently state:

> Not all aspects of the human organism are necessarily in close synchrony in the process of aging. While an individual may be declining physically in the later years, he may show an expansion in the psychological domain. Therefore, in describing an individual it may be useful to distinguish three ages—biological age, referring to life expectancy; psychological age, referring to adaptive, behavioral capacities of the individual; and social age, referring to the social roles of an individual with regard to the expectations of his group and society for someone of his age. (P. 5)

Conclusion

As the research reviewed in this chapter demonstrates, defining what is the typical and expectable experience of people over age sixty-five is a complex and challenging undertaking. The diversity within this age group, its transitional status within Western society, the inaccessibility of subjects, and the methodological problems involved in studying cohorts of older people contribute to the difficulty of defining normality in late life. However, a base of empirical studies on cognitively intact, psychologically and physically healthy older adults is developing. These data

provide a basis for challenging the long-established myths and stereotypes about old age that grew out of clinical involvement with institutionalized and hospitalized impaired elderly patients.

In contrast to these myths, on reaching age sixty-five or seventy the
individual is not typically confronted with incapacitating illness or dementia. Older adults are not preoccupied with loss, death, failure, or
disappointment. In contrast to stereotypes of late life as a time of rigid
reentrenchment in personality, coping methods, and attitudes, older
adults show remarkable capacity to confront, adapt to, and learn from
late-life experiences. In coping with these experiences, the individual has
a long lifetime of experiences on which to draw.

The literature reviewed in this chapter indicates three major issues as
shaping the normal experience for this phase of life. The first issue is the
diminishing impact of life structures and social responsibilities. Although
many older adults continue to play an active role in work and social
activities, there is for most people a sense of choice about either continuing these commitments or developing new outlets for time and energy.
Whereas in middle adulthood, when responsibility for the care of others,
such as one's children and aging parents, predominates, caring for and
maintaining one's own life becomes the important issue in late life. Western culture's work-oriented ethic contributes to the elderly being viewed
with disdain and as expendable when instrumental role functions become less important to them. However, this is a simplistic and age-biased
view. The freedom that accompanies this loosening of work-oriented role
demands can allow for the development of new life interests and perspectives. The challenge for the aging individual is to constructively
make use of this freedom; the challenge for Western society is to learn
from, and to integrate, this shift in values into its cultural heritage.

A second important issue in the life period after age sixty-five is the
individual's personal confrontation with the impact of the aging process.
Although pessimistic beliefs that old age is necessarily accompanied by
rapid and pervasive physical, cognitive, and psychological deterioration
have proven to be unfounded, changes accompanying aging do impact
on the individual. Research suggests that not only do individuals actively
adapt to these changes, but that the changes themselves can be adaptive.
In addition, older adults must be able to maintain a sense of what is
constant and essential in their own self-view—an awareness and acceptance of the essential self that developed during youth and adulthood—
and be able to integrate into that core self-concept the new experiences
and resulting self-awareness that occurs in late life.

The third issue that shapes late-life experiences is closeness to death.
Aging individuals confront not only their own death, but that of family,

friends, and generation. Evidence that older people demonstrate less fear of death than do younger adults suggests that psychological and physiological preparation for this event takes place in late life. The gradual slowing down of physiological systems may reflect a biological preparation for death. The deaths of friends and family make the process more familiar, less frightening, and increasingly accepted as an "age-appropriate" event. Psychologically, the aging adult engages in a process of putting his or her own life in order through reminiscence and reflection. This life review process provides an opportunity for further psychological growth and self-understanding.

It can be argued that late life is the most challenging life stage. With the exception of adolescence, there is no other period in which the individual confronts so many changes that challenge the self-concept and personal worldview, both within the body and in relation to social expectations. It is not surprising that when confronted with so much internal and external instability, personality and coping styles that have developed across the life span provide the one consistent element of strength and stability. It is also not surprising, in light of many years of very diverse experiences prior to age sixty-five, that the later years is the period that finds the greatest variety, richness, and diversity among people.

REFERENCES

Adams, D. L. 1971. "Correlates of Satisfaction Among the Elderly." *Gerontologist* 2:64–68.

Adelman, R. C. 1972. "Age Dependent Control of Enzyme Adaptation." In *Advances in Gerontological Research*, ed. B. L. Strehler, pp. 1–23. New York: Academic Press.

Atchley, R. C. 1975. "Dimensions of Widowhood in Later Life." *Gerontologist* 15:176–78.

Benedek, T. 1970. "Parenthood During the Life Cycle." In *Parenthood: Its Psychology and Psychopathology*, ed. E. J. Anthony and T. Benedek, pp. 185–206. Boston: Little, Brown.

Bengtson, V. L., and Treas, J. 1980. "The Changing Family Context of Mental Health and Aging." In *Handbook of Mental Health and Aging*, ed. J. Birren and R. B. Sloane, pp. 400–428. Englewood Cliffs, N.J.: Prentice-Hall.

Bengtson, V. L.; Kasschau, P. L.; and Ragan, P. K. 1977. "The Impact of Social Structure on Aging Individuals." In *Handbook of the Psychology of Aging*, ed. J. E. Birren and K. W. Schaie, pp. 327–53. New York: Van Nostrand Reinhold.

Bengtson, V.; Olander, E. B.; and Haddad, A. 1976. "The 'Generation Gap' and Aging Family Members: Toward a Conceptual Model." In *Time, Self, & Roles in Old Age*, ed. J. F. Gubrium, pp. 237–63. New York: Human Sciences Press.

Birren, J. E. 1969. "Age and Decision Strategies." In *Decision Making and Age*, ed. A. T. Welford and J. E. Birren, pp. 23–36. Basel: S. Karger.

Birren, J. E., and Renner, V. J. 1977. "Research on the Psychology of Aging: Principles and Experimentation." In *Handbook of Aging and the Individual*, ed. J. E. Birren and K. W. Schaie, pp. 3–38. New York: Van Nostrand Reinhold.

Birren, J. E.; Woods, A. M.; and Williams, M. V. 1980. "Behavioral Slowing with Age:

Causes, Organizations, and Consequences." In *Aging in the 1980's: Psychological Issues*, ed. L. W. Poon, pp. 293–308. Washington D. C.: American Psychological Association.

Birren, J. E., et al., eds. 1963. *Human Aging: A Biological and Behavioral Study*. Washington, D.C.: U.S. Government Printing Office.

Blum, J. E.; Clark, E. T.; and Jarvik, L. F. 1973. "The New York State Psychiatric Institute Study of Aging Twins." In *Intellectual Functioning in Adults*, ed. L. F. Jarvik, C. Eisdorfer, and J. E. Blum, pp. 13–19. New York: Springer.

Bondareff, W., and Narotzky, R. 1972. "Age Changes in the Neuronal Microenvironment," *Science* 176:1135–36.

Botwinick, J. 1973. *Aging and Behavior*. New York: Springer.

_____. 1977. "Intellectual Abilities." In *Handbook of the Psychology of Aging*, ed. J. E. Birren and K. W. Schaie, pp. 580–605. New York: Van Nostrand Reinhold.

_____. 1981. "Neuropsychology of Aging." In *Handbook of Clinical Neuropsychology*, ed. S. B. Filskov and T. J. Boll, pp. 135–71. New York: John Wiley & Sons.

Boyd, R. 1969. "The Valued Grandparent: A Changing Social Role." In *Living in the Multigenerational Family*, ed. W. Donahue, J. J. Kornbluh, and L. Power. Ann Arbor: Institute of Gerontology, University of Michigan.

Britton, J. H., and Britton, J. O. 1972. *Personality Changes in Aging: A Longitudinal Study of Community Residents*. New York: Springer.

Bultena, G., and Powers, E. 1976. "Effects of Age-grade Comparisons on Adjustments in Later Life." In *Time, Roles, and Self in Old Age*, ed. J. F. Gubrium, pp. 165–78. New York: Human Sciences Press.

Burnet, F. M. 1970. "An Immunological Approach to Aging." *Lancet* 2:358.

Burr, W. 1970. "Satisfaction with Various Aspects of Marriage over the Life Cycle: A Random Middle-class Sample." *Journal of Marriage and the Family* 32:29–37.

Busse, E. W. 1981. "Old Age." In *The Course of Life: Psychoanalytic Contributions Toward Understanding Personality Development*, ed. S. I. Greenspan and G. H. Pollock, pp. 519–44. Washington, D.C.: U.S. Government Printing Office.

Butler, R., and Lewis, M. 1977. *Aging and Mental Health: Positive Psychological Approaches*, 2nd ed. St. Louis: C. V. Mosby.

Carp, F. M. 1975. "Ego-defense or Cognitive Consistency Effects on Environmental Evaluation." *Journal of Gerontology* 30:707–11.

Cath, S. H. 1976. "Functional Disorders: An Organismic View and Attempt at Reclassification." In *Geriatric Psychiatry: A Handbook for Psychiatry and Primary Care Physicians*, ed. L. Bellak and T. B. Karasu, pp. 141–72. New York: Grune & Stratton.

Cerella, J.; Poon, L. W.; and Williams, D. M. 1980. "Age and the Complexity Hypothesis." In *Aging in the 1980's: Psychological Issues*, ed. L. W. Poon, pp. 332–40. Washington, D.C.: American Psychological Association.

Chiriboga, D. A., and Cutler, L. 1980. "Stress and Adaptation: Life Span Perspectives." In *Aging in the 1980's: Psychological Issues*, ed. L. W. Poon, pp. 347–62. Washington. D.C.: American Psychological Association.

Clarkson, P. M. 1978. "The Relationship of Age and Level of Activity with the Fractionated Components of Patellar Reflex Time." *Journal of Gerontology* 33:650–56.

Craik, F.I.M. 1977. "Age Differences in Human Memory." In *Handbook of the Psychology of Aging*, ed. J. E. Birren and K. W. Schaie, pp. 384–420. New York: Von Nostrand Reinhold.

Craik, F.I.M., and Simon, E. 1980. "Age Differences in Memory: The Roles of Attention and Depth of Processing." In *New Directions in Memory and Aging: Proceedings of the George Talland Memorial Conference*, ed. L. W. Poon et al., pp. 95–112. Hillsdale, N.J.: Lawrence Erlbaum Associates.

Cumming, E., and Henry, W. E. 1961. *Growing Old*. New York: Basic Books.

Dilman, V. M. 1971. "Age-associated Elevation of Hypothalmic Threshold to Feedback Control and Its Role in Development, Aging and Disease." *Lancet* 1:1211–19.

Dowd, J. J. 1975. "Aging as Exchange: A Preface to Theory." *Journal of Gerontology* 30:585–94.

Dressler, D. M. 1973. "Life Adjustment of Retired Couples." *International Journal of Aging and Human Development* 4:335–49.

Eisdorfer, C., and Wilkie, F. 1977. "Stress, Disease, Aging and Behavior." In *Handbook of the Psychology of Aging*, ed. J. E. Birren and K. W. Schaie, pp. 251–75. New York: Van Nostrand Reinhold.

Erikson, E. H. 1963. *Childhood and Society.* New York: W. W. Norton.

Finch, C. E. 1973. "Catecholamine Metabolism in the Brains of Aging Male Mice." *Brain Research* 52:271–76.

Fiske, M. 1980. "Tasks and Crises of the Second Half of Life: The Interrelationship of Commitment, Coping and Adaptation." In *Handbook of Mental Health and Aging,* ed. J. E. Birren and R. B. Sloane, pp. 337–73. Englewood Cliffs, N.J.: Prentice-Hall.

Flavell, J. H. 1970. "Cognitive Changes in Adulthood." In *Life-span Developmental Psychology: Research and Theory,* ed. L. R. Goulet and P. B. Baltes, pp. 247–53. New York: Academic Press.

Fozard, J. L. 1980. "The Time for Remembering." In *Aging in the 1980's: Psychological Issues,* ed. L. W. Poon, pp. 273–87. Washington, D.C.: American Psychological Association.

Friedmann, E., and Orbach, H. L. 1974. "Adjustment to Retirement." In *American Handbook of Psychiatry,* 2nd ed., ed. S. Arieti, vol. 1, pp. 609–45. New York: Basic Books.

Frolkis, V. V. 1966. "Neurohumoral Regulations in the Aging Organism." *Journal of Gerontology* 21:161–67.

———. 1968. "Regulatory Process in the Mechanism of Aging." *Experimental Gerontology* 3:113–23.

Giambra, L. M., and Arenberg, D. 1980. "Problem Solving, Concept Learning, and Aging." In *Aging in the 1980's: Psychological Issues,* ed. L. W. Poon, pp. 253–59. Washington, D.C.: American Psychological Association.

Glamser, F. D. 1976. "Determinants of a Positive Attitude Toward Retirement." *Journal of Gerontology* 31:104–7.

Goldfarb, A. 1968. "Marital Problems of Older Persons." In *The Marriage Relationship,* ed. S. Rosenbaum and I. Alger, pp. 105–20. New York: Basic Books.

Granick, S., and Patterson, R. D., eds. 1971. *NIMH: Human Aging II: An 11 Year Follow-up, Biomedical and Behavioral Study.* Washington, D.C.: U.S. Department of Health, Education, and Welfare.

Green, S. K. 1981. "Attitudes and Perceptions About the Elderly: Current and Future Perspectives." *International Journal of Aging and Human Development* 13:99–119.

Gusseck, D. J. 1972. "Endocrine Mechanisms and Aging." In *Advances in Gerontological Research,* ed. B. L. Strehler, pp. 105–66. New York: Academic Press.

Gutmann, D. L. 1964. "An Exploration of Ego Configurations in Middle and Later Life." In *Personality in Middle and Late Life: Empirical Studies,* ed. B. L. Neugarten, pp. 114–48. New York: Atherton Press.

———. 1971. "Dependency, Illness, and Survival Among Navajo Men." In *Prediction of Life Span: Recent Findings,* ed. E. Palmore and F. C. Jeffers, pp. 181–98. Lexington, Mass.: D. C. Heath.

———. 1980a. "Observations on Culture and Mental Health in Later Life." In *Handbook of Mental Health and Aging,* ed. J. Birren and R. B. Sloane, pp. 429–47. Englewood Cliffs, N.J.: Prentice-Hall.

———. 1980b. "Psychoanalysis and Aging: A Developmental View." In *The Course of Life: Psychoanalytic Contributions Toward Understanding Personality and Development, Vol. 3: Adulthood and the Aging Process,* ed. S. I. Greenspan and G. H. Pollock, pp. 489–517. Washington, D.C.: U.S. Government Printing Office.

Hall, E. H., et al. 1972. "Intellect, Mental Illness, and Survival in the Aged: A Longitudinal Investigation." *Journal of Gerontology* 27:237–44.

Hartley, J. T.; Harker, J. O.; and Walsh, D. A. 1980. "Contemporary Issues and New Directions in Adult Development of Learning and Memory." In *Aging in the 1980's: Psychological Issues,* ed. L. W. Poon, pp. 239–52. Washington, D.C.: American Psychological Association.

Havighurst, R. J. 1968. "Personality and Patterns of Aging." *Gerontologist* 8:20–23.

Hayflick, L., and Moorhead, P. S. 1961. "The Serial Cultivation of Human Diploid Cells." *Experimental Cell Research* 25:585–621.

Hill, R., et al. 1970. *Family Development in Three Generations.* Cambridge, Mass.: Schenkman Publishing Co.

Holmes, T. H., and Rahe, R. H. 1967. *Schedule of Recent Experiences.* Seattle: School of Medicine, University of Washington.

Hoyer, W. J., and Plude, D. J. 1980. "Attentional and Perceptual Processes in the Study of Cognitive Aging." In *Aging in the 1980's: Psychological Issues,* ed. L. W. Poon, pp. 227–38. Washington, D.C.: American Psychological Association.

Hulicka, I. M. 1967. "Age Changes and Age Differences in Memory Functioning." *Gerontologist* 7:46–69.

Jarvik, L. F. 1973. "Discussion: Patterns of Intellectual Functioning in the Later Years." In *Intellectual Functioning in Adults*, ed. L. F. Jarvik, C. Eisdorfer, and J. E. Blum, pp. 65–67. New York: Springer.

Jarvik, L. F., and Falek, A. 1963. "Intellectual Stability and Survival in the Aged." *Journal of Gerontology* 18:173–76.

Johnson, E. S., and Bursk, B. J. 1977. "Relationships Between the Elderly and Their Adult Children." *Gerontologist* 17:90–96.

Jung, C. G. 1960. "The Stages of Life." In *The Collected Works of C. G. Jung. vol. 8: The Structure and Dynamics of the Psyche*, ed. H. Read, M. Fordham, and G. Adler, pp. 384–403. New York: Pantheon.

Kaack, B.; Ordy, J. M.; and Trapp, B. 1975. "Changes in Limbic, Neuroendocrine and Autonomic Systems, Adaptation, Homeostasis During Aging." In *Neurobiology of Aging*, ed. J. M. Ordy and K. R. Brizze, vol. 16, pp. 209–31. New York: Plenum.

Kahana, B., and Kahana, E. 1970. "Grandparenthood from the Perspective of the Developing Grandchild." *Developmental Psychology* 3:98–105.

Kahana, E., and Kahana, B. 1971. "Theoretical and Research Perspectives on Grandparenthood." *Aging and Human Development* 2:261–68.

Kidwell, I., and Booth, A. 1977. "Social Distance and Intergenerational Relations." *Gerontologist* 17:412–20.

Kohut, H. 1966. "Forms and Transformations of Narcissism." *Journal of the American Psychoanalytic Association* 14:243–72.

———. 1971. *The Analysis of the Self*. New York: International Universities Press.

———. 1972. "Thoughts on Narcissism and Narcissistic Rage." *Psychoanalytic Study of the Child* 27:360–400.

———. 1977. *The Restoration of the Self*. New York: International Universities Press.

Kohut, H., and Wolf, E. 1978. "The Disorders of the Self and Their Treatment: An Outline." *International Journal of Psycho-Analysis* 59:413–25.

Kuypers, J. A., and Bengtson, V. L. 1973. "Social Breakdown and Competence: A Model of Normal Aging." *Human Development* 16:181–201.

Labouvie-Vief, G., and Gonda, J. N. 1976. "Cognitive Strategy Training and Intellectual Performance in the Elderly." *Journal of Gerontology* 31:327–32.

Lachman, J. L., and Lachman, R. 1980. "Age and the Actualization of World Knowledge." In *New Directions in Memory and Aging: Proceedings of the George A. Talland Memorial Conference*, ed. L. W. Poon et al., pp. 313–43. Hillsdale, N.J.: Lawrence Erlbaum Associates.

Layton, B. 1975. "Perceptual Noise and Aging." *Psychological Bulletin* 82:875–83.

Lazarus, L. W. 1978. "The Psychiatrist's Role in the Management of Elderly Patients with Organic Brain Syndrome." *Psychiatric Annals* 8:84–99.

———. 1980. "Self Psychology and Psychotherapy with the Elderly: Theory and Practice." *Journal of Geriatric Psychiatry* 13:69–88.

Lehr, U., and Schmitz-Scherzer, R. 1976. "Survivors and Nonsurvivors—Two Fundamental Patterns of Aging." In *Patterns of Aging: Findings from the Bonn Longitudinal Study of Aging*, ed. H. Thomae, pp. 137–56. Basel: S. Karger.

Lemon, B. W.; Bengtson, V. L.; and Peterson, J. A. 1972. "Activity Theory and Life Satisfaction in a Retirement Community: An Exploration of the Activity Theory of Aging." *Journal of Gerontology* 27:511–23.

Levinson, D. J. 1978. "Eras: The Anatomy of the Life Cycle." *Psychiatric Opinion* 15(9):10–48.

Lieberman, M. A. 1975. "Adaptive Processes in Late Life." In *Life-span Developmental Psychology: Normative Life Crises*, ed. N. Datan and L. Ginsberg, pp. 135–59. New York: Academic Press.

———. 1978–79. "Social and Psychological Determinants of Adaptation." *International Journal of Aging and Human Development* 9:115–26.

Lipton, M. A., and Nemeroff, C. B. 1978. "The Biology of Aging and Its Role in Depression." In *Aging: The Process and the People*, ed. G. Usdin and C. K. Hofling, pp. 47–95. New York: Brunner/Mazel.

Loeb, M. B. 1975. "Adaptation and Survival: New Meanings in Old Age." In *Life-span*

Developmental Psychology: Normative Life Crises, ed. N. Datan and L. H. Ginsberg, pp. 161–84. New York: Academic Press.

Lopata, H. Z. 1975. "Widowhood: Societal Factors in Life-span Disruptions and Alternatives." In *Life-span Developmental Psychology: Normative Life Crises,* ed. N. Datan and L. H. Ginsberg, pp. 217–34. New York: Academic Press.

Lowenthal, M. F., and Chiriboga, D. 1973. "Social Stress and Adaptation: Toward a Life-course Perspective." In *The Psychology of Adult Development and Aging,* ed. C. Eisdorfer and M. P. Lawton, pp. 281–310. Washington, D.C.: American Psychological Association.

McGeer, D. G., et al. 1971. "Aging and Brain Enzymes." *Experimental Gerontology* 5:391–96.

McKee, P. L. 1980–81. "Consummation: A Concept for Gerontologic Theory." *International Journal of Aging and Human Development* 12:239–49.

McNamara, M. C., et al. 1977. "Age-related Changes in the Effect of Electroconvulsive Shock (ECS) on the In Vivo Hydroxylation of Tyrosine and Tryptophan in Rat Brain." *Brain Research* 131:313–20.

McTavish, D. G. 1971. "Perceptions of Old People: A Review of Research Methodologies and Findings." *Gerontologist* 11:90–101.

Mathey, F. J. 1976. "Psychomotor Performance and Reaction Speed in Old Age." In *Patterns of Aging: Findings from the Bonn Longitudinal Study of Aging,* ed. H. Thomae, pp. 36–50. Basel: S. Karger.

Meissner, W. W. 1976. "Normal Psychology of the Aging Process Revisited—I: Discussion." *Journal of Geriatric Psychiatry* 9:151–59.

Monge, R. H. 1975. "Structure of the Self-concept from Adolescence Through Old Age." *Experimental Aging Research* 1:281–91.

Morgan, L. A. 1976. "A Re-examination of Widowhood and Morale." *Journal of Gerontology* 31:687–95.

Munnichs, J.M.A. 1979. "Chronological, Social and Psychological Time." In *Proceedings of World Conference on Aging: A Challenge to Science and Policy,* ed. J. E., Birren, J. M. Munnichs, and H. Thomae. Oxford: Oxford University Press.

Nandy, K.; Fritz, R. B.; and Threatt, J. 1975. "Specificity of Brain-reactive Antibodies in Serum of Old Mice." *Journal of Gerontology* 30:369–74.

Neugarten, B. L. 1964. *Personality in Middle and Late Life: Empirical Studies.* New York: Atherton Press.

———. 1971. "Personality Change in Late Life: A Developmental Perspective." In *The Psychology of Adult Development and Aging,* ed. C. Eisdorfer and M. P. Lawton, pp. 311–35. Washington, D. C.: American Psychological Association.

———. 1974. "Age Groups in American Society and the Rise of the Young-Old." *Annals of American Academy,* September, pp. 187–89.

———. 1977. "Personality and Aging." In *Handbook of the Psychology of Aging,* ed. J. E. Birren and K. W. Schaie, pp. 626–49. New York: Van Nostrand Reinhold.

———. 1979. "Time, Age and the Life Cycle." *American Journal of Psychiatry* 136:887–94.

Neugarten, B. L., and Datan, N. 1973. "Sociological Perspectives on the Life Cycle." In *Life-Span Developmental Psychology: Personality and Socialization,* ed. P. B. Baltes and K. W. Schaie, pp. 53–69. New York: Academic Press.

Neugarten, B., and Weinstein, K. 1964. "The Changing American Grandparent." *Journal of Marriage and the Family* 26:199–204.

Palmore, E., ed. 1970. *Normal Aging, Reports from the Duke Longitudinal Study, 1955–69.* Durham, N.C.: Duke University Press.

Palmore, E., and Kivett, V. 1977. "Changes in Life Satisfaction: A Longitudinal Study of Persons Aged 46–70." *Journal of Gerontology* 32:311–16.

Pfeiffer, E. 1971. "Physical, Psychological and Social Correlates of Survival in Old Age." In *Prediction of Life Span—Recent Findings,* ed. E. Palmore and F. C. Jeffers, pp. 228–36. Lexington, Mass.: D. C. Heath.

Powell, A. H.; Eisdorfer, C.; and Bogdonoff, M. D. 1964. "Physiologic Response Patterns Observed in a Learning Task." *Archives of General Psychiatry* 10:192–95.

Rabbitt, P. 1977. "Changes in Problem-solving Ability in Old Age." In *Handbook of the Psychology of Aging,* ed. J. E. Birren and K. W. Schaie, pp. 606–25. New York: Van Nostrand Reinhold.

Reichard, S.; Livson, F.; and Petersen, P. G. 1962. *Aging and Personality: A Study of Eighty-seven Older Men.* New York: John Wiley & Sons.

Reimanis, G., and Green R. F. 1971. "Imminence of Death and Intellectual Decrement in the Aging." *Developmental Psychology* 5:270–72.

Riegel, K. F., and Riegel, R. M. 1972. "Development, Drop, and Death." *Developmental Psychology* 6:306–19.

Roberts, W. L. 1979–80. "Significant Elements in the Relationship of Long-married Couples." *International Journal of Aging and Human Development* 10:165–72.

Robertson, J. F. 1976. "Significance of Grandparents." *Gerontologist* 16:137–40.

Robinson, D. S., et al. 1972. "Aging, Monoamines and Monoamine Oxidase." *Lancet* 1:290–91.

Rochlin, G. 1965. *Griefs and Discontents: The Forces of Change.* Boston: Little, Brown.

Rollins, B., and Feldman, H. 1970. "Marital Satisfaction over the Family Life Cycle." *Journal of Marriage and the Family* 32:20–27.

Rosenfeld, A. H. 1978. *New Views on Older Lives.* Rockville, Md.: National Institute of Mental Health.

Rosow, I. 1974. *Socialization to Old Age.* Berkeley: University of California Press.

Roth, G. S. 1975. "Age-related Changes in Corticoid Binding by Rat Splenic Leukocytes: Possible Cause of Altered Adaptive Responsiveness." *Federation Proceedings* 34:183–85.

Ryff, C. D., and Baltes, P. B. 1976. "Value Transition and Adult Development in Women. The Instrumentality-terminality Sequence Hypothesis." *Developmental Psychology* 12:567–68.

Samorajski, R. 1975. "Age-related Changes in Brain Biogenic Amines." In *Aging,* ed. H. Brody, D. Harman, and J. M. Ordy, pp. 199–214. New York: Raven Press.

Sands, J. D., and Parker, J. 1979–80. "A Cross-sectional Study of the Perceived Stressfulness of Several Life Events." *International Journal of Aging and Human Development* 10:335–41.

Schaie, K. W. 1977–78. "Toward a State Theory of Adult Cognitive Development." *International Journal of Aging and Human Development* 8:129–38.

Scheibel, M. E., and Scheibel, A. B. 1975. "Structural Changes in the Aging Brain." In *Aging,* ed. H. Brody, E. Harman, and J. M. Ordy, pp. 11–37. New York: Raven Press.

Shanas, E., and Maddox, G. L. 1976. "Aging, Health, and the Organization of Health Resources." In *Handbook of Aging and the Social Sciences,* ed. R. H. Binstock and E. Shanas, pp. 592–618. New York: Van Nostrand Reinhold.

Sheppard, H. L. 1976. "Work and Retirement." In *Handbook of Aging and the Social Sciences,* ed. R. H. Binstock and E. Shanas, pp. 286–309. New York: Van Nostrand Reinhold.

Shock, N. W. 1972. "Energy Metabolism, Caloric Intake and Physical Activity of the Aging." In *Nutrition in Old Age, (X Symposium of the Swedish Nutrition Foundation),* ed. L. A. Carlson, pp. 12–23. Uppsala: Almquist and Wiksell.

———. 1977. "Systems Integration." In *Handbook of the Biology of Aging,* ed. C. E. Finch and L. Hayflick, pp. 639–65. New York: Van Nostrand Reinhold.

Stinnett, N.; Collins, J.; and Montgomery, J. 1970. "Marital Need Satisfaction of Older Husbands and Wives." *Journal of Marriage and the Family* 32:428–32.

Streib, G., and Schneider, C. J. 1971. *Retirement in American Society.* Ithaca, N.Y.: Cornell University Press.

Sussman, M. 1965. "Relationships of Adult Children with Their Parents in the United States." In *Social Structure and the Family: Generational Relationships,* ed. E. Shanas and G. Streib, pp. 62–92. Englewood Cliffs, N.J.: Prentice-Hall.

———. 1976. "The Family Life of Old People." In *Handbook of Aging and the Social Sciences,* ed. R. H. Binstock and E. Shanas, pp. 218–43. New York: Van Nostrand Reinhold.

Sussman, M., and Burchinal, L., 1962. "Family Kin Network: Unheralded Structure in Current Conceptualizations of Family Functioning." *Marriage and Family Living* 24:231–40.

Thomae, H. 1970. "Theory of Aging and Cognitive Theory of Personality." *Human Development* 13:1–16.

———. 1976. "Patterns of 'Successful' Aging." In *Patterns of Aging: Findings from the Bonn Longitudinal Studies of Aging,* ed. H. Thomae, pp. 147–61. Basel: S. Karger.

———. 1980. "Personality and Adjustment to Aging." In *Handbook of Mental Health and Aging,* ed. J. Birren and R. B. Sloane, pp. 285–309. Englewood Cliffs, N.J.: Prentice-Hall.

Timaras, P. S., and Vernadakis, A. 1972. "Structural, Biochemical and Functional Aging of the Nervous System." In *Developmental Physiology and Aging*, ed. P. S. Timaras, pp. 502–26. New York: Macmillan.

Trimakas, K. A., and Nicolay, R. C. 1974. "Self-concept and Altruism in Old Age." *Journal of Gerontology* 29:434–39.

Troll, L. E. 1980. "Grandparenting." In *Aging in the 1980's: Psychological Issues*, ed. L. W. Poon, pp. 475–81. Washington, D.C.: American Psychological Association.

Troyer, W. G., et al. 1966. "Free Fatty Acid Responses in the Aged Individual During Performance of Learning Tasks." *Journal of Gerontology* 21:415–19.

Tuttle, R. S. 1966. "Age-related Changes in the Sensitivity of Rat Aortic Strips to Norepinephrine and Associated Chemical and Structural Alterations." *Journal of Gerontology* 21:510–16.

U.S. Bureau of the Census. 1981. *Statistical Abstract of the United States: 1981*, 102d ed. Washington, D.C.: U.S. Government Printing Office.

U.S. Department of Health, Education, and Welfare, Health Resources Administration, National Center for Health Statistics. 1975. *Health Interview Survey*. Washington, D.C.: U.S. Government Printing Office.

Walford, R. 1969. *The Immunological Theory of Aging*. Copenhagen: Munksgaard.

Wechsler, D. 1958. *The Measurement and Appraisal of Adult Intelligence*, 4th ed. Baltimore: Williams & Wilkins.

Weinberg, J. 1973. "The Inner Life of the Elderly." Unpublished.

———. 1975. "Geriatric Psychiatry." In *Comprehensive Textbook of Psychiatry*, 2nd ed., vol. 2, ed. A. M. Freedman, H. L. Kaplan, and B. J. Sadock, pp. 2405–20. Baltimore: Williams & Wilkins.

Willis, S. L., and Baltes, P. B. 1980. "Intelligence in Adulthood and Aging: Contemporary Issues." In *Aging in the 1980's: Psychological Issues*, ed. L. W. Poon, pp. 260–72. Washington, D.C.: American Psychological Association.

Wood, V., and Robertson, J. F. 1976. "The Significance of Grandparenthood." In *Time, Roles, and Self in Old Age*, ed. J. F. Gubrium, pp. 278–304. New York: Human Sciences Press.

PART II

THEORETICAL AND METHODOLOGICAL PERSPECTIVES

Psychoanalytic Perspectives on Normality

Historical Origins

Psychoanalysis has its origins in nineteenth-century medicine and neurology and in the study and treatment of patients who were suffering from pathologic conditions. Before psychoanalysis, normal individuals were of little interest to psychiatry. There was no concern with those who did not seek or need help, while those who did had symptoms that were understood as signifying some underlying disease. The various clinical syndromes were categories of pathology, with the residual category, without symptoms or disease, understood as normal. The relative magnitude of the various disease categories was a matter for investigation, but it was implicit that with nineteenth-century notions of mental illness, the great majority of individuals were normal—that is, without mental illness (Michels 1983a).

Psychoanalysis began with the investigations of Breuer and Freud on hysteria. This had previously been understood as a pathologic syndrome, affecting patients who were "abnormal" just like the other patients of the nineteenth-century neurology and medicine, patients with dementia paralytica (syphilis) or dementia praecox (schizophrenia), with multiple sclerosis or epilepsy or manic depressive psychosis. However, Freud's brilliant reconceptualization of hysteria did far more than enrich our understanding of a specific type of pathology; it provided a new paradigm for considering mental states, including both those that had been regarded as pathologic and others that had not, and thus radically altered the conceptual relationship between the clinical pathologic syndromes of psychiatry and normality. Freud believed that hysterical patients were fundamentally normal and that the psychological mechanisms leading to their symptoms were normal mechanisms that could be recognized in anyone. The distinction between a hysterical patient and any *other* normal individual was of quantity, not quality, or at most was based on the social appraisal of a surface differentiation that overlay a hidden, deeper commonality. Anyone was capable of constructing a hysterical symptom, and such symptoms could be traced to universal themes and structures in mental life. Psychoanalysis was the tool for translating the apparently pathologic phenotype that seemed to be qualitatively different from normal to the deeper mental life that had created it. Furthermore, the deeper mental life that was first discovered in the treatment of neurotic patients was not only characteristic of the normal mind as well, but actually became the key for unlocking the secrets of normal psychological development. In 1895 Freud wrote that he intended "to extract from psychopathology a yield for normal psychology. It is in fact impossible to form a satisfactory general view of neuro-psychotic disorders unless they can be linked to clear hypotheses upon normal psychical processes" (1966, pp. 283–84). The focus of interest shifted from studying the various categories of pathology and the characteristics that differentiated each from the others to studying the universal mechanisms of all behavior, whether clinical syndrome or mundane experience, with the recognition that normality and pathology were expressions of the same fundamental processes and that individuals were neither one nor the other but rather both.

The terms and labels of pathology continued to be used by psychoanalysis, but they were relegated to a relatively minor role, referring to quantitative variations in the importance of the several determinants of behavior, to disturbances in the integration of these determinants, or to social attitudes toward the behavior itself. More important than the discarding of this older categorizing tradition, psychoanalysis came to regard the clinical syndromes of psychiatry in a new way. Hysterical or obsessional symptoms were not seen as similar to the tremors and palsies and convulsions of neurological disorders. Rather they were studied together with phenomena that had never been regarded as abnormal—dreams, jokes, artistic creativity, and parapraxes. The fundamental distinction underlying nineteenth-century medicine, that between normal and pathologic, had been replaced by the fundamental distinction that defines the domain of psychoanalysis, between meaningful and meaningless. The same mechanisms that had first been discovered in such bold relief in the neurotic conditions formerly considered to be pathologic were studied in every area of behavior. Wishes, fears, defenses, conflicts were characteristic of what had been regarded as pathology, but more important, they were characteristic of the human condition (Michels 1981a). Freud repeatedly emphasized that "psycho-analytic research finds no fundamental, but only quantitative, distinctions between normal and neurotic life" ([1900–1901] 1953, p. 373), that "there is no fundamental difference, but only one of degree, between the mental life of normal people, of neurotics and of psychotics" ([1913] 1958, p. 210). The categories of mental illness, or at least of those mental illnesses that could be studied and comprehended by psychoanalysis, were categories of surface manifestations. Deeper mental structures were not usefully classified as normal or pathologic.

Psychoanalysis as a science of behavior thus bears the same relationship to concepts of normality and pathology in psychiatry that the basic sciences of biochemistry or physiology have to normality and pathology in medicine. Psychoanalysis, like biochemistry and physiology, attempts to understand and describe the mechanisms and processes that form the basis for all function, both normal and pathologic, and psychoanalytic understanding is essential to a full comprehension of both normal and pathologic mental life, but the distinction between normal and pathologic mental processes is not based on psychoanalytic concepts any more than the distinction between normal and pathologic physical states is based on biochemical or physiologic concepts. Normality and pathology refer to psychiatric and medical categories.

However, unlike biochemistry or physiology, the term psychoanalysis refers to a method of treatment in psychiatry as well as to a science of behavior, and it is difficult to imagine a treatment that does not imply some decisions about indications and goals, decisions that inevitably involve questions of normality and pathology (Hartmann 1939).

Some have argued that psychoanalysis must be kept pure of psychiatric contamination and that questions of health are actually antithetical to the essence of psychoanalysis, which is more properly concerned with a value-free search for meaning than with decisions about what is normal and what is pathologic. The central paradox of psychoanalysis is that it is a medically derived treatment that requires for its success a suspension of external therapeutic goals and that it is best conducted as an inquiry that proceeds without concern for normality or pathology (Michels 1980).

Psychic Reality

The earliest formulations of psychoanalysis traced symptoms and pathologic conditions to traumatic occurrences and the individual's response
to them. This model was a familiar one for a medical world that had
recently been revolutionized by the discovery of microbiology and advances in the study of infectious disease. Where nineteenth-century psychiatry had been built on the model of degenerative processes that affected the nervous system and therefore the mind, as suggested by the terms
"neur-osis" and "psych-osis," psychoanalysis shifted to studying the
mental response to stimulation and trauma, based on the model of the
organism's defensive processes. Freud should have shifted to the term
"psych-itis"—although tradition, desire for historical continuity, and
Freud's efforts to retain a neurobiological component in his theoretical
model led to "psycho-neur-osis" instead. This first psychoanalytic model
of pathology shifted attention from predisposing individual traits to pre-
cipitating exogenous factors and the mental states in which they occurred, from character as a cause of pathology to symptom as an expression of meaning (Michels 1983a).

In the initial formulation of this early model, the traumatic events were
believed to have occurred in adult life. However, the data quickly led to
two modifications in this view. First, the more recent traumatic events
were discovered to be superimposed on a series of earlier and earlier
experiences that inevitably led back to childhood. Second, and far more
important to the fundamental theory, the critical childhood events turned
out never to have occurred at all but rather to have been invented by
patients as the result of subjective experiences that were determined
more by their inner mental life during childhood than by the occurrences
in the world around them. Thus the model changed, with the interest in
external reality shifting to an interest in an inner psychic reality, the
interest in precipitant shifting back to an interest in predisposition, and
the interest in state being accompanied by an interest in persistent traits.
These traits both determine and are determined by childhood states, and
they are important predisposing factors to adult states. Symptoms remained an important concern in this new theory, but character returned
to central interest as well. Differences among individuals—not really normality as opposed to pathology but rather the array of symptoms and
traits, more or less adaptive or maladaptive, that characterized each individual—were explained as the result of a complex multifactorial set of
determinants, external events, inner predispositions, and the timing and
relationships among them.

The Focus of Psychoanalytic Theory

The data on which these theories were based were the data of clinical psychoanalysis, the stories that patients told, and the events that transpired in the consulting rooms of psychoanalysts. The great majority of psychoanalytic patients were, and continue to be, young adults. It was many years before children were seen by psychoanalysts, and even today they comprise only a small fraction of psychoanalytic patients, certainly disproportionate to the role of childhood in psychoanalytic theory. This means, of course, that the childhood of psychoanalytic theory is to a great extent not the childhood of children but rather the childhood remembered and reconstructed by adult patients and their psychoanalysts, the childhood that persists unconsciously throughout our lives rather than that which comes to an end with puberty and adolescence. Anna Freud (1976) reminds us of this when she says that

> reconstruction from adult analysis is inevitably weighted towards pathology, to the neglect of normal developmental happenings; . . . it is always the conflictual and unsolved which does not come to rest in the individual's mind, welcomes the opportunity to re-establish itself in the transference situation, and thus captures and monopolizes the analyst's attention. In contrast, the satisfied impulses, the successful adaptive conflict solutions disappear from view by entering the fabric of the personality. They are outgrown, with little incentive left for revival at a later date. (P. 402)

This preoccupation of psychoanalytic theory extends beyond its view of childhood. The major function of the theory is to facilitate the psychoanalytic treatment of patients. The treatment is conducted by the patient describing and sharing his or her inner mental experience with the analyst and the analyst offering comments and interpretations, speculations, and suggestions that help the patient to gain a new perspective on that experience, to conceptualize and organize it in different and more adaptive ways. Psychoanalytic theory, whether it be theory of the biological drives that underlie psychic motivation, of child development, or of sexuality or interpersonal relationships, is first and foremost a theory that guides the analyst in making interpretations. The test of the theory is not whether it explains the data of motivation, childhood, sexuality, or interpersonal relationships to a scientist, or to any other outside observer, but rather whether it helps patients to reexperience and understand their own motives or childhood memories, sexual feelings or human relationships during their analyses (Michels 1983b). This means that the theory must be highly selective, ignoring themes that are not important in the mental experience of adults, no matter how central they might have been in childhood itself or how important they might be to a comprehensive scientific understanding of behavior. Psychoanalytic theory emphasizes and exaggerates those themes that play the greatest role in the persisting fantasies of adults, particularly of adult psychoanalytic patients. These are themes of dramatic conflict, of passions and wishes and fears, rather than themes of the commonplace or mudane. The psychoanalytic version of childhood, or for that matter of anything, is thus quite different from the sociologic or the behaviorally oriented version, just as we might find quite different views of Elizabethan England in contemporary civil documents, in a textbook of history, and in a play of Shakespeare. None of these is false, but each provides a different perspective and serves a different function. There is little point in evaluating one by criteria more appropriate for the others. Psychoanalytic theories of childhood, or adolescence, or adults, are models for helping patients reorganize their inner experiences. They are not designed to be veridical replicas of developmental events, or to provide balanced representation to the various components of psychological life, some tranquil or unregistered, others dramatic or conflictual. A balanced comprehensive theory that might be of greatest value to students of normal personality development would be less useful to psychoanalysts. Psychoanalytic theory can provide valuable guidance for scholars in other disciplines if these characteristics are taken into account. It does have something to say about both normal and pathological mental life, but it is not primarily concerned with the distinction between normality and pathology, and it does not provide valid descriptions of either normal or pathologic behavior as observed from the outside (Jones [1931] 1942; Hartmann 1960).

These characteristics of psychoanalytic theory must be kept in mind as we explore the value of psychoanalytic thinking in our understanding of normality. Psychoanalysis is primarily about inner mental life and only secondarily about behavior viewed from outside, the social or biologic aspects of the individuals' functioning. Psychoanalytic theory may draw on biologic theory (Freud's favorite source of hypotheses), developmental observations (a popular source for contemporary theorists), psychology, anthropology, literature, or history, but these are only *sources* for ideas. The theory itself is basically a theory that guides interpretations in clinical psychoanalysis, and when it is drawn on by those same disciplines that provided its origins, its primary function must be remembered. Adolescents who are studied by questionnaires administered to samples of large populations may not look at all like the adolescents portrayed in psychoanalytic theories of development, but this only means that the model that is the most valuable framework for the psychoanalytic interpretations that patients find useful in integrating their memories of adolescence is not also the most useful in describing the self-reports of contemporary adolescents. This is an important finding, but one that should neither surprise nor dismay us (Sachs 1977).

From Pathology to Developmental Predisposition

The shift of attention from the immediate external precipitants of psychopathology to the internal childhood processes that predisposed to it naturally led to an interest in early psychological development. The traumatic experiences of childhood that were formerly seen as the results of unfortunate events were increasingly understood as stemming from the maturational unfolding of the child's innate potentials. This meant that pathology was again seen as the product of innate predisposition, but unlike the views of prepsychoanalytic psychiatry, the predisposition developed and was transformed through complex interactions between nature and nurture that determined the traits the individual brought to adult life. Indeed, the recognition of the manifold possibilities for developmental difficulties shifts the central question in understanding pyschopathology from "What are the mechanisms that lead to disturbances?" to "How does the individual cope with and correct the many potential disturbances that threaten a normal outcome?" with the proviso that on relatively infrequent occasions these coping capacities may not be sufficient and a pathologic outcome may result.

The psychoanalytic developmental theory that emerged is of a series of sequential stages, each determined by the biological givens of the individual, the experiences that occur during that stage, and the results of earlier stages. Each stage integrates and transforms prior experiences, so that it is generally not possible to trace the direct impact of infantile events on the adult but rather only to trace adult characteristics back to the transformations of the most recent major stage. The central role accorded to the oedipal stage in the development of neuroses in "classical" psychoanalytic theory stems in part from its importance as the last great transforming epoch in child development. The theory argues not that preoedipal or postoedipal events are irrelevant or even unimportant, but that a major pathway of their effect is indirect, through their impact on the oedipal period and on the psychological structures that emerge from it. Later refinements of the developmental theory emphasize the special contributions of other transforming stages, such as separation-individuation or adolescence, and the importance of separate developmental lines, while recognizing that each may have different critical periods of transformation and crystallization.

From the point of view of the risk for pathology, each of the major developmental stages offers an opportunity for a new integration that encompasses all of the previous determinants of psychological functioning, both biologic and psychologic, and thus each offers the potential for health, with the previous risk factors being transformed into nonpathologic characteristics that provide the unique flavor of individual character, persisting as potential predispositions to psychopathology, or, on occasion, if the integrative attempt fails, persisting as areas of pathologic functioning (Abrams 1979).

Psychodynamic Aspects of Adulthood

The psychoanalytic treatment and study of young-adult patients as a primary source of data led to a theory that not only exaggerated the conflictual aspects of earlier development but also tended to view adult mental life as relatively static—the product of earlier experiences rather than a continuing and evolving process. Although there has been very little clinical experience with the psychoanalysis of older patients, those psychoanalysts who became interested in the psychology of aging did become aware of the developmental transformations that characterized later life. However, the implicit model of most psychoanalytic developmental thinking has continued to be that of a series of intense and tumultuous stages of development culminating in the transformations of adolescence and a relatively long period of adult quiescence, punctuated only by pathologic upheavals or the iatrogenic disruptions of psychoanalysis itself, until a final series of developmental stages mark the process of aging and decay. Only in recent years have psychoanalysts recognized that the general pattern of this model tells us more about the setting in which it was constructed than the processes it attempts to explain (Michels 1981b).

Of course, the impact of the purpose for which a theory is constructed on its general form is not unique to psychoanalysis. The very young and the very old are more likely to come to medical attention than those of intermediate age, and social scientists have traditionally been most interested in those adults who conduct the various vital functions of the social system. One result is that each discipline tends to regard certain developmental stages as the implicit model for all others, and "experts" with

interests in specific developmental epochs are likely to have related theoretical biases. The concept of normality also changes meaning with development. It may seem more "normal" to be "normal" at age twenty-three
than to be a "normal" premature infant or a "normal" ninety-two-year-
old. The area of expected deviance, the probability of its occurrence, and
the degree to which it is integrated into our concept of normality all vary
with the stage of development.

One can see these factors at work in the preceding chapters. The discussions are not only about different epochs in the life cycle, but they are
about different aspects of the person—generally those that have attracted
the greatest attention from students of that epoch. From a psychoanalytic
perspective, it is striking that it is possible to discuss adulthood or aging
without recourse to the introspective accounts of subjective experiences
and the inferences that have been made from them. Certainly it is difficult to ensure objectivity and reliability in such data, but the cost of
excluding them may be the cost of ensuring limited relevance. It is also
easier to be objective in describing color and shape than meaning, but
few would attempt to discuss a painting without regard to the subjective
experience of the viewer.

The Importance of External Reality

The early psychoanalytic concern with external reality both diminished
and shifted. The world, particularly the social world, was seen as both an
important substrate for normal development and an important source of
potential pathogenic factors. Concepts such as the "average expected environment" or "good-enough mothering" emphasize this view, although
they tend to suggest that external reality is an enabling factor, that a
certain minimal requirement must be met, rather than see it as a primary
determinant of outcome—whether normal or pathologic, equivalent in
importance to drive endowment or the constitutional precursors of the
ego and the adaptive capacities. To some extent this emphasis resulted
from the power of the early discoveries of psychoanalysis, the role of
inner factors in determining the meaning of events, the importance of
drives, developmental stages, and unconscious psychodynamic factors in
giving meaning to experience. The obvious importance of the real people
in the child's world was rediscovered by psychoanalysis through the
study of genetic reconstructions in the analysis of adults, the growing
interest in the analysis of children, and the derivative interest in the

direct observation of children. At the same time, the shift of interest from psychoanalysis as the study of drives and their derivatives to psychoanalysis as a more comprehensive psychology, with attention devoted to affects, fantasies, identifications, and patterns of coping and integration, allowed the real figures of the child's life to be more than gratifiers or frustrators of the child's wishes and recognized their primary importance in contributing to the form of the child's personality. This recognition that character was shaped not only by biology but also by experience—particularly the critical experiences with parental caretakers—opened important new issues for the concepts of health and pathology. The individual would grow up to be more or less like his or her parents, and if the process worked well and they were more or less well adapted to their environment the individual would be more or less well adapted as well. In many ways this is simply a psychological equivalent of a simple genetic model of the transmission of adaptive traits. However, a vital assumption is that the external reality to which the individual must adapt is more or less similar to the external reality of the parents. In other words, the adaptive value, the health, of a characteristic is a function of context, and the mechanisms of personality development produce children who generally develop the traits that were adaptive and healthy in the context of their parents' world. If the child leaves that world—shifts to another culture or lives in an epoch in which history moves so rapidly that the culture of one generation is inevitably discordant with the culture of the previous one—the normal developmental processes with healthy parents and healthy biologic predispositions may lead to a maladaptive response. Flexibility in modes of adaptation is one feature of psychological health and may offer limited protection from this difficulty (Kubie 1954), but psychological development and the transmission of personality characteristics are fundamentally conservative processes, and if the world is changing very rapidly, psychopathologic disruptions may be an inevitable result (Michels 1972).

Determinants of Health

Psychological health or the quality of adaptation thus depends on a number of different factors. Psychoanalysis has continued to see drive endowment as important. In addition, there are a variety of other constitutional factors, including the precursors of autonomous ego capacities, defenses, emotional responses, and other regulating and controlling functions. Early experiences, particularly interactions with primary caretakers, are critical determinants of personality. Accident and trauma are important, particularly when understood in relation to the specific meaning attached to them according to the stages of the child's psychological development. The relationship between the world of the child's development and the later world of the adult's life, their congruences and incongruences, are vital. Finally, the entire process of development is marked by a series of stages, each of which consists of a new integration of these various themes, transforming the structures that resulted from the last stage into a new set of structures that will determine the dominant style of adaptation until the next one and will persist as a potential mode of adaptation for the rest of the individual's life. This means that any potential pathogenic factor is always only a potential until one knows how it has been integrated into subsequent development phases and also which of those phases has become dominant in shaping the individual's adaptation.

Psychoanalysis and Normality

The meaning of normality and pathology are different at different developmental epochs. In infancy, normality is generally used to mean the biological capacity for healthy psychological development. With each subsequent developmental epoch, experiences interact with that capacity to lead to an ever narrowing range of potential outcome. At each of these stages, normality continues to mean that an eventual healthy outcome is possible, that the psychological structures that emerge from that stage have sufficiently integrated the pathologic predispositions and problems that preceded them so that adaptive functioning can occur. But normality of course means more than this. It also means that the individual is reasonably free of symptoms, reasonably flexible in the face of stress, and reasonably capable of personal and social happiness and creativity.

If pathology in infancy usually reflects biological limitations that restrict the possibility for developmental resolution, pathology that emerges later in life more often reflects developmental processes that have failed to integrate what has gone before. Psychoanalysis studies that process and attempts to create new opportunities for resolving what has not been adequately resolved—in effect, to provide an additional developmental stage that might be able to pick up some of the pieces that have not been integrated before and that have led to pathologic results.

Patients are selected for psychoanalysis because they have pathology or are at risk for developing it, but this decision is really more a psychiatric than a psychoanalytic one. The psychoanalyst's attention is directed not to pathology per se but rather to psychic conflict, to the powerful psychological factors that shape the patient's inner world. Psychoanalytic theory is specifically focused on these factors, and in that sense it is not a comprehensive theory of mental functioning, either normal or pathological, although it has an important contribution to make to our understanding of the role of these powerful inner forces in both normal and pathologic mental life. There are multiple criteria for concluding a psychoanalysis. These include criteria intrinsic to the psychoanalytic process—whether the inquiry has been reasonably fruitful—as well as criteria external to the psychoanalysis—whether the patient has regained health and is likely to sustain it. The latter certainly involves issues of normality and pathology, but again these are really psychiatric issues rather than psychoanalytic ones.

In addition, psychoanalysts have provided us insight into one special aspect of normality, that is, the façade of normality that can be a symptom of underlying conflict. This is normality used as a defense against more authentic but less acceptable and therefore disavowed inner experience. It has been discussed as a character type (Tartakoff 1966), a form of transference (Reider 1950), and a residual form of pathology after psychoanalysis (Schmideberg 1938).

Thus psychoanalysts come up against questions of normality in pursuing their work, but except for this symptomatic normality their core psychoanalytic theory offers them little assistance and they must turn to traditional psychiatric or medical notions for guidance (Jones [1931] 1942; Joseph 1982; Weinshel 1970). Psychoanalytic theory offers an important insight into the normal as well as the pathologic mind, but it is not particularly helpful in explaining the essential characteristics that differentiate each from the other, and it generally disavows the distinction. Psychoanalytic models of development are likely to be misleading in studying the developmental aspects of normality unless it is recognized that the psychoanalytic theory is not of all development, but rather of the development of the great passions, fears, and fantasies that shape our inner mental life from earliest childhood.

REFERENCES

Abrams, S. 1979. "The Psychoanalytic Normalities." *Journal of the American Psychoanalytic Association* 27:821–35.

Freud, A. 1976. "Psychopathology Seen Against the Background of Normal Development." *British Journal of Psychiatry* 129:401–6.

Freud, S. [1895] 1966. "Project for a Scientific Psychology." In *The Standard Edition of the Complete Psychological Works of Sigmund Freud* (hereafter *Standard Edition*), ed. J. Strachey, vol. 1, pp. 283–397. London: Hogarth Press.

———. [1900–1901] 1953. "The Interpretation of Dreams." In *Standard Edition*, ed. J. Strachey, vol. 5, pp. 339–751. London: Hogarth Press.

———. [1913] 1958. "On Psycho-Analysis." In *Standard Edition*, ed. J. Strachey, vol. 12, pp. 207–11. London: Hogarth Press.

Hartmann, H. 1939. "Psychoanalysis and the Concept of Health." *International Journal of Psycho-Analysis* 20:308–21.

———. 1960. "Towards a Concept of Mental Health." *British Journal of Medical Psychology* 33:243–48.

Jones, E. [1931] 1942. "The Concept of the Normal Mind." *International Journal of Psycho-Analysis* 23:1–8.

Joseph, E. D. 1982. "Presidential Address—Normal in Psychoanalysis." *International Journal of Psycho-Analysis* 63:3–13.

Kubie, L. S. 1954. "The Fundamental Nature of the Distinction Between Normality and Neurosis." *Psychoanalytic Quarterly* 23:167–204.

Michels, R. 1972. "Cultural Changes and Their Impact on Psychic Functioning." *Psychiatric Quarterly* 46:572–76.

———. 1980. "Character Structure and Analyzability." *Bulletin of the Association for Psychoanalytic Medicine* 19(3):81–86.

———. 1981a. "The Psychoanalytic Paradigm." In *Models for Clinical Psychopathology*, ed. C. Eisdorfer et al., pp. 5–12. New York: Spectrum Publications.

———. 1981b. "Adulthood." In *The Course of Life: Psychoanalytic Contributions Toward Understanding Personality Development. Vol. III: Adulthood and the Aging Process*, ed. S. Greenspan and G. Pollock, pp. 25–34. Adelphi, Md.: National Institute of Mental Health (Mental Health Study Center).

———. 1983a. "The Basic Propositions of Psychoanalytic Theory." In *Introduction to Psychoanalytic Theory*, ed. S. Gilman, pp. 5–15. New York: Brunner/Mazel.

———. 1983b. "The Scientific and Clinical Functions of Psychoanalytic Theory." In *The Future of Psychoanalysis*, ed. A. Goldberg, pp. 125–35. New York: International Universities Press.

Reider, N. 1950. "The Concept of Normality." *Psychoanalytic Quarterly* 19:43–51.

Sachs, D. M. 1977. "Current Concepts of Normality." *Journal of the American Psychoanalytic Association* 25(3):679–92.

Schmideberg, M. 1938. "After the Analysis." *Psychoanalytic Quarterly* 7:122–42.

Tartakoff, H. H. 1966. "The Normal Personality in Our Culture and the Nobel Prize Complex." In *Psychoanalysis—A General Psychology: Essays in Honor of Heinz Hartmann*, ed. R. M. Lowenstein et al., pp. 222–52. New York: International Universities Press.

Weinshel, E. 1970. "The Ego in Health and Normality." *Journal of the American Psychoanalytic Association* 18:682–735.

9

Arnold J. Mandell and Jonas Salk

Developmental Fusion of Intuition and Reason: A Metabiological Ontogeny

Introduction

Geometric patterns latent in thought reveal our personal perceptions of processes in nature. Recurrence and continuity in natural and human phenomena are frequently seen and expressed as the sine wave, the limit cycle, the rise and fall motion of stable oscillatory mechanisms. The unfolding of compactly coded structures, seen as a half-wave in the time-dependent oscillations, has become the most prominent metaphor in biology, used by genetic theorists and molecular biologists in dealing with regulatory phenomena from transport to expression of genetic information. An alternative image, perhaps better suited to the dynamics of emergent evolutionary processes, is the density-dependent, parabolic-differential, sigmoid-integral curve (Salk 1973, 1983; Salk and Salk 1981). It may be seen as a geometric pattern formed by apparently random processes that self-organize in time, becoming complex yet stable structures (Collet and Eckmann 1980; Lorenz 1963). In dynamic psychiatry this

This chapter is supported in part by a grant in integrative neuropsychobiology from the W. M. Keck Foundation.

model can also be applied to the sequential emergence of new modes of psychic organization, as represented in the work of Erikson (1946).

Concepts used to describe ego apparatus have gone through several stages. The repressive amnesia of the defense neuropsychoses (Breuer and Freud [1893] 1957) became: (1) ego instincts (Freud [1914] 1957); (2) secondary process serving reality testing (Freud [1911] 1957); (3) an organization of mental processes composed of an integrated organization of internalized lost objects (Freud [1923] 1957); (4) an anxiety-signaled autonomous armamentarium (inborn ego roots independent of instinctual drives) for dealing with internal and external disturbances (Freud [1926] 1957, [1937] 1957); (5) primary coping mechanisms such as motility, perception, and memory transformed into characteristic adaptive states (Hartmann 1958; Hartmann, Kris, and Loewenstein 1946); and finally (6) Erikson's (1946) epigenetic approach symbolizing transitions in style (psychic structures) used in relating to changing external realities.

Adaptational modes disconnected from their instinctual origins were postulated to move through a sequence of transformations that adjudicated the balance between symmetric polarities of *environmentally derived* developmental tasks such as those involving dependence (trust versus mistrust), pride (autonomy versus shame), courage (initiative versus guilt), and meaning (integrity versus despair) (Erikson 1950). Modern calculus and topology have shown us that such discontinuities may be built into the original equations of state and not require external perturbation for their realization (Thom 1975).

Since their beginnings, theories of brain mechanisms have been dominated by anatomical places and connections, and a climate of radical reductionism and logical positivism plus the emergence of linear codes in both kinds of macromolecules that conduct the body's business (Pauling, Corey, and Branson 1951; Watson and Crick 1953) have left little room for the idea of dynamical brain structures ordered principally in time, distributed properties configuring the function of brain systems in the way that personality style shapes the appearance of all an individual's activities. Phenomena abstractable from real data, reflecting latency, hysteresis, and nonmanifest order were understandably rejected by academic psychology as not objectively verifiable metatheoretical concepts (Koch 1959). Analogously, the persistence of immunity as a latent dynamical process, manifest in immunological memory in the absence of measurable circulating antibody, has not yet been widely accepted (Salk 1960).

Early Simplifying Assumptions About Dynamical Biological Systems

Before computers and the modern theory of complex systems, biological mechanisms were approached using a multivariate calculus that permitted analytic solution only after many simplifying assumptions. Strategies for solution tended to: (1) eliminate instability-dependent autonomous motion ("intrinsic noise"); (2) ensure stability by using contrived coefficients; (3) keep force terms small and simply periodic; (4) eliminate the phasing aspect of the cause-effect interactions—perhaps the most important order parameter in biological dynamical systems; (5) assume an immediacy of response with no memory of previous interactions; and (6) heavily damp the system so that in expansions it was justifiable to keep only the leading and linear terms. Complex systems were assumed to be linear, independent, monomodal, memoryless, phaseless, and stable so that differential equations might be tractable. Such modes of thought found resonance in the linear-causal thinking of molecular biologists, and algebraic maneuvers were transformed from necessary mathematical simplifications to restrictions on theories of biological mechanisms.

Since that time, advances in several areas of physical research and in the theory of complex evolutionary systems offer an alternative to the point-to-point printing of a sequence code unfolding in time as the molecular image of ontogeny. They also lead away from the metaphor of a continuous biological progression up a ladder of developmental stages and from the regressive backsliding to fixation that is presumed to occur in psychiatric disease. Discontinuities, reordering of latent patterns, the sudden emergence of new forms, and the occurrence of global disorder among healthy and well-functioning individuals are examples of phenomena well known to psychosocial clinicians. Such observations cause conceptual difficulties when an attempt is made to explain them according to the theory of an unrolling predetermined pattern and have led to emphasis on a nonphysical, psychosocial determinism to account for the appearance of nonlinearities, including singular events and phase transitions, in people's lives. According to the traditional model, a new behavior is attributed to a recent environmental perturbation.

Unpredictability in Complex Biological Systems

Unpredictability in complex systems may be separated into deterministic and random components. In the language of multidimensional molecular structure, nucleic acid codes for many enzymatic proteins are composed of smaller regions of fixed sequences and even larger ones with random arrangements (Eigen and Winkler-Oswatitsch 1982), findings consistent with early reports that gene mutations can result in amino acid substitution away from the active site, which continues to manifest catalytic capacity (Yanofsky 1963). A significant amount of variability in many regions of immunoglobulin chains has been well documented (Kabat, Wu, and Bilofsky 1977), as has the similarity of quasi-stable folding intermediates in globins with widely differing amino acid sequences (Lesk and Chothia 1980). The variable component of amino acid composition contributes significantly to the dynamic characteristics of the autonomous motions of globular proteins in solution (Gurd and Rothgeb 1979; Karplus 1981).

The water of the heat bath is a nonlinear cooperative, dissipative system. The charge distribution within the participating monomers following the formation of one hydrogen bond changes such that the hydrogen bond acceptor becomes a better donor, and the inverse, up to a maximum polymer length, suggesting a density-dependent parabolic function (Stillinger 1980). A comparison of the second and third virial coefficients in steam demonstrates attractive forces among three molecules that are not present between two (Eisenberg and Kauzmann 1969). Although not a perfect harmonic heat bath, the dynamic structure of water is not random. Manipulation of the stability properties of proteins by changing solvent viscosity alters Arrhenius plots and reaction rates for both binding and catalysis (Beece et al. 1980; Gavish 1980), quasi-systematic changes in the "random" component leading to predictable functional outcomes. At the finest molecular level of chemical reaction theory, what was once thought to be ergodic exploration of vibrational phase space by anharmonic modes confirms the Kolmogorov-Arnold-Moser theorem that (below critical temperatures) coupled anharmonic oscillators generate strong quasi-periodic actions, not randomness (Noid, Koszykowski, and Marcus 1981).

The foregoing leads us to conclude for both structure and function that macromolecular identity appears to involve a deterministic capacity (potential) in addition to statistical fluctuations with the tendency to organize in a way that determines function. A point-to-point unfolding of a

DNA-determined process ("one gene:one enzyme") with a linear response characteristic must be mixed with statistically stable but individually varying structures with dynamic nonlinearities and cooperativities
in a binary ontogeny of biological process. It has been shown that discontinuities and emergent forms unfold in the noise and may come to domi-
nate what have been regarded as deterministic functions of the system
(Haken 1975). Changes in this latent structure, folded in via small biases
in the probabilities, configure an (initially) nonmanifest distributed order
in context.

A Predictive Aspect of Unpredictability: Stability

Efforts toward qualitative description of this "random" germinative context take the form of assessments of a system's stability. New dynamic
structure emerges from the tails of a probability distribution when ordered processes symbolized by the "deterministic" mean change their
stability. Approached from the standpoint of the emergent dynamics of
phase, the question becomes What happens to the distance between two
nearly but not identical values entering a differential equation set at the
same time? This sensitivity of a system to initial conditions is called its
"mixing" properties (Arnold and Avez 1968). Generalizing the metaphor
to a more complex physiological system manifesting recurrence (every
physiological event happens again), it is possible to study the consistency
in the behavior of orbits in the neighborhood of a given periodic orbit,
that is, to describe the system in terms of local stability properties, with
eigenvalues indicating divergence. A more global approach can be made
to system stability by means of characteristic exponents as descriptors of
the dynamical behavior decomposed into the coordinates (dimensions) of
phase space. A system can be stable to small perturbations in some directions and not in others. The Lagrange-Dirichlet theorem applied to a one-
dimensional potential function indicates that the equilibrium positions of
a time-independent solution of Lagrangian differential equations are stable at energy minima, and Lyapounov proved that they are unstable if
the potential energy has no minimum there (Minorsky 1962). More complex description is required when dealing with the unfolding of N-dimensional attractors. The spectrum of Lyapounov characteristic exponents (N
of them representing N dimensions) offers a more comprehensive qualitative picture of a system's stability (Farmer 1982).

Qualitative Dimension and Transition

Dimensional decomposition of a complex dynamical system changes the image of its distribution function from that of a dominant mean "real" value surrounded by measurement error (and irrelevant noise) to one showing equilibrium or nonequilibrium, quasi-periodic or nonperiodic recurrence that can be described by a spectrum of N-complex numbers (characteristic exponents) portraying the behavior of tangent subspaces (Peixoto 1962). The statistical mean changes from a quantitative index reflecting deterministic mechanism (e.g., affinity, V_{max}, K_d, etc.) to a compromise of an N-dimensional dynamical struggle, the "noise" in the tails representing not error but the anlage of future order. In the metaphor of our title, reason is a composite structure with only apparent sequential stability that derives from the interactions among unstable elements of an N-dimensional system whose latent structure, the context, is (affectively coded) intuition.

These dynamical descriptors can be extended beyond equations of motion in Euclidean time and space by generalization to dimensionalized qualities. Whereas quantities are susceptible to addition (arithmetic measurement along a number line, a value being more or less), markers of intensity of qualities may emerge as singularities, often signaling transitions to other states—for example, fluid turning from clear to opalescent at the critical point or Ising magnetization below T_c (Stanley 1971). In this ontogenetic realm, more becomes different. Qualities can be decomposed into their subspaces, the aggregate of their projections composing the cohesive and multidetermined neighborhood of continuous partial differential equations representing the dynamical system. These "hidden" qualitative subspaces compose the invariant dimensions (Alexandroff 1960; Lefschetz 1949) of the manifold upon which the trajectories play. They are analogous to the harmonic and rhythmic structure underlying the theme and variations of musical composition and the qualities of personality style that configure abstract dimensions of behavioral particulars similarly. In the context of qualitative description, a categorical diagnosis may be an illusion arising from a temporary and multidetermined statistical compromise of interacting dimensional coordinates, and the fine-grained variations called indeterminacy and error may provide a more predictable font of emergent coarse-grained dynamic structure. It may be that in many biological systems the manifold underlying the variational behavior is more pervasive and stable than the mean of the trajectory thought to represent physical mechanisms. Thom's (1975) patterns of emergent discontinuities in gradient systems depend only on the number of controls, the system's dimensions.

How the observable behavior at the surface of a dynamic structure is configured by the complexity of its underlying dimensionality can be visualized from the following example (Manin 1981). Removing the middle 90 percent of a line (dim = 1) of unit length leaves 10 percent at the "surface" of the two ends; removing a circle of diameter 0.9 from the unit disc (dim = 2) leaves about 20 percent at the surface; in dim = 3 the removal of a concentric ball of diameter 0.9 from the unit sphere leaves 28 percent at the surface. In the limit, the internal volume of a geometric object of diameter 0.9 and dimension D (0.9^D) goes to 0 as D goes to infinity. In the geometry of multidimensional volumes, the higher the dimensionality, the greater the arc length of the perimeter relative to its volume, that is, the rougher the surface. Its measure, the minimum number of arbitrarily fine unit coverings required, increases with integer dimensionality as D + 1 (Alexandroff 1960).

Emergent Biological Patterns

Infinite dimensional dynamical systems are dominated by the manifold geometry of low dimensional attractors, and order emerges in the transversals of flows (Abraham and Marsden 1978; Birkhoff 1927). In recent approaches to ontogenetic pattern formation, a similar hidden positional information-supplying coordinate system has been hypothesized as controlling patterns that arise in biochemical reaction-diffusion systems generating transverse gradients in growing asymmetrical tissue domains (Kauffman and Ling 1981; Wolpert 1969). The earlier model of the prepatterning of developmental fields via the inhomogenous spatial distributions of morphogen peaks, each inducing an element in the overall pattern (Weiss 1939), is analogous to the deterministic mapping of the one gene:one enzyme scheme.

Recent epimorphic studies of the reformation of missing pattern elements after truncation of developing parts, as well as other experimental approaches to embryologic developmental sequencing, suggest that cellular actions are based on assessments of position with respect to dimensional coordinates configuring manifold geometries (Bryant, Bryant, and French 1977), spherical and/or cartesian varieties (Kauffman 1981). Prepatterning in this context is viewed as appearing spontaneously from initial homogenous distributions via bifurcations of the chemical kinetic reaction-diffusion equations (nonlinear partial differential equations) subject to stability properties determined by the geometry of their manifolds and the boundary conditions.

A startling recent example of this nondeterministic self-organization in embryogenesis is the spindle-free nuclear division, poleward migration, and other normal chromosomal organization in protozoa, an orderly bipolarity without centriolar structures to configure it, which has been successfully modeled using a nonlinear diffusion system in a three-dimension sphere (Hunding 1981; Hunding and Billing 1981). Such spontaneous emergence of organization through dynamic variation and mode selection has been observed as well in template-free self-replication of polynucleotides *in vitro* in simulations of prebiotic chemistry (Schuster and Sigmund 1980). Morphogens are discontinuities in chemical, physical, or dynamic (i.e., phase) gradients that unfold from latent dynamic structure, not from substances or center sending organizing signals (Thom 1975; Zeeman 1974). As a developmental code, characteristic instabilities in the apparently random motions of complex systems reflecting the invariant geometric character of the underlying multidimensional manifold stand in contrast to a deterministic sequence.

Fine-structure indeterminism comprising more coarse-grained order juxtaposes the polarities of dynamical system description. A study of the characteristics of forced dissipative motion in an anharmonic oscillator over period-doubling regimes suggests different kinds of stability at the two extremes of the bifurcation gap caused by the noise driving: (1) a limit cycle regime with a narrow range of potentially new behavior and a rigid maintenance of sequence versus (2) a phaseless regime of emergent geometric structure without sequential order (Crutchfield and Huberman 1980). Whereas we have tended to think since Mendel's work that the linear, phase-dependent, circular flow of genetic information of single qualities such as the color of flowers or eye pigment could be generalized to account for the stability across time of more complex phenomena, an argument can be made that the metaphor of a multidetermined, self-organizing dynamic structure is both more realistic with respect to the organization of developmental fields and theoretically more stable. If a low-dimensional message arises from interactions of many different kinds of contributors, a few elements missing will make little difference. The abstract dynamic that serves as the organizing mechanism can use relatively nonspecific substitutes that will be pulled into the prepotent mythic process. The higher the number of coordinates (contributing dimensions), the better located the system, so a multidimensional geometric volume may be more precise as well as more stable.

The Parabolic Manifold and Biological Dynamics

By describing an infinite dimensional differential system that can be reduced to a one-parameter nonlinear difference equation without significant loss of its qualitative features, perhaps we can demonstrate: (1) the power of a low-dimensional ("hidden") organization to configure what in a linear-sequential context appears as unpredictable evolutionary behavior; (2) the generalizable character of the dimensionless numbers constituting the parametric control over its evolution; and (3) the coarse-grained predictability of sudden and dramatic discontinuities in macroscopic behavior in the face of unpredictable sequencing. The Lorenz (1963) attractor representing emergent hydrodynamic turbulence may replace the polynucleotide molecule as a symbol of a new kind of biological determinism, the flow of water coming to represent the dynamics of a generalized complex interactive system unfolding over time. Although the governing equations grow impossibly complex as terms representative of reality are added (density, temperature, thermal diffusivity, gravity, volume expansion, height, etc. [Rössler 1976; Saltzman 1962]), using sequential maxima, Lorenz (1963) found a simple parabolic, tentlike return map in the Poincaré section of the equation set.

Parabolic in differential and sigmoid in integral form, the invariant manifold geometry underlying density-dependent dynamics (Grossman 1982) has been generalized by Salk (1973, 1983; Salk and Salk 1981) to all evolutionary processes—for example, a population of elements that at low densities grows by a multiplicative factor but at high densities manifests either phase transition or cataclysmic decline, as with the exponential fall in population during an epidemic (May 1976). Figure 9.1 shows that, depending on the value of the force term r, the temporal evolution simulated by computer iterations of a simple difference equation (May 1976) manifests nonlinear instability with sequential emergence of qualitatively different regimes that are unpredictable from the standpoint of deterministic differential equations but stable and predictable from the standpoint of a statistical geometry. An underlying law in the form of an invariant manifold gives deep and stable structure to the time-dependent, "random" variations of the motions upon it.

The generalized force term r serves as a geometrical property like ratio, proportion, or similarity, regardless of the units of measurement. The Reynolds r is the ratio of inertial to viscous forces; the Prantl r, that of vorticity to thermal diffusivities; the Rayleigh r, the free energy available from buoyancy reduced by its dissipation by conduction and viscous drag (Monin and Yaglom 1965; Whitehead 1975). In a general way, r can be

FIGURE 9.1
Effect of Force Parameter on a Model Dynamic System

$$X_{t+1} = X_t \exp[\, r\,(1 - X_t)\,]$$

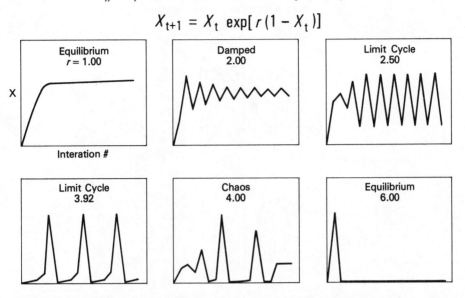

seen as a dynamic balance between a numerator generating nonlinearity and a denominator dispersing it via molecular diffusivity; adjoint ratios within critical parameter ranges produce dramatically different system dynamics. Time-dependent evolutions have different patterns at different values of r (see figure 9.1).

One of the best studied scenarios using a one-dimensional equation is the subharmonic route to turbulence, a sequence of period-doubling bifurcations over increasing r, represented schematically in figure 9.2. Longer and longer periodicity is generated until a critical value of infinite wavelength is reached (critical slowing), then there is a sudden transition to an invariant geometric object without sequential order, a phaseless attractor.[*]

Coding via a latent multidimensional invariant manifold such that structure arises autonomously from the superficially random motions of complex cooperative systems suggests that "intuitive" statistical field properties may be the source of more linear "reason." It also suggests a general mechanism underlying Eriksonian emergence, one composed of multiple phase transitions that can be sudden and discontinuous without new environmental demands. Perhaps the most pervasive suggestion to be derived from this metaphor is that problems arising from the intrinsic manifold of evolution, the density-dependent parabolic-differential, sig-

---

[*]See Coullet and Tressor (1978); Feigenbaum 1979; Geisel and Nierwetberg (1982); and Grossmann and Thomae (1977).

FIGURE 9.2

*The Subharmonic Route to Turbulence, a Sequence of Period-doubling Bifurcations
Over an Increasing Force Term, r.*

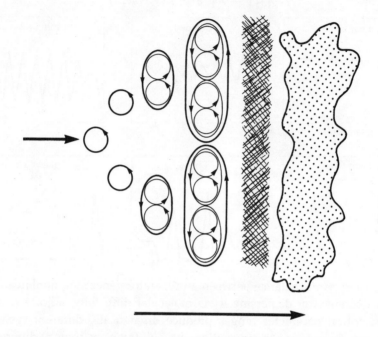

moid-integral curve (Salk 1973; Salk and Salk 1981) may be solved by
further evolution (Salk 1983), emergent new systems serving as transcen-
dent solutions for apparently hopeless endstates. This may be happening
today to theories of biological process.

REFERENCES

Abraham, R., and Marsden, J. E., eds. 1978. *Foundations of Mechanics.* Reading, Mass.:
Benjamin Cummings.

Alexandroff, P. 1960. *Elementary Concepts of Topology.* New York: Dover.

Aronold, V. I., and Avez, A. 1968. *Ergodic Problems of Classical Mechanics.* New York:
Benjamin.

Beece, D., et al. 1980. "Solvent Viscosity and Protein Dynamics." *Biochemistry* 19:5147–
57.

Birkhoff, G. D. 1927. "On the Periodic Motions of Dynamical Systems." *Acta Mathema-
tica* 50:359–79.

Breuer, J., and Freud, S. [1893] 1957. "Studies in Hysteria." In *The Standard Edition of the
Complete Psychological Works of Sigmund Freud* (hereafter *Standard Edition*), ed J. Strachey,
vol. 1, pp. 1–182. London: Hogarth Press.

Bryant, P. J.; Bryant, S. V.; and French, V. 1977. "Biological Regeneration and Pattern Formation." *Scientific American* 237:66–72.

Collet, P., and Eckmann, J-P. 1980. *Iterated Maps on the Interval as Dynamical Systems.* Boston: Birkhauser.

Coullet, P., and Tressor, J. 1978. "Iterations d'endomorphismes et groupe de renormalisation." *Journal de Physique C* 5:25–34.

Crutchfield, J. P., and Huberman, B. A. 1980. "Fluctuations and the Onset of Chaos." *Physics Letters A* 77:407–10.

Eigen, M., and Winkler-Oswatitsch, R. 1982. "Experiments in Biogenesis." In *Evolution of Chaos and Order*, ed. H. Haken, pp. 6–25. Berlin: Springer-Verlag.

Eisenberg, D., and Kauzmann, W. 1969. *The Structure and Properties of Water.* London: Oxford University Press.

Erikson, E. H. 1946. "Ego Development and Historical Change—Clinical Notes." *Psychoanalytic Study of the Child* 2:359–96.

————. 1950. *Childhood and Society.* New York: W. W. Norton.

Farmer, J. D. 1982. "Chaotic Attractors of an Infinite-dimensional Dynamical System." *Physica D* 4:366–93.

Feigenbaum, M. 1979. "Quantitative Universality for a Class of Nonlinear Transformations." *Journal of Statistical Physics* 21:669–706.

Freud, S. [1911] 1957. "Formulations on the Two Principles of Mental Functioning." In *Standard Edition*, ed. J. Strachey, vol. 12, pp. 213–26. London: Hogarth Press.

————. [1914] 1957. "On Narcissism: An Introduction." In *Standard Edition*, ed. J. Strachey, vol. 14, pp. 73–102. London: Hogarth Press.

————. [1923] 1957. "The Ego and the Id." In *Standard Edition*, ed. J. Strachey, vol. 19, pp. 13–68. London: Hogarth Press.

————. [1926] 1957. "Inhibitions, Symptoms, and Anxiety." In *Standard Edition*, ed. J. Strachey, vol. 20, pp. 87–174. London: Hogarth Press.

————. [1937] 1957. "Analysis Terminable and Interminable." In *Standard Edition*, ed. J. Strachey, vol. 23, pp. 209–54. London: Hogarth Press.

Gavish, B. 1980. "Position-dependent Viscosity Effects on Rate Coefficients." *Physical Review Letters* 44:1160–63.

Geisel, T., and Nierwetberg, J. 1982. "Onset of Diffusion and Universal Scaling in Chaotic Systems." *Physical Review Letters* 48:7–10.

Grossmann, S. 1982. "Diversity and Universality in the Spectral Structure of Discrete Time Evolution." In *Evolution of Chaos and Order*, ed. H. Haken, pp. 164–73. Berlin: Springer-Verlag.

Grossmann, S., and Thomae, S. 1977. "Invariant Distributions and Stationary Correlation Functions of One-dimensional Discrete Processes." *Zeitschrift für Naturforschung Teil A.* 32:1353–63.

Gurd, F.R.N., and Rothgeb, T. M. 1979. "Motions in Proteins." *Advances in Protein Physics* 33:73–165.

Haken, H. 1975. "Cooperative Phenomena in Systems Far from Thermal Equilibrium and in Non-physical Systems." *Reviews of Modern Physics* 47:67–121.

Hartmann, H. 1958. *Ego Psychology and the Problem of Adaptation.* New York: International Universities Press.

Hartmann, H.; Kris, E.; and Loewenstein, R. M. 1946. "Comments on the Formation of Psychic Structure." *Psychoanalytic Study of the Child* 2:11–38.

Hunding, A. 1981. "Possible Prepatterns Governing Mitosis: The Mechanism of Spindle-free Chromosome Movement in *Aulacantha scolymantha*." *Journal of Theoretical Biology* 89:353–85.

Hunding, A., and Billing, G. D. 1981. "Spontaneous Pattern Formation in Spherical Nonlinear Reaction-diffusion System: Selection Rules Favor the Bipolar Mitosis Pattern." *Journal of Chemical Physics* 75:486–88.

Kabat, E. A.; Wu, T. T.; and Bilofsky, H. 1977. *Variable Regions of Immunoglobulin Chains.* Cambridge, Mass.: Medical Computer Systems.

Karplus, M. 1981. "Aspects of Protein Dynamics." *Annals of the New York Academy of Sciences* 367:407–18.

Kauffman, S. A. 1981. "Bifurcations in Insect Morphogenesis I." In *Nonlinear Phenomena in Physics and Biology*, ed. R. H. Enns et al., pp. 401–50. New York: Plenum.

Kauffman, S. A., and Ling, E. 1981. "Regeneration by Complementary Wing Disc Fragments of *Drosophilia melanogaster*." *Developmental Biology* 82:228–41.

Koch, S. 1959. "Introduction to the Series." In *Psychology: A Study of a Science*, ed. S. Koch, vol. 1, pp. 1–19. New York: McGraw-Hill

Lefschetz, S. 1949. *Introduction to Topology*. Princeton, N.J.: Princeton University Press.

Lesk, A. M., and Chothia, C. 1980. "Solvent Accessibility, Protein Surfaces, and Protein Folding." In *Second Biophysical Discussion*, ed. V. A. Parsegian, pp. 143–47. New York: Rockefeller University Press.

Lorenz, E. N. 1963. "Deterministic Nonperiodic Flow." *Journal of Atmospheric Science* 20:130–41.

Manin, Y. I. 1981. *Mathematics and Physics*. Boston: Birkhauser.

May, R. M. 1976. "Simple Mathematical Models with Very Complicated Dynamics." *Nature* 261:459–67.

Minorsky, N. 1962. *Nonlinear Oscillations*. New York: Van Nostrand Reinhold.

Monin, A. S., and Yaglom, A. M. 1965. *Statistical Fluid Mechanics: Mechanics of Turbulence*, vol. 1. Cambridge: M.I.T. Press.

Noid, D. W.; Koszykowski, M. L.; and Marcus, R. A. 1981. "Quasiperiodic and Stochastic Behavior in Molecules." *Annual Review of Physical Chemistry* 32:267–309.

Pauling, L.; Corey, R. B.; and Branson, H. R. 1951. "The Structure of Proteins: Two Hydrogen-bonded Helical Configurations of the Polypeptide Chain." *Proceedings of the National Academy of Science* 37:205–11.

Peixoto, M. M. 1962. "Structural Stability on Two-dimensional Manifolds." *Topology* 1:101–20.

Rössler, O. E. 1976. "An Equation for Continuous Chaos." *Physics Letters A* 57:397–98.

Salk, J. 1960. "Persistence of Immunity After Administration of Formalin-treated Polio Virus Vaccine." *Lancet* 1:715–23.

————. 1973. *The Survival of the Wisest*. New York: Harper & Row.

————. 1983. *Anatomy of Reality: Merging of Intuition and Reason*. New York: Columbia University Press.

Salk, J., and Salk, J. 1981. *World Population and Human Values: A New Reality*. New York: Harper & Row.

Saltzman, B. 1962. "Finite Amplitude Free Convection as an Initial Value Problem." *Journal of Atmospheric Science* 19:329–41.

Schuster, P., and Sigmund, K. 1980. "Self-organization of Biological Macromolecules and Evolutionary Stable Strategies." In *Dynamics of Synergetic Systems*, ed. H. Haken, pp. 156–69. Berlin: Springer-Verlag.

Shaw, R. 1981. "Strange Attractors, Chaotic Behavior, and Information Flow." *Zeitschrift für Naturforschung Teil A* 36:80–112.

Stanley, H. E. 1971. *Introduction to Phase Transitions and Physical Phenomena*. New York: Oxford University Press.

Stillinger, F. H. 1980. "Water Revisited." *Science* 209:451–58.

Thom, R. 1975. *Structural Stability and Morphogenesis*. Reading, Mass.: Benjamin.

Watson, J. D. and Crick, F. H. C. 1953. "Molecular Structure of Nucleic Acids." *Nature* 171:737–38.

Weiss, P. 1939. *Principles of Development*. New York: Holt, Rinehart.

Whitehead, J. A. 1975. "A Survey of Hydrodynamic Instabilities." In *Fluctuations, Instabilities, and Phase Transitions*, ed. R. Riste, pp. 153–80. New York: Plenum.

Wolpert, L. 1969. "Positional Information and the Spatial Pattern of Cellular Differentiation." *Journal of Theoretical Biology* 25:1–47.

Yanofsky C. 1963. "Amino Acid Replacements Associated with Mutation and Recombination in the A Gene and Their Relationship to In Vitro Coding Data." *Coldspring Harbor Symposia on Quantitative Biology* 28:581–88.

Zeeman, E. C. 1974. "Primary and Secondary Waves in Developmental Biology." *American Mathematical Society Lectures in Mathematics and Life Science* 7:69–161.

10 Gerald L. Klerman and Myrna M. Weissman

An Epidemiologic View of Mental Illness, Mental Health, and Normality

Introduction

According to the World Health Organization (WHO), "Health is a state of complete physical, mental and social well-being and not merely the absence of infirmity" (Rosen 1968, p. 248). This definition embodies a utopian vision of normality, using the concepts put forth by Offer and Sabshin. Within their framework, the WHO definition blurs the distinction between normality as health and normality as utopia. It redefines health into a utopian goal. The conventional definition of normality as health, as elaborated by Offer and Sabshin, sees health as the absence of definable illness. The WHO definition extends that definition of health to include positive health.

For the most part, epidemiology has not focused on defining health but has been concerned with illness and problems of sampling measurement related to the definition of mental disorders. As such, the definition of normality in classic epidemiology would fall into Offer and Sabshin's concept of normality as health, health being the absence of illness. Epidemiologic research and thinking has not devoted explicit attention to the utopian definition of normality as health. This is not to say, however, that epidemiologic methods are not potentially applicable to issues of normal development, coping with stress, or feelings of satisfaction and happiness. In this chapter, we review some of the basic principles of the epidemiologic approach and method and summarize recent trends in psychiatric epidemiology that have contributed to better estimates of the occurrence of mental disorder in American society. Based on this review, we will explore some of the unresolved issues in definitions of normality that go beyond the occurrence of illness and explore the potential value of epidemiologic approaches to the definition of mental health and normality.

The Epidemiologic Approach

According to its classic definition, epidemiology is the study of the distribution of specific disorders in man and the factors that influence that distribution (MacMahon and Pugh 1970). Epidemiologic studies generate at least three types of information about a disorder: (1) the rates of its occurrence (prevalence and incidence); (2) the variation of these rates by person, time, and place; and (3) identification of risk factors that increase or decrease the probability of developing the disorder.

The origins of epidemiology are to be found in the ancient Mediterranean and Middle Eastern civilizations. Early observations about contagious diseases were codified by Hippocrates and other Greek and Roman physicians. As a scientific discipline, epidemiology emerged in the late nineteenth and early twentieth century, concerned mainly with infectious diseases and their control through public health measures.

In recent decades, the scope of epidemiology has expanded from the study of infectious diseases to include chronic noninfectious conditions such as coronary heart disease, hypertension, and cancer. Most recently the field has been broadened to encompass mental disorders, social disability, and/or emotional impairment.

As the methods and approaches that have proven so successful in the control and prevention of infectious disease have been applied to cancer, heart disease, and other chronic illnesses, significant public health benefits have become apparent. For example, the demonstration of a relationship between tobacco smoking and cancer has led the way to preventive interventions, even though the causative agent in tobacco responsible for carcinogenesis has not been identified. Similarly, identification of environmental carcinogens often related to industrial pollutants has contributed to opportunities for prevention and control. The identification of significant risk factors such as diet, cigarette smoking, exercise, level of sedentary activity, and personality type has been associated with a dramatic decline in the death rate from cardiovascular disease and has offered hope that further advances can be found.

The epidemiologic approach involves an attitude—a point of view toward illness—and a set of methods. The epidemiological attitude is predominantly empirical and even at times skeptical. Relatively little effort is given to speculation. In general, epidemiologists are hesitant to wander too far from the available data. The emphasis is placed on determining quantitative relationships between rates of illness and associated "risk factors." However, the availability of information about rates and risk factors, while based on quantitative empirical data, is not an end in itself. Experience with infectious diseases, cancer, and cardiovascular disease demonstrates that such information can generate new hypotheses about etiology and pathogenesis although methods other than those of epidemiology would be required to establish the scientific validity of these hypotheses.

Moreover, epidemiological knowledge can provide insights to improve clinical practice and health planning and provide a more scientific basis for public policy in health and social welfare.

It is often asserted that epidemiologic findings are entirely empirical and "just statistical" and that they cannot provide definitive information as to causation and pathogenesis. Such knowledge requires experimental studies of pathology, biochemistry, and so on. This assertion is, for the most part, true. For example, the finding from epidemiologic data of a relationship between tobacco smoking and cardiac disease and cancer has intensified efforts to identify the carcinogenic and cardiotoxic components of cigarettes. Nevertheless, even though these agents have not been specifically identified, the validity of the epidemiologic evidence has led to opportunities for intervention and control. This illustrates one of the major achievements of the epidemiologic approach: it is possible to initiate public health interventions directed at individuals or groups to control and prevent illnesses even though their causation may not be definitively established by laboratory methods.

For the most part, the epidemiologic approach has been applied to discrete disorders and has seldom been applied to matters of health or "normalcy."

Application of Epidemiologic Approaches to Mental Illnesses and Psychiatry

Observations and speculation about issues related to what today would be called psychiatric epidemiology have gone on for many centuries. In previous eras, "lunacy," "insanity," "nervousness," and related conditions have been associated with diet, civilization, climate, astrological phenomena, witchcraft, and numerous other factors, usually those related to the values and beliefs of the particular society or, in the case of Western civilization, to different historical periods. Psychiatric epidemiology did not emerge as an identifiable scientific field until after World War II. As will be discussed, in the United States the focus of psychiatric epidemiology has been primarily on demonstrating the relevance of psychosocial and cultural factors to understanding mental health. In this effort, the hope is that the application to mental health of medical epidemiology's approach and techniques will not only help resolve controversies as to the nature of mental illnesses and their causation but also lead to preventive interventions.

Psychiatric and medical epidemiology have tended to develop in separate directions; psychiatric epidemiology has tended to be separate from the "mainstream" of epidemiology in the types of risk factors it has studied and the methods of measurement and the statistical methods applied to data. Only very recently have there been attempts to bring psychiatric epidemiology closer to the main trends in epidemiology. In general, psychiatric epidemiology has tended to be more broad based, paying considerable attention to psychosocial variables as causal. For example, American psychiatric epidemiology has studied the impact of social stress, social class, family experience, and life events, whereas medical epidemiology has been mainly concerned with infection, nutrition, genetics, and other biological factors.

Regarding measurement and statistical techniques, psychiatric epidemiology has relied on nonparametric techniques, such as chi-square and regression methods derived from sociology and psychology, and has seldom expressed rates in terms of standard indices of incidence or prevalence or estimated magnitude of risk, such as relative risk or attributable risk. However, recently there have been interesting lines of convergence. Genetic investigations have become more prominent in American psychiatric research. As already mentioned, in the epidemiology of cardiac disease, increasing attention is being paid to life style, level of sedentary activity and exercise, nutritional and diet patterns, and personality style. In the epidemiology of cancer, greater attention is being paid to the environment, particularly the role of tobacco smoking and exposures to toxins in industrial and occupational settings.

In order to obtain accurate estimates of the distribution and risk factors for any disorder, epidemiologic studies are usually undertaken in the general population. In this way true estimates of a disorder, independent of help seeking, can be obtained (i.e., a sample of persons who may or may not have received treatment for the disorder under study is sought).

As a result, a major technical problem in any epidemiologic study is the definition of a case and, therefore, determining the boundaries between normal and abnormal, ill and not ill, or ill and healthy. MacMahon and Pugh (1970) have identified at least two types of criteria used to categorize cases. These are:

1. *Manifestational criteria.* The ill persons are grouped according to their similarity with respect to symptoms and signs and changes in body fluids, physiologic function, and behavior. Examples include cervical cancer, diabetes mellitus, and schizophrenia.
2. *Causal criteria.* The ill persons are defined in terms of similarity with respect to a specified characteristic believed to be a cause of the illness. Examples include birth trauma, lead poisoning, silicosis, syphilis.

The epidemiologic study of psychiatric phenomenon is primarily based on what MacMahon and Pugh (1970) term manifestational disorders. In the absence of biologic criteria, the studies rely exclusively on subjective reports of signs, symptoms, and behavior and to some lesser extent on prognosis.

In the absence of knowledge of causal factors, manifestational criteria provide the major basis for diagnosis and classification. Consequently, the setting of boundaries of disorders can be seen as highly intuitive or arbitrary. The underlying assumption is that the greater the similarity of the manifestations, the more likely the persons showing the manifestations may be considered an entity. Defining a disorder in manifestational terms creates problems in determining boundaries. While the boundary between normal and abnormal or healthy and ill is a major issue in epidemiologic research, the focus in epidemiology is usually on disease or ill health.

Objective criteria are essential for definition of a case (diagnosis) and assignment to some grouping (classification). The reliability and validity in psychiatric diagnosis and classification had, until recently, been so limited as to hinder progress in estimating rates of specific disorders and establishing risk factors. Recent progress in psychopathology and other fields of psychiatric research have rendered these difficulties less severe, so much so that large-scale community surveys have taken on new momentum.

Psychiatric Epidemiology in the United States

In previous writings we have noted four phases in the development of American psychiatric epidemiology (Weissman and Klerman 1978): (1) the period prior to World War II; (2) World War II; (3) the "golden era" of social epidemiology following World War II; and (4) the current renaissance of epidemiology of mental disorders.

THE PERIOD PRIOR TO WORLD WAR II

The first partially completed attempt to investigate the true prevalence of mental disorders—that is, both treated and untreated cases— in a community in the United States was conducted in Massachusetts in 1855. Dr. Edward Jarvis surveyed key community leaders as well as hospital and other official records to determine the frequency of insanity and idiocy, the major psychiatric nosological distinction at that time. The national census of 1880 also incorporated this distinction and provided the first national estimates of mental disorder.

Indirect procedure of ascertainment from medical records and key informants characterized subsequent United States studies up to World War II. Representative studies using these methods were reported by Lemkau and associates (1942) in the Eastern Health District of Baltimore in 1933 and 1936, and by Roth and Luton (1943) in Williamson Country, Tennessee, in 1935. Lemkau and associates supplemented these procedures with data from direct interviews determining frequency of "nervousness" that had been conducted coincidentally by the National Health Survey in the same district.

Although not a community survey, the pioneering study of Faris and Dunham (1967) examined the ecological distribution of first admissions to mental hospitals in Chicago in the 1930s. Diagnosis from hospital records was related to the patients' area of residence. The highest rates of hospitalization for mental illness occurred in residents from areas with the highest social disorganization. This careful study demonstrated the importance of social variables in mental illness.

These studies, although advanced for their time, had two major limitations: case ascertainment was incomplete, and clinical diagnoses were given at face value, with little attention to issues of reliability or validity.

WORLD WAR II EXPERIENCE

Although World War II produced a moratorium on community surveys, the mental health experiences of the selective service and the armed forces were to have an important impact. During World War II, the

Selected Service System rejected large numbers of young men for psychiatric reasons; in fact, psychiatric reasons accounted for the largest proportion of nonacceptance. It is notable that a large number of men rejected on psychiatric grounds were intellectually deficient, "the mentally retarded," as well as those who were mentally ill or emotionally troubled. After the war, the scientific and military justifications for the rejection policy were criticized and the accuracy of the diagnostic procedures was questioned; nevertheless, the publicity given to the high rates of psychoneurosis, personality disorders, and psychosomatic problems focused public attention on mental health problems and supported efforts to obtain more information on the rates of psychiatric disability.

Neuropsychiatric specialists were widely dispersed in the military medical services and contributed clinical description and statistical documentation of mental disorders, such as combat fatigue, transient functional psychoses, dissociative states, and stress reactions. Whereas the rates of psychoses in the military remained relatively stable, the rates of psychoneuroses and personality reactions fluctuated and were related to combat and other situational stresses, such as the extreme deprivation of concentration camps.

In the U.S. Army, a group of talented social scientists was organized. Using the best available sampling methods, survey techniques, and statistical analyses, this group conducted a wide range of studies and developed neuropsychiatric screening questionnaires to relate neurotic symptoms to combat stress and morale problems (Stouffer et al. 1949). These scales were forerunners of the impairment scales used in community surveys after the war.

The observation that the frequency of psychiatric reactions varied in direct relation to combat stress was of practical and theoretical importance. These combat reactions occurred in psychiatrically screened young men, among whom preexisting disability would seem to have been eliminated. From today's vantage point, the methods for screening were far from ideal. However, for the post–World War II phase, they were of great importance. The planners of epidemiologic research in the post–World War II periods were impressed by the selective service and military experience and concluded that predisposing vulnerability and concurrent mental and physical illness had been adequately screened. Therefore, it seemed reasonable at that time to conclude that precipitant stress, rather than predisposition or vulnerability, was a major factor in the men's psychiatric illness. The role of stress as an immediate precipitant of mental illness was supported powerfully by these observations, and stress was to become a major unifying concept in the post–World War II studies in civilian settings. Poverty, urban anomie, rapid social change, and social class were to become in civilian life equivalent to stress of combat and the threat of death in the military.

THE GOLDEN ERA OF SOCIAL EPIDEMIOLOGY

After World War II, the experience gained by the military and the growing public awareness of the high incidence of mental illness stimulated new epidemiologic studies of the general population. Moreover, governmental, financial, and policy support for community surveys became available when the National Institute of Mental Health was created legislatively in 1946, and became operational in 1949 (Weissman and Klerman 1978).

Studies representative of the community surveys of this period were the Midtown Manhattan survey conducted by Srole, Langer, and Rennie (1962), which assessed the impact of urban life on mental health based on interviewing more than one thousand adult residents, selected by probability sampling in Midtown Manhattan; the nationwide survey of mental health by Gurin and associates (1960) of the University of Michigan Survey Research Center in which more than two thousand adult Americans also selected by probability sampling were interviewed; and the cross-cultural studies of Leighton and coworkers (1963) based on Leighton's research among the Japanese-American internees in California during World War II, and subsequently undertaken in the 1950s in Nigeria, northern Canada, and southwestern United States. Leighton and associates' well-known study assessed the impact of social and economic change on the mental health of a previously stable community.

Many of the American social scientists and psychiatrists conducting these studies explicitly rejected the "medical model" of multiple discrete psychiatric disorders due to diverse, but specific, causes. In this respect, there was considerable difference between the post–World War II American approach and that of continental Europe and Scandinavia, which grew out of the Kraepelinian tradition. Their use of traditional psychiatric diagnostic categories was based on the assumption that each illness had a different underlying etiology, syndrome, course, and treatment, and that biological (genetic, biochemical) factors rather than social and environmental stress most likely would explain the cause of different syndromes, at least for the major psychoses.

The unitary concept of mental illness in the United States was consistent with theories of social causation of mental illness. These theories emphasized the importance of life experience for understanding the psychopathology of individuals and the role of economics, social class, and social stress in the etiology of mental disorders. The American approach was heavily influenced by the teachings of Adolph Meyer of Johns Hopkins University (Klerman 1979). Diagnostic groups were considered quantitatively different manifestations of the same causes of mental functioning since common etiological factors, and social stress, underlay psychiatric disorders. Mental health and mental illness, it was postulated, fell along a gradient. The most succinct expression of this viewpoint was offered in 1955 by the National Advisory Mental Health Council. "The concept of etiology as embraced by modern psychiatry," it said, "differs from the simple cause and effect system of traditional medicine. It subscribes to a 'field theory' hypothesis in which the interactions and transactions of multiple factors eventuate in degrees of health and sickness" (Lin and Standley 1962, p. 65). Less emphasized as etiologic in the American studies were genetics, birth defects, nutrition, infection, and biological variations. Having rejected the use of discrete psychiatric disorders and conventional psychiatric diagnostic procedures, the American investigators conducting epidemiologic studies adopted inventories developed during World War II that measured non-differentiated severity of psychiatric impairment.

The rejection of categories of psychiatric diagnosis and the use of measures of impairment was expressed in views proposed at the series of influential conferences on psychiatric epidemiology sponsored by the Milbank Memorial Fund, and by the World Health Organization as early as 1956. For example, Lin and Standley (1962), in a report published by the WHO, noted the reliability problem in psychiatric diagnosis and suggested that instead of attaching a firm diagnosis to each patient, the physical, psychological, and psychiatric findings could be used to isolate symptom or personality traits that go together and new labels could be applied to such aggregates. This approach had been advocated by workers who were skeptical of psychiatric diagnosis and had been applied in psychological rather than psychiatric investigation. It was felt worth trying to see how much psychiatry could gain from it, even though it implied reversion to pre-Kraepelinian ideas. The quantitative aspect of morbid psychiatric states—the degree of impairment—an aspect neglected in the past, also gained new attention.

These American surveys made important contributions to research. They introduced rigor to community surveys of mental illness by giving attention to sampling and by the use of standardized questionnaires to systematize the collection of data and of sophisticated statistical techniques for their analysis. They enlarged the domain of independent variables in epidemiology to include psychosocial factors, help-seeking behavior, and social role as factors in illness, and they improved measurements of these new variables, such as recent life events, social class, and personality. They sensitized researchers to the influences of psychosocial variables in many medical disorders, as is now reflected in evidence relating stress and personality to cardiovascular disease.

Although the epidemiologic surveys of the 1950s and the 1960s generated a considerable body of information on mental health and impairment in the United States, those studies had limitations. Most important, they did not generate rates of specific psychiatric disorders. The impairment rates that were reported were independent of diagnosis and obscured diagnostic variations. Impairment rates could not be translated into equivalent clinical diagnostic categories, and studies subsequently showed that the relationship between impairment rates and rates of specific diagnoses was poor (Schwartz 1973). As a consequence of these limitations, no rates of treated and untreated specific psychiatric disorders were available that could be used to resolve issues of scientific and public policy concern in the 1970s.

THE CURRENT RENAISSANCE OF EPIDEMIOLOGY OF MENTAL DISORDERS

Progress in American psychiatric epidemiology drew to a halt in the late 1960s. There were few new findings, although controversy continued over previously generated theories. For example, debate continued as to whether the relationship between low social class and schizophrenia was a direct social cause or a reflection of social drift (Kohn 1976).

Meanwhile, in other areas of psychiatric research—psychopharmacology, genetics, psychopathology, and neurobiology—considerable progress was underway. Developments in these fields led to advances in validity and reliability of diagnoses and to a strengthening of the evidence for biological factors in the etiology of mental illness. Both these occurrences contributed to the redefinition of the traditional "medical" model as being relevant to psychiatry and, therefore, to psychiatric epidemiology. These developments have led to a renaissance of studies of the epidemiology of specific mental disorders and, more specifically, to the NIMH Epidemiologic Catchment Area Study begun in 1980.

ADVANCES IN GENETICS AND NEUROBIOLOGY

Research in genetics strengthened evidence for the biological factors in the causation of mental illness. The studies by Heston (1966), and those done in Scandinavia by Mednich and associates (1974) and Rosenthal and Kety (1968), using the cross-rearing adoptive technique, established the high likelihood that genetic factors were involved in schizophrenia. In the 1960s independent research groups in the United States, Europe, and Scandinavia studied primary affective disorders and found that by dividing their population into unipolar and bipolar groups based on the presence of a history of manic episode, strong familial association was found that supported a genetic transmission for the primary affective disorders, especially the bipolar forms (Perris 1966).

Evidence for biological factors in psychiatric disorders also emanated from studies in mental retardation, where the classical medical strategy led to discovery of new nosological subclasses. Using laboratory methods, the large group of mental retardations could be divided on the basis of origin, particularly subclasses due to aminoacidurias and to chromosomal abnormalities. However, in the other mental disorders, particularly schizophrenia, affective states, and anxiety states, evidence for biological factors has been slower to emerge, and what evidence there is derives indirectly from psychopharmacology. In studies of the modes of action of these drugs, the neurotransmitters, particularly the catecholamines, have been implicated in the pathogenesis of various disorders.

ADVANCES IN PSYCHOPHARMACOLOGY

The introduction of psychotropic drugs in the mid-1950s led to changes in the scientific investigation and in the treatment of psychiatric disorders. The initial research contribution of modern psychopharmacology was to stimulate the development of methodology for systematic assessment of patient's symptoms, social function, and diagnosis. Case reports and clinical experience could no longer be relied on to evaluate the flood of new agents that followed the introduction of chlorpromazine. The need to establish efficacy led to controlled clinical trials. Randomized designs, double-blind techniques, and placebo controls became the standards for therapeutic evaluation. These studies demonstrated that the new drugs, which had been shown to have varying neuropharmacologic modes of action, had different patterns of clinical efficacy, explainable partially by diagnostic type (e.g., schizophrenic patients responded to phenothiazines, whereas depressed patients responded to tricyclic antidepressants and the bipolar subtype showed response to lithium carbonate). These findings supported the concept that psychiatric disorders were discrete and heterogeneous and prompted reevaluation of diagnosis.

ADVANCES IN PSYCHOPATHOLOGY

By the mid-1960s, there was growing awareness among clinicians and researchers that the absence of an objective and reliable system for describing psychopathology and for psychiatric diagnosis limited research. In 1965, the NIMH Psychopharmacology Research Branch sponsored a conference on classification in psychiatry. In the decade since that conference, there have been major achievements in three areas: understanding sources of cross-national differences in diagnostic practices, improving their precision and reliability, and developing methods for their validation.

Cross-National Differences in Diagnosis. Two major studies clarified diagnostic practices and led to comparable data on mental disorders in different countries. The United States–United Kingdom (US-UK) study organized by Kramer and Zubin investigated whether reported differences in diagnostic distributions between patients admitted to mental hospitals in the United States and the United Kingdom were real or artifacts due to different diagnostic criteria. The findings showed that the reported large differences between American and British rates of depression and schizophrenia were mainly a function of different diagnostic usage (Kramer 1969; Zubin 1969). American psychiatrists tended to diagnose as schizophrenic, patients who would be considered depressed or manic by British psychiatrists.

Stimulated in part by the findings of this study, the World Health Organization undertook to determine whether comparable cases of schizophrenia could be identified in various nations with different political and social characteristics (Wing 1974). The results of the US-UK and the WHO studies demonstrated that criteria and methods could be developed for the collection of reliable, uniform, and comparable diagnoses under varying conditions.

Reliability of Diagnosis. Considerable progress in psychopathology research helped to identify sources of variance that contributed to unreliability of diagnosis among clinicians. Five sources of variance in the diagnostic process were identified: subject—the patient actually has different conditions at different times; occasion—the patient is in a different stage of the same condition at different times; information—clinicians have different sources of information; observation—clinicians presented with the same stimuli differ in what they observe; and criteria—the formal inclusion and exclusion criteria that clinicians use to summarize patient data into psychiatric diagnosis differ.

Methods were evolved to reduce these sources of variance. A structured clinical interview was developed to elicit the patient's signs and symptoms in a systematic fashion and to reduce that portion of variance due to different interviewing styles and coverage (Endicott and Spitzer 1978). A set of operational definitions, with specific inclusion and exclusion criteria for a variety of nosological groups, was developed for reducing the criterion variance that was shown to account for the largest source of error Spitzer, Endicott, and Robins 1978).

The Research Diagnostic Criteria (RDC) evolved from a decade of research on diagnosis, particularly by the group at Washington University, St. Louis (Robins and Guze 1972). The conditions included were usually chosen because they had the most evidence of validity in terms of clinical descriptions, consistency over time, and increased familial incidence.

Spitzer, Endicott, and Robins (1978) and Wing (1974) and others have shown convincingly that the use of these methods increased the reliability of psychiatric diagnosis. Although the RDC has received attention in the United States, parallel work in Great Britain, Scandinavia, and continental Europe—particularly the Present State Examination (PSE), developed by Wing and associates (1974)—led to similar improvement of reliability. These efforts demonstrated that respectable levels of concordance in psychiatric diagnosis could be achieved among clinicians and researchers.

Validity of Diagnosis. Whereas the validity of a classification is limited by its reliability, reliability per se does not establish validity. Validity of nosological classes in psychiatry requires correlation of the clinical phenomena with other domains of variables, such as long-term outcome, response to treatment, familial associations, and so on.

The usual approach to validity in psychiatry has been to base diagnostic classification on the best clinical judgment of experienced psychiatrists largely based on a prior principle rather than systematic study. Robins and Guze (1972) put forth methods for establishing diagnostic validity in psychiatry on a scientific basis. The methods they identify are careful clinical description, delimitation from other disorders, laboratory studies, follow-up studies, family and genetic studies, response to treatment, and correlation with independent psychological or social variables.

With these principles in mind and concentrating primarily on follow-up and family studies, various research groups have studied carefully defined psychiatric disorders. These studies have lent further support to the heterogeneity of psychiatric disorders. Using the validity procedures described, investigators have demonstrated that different psychiatric disorders have different clinical pictures, natural history, family aggregation, and response to treatment. Moreover, this approach is leading to even finer differentiation of the diagnostic criteria.

With these advances, a new model of psychiatric epidemiology was possible in the United States. This model integrates advances from psychiatric research with the achievements derived from survey research in the 1950s and 1960s. This model is not new in epidemiology; it is implicit in the tradition of epidemiology applied to nonpsychiatric chronic diseases and it involves the following components: (1) a sharp distinction is made between the dependent and independent variables; (2) the major dependent variables are the multiple categories of discrete psychiatric disorders; (3) the independent variables are multiple and include biological (genetic, biochemical, nutritional) and psychosocial factors (social stress, social class, migration, urbanization, economic change); (4) specific modes of causal explanation need to be explicated for relating the independent and dependent variables. In these explanations, multifactorial and multidimensional approaches are being developed mathematically and tested empirically to supplement classical explanation by necessary and sufficient, single antecedent factor models.

THE NIMH EPIDEMIOLOGIC CATCHMENT AREA PROGRAM

In 1979, the National Institute of Mental Health started a five-year program involving a number of Epidemiologic Catchment Areas (ECA) (Eaton 1981). The ECAs will operate for a minimum of five years and investigate populations at least as large as that covered by a comprehensive Community Mental Health Center (CMHC). Each ECA study has a degree of autonomy in collecting specific data for its area, but all centers collect the same core of basic material. The objectives of the multisite longitudinal study are to provide: (1) information on the prevalence and incidence of specific mental disorders in the community by means of appropriate surveys in single family households, multiple dwelling units, group quarters, and institutional settings such as nursing homes, homes for the aged, prisons, schools, and mental institutions; (2) estimates of the number of people in need of treatment; how many people are in treatment; where services are received and when treatment is first initiated; and if not in treatment, the reasons for not seeking and/or receiving treatment; and (3) for incidence of newly developed mental disorders, the concomitant factors associated with or causative of the disorder. This information has practical public health potential for initiating intervention programs aimed at primary and secondary prevention.

The catchment areas have at least 200,000 inhabitants and have boundaries that coincide with one or more contiguous comprehensive CMHC catchment areas. Because of the large number of persons surveyed (a minimum of three thousand per site on two to three occasions), the method of diagnostic assessment developed had to be suitable for use by lay interviewers.

The NIMH Division of Biometry and Epidemiology initiated the development of an adaptation of the Schedule for Affective Disorders and Schizophrenia (SADS) and Renard Diagnostic Interviews for use in general population studies by lay interviewers (Robins et al. 1977). This new instrument, the Diagnostic Interview Schedule (DIS), is now being used in the ECA study. The history, characteristics, and validity of the DIS have been described by Robins, Helzer, Croughan, and Ratcliffe. Briefly, the DIS is a highly structured interview designed for use by lay interviewers in epidemiologic studies and capable of generating computer diagnoses according to some DSM-III, Feighner, or Research Diagnostic Criteria. It is possible to make diagnoses by all three systems with a single interview because the systems share a common heritage by addressing diagnoses from a descriptive rather than etiologic perspective.

The DIS elicits the elements of a diagnosis, including symptoms, their severity, frequency, distribution over time, and whether they can be explainable by physical illness, drug, or alcohol use or another psychiatric diagnosis. Structured both for the questions and the probes, it is precoded so that after editing, answers can be directly entered into a computer. The DIS takes forty-five minutes to one hour to administer. Diagnoses can be generated both currently (last two weeks, one month, six months, one year) and over a lifetime. The DIS is relatively economical because it does not require a clinician, external data, extraneous coders, or a lengthy training program.

In summary, the ECA study is unique in that it is the first time in the United States that a complete cross-sectional sample has been studied that includes both household and institutional cases. In the past, studies included one or the other but not both. In addition, the study is longitudinally immature and uses diagnostic instruments that can generate diagnoses similar to those used in clinical practice in the United States.

As of this writing, over twenty thousand interviews have been completed in three of the five ECA sites. The Yale University site, which was the first in the field, reported preliminary findings at the American Psychiatric Association Annual Meeting in New Orleans, 1981. The Yale ECA consists of the New Haven Standard Metropolitan Statistical Area of 427,000 people (1970 census). During the three-year survey, there are three field periods with an initial interview and two interviews of a household sample after six months each. In the first interview wave, begun in July 1980, a systematic probability community sample of 4000 adults (eighteen years of age and over) were contacted in order to complete at least three thousand interviews, and an additional sample of nearly 2,700 persons sixty-five years of age and over to complete two thousand such interviews.

Sampling was based on electric meter listings supplemented by city directory and telephone book information. One household in thirty-one was selected for the community sample and one person eighteen years of age or over was selected at random (according to the Kish grid method), from the household for inclusion in the sample. In addition to the household sample, an institutional sample of about five hundred is being interviewed.

An in-person interview (averaging about seventy minutes in length) was conducted for each respondent. The materials in the interview schedule included specific questions on: psychiatric diagnosis and mental status (DIS); general health status and functional disability; sociodemographic characteristics; barriers to care and stigma attached to mental illness; utilization of general medical, mental health, and human service facilities; and role-performance activities. Interviews were conducted by survey research interviewers who received six days of formal training plus practice interviewing.

Preliminary results from the Yale ECA replicate some of the findings in the 1975 survey in New Haven (Weissman and Myers 1978). About 15 percent of the adult population suffers from a definable alcohol, drug, or mental disorder within a given year. Moreover, the disorders with the highest prevalence are alcoholism, depression, related affective disorders, phobia, and related states. Schizophrenia and other major psychoses account for only about 1 percent of annual prevalence.

The findings also replicate some of the early estimates of Regier and associates (1978) and Dohrenwend and associates (1971) in material prepared for the President's Commission on Mental Health in 1977 based on extra populations from earlier studies and from treated prevalence. At that time they estimated that about 15 percent of the adult population had some mental disorder. The majority of these persons were being treated but not, as might be expected, in the specialty mental health sector, but rather in the general health sector.

At this point, the most important aspect of the ECA project is not the establishment of specific rates. The rates presented are likely to change as the DSM-III criteria are more closely approximated and after data from individuals residing in institutional settings are analyzed. The most significant result of the Yale study is the demonstration that it is possible to train lay interviewers to administer a sophisticated assessment instrument in a community survey, and produce diagnostic equivalents very similar to that found in studies using more clinical instruments and clinical interviewers. Whatever the specific data findings of the ECA project, it is clear that we have just entered a new era in psychiatric epidemiology.

The Epidemiology of Mental Disorders, Mental Health, and Normality

If 15 percent of the population, or about 32 million individuals, have a mental illness, what about the other 85 percent? Are they to be considered "mentally healthy"? From the point of view that defines normality or mental health as the "absence of a diagnosable disorder," those 85 percent are to be regarded as "normal" or "mentally healthy." However, very few mental health professionals or social scientists would accept this conclusion. Rather, it is widely accepted that health is not just the absence of disorder. The mental health field and, increasingly, the general health field are not satisfied with the goals of reduced mortality or morbidity or even the elimination of illness; they have attempted to define more positive goals—the enhancement of health.

When applied to mental health, this goal has generated considerable discussion and, at times, controversy. How is mental health to be defined? By what criteria? Are there objective criteria, free of social values or cultural bias?

There is no consensus on how to define normality and health, other than by identifying them with the absence of disease. One prominent approach within the normality as utopia framework has been to derive listings of attributes and characteristics of hypothesized ideally "healthy" persons. This approach was summarized in the volume by Marie Jahoda prepared for the Joint Commission on Mental Health and Mental Illness in the late 1950s. However, there is general consensus that these judgments—on the competence, rationality, flexibility, capacity to cope, or level of psycho-social fixation of respondents—lack any empirical basis and reflect the theoretical values of the writer.

An alternative approach has been to relate normality to the life cycle and build on developmental psychology. This is embodied in the writings of Erikson (1968), Levinson (1978), Vaillant (1977), and Neugarten (1975), who seem to define normality and mental health as the capacity to adapt successfully and to master the developmental tasks of life-cycle stages or other age-appropriate decisions and tasks.

Another approach has been suggested by one of us (Klerman) and attempts to define alternative sets of criteria for ever-widening groups of actual or potential populations. The following text explains this approach.

THE CORE POPULATION: INDIVIDUALS WITH MENTAL DISORDERS

At the core are the 15 percent of the population with definable and diagnosable mental disorders. Some psychiatrists would argue that within this core there is a further "inner core" of individuals with chronically disabling mental illness, particularly schizophrenia, other psychoses, and severe alcoholism.

Psychiatry began with psychotic patients, particularly those chronically disabled and requiring institutionalization, usually under public and governmental auspices. In a study prepared for the United States Department of Health and Human Services Task Force on the chronically ill, chaired by Richmond and Klerman (1982), it was estimated that there are about 1.5 million chronically mentally ill. It is this chronic group that has historically been the main concern of psychiatry, as psychiatry began as a group of physicians specializing in the care of institutionalized mentally ill in the nineteenth century. Not only does this "inner core" reflect the historical origin of the field, but it represents a group with greater social cost because of the high level of disability, demand for residential and financial supports, economic and vocational maladjustments, and frequent use of institutional settings.

Since the turn of the century, the scope of mental illness has increased so as to include various categories of neuroses, depressions, and personality disorders in addition to the psychoses. The epidemiologic evidence indicates that about 15 percent of the population in any one year suffers from such a disorder.

While 15 percent of the population represents current prevalence, epidemiologists are also interested in lifetime expectancy. Although full data are not available, it appears that about 40 percent of the population will experience some diagnosable mental illness during their lifetime. For example, the life expectancy for depression for women is about 25 percent and for men about 12 to 15 percent (Weissman and Myers 1978). To this can be added expectancies of about 10 percent alcoholism for men and various episodes of anxiety, phobia, and so forth, and it becomes clear that 40 percent is a conservative estimate. In any one year, about 15 percent of the population experiences a psychiatric illness diagnosable according to DSM-III. Over a lifetime, about 40 percent of individuals will experience some episode of diagnosable disorder; relatively few individuals will not have symptoms of anxiety, tension, or sadness at some time in their life, but they need not necessarily reach the criteria of intensity and duration that would qualify a diagnosis of a psychiatric disorder.

We do not have comparable estimates of familial prevalence. It is likely that in at least 50 percent of families, at least one family member will suffer a definable mental illness at some time during the "life of the family." The impact on family functioning and social and economic status remains to be investigated.

In addition to this core population of individuals with diagnosed illness, figure 10.1 identifies two other populations of interest. The second population includes the large numbers of individuals coping with stress and life events and the third, individuals attempting to enhance their life and achieve happiness and personal fulfillment and satisfaction.

FIGURE 10.1
Boundaries Between Mental Illness and Mental Health

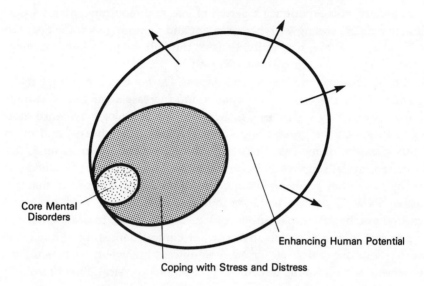

Core Mental
Disorders

Enhancing Human Potential

Coping with Stress and Distress

THOSE COPING WITH STRESS AND LIFE EVENTS

A major achievement in psychiatric research since World War II has been the clarification of the concept of stress and the development of quantitative measures for the assessment of life events and other stressors. A key advance in this research was Holmes and Rahe's development of the scale for quantitative rating of life events. Their scale has been used in a large number of clinical studies, social surveys, and in much epidemiologic research. Based on this approach, it is now possible to estimate that between 30 and 50 million persons in the United States each year experience a stressful life event that immobilizes their capacity to cope.

It should be emphasized that experiencing a stressful life event does not necessarily result in an episode of diagnosable mental illness. However, the evidence is increasingly strong that individuals coping with these life events are at greater risk for symptoms of distress and illness and are likely to increase their utilization of the health-care system during the period of coping. Moreover, a significant fraction will fail to cope adequately; this will be reflected in their subsequent higher rate of medical illness in general, and mental illness in particular.

For example, there are about one million deaths in the country each year. Assuming that each person who dies has one to three close relatives and friends who experience a period of loss and mourning, about 4 million people are coping with bereavement and mourning over the death of a loved one. As bereaved individuals go through the period of mourning, there is an increase in distress reflected by poor sleep, loss of appetite, bodily complaints, and feelings of sadness. During this period they make greater use of the health-care system and increase their use of various drugs, particularly sedatives. Furthermore, epidemiologic evidence indicates that men are greater at risk for cardiovascular disease and other manifestations of increased mortality during a period of mourning. Assuming Clayton's figures indicating that about 85 percent of individuals are symptom free at the end of one year of mourning are correct, that still leaves about 15 percent with continuing symptoms. The work of Paykel and others, based on data from a case control study, indicates that bereavement increases the relative risk for clinical depression. Similar investigations are underway for other significant life events such as unemployment and economic difficulties and serious physical illness resulting in hospitalization, divorce, and separation. (See table 10.1.)

Adding up the numbers of individuals experiencing the major events in the Holmes and Rahe (1967) listing provides a crude estimate of a minimum of 30 million, to a maximum of possibly 50 million persons who will experience a major life event of sufficient magnitude to require some coping response.

In addition to these life events, there are significant circumstances of a chronic and enduring nature that also stimulate the coping capacity of individuals. Pearlin (1977) documents the extent to which enduring adverse circumstances, such as poor marriages or economic and financial difficulties, produce an increased risk for depressive symptoms.

TABLE 10.1
Epidemiology of Life Stress

Stressful Life Event	Estimated Prevalence of Persons Directly Affected	Estimated Prevalence of Persons Indirectly Affected per Year
Death	1.5 million	4 million
Divorce	3 million	6 million
Retirement	10 million	20 million
Unemployment	7 million	20 million
Chronic Medical Illness	10 million	20 million
Others ?	?	?

The growing epidemiologic and social survey research on stress has been paralleled by sophisticated endocrine and physiologic research that has elucidated mechanisms by which adverse environmental events can influence physiologic functioning. The three main mechanisms are the hypothalamic-pituitary-adrenal systems, the autonomic nervous system, particularly its sympathetic components, and the immune system.

Studies are needed to extend the epidemiologic approach to life events and to determine more precisely the incidence of adverse life events. If one thinks of these events as an infectious organism or chemical toxic agent, one could then apply epidemiologic measures such as exposure rate and other quantitative techniques to estimate not only the frequency of these events in various population groups, but also the extent to which they impact on the health behavior. The epidemiologic hypothesis would be that exposure to these life events would result in increased morbidity, as measured by both emotional and physical symptoms; increased utilization of the health-care system including outpatient visits, hospitalization, laboratory tests, and drug ingestion, both with and without prescription; and also a greater risk for subsequent illness, such as cardiovascular disease, depression, and alcoholism.

ENHANCEMENT OF PERSONAL POTENTIAL: THE SEARCH FOR PERSONAL HEALTH AS A UTOPIAN IDEAL OF NORMALITY

In addition to the two large groups of individuals suffering from definable mental disorder and those coping with stressful life events, there is a third group as shown in figure 10.1. These are individuals who are not overtly ill or even attempting to cope with adverse life events but who seek to enhance their personal potential and satisfaction and happiness. This group comes closest to the WHO view of health as utopian or as a state of complete well-being.

In the United States today, there are increasing numbers of organized efforts to meet the needs of these people through EST and other human potential groups. Many of these groups operate outside the health-care system and use various kinds of weekend seminars or quasi-educational methods, and often charge fees for service. The origins of this help-seeking are multiple and have been variously discussed in the sociologic and popular literature as the "me generation," in Lasch's (1979) work on narcissism, and in the writings about the extension of modernity since the seventeenth-century Enlightenment.

Increasing numbers of individuals seek assistance from mental health professionals to enhance their state of well-being, to actualize their potential, and to increase their competence in interpersonal relations. It is estimated that about 6 to 10 percent of the population saw some mental health professional in 1980 and that a significant proportion of these individuals would not meet the DSM-III Axis I criteria for definable disorder. The human potential movement has, since its early writings by Perls, Maslow, and Rogers, emphasized its non-health orientation. Moreover, it has been critical of the health orientation of much of clinical psychology and psychiatry and the "medical model" in particular. Clinical approaches are criticized as emphasizing the limitations and symptoms of individuals rather than the individual's potential for growth and development. Given this view, the human potential movement has defined itself as outside of the health field.

Some advocates of personal enhancement have attempted to justify their approach in terms of prevention, arguing that involvement in psychotherapy and counseling to enhance personal potential would prevent the later occurrence of definable mental illnesses such as alcoholism, depression, or anxiety states. This may be true, but further research is required to document that assertion. Such documentation would provide a more scientific basis for justifying these applications of psychotherapy as relevant to health and suitable for reimbursement under health insurance.

However, from a theoretical point of view, it is important to reiterate that the founding theorists of the human potential movement were explicit in their rejection of the health approach and justified the goals of psychotherapy and counseling as enhancing personal development and happiness, independent of whether or not these interventions have possible value in preventing mental illness.

It is apparent, at least to us, that the psychotherapy field has developed forms of soft "technology" that have applicability beyond the treatment of symptoms and defined disorders. Increasing segments of the population, particularly those who are young, better educated, and upwardly mobile as well as geographically separated from their family and friends, seek these "technologies" not for the treatment of illness but for enhancement of personal satisfaction. The individuals wish to become more articulate, more attractive, more satisfied, enlarge their circle of friends, develop more intimacy, be a better parent, and they believe that these goals can be accomplished through some form of psychotherapeutic help and/or counseling. While we do not have accurate data as to the frequency of these efforts, the recent report from the University of Michigan Survey Research Center indicates a dramatic increase in the number of people willing to see the mental health field as relevant for these concerns (Veroff, Douvan, and Kulka 1981).

THE EPIDEMIOLOGY OF SATISFACTION AND HAPPINESS

Another possible approach to the epidemiology of normality would be to study feelings of happiness and satisfaction and to apply the epidemiologic method to the collection and interpretation of such data. While questions of happiness and satisfaction have been of considerable interest to sociologists, psychiatrists, philosophers, and economists, the design of experiments and data collection and data analysis have seldom, if ever, used epidemiologic concepts such as population rates or identification of the magnitude of "risk." In principle, the methods of sampling, rating scales, multivariate statistics, and so forth that are employed in social science research, particularly survey research, are isomorphic with epidemiologic methodology.

Some scattered data is of interest and, more importantly, points the way for avenues of future research. Assessments of satisfaction and happiness are usually based on individual self-perception. Cross-national data indicate that the ratings of individual happiness correlate with income across nations. However, in this sense, income would be a "risk factor" for happiness. The relationship between happiness and income is not direct and there are considerable individual variations within social groups. Easterlin (1973) has reviewed some of this data from the United States and reports that self-ratings of happiness have varied since 1946. Reported happiness ratings peaked around 1957 and dropped thereafter such that by the 1970s they had returned to the levels of reported happiness of the early 1950s. Easterlin interprets the data to mean that the relationship between happiness and income is not direct but is mediated by perception of need. Put another way, there is a level of expectation that varies across individuals in groups and is heavily determined by historical zeitgeist as well as by social class and ethnic and sex differences. The work of Easterlin (1980) and that of others suggests that while happiness and satisfaction are not in themselves illnesses suitable for diagnosis, the epidemiologic techniques of sampling, looking for trends over time, and seeking correlates with antecedent or concomitant risk factors provide a potential avenue for the investigation of normality.

Integrating Life-cycle and Epidemiological Approaches

AGE AND DEVELOPMENT

Age has always been a major variable for the analysis of data. However, for the most part, age has been treated in a statistical manner rather than being regarded as part of a broader conceptualization. Where conceptualization has been involved, it has usually been implicitly biological, namely age being a proxy variable for biological growth and development in children and maturation and aging in adults. Current thinking regards age as related to stages of personal development through the life cycle, rather than exclusively as a biological timetable.

Relatively infrequently have attempts been made to link and integrate the recent developments in the epidemiology of mental health and mental disorders with the rapid development in thinking and research on personal development, particularly the recent trend toward enlarging the developmental concept to encompass the total life cycle. One potentially unifying concept would be to regard transitions in the life cycle as periods of risk before the development of psychopathology. Implicit in this concept is the thesis that each stage in the life cycle carries with it certain demands on the organism for adaptation, specifically to accomplish age-specific life-cycle tasks of development and maturation. Psychopathology is related to these tasks in two ways: (1) during the period of transition, there are often lapses to episodes of depression, anxiety, tension, and perhaps an increase in the use of alcohol, and central nervous system drugs, and consultation with physicians and other health providers; (2) failure to adequately resolve these transitions and to achieve the appropriate life-cycle tasks, it is hypothesized, renders the individual susceptible to the subsequent development of psychopathology.

From the epidemiologic point of view, these life-cycle-specific transitions are to be regarded as risk factors increasing the likelihood of specific psychopathology. In fact, the concept of risk provides a bridge between epidemiologic research and current interest in life events and stress, since many of the significant stressors are related to life cycle development. For example, in adolescence such stressors are the onset of puberty and the transition from junior to senior high school; in early adulthood the stressor is the transition to college, which is often the first protracted period of separation from parents, and the challenge of development of autonomy and intimacy, particularly for middle-class young adults. For working-class adults the transition stressor is the move into the workforce or into the military.

At each stage of the life cycle there are different transitions, such as entrance into a labor force, marriage, birth of first child, geographic mobility, economic privation as with unemployment or career development, retirement, and so forth. Transitions often involve shifts from one social role to another.

At this time, there exists a social epidemiology neither of life stress nor of life-cycle developments. Two requirements for such an epidemiology are objective and valid criteria for each developmental stage, and appropriate knowledge of the frequency of occurrence of stressful events and of the likelihood of the development of short- and long-term psychopathology.

In recent years there has been significant research not only on life stress in general, but on how some of the specific stressors impact on people in different stages of the life cycle. For example, the best study examines the stressors of mourning and grief. Evidence indicates that the likelihood of developing difficulty seems greatest for men compared to women, and for young compared to older people. As the life cycle progresses, loss through bereavement occurs increasingly and comes to be accepted as part of life's vicissitudes. However, loss of a spouse during early years poses considerable burden upon the survivor, particularly if there are young children. Another developmental life stress that has been studied recently is that of marital separation.

While it is possible to project into the future a program of research linking epidemiology of mental disorders and mental health to the life-cycle approach, this is more of a promise than an actual attainment.

COHORT EFFECTS

The concept of cohort has been a standard one in demography and epidemiology. "Cohort" is usually defined as "those born in the same year or decade." A major source of confusion arises from the need to disentangle aging effects from cohort effects. This is particularly a problem in cross-sectional data since differences in age groups may be due to some complex interaction of aging effects related to increasing years or of cohort efforts related to year of birth and common experience.

This has become of particular interest in view of the attention being given in demography and economics to the effects of birth cohort size on economic and social experience. Richard A. Easterlin (1980) has provided powerful evidence for the effect of birth cohort size upon subsequent economic and educational experience. Briefly stated, Easterlin's thesis is that individuals born into large birth cohorts experience relative disadvantage when they enter the labor force, and this is reflected in high rates of unemployment among young people, delayed entrance into paid occupations, lessened earnings, and greater competition. He has applied this concept to the experience of the baby boom group, those born between 1947 and 1962.

This concept has recently been applied to psychiatric variables. Three groups of data are relevant. One are studies relating homicide to the birth cohort size. Second, and more significant, are the recent findings that suicide rates among young people fluctuate over time related not only to the absolute size of the birth cohort but even more powerfully to the relative proportion of young people in the total adult population. (Holinger and Offer 1982).

It is interesting to speculate on the impact of this on feelings of satisfaction, frustration, optimism, and alienation. Contrast the relationship between expectations and opportunity of individuals born during the late 1920s and early 1930s, periods of low birth and economic depression; for those individuals, expectations were low, yet when they entered the labor force in the early 1950s, they experienced an unprecedented economic expansion and unique opportunities. In contrast, their children, born during the baby boom, were raised during periods of high expectations and they entered the labor force at a time when opportunities were constricted. One hypothesis is that depression occurs when there is a gap between expectation and opportunity, and this would seem to predict a rise in depression, particularly among young adults (Easterlin 1980). How this interacts with the differences between men and women, economic changes such as high unemployment, and changes in age of marriage and family size is currently the subject of considerable debate. Offer and Sabshin have alluded to the generational cohort effects, particularly as they impact on adolescents and young adults (see chapter 3).

Cohort analysis has been widely used in infectious and in chronic disease epidemiology but has infrequently been applied to psychiatric epidemiology. A notable exception is the recent report by Srole and Fischer (1980) of changes in the self-report of mental health status of women, based on a twenty-year follow-up for the Midtown Manhattan study. A number of similar cohort analyses are underway.

Critics of the life-cycle approach have suggested that rather than see personality development in adulthood as resulting from a fixed sequence of stages, one must look at the timing of crucial decisions such as age of leaving home, entrance into the labor force, marriage, birth of first child, and so on. Evidence indicates that the expected timing of these events in the transition from adolescence to young adulthood varies considerably over historical times, more for women than for men.

Conclusion

In the introduction to this volume, Offer and Sabshin propose four definitions of normality. Within that framework, the epidemiologic approach would appear, at first glance, to be mainly concerned with normality as average since epidemiologic research is heavily based on quantitative assessments of "actual" empirical phenomena and their distribution within the population. However, epidemiologists seldom regard the statistical norm as sufficient for their interest. More traditionally, epidemiologists have been concerned with using distributional statistical data to study illness, with "illness" being defined primarily in terms of clinical and medical criteria. In this sense epidemiology has been classically concerned with the definition of normality as health, where health is defined as the absence of diagnosable illness.

In recent years, it has been proposed that health be redefined as not just the absence of illness, but to include more positive criteria. As discussed previously, the most general definition of positive health is embodied in the preamble to the World Health Organization Constitution; the WHO definition of health is identical to the concept of normality as utopia, where normality is defined as positive health. Similar approaches to broadening the definition of health have been employed by mental health theorists who have argued for the distinction between mental illness and mental health and have attempted to study various aspects of psychological and social functioning in individuals other than those with definable mental disorders. Efforts at promoting health as part of a prevention program in public health and concepts of positive mental health and preventive mental health attest to the utopian definition of mental health as normality and are a further expression of the recent expansion of the field of health in general, and mental health in particular.

Epidemiologic research has recently been extended to issues of mental health and mental illness with increasingly encouraging results. With the availability of new techniques for reliable and valid diagnostic criteria, a new wave of community surveys is generating valuable data as to the prevalence and incidence of specific mental disorders. In this trend, psychiatric epidemiology is converging with the mainstream of medical epidemiology.

Although the mental health field has devoted considerable attention to conceptualization and theorizing about normality, positive mental health, and related concepts, relatively little empirical data are available on the subject. What empirical data are available have not employed epidemiologic methods for the estimates of rates and the calculation of associated risk factors, and their magnitude and interaction. In principle, many of the techniques used in social surveys and in clinical research to study non-ill or normal populations or to ascertain levels of symptoms, feelings of satisfaction and happiness, and levels of functioning are parallel to techniques used in epidemiology. The difference, however, lies in how the problem is approached and which statistical methods are used to approximate these different models.

Projecting into the future, we will likely see a further convergence between epidemiology and clinical psychiatry, personality research, and developmental approaches to the life cycle. Increasing data are likely to become available about how different social groups, historical eras, and philosophical orientations define the concept of normality for different developmental phases. The approach to developmental stages and phases in the life cycle that is widely accepted in many of the chapters of this volume is itself reflective of current social expectations and the values of the modern historical era. As has been pointed out repeatedly in other chapters, most of the conceptualization and data about the life cycle is derived from the study of white, middle-class males in the post–World War II era, an era particularly associated with population growth, rising affluence, and feelings of optimism. Theories of personal enhancement and emphasis on satisfaction and individual growth are more likely to gain acceptance in a period of social and economic growth, where opportunities and optimism are reflected in changes in population and income.

The methods of epidemiology, with their emphasis on the techniques of sampling, quantitative measures, and the use of longitudinal data to disentangle secular trends, the influence of aging, and cohort or generational effects, are highly appropriate to these issues. However, in the long run, the criteria to be employed do not derive from the data themselves but must be deduced from the empirical data. The distinction between fact and value that originates in the philosophical writings of Hume and has been carried forward through modern philosophy of science is highly pertinent here. Ultimately, the criteria to be employed to define normality are those of value and cannot be expected to derive from data per se. This is not to say that judgments as to values—whether they be the value of mental health, normality, positive mental health, or rationality—are derived from larger societal concerns and the judgments of individuals and groups, or that the study of values cannot be made reasonable, rational, even empirical. In the final analysis, determinations as to mental health and normality are based on considerations other than those that derive exclusively from empirical knowledge.

REFERENCES

Dohrenwend, B. P.; Egri, G.; and Mendelsohn, F. S. 1971. "Psychiatric Disorder in General Populations: A Study of the Problem of Clinical Judgment." *American Journal of Psychiatry* 127:1304–12.

Easterlin, R. A. 1973. "Does Money Buy Happiness?" *Public Interest* 30:3–10.

———. 1980. *Birth and Fortune.* New York: Basic Books.

Easterlin, R. A., and Schapiro. M. O. 1979. "Homicide and Fertility Rates in the United States: A Comment." *Social Biology* 26:341–43.

Eaton, W. W., et al. 1981. "The NIMH Epidemiologic Catchment Area Program." In *Community Surveys,* vol. 4, ed. M. M. Weissman, J. K. Myers, and K. Ross. In *Monographs in Psychosocial Epidemiology.* New York: Neale Watson Academic Publications.

Endicott, J., and Spitzer, R. L. 1978. "A Diagnostic Interview: The Schedule for Affective Disorders and Schizophrenia." *Archives of General Psychiatry* 35:838–44.

Erikson, E. 1968. *Identity: Youth and Crisis.* New York: W. W. Norton.

Faris, R.E.L., and Dunham, H. W. 1967. *Mental Disorders in Urban Areas: An Ecological Study of Schizophrenia and Other Psychoses.* Chicago: The University of Chicago Press.

Gurin, G. J.; Veroff, J.; and Feld, S. 1960. *Americans View Their Mental Health: A Nationwide Interview Study.* New York: Basic Books.

Heston, L. L. 1966. "Psychiatric Disorders in Foster Home Reared Children of Schizophrenic Mothers." *British Journal of Psychiatry* 112:819–25.

Holinger, P. C., and Offer, D. 1982. "Prediction of Adolescent Suicide: A Population Model." *American Journal of Psychiatry* 139:302–6.

Hollon, C. P., and Solomon, N. I. 1980. "The Changing Profile." *Archives of General Psychiatry* 37:505–11.

Holmes, T. H., and Rahe, R. H. 1967. "The Social Readjustment Rating Scale." *Journal of Psychosomatic Research* 11:213–18.

Illich, I. 1976. *Medical Nemesis: The Expropriation of Health.* New York: Pantheon.

Jahoda, M. 1959. *Current Concepts of Mental Health.* New York: Basic Books.

Jones, L. Y. 1981. *Great Expectations.* New York: Ballantine.

Klerman, G. L. 1979. "The Psychobiology of Affective States: The Legacy of Adolph Meyer." In *Research in the Psychobiology of Human Behavior,* ed. E. Meyer and J. V. Brady, pp. 115–31. Baltimore: Johns Hopkins University Press.

———. 1982. "The Psychiatric Revolution of the Past Twenty-five Years." In *Deviance and Mental Illness,* ed. W. Gove, pp. 177–98. Beverly Hills, Calif.: Sage Publications.

Kohn, M. L. 1976. "The Interaction of Social Class and Other Factors in the Etiology of Schizophrenia." *American Journal of Psychiatry* 133:177–80.

Kramer, M. 1969. "Cross-national Study of Diagnosis of the Mental Disorders: Origin of the Problem." *American Journal of Psychiatry* 25(1):(suppl)1–11.

Lasch, C. 1979. *The Culture of Narcissism.* New York: W. W. Norton.

Leighton, D. C., et al. 1963. "Psychiatric Findings of the Stirling County Study." *American Journal of Psychiatry* 119:1021–26.

Lemkau, P.; Tietze, C.; and Cooper, H. 1942. "Complaint of Nervousness and the Psychoneuroses." *American Journal of Orthopsychiatry* 12:214–23.

Levinson, D. J. 1978. *The Seasons of a Man's Life.* New York: Alfred A. Knopf.

Lin, T. Y., and Standley, C. C. 1962. *The Scope of Epidemiology in Psychiatry,* p. 65. Geneva, World Health Organization.

MacMahon, B., and Pugh, T. F. 1970. *Epidemiology.* Boston: Little, Brown.

Mednick, S. A.; Schulsenger, F.; and Higgins, J., eds. 1974. *Genetics, Environment, and Psychopathology.* New York: North Holland.

Murphy, G. E., and Wetzel, R. D. 1980. "Suicide Risk by Birth Cohort in the United States, 1949 to 1974." *Archives of General Psychiatry* 37:519–23.

Murphy, J. M. 1980. "Continuities in Community-based Psychiatric Epidemiology." *Archives of General Psychiatry* 37:1215–23.

Neugarten, B. L. 1975. "Adult Personality: Toward a Psychology of the Life Cycle." In *The Human Life Cycle,* ed. W. C. Sze. New York: Jason Aronson.

Pearlin, L. I., and Johnson, J. S. 1977. "Marital Status, Life-strains and Depression." *American Sociological Review* 42:704–15.

Perris, C. 1966. "A Study of Bipolar (Manic Depressive) and Unipolar Recurrent Depressive Psychoses." *Acta Psychiatr Scands* 42:9–189.

Regier, D. A.; Goldberg, I. D.; and Taube, C. A. 1978. "The De Facto U.S. Mental Health Services System." *Archives of General Psychiatry* 35:685–93.

Robins, E., and Guze, S. B. 1972. "Classification of Affective Disorders. The Primary-secondary, the Endogenous-reactive, and the Neurotic-psychotic Concepts." In *Recent Advances in the Psychobiology of the Depressive Illness*, ed. T. A. Williams, M. M. Katz, and J. A. Schield, pp. 283–93. Washington, D.C.: U.S. Government Printing Office.

Robins, L., et al. 1979. *NIMH Diagnostic Studies*. Bethesda, M.D.: National Institute of Mental Health.

Rosen, G. 1968. *Madness in Society*. New York: Harper Torchbooks.

Rosenthal, D.; Kety, S. S. 1968. *The Transmission of Schizoprenia*. New York: Pergamon Press.

Rossi, A. 1980. "Life Span Theories and Women's Lives." *Signs* 16:4–32.

Roth, W. F., and Luton, F. H. 1943. "The Mental Health Program in Tennessee." *American Journal of Psychiatry* 99:662–75.

Schwartz, C. C.; Myers, J. K.; and Astrachan, B. M. 1973. "Comparing Three Measures of Mental Status: A Note on the Validity of Estimates of Psychological Disorder in the Community." *Journal of Health and Social Behavior* 14:265–73.

Solomon, M. I., and Hellon, C. P. 1980. "Suicide and Age in Alberta, Canada, 1951 to 1977." *Archives of General Psychiatry* 37:511–13.

Spitzer, R. L.; Endicott, J.; and Robins, E. 1978. "Research Diagnostic Criteria: Rationale and Reliability." *Archives of General Psychiatry* 35:773–82.

Srole, L., et al. 1962. *Mental Health in the Metropolis*. New York: McGraw-Hill.

Srole, L., and Fischer, K. 1980. "The Midtown-Manhattan Longitudinal Study vs. 'The Mental Paradise Lost' Doctrine." *Archives of General Psychiatry* 37:209–21.

Stouffer, S. A., et al. 1949. *The American Soldier: Combat and its Aftermath, Vol II*. New York: John Wiley & Sons.

Vaillant, G. E. 1977. *Adaptation to Life*. Boston: Little, Brown.

Veroff, J.; Douvan, E.; and Kulka, R. A. 1981. *The Inner American*. New York: Basic Books.

Weissman, M. M., and Klerman, G. L. 1978. "Epidemiology of Mental Disorders." *Archives of General Psychiatry* 35:705–12.

Weissman, M. M., and Myers, J. K. 1978. "Affective Disorders in a U.S. Urban Community: The Use of Research Diagnostic Criteria in an Epidemiological Survey." *Archives of General Psychiatry* 35:1304.

Wing, J. K.; Cooper, J. E.; and Sartorious, N. 1974. *The Measurement and Classification of Psychiatric Symptoms*. London: Cambridge University Press.

World Health Organization. 1946. *The Preamble to the Constitution of the World Health Organization*. Geneva.

Zubin, J. 1969. "Cross-national Study of Diagnosis of the Mental Disorders: Methodology and Planning." *American Journal of Psychiatry* 25:(suppl)12–20.

11   Boris M. Astrachan
          and Gary L. Tischler

Normality from a Health Systems Perspective

The social context in which medical practice occurs is one that fosters competition for resources. In this competition medicine defends its unique importance from two perspectives: humanistic and scientific. From the humanistic perspective medicine argues that society has the responsibility for caring for its members who are ill. From a scientific perspective medicine argues that it possesses an enlarging knowledge base that enables practitioners to understand and effectively treat illness. Considerations about normal development have not generally served as part of the scientific base from which medical and mental health policy have evolved. Instead, individual and group *beliefs* about normality have helped to shape humanitarian goals. These goals in turn influenced the formulation of policy. While health and mental health policy have been significantly affected by beliefs about normality, those beliefs have rarely reflected research based knowledge of normal development.

Within this chapter one model for understanding the evolution of policy is described and the utility of constructs about normality to the development of health policy is explored. In this process the manner in which knowledge of normal development may be used to inform policy is examined.

Policy Formulation: Coalitions and Ultimate Objectives

Those of us involved in formulating social policy, in developing programs that transform policy into operational formats, and in managing established programs frequently bring a health systems approach to the task at hand. The approach requires the constant examination of a complex equation in which program implementation is dependent on the interaction of several factors including: the nature and magnitude of the problem being addressed; the knowledge base that contributes both to our understanding of the problem and to the elaboration of appropriate intervention strategies; the state of the art as it defines which problem-solving techniques are acceptable for clinicians to use; and the availability of resources—funds, manpower, facilities, and the like—to perform the task. Examining the equation demands grounding in economics, political science, and sociology. It draws on a working knowledge of the distribution of illness, disease processes, and the effectiveness of available curative and rehabilitative therapies derived from the behavioral and biological science and the field of epidemiology. It also requires a degree of humility tempered by a healthy skepticism.

The humility and skepticism reflect realities inherent in policy development and program implementation. We frequently assume that policy and program evolve in response to identified needs or problems but rarely acknowledge the highly politicized context within which the process occurs. The identification of need may be based on highly subjective experiences or on evidence that meets criteria of scientific proof. If the proponents of need form a coalition that is sufficiently large, articulate, or influential, the executive and legislative arms of government responsible for developing policy are unlikely to make distinctions between the modes of problem identification. They are equally unlikely to distinguish situations where problem specification reflects a statement of wants as opposed to needs. In the political arena, the need to make such distinctions is minimal because policy speaks to ultimate objectives that can be framed in the broadest of terms.

The development and implementation of the Community Mental Health Centers (CMHC) Act provides an example that allows us to track the identification of a problem and the evolution of policy into a system of care. In February 1963 President John F. Kennedy identified a major problem in his stirring address to the Congress. He insisted that mental illness was an issue of great national concern, that too many Americans suffered from the ravages of mental illness, that the skills and tools were available for reducing its ravages, and that the time had come for the nation to devote its energies to the issue. An aura was created that allowed diverse groups to coalesce around a problem. Few questioned the accuracy of the President's assessment of either the problem or the means to deal with it. Thus the stage had been set for a powerful coalition to press forward.

Program Development: A Conspiracy of Silence

When the time comes to translate policy into an operational format, emphasis shifts from ultimate to programmatic objectives. To the extent that these objectives speak to the outcomes anticipated from a program's efforts, they should take into account factors that constrain the achievement of ultimate objectives.

Since ultimate objectives provide the societal justification for program, this is easier said than done. Establishing public policy often involves extended debate and can generate political disruption. Once the policy is established, reopening debate to air legitimate differences concerning the relative merit of various problem-solving techniques as vehicles for achieving programmatic objectives may be discouraged by policy advocates. The rationale usually provided is that the debate may reactivate political disputes among the factions forming a coalition even before the program is implemented.

Returning to our example of the CMHC program, a strategy similar to that advocated in *Action for Mental Health* might have been adopted (Joint Commission on Mental Illness and Health 1961). This would have involved organizing local clinics, general hospital inpatient units, and state hospitals into a system of care. The strategy—building on existing structures and augmentation when the structures are not entirely suitable for the task at hand—is not unlike that recommended seventeen years later in the *Report of the President's Commission on Mental Health* (1978). Alternatively, the quest for categorical funds to create new centers for mental health care could have been set aside in favor of a vigorous pursuit of expanded mental health benefits through private and public insurance programs. Still another option would have been to accept the premise that the problem would remain relatively intractable if clinical intervention alone were relied upon. This premise was advanced by those who believed only massive social change could lead to a mentally healthy nation. Musto (1975) has portrayed some of the differing strategies explored as ultimate ends when translated into progammatic objectives. His analysis indicates that the exploration of alternative strategies was minimal.

Program Implementation: The Art of Overstatement

When the time comes to transform objectives into an organized set of responses to reduce or eliminate problems, attention shifts from ends to means. Initially, primary consideration is given to the issues of resource availability and program structure. Managers are mindful of the necessity to balance an organization's requirements for self-renewal and stability. They are reluctant to jeopardize growth by generating public doubt concerning a program's worth. They are equally reluctant to compromise organizational stability by stimulating disagreement within the staff that may lead to internal dissonance and diminished productivity. By overstating the importance of structure and resources as means to ends, they are able to mask the limits imposed by existing knowledge and technology on the achievement of programmatic objectives.

The final CMHC Act and the rhetoric surrounding it provide an excellent example of the art of overpromising. As the legislation was amended and regulations promulgated, managers were charged with addressing many more problems than they could conceivably attend to. As various populations at risk became program foci, and the list of "essential" services expanded, the image of the CMHC as an institutional panacea was reinforced. Since monitoring systems were rudimentary, problems in implementation could not be easily identified. The question of whether adequate resources were available to accomplish assigned responsibilities largely escaped examination. If there was tension between advocates of social change versus clinical strategies, program budget made it clear that allocations of funds to consultation and prevention were minimal.

Social Policy, Ideology, and a Health Systems Approach

The factors that we have identified create a set of circumstances where the reach of social policy can extend beyond the limits of knowledge and technology. As Mechanic (1969) points out, this dilemma is particularly apparent in the mental health field. It is a field where intervention strategies are often based on a theory or set of theories that have achieved only a modest level of scientific confirmation. As a result, there is a real danger that opinions will be represented as fact. Under such circumstances, ideologies and ideologues may abound. In the process of proselytizing their beliefs, the ideologues band together as a constituency intent on transforming a belief system into an action system. The end result may be social policy that reflects values and aspirations to a far greater degree than knowledge, understanding, or technology.

All this is not to say that a health systems approach is without values or aspirations. These include: (1) addressing those conditions that cause greatest burden both to the individual and society; (2) providing curative therapies when they are available, but, when not, providing for care that limits deterioration of function; (3) providing for equity in access to care; and (4) providing care that meets individual needs in a manner congruent with individual rights. The values are not conceived of as ends in themselves. Rather they provide a framework within which to practice the art of the possible.

In practicing the art of the possible, it soon becomes apparent that society is unable to support simultaneously an unlimited number of ultimate objectives. The competition among sectors to secure societal support for the objectives they espouse and the resources required to achieve them also becomes abundantly clear. As a result, proponents of the health systems approach begin to think in terms of what can reasonably be achieved.

The Clinical versus the Health Systems Approach

The question for the *reasonable* as opposed to the *optimal* is a major characteristic differentiating a health systems and a clinical approach. Clinicians have been brought up to accomplish what is optimal, not what is reasonable. The quest for the optimal is consistent with the clinicians' identity as a professional. Eliot Friedson (1970) identifies a profession as "an occupation which has assumed the dominant position in the division of labor, so that it gains control over the determination of the substance of its own work" (p. xvii). While willing to accept the constraints that existing knowledge and technology place upon practice, clinicians are unsympathetic to the notion that nonclinical factors may impede their efforts at providing every patient optimal care.

Proponents of clinical and health systems approaches differ in two other ways: in the importance ascribed to individual needs versus the needs of a collective and in the temporal perspective governing their work. Clinicians focus on the person. Their worldview tends to be particularistic, and their work with individuals is clearly circumscribed by the period of illness. They prefer to treat illness early and disengage as soon as it is arrested or cured. Proponents of a health systems approach are concerned with groups or populations. Their worldview is universalistic. In considering strategies to meet the needs of the collective, they balance current knowledge and technology against the prospects for the future. What is put in place today will require and support modifications as existing knowledge and technology is refined and the new knowledge and technology are generated. Their temporal perspective is evolutionary, hence less circumscribed.

Normality and the Health Systems Approach

Despite these differences, advocates of both approaches encounter similar problems in dealing with the concept of normality. It is not an alien concept to either group. It is merely one with which they are less familiar than those of illness, or deficit, or, in the mental health area, deviance. The concept of normality is utilitarian only to the extent that it helps define the abnormal with greater precision or assists, by exclusion, in more rigorously demarcating domains of legitimate professional concern.

Let us now consider the manner in which the constructs articulated by Offer and Sabshin (1974) influence the development of policy and program and help delimit practice. The taxonomy of psychiatric tasks developed by Astrachan, Levinson, and Adler (1976; Adler, Levinson, and Astrachan 1978; Adler, Astrachan, and Levinson 1981) is particularly useful for grappling with this issue. Their taxonomy permits an examination of practice by identifying four major clinical task areas within which the profession of psychiatry must act.

1. *The Medical Task Area*—diagnosis, curing, and limiting illness.
2. *The Rehabilitative Task Area*—reducing defect and enabling those with defects to live more normal lives.
3. *The Societal/Legal Task Area*—controlling socially deviant behavior.
4. *The Education/Developmental Task Area*—fostering growth and competence.

The Medical Tasks of Psychiatry

The concept of disease is central to the medical task area. Those who use services are called patients. Work involves the assessment of symptoms and pathology, the diagnosis and differential diagnosis of illness, and the treatment of conditions such as the schizophrenias, major affective disorders, organic brain syndromes, somatoform disorders, and acute stages of neuroses and the addictions. Within this task area, medicine is the prepotent profession. Although the profession's influence on other groups is mediated by established rules and protocols, the integration of curing efforts is directed by the physician's prescription, and the physician retains overall responsibility for patient care.

Of the various constructs, normality as health is best suited for conceptualizing work in the medical task area. It insists on clarity in segregating health from illness and in defining which practitioners have the privilege and right to attempt to heal the ill. As a result, commonly occurring variants of behavior are not perceived as illness and do not require medical intervention. For example, an important minority of late adolescents may be in some turmoil while beginning to separate from home. If the turmoil is a variant of healthy behavior, it should not be labeled illness. Medical interventions would be appropriate only if an underlying disease was diagnosed or if the interventions were known to prevent the development of illness in members of the group in question. Absent compelling documentation speaking to these points, one should question the legitimacy of assigning the health care sector responsibility for dealing with adolescent turmoil.

The construct of normality as health frequently has utility in making allocative decisions. Emde and Sorce (see chapter 1) provide an elegant description of a strategy for identifying high-risk infants. They suggest that subtle signs of later behavioral problems are not reliably available in infancy. Rather, ongoing observation for potential difficulties should occur in the perinatal period. It should concentrate on children exposed to a number of high-risk factors, such as those with either a serious illness or defect or exposure to neglect, deprivation, or abuse. The health system implications of these observations are profound. Through specifying an optimal time for observation and identifying the risk matrix that should receive priority, a program focus is provided that allows targeting limited resources for maximum benefit.

Normality as health is also a useful construct for focusing on life-cycle and developmental issues within the medical task area. Knowledge of normal development may be quite helpful in eliciting patient compliance.

An awareness of the adaptive tasks common to a particular life-cycle phase can enable the physician to combine the "art" and science of practice more effectively. In working with elderly patients, for example, awareness of biological and psychological changes helps guide treatment strategies (see chapter 7). Clinicians know that it is important to use cues to stimulate memory tasks, to be clear about instructions and limit concurrent task instruction, to build on past coping strategies and adaptive skills in mastering present problems and incapacities, and to be aware of the willingness of the elderly to be attentive to advice.

The Rehabilitative Task Area

The concept of defect is central to the rehabilitative task area. The term refers to an impairment or deficiency in adaptive functioning. By adaptive functioning we mean the ability to perform essential life tasks and to meet specific role requirements. The performance deficit may be physical, psychological, occupational, or social. It may result from genetic or biochemical causes or follow trauma or disease. In some instances the defect will remit spontaneously; in others, intervention will be required to minimize or prevent deterioration of function or to stabilize or restore function. While medicine and psychiatry, as medical disciplines, play a rehabilitative as well as curative role, they possess no monopoly on practice. Depending on the nature of the defect, a host of disciplines have legitimate and established roles in this task area. Psychiatry, for example, may be called on in a consultant capacity when questions exist concerning the psychological rehabilitation of patients with medical disorders. Conversely, psychiatry will draw on the disciplines of occupational therapy, vocational rehabilitation, recreational therapy, and social work—to name but a few—to deal with the defects in adaptive functioning that are so frequently concomitants to severe mental illness such as the psychoses, organic mental disorders, and mental retardation.

Of the constructs, normality as health seduces practitioners into defining performance deficits as illness and prescribing medical interventions to assure adaptive functioning. An extreme example of such an outcome occurred during the 1960s. It was clearly identified that major compromises of adaptive functioning were corollaries of poverty. Poverty was identified as a disease, the effects of poverty were viewed as symptoms— ergo the effects of poverty could be treated through the use of intervention strategies derived from public health infectious-disease models.

While syllogistic, the logic was compatible with the social ethic of the time. It enabled the profession to act as a responsive member of the community.

Applying utopian constructs to the rehabilitative area can have the opposite effect by encouraging the use of strategies that maximize benefits for an elite. Here, quite limited improvements in the functioning of teachers, politicians, psychiatrists, and the like might be accorded higher priority than improvement of serious physical or mental disability in factory workers or the unemployed. The logic is that of an assumed transfer of benefit. For example, one teacher will impact upon many lives; therefore, enhancing the teacher's functioning will lead to improved functioning in large numbers of students and is societally more "efficient" than efforts directed toward individuals who may have less ability to contribute.

Normality as average presents a different set of problems. By using deviations from a mean to define a group of exceptions, one runs the risk of casting too wide a net and inappropriately identifying certain groups as deviant. Labeling theorists, for example, have written about the ways that some individuals who just meet standards of legal blindness become enmeshed in a rehabilitative matrix that socializes them into the role of the severely impaired and forces them to surrender an unwarranted degree of autonomy (Scott 1966; Wessen 1966).

Perhaps the most useful construct for considering work in the rehabilitative task area is normality as transactional system. It encourages a longitudinal perspective and takes into account multiple variables. One can factor into the equation the nature of the defect, individual coping styles, age-specific role requirements, and essential life tasks. These can, in turn, be considered within a political context by examining the relationship between intervention strategies and societal goals.

The Educative-Developmental Task Area

Within this task area, those who use services are clients engaged in a personal search to become "more fully human," more effective, or more self-aware. The practitioner's task is to help individuals in their struggle to be the best they can be. Treatment evolves from an educational philosophy and emphasizes the struggle to be "weller than well" (Menninger, 1963, p. 406). Techniques ranging from psychoanalysis through counseling to encounter groups may be used in a variety of settings, such as practitioners' offices, university counseling services, drop-in centers, EST courses, and the like. Clients are considered to be competent enough to assume responsibility for their personal growth.

The construct of normality as utopia is most suitable to this task area. Definitions of ideal or utopian behavior, however, are heavily influenced by cultural dynamics. They frequently reflect the interaction of social, political, economic, psychological, and ethical views of behavior. To the extent that one believes that efforts at enhancing individual potential will impact on larger social structures to create a "better" society, differing views of utopia will compete for primacy. Nor is it unusual for competing worldviews to be pursued simultaneously. For example, some educators insist that all children, regardless of capability or disability, should receive equivalent education. They argue that resources should be committed toward ensuring that severely handicapped children grow as normally as others. Others insist that individuals of unique talent ought to be allowed to express that talent for their own good and that of society. They would commit resources to special schools for the gifted. Still others view individualistic striving as injurious. They emphasize group-oriented goals and would structure education in ways to minimize competition and assist each child to find his or her way in the context of family, social groups, and the like.

Attempts at applying the construct of normality as health to this task area are problematic. The definition of health most commonly used is a subjective state of physical, mental, and social well-being, not merely the absence of the symptoms that constitute illness, the pathologic reactions labeled as disease, or the performance deficits characteristic of impairment. Datan and Thomas (see chapter 6), in much the same vein, suggest that clinical interventions may be useful in dealing with important transitions, including achievement of intimacy between spouses, autonomy for both partners, identification of new sources of interest for women whose children are graduating from high school, and difficulties in coping with bereavements and/or disability of the aged parent.

While these issues may be ameliorated by competent counseling, it is not clear whether one is engaged in a quest for health, welfare, or happiness. In "treating" transitional states, are we dealing with disorder or the natural state of affairs? To what extent is each of us entitled to a reasonable amount of disease before society is compelled to assume responsibility for our well-being? If we subsume such issues under the mantle of a medical or rehabilitative perspective, to what extent do we conspire in depriving the severely ill and disabled of such resources or subvert alternative problem-solving approaches? Does using a definition of normality as health to justify a set of activities more consonant with an educative-developmental than medical or rehabilitative perspective misshape practice in the health-care area and lead to a chaotic redefinition of priorities?

Questions such as these underlie the ongoing debate concerning health insurance coverage for the psychotherapies (Sharfstein and Taube 1982). Those responsible for policy development now insist that there be clear medical or rehabilitative indications for treatment. They express grave concern that health dollars are being diverted from required care for the ill to elective care for individuals who wish to enhance their personal growth and individual capacities.

The Societal-Legal Task Area

Each society segregates behavior into that which is desirable and that which is reprehensible. We usually identify desirable behavior as "good," "healthy," or normal. Undesirable behaviors are categorized as "bad," "sinful," or "mad." In the United States, psychiatry is often called on by the justice and corrections systems in their efforts to deal with social deviance that is considered an extension of mental illness. The social control task area of psychiatry involves treating persons committed or remanded to its care because they have been found to be dangerous or gravely disabled, because they have been tried for criminal behavior but diverted to the psychiatric system following a judgment of not guilty by reason of insanity, or because their antisocial behaviors are felt best dealt with in a therapeutic rather than correctional context (drug addicts, sexual deviates, and alcoholics).

The work of psychiatry in this task area is complicated by the fact that society acts from two separate and often conflicting positions. In the *parens patrie* tradition it responds benevolently and attempts to care for those who cannot care for themselves. In a second tradition, police responsibility is exercised in order to protect the social order. When the "bad" are permitted full protection of the law and the "mad" not, or when diversion to psychiatric facilities is seen as exercise of police power not *parens patrie* responsibility, institutional systems are forced into confusion. Equally, when the "bad" are redefined as "mad" in order to allow them to escape responsibility for their acts and from punishment, society becomes confused.

Unfortunately, the varying constructs of normality provide little assistance in reconciling the confusion that abounds in an area where legal, social welfare, and health-care policy interact and strive for primacy. The construct of normality as average, for example, invites the use of statistical criteria for identifying deviant behaviors and results in the identification of categorical minorities as target populations. Subgroup norms are either unattended to or mislabeled when they fall several standard deviations from societal norms. Without a careful definition of acceptable variations from an "average," there is always the risk of applying the construct in a manner that obscures individual rights in order to protect the larger society.

The same dilemma exists when the concept of normality as health is applied to this task area. While it can provide an anchor point for identifying certain deviant behaviors as "illness" as opposed to "evil," a major ethical issue occurs when the redefinition is done to discredit deviant positions or provide coerced treatment. This, of course, is an underlying argument in the efforts to discredit the rule of psychiatry in totalitarian states such as the USSR or, in this country, when the profession is called on to assess individuals whose acts of social protest have brought them to the attention of the criminal justice system. Similarly, the application of the construct of normality as utopia may allow the state to insist that individuals who have been diverted from the criminal justice system to psychiatric care are required to achieve a level of rehabilitation that is difficult, if not impossible, to attain. Thus such diversion might conceivably result not in appropriate care and rehabilitation but in indeterminate incarceration.

The construct of normality as a transactional system has the advantage of allowing one to consider a host of variables simultaneously when dealing with an individual case—for example, illness and capacity for recovery, deviance and threat to society, individual rights and their protection. In some ways, it is best suited for helping us conceptualize an area where jurisdictional boundaries are contested and altering values can lead to rapid reequilibration in the balance of correctional versus therapeutic approaches for dealing with deviance. As with other constructs, however, applications must be carefully monitored to assure that they are not used to mask the proliferation of programs that solely serve the goal of segregating a deviant population without providing promised treatment.

Conclusion

We live in an era where our use of the English language often is an exercise in subterfuge. There are no "wars," only "police actions"; no "criminals," only "perpetrators." "Senior citizens" never die. They move to "happier pastures." Through carefully selecting the words we use, we may yet succeed in speaking a perfect world. But that speech blurs reality.

Within this nation, most health policy is illness policy. It is concerned with the accessibility, availability, appropriateness, adequacy, acceptability, effectiveness, and efficiency of services provided the ill. It is preoccupied with the inordinate cost of these services. Within such a context, perspectives of normality do not adequately inform us about the critical choices that must be made as we evolve policy, translate policy into program, and implement program. These choices will most strongly influence the nature of work within the medical and rehabilitative task areas.

Normality as utopia overpromises. While promoting strategies for enhancing "fulfillment," it does not provide a framework within which to conceptualize disease. The construct is most relevant to work within the educational-developmental task area. Normality as average identifies deviant groups and points out the corollaries of membership in such programs. It does not identify the causes of the deviance, specify its societal importance, or suggest intervention strategies. Normality as a transactional system provides a longitudinal perspective and takes into account the interaction of a host of variables that promote homeostasis. As such, it is useful in developing strategies for coping and adaptation—adjuncts to the medical task area. Normality as health helps define issues of concern to the medical task area but does so by exclusion. In planning services, it is illness and not normality and health that require attention.

Constructs of normality are of importance in framing social and educational policy. An understanding of child, adolescent, and young-adult development is critical to the design of effective educational programs. Awareness of normal adult development can be useful in considering family and social welfare policy. Those of us concerned with formulating illness policy and in developing and implementing programs for the ill and the disabled, however, must look towards definitions that can separate out those conditions requiring attention from those that do not; that can specify which conditions can be improved and at what cost; and that can permit one to contrast the outcome and the costs of various intervention strategies. The concept of normality is of limited utility in achieving these aims.

REFERENCES

Adler, D. A.; Astrachan, B. M.; and Levinson, D. J. 1981. "A Framework for the Analysis of Theoretical and Therapeutic Approaches to Schizophrenia." *Psychiatry* 44:1–12.

Adler, D. A.; Levinson, D. J.; and Astrachan, B. M. 1978. "The Concept of Prevention in Psychiatry." *Archives of General Psychiatry* 35:786–89.

Astrachan, B. M.; Levinson, D. J.; and Adler, D. A. 1976. "The Impact of National Health Insurance on the Tasks and Practice of Psychiatry." *Archives of General Psychiatry* 33:785–94.

Friedson, E. 1970. *Profession of Medicine: A Study of the Sociology of Applied Knowledge.* New York: Dodd, Mead.

Joint Commission on Mental Illness and Health. 1961. *Action for Mental Health.* New York: Basic Books.

Mechanic, D. 1969. *Mental Health and Social Policy.* Englewood Cliffs, N.J.: Prentice-Hall.

Menninger, K. 1963. *The Vital Balance.* New York: Viking Press.

Musto, D. F. 1975. "Whatever Happened to 'Community Mental Health'?" *Public Interest* 39:53–79.

Offer, D., and Sabshin, M. 1974. *Normality: Theoretical and Clinical Concepts of Mental Health.* New York: Basic Books.

Report of President's Commission on Mental Health. 1978. Washington, D.C.: U.S. Government Printing Office.

Scott, R. 1966. "Comments About Interpersonal Processes of Rehabilitation." In *Sociology and Rehabilitation,* ed. M. B. Sussman, pp. 132–38. Washington, D.C.: American Sociological Association in collaboration with Vocational Rehabilitation Administration.

Sharfstein, S. S., and Taube, C. A. 1982. "Reductions in Insurance for Mental Disorders: Adverse Selection, Moral Hazard, and Consumer Demand." *American Journal of Psychiatry* 139:1425–30.

Wessen, A. F. 1966. "The Rehabilitation Apparatus and Organization Theory." In *Sociology and Rehabilitation,* ed. D. Sussman, pp. 148–78. Washington, D.C.: American Sociological Association in collaboration with Vocational Rehabilitation Administration.

PART III

TOWARD AN INTEGRATIVE APPROACH TO NORMALITY AND THE LIFE CYCLE

In this, the third section of the book, we wish to express our own thoughts concerning normal behavior.* We will integrate the voluminous empirical data presented in this volume from our vantage point, that of psychiatrists who are deeply invested in the care of the mentally ill. A better empirical understanding of normal behavior will present us with a new vision of the potentials of man- and womankind. It will ultimately lead to newer themes concerning human development.

We believe that men and women have excellent potential of understanding themselves as far as their own physical makeup and their psychological mindedness will allow them. We obviously do not know what the limits of our knowledge are; now, in A.D. 1984, there seem to be no limits. Men and women have always tried to understand themselves using all the "tools" in their possession, be they religion, art, imagination, or science. They were in search of, to put it simply, the meaning of life. It is not possible to focus on all the fascinating aspects of human development in one book. In different eras throughout history men and women focused on specific characteristics that interested them. Plato

*We are grateful to Jean Carney, M.A., for her considerable help in the writing of these chapters.

concentrated on the rational person. Later Plutarch discussed lives of great men in Greece and Rome from the point of view of ambition, greed, and virtue, and his man can be described as the honorable man. Marx described men and women mainly in economic terms. Freud focused on guilt, sexuality, and aggression and also on the darker side of man- and womankind. Kohut (1971) described modern men and women as a tragic people who continuously struggle to find their true selves. Many adjectives can be used to describe other foci of interest—rational, instinctional, mystical, moral, and social men and women. Our focus has been and is on the *empirical* man and woman. This person is conceptualized from observations and experimentations rather than by deduction from general principles. The observations come from direct behavioral measurements, as well as from psychological (i.e., emotional) assessment. We are interested in all of the factors that affect human development—biological, social, or psychological. We call our woman or man "empirical" because the first seven chapters describe what is empirically known about normal human development from infancy to old age. Our interest in theory about normal human development is meaningful only if it helps us better understand the laws (if any) that govern human development. In other words, our interest is to try to understand development by discovering what causes change and what affects stability over time and across a multitude of circumstances. The purpose of behavioral science may be said to be the construction of a "map" that describes relationships between sets of phenomena over time. Concepts delimit a band or range of phenomena that can be clearly described in such a way (Offer, Ostrov, and Howard, 1981).

The broad field of mental health has finally come of age. No longer need mental health professionals hide in faraway state hospitals, sanitariums, or clinics. They are practicing everywhere: in general hospitals, universities, primary and secondary schools, industry, businesses, banks, and the armed forces. In short, they have become part of mainstream America: the Establishment. Despite some rather strong criticism from within the profession (Szasz 1961; Torrey 1974) and from outside (Illych 1976), Veroff, Douvan, and Kulka (1981) state that a considerably broader segment of Americans utilized mental health services in 1976 than in 1956. It seems that the time is ripe for doing extensive normative developmental research. As we have stated elsewhere (Offer and Petersen 1982), it is easier to conduct normal developmental research with children, adolescents, and adults now than it was in 1962.

We conclude this volume with recommendations for furthering the study and understanding of the normal man and woman in a new field entitled *normatology*.

REFERENCES

Illych, I. D. 1976. *Medical Nemesis: The Expropriation of Health.* New York: Pantheon Books.

Kohut, H. 1971. *The Analysis of the Self.* New York: International Universities Press.

Offer, D., and Petersen, A. C. 1982. "Adolescent Psychiatry: A Brief Research Note." *Journal of the Academy of Child Psychiatry* 21:86–87.

Offer, D.; Ostrov, E.; and Howard, K. I. 1981. *The Adolescent: A Psychological Study.* New York: Basic Books.

Szasz, T. S. 1961. *The Myth of Mental Illness.* New York: Harper & Row.

Torrey, E. F. 1974. *The Death of Psychiatry.* Radnor, Pa.: Chilton Book Co.

Veroff, J.; Douvan, E.; and Kulka, R. A. 1981. *The Inner American.* New York: Basic Books.

12   Daniel Offer
and Melvin Sabshin

Culture, Values, and Normality

Throughout history formulations of concepts of normality have been influenced by value patterns in the larger cultural surroundings. Over the centuries philosophers, historians, and artists have reflected the changing attitudes. With a view toward comprehending the roots of the various contemporary scientific approaches to normality, we will discuss certain philosophic and religious influences. Then, using the arts as an example, we will indicate how some concepts of normality have been affected by social attitudes. In the latter part of the chapter we shall focus more on the current social scene and discuss modern mental health issues in relation to their historical roots and the social values that influence their direction.

The term normal itself was not coined until the time of the ancient Romans.* The growth of this concept, however, had begun in Greek antiquity, when efforts to redefine concepts of health became central philosophical issues. To many Greek thinkers, health appeared to be synonymous with happiness. Happiness, in turn, was viewed from ethical and political perspectives. Plato and Aristotle were, perhaps, the theoreticians most responsible for the development of these perspectives.[†]

---

*The word normal comes from the Latin *normalis*, which means "made according to rule." It also means "conforming to the standard or the common type; regular, usual, natural."

†For a scholarly discussion of the classical roots of modern psychiatry in ancient Greece, see Simon (1980).

The Ancient Roots of Normality*

Plato developed the concept of health as both a moral and a natural ideal toward which all men strive. The attainment of this ideal is difficult for the masses, who are led astray by the glitter of false suns. In the following selection from Plato's *Phaedrus* (Jowett 1937), the perfect harmony of mental structure and function that is necessary for the attainment of happiness is presented:

> As I said at the beginning of this tale, I divided each soul into three—two horses and a charioteer; and one of the horses was good and the other bad: the division may remain, but I have not yet explained in what the goodness or badness of either consists, and to that I will proceed. The right hand is upright and cleanly made; he has a lofty neck and an aquiline nose, his color is white, and his eyes dark, he is a lover of honour and modesty and temperance, is guided by word and admonition only. The other is a crooked lumbering animal, put together anyhow; he has a short thick neck; he is flat faced and of a dark color, with gray eyes and blood-red complexion; the mate of insolence and pride, shag-eared and deaf, hardly yielding to whip and spur. Now when the charioteer beholds the vision of love and has his whole soul warmed through sense, and is full of the prickings and ticklings of desire, the obedient steed, then as always under the government of shame, refrains from leaping on the beloved; but the other, heedless of the pricks and of the blows of the whip, plunges and runs away, giving all manner of trouble to his companion and the charioteer, whom he forces to approach the beloved and to remember the joys of love.
>
> After this their happiness depends upon their self-control; if the better elements of the mind which lead to order and philosophy prevail, then they pass their life there in happiness and harmony—master of themselves and orderly— enslaving the vicious and emancipating the virtuous elements of the soul, and when the end comes, they are light and winged for flight, having conquered in one of the three heavenly or truly Olympian victories; nor can human discipline or divine inspiration confer any greater blessing on man than this. If, on the other hand, they leave philosophy and lead the lower life of ambition, then probably, after wine or in some other careless hour, the two wanton animals take the two souls when off their guard and bring them together, and they accomplish that desire of their hearts which to the many is bliss; and this having once enjoyed they continued to enjoy, yet rarely because they have not the approval of the whole soul. (Pp. 257–58)

In his horse and charioteer analogy, Plato has set the stage for the psychoanalytic description of conflict and the balance of internal forces formulated many centuries later. In psychoanalytic theory, normality or health is seen in the flexibility and harmony among the various parts of the psychic apparatus. The Platonic concept that only the philosopher-

*Parts of this section were published in a previous book (Offer and Sabshin 1974).

kings may approach the attainment of the ideal has served at least in part as a prototype for current concept of self-actualization of the few. According to Plato, the philosopher-king alone could climb the ladder of knowledge, while the average man remained chained by ignorance and "ignoble" desires.

Moral ascendancy, according to Plato's *Gorgias*, should be the proper qualification for political ascendancy. Just as the physician's knowledge qualifies him to attend to the health or right ordering of the body, so should the philosopher, with his thorough knowledge of the healthy soul, be the person to prescribe medications to society. The philosopher, rather than the people themselves, should be entrusted with diverting their actions, irrespective of their particular desires. Hence to the extent that doctors govern the sale of drugs and determine certain sanitary rules, so, according to Plato, should philosophers (or the modern physician, including the psychiatrist?) be allowed to establish the laws for the running of society.

The attainment of knowledge implied the right ordering of one's own soul as well as the ability to govern others. If this line of reasoning is valid, must it logically follow that the present-day psychiatrist, who has been trained in the "ordering of the mind," and the psychoanalyst, who has undergone personal psychoanalysis, should consider it their moral duty to direct the mental health of the populace? Did not Plato pave the way for the psychiatrist to behave like a philosopher-king and thus be vulnerable to criticism from those who oppose this kind of explicit or even implicit elitism?

In Plato's writings, the question of "normal for whom?" is asked in a pre-Roman vocabulary. If only the few could attain true health, then the masses must settle for lesser degrees of health, toward which their more limited perspectives could be oriented most successfully. Thus was designed Plato's *Republic*, where one best suited by temperament to being a carpenter should be a carpenter. In this work, health for the many meant adequate but not ideal adjustment. The decision of what was healthy for whom was a political one.

In his *Ethics*, Aristotle, too, defines a superior type of happiness and lesser types suitable for less gifted persons. He designates types of happiness for which different groups yearn: first, the common people, who identify happiness with sensual pleasure; second, the superior people, who equate happiness with honor or political life; and third, the only truly happy people, those who lead a contemplative life. In the contemplative life, man does not completely suppress all emotions but rather trains his emotions by reason. These divisions manifest Aristotle's lack of belief in an absolute golden rule for happiness for all men. Concepts of happiness are graded. Terms such as "suitable" and "adequate" are used along with "ideal" as assumed modifiers of normality in many of its later usages.

Aristotle proceeds, in his *Ethics*, to discuss several components of happiness. The desirable characteristics are ranges of moderation between two extremes. Nonetheless, one extreme will often be judged less desirable than its opposite; thus the mean for happiness will not be a statistical middle point between two poles. The degree of virtue that each man must perfect within himself for his own happiness is relative to each individual, his intellect, and his social position.

Aristotle postulated no single Platonic ideal of goodness of which all lesser goods partake, but rather many relative goods determined by practical wisdom. He singles out one good that is significantly different from all others. Not all ends (goods) are final ends, but this chief good, the principle of rationality, is always desirable for itself. God's virtue consists of his total exercise of the power of thought. While no man, being a political animal, can ever lead a life of pure contemplation, it is every man's duty to live according to the highest in him, that which he shares with God (see Guthrie 1960).

Although happiness may be regarded as other than an absolute ideal, Aristotle was not the forerunner of our normality as average perspective. In *Ethics*, Aristotle says, "Now the mass of mankind are evidently quite slavish in their tastes, preferring a life suitable to beasts . . . " (Ross 1942). With criteria such as "courage," "temperance," "proper pride," and "proper ambition," Aristotle anticipated the conception of normality as a state of health lacking any great sins of extremism. While differing from Plato's philosophic bases, Aristotle reinforced the "happiness as an ideal" concept.

While ethical and political precedents were being established by these great rational thinkers, the forces of religion and mysticism were fostering moral conceptions of the "abnormal" of which our society still finds residues and recurrences. On the one hand, "normality" is regarded as happiness and good fortune. On the other hand, it is often considered as mediocrity. Ethical approval and disapproval both contribute to the ambiguity of the term. Throughout history, examples of the exaltation of abnormality are prevalent. In the Grecian and Hebraic eras, the delusional person was regarded as one possessed by supernatural, godlike powers. He was often seen as a prophet or a messenger from God. As Socrates says in *Phaedrus* (Jowett 1937):

> It might be so if madness were simply an evil; but there is also a madness which is a divine gift, and the source of the chiefest blessing granted to men. For prophecy is a madness, and the prophetess at Delphi and the priestess at

Dodona when [they are] out of their senses have conferred great benefits on Hellas, both in public and private life, but when [they are] in their senses few or none. (Pp. 244–45)

The unpredictability of the mad was awesome, and it was that which made them so powerful. Next to them the normal was the one who lacked the divine gift and therefore could not be endowed with genius or creativity. Thus when Epicurus says that the aim of life is the pleasure of being free from pain of body and anxiety of mind, the aim does have an ordinary sound to it (Wheelright 1954).

Even in ancient times there was a tendency to consider mental illness in light of its adaptation within the existing society; abnormality was given a value meaning based on its context. "Abnormal," when not equated with "holy," was associated with the opposite quality and seen as the incarnation of all evil. Demonic powers were attributed to the psychotic individual. Even those who rationally disagreed with a particular, prevalent philosophy were frequently accused of being marked by evil spirits (Bromberg 1959). Both they and the disruptive psychotics were considered abnormal, not medically, but religiously.

In yet a different interpretation of man's normal striving, Virgil discusses piety (devotion) in the *Aeneid*. Virgil describes an idealized version of a good Roman. This person, Aeneid, is devoted to his country, his nation, his home, and his family. This devotion is all-consuming and is observed in what many today would call mentally healthy individuals.

It is important to note the ancient roots of the idealization of political leaders and their implications for the definition of normality. Plutarch describes the leading political figures of ancient Rome and Greece in his monumental work, *Lives*. His aim was to give the reader a detailed description of their military, political, and personal characteristics. Plutarch had strong convictions of what was morally right or wrong. According to him, more often than not, the success of a particular leader was dependent on how good a person he was and whether he respected the laws of the land. Plutarch described man as a most complex psychological being who is continuously faced with conflicts not only between virtue and evil but often also between conflicting emotional states. The way he resolves these conflicts either makes or breaks him. While Plutarch does not describe the ordinary man of his day, it seems fair to say that he believed that mentally healthy individuals were those who cared for others as well as for themselves. They were balanced emotionally and could postpone gratification. They were law-abiding citizens who were virtuous yet ambitious. They had a happy childhood, free of major traumas (such as a loss of a parent), and they were physically healthy, strong, and competent.

In the Middle Ages, in Western culture, the basic orientation toward madness was similar to the one in ancient Greece; it was seen as having religious significance. However, the mad were treated as enemies of civilization, and bad, during this time. They had no power to bless, but rather they were possessed by devilish (anti-Christ) powers. Hence, according to Veith (1958), medieval dogmatism viewed all behavior that deviated from its rigid structures as a religious offense: "The problem was met with exorcism, intended to bring about recantation of an unholy alliance, and frequently, if the patient's type of dementia did not lend itself to a public disavowal, he was, for the good of his own soul, tortured to death or burned outright" (p. 9).

On first glance, a review of the ancient roots of normality may seem to involve concepts and issues different from those that we are currently debating. On more careful review, however, the pertinence of the ancient debate becomes more and more apparent. In fact, as one strips away the philosophic and religious language it is amazing how relevant the ancient debates are to many important current issues of values and our definitions of normality. The differences between Plato and Aristotle, for example, have implications for today's policy debates. Aristotle's gradation of normality may be important in elucidating the boundaries between health and illness. Plato's strong emphasis on the ideal, on the other hand, may inhibit empirical investigation of normal behavior. Plato's concepts were the original source of the normality as utopia perspective, which has been challenged extensively during the past decade. It is questionable whether we have been more successful in solving some of the basic conceptual problems than our colleagues 2,500 years ago. The ancient philosophers defined the questions to be debated and provided part of the answers. In this chapter and in the book as a whole, our emphasis is on how these questions might be debated, discussed, and at least partially solved through scientific research.

The Artistic Connotations of Normality

Despite efforts to eliminate ethical judgments from scientific language, scientists often unconsciously accept these same judgments before they begin to select criteria for defining normality. They must decide whether their "normality" is a prized or a disdained one.* They must also decide whether they can establish criteria for a permanent definition of normality or whether they must take into account the cultural changes in attitude whereby the normal for today is the abnormal of yesterday and vice versa. In making these decisions, scientists can profitably turn to the field of aesthetics, because the arts may reveal many subtle aspects of the relations between connotations of normality and changing value systems. Our discussion of aesthetics is intended to heighten the awareness of such relationships as they pertain to the various scientific disciplines involved in the definitions of normal or healthy behavior.

In the arts, the bizarre, the unusual, of a generation might later be called the average or normal of the same generation that had rejected it. Although this conception of change is common to many fields, artists stand in the particular position of bringing to our eyes that which, they believe, relates to the essence of life without need of absolute proofs. They need not be objective; they can immerse themselves in subjectivity. As is true in philosophy, artists will bring to the fore ideas that, if valid, will lend themselves to development in fields ordinarily perceived as far distant from aesthetics. Thus from the artist comes a personal and subjective view of man as he is and man as he ideally might be.[†]

How does art reveal the normal actions and emotions of man? Each artist portrays his conceptions of what man is or of how he, as a man, views the universe. He tries to capture those criteria that are most important to him in expressing man's essential being.

In our opinion, our four perspectives of normality described in the preface and throughout this book can help in further understanding our

---

*An example of the latter is masterfully illustrated in the following quotation from Dostoyevsky's *Notes From the Underground* ([1864] 1961):

> In my view, such a spontaneous man—the real, normal man—is the fulfillment of the wishes of his tender mother, Nature, who so lovingly created him on this earth. I envy that man. I'm bilious with envy. He's stupid, I won't dispute that, but then, maybe a normal man is supposed to be stupid; what makes you think he isn't? Perhaps that's the great beauty of it. And what makes me even more inclined to suspect this is that if we take the antithesis of a normal man, the man of heightened consciousness, who is a test-tube product rather than a child of nature (this is almost mysticism, my friends, but I have a feeling that it is so), we find that this test-tube man is so subdued by his antithesis that he views himself—heightened consciousness and all—as a mouse rather than a man. So, even if he's a mouse with a heightened consciousness, he's still nothing but a mouse, whereas the other is a man. So there. And, what's more, he regards himself as a mouse; no one asks him to do so. This is a very important point. (Pp. 96–97)

†In the past, the vast majority of artists were males. Their presentation of the world is theoretically different from that of a group of female artists, and for that reason we use the male pronoun when referring to the artists. Can we assume that the norms or ideals of productions of female artists could result in different themes or variations of life and the pursuit of happiness in womanhood? The answer to this most interesting question is not yet available.

view of the arts. There are artists whose productions reflect the normality as average perspective. Their artistic creations are easily understood and appreciated by most people living within their culture. As the years go by the creations no longer reflect the social norm, so they can no longer be widely appreciated. Often artists who cater to a particular subgroup reflect the normality as health perspective. Only those individuals within a narrow band appreciate their art. Possibly these artists reflect what we have called the symptomatic group. In other words, their art communicates well with those individuals in the social system who are deviant for one reason or another. They, too, are more often than not forgotten when the next generation constructs its norms. The new deviants (or whatever one would call them) would not find the old art meaningful. Artists whose creations resonate with a basic human ideal that cuts across culture and generations subscribe to either the normality as utopia or the normality as transactional systems perspective.

A discussion of the criteria that could be used to distinguish between artists is well beyond the scope of this work. Offer and Stine (1960) have shown that artistic productions can indeed be objectively classified. Whether this approach can be generalized in the way we suggested is an open question.

An artist often illustrates through his work that which he considers essential or significant in man. His art communicates a large variety of social and cultural norms. The following examples illustrate our point concerning the artist who transcends his own social norms.

Rembrandt can be seen through his paintings as having conceived of man as a spirit radiating through the bodily frame. Edgar Degas stresses the gawkiness that is part of man. Beethoven's music implies strength and shows the force of man's hopes and inspirations. Wolfgang Mozart's music has an angelic quality that conveys a legendary aura of fantasy and beauty in the abstract. Thomas Mann's *Buddenbrooks* illustrates man's desire to carry on family tradition and conform to his social environment in everyday life. Of course, these artists' creations are tremendously more complex than our capsule characterizations suggest, but even such gross oversimplifications convey the fact that the genius of the great artist reflect his personal view of man.

As their work becomes known, the artists' revelations may be accepted as descriptions of man in his relation to the universe. Whose work, though, can be said to represent the normal (in the sense of any of our four perspectives) at any given time? If a contradiction exists, shall we go to the most popular or greatest artists of the time for a true picture of a particular period in history? Though Johann Sebastian Bach was highly regarded as an organist during his lifetime and made a comfortable living as a musician, he was not considered a great composer. It was his son, Karl Philipp Emanuel Bach, who was known during his lifetime as "the great Bach." He functioned well within his culture and, following our classifications, communicated the normality as average perspective to his audience. J. S. Bach was forgotten after his death for a time. Eighty to one hundred years later, an interest in his music was revived, notably by Felix Mendelssohn. It took another eighty to one hundred years before J. S. Bach's music became a part of the established repertoire of the great music of the Western world.

The effect of the passage of time can be illustrated by still another example from the history of music. Gustav Mahler is said to have told Reik (Reik 1954) that his teacher and friend, Hans Von Bulow, who was both a distinguished conductor and a leading music critic of the nineteenth century, told him: "If this [Mahler's second symphony] is still music, then I do not understand anything of music anymore."

When there is a distinction between popular art and great art, both types of art will affect the concept of normality. That which is depicted most frequently will indicate the generally accepted patterns of normality at a particular time, or normality as average. The great artists' insights will operate not only on the concepts of normality for a more extended period of time, but also may penetrate areas of scientific endeavor. Great creations may reflect, however, something innate and characteristic of man, while the majority of contemporary art depicts surface judgments more acceptable to society. The new ideas the great artist brings to light might frighten the populace because of its preconceptions of what ought to be, that is, normality as utopia. Thus time must often elapse before people can incorporate the artist's revelations into their ordinary, average, ideal perspectives on normality. According to Sterba (1960), the real artist who expresses the Zeitgeist of his period is never appreciated in his own time because his sensitivity to the currents of the era make it possible for him to express them in his art long before the public becomes aware of them.

Sterba describes only one kind of artist, the one who was able to communicate normality as ideal. A significant number of psychoanalysts and clinicians from all mental health disciplines subscribe to this idea. The assumption is that by studying the lives of "great men," we will discover the psychological mechanisms that the ordinary man uses to resolve his conflicts (see the discussion of Erikson's study on identity through the case of Martin Luther in chapter 13). In our opinion, this view of the artist as depicting the "true" nature of man's fundamental problems endows the artist with supernatural (divine) powers. How can we tell when he is (or was) simply wrong? After all, the artist cannot always be right! Furthermore, different artists, in the same historical time period, create different imageries. Do we select the artist who agrees with us, or do we wait until the majority has swung our way? And how long should we wait? A generation is simply not enough, and for those currently alive, one hundred years is too long to wait. Surely we in the mental health field do not want to be accused of favoring an elitist psychology, one relevant only to the upper echelon of our culture. Artists, poets, and other great men in our history might reflect universal struggles. But so can every man. The authors question the validity of placing artists (even great ones) on a conceptual or scientific pedestal. An acceptance, without scientific checks and balances, of great artistic creations as reflectors of psychological changes may cause qualities formerly considered deviant to be recategorized. For example, through the force of subjective artistic portrayals, loneliness, rigidity, or brashness could become considered characteristic of a particular period or of the human condition.*

The legend of the artist himself, as a deviant living on the periphery of society, has supported the association between abnormality and superiority. In reality, however, many highly creative artists work quietly and effectively within their own social milieu. Nonetheless, creativity and genius are frequently seen as being enriched by social deviance or neuroses.† It may be that society wishes to alienate itself from its artists so that it will not have to view their creations seriously. Indeed some societies—such as Nazi Germany or Mussolini's Italy—view artists as threats to the social order.

Society's intense ambivalence toward its artists can be likened to the attitude of the Greeks toward Philoctetes, the expert archer. In Sophocles' *Philoctetes*, the hero is bitten by a snake while performing a public sacrifice. His groans and the horrible smell emanating from the wound so disturb his companions that he is banished to a neighboring island and not recalled until ten years later upon the advice of a Trojan soothsayer. Upon his return, a physician heals the disturbing wound. Likewise, when artists condemn aspects of their own society, there is a tendency in almost all societies to label them as deviants. This fact is reminiscent of the insistence of some sociologists that society rejects delinquents because delinquents point to certain weaknesses within the social system.

The label "deviant" as applied to the artist and/or his works encour-

---

*Indeed, Laing (1967) at one point implied that certain conditions deemed to be mental illness were in reality creative reactions of larger social conflicts.

†For a possible relationship between neurosis and creativity, see, for example, Eissler (1962, 1963); Freud ([1910], 1932, [1928], 1959); Kris (1952); Kubie (1958); Phillips (1957); and Rank (1932). We believe with Kubie that although highly creative people are sometimes emotionally disturbed, they are creative despite their neuroses rather than because of them.

ages some people to have negative reactions to the label "normal." Normality as average or normality as health becomes normality as conformist or earthly. It is surprising how many people equate normality with passive conformity to a social order. Indeed the authors have been criticized occasionally for their involvement with studies on normality by those who believe that such studies implicitly advocate social conformity. On the other hand, revelations of a norm, in the sense of an unprecedented insight into the average, healthy, ideal, or process conception of man, are highly valued. Normality in this context is associated with basic truths. To be normal is to share a communality with the artistic portrayal. The negative and the positive values of normality flow from the image that is projected by the artist and his creative works. Further, the fluidity of the term normality must be emphasized. Changing attitudes toward the artist's revelations highlight the transitoriness of descriptions of man and his environment. To the extent that normality relates to that which exists or is thought to be most advantageous, changing descriptions of man will cause reevaluations of the boundaries of normality.

The various discussions of human values thus far presented pertain to the fully functioning adult male. In the past, males served as the idealized models depicting what the rest of humanity should strive to become. Until the modern era, women rarely have served in this role. Earlier in history the time was not ripe to differentiate individuals at varying stages of the life cycle as prototypes for the happy or normal *man* or the happy or normal *woman*.

Culture and Normality

Artists and philosophers have made brilliant personal contributions to our perceptions and understanding of normality throughout history. Nevertheless, each genius was naturally also influenced by his (or her) social environment. The relationship, then, between the social environment and all individuals within it is a most important matter. Normality is, in part, a cultural construct based on social consensus (or social norms). These norms are fluctuant; they change from one social setting to another and over time. Continuously changing cultural norms make it difficult for investigators to undertake hypothesis-testing predictive studies because it is almost impossible to know which intervening variables will have the most influence on the functioning of people in the future.

At times the intervening variables are weak or not even extant when a longitudinal study begins; for example, the Women's Liberation Movement has had a much greater recent impact on the behavior and psychology of a segment of both men and women in our society than had previously been anticipated.

The larger historical changes related to female and male development are reflected in changes over the whole life cycle. Recent work by Brenner (1979) and Easterlin (1980) has clearly demonstrated that economic factors such as birth rate, unemployment, and density of population have a direct and significant impact on physical and mental health and illness. Furthermore Holinger and Offer (1982) have demonstrated that the ratio of adolescents in the population is directly related to adolescent suicide rate. They examined epidemiological data concerning adolescent suicide and population densities from 1933 to 1978. They found that the higher the ratio of adolescents in the total population, the higher the rate of adolescent suicide. This finding was not related to the absolute number of adolescents, only to their ratio in the total population. Other concerns, such as war or the threat of war, can also affect social expectation and behavior of groups of individuals. Beardslee and Mack (1982), for example, have studied the threat of nuclear war on children and adolescents.

We have also seen the opposite; namely, charismatic individuals with strong goals and objectives change (at times tragically so) the subsequent development and even existence of others whom they control through a variety of means. While the names Hitler and Stalin come readily to mind, numerous others—such as the leader of the People's Temple movement, Jim Jones—have the power to change the social environment of many individuals. We assume that in a relatively stable society, only those individuals with specific problems will be changed by leaders who can manipulate the social environment and hence change the social norms. Those individuals who do not change are assumed to be psychologically stronger.

Social, political, and economic forces can have an impact on all phases of the life cycle. Currently, for example, there are strong efforts by groups representing older people (e.g., Gray Panthers) to change the status and the self-image of the elderly. We also know from the recent studies of Offer, Ostrov, and Howard (1981a) that there have been significant changes in adolescent self-image from 1962 to 1980. The 1962 adolescent group had more positive and stable self-concept. It is important to note that we have also seen yearly but smaller fluctuations in adolescent self-image (see, e.g., Nesselroade and Baltes [1974] and Ostrov, Offer, and Howard [1983]). As self-concept changes, so do the norms that accompany it.

An additional change that has taken place is the decreasing importance that people are placing on marriage during the past two decades. The increase in the divorce rate in the United States, its relative emotional acceptance, together with less isolation of single individuals, has, to some extent, changed our perception of the family. Veroff, Douvan, and Kulka (1981) described this process in the following way:

> Certainly marriage remains a critical area of gratification and problems. We have seen that married people look to the role of spouse for realization of their central values and attribute great salience to the role. But it can hardly be said in 1976 that we automatically assume that "the person deprived of the marriage role" will have extreme psychological problems. (P. 156)

It can no longer be said without qualifications that we think of the un-married person as "deprived." The individualization of the concepts of mental health and happiness is perhaps most felt in the fact that mental health is no longer assumed to depend on the realization of all possible normal adult roles. In 1957 many mental health professionals and the population at large assumed that not being married or not having chil-dren would make a person unhappy at the least and probably psycholog-ically maladjusted. Veroff, Douvan, and Kulka's data showed that this is no longer the case (see chapters 5 and 6 herein). Today most people think that an unmarried person can have a happy life. And it ill behooves anyone to attribute "extreme psychological problems" to all those people who choose not to marry or who give up the married state. Such a posi-tion would require labeling too many of one's friends and neighbors "pathological." While in 1957 failure to assume and maintain the spouse role was taken to be a symptom of psychological problems, by 1976 marriage had come to be seen by some as only a potential mechanism for increasing happiness and psychological well-being. Individual marriages are judged by the criterion of their realization of these individual out-comes. In 1957 it was rather the individual who was judged by his or her ability to form and maintain a marriage.

The balance between the social norms and personality development is exquisite. The slightest shift in one variable has reverberating effects (of greater or lesser extent) throughout the whole living system made up of bio-psycho- and social variables.

It is not our goal to discover how social norms are transmitted to indi-viduals. No study, to our knowledge, has effectively done so. In their classic social-psychiatric study of mid-Manhattan, Srole and his col-leagues (1963) found that cultural values are idiosyncratically internal-ized by individuals as they interact with members of their families. Thus lower-class children may come to disparage themselves as they internalize self-disparaging attitudes that their parents have adopted from the culture. As an example:

> That the parents of the slum child may themselves be behaving under this self-defeating mechanism could account for the atmosphere of malaise often observed in such homes and for the affectional fractures discerned . . . in the father-mother and parent-child relationships. Given this kind of disarticulated family setting in infancy and early childhood, given the assaults on body, mind, and spirit in early and late childhood, and given the double-barreled, destructive conflict of self-image during adolescence, we can judge that chance and society have saddled the lower class child with a cumulatively oppressive series of burdens. Compared with the more privileged child, we originally hypothesized that as an adult he would be more defenseless against the crises of life and therefore more susceptible to mental morbidity. (P. 305)

Much has been written by Kardiner (1939, 1945) about the relationship between a "basic personality structure" of a particular culture and an individual's sense of coherence or identity. However, to begin with, the basic personality structure approach overlooks the fact that cultures require conventionality but say little about how the individual actually will feel when conforming. Thus there is no predictable correspondence between a child-rearing practice and a child's behavior (including attitudes, such as "sense of coherence"). One has to consider the meaning of the practice to the particular child at the particular time—the child's subjective experience of the practice—rather than some postulated objective practice. Different from Kardiner's approach is the recent work of Clifford Geertz (1973), which emphasizes the role of culture in creating reality for the individual by defining collectively what is to be taken as real and valuable. This approach lends itself to a search for the linkages between individuals and their culture, to an avenue of approach that seems more solid theoretically and methodologically: an examination into the ways that individuals idiosyncratically internalize, organize, and manipulate the symbols provided them by their culture.

In this section we have emphasized the fundamental importance of cultural factors on a variety of developmental patterns including the basic personality structure. Cultures vary in how they perceive the significance of age as an independent variable. We are particularly interested in the degree to which the past is of significance in psychological development.

In order to study the importance of age as a social variable in human development, it must be kept in mind that the "biological clocks" may not be synchronous with the "social clock." Neugarten's concept of "on-time" and "off-time" events is central to her work:

> In considering the life course, the emphasis will be upon social timetables, and how social age regulates the individual's behavior and self-perceptions. Indi-

viduals develop a mental map of the life cycle; they anticipate that certain events will occur at certain times; and they internalize a social clock that tells them whether they are on time or off time. They also internalize other cultural norms that tell them if their behavior in various areas of life is age-appropriate. (Neugarten and Hagestad 1976, p. 35)

The passage of time cannot be validly considered apart from the events that are taking place in the lives of individuals during those years. In order to understand development, one needs to understand an individual's personal experience of the passage of time—that is, personal events and their idiosyncratic meaning. For example, very little is known of the impact of unexpected loss on the remaining family members. Studies have usually confined themselves to finding out what the immediate response to the trauma were. When a woman becomes a widow at age thirty, very much "off-time," very little is known on how it affects her development and coping abilities one decade later. Likewise, one needs to know the cultural meanings attached to age periods in a society, since these form the basis of the social expectations with which the individual is expected to conform. Since the society "pushes" people into behaviors and attitudes considered appropriate for their age, individuals must be viewed in the context of such social pressure.

An example of the influence of social norms of psychiatric practice comes from the examination of an empirical text such as the *Diagnostic and Statistical Manual of Mental Disorders* (DSM-III) (1980). It will have to change its diagnostic profiles in order to keep up with ongoing social changes. DSM-III's Antisocial Personality Disorder includes in its descriptors, for example, "repeated sexual intercourse in a casual relationship." The item from the DSM-III will still be considered a pathological factor even though for a large segment of the population, adult sexual behavior patterns have changed dramatically during the past two decades. Obviously the diagnosis will be less reliable under these circumstances.

A Perspective on Psychological Time

While we have emphasized the significance of current sociocultural forces affecting human behavior, we do not subscribe to the point of view that normal and abnormal behaviors are simply a product of these forces. Indeed in the first part of this chapter we emphasized the impact of past historical events. In stressing normality throughout the entire life cycle, we adopt a deterministic approach in which prior events affect behavior throughout the time of the individual's life.

From a psychological point of view, time has multiple meanings. Freud, for example, did not believe that man is basically capable of changing his animal nature. Freud also strongly believed that the unfolding of events is not coincidental. One is never completely free from one's past, and time has a definite though differential impact on individuals. It is because of this belief in psychological determinism that classical psychoanalytic theory has basically focused its developmental (Freudian) theory on the resolution of past conflicts. For example, the adolescent has to re-solve conflicts that had been repressed during latency and that, during adolescence, reemerge. This is, in part, why Blos calls adolescence the second individuation stage. Adolescents, according to Blos (1962), reexperience their older, past conflicts and do not have a chance to really resolve them. The only way to resolve them is by a major crisis in behavior that has serious repercussions in affect, cognition, and other internal states. The underlying theoretical premise of psychoanalysis and other child-centered developmental theories is that the present is a necessary outcome of what took place in the past. We agree that events in each person's past has a differential impact on his or her present functioning and feelings. We question, however, whether it is always necessary to recreate the past before developmental advance can take place. A person has to accept and integrate the past to function adequately in the present. In normal development it is less likely to see early relationships emerge and continuously disrupt the present functioning of the individual. The conflicts and tasks specific to each developmental stage may be coped with slowly, allowing for stability of personality configuration. Social and cultural structures also help individuals maintain their emotional equilibrium. Normal individual adolescents, then, are more hopeful, positive, and future oriented. Neugarten and Hagestad (1976) are interested in the price paid by the individual in relation to age-related convention, whether exacted by deviance or conformity. They suggest that whether the individual perceives personal milestones as being on-time or off-time, self-esteem is enhanced. According to them, if the individual is felt by other members of society to be on-time, social support is more likely.

Gubrium and Buckholdt (1977) have also focused their attention on age-related variables and discuss them from a social phenomenological point of view. Similar to Neugarten and Hagestad, they state that a person is either on course of off course. Here again the appeal of a "neat" theory seems to favor a universal statement about development. As will be discussed in the next chapter, both theories lack compelling empirical evidence to support them. Is it not possible that some "off-time" poignant events are perceived by others as tragic and hence elicit even more support from the social and cultural surroundings?

Since the Renaissance, the concept of time in Western society has implied progress. It is development toward a goal. It also seems to imply that there is an underlying order to developmental events—give man enough time and he will solve almost everything. As correct as this has been from a technological point of view, it is more questionable in the social sciences. As early as the last century, Macaulay (1968) wrote about his interpretation of history, which was later termed the Whig interpretation of history. Since Macaulay believed England in 1850 to be a "perfect society," he wanted to study the historical processes that helped make English society so good. Similarly, in the 1960s and 1970s architects of some community mental health programs believed that with time mental illness could be eradicated (see chapter 11). Now, in the 1980s, in part because of economic problems, people are less optimistic about society's ability to solve its social problems.

Erikson's (1968) approach, like that of classical psychoanalysts, is basically retrospective. "As is usual in psychoanalysis, we learned first of the 'basic' nature of trust from adult psychopathology" (p. 97). It is not generally accepted, based on empirical evidence, including the work of Vaillant (1977) and of Elder (1974), that adult memories differ from events as actually recorded in the past at the time of longitudinal studies. Furthermore, it is possible to envision past conflicts as exerting influence on present life without assuming that the conflicts remain in layers accessible as they were in the past. An interpretation of this phenomenon is Cohler's (see chapter 5) idea that adults reconstruct their life stories in light of *present* needs, so that memories may shed more light on where the individual is headed than on where he or she actually has been.

Kagan (1979a,b) minimizes the importance of infantile roots in people's personality development. Like Offer, Ostrov, and Howard (1981a), he focuses on the present, based on the structural molding of the past. In normal development it is *less* likely to observe early relationships emerging later on and having a continuously disruptive influence on the person.

Finally, Livson and Peskin (1980) state that the discipline of adult development disputes the axioms of much child-centered personality theory that the past necessarily determines current behavior.

In much of developmental research individuals are interviewed about their past experiences. The subjects are asked to construct life stories. This raises the question of whether life follows art or art follows life. The literary genre of the narrative is a powerful, interesting, and well-established influence in our culture. But to what extent do individuals actually reconstruct memories, in the process of revising their current self-images for present and future purposes, according to culturally dominant literary conventions? The typical story has a beginning, middle, and end, with causal explanations linking events in chronology. Above all, the story *must make sense*, that is, everything that has come before must make sense in light of the outcome. To tell subjects that their task is to tell stories may accentuate this culturally induced tendency. Thus it is an open question: To what extent are many of the studies presented herein a true reflection of life and to what degree are the findings an artifact of literary convention?

Values and the Definitions of Mental Health and Illness

The philosophic, religious, aesthetic, and cultural standards of normality are illustrative of the many forces that have shaped the term. Can the behavioral scientist study normality without being burdened by ethical commentaries? Throughout history the term normality has steadily become more significant scientifically despite its quasi-religious and even mystical connotations. When, for example, the ancient Greeks regarded the epileptic as a holy man, they obviously would not have considered therapy for him. Hippocrates challenged the ethical supremacy of the epileptic, and his observations of epileptic behavior led him to establish scientific procedures unwarranted by existing religious judgments. In "On the Sacred Disease," Hippocrates refers to epilepsy as an affliction caused by a brain disorder. Examples of such courageous thinking are infrequent. Not until the middle of the sixteenth century did belief in witchcraft begin to diminish. Belgian physician Johann Weyer published, in 1563, the classical treatise entitled *De Praestigiis Daemonun*, in which he was one of the first to demonstrate the fallacies of witchcraft and demonology. Paradoxically, however, Weyer, unable to ascribe natural causes to his patients' symptoms, attributed them to the influence of the devil on individuals weaker than others (Mora 1963). Despite his own internal struggle with the concept of demonology, Weyer's predominantly naturalistic explanation was a second major achievement in defining unconventional behavior as ethically neutral phenomena.

It was not until almost two and a half centuries later, in 1793, that the French physician Philippe Pinel removed the chains of the mentally ill in Bicétre. This act dramatically demonstrated the end of the long popular equation of mental illness with demoniacal possession. Pinel also did away with treatments such as bleeding, purging, and blistering and instead recommended friendly contact with patients and physical activities and discussions of their difficulties. Pinel, considered by many to be the founder of modern psychiatry, ascribed mental illness to social, psychological, physiological, and genetic causes. He facilitated psychiatry's firm entrance into the field of medicine and did away with the idea that the supernatural caused mental illness.

The dramatic changes in the treatment of the mentally ill that originated with Pinel have had many far-reaching consequences, including perhaps a number of unintended ones. As Foucault (1965) has pointed out, it ultimately led to the confinement of a much larger number of mentally ill persons who previously had been taken care of in their community. How well they were taken care of while living with their families and in their communities is a question for which neither Foucault nor any other psychiatric historian has a convincing answer. Foucault claims that as a result of freeing a small number of "mad" patients in Bicétre and Bedlam, the human spirit of a much larger group of individuals was destroyed by confining them to large private and governmental sanitariums and state hospitals. According to Stone (1982), there were relatively few individuals in mental hospitals in the eighteenth and early nineteenth centuries. For example, he states that in England in 1810, the total number of mad people in confinement was 2,500 out of a population of 9 million, or about 30 per 100,000. It did not begin to rise rapidly until the 1830s. He also states that before the Enlightenment, from the early sixteenth century until the early eighteenth century only the few dangerously mad patients were locked up in cages like animals. Only twenty-odd manacled madmen were gibbering and rattling their chains in their filthy cages in Bedlam, one of the great tourist attractions of London. It was one of the standard sights of the city, on a par with the royal tombs at Westminster Abbey, the lions prowling in the moat by the Tower of London, the flogging of half-naked whores in Bridewell, and the bull-and-bear baiting over the river at South-Lark.

During the two centuries since Pinel, much progress has been made in psychiatry. Nevertheless, many of the advances have also continued to elicit unintended consequences. Certainly, the symptoms of the severely mentally ill have been controlled more efficiently by chemicals than by chains. As a result, there are fewer patients in mental hospitals today than were twenty years ago. However, as Begun (1981), the Chair of New York City's Community Mental Health Board, has recently pointed out, in New York City alone there are over 30 thousand "street people" who have a history of serious mental illness. We have, according to Begun, done a tremendous disservice to these people by giving special weight to civil liberties as against human dignity. They are kept in almost unbelievable human misery under the pretext of protecting their civil liberties.* And so the argument goes on as to who has helped and hurt the mentally ill most, when, and where.

Pinel's dramatic actions made psychiatric patients accessible to naturistic and behavioristic studies. As part of the Enlightenment, in 1725, G. Vico's *New Science* appeared, which was the first break with the accepted theological interpretation of human history. In 1830 Comte paved the way for social studies of man through empirical observations. Objective observations were thus made possible. It is our contention that once the supernatural was no longer considered as causing mental illness, the climate was ripe for biopsychosocial investigations. Every individual had a personality with specific psychological characteristics; when a person became "mad," he was simply an extreme case—an ill person with specific signs and symptoms. Over the next 120 years the boundaries between mental health and mental illness continued to diminish. As time progressed, it became apparent that so-called normal individuals can also have psychological difficulties. Psychoanalytic clinical investigations have shown dramatically that psychological defenses such as repression, regression, and projection are common to all. What differs is the extent of the utilization of the defense and how it is coped with. The boundaries between mental health and mental illness continued to become fuzzier and fuzzier, until in the 1950s and 1960s they disappeared altogether in some quarters.

Values and Psychotherapy

The attempt to isolate behavioral and social variables related to mental illness has, on the whole, been more successful than the attempt to better understand normality and mental health. There is, however, no question but that the professional judgments of behavioral and social scientists are still influenced by a combination of currently accepted social values and centuries of past ethical associations. Psychotherapists, perhaps more often than any other behavioral scientists, are criticized for incorporating their own or their group's ethical prejudice into their professional judgments. Since one of the major functions of psychotherapists is to correct

---

*Segdwick (1982) has made this point in a convincing monograph, in which he discusses the abuse psychiatry has taken during the past two decades from its critics, from both the political right and the political left.

personality defects, they should be fully qualified to act with scientific objectivity. In a young field with many areas yet to be investigated and only a minimal amount of objectively verifiable data, the judgment of psychotherapists is often suspect. In addition, given the influence of personal values on therapy, to what extent can psychotherapists be authorities on the behavior of others? Most other (nonmedical) behavioral scientists are interested primarily in diagramming and understanding. Altering existing conditions is only secondary. Thus in these fields an intermingling of subjective values with professional skills is not subject to a corresponding degree of attack. It is not our goal to provide an extensive discussion of the place of values in psychotherapy. This complex question has been exhaustively discussed by others. Suffice it for us to say that psychotherapists should be aware of their patients' notions of normality in order to compare them with their own (see, e.g., Favazza 1982).

In the recent past, mental health professionals have expanded their services to the community at large. Many community mental health centers have developed preventive programs and have provided services to populations for marital, vocational, and school adjustments problems. This fact has intensified concern with boundaries and priorities and, at least implicitly, has raised questions about the operational definition of illness and normality in each community. Must a belief that certain psychiatric concepts can explain the composition of normality logically lead to a belief that mental health professionals should be given full power to care for the mental health of man- and womankind?* And whose concepts should one use? The psychiatrist-psychotherapist should be to mental health what other physicians are to physical health. In discussing philosophic implications of this issue, R. P. Wolff (pers. com. 1963) stated that the psychiatrist's position vis à vis his or her patients must logically support an analogous position vis à vis the individuals who have not expressed their desire for psychiatric treatment. In referring to psychiatry, Wolff stated:

> Modern-day psychiatrists don't realize the immensely powerful implications of their theory of mental health, whereas Plato *did* realize the implications of his analogous theories. Both Plato and psychiatrists feel confident in telling a person that he is not really happy, even though he thinks he is. And this is done on the basis of observable phenomena which can be confirmed by repeated examinations of patients. . . .
>
> If mental health is a reality, then psychiatrists should be the judges of matters pertaining thereto, for they are the most knowledgeable people in this area. In fact, just such a trend has developed. With regard to juvenile delin-

---

* Indeed there is reason to believe that the antipsychiatry movement began to grow in the United States in reaction to the expanded functions of psychiatry and the perceived power thought to be implicit in that expansion.

quency, certain forms of adult crime, aspects of education, and so forth, we have begun to treat the issues as amenable to expert judgment, like questions of fluoridation, inoculation, and so forth.

Psychiatry, as described by Wolff, would transcend the fields of law, politics, and economics on the one hand, and ethics, religion, and philosophy on the other. Although at certain times in the past philosophy was a combination of all of these areas—for example, with Aristotle—most psychiatrists and psychoanalysts do not see themselves as a present-day incarnation of the Greek philosopher. Rather they limit themselves to the behavioral sciences, where their specific knowledge of human psychopathology and psychotherapy gives them a basis to help those who ask for guidance. As mentioned earlier, if psychiatrists were to act as judges of the mores of society, their scientific judgment would have to be comparatively free of the current standard of society.

Psychoanalysts have often discussed the relationship between their own personal values and that of the style, technique, and content of their therapeutic method. Yet they have shown only limited interest in understanding the concept of normality. One can, however, obtain a fairly good notion of their concept of it by studying the criteria they set for successful termination of psychoanalytic treatment. While it is one of the most widely discussed areas, ambiguities and controversies still exist and criteria for termination are insufficiently objectified. Thus in a symposium on psychoanalytic education and training analysis, participants took a strong position concerning different goals of psychoanalytic treatment for different individuals. In this conference,

> there was an attempt to compare and contrast termination criteria between a therapeutic analysis with a layman and a didactic analysis with a candidate. The focus was on how much neurotic difficulty is acceptable at the end of analysis. For instance, a businessman ending analysis with some superego lacunae might do well intrapsychically and in the community, since the business community might allow shades of immorality which the analytic community would not. Thus, there was considerable reluctance to end the analysis of a candidate if such a state existed. The danger of a candidate's corruptibility in exploiting patients is too serious to allow such a man to finish. We hope to accomplish more in the super-ego-ego-ideal areas with a candidate than with a layman. (Seidenberg 1973, p. 95)

Some psychoanalytic educators set up different qualitative standards for their trainees and other individuals undergoing psychoanalytic treatment. In the preceding example, it sounds very much as if the psychoanalyst is set up as an ideal, who is a better person (i.e., more ethical) than other individuals. Perhaps unintentionally, the psychoanalyst emerges in this example as a moral torch carrier of our society.

Whether such scientific objectivity is possible in areas of human behavior is debatable. It could be contended that, instead of acting as a judge and being above the mores, the psychotherapist actually is part of the mores and, thereby, creates conformist standards for society.

A recent study has shown that, at least for adolescents, mental health professionals (psychiatrists, psychologists, psychiatric social workers, and psychiatric nurses) were not able to predict how normal (i.e., nonpatient) teenagers described themselves (Offer, Ostrov, and Howard 1981b). The results of the study highlight the problem that mental health professionals who are actively engaged in clinical work with adolescents have in conceptualizing the self-image of normal, mentally healthy individual adolescents.

This research poses a challenge to leaders in the field of mental health. More attention must be paid to diagnosis, and new empirical data must be kept up with as they are continuously presented. Psychiatrists treating patients have an obligation to broaden their knowledge base. But unless a major effort is made to study normal adolescent development, our trainees in the different mental health specialties, including psychiatry, will persist in upholding Anna Freud's idea that "to be normal during the adolescent period is by itself abnormal" even though normal adolescents do not in fact view themselves as a variation of the disturbed.

A possible advantage to clinicians of viewing normality as part of a psychopathological system is that they may find it easier to work with psychiatrically disturbed individuals. Clinicians have to have a high tolerance for deviance in order to be able to successfully treat severely disturbed individuals. In a study of psychotherapists, one-third of whom were practicing psychiatrists, another third clinical psychologists, and one-third psychiatric social workers, Goldman and Mendelsohn (1969) found that psychotherapists in all three professions saw themselves as being more like their patients than like "normal" individuals. These findings are consistent with our own. Psychotherapists identify with their patients more than with "normal" people. They concentrate on the psychopathology they observe in their patients as well as in themselves. While the normal person seems a distant, unattainable ideal, therapists exhibit a readiness *not* to distance themselves from the patient. In this context psychotherapists are not people to whom we can reasonably turn for valid and reliable data about normal behavior or normal development.

Suchar and Markin (1983) discuss deviance from a different perspective. Their model attributes to a particular mode of storytelling processes that organize thoughts, feats, insights, and data into a particular narrative which contains a moral plot. This plot is a cultural product of criteria interpreted according to the values and ideals of that society. Hence morality and madness or normality and abnormality are culturally determined by the type of narrative that the respondents choose in order to tell their story.

Values and the Healer

After this very brief discussion of psychotherapy, let us examine how clinicians have discussed theoretical notions of behavior and development (see also chapter 8). Certain psychiatrists, psychoanalysts, and psychologists have attempted to broaden the implication of, for example, the findings of psychoanalytic psychology and would accept implicitly the role of "philosopher-king," which, according to Wolff (pers. com. 1963), is the logical conclusion of their theories. Following in a Platonic tradition, Fromm (1960) and Meerloo (1962) try to establish certain rules for "the Sane Society" based on their expert knowledge of psychopathology and their notion of normal or healthy psychology. On the other hand, Szasz (1963) cautions against what he calls excessive and unwarranted "social engineering." He warns society at large of the implications of giving the psychiatrist just the kind of "expertness" that we have described. Szasz feels that the psychiatrist's knowledge is not necessarily the knowledge requisite to the good functioning of society. The psychiatrist can help the individual make peace with him- or herself but cannot, and should not, determine the order of peace within society at large.

Szasz (1961) finds a fallacy in the parallels drawn between the medical physician and the psychiatrist. According to his theories, psychiatry is culture-bound, whereas medicine is universal. He claims that psychiatrists use the verbiage of medicine only as a cover-up for essentially unscientific value-laden judgments. Szasz states that in medicine proper, we have certain criteria by which people of varying backgrounds and value systems can agree on what constitutes health and disease (Szasz 1963). According to Szasz, such criteria are specifically missing in psychiatry.

This statement is highly oversimplified. Differences of opinion among physicians in organic medicine do not differ markedly from those among psychiatrists when similar types of cases are compared. For example, the accuracy of the diagnosis of severe mental illness (e.g., psychosis or severe depression) has the same reliability as that of severe physical illness (e.g., see Beck [1962] and Beck et al. [1962], and the more recent studies using criteria cited in the DSM-III). In less severe mental illnesses the reliability is not as good when compared to physical illness. The reason for this discrepancy is, in our opinion, due to the fact that in psychiatry the boundaries between mental health and mental illness are not as concise. Furthermore, recent discoveries regarding the biological aspects of mental illness have rendered Szasz's arguments almost pointless. We need not dwell on recent biological advances here, since they have been widely publicized. The "remedicalization" of psychiatry is a fact.

In order to define normality scientifically, we need to be able to clearly distinguish between mental health, or normality, and mental illness. Biological variables, though of tremendous help, will not suffice. We need to be able to establish the place of concise, measureable, and reproducible psychosocial variables in the distinction between normality and mental illness. Instead of asserting the scientific supremacy of psychiatric judgments of human behavior, perhaps we could reassert the interrelatedness and interdependence of psychiatry with prevailing ethical and social values. Accordingly, Hoffman (1960) emphasizes the power of the social environment upon all definitions of health:

> Our attempt to define "health" in psychiatry has not really produced satisfactory results, *and* we always have to define "health" within a specific cultural context of *values*. It would seem that our difficulty in defining "mental health" is due precisely to the fact that it is not properly a scientific term. In fact, it can only be meaningful when ultimate values have already been postulated by some extra-scientific (for example, religious, cultural) means. It may be doubted whether any two theorists in the field will ever agree on the same order of ultimate values. Consequently we shall never have a "true" definition of "justice." (P. 207)

Perhaps, as Hoffman suggests, an ideal definition of health can never be attained, just as an ideally healthy man can never be brought into existence. This should not, however, impede efforts to perfect the use of the concept of normality by further defining it. The cultural connotations of normality can be retained so long as there is an awareness of the influence of nonscientific values and an ability to distinguish the moral from the scientific. In their contributions, Hippocrates, Weyer, and Pinel kept these influences in their proper perspective. According to London (1962):

> Science and morality have generally been confounded in psychotherapy—willy nilly, by the unwitting imposition of value and fact upon each other, by the causal assumption that there exist norms which suit values when the former have not been measured and the latter not defined, by the failure to weigh means (technique) against ends (goals) and both against fact. (P. 45)

In order to avoid this "willy nilly" confusion, definitions of terms and evaluations of the scientific worth of the definitions are needed. In this direction, Grinker (1963) suggests the following as values to which the psychiatrist in our society appears to subscribe:

> Upward mobility regardless of intellectual, aptitudinal or social fit, doing and becoming which is operationally goal-changing rather than goal-seeking, permissiveness rather than boundary fixing of behavior, work, strict religious belief, and discipline; and child-rearing according to the latest fact based on current theory. (P. 128)

The discussions on the place of values in the behavioral and social science have not abated. The humanistic psychology movement has continuously struggled with these important issues, and there have been a number of other important recent contributions.* It is not our intention to offer even a partial solution to the problem of values and normality, but rather to illustrate how it influences various aspects of our practices and our theoretical formulations. Obviously, the impact of values on psychiatry and the behavioral sciences in general is considerable.

In order to study people separate from their own social and cultural milieu, investigators need to be aware of their own values and those of the people whom they study. Only then will they approach what is necessary for reasonably objective investigators. For example, it is well known that almost all the psychological and psycho-historical research on Nazism has been done by persons with a relatively strong Jewish identity. Whatever the reasons for the lack of non-Jewish research into Nazism, they need to be openly stated and explored in order to give the data a more meaningful psychological perspective.

It is apparent that any definition of normality will be affected by values influenced by philosophic aesthetic and cultural theories. A scientist's original choice of one of the four perspectives of normality may be motivated by his or her past conditioning. Correspondingly, behavioral scientists' criteria of normality, which they proceed to establish experimentally or clinically, may not differ greatly from the criteria they have absorbed from the philosophic, religious, or aesthetic values of their culture. Psychotherapists especially need to be aware of their patients' values and of when they conflict with their own, before open and meaningful communication can be established. The nonscientific use of the term normality has not invalidated its use in the behavioral sciences. Social judgments on the boundaries of normality have merely made the concept a more complex one. It becomes even more important to have clear definitions of normality.

*See Buhler (1971); Madsen (1971); Maslow (1966); Smith (1978); and Wilder (1969).

Conclusion

Many chapters of this book include a discussion of value orientation, for we and the contributors recognize that larger sociopolitical and economic forces influence our value system. Our value system has influenced and will continue to influence psychiatric practice.

We believe that the mental health field (above and beyond psychiatry) has an obligation to transcend values, ideologies, and humanistic influences in an effort to develop a more rational and empirical approach to the studies of human development. In order to transcend these influences, there needs to be widespread awareness of their implication and their influence.

We advocate such an approach for its own sake, but also, as discussed in the next chapters, the accountability demands of our current historical period require a more rigorous scientific rationale for our concepts of normality and illness.

REFERENCES

Beardslee, W., and Mack, J. 1982. "The Impact on Children and Adolescents of Nuclear Developments." *Psychological Aspects of Nuclear Development.* Washington, D.C.: American Psychiatric Association.

Beck, A. T. 1962. "Reliability of Psychiatric Diagnosis: 1. A Critique of Systematic Studies." *American Journal of Psychiatry* 119:210–16.

Beck, A. T., et al. 1962. "Reliabilty of Psychiatric Diagnosis: 2. A Study of Consistency of Clinical Judgments and Ratings." *American Journal of Psychiatry* 119:351–57.

Begun, M. S. 1981. "W.P.A. Speaker Denounces Deinstitutionalization Impact." *Psychiatric News* 16:1.

Blos, P. 1962. *On Adolescence.* New York: Free Press.

Brenner, M. H. 1979. "Mortality and the National Economy: A Review, and the Experience of England and Wales 1936–76." *Lancet* 2:568–73.

Bromberg, W. 1959. *The Mind of Man: A History of Psychotherapy and Psychoanalysis.* New York: Harper Torchbooks.

Buhler, C. 1971. "Basic Theoretical Concepts of Humanistic Psychology." *American Psychologist* 26:378–86.

Diagnostic and Statistical Manual of Mental Disorders (DSM-III), 3rd ed. 1980. Washington, D.C.: American Psychiatric Association.

Dostoyevsky, F. [1864] 1961. *Notes from the Underground.* New York: New American Library.

Easterlin, R. A. 1980. *Birth and Fortune.* New York: Basic Books.

Eissler, K. R. 1962. *Leonardo da Vinci: Psychoanalytic Notes on the Enigma.* New York: International Universities Press.

———. 1963. *Goethe: A Psychoanalytic Study 1775–1776*, vol. 1. Detroit: Wayne State University Press.

Elder, G. 1974. *Children of the Great Depression.* Chicago: University of Chicago Press.

———. 1968. *Identity: Youth and Crisis.* New York: W. W. Norton.

Favazza, A. R. 1982. "Modern Christian Healing of Mental Illness." *American Journal of Psychiatry* 139:728–35.

Foucault, M. 1965. *Madness and Civilization: A History of Insanity in the Age of Reason.* New York: Pantheon Press.

Freud, S. [1910] 1932. *Leonardo da Vinci: A Psychosexual Study of an Infantile Reminiscence.* New York: Dodd and Mead.

———. [1928] 1959. "Dostoyevsky and Parricide." In *Collected Papers of Sigmund Freud,* vol. 5, ed. J. Strachey, pp. 222–43. New York: Basic Books.

Fromm, E. 1960. *The Sane Society.* New York: Rinehart and Company.

Geertz, C. 1973. *Interpretation of Cultures.* New York: Basic Books.

Goldman, R. K., and Mendelsohn, G. A. 1969. "Psychotherapeutic Change and Social Adjustment: A Report of a National Survey of Psychotherapists." *Journal of Abnormal Psychology* 74:164–72.

Grinker, R. R., Sr. 1963. "A Dynamic Story of the 'Homoclites.'" In *Science and Psychoanalysis,* vol. 6, ed. J. H. Masserman, pp. 115–34. New York: Grune & Stratton.

Gubrium, J. F., and Buckholdt, D. R. 1977. *Toward Maturity.* San Francisco: Jossey-Bass.

Guthrie, W.K.C. 1960. *The Greek Philosophers, From Thales to Aristotle.* New York: Harper Torchbooks.

Hoffman, M. 1960. "Psychiatry, Nature and Science." *American Journal of Psychiatry* 117:205.

Holinger, P. C., and Offer, D. 1982. "Prediction of Adolescent Suicide: A Population Model." *American Journal of Psychiatry* 139:302–7.

Jowett, B., trans. 1937. *The Dialogues of Plato,* vol. 1. New York: Random House.

Kagan, J. 1979a. "Overview: Perspectives on Human Infancy." In *The Handbook of Infant Development,* ed. J. Osofsky, pp. 1–25. New York: Wiley-Interscience.

———. 1979b. "The Form of Early Development." *Archives of General Psychiatry* 36:1047–54.

Kardiner, A. 1939. *The Individual and His Society.* New York: Columbia University Press.

———. 1945. *The Psychological Frontiers of Society.* New York: Columbia University Press.

Kris, E. 1952. *Psychoanalytic Exploration in Art.* New York: International Universities Press.

Kubie, L. S. 1958. *Neurotic Distortions of the Creative Process.* Lawrence, Kans.: University of Kansas Press.

Laing, R. D. 1967. *The Politics of Experience.* New York: Pantheon.

Livson, N., and Peskin, H. 1980. "Perspectives on Adolescence From Longitudinal Research." In *Handbook of Adolescent Psychology,* ed. J. Adelson, pp. 47–98. New York: John Wiley.

London, P. 1962. The Sources of Therapeutic Morality. *Columbia University Forum* 3:45–46.

Macaulay, T. B. 1968. *The History of England.* New York: Washington Square Press.

Madsen, K. B. 1971. "Humanistic Psychology and the Philosophy of Science." *Journal of Humanistic Psychology* 11:1–10.

Maslow, A. H. 1966. *The Psychology of Science: A Reconnaissance.* New York: Harper & Row.

Meerloo, J.A.M. 1962. *Suicide and Mass Suicide.* New York: Grune & Stratton.

Mora, G. 1963. "On the 400th Anniversary of Johann Weyer's *De Praestigiis Daemonum*—Its Significance for Today's Psychiatry." *American Journal of Psychiatry* 120(5):417–29.

Nesselroade, J. R., and Baltes, P. B. 1974. "Adolescent Personality Development and Historical Change: 1970–1972." In *Monographs of the Society for Research in Child Development,* serial no. 154, vol. 39(1). Chicago: University of Chicago Press.

Neugarten, B. L., and Hagestad, G. O. 1976. "Age and the Life Course." In *Handbook of Aging and the Social Sciences,* ed. R. H. Binstock and E. Shanas, pp. 35–55. New York: Van Nostrand Reinhold.

Offer, D., and Sabshin, M. 1974. *Normality: Theoretical and Clinical Concepts of Mental Health.* New York: Basic Books.

Offer, D., and Stine, D. 1960. "Function of Music in Spontaneous Art Production," *Archives of General Psychiatry* 3:490–503.

Offer, D.; Ostrov, E.; and Howard, K. I. 1981a. *The Adolescent: A Psychological Self-Portrait.* New York: Basic Books.

————. 1981b. "The Mental Health Professional's Concept of the Normal Adolescent." *Archives of General Psychiatry* 38:149–52.

Ostrov, E.; Offer, D.; and Howard, K. I. 1983. "Historical and Developmental Changes in Adolescent Self-Image." Unpublished. Chicago, Ill.

Phillips, W., ed. 1957. *Art and Psychoanalysis.* New York: Criterion Books.

Rank, O. 1932. *Art and Artists.* New York: Knopf.

Reik, T. 1954. *Listening with the Third Ear.* New York: Farrar and Straus.

Ross, W. D., ed. 1942. *The Student's Oxford Aristotle: Ethics,* vol. 5. London: Oxford University Press.

Sedgwick, P. 1982. *Psycho-Politics.* New York: Harper & Row.

Seidenberg, H. 1973. "Effect of the Teaching, Administration and Recruiting Roles of the Training Analyst." In *Training Psychoanalysis: A Report on Psychoanalytic Education,* prepared by I. Ramzy. Topeka, Kansas: Topeka Institute for Psychoanalysis.

Simon, B. 1980. *Mind and Madness in Ancient Greece.* Ithaca, N.Y.: Cornell University Press.

Smith, M. B. 1978. "Psychology and Values." *Journal of Social Issues* 34:181–99.

Srole, L., et al. 1963. *Mental Health in the Metropolis: Manhattan Studies.* New York: McGraw-Hill.

Sterba, R. F. 1960. "Therapeutic Goal and Present-Day Reality." *Journal of the Hillside Hospital* 9:4.

Stone, L. 1982. "Madness." *New York Review of Books,* November, pp. 28–36.

Suchar, C. S., and Markin, R. M. 1983. "Morality, Madness and Biography: Deviance as Narrative (An Abstract)." Unpublished. Chicago: Michael Reese Hospital and Medical Center.

Szasz, T. S. 1961. *The Myth of Mental Illness.* New York: Harper & Row.

————. 1963. "Some Implications for Law of the 'Myth of Mental Illness.'" Paper delivered at the Illinois Psychiatric Society meeting, March.

Vaillant, G. E. 1977. *Adaptation to Life.* Boston: Little, Brown.

Veith, I. 1958. "Glimpses into the History of Psychotherapy." In *Progress in Psychotherapy,* vol. 3, ed. J. H. Masserman and J. C. Moreno, pp. 1–20. New York: Grune & Stratton.

Veroff, J.; Douvan, E.; and Kulka, R. A. 1981. *The Inner American.* New York: Basic Books.

Vico, G. [1725] 1970. *The New Science.* Ithaca, N.Y.: Cornell University Press.

Wheelright, P. E. 1954. *The Way of Philosophy.* New York: Odyssey Press.

Wilder, J. 1969. "Values and Psychotherapy." *American Journal of Psychotherapy* 23:405–14.

13   Daniel Offer
                    and Melvin Sabshin

Patterns of
Normal Development

The Meaning of Development

We have come to the point in the book where it is reasonable to pose the following two questions: (1) Are there normal patterns of human development that can be distinguished from abnormal patterns?; and (2) What theory of normal development do we espouse?

Obviously, many people have always been eager to form theories concerning the phenomena in and around them. They felt that once they had a "theory" concerning events, they could not only understand the event better but eventually control it. When theories were proven wrong, new ones replaced old ones.*

In our opinion, a theory concerning normal human development has tremendous appeal for the following reasons:

First, it will help us make "sense" of our personal lives. We will know what to expect in each stage and we will be better prepared for potential crises. Furthermore, it will enable us to better understand our children and our parents and to help them when necessary. We will also know when someone deviates from the normal pattern; in other words, we will recognize when he or she needs outside, professional help in order to get

---

*Obviously we will not deal here with this most interesting aspect of philosophy of science. We will merely briefly discuss some overriding issues specific to theory-building in the behavioral sciences as applied to normal development. We will then give some relevant examples.

back on track. We will also know when the outside professional help is sufficient and we can continue developing by ourselves. A theory will also allow us to optimally control our future and permit us to make better decisions concerning ourselves, our families, and our friends. In short, it will, or should, make us feel better.

Second, in this best of all possible worlds, theory would be based on knowledge. Knowledge would be the sum part of bits of data. Each of these bits of data would be defined, classified, and, most important, *measurable*. After all, we can only make reasonable predictions if we can measure the variables on which we have to base our predictions.

These issues have interested philosophers of science ever since Comte, whose works were published in the 1830s (1830–1842), maintained that the social sciences should proceed from observation to general laws, like the physical sciences. He was unsure whether psychology could become a "real" science since he maintained that in attending to one's own mental states, these same mental states would be irrevocably altered and distorted. He believed, therefore, that the only sciences of behavior that deal with observable and measurable phenomena were sociology and physiology. In his insistence on objective observations, Comte was in some respects the forerunner of the twentieth-century logical positivists, who insisted on verifiability criterion of factual meaningfulness. For them, an observation has meaning only if there is a difference, or principle, open to tests and observations, between acceptance or rejection of a given premise. One century after Comte, Karl R. Popper ([1935] 1959) differentiated between the scientific, or empirical, and the metaphysical, or transempirical.

Empiricism has usually been defined as the attitude that beliefs are to be accepted and acted on only if they first have been confirmed by actual experience—a definition that accords with the derivation of the term from the Greek word *empeiria*, "experience." Empiricism is also the antithesis of rationalism. The latter asserts that there are a priori concepts, such as the belief that everything must have a sufficient reason, and that everything can rise from intellectual intention. To rationalists, there are, for example, self-evident truths that one can arrive at from purely deductive reasoning. Empiricists take nothing for granted. Not only do theories have to be proven, but they exist only as long as they are not disconfirmed. Popper called his scientific theory logical empiricism. In his view, one can never complete the process of confirming a hypothesis. More important, it is the extent to which it resists attempts at falsification that keeps a hypothesis viable.

Popper's appeal comes, in part, from his being, according to Lieberson (1982) a Romantic rationalist. As Lieberson says, "throughout his [Popper's] work we found the image of scientists trying to impose their theories on nature and then awaiting the voice of nature in response." Lieberson feels that by rejecting our "inductive intuition" and replacing it with a method by which we learn from our mistakes, Popper did not appreciate how firmly the inductive method has been established in our everyday scientific work. We are not recommending acceptance of Popper's (or logical positivists') philosophies. We believe that we need to undertake considerably more empirical research before we can even attempt to conceptualize a universal theory of normal and/or deviant development. As has been pointed out over and over in this volume, we cannot only study *deviant* samples and *theorize* about normal development.

Rules and regulations in a culture change from one time to another. That is one reason why long-term predictive studies (despite massive data accumulated) tend to be so disappointing. In addition, investigators always select what (to them) are the most significant facts. As correct as they often are, they can also fail dramatically, since two decades later the culture has shifted and values, goals, fantasies, and behaviors have also changed. Hence data collected during time one may not be relevant to those living in time two. In addition, since the new values and behaviors were not present at time one, they were not measured. Just measuring coping styles is not enough either, since various life crises—war, economic depression, parent loss—bring to the foreground different coping styles in different individuals. Also, as we have shown in chapter 12, coping with divorce is a different psychological phenomenon in the 1980s than it was in the 1950s. Hence it has different ramifications even for psychologically similar individuals at different points in a culture's history.

It seems to us that there is no straight path (linear causality) by which one necessarily can move from the data base of observation to arrive at theory. There has to be some multivaried correlation between the two (data and theory).

Obviously we recognize that we are light-years away from predicting the course of development from our theoretical (or empirical) knowledge. There simply are too many variables, and their relationship with each other, as well as with chance occurrences, throws a continuous monkey wrench into our "near" attempt. We cannot confirm or deny our hypothesis, but we can use our empirical data to help us narrow the field of possible theories.

Despite the obvious limitations to a current overall theory of development, there are many theories of normal human development. The wish to know ourselves is understandable, but the consequences are often ignored. We believe that we need to weigh the consequences of our beliefs in order to understand our actions better. One of the problems that often surfaces is that after a theory is postulated (often based on personal experiences), there is an immediate need to generalize it to everyone, because "if it fits me, it just must fit her or him too." Only too often do we spend the rest of our lives justifying our personal experiences.

Many social and behavioral scientists as well as many others (e.g., moral philosophers, theologians) strongly cling to their own notion of development. It is important to examine, scientifically, whether commonly held folk notions about the developmental relationship between infancy and childhood are correct. As Kagan (1979a,b) has shown, the variation in psychological profiles that exists at age two years does not seem to be very predictive of behavior a decade later. Emde and Sorce (see chapter 1) have stated the same thing. They demonstrate that tests like the Brazelton Neonatal Assessment Scales (1973) can correctly predict problems in development in only a very small percentage of infants (under 10 percent) and for a small number of variables.

As we have stated, it is not our intent to summarize the extensive review of the various theories of normal human development. This has been attempted in the first seven chapters of this book. What we want to do is to discuss the assumption that we believe behavioral and social scientists make when they present us with their theories of normal human development. In other words, we shall discuss the values implicit in the developmental theories already presented in the volume.

Continuity and Discontinuity in Normal Development

The main focus throughout the book has been an empirical one. What do we know about normal human development? What are the affective cognitive, interpersonal variables that lead to normal behavior in different ages? We have not concerned ourselves with deviant development, cross-cultural or cross-ethnic variations, historical or evolutionary differences, or the biological underpinning of normal behavior. Within our field of interest, there are basically two theories about the patterns of human development. According to the first theory, development is continuous, stable, and cumulative. One might say that, in addition, it is hierarchial as well, where certain psychological elements have differential impact on a person at different ages. According to the second, development is discontinuous, unstable, and cyclical. The cyclical part refers to people's propensity to attempt to resolve similar (if not identical) conflicts at different periods of their life. These two theories are not mutually exclusive (see chapter 9). Each period of life has certain basic psychological elements that continue from one period to another (e.g., temperament, self-image). It also has other factors that are less stable and are discontinuous from one period to another (e.g., memories, patterns of relationship). Here we shall attempt to examine some of the conceptual foundations behind each of these two basic assumptions about development.

It is our contention that most theories underlying the continuous and discontinuous notions about development are conceptual rather than empirical. The difference between the two theories is more apparent than real. As we have mentioned, certain aspects of one's personality are relatively stable across time and other aspects are not. As far as we are concerned the question is an empirical, not a theoretical, one. Certain empirical studies discussed in this volume focused on continuity; others stressed discontinuity. It is important to emphasize that the interplay between internal (psychological), external (social), and physical (biological) variables is so fluid and changing that longitudinal studies will probably not answer our questions. Concerning continuity and discontinuity, we also cannot do human subject research without interfering to a certain extent with our subjects' development. The "research alliance" so needed for longitudinal research often turns into a "therapeutic alliance," with the investigator doing what has been called "miniature psychotherapy" (Offer 1969).

It seems to us that the differences between studies that focus on continuity in development and those that stress discontinuity are often dependent on the variables studied rather than on basic inherent differences in the findings of the research. In chapter 1 Emde and Sorce show that studies of IQ, temperament, and activity/passivity in infants are not stable over time. In chapter 3 we discuss the stability of the self-image throughout the adolescent years. We also discuss the stability of adolescents' relationships with their parents. It is possible that studies of similar variables in different age groups will yield similar results. Such studies have rarely been done because the variables do not have the same significance at different stages in the life cycle. A good example of the problems associated with doing longitudinal-development research can be seen by comparing young adults and adults. For example, in chapter 4 Arnstein discusses the clinical psychoanalytic theory of mental health among young adults. For a young adult to become mentally healthy, he or she has to disengage from his or her infantile-internalized objects. Obviously, this behavior is specific for late adolescents. In chapter 5 Cohler and Boxer discuss factors that contribute to mental health during midlife. While factors such as the relationship of childhood socialization to adult adjustment could be studied during all stages of adulthood, the relationship between aspiration and achievement is more meaningful in mid-life than any other stage. Therefore comparison across other stages would not be as meaningful. Certain social and/or psychological factors could be studied longitudinally. Self-image, cognitive abilities, IQ (past childhood), and verbal and mathematical abilities are only a few variables that can be meaningfully compared across the different stages of the life cycle. Yet as Cohler and Boxer have so clearly shown, even these variables have to be studied within their historical and generational context in order to be understood.

Psychologists have spearheaded the studies in developmental research. Psychiatrists have been interested in the natural course of psychiatric illness (e.g., juvenile delinquency and schizophrenia); with the few exceptions noted in the preface, psychiatrists have traditionally not studied normal development. Psychologists have been most interested in normal developmental research for some time. Gergen (1981) examines life-span research and discusses the crisis that he believes has emerged recently in the field of life-span study. According to him, three theories of development have emerged. The first, which he termed stability account, focuses on behavioral constancy, stabilized patterns of personal identification, cognitive and emotional processing, and so on. This theory is dominant among psychoanalytic theoreticians and investigators of longitudinal psychological research. In the second, called the ordered change account, an individual passes through a series of predetermined, epigenetic stages. Examples of theoreticians who favor this orientation are Erikson, Piaget, and Kohlberg. Critics have argued that neither approach has had broad enough data base and that the researchers' methodologies were often value-laden. Gergen added a third approach, called the aleatoric (autonomous) account. This account focuses on the flexibility of developmental patterns and emerges from the study of the broad diversity of developmental patterning. According to Gergen (1981):

> Existing patterns appear potentially evanescent, the unstable result of the peculiar juxtaposition of contemporary historical events. For any individual the life course seems fundamentally open-ended. Even with full knowledge of the individual's past experience, one can render little more than a probabilistic account of the broad contours of future development. (Pp. 34–35)

He goes on to state that the most systematic support for his aleatoric position is the data that have come from cohort differences in life-span development.

In our opinion, the theoretical perspective of the developmental researcher is of secondary importance. Of crucial importance is the empirical data sought. Different research methods will harvest different sets of data. If those sets of data are contradictory, it might be necessary to undertake new research to settle the differences. They cannot and should not, as we have seen, be settled theoretically. Normal development has many patterns. It is up to the scientist to discover what they consist of.

Psychosocial Aspects of Normal Development

Modern understanding of normal human development from a psychosocial point of view has been uniquely influenced by Erik Erikson. This influence has been twofold: he stimulated new empirical research on *many* developmental stages; he also considerably influenced our theories concerning human development.

Erikson is best known for his work on youth and the popularization of the concept of identity. The term identity, of course, is not new. It has been in use for over one thousand years. The Oxford English Dictionary defines the term psychologically: "The sameness of a person or thing at all times or in all circumstances; the condition or fact that a person is his self and not something else." Erikson traces the origin of the concept identity to Freud and William James. Freud used the term inner identity when he addressed the B'nai B'rith Society in Vienna in 1926. In that setting he emphasized the term identity, which had been rooted in tradition. James described identity as "a subjective sense of an invigorating sameness and continuity" (1892, p. 675). Although not the originator of the term, there is no question but that Erikson launched its psychological use in the Western world. Erikson's own definition of identity is based on "the perceptions of the self-sameness and certainty of one's existence in time and place." As the historian Strozier (1984) puts it:

> Unless we have been under a rock for the last generation, few of us can escape the term identity. In fact, the identity crisis is now almost a rite of passage for adolescents who seem to wear their crises, as Erikson once noted, on their sleeves, Edwardian or leather. But it is worth stressing that the detailed cases Erikson provides to illustrate the precise meaning of the identity crisis are historical. Martin Luther, one of the first Erikson described, remains the most interesting. In 1505 on his way home from college, going to his father's choice of bride and career, Martin heard God call him to the faith during a thunderstorm. He fled into the Augustinian Order without so much as a postcard home. In the monastery a kindly superior, Father Staupitz, listened patiently to Martin's compulsive confessions, guided him to think critically about the scriptures, and, as it seems, fell in love with him. Martin weathered many emotional

storms within himself as he gathered together his ferocious creativity that led
to the posting of the 95 theses on the Wittenberg Church door. (P. 4)

Erikson (1958) states that the struggles between young Martin Luther and
his father were not unique. Rather:

> Millions of boys face these problems and solve them in some way or another—
> they live, as Captain Ahab says, with half of their heart and with only one of
> their lungs, and the world is the worse for it. Now and again, however, an
> individual is called upon (called by whom, only the theologians claim to know,
> and by *what*, only bad psychologists) to lift his individual patienthood to the
> level of a universal one and to try to solve for all what he could not solve for
> himself alone. (P. 67)

The "collective patienthood" Erikson evokes here is the crisis of Western Christendom over man's relationship to God the Father, which found
its direct political analogue in struggles with earthly fathers, princes, and
popes. Luther did the dirty work of his age, Erikson concludes. And ever
since we have all benefited from an enhanced sense of self. Erikson
makes the controversial decision to generalize from the study of the great
man to the mechanism by which all of us resolve our developmental
crises.

But the notion of "identity crisis" is not unique anymore to adolescents. As we have seen, particularly in chapters 3 to 7, many developmentalists are eager to interpret their findings from the following point of
view: Emotional growth cannot occur smoothly. It is, by definition, produced out of conflict. Once the conflict is experienced and resolved (i.e.,
once a crisis has taken place), development can occur. Yet the empirical
evidence for this concept is not as strong as many developmentalists
believe. Furthermore, the perspective comes with its own bias—a particular middle-class orientation that sees crisis resolution in terms of specific
goals to be achieved (e.g., vocational choices).

Erikson's (1968) stages of life captures his philosophy of development;
namely, that human development is a psychosocial process that changes
over time. He further states that there is no such thing as development in
a vacuum; the agenda for individual development, while biologically
paced, is set by the culture in which the individual is raised. A person's
development can be understood fully only in the context of that individual's society and culture.

A given life history unfolds epigenetically according to a coded psychosocial "plan," and a hierarchy of "virtues" occur for those individuals
who pass muster at the natural points of crisis in their development. The
model of layers of personality, a succession of products that build one
upon the other, comes from the ancient conception of the life cycles

characterized by stages. According to Roazen (1980), Aristotle proposed three phases and in the Middle Ages the individual life was divided into four to ten stages. Roazen believes that not only has Erikson underemphasized the continuity of his theories from these predecessors, but he tends to formulate a life-cycle theory to fit American mechanistic and optimistic perspectives.

The other tradition that contributed to Erikson's notion of stages is from biology and, in particular, from embryology. Erikson (1968) described his notions in the following way:

> Whenever we try to understand growth, it is well to remember the *epigenetic principle* which is derived from the growth of organisms *in utero*. Somewhat generalized, this principle states that anything that grows has a ground plan, and that out of this ground plan the parts arise, each part having its time of special ascendancy, until all parts have arisen to form a functioning whole. This, obviously, is true for fetal development where each part of the organism has its critical time of ascendance or danger of defect. At birth the baby leaves the chemical exchange of the womb for the social exchange system of his society, where his gradually increasing capacities meet the opportunities and limitations of his culture. How the maturing organism continues to unfold, not by developing new organs but by means of a prescribed sequence of locomotor, sensory, and social capacities, is described in the child-development literature. . . . psychoanalysis has given us an understanding of the more idiosyncratic experiences, and especially the inner conflicts, which constitute the manner in which an individual becomes a distinct personality. But here, too, it is important to realize that in the sequence of his most personal experiences the healthy child, given a reasonable amount of proper guidance, can be trusted to obey inner laws of development, laws which create a succession of potentialities for significant interaction with those who tend to respond to him and those institutions which are ready for him. While such interaction varies from culture to culture, it must remain within "the proper rate and proper sequence" which governs all epigenesis. Personality, therefore, can be said to develop according to steps predetermined in the human organism's readiness to be driven toward, to be aware of, and to interact with a widening radius of significant individuals and institutions. (Pp. 92–93)

This biological stage model breaks down, however, if we generalize it to psychosocial development because embryonic development differs in key ways from psychosocial development. A central difference is the relative predictability of the environment. A normal infant can develop only within a narrow range of intrauterine conditions. The embryo has comparatively little impact on its environment. There are fetal-maternal feedback mechanisms, of course, but these function in a relatively narrow range to ensure normal development. The embryo can be said to be growing toward a fixed goal in an environment to which evolution has tightly adapted it.

In sharp contrast to the intrauterine environment, the psychosocial environment varies widely from culture to culture, as Erikson acknowledges, but also from family to family within the same culture and even from child to child within the same family. In part, this is because children exert such powerful influences in creating their environment. They start with constitutional factors that elicit responses from parents, which in turn confirm the children in behavior. The psychosocial environment is also a *perceived* environment. What may look like a uniform environment across individuals to the experiencing individual is very different, depending on idiosyncratic perceptions influenced by constitutional factors, personal experience, and feedback mechanisms within the family.

Erikson has serious problems applying the stage model from embryology because he does not appear to give sufficient emphasis to the evidence that the relationship between individuals and their environment differs within the same culture. At times he seems to assume that culture is like the intrauterine environment, relatively uniform, or at least expectable, across individuals. He does not take into account the fact that while culture exerts a powerful influence on individual development, the nature and extent of cultural influences on different individuals is a matter to be explored, not assumed.

Another model of development that is frequently used states that each different period has its unique tasks with which individuals have to cope successfully before they can move on to the next stage of development. Thus Levinson and associates (1978) say that since the developmental tasks have so much to do with building and rebuilding the life structure, it becomes important to define and evaluate the "satisfactoriness" of a structure. During a stable period, people try to build a structure that will in some sense be satisfactory to them. During a transitional period, they try to reappraise the current structure and to move toward a new and more satisfactory one. But who is to do the evaluations, and what does "satisfactory" mean psychiatrically or psychologically? At no point in their work do Levinson and his co-workers clearly state how one can behaviorally operationalize their concepts about "satisfactory" and "unsatisfactory." It is either left up to readers to decide for themselves or it is assumed that "everyone" must be familiar with the ideas so no restatement is necessary. This latter viewpoint seems to be shared among many investigators. Levinson's work is often regarded as an example of some of the best clinical research on normal development. It is similar in perspective to the work of Gould (1978) and Vaillant (1977). Their view of what constitutes ideal development is so well defined that one wonders to what extent they imposed their vision of ideal man onto the lives of their subjects. Their presentation of theory, secondarily supported by case histories, suggests that the biographies have been used to illustrate a vision of ideal development. Their books are unsparingly evaluative in depicting their subjects' lives. While we recognize that some patterns of living are more effective than others, we question the extent to which the researchers' immersion in their own version of normality as utopia may have influenced their findings.

In reviewing investigators' pet descriptions of their area of interest, we found that many of the terms used were not specific to a particular period of development. Rather they typified an ideology. The psychological, behavioral, and social terms used could have described a number of periods. For example, the following statement (Levinson et al., 1978) could describe any of the periods of the life cycle with the possible exception of infancy:

> The transition from A to B contains a remarkable gift and burden. It provides an opportunity to work on the flaws in the life structure formed during the previous period, and to create the basis for a more satisfactory structure that will be built in the following period.

Throughout Levinson and associates' book such descriptions are presented as being "typical" of the particular age or period under discussion. Also common are such statements as:

> Having a crisis at this time is not in itself pathological. Indeed, the person who goes through this period with minimal discomfort may be denying that his life must change, for better or worse. He is thus losing an opportunity for personal development. (Levinson et al. 1978, p. 26)

When one reviews the vast literature on development through the life cycle, these statements lose their specific meaning, because almost all investigators use them for "their" stage of development. It does bring us up against a basic ideological underpinning shared by many social and behavioral scientists—that only through emotional turmoil can "real" growth or development take place.

Turmoil, Crisis, and Human Development

Turmoil is defined as an emotional condition that represents a significant disruption in psychological equilibrium leading to fluctuation in moods, confusion in thought, rebellion against established values, and changeable and unpredictable behavior. Many investigators see this concept, which was originally ascribed mostly to adolescents, as representing other developmental periods. At times investigators, so confident of their theory, state unequivocally that if individuals say they are not in turmoil, they are either denying it or losing an opportunity for personal growth (see, e.g., Levinson et al. 1978). This illustrates how strongly rooted romantic ideology is among psychoanalytically oriented developmental researchers.* As Levinson's theory of stages coalesced, he seemed to view his subjects from a preconceived notion about what people should and should not experience. We believe that he did not necessarily see and experience the world as his subjects did. And because he is a mental health professional, his judgment as to who is "sick" and who is "healthy" is assumed to be the correct one. Levinson and associates (1978) say that:

> Because a man in this [mid-life] crisis is often somewhat irrational, others may regard him as "upset" or "sick." In most cases, he is not. The man himself and those who care about him should recognize that he is in a normal developmental period and is working on normal mid-life tasks. The desire to question and modify his life stems from the most healthy part of the self. The doubting and searching are appropriate to this period; the real question is how best to make use of them. The problem is compounded by the fact that the process of reappraisal activates unconscious conflicts—the unconscious baggage carried forward from hard times in the past which hinders the effort to change. The pathology is not in the desire to improve one's life but in the obstacles to pursuing this aim. It is the pathological anxiety and guilt, the dependencies, animosities and vanities of earlier years, that keep a man from examining the real issues at mid-life. They make it difficult for him to modify an oppressive life structure. (P. 199)

It is obvious that the notion of crisis as used by Levinson, Erikson, and many others is better understood from the observer's perspective. Whether the person observed experiences the event described by the observer as a crisis is an entirely separate question. It may be that only in retrospect, and from the perspective of an outsider, is "crisis" experienced. That is, there comes a point in time when observers decide, in order to make sense of the events observed, to call the subject's experience by another name. But this is a conceptual event, going on in the

---

*The romantic ideology stems from Hall's (1904) two-volume treatise *Adolescence*, in which he introduced the phrase *Stürm und Drang* (storm and stress) to characterize the universal developmental psychology of adolescents. *Stürm und Drang* comes directly from the nineteenth-century German romantic literary movement that stressed idealism, romanticism, rebellion against the established ways, and the expression of deep passions, and is represented in the works of Goethe and Schiller, among others. Later Hall re-translated the German term to "adolescent turmoil." We are impressed with how deeply people feel about the notion of storm and stress, or adolescent turmoil. Strong (political) ideological forces are at play here. In our empirical approach we attempt to sidestep some of these ideological conflicts. In so doing, it may seem to some that we are also taking an ideological stand.

mind of understanding observers. It is not to be confused with the actual experience of the observed subject as he or she experiences life from day to day. Furthermore, the two realities (of the observer and of the observed) can both be correct in their own universe of emotional experiences. Each one has its own reality. We in the behavioral sciences encounter a problem when we attempt to use and transfer the observations and measurement from one reality to the next.

Because the discussion of crisis is such a central one for our argument about the need for empirical data, we will briefly examine it from another perspective. All theories concerning behavior and/or development are eventually proven or disproven in the crucible of "what really happens." For example, unconscious conflicts by themselves are only meaningful if they are correlated with behavior. People who have not separated from their "unconscious internalized objects" would, by definition, relate more poorly to important persons in their life than these people who have successfully separated from their "unconscious internalized objects." If these people have identical transient and/or lasting interpersonal relationships, then the theory would be very suspect. Similarly, when considering "crisis," it is incumbent upon the theoretician to outline the behavioral consequences of her or his theory of crisis. As we have seen, studies of the behavior of a group of normals (i.e., nonpatients) did not manifest these behavioral consequences. A large percentage of the normal group grow up without showing the behavioral consequences ascribed to adolescents in crisis by many theoreticians. Obviously adolescents have internal and external conflicts. They usually are able to cope with the conflicts successfully and without concomitant crisis as represented by overt behavioral problems. Crisis has always been defined as dramatic shifts in affect, cognition, interpersonal relationship and behavior. If these manifestations do not take place, then no crisis is present.

Erikson and other psychosocial theoreticians appreciate the culturally constructed and shared conceptual categories by which we jointly organize and construct our experiences. Thus he and other investigators report that some young people familiar with his ideas expect to have an identity crisis. Cultural constructs seem to affect individuals' expectations about their inner experience since, in a sense, giving a culturally provided name to an experience makes it real to the individual. However, in using a conceptual tool such as "stage" or "crisis," one has to consider: from whose perspective? It makes a difference whether the perspective is subjective or objective and, as Offer, Ostrov, and Howard (1981) have shown, whether the perspective is that of a member of one age group (adolescent) or another (adult). Erikson and others look at the life-span stages from the perspective of an outside adult observer. Theories built on subjective reports of people about their present life experience, at different life stages, might well be different.

It is of interest to note that the turmoil theory seems to conflict with much of classical psychoanalytic theory of child development (see chapters 8 and 12). The continuity of one's past with one's present and future functioning and behavior seems to be taken for granted. Psychoanalytic theories of adulthood are less developed, since there has been considerably less interest in it.

Other Psychosocial Theories of Development

A psychosocial theory of development, termed by Cohler (1981; see also chapter 5) a "personal narrative," is another popular developmental theory. Cohler describes his perspective in the following way:

> Studies of lives have suggested that the course of development may be much less predictable and well ordered than previously realized. Rather than viewing personality development either in terms of continuing stability over time or in terms of a number of well-ordered phases or stages, lives seem to be characterized by often abrupt transformations determined both by expected and eruptive life events and by intrinsic, but not necessarily continuous, developmental factors, including biological aging. These events taking place across the life course are later remembered as elements of a narrative which provides a coherent account of this often disjunctive life course. The form of this narrative is based upon a socially shared belief in Western culture that all narratives, including history, literature, and biographies, must have a beginning, a middle, and an end related to each other in a meaningful manner.
>
> Both the person creating a personal narrative and others studying lives rely upon the same shared criterion for judging the adequacy of the interpretation of this personal narrative. The interpretation is selected which provides the most coherent or internally consistent account of the life course. From this perspective, there are no events or facts regarding lives which are independent of interpretations which are made of them, just as, in studying history more generally, concern is with the adequacy of the narrative or interpretation, rather than with the actuality of the events.
>
> Three particular transformations appear to have special significance in the life course: (a) from early to middle childhood, (b) from childhood to adolescence and young adulthood, and (c) from adulthood to middle age. As a result of such transformations, not necessarily representing an ordered and predictable timetable of development, earlier memories change. Together with the changing context of time and situation, these earlier memories are continually revised so as to maintain a sense of continuity across the life course. The first of these three transformations, from early to middle childhood, has been particularly well studied because of Sigmund Freud's genius in recognizing the impor-

tance of this period of life in the reorganization of memory. Similar detailed inquiry is required for each of the other transformations, together with the somewhat less often experienced transition from middle age to old age. (Pp. 227–28)

Cohler describes himself as a person who believes in the subjective (i.e., the individual's perception) point of view. The core of the personality stays on while the landscape (images) are continuously on the go.

The Berkeley Guidance Study was a four-decade-long study on consistency and change in women's characteristics, conducted by Mussen and associates (1980). This was an unusual opportunity, for no studies exist that span such a long period. In the study, the researchers focused on psychological and personality characteristics. They found, through an innovative stationary factor analysis, which factors were stable over time as well as those that were specific to each period. In contrast to Elder (1974), who found that factors seem to decrease in importance with the ensuing years, Mussen and associates, found that certain factors were quite stable. (It is not quite clear whether Mussen believes that the older women are still influenced by their earlier experiences, or whether they simply continue to have the same patterns of coping and cognition.) The following psychological factors were relatively consistent over forty years: intelligence, mental alertness, speed of mental processes, use of language, accuracy in thinking, and other personality-social characteristics such as cheerfulness. Retaining of self-assurance, attitude toward child, and satisfaction with life showed little stability over this long interval. One could argue, and the authors do, that the former have strong genetic elements in them and that the factors that are not stable over time are more influenced by the environment.

Another recent work critical of the developmentalist approach is that of Gubrium and Buckholdt (1977). They too state that they do not assume that life inherently cycles in some ordered or progressive fashion. Rather they believe that the important questions for us are: "What ideas are held about the advance of life, how do people use these ideas to construct and control each other's lives in terms of time, and how do they come to think and talk about movement from one stage of life to another?" (p. xxi). Their social phenomenological approach studies behavior from its social interactional point of view. They are interested in the meaning of the behavior or the social level. Similar to Cohler, they also pay much attention to the personal narrative. Cohler and Gubrium and Buckholdt seem to underemphasize the vast existential literature about the meaning of life (e.g., Dostoevsky, Kafka, Camus, Kierkegaard) and their theories seem to be relevant primarily to a segment of the middle class. For many people, life might not have meaning in the sense that Cohler and Gubrium and Buckholdt imply. It might be very difficult for many of these people to tell their stories. Therefore, we question the universal applicability of the personal narrative.

Investigators who subscribe to the theory that people do want to make sense of their lives counter with the argument that existentialists know that most people believe in order. The existentialists simply choose to ignore it. The argument proceeds further: most people have a concept of what is considered success or failure in one's culture. Similarly, people also search for meaning in their lives. They want to know whether they fit in the success picture. Are they, as Neugarten said, "on-time" or are they "off-time"? If they are "on-time" then they will feel better about themselves and be closer to what the people consider normal. We feel that the argument should eventually be settled empirically. However, studies will have to be formulated that do not organize subjects' lives according to investigators' preconceived notions. If investigators ask a person to recount his or her "life's story," the implication is that there indeed is a story to tell. Interview techniques and psychological instruments are too often organized around the investigator's value system to answer the type of question the investigator is interested in. In order to overcome what Murphy (1979) calls the "difficulty of detachment in behavioral research," we in psychological research need to develop a type of double-blind method of investigation similar to those developed in biology.

In evaluating theories of development, we need to take into account the values of the total culture, not just part of it. If we were not so eager to find "meaning" everywhere, we might more be able to decipher whatever does exist out there. (See also chapter 9 for a different perspective on this issue.)

Psychoanalysis and Normal Development

Psychoanalysis as a theory of normal human development has had considerable influence on all investigators working in the field. Psychoanalysts beginning with Freud tended to subscribe to the normality as utopia perspective. In other words, all men were created to be neurotic and normal functioning is considered as an ideal fiction (Freud [1937] 1959). According to Michels (see chapter 8), Freud believed that the psychological mechanisms that led to his patients' symptoms were normal mechanisms present in every man. The distinction between a patient and any other (normal) individual was one of quantity or, at most, based on the social appraisal of a surface differentiation that overlay a hidden, deeper commonality. Psychoanalysis was a tool for translating the apparently psychopathologic phenotype that *seemed* to be qualitatively different from normal to the deeper mental life that had created it. Furthermore, the deeper mental life that was first discovered in the treatment of neurotic patients was not only characteristic of the normal mind but actually became the key for unlocking the secrets of normal psychological development.

Classical psychoanalytical theory is based on the premise that childhood experiences leave significant marks on the adult. The theory further states that all adults carry within them the residues of their childhood. The continuity between the child, the adolescent, and the adult can be seen in the normal, in the neurotic, and in the psychotic individual and is seen, for example, in personality typologies, temperament, unresolved conflicts, and defense mechanisms.

The relationship between progress along normal developmental lines and psychopathology is most clearly seen in Anna Freud (1965) and Mahler (1968). The normal and pathological developmental lines are theoretically and clinically intertwined. If a child's environment produces difficulty in one or several lines of development, it is assumed that the child now has a psychopathological problem. Psychotherapy is recommended for the psychopathological state. The goal of psychotherapy is the removal of the blockage and the easing of the child back into normal, or healthy, development. Because both approaches are based on extensive clinical experience with seriously disturbed children, the child is easily labeled psychopathological. Almost any trauma can force the child out of normal developmental lines. In these situations, children could potentially cope successfully if there was any external (psychotherapeutic) intervention. Unfortunately, there is insufficient data to confirm either point of view.

As Michels has stated in chapter 8, psychoanalysts have assumed that the difference between normal and disturbed individuals is one of degree of experiencing and defending against troubles rather than a substantive difference in quality of experience. Psychopathology is marked by the same troubles as normality, only worse. Current biological thinking takes a major exception to this statement. Many leading biological psychiatrists feel that mental illness is present in individuals only when, or if, distinct biological markers are present. Or to put it differently, individuals are mentally healthy, or normal, from a medical-psychiatric point of view if all the present and future biological tests (endocrinological, electrophysiological, biochemical, etc.) cannot distinguish them from a nonpatient population. It is important to add that the risk for mental illness is also part of the biological perspective. Hence if a person has one parent who suffered, for example, from an affective disorder, that person will have certain discernible genetic biological findings. (See chapter 10 for a detailed discussion.) Biological psychiatrists utilize the normality as health perspective, which suggests a qualitative difference between the mentally healthy and the mentally ill. We are in agreement with Michels about psychoanalysis being primarily about inner mental life and only secondarily about behavior. Thus we assume that psychoanalysis is limited in what it can state about social and/or biological aspects of behavior, for its theory does not have the data base to be applicable to the full range of normal development. In this context, psychoanalytic theory cannot be a general psychology.

Psychoanalysts can, of course, from their in-depth experience with psychiatrically disturbed patients, present us with important hypotheses that can be tested using other behavioral science methods. This give-and-take between psychoanalysis and other behavioral and social sciences can be optimal for the development of newer theories of human development. The fact that psychoanalytic theory has often been used as a baseline for normal development has, at times, served to confuse those investigators who attempted to separate data from theoretical speculation. In addition, if, as Michels feels, the major function of psychoanalytic theory is to facilitate the psychoanalytic treatment of patients, further questions can be raised concerning the relevance of psychoanalytic theory to a theory of normal development. Psychoanalytic psychotherapy is a procedure aimed at understanding and helping individuals. It is difficult to envision a theory that purports to be so all-encompassing that it can explain clinical practice, psychopathology, and normal development, all with one broad conceptual swoop.*

Finally, we believe that there is an additional problem in generalizing from psychoanalytic data to the whole life cycle. The vast majority of psychoanalytic data come from direct clinical contact with individuals during the third and fourth decade in life. Relatively few children and adolescents, and virtually no infants and senior adults, have ever been psychoanalyzed. Hence there is little direct clinical data from which to draw conclusions about these populations. Psychoanalysis is a complex treatment applicable to only very specific situations. It cannot be considered an in-depth, random study of the men and women of the world, or even the Western world. Psychoanalysis has taught us much about hu-

---

*In a recent paper Wallerstein (1983) compares psychoanalytic therapy with other forms of treatment. Wallerstein discusses the lack of congruence between theory and practice in psychoanalysis.

man being's inner world, but the breadth of its applicability remains to be studied empirically.

Two articles discuss the meaning and relevance of the concept of normality for psychoanalytic treatment and theory (Abrams 1976; Joseph 1982). Similar to Michels, Abrams and Joseph believe that the term normality is confusing and is used to convey a host of different meanings. Abrams in particular believes that the concept is misleading because it is borrowed from other disciplines. In psychoanalysis proper normality is in continuous flux both internally and in its various interactive modalities with the environment. Abrams is unable to distinguish clinical (i.e., psychopathological) phenomena from normal (i.e., nonpatient-based) phenomena. Hence he has not succeeded in developing a nonpathologically-based concept of normality. On the other hand, Joseph is much more aware of the complexities of the term's usage. He, too, uses clinical example to highlight his interest in the concept. However, he carefully describes all four perspectives of normality and shows how they are relevant to psychoanalytic theory. Joseph finds the normality as transactional processes perspective the most relevant for current psychoanalytic theory, although he can see the usefulness of each of the others for cross-sectional studies. Both Abrams and Joseph believe that psychoanalytic theory of normality has to be brought up to date. However, neither indicates that psychoanalysis is a discipline that can benefit significantly from data obtained from other behavioral sciences. They believe that whatever the problem is, psychoanalysts should be able to solve it, using their method and their theory.

Adaptation: Whose Concept Is It?

Much current theory-building in normal human development prescribes for individuals how they should adapt. This is done in order to ensure both that the individual *fits* in and that society runs smoothly. Theories of culture and personality and of ego psychology emphasize successful adaptation to the external world of reality, a process that begins early and continues throughout life. Development is then conceived of as a series of stages through which all individuals pass, some progressing further than others. For example, consider the work of the following researchers with individuals from a variety of age groups: Blos (1962); Brazelton (1961); Erikson (1968); A. Freud (1965); Guttmann (1977); Keniston (1968); Levinson et al. (1978); Loevinger (1976); Piaget (1950); and Vaillant (1977). The emphasis in these studies and the theoretical treatise built on them is on invariant sequences of steps common to all people. The evidence for this sequencing, and, more important, its universality, is not strong. An individual who progressed successfully through the Eriksonian stages would move from infancy through childhood, adolescence, and young adulthood toward the occupational community where autonomy, initiative, and industry are highly valued. The person would be resourceful and self-reliant, virtues that well served frontier Americans and that are deeply entrenched in the Protestant work ethic. How such an independent individual would do in relating to other people in mentally healthy adult mutual dependence, in sharing closely in other people's lives, is another question. Erikson (1950) defines intimacy, his stage for young adulthood, as "the capacity to commit [oneself] to concrete affiliations and partnerships and to develop the ethical strength to abide by such commitments, even though they may call for significant sacrifices and compromises" (p. 263). That is calculated language indeed to describe intimacy, terms that sound more like a legal contract in which morally binding obligation is the defining factor.

Adaptation became a concept central to ego psychology when Freudian thought emigrated to the United States (Hartmann [1938] 1958). The idea of adaptation is eminently American. The United States has been seen as the land of immigrants, the melting pot where diverse peoples have striven not only to be equal but in a sense to be alike. In the United States, ego psychologists made their goal of psychotherapy a reflection of the culturally encouraged virtue of fitting in—getting the patient to adapt to the environment.

When adaptation is the therapeutic goal, the obvious question becomes: To what should the patient adapt? What is a healthy environment? Neurosis is adaptation to reality, but it is not advocated as health. Simply to adapt successfully to an environment by definition makes for individual adjustment, but it may not make for personal experience that is felt to be desirable. How does one decide what reality is best for healthy adaptation? The values underlying Erikson's ideal environment and his ideal route toward adaptation are all-American. They are the values of the United States, the land of unlimited opportunity, where moving up the ladder of success is a dominant theme, whether that ladder be career, marriage market, or individual development.

Erikson's theories were intricately shaped by the political climate of his youth. World War I, the war to end all wars, was concluded with a strong note of optimism that uplifted the general population. Theories about human nature rejected the pessimistic Freudian view about man. They allowed one to think optimistically about the future and seemed to give ethical mandate for individuals. This system, although not empirically based, became the one Erikson found so appealing in American culture two decades later.

However, it would be a mistake to ascribe all the "positive" concepts about human development to Erikson. Carl Rogers (pers. com. 1982) was known to have said that his theories concerning self-actualization and the ultimate goodness of man came at the right historical time, because after World War II people were tired of hearing about Freud's death instinct. They wanted to hear something more positive. The same can also be said about Kohut (1971, 1977), whose theories about human psychology and development have a definite optimistic ring to them. Kohut speaks out strongly against a basic aggressive drive, and he stresses the positive transformation of drive and affect in the course of the life cycle.

The American values espoused by Erikson and others were embedded in the language of ego psychology. For ego psychologists, the task of development—and they emphasize *task*, in the sense of a job well done, work to be completed—is the promotion of ego autonomy, an adaptive state in which the individual continually struggles to maintain relative independence in the face of potentially conflictual forces arising from within and without. This beleaguered individual is a Freudianized version of the American pioneer, heading for the unknown of the West, unaided and undeterred. American pragmatism always carried with it the belief that anything was "do-able" and within reach. If it also had a slight cheery tune to it, it was only because of the American's blanket rejection of "man's darker side."* Of course, there is great reward for American individuals to internalize such attitudes—they are valued highly in the occupational system. However, the point is that Erikson's stages are rooted in the values of ego psychology, American style. These values are not right or wrong. They are relative. Another set of values could lead to the positing of a different series of stages, different sets for ideal development, seen as successful adaptation to culture. In fact, even as cultural constructs, Erikson's stages are cohort-bound and would have to be revised in light of changing cultural values. Erikson builds his theoretical system on his notions of the social constructs, the norms, values, and expectations inherent in ego psychology and compatible with American ideals. It is an open question to what extent and in what ways individuals actually internalize these social constructs. Only by studying diverse

* Bertrand Russell was once asked to compare American and French character. He replied: "A French farmer would *do* things for money that an American farmer has not even dreamt of!"

groups of normal and disturbed individuals and observing their personalized interactions with the micro- and macrosocial order will it be possible to build a comprehensive theory of human development.

The Family in the Context of Human Development

In the context of the microsocial order, it is obvious that the family also has to be carefully investigated for its role in human development. Each family has its own structure that shapes the functions of its individual members. The family is more than a passive conveyer of cultural norms. It interacts with its individual members, helping some grow, inhibiting maturation of others, and being on the emotional sidelines for still others. Developmental processes, then, have to be seen as being continuously influenced and influencing a host of biopsychosocial variables over time.

A review of the clinical literature of the past three decades clearly indicates that families containing disturbed children and adolescents have been described as disturbed social systems. The inability to communicate basic values, beliefs, and affect within the family has long been thought to be a corollary of mental illness and deviant behavior. Most of the research in the area of family functioning, however, has been on disturbed families. The assumption has been that well-functioning families are the antithesis of those with overt psychopathology. Only recently has a systematic attempt to discuss the normal family begun. Obviously an understanding of normal family processes is essential to the understanding of families with disturbed children and adolescents, since there is a continuing need for the diagnosis and treatment of mentally ill children, adolescents, and their parents. If mental health professionals are not aware of what normal family processes are, it will be difficult indeed for them to determine what is psychopathological.

Similarly, there have been recent attempts to better understand the process of parenthood. In a recently published book, one of us wrote:

Parenthood as a specific psychological event for *both* generations has been an extremely difficult phenomenon to observe and/or study. There have been studies on the impact that being a parent has on parents. There have been many studies on how parents influence their children. However, we do not have, to date, direct observational studies on reciprocal relationships between children and their parents and how the nature of the interaction influences mental health or mental illness in either parent and/or child. From an experimental research point of view, then, parenthood remains a phenomenon as it was in years gone by. Before we can seriously embark on new ventures in raising children and improving the parent-child relationship, it is incumbent upon us to find methods which will enable us to study parenting. These methods are needed in order to help us determine what went wrong and why in a particular family. For example, why do certain children seem to be relatively healthy despite growing up in a disturbing familial environment? Once we understand the complexities of the present situation better, we should be able to raise a generation which can cope better with modern life than their parents did. (Offer 1984, p. 4)

It is essential for us, as behavioral and social scientists, to develop appropriate methodology in order to discover how the normal parent or family affects its members, how a normal individual grows up within a disturbed (or deviant) family.*

Toward a Multiple Pathway Theory of Normal Development: Examples from Studies of Adolescents

INTRODUCTION TO THE ADOLESCENT PROJECT

According to the mythology of our field, deviant development is more complex, interesting, and has a larger number of different patterns (diagnoses) than normal development. But where did this mythology come from?

First, it is apparent that the relative paucity of studies of normal populations have led to a notion that these people essentially are a homogenous group who do not need much investigation. Embedded within this concept is the notion that people with psychopathology exhibit much more mercurial behavior and show extraordinary variance in all sorts of behavioral variables. It is assumed that normals, showing less variation, are much more similar to each other.

Second, it is apparent that many, following Dostoevsky's lead, view the normal person as uninteresting, boring, and plodding. This view is still very common, even in American society. It's as if the world consists of an elite who are exciting and far different from the ordinary or normal person. The normal person, hence, must be relatively simple and be part of a homogenous group. For all of these reasons, and in the absence of empirical studies, the mythology has tended to persist; and in this volume we have indicated why this mythology needs debunking.

---

*See Cohen, Weissman, and Cohler, (1984); Lewis et al. (1976); and Walsh (1982), all works that grapple with these most interesting dilemmas.

It should also be noted that gross heterogeneity of normal populations can be seen by looking cross-culturally. The variation in normal behavior from rural parts of the third world (e.g., a farmer living in rural Pakistan) to a wealthy businessman in New York City is quite obviously large. The mythology and perhaps theoretical blind spots have made us underemphasize that difference. In fact, it is quite likely that cross-cultural studies of normal populations would show almost an infinite variation in combinations of psychosocial variables. In fact, it may be that there is greater homogeneity in the severely ill patient population because of the greater impact of biological factors in illness. An illness may be seen as a constricting phenomenon that limits varieties of behavior rather than as something leading to more diverse, mercurial, and heterogeneous behavior.

To put it in a different context, the third edition of the *Diagnostic and Statistical Manual of Mental Disorders* (1980) describes many different psychiatric diagnoses. These diagnoses cover approximately 5 percent of the American population. In order to have a reasonable understanding of the complexity of social and behavioral charateristics of the remaining 95 percent of the people living in the United States, we would need nineteen additional volumes.

Other mental health theoreticians have made note of this same observation. For example, Kohut (1983) has stated: "First of all, it must be admitted that Normality is often a (almost unfathomably) complex state—more complex at any rate than those forms of psychopathology which rest on regression and primitivization" (p. 3). Garmezy (1982) has said: "'Vulnerables' have long been the province of our mental health disciplines; but prolonged neglect of the 'invulnerable' child—the healthy child in an unhealthy setting—has provided us with a false sense of security in erecting prevention models that are founded more on values than on facts" (p. 5).

ᵥIt has also generally been assumed that there is one route for normal development. Very few studies (Block 1971; Offer and Offer 1975) suggest that there is more than one developmental pattern for normal individuals. An example from our research will illustrate the variety of growth patterns among a group of essentially normal adolescents. We will not discuss here the selection of the group, the methodology, and the problems with the research as this has been discussed extensively in previous publications (Offer 1969; Offer and Offer 1975). We will briefly outline the background of the research, summarize the major findings, and finally discuss the implications of the results.

The purpose of the research program was to investigate the psychosocial development of normal adolescent males. The subjects were selected based on the normality as average perspective. In addition, they were physically healthy individuals. Within this psychosocially relatively uniform group of individuals, three normal developmental lines unfolded over the decade. The normality as health perspective would not be adequate for describing the three routes. The selected subjects were not ideal types, constructed as prototypic of what theoretically should take place. In addition, there were three distinct groups so that depending on one's ideology and philosophy of life, one group might be chosen over the other. But that would clearly violate a scientific dictum, that the observer should not make ethical or value judgments concerning the data. The reader, or the public, should be left with this prerogative. The normality as utopia perspective would not describe our empirical findings either. The three normal growth patterns were identified through statistical scores on a variety of tests and measurements. They combined factors such as childrearing practices; genetic background; experiential and traumatic factors; cultural, social, and familial surroundings; coping mechanisms; ideals; peer relationships; fantasy life; and basic personality structure. These three groups are only operational in the sample of normal, white, middle-class American male adolescents. How generalizable the theory is, is open to empirical testing.* The important fact is that there is more than one development route for normal subjects. We do not have an all-encompassing theory to account for all three routes. We believe that the discussions in the developmental psychology literature regarding continuity versus discontinuity in development is a moot one, since our data clearly show that both developmental routes are present in normal individuals.

Continuous Growth.   Among our adolescent subjects this pattern reflected the purest of the normality as health perspective. The subjects presented with an absence of even a mild behavioral or emotional crisis. They progressed throughout adolescence and young manhood with a smoothness of purpose and a self-assurance of their progression toward a meaningful and fulfilling adult life. These subjects were favored by environmental circumstances. Their genetic and familial backgrounds were excellent. Their childhood had been unmarked by death or serious illnesses of a parent or sibling, and the nuclear family remained a stable unit throughout their childhood and adolescence. The continuous-growth subjects had mastered previous developmental stages without serious setbacks. They were able to cope with internal and external stimuli through an adaptive combination of reason and emotional expression. These subjects accepted general cultural and societal norms and felt

---

*In a recent study of normal early adolescent (ages eleven to thirteen) females, Petersen (1982) has found similar routing patterns.

comfortable within this context. They had a capacity to integrate experiences and use them as a stimulus for growth.

The parents of these subjects were able to encourage their children's independence; the parents themselves grew and changed with their children. Throughout the study, there was basic mutual trust, respect, and affection between the generations. The sense of gratification was reciprocal, with the son gaining from the parents; and the parental willingness to allow their sons to create their own individual lives outside of the household made the parents feel good about themselves. The value system of the subjects in this group dovetailed with that of their parents. In many ways, the young men were functioning as continuations of the parents, living out not so much lives the parents had wished for but not attained but rather lives similar to those of the parents.

In their interpersonal relationships, the subjects showed a capacity for good object relationships. They had close male friends in whom they could confide. Relationships with the opposite sex became increasingly important as they reached the post–high school years. By the subjects' fourth post–high school year, intimacy with the opposite sex was developing and was a goal toward which these subjects strove.

Subjects described by the continuous-growth pattern acted in accordance with their consciences, developing meaningful ego ideals, often persons whom they knew and admired within the larger family or school community. These subjects were able to identify feelings of shame and guilt, and proceeded to explain not only how the experiences provoking these responses had affected them but also how they brought closure to the uncomfortable situations. If a second similar experience was described by these young men, it was one that they had been prepared to handle better, putting the earlier upsetting experience into a past time frame of immaturity conquered.

The young men's fantasy lives were relatively active, almost always giving in to reality and action. They could dream about being the best in the class academically, sexually, or athletically, although their actions would be guided by a pragmatic and realistic appraisal of their own abilities and of external circumstances. Thus they were protected from meeting with repeated disappointments.

The subjects were able to cope with external trauma, usually through an adaptive action orientation. When difficulties arose, they used the defenses of denial and isolation to protect their ego from being bombarded with affect. They could postpone immediate gratification and work in a sustained manner toward a future goal. They were generally successful in responding to their aggressive and sexual impulses without being overwhelmed or acting-out in a self-destructive manner. Their delay mechanisms including temporary suppression of affect (rather than repression) worked successfully. They did not usually experience prolonged periods of anxiety or depression, two of the most common affects described by the entire subject population, including this subgroup. In general, these young men had an order to their lives that, while it could be interrupted, would not yield to states of symptomatology or chaotic behavior as they grew older and matured cognitively and emotionally.

Surgent Growth. Subjects in this growth pattern showed some quantitative changes as they moved through adolescence. However, they still exhibited a significant lack of behavioral or emotional crisis. The surgent-growth group, although functioning as adaptively as the first group, was characterized by important enough differences in personality, background, and family environment to present a different cluster and thus be defined as a different subgroup. Developmental spurts are illustrative of the pattern of growth of the surgent-growth group. These subjects differed in the amount of emotional conflict experienced and in their patterns of resolving conflicts. They directed more concentrated energy toward mastering developmental tasks than members of the continuous-growth group. At times, these subjects were adjusting very well, integrating their experiences and moving ahead, and at other times, they seemed to be stuck at an almost "premature closure" and unable to move forward. A cycle of progression and regression is more typical of this group than of the first group. The defenses they used, anger and projection, represent more potential psychopathology in the sense that they represented poorer impulse control.

One of the major differences between the surgent-growth subjects and those in the continuous-growth group was that their genetic and/or environmental background was not as free of problems and traumas; the nuclear family of surgent-growth group members was more likely to have been affected by separation, death, or severe illness.

The affects of these subjects, which were usually flexible and available, would become stringently controlled at times of crisis, such as the death of a close relative. This, together with the fact that they were not as action oriented as the first group, made surgent-growth group members slightly more prone to depression. The depression would accompany or openly follow the highly controlled behavior. On other occasions when their defense mechanisms faltered, they experienced moderate anxiety, and a short period of turmoil resulted. When disappointed in themselves or others, they tended to use projection and anger.

These subjects were not as confident as were the young men in the continuous-growth group; their self-esteem wavered. They relied on positive reinforcement from important others, such as parents and/or peers.

When this was not forthcoming, they often became discouraged about themselves and their abilities. As a group, they were able to form meaningful interpersonal relationships, similar to those of individuals in the continuous-growth group. The relationships, however, would be maintained with a greater degree of effort.

For surgent-growth group members, relationships with parents were marked by conflicts of opinions and values. There were areas of disagreement between father and mother concerning basic issues, such as the importance of discipline, academic attainments, or religious beliefs. In several cases the parents came from different backgrounds. The mothers of some of these subjects had difficulty in letting their children grow and separate from them.

Some subjects in this group were afraid of emerging sexual feelings and impulses. For most of these young adults, meaningful relationships with the opposite sex began relatively late; a small subgroup of these adolescents started experimenting with sexuality early in high school, possibly due to a counterphobic defense. These early sexual relationships were not lasting, although they could be helpful in overcoming anxiety concerning sexuality.

The group as a whole was less introspective than either the first or the third group. Overall adjustment of these subjects was often just as adaptive and successful as that of the first group. The adjustment was achieved, though, with less self-examination and a more controlled drive or surge toward development, with suppression of emotionality.

Tumultuous Growth. Subjects in this growth pattern showed qualitative changes in development through adolescence. Thus we have, with this group of adolescents, subjects *within the normal sample* who definitely show a crisis in their behavior and/or emotional state. The pattern, was continuously tumultuous. The subjects, did not change behaviorally or emotionally as they grew into young-adulthood. Whether this pattern will be with them throughout their lives we do not know. This growth group is almost identical to the adolescents so often described in psychiatric, psychoanalytic, and social science literature. These are the children who go through adolescence with much internal turmoil that manifests itself in overt behavioral problems in school and at home. Subjects characterized by a tumultuous growth pattern were those who experienced the years from fourteen to twenty-two as a period of discordance, as a transitional period for which their defenses needed mobilizing and their adaptations needed strengthening.

The subjects demonstrating tumultuous growth patterns came from less stable backgrounds than did subjects in the other two groups. Some of the parents in this group had overt marital conflicts, and others had a history of familial mental illness. Hence the genetic and environmental backgrounds of subjects in the tumultuous-growth group were decidedly different from those of the other two groups.

The tumultuous-growth group experienced more events as major psychological trauma. Difficulties in their life situations were greater than satisfactions. Their defenses for handling emotionally trying situations were not well developed. Strong family bonds, however, were present within the tumultuous-growth subjects, as they were within each of the other groups.

Many subjects in this group were highly sensitive and introspective. They were usually aware of their emotional needs. Academically, they were less interested in science, engineering, law, and medicine, and preferred the arts, the humanities, or the social and psychological sciences.

Those adolescents in this group experienced more psychological pain than did the others; however, as a group they were no less well adjusted in terms of overall functioning within their respective environmental settings than were the persons in the continuous- and surgent-growth groups. They were less happy with themselves, more critical of their social environment, but just as successful academically or vocationally.

In this group action was accompanied by more anxiety and depression than in the other two groups. Emotional turmoil was part of these adolescents' separation and individuation process. Without the tumult, growth toward independence and meaningful interpersonal relationship was doubtful. Subjects showed mood swings in statements indicating their search for who they were as separate individuals and their questioning whether their activities were worthwhile. This group often expressed feelings of mistrusting the adult world. Affect was available and created both intensely pleasurable and painful experiences. Changes in self-concept could precipitate moderately severe anxiety reactions. These subjects were considerably more dependent on peer culture than were their age-mates in the other groups, possibly because they received less gratification from their relationships within the family.

The tumultuous-growth group subjects began dating activities at a younger age than had their peers in the first two groups. In early adolescence, their relationships with females were dependency relationships, with the females being a substitute for a mothering figure. In late adolescence, for some, heterosexual relationships gained meaning, and they were able to appreciate the personal characteristics of their female friends and move toward intimate relationships with members of the opposite sex.

GENERAL FINDINGS OF THE ADOLESCENT PROJECT

The subjects presented differ in affect, defenses, openness, interpersonal relationships as well as environmental circumstances. We might hypothesize an ideal that would be chosen from among the characteristics of all three groups, but we do not know enough about the realities of adolescence and young manhood, let alone the ideals. If we opt for contentment with self as a valid ideal, then the continuous-growth group may well be the group to be emulated. If we choose to say that maturity comes from growth through conflict, then both the surgent- and tumultuous-growth groups become the ideal. If we are after artistic talent, then the tumultuous group is our choice; and if we look for the future leaders in business, law, and engineering, the continuous-growth group is our choice.

In the study we divested ourselves of the notion that there exists *one* group of normal adolescent males. Even though our group was relatively uniform socioeconomically, we were looking for diversity among the normal adolescent, middle-class male population. We found three different growth patterns. We strongly believe that the diversity would grow exponentially as we expand our studies to include other age groups, both genders, all socioeconomic and ethnic strata, and the main cultures in the world today.

Every stage of life brings new challenges and opportunities. Meeting them leads to changes in one's basic personality structures that are a function of the successes and failures during that stage. Many developmental theorists view adolescence as a transitional stage, a period that stresses change rather than stability. But we maintain that this viewpoint is not helpful, it leaves many questions unanswered. It makes it much harder to arrive at psychiatrically meaningful diagnosis and end points for psychotherapeutic interventions. Meaningful psychiatric yardsticks seem to disappear with a notion that emotional turmoil is the password for adolescence or any other transitional stage. While it is true that, for example, adolescents have to learn how to cope with special problems that come their way during the high school years, most are stable and cope well. Adolescence is probably no more "transitional" in nature than other times in the life cycle when the individual has to meet special problems, such as midlife, menopause, or retirement. Much has been written in this book about childhood, adolescence, and the stages of adulthood. However, it is apparent that in both infancy and old age people have much more "objective" crises to overcome than any other stage in the life cycle. At any stage in life, psychiatric difficulties more often than not have roots in the past. For example, if an individual is unable to develop meaningful and gratifying interpersonal relationships at a particular stage in life, then it is assumed that he or she most probably had a poor relationship with parents in the past. A lonely, isolated, depressed person often needs to recreate his or her personal past and resolve it before current psychiatric difficulties can be overcome. In making these statements we are aware that our clinical experiences with disturbed adolescents come to the fore. The degree of applicability to normal adolescents, however, is much more difficult to deduce and awaits further empirical clarification.

Fundamentally, we believe that case examples about normality pose special problems. We argue against the use of "great men" examples as typifying normal development. We emphasize the diversity among normal individuals, a diversity that is at least as complex as the one found in the DSM-III for psychiatric patients. Also, we argue for a pluralistic theory of normal development throughout the life cycle. When investigators divest themselves of homogenous developmental theory and study the normal population over a significant time span, the empirical evidence tends to support the multiple pathway theory.

Certainly we recognize that lives of normal people may be quiet and rather ordinary. Some people may show stability of character, affect, and cognition, and others may not. It is one of the tasks of the mental health professional of the future to discover who is stable and who is not, under which circumstances, and why. We reject the notion that the prototypic normal person is dull and unimaginative, just as we reject the "great man" theory (i.e., that only great men can have "meaningful" experiences with universal significance). We do not believe, as Dostoyevsky said in *Crime and Punishment*, that "A normal man, it is true, hardly exists." Rather we believe that there are variegated typologies of normal behavior. They are out there and they await our discovery.

REFERENCES

Abrams, S. 1976. "The Psychoanalytic Normalities." Paper presented at the American Psychoanalytic Association's Panel, New York City, December 17.

Block, J. 1971. *Lives Through Time*. Berkeley, Calif.: Bancroft Books.

Blos, P. 1962. *On Adolescence*. New York: Free Press.

Brazelton, T. B. 1961. "Psychophysiologic Reaction in the Neonate. II. The Effects of Maternal Medication on the Neonate and His Behavior." *Journal of Pediatrics* 58:513–18.

———. 1973. "Neonatal Behavioral Assessment Scale." *Clinics in Developmental Medicine* 50. London: Spastics International Medical Publications.

Cohen, R.; Weissman, S.; and Cohler, B. J. eds., 1984. *Parenthood as an Adult Experience.* New York: Guilford Press.

Cohler, B. J. 1981. "Personal Narrative and Life-Course." In *Life-Span Development and Behavior,* vol. 4, ed. P. Baltes and O. G. Brim, Jr., pp. 205–41. New York: Academic Press.

Diagnostic and Statistical Manual of Mental Disorders (DSM-III), 3rd ed. 1980. Washington, D.C.: American Psychiatric Association.

Elder, G. 1974. *Children of the Great Depression.* Chicago: University of Chicago Press.

Erikson, E. H. 1950. *Childhood and Society.* New York: W. W. Norton.

————. 1958. *Young Man Luther: A Study in Psychoanalysis and History.* New York: W. W. Norton.

————. 1968. *Identity: Youth and Crisis.* New York: W. W. Norton.

Freud, A. 1965. *Normality and Pathology in Childhood.* New York: International Universities Press.

Freud, S. [1937] 1959. "Analysis Terminable and Interminable." In *Collected Papers of Sigmund Freud,* vol. 5, ed. J. Strachey, pp. 316–58. New York: Basic Books.

Gergen, K. J. 1981. "The Emerging Crisis in Life-Span Development Theory." In *Life-Span Development and Behavior,* vol. 3, ed. P. B. Baltes and O. G. Brim, Jr., pp. 31–63. New York: Academic Press.

Gould, R. L. 1978. *Transformations: Growth and Change in Adult Life.* New York: Simon & Schuster.

Gubrium, J. F., and Buckholdt, D. R. 1977. *Toward Maturity.* San Francisco: Jossey-Bass.

Guttmann, D. 1977. "The Cross-Cultural Perspective: Notes Toward a Comparative Psychology of Aging." In *Handbook of the Psychology of Aging,* ed. J. Birren and K. W. Schaie, pp. 302–26. New York: Van Nostrand Rinehold.

Hall, G. S. 1904. *Adolescence.* New York: Appleton.

Hartmann, H. [1938] 1958. *Ego Psychology and the Problem of Adaptation.* New York: International Universities Press.

James, W. 1892. *Psychology, Briefer Course.* New York: Henry Holt.

Joseph, E. D. 1982. "Presidential Address." *International Journal of Psychoanalysis* 63:3–13.

Kagan, J. 1979a. "Overview: Perspectives on Human Infancy." In *The Handbook of Infant Development,* ed. J. Osofsky, pp. 1–25. New York: Wiley-Interscience.

————. 1979b. "The Form of Early Development." *Archives of General Psychiatry* 36:1047–54.

Keniston, K. 1968. *Young Radicals: Notes on Committed Youth.* New York: Harcourt, Brace.

Kohut, H. 1971. *The Analysis of the Self.* New York: International Universities Press.

————. 1977. *The Restoration of the Self.* New York: International Universities Press.

————. 1983. "On Courage." Unpublished. Chicago, Ill.

Lieberson, J. 1982. "The Romantic Rationalist." *New York Review of Books,* December 2.

Levinson, D., et al. 1978. *The Seasons of a Man's Life.* New York: Knopf.

Lewis, J. M., et al. 1976. *No Single Thread: Psychological Health in Family Systems.* New York: Brunner/Mazel.

Loeninger, J. 1976. *Ego Development: Conceptions and Theories.* San Francisco: Jossey-Bass.

Mahler, M. 1968. *On Human Symbiosis and the Vicissitudes of Individuation.* New York: International Universities Press.

Murphy, E. A. 1979. "The Epistemology of Normality." *Psychological Medicine* 9:409–15.

Mussen, P., et al. 1980. "Continuity and Change in Women's Characteristics Over Four Decades." *International Journal of Behavioral Development* 3:333–47.

Offer, D. 1969. *The Psychological World of the Teenager: A Study of Normal Adolescent Boys.* New York: Basic Books.

————. 1984. Preface to *Parenthood as an Adult Experience,* ed. R. Cohen, S. Weissman, and B. J. Cohler. New York: Guilford Press.

Offer, D., and Offer, J. B. 1975. *From Teenage to Young Manhood: A Psychological Study.* New York: Basic Books.

Offer, D.; Ostrov, E.; and Howard, K. I. 1981. *The Adolescent: A Psychological Self-Portrait.* New York: Basic Books.

Peterson, A. C. 1982. "The Early Adolescent Girls." Paper presented at the Department of Psychiatry Meeting of Michael Reese Hospital and Medical Center, Chicago, Ill., January.

Roazen, P. 1980. "Erik H. Erikson's America: The Political Implications of Ego Psychology." *Journal of History of Behavioral Science* 16:333–41.

Strozier, C. B. 1984. "Erikson's Notions on Psycho-History." In *Psychoanalytic Studies of Leadership*, ed. C. B. Strozier, and D. Offer. New York: Plenum. In press.

Vaillant, G. E. 1977. *Adaptation to Life*. Boston: Little, Brown.

Wallerstein, R. S. 1983. "Psychotherapy and Psychoanalysis: Change Agents in Adulthood." Presented as a Plenary Address at the conference on creativity and challenges of the adult experience, Michael Reese Hospital and Medical Center, Department of Psychiatry, Chicago, Ill., March 19.

Walsh, F. ed., 1983. *Normal Family Process*. New York: Guilford Press.

Daniel Offer
and Melvin Sabshin

Implications and New Directions

Normality and Psychiatric Care in the 1980s

The policy implications of the concept of normality penetrate deeply into the fabric of social and economic forces affecting psychiatric treatment in the United States and, indeed, in every country in the world. In the United States, the boundaries of psychopathology have tended to be defined more broadly than anywhere else. As fiscal expenditures for psychiatric treatment have risen, concerns by governmental agencies and insurance carriers have become stronger and more vehement. Frequently representatives of the insurance industry have characterized psychiatric illness as a "bottomless pit"; their insistence on objective criteria for reimbursement and for a more precise nosology have become more pronounced.

A current study (Veroff, Douvan, Kulka 1981) found that in the last two decades (1956–1976) there has been a dramatic increase in the number of people seeking professional help in the mental health field. There has also been a decrease in the number of people who deny that there are problems in their lives. This reflects what the authors call the current "psychological error" in which mental health professionals have been invested with tremendous expectations that they can indeed help people improve their lives. Most interesting, Veroff, Douvan, and Kulka have also found that considerably more lower-class people get psychotherapy now than ever before. The need to conduct epidemiological investigations of prevalence and incidence of the full range of mental health *and* illness across class lines is even more apparent. Knowledge of incidence will assist health planners, insurance agencies, and governmental bodies to make more rational decisions.

In defending the 1981 cutbacks at a May congressional hearing, the Office of Personnel Management's Gary Nelson (1981) said that "mental conditions do not lend themselves to definitive diagnoses or courses of treatment, making it virtually impossible to effectively control utilization." Many insurers share this view. Although most patients would resist inappropriate inpatient psychiatric care, one insurance executive noted, the use of outpatient psychotherapy is almost impossible to control; it could continue twice a week for the next ten years. Fears were also expressed that many people interested in "personality enhancement" would create totally unpredictable demand. One suggested solution was that Blue Cross and Blue Shield Insurance Company programs for federal employees "own" a 50 percent co-payment to assure that the patient assumed a large enough share of the burden to guarantee seriousness of intent.

In response, the American Psychiatric Association points out (McGrath 1981) that within the Blue Cross and Blue Shield federal program, the cost for psychiatric services has remained constant for ten years. Furthermore, diagnoses are becoming more exact due to the DSM-III; studies show that three out of four persons who see a psychiatrist have moderate-to-severe diagnoses and psychotherapy is an effective treatment. In addition, psychiatrists point to a number of studies (e.g., Schlesinger et al. 1983) suggesting that patients receiving psychotherapy actually use fewer other medical services as a result. This offset may be due to the emotional origins of many physical disorders. Therefore, a reduction in mental health benefits actually could result in greater costs because of the increased use of other medical services.

Over and over again, governmental health policy planners have alleged that too many psychiatrists are working with the "worried well." Fears of a bottomless pit in diagnostic criteria and treatment results have escalated into restrictions on who can be reimbursed for psychiatric treatment. Recently psychologists, social workers, nurses, marriage counselors, ministers, rabbis, and priests as well as nonpsychiatric physicians have all been treating mentally ill patients. Most, if not all, of these professionals have competed with psychiatrists on the open "therapeutic market." They all want part of the insurance dollar. Some work under the supervision of psychiatrists, others work within their own professional milieu. It is an open question whether the different professionals treat patients whose diagnosis or extent of psychopathology is similar. While a comparative study has not been done, it would be of great interest. Or, to put it differently, do some mental health professionals treat essentially normal individuals who are in the process of educating themselves in order to maximize their potential? Obviously one's definition of normality is crucial in determining answers to this question.

One of the basic proposals of this book is for increased research and greater precision in the definition of both mental health and mental illness in a developmental context. Administrators of health delivery systems have a genuine concern that, if psychiatrists and other mental health professionals fail to develop clearer standards, normality as utopia will be perceived as the mode and the fear that there will be no limits to potential costs for psychiatric coverage will prevail.

Since World War II, the broadening boundaries of psychiatry have become reflected in the wider use of the term mental health as a synonym for psychiatry. The growth of a number of mental health disciplines other than psychiatry has indeed been pronounced. Many psychiatrists have become critical of the way the words mental health have been used; and some suggest that it has become an "Achilles' heel" for psychiatry. The criticism comes from the legal-minded psychiatrists whose main concern is the patient's civil rights and not his or her personal welfare (e.g., Szasz 1961). It has recently also come from psychiatrists who see psychiatry as a medical discipline (e.g., Ludwig 1975). They believe that psychiatrists have no business meddling with the patient's psychosocial world. At times, the use of the very term mental health may be utilized in contradictory fashion; when a person receives *mental health* rather than psychiatric treatment, it might be questioned why he or she needs treatment if he or she is mentally healthy. When there is discussion of *mental health* policy, there is ambiguity about whether one is speaking about maintenance of mental health or about treatment of people with severe psychiatric illness. On a worldwide level, using the World Health Organization definition of health, "a state of complete physical, mental and social well-being and not merely the absence of infirmity," as equivalent to our normality as utopia has caused massive policy problems. Even in the United States it would be difficult to envisage, let alone to finance, optimal health for the entire population. In many countries where psychiatry is still at an early stage of development, the talk of optimal health may lead to expectations that are impossible to achieve in the foreseeable future. In many underdeveloped countries, reported incidence and prevalence of neuroses is quite low as compared to the United States. Because of the lack of empirical data, it is highly likely that these discrepancies in incidence and prevalence reflect national policies rather than true incidence. The question of whether these low incidences of patients with psychological problems is only observed in underdeveloped countries has been further complicated by MacDonald's (1982) recent book. MacDonald classifies the cases treated by the Reverend R. Napier from 1597 to 1634 in England. Altogether Napier described 60 thousand consultations of both physical and psychiatric nature. MacDonald classifies only 5 percent of Napier's patients as suffering from mental, as opposed to physical, illness. The mental health picture in preindustrial England is similar to what is observed nowadays in underdeveloped countries. It is important to note that, according to Stone (1982), preindustrial England was also: ". . . a world of suspicion, intrigue, petty jealousy, sudden brawls, and vindictive revenges for assumed slights or injuries." One might even speculate paradoxically whether the relatively low incidence of mental illness was related to the relatively high incidence of violence and antisocial aggression.

As psychiatrists and other behavioral scientists continue to investigate the incidence of mental health and mental illness in underdeveloped countries, it would be of interest to discover whether the rate of mental illness increases as these countries become more industrialized. At the present time there is little likelihood that psychiatrists in China, India, and other underdeveloped nations will deal with the "worried well"; their emphasis has to involve adequate systems of treatment for those with gross mental symptomatology.

In addition to the scholarly and research benefits from studies of normality through the life cycle, failure to focus on questions we have raised could lead to arbitrary cuts in support of psychiatric treatment. Empirical investigations leading to data-based projections could make a significant difference in the psychiatry of the 1980s, 1990s, and beyond.

As detailed in this book, the vast majority of the samples studied have indeed adjusted well to the environment in which they lived. They coped with the stresses and strains that came their way. They had good relationships with important individuals in their lives and they moved from one stage in the life cycle to another without undue problems. Specifically, in Offer, Ostrov, and Howard study of normal adolescents (1981a), it has been shown that 85 percent of all adolescents studied were reasonably happy and adjusted well to their internal and external environment. The fear that insurance companies and governmental agencies have about a very high percentage of disturbed individuals in the population is empirically unfounded. Indeed, the results gained from the study of adolescents are not isolated findings (see chapter 10). There is good reason to believe that studies throughout the life cycle will support this distinction between health and illness except perhaps for very late old age. Ultimately, the type of data presented herein should have a profound impact on policymakers.

There is also reason to believe that other debates within the mental health professions hinge on the concept of normality. For example, we believe that the debate on whether homosexuality must be classified as an illness hinges in part on underlying concepts of health and normality. Obviously, those who argue for the ubiquity of mental illness would perceive all homosexuals as sick whatever the alleged psychodynamics. There is a need to conduct demographic studies of homosexuals as well as others in the general population throughout the life cycle. Similar policy debates are seen in questions about the incidence and prevalence of mental health in women and in minorities. Both groups have correctly argued against stereotyping and have been very concerned about a reported high incidence of psychopathology; for example, feminists have reacted negatively to assumptions about the ubiquity of mental disease during menopause. At the same time, feminists and minority groups have argued that prejudice, institutional racism, and sexism have produced higher incidence of mental illness. Definitions of mental illness and of normality are crucial to these very important allegations. The need for empirical investigations should also be apparent.

In addition to advocating better epidemiological data for normal behavior and development, we have emphasized that despite their limitations, predictive studies from one developmental stage to the next can add much to our knowledge. For example, what impact does adaptation to crises early in life have on the adaptation to later developmental and adventitious crises? In an interesting study entitled *Vulnerability and Invincibility*, Werner and Smith (1982) studied a group of children born to blue-collar parents of different races. They found that despite backgrounds that some people view as causing vulnerability, their subjects coped well with their internal and external environment. Other studies in different stages of the life cycle have been undertaken. One question they have asked is, Does knowledge about behavior in adolescence prove important in predicting healthier adaptation later in life? The work of Block (1971), Elder (1974), Mussen and associates (1980), and Vaillant (1977), among others, shows the continuity of adaptation from adolescence to adulthood. Much more empirical work is necessary to establish this fact for all stages of the life cycle.

It is noteworthy that a number of critics have tended to project their own concepts that normal people must be dull, conforming, and noncreative (see chapter 12). Occasionally potential investigators resist studies of normality because of this projection. Over and over again in this book the contributors have postulated the heterogeneity and the complexity of normal behavior throughout the life cycle. While relatively homogenous basic personalities may be found in some isolated cultures (Kardiner 1939) overwhelming evidence for diverse pathways exists throughout most of the world. The importance of the policy deliberations makes it necessary for us to attempt to deal with this complexity rather than avoid the problem or project simpleminded values about the concept of normality.

The wide use of psychotherapy (including psychoanalysis) in the United States also poses policy issues that directly relate to our definitions of health and normality. If the end point of psychotherapy is the reestablishment of prior equilibrium, psychotherapy can be briefer and more sharply defined. Those who advocate a more ambitious goal of treatment can be subsumed under the human potential movement. As has been discussed in chapters 10 and 11, this type of treatment, in which well people are helped to become even better adjusted, in an extreme form could be seen as educational counseling rather than psychiatric treatment. However, in the case of a neurosis where an individual functions, but functions poorly, the boundary is fuzzy. The ambitious goal of reducing the vulnerability for future illness for individuals receiving psychotherapy and the equally ambitious goal of optimizing the patient's function at the end of treatment may be resisted by those who pay for those treatments. We do not oppose resources allocated for this purpose, but we are fearful that implicit definitions of normality as utopia can lead to interminable policy problems. If prevalence of mental illness is close to 100 percent, no insurance program could afford the treatment. No country in the world can afford to support psychotherapy for such a large number of potential patients. Furthermore, the normality as utopia perspective can play a role in prolonging psychotherapy and rendering it interminable. Decision makers tend to respond to such ambiguity by making arbitrary decisions for psychiatric coverage. Unless objective criteria, supported by empirical data, can be developed for the small number of individuals who need long-term therapy, we are fearful of preemptory limitations. More explicit criteria for outcome in psychotherapy derived from empirical studies will become even more important in the 1980s. Similar methodological and conceptual problems are present in defining outcome as in carrying out epidemiological studies in the so-called normal population.

Only when we are able to improve the reliability and validity of the criteria for outcome in our treatment modalities will we be able to argue for financial support from governmental and private sources for our efforts. Does intensive psychotherapy (e.g., psychoanalysis) decrease the potential risk for physical illness one, two, or three decades after the treatment has been terminated? There is some evidence that it does (Sharfstein 1978). We need more studies in order to effectively argue our case. We also need more sophisticated financial system analysts who can demonstrate that a successful treatment of a "success-neurosis" saves society money by (1) removing a person from the list of the unemployed; and (2) creating a new source of revenue for society (by enabling the person to pay higher taxes). It is incumbent on psychiatry and the other mental health disciplines to work toward better differentiation of affective treatment, prognosis, and reasonable expectations. The latter is a most difficult question, because what is reasonable for one individual may not be for another. Despite the problems involved, this differentiation is a major priority for our field in the 1980s.

These policy questions are important for a significant number of mental health professionals. Traditionally, normal developmental psychology has been the domain of the psychologist. We expect that psychologists and other mental health professionals will continue to contribute to this field, but we also believe that psychiatrists should participate even more fully with these policy and research questions. Indeed, we believe that psychiatrists' understanding of the full range of psychopathology may help in understanding and classifying more subtle questions of the definitions of normality. On the one hand, psychiatrists have tended to err in emphasizing psychopathology rather than adaptation; greater awareness of this problem should reduce that tendency. On the other hand, psychologists and social workers have tended to shy away from treating the very disturbed (e.g., acutely psychotic or dangerously suicidal). Under these conditions, more subtle and refined assessments of the boundaries between psychopathology and healthy behavior can be accomplished.

It seems important to mention the field of forensic psychiatry. The forensic psychiatrist's or psychologist's definition of normality has direct consequences for understanding patients, the legal ramifications of the case and its impact on society. A current policy debate hinges on one's definition of normality. For example, in some countries opposition to the national political system indicates the presence of psychiatric illness. Even more broadly, the equation of delinquency and crime with mental illness in certain quarters poses similar questions; for example, are all criminals mentally ill? What are the boundaries between mental illness and mental health and criminals? This has also been apparent in aspects of the field of psychiatry and law. The recent trial of John Hinckley has evoked wide national commentary on this question. Just as the definition of psychopathology has broadened steadily in the United States, the definition of "not guilty by reason of insanity" has similarly broadened.

While we respect the judicial system and separate the fundamental role of jurors from experts, we are concerned that differences among psychiatric experts in their definition of normality have tended to affect their testimony more than has been realized. In federal courts, where the burden is placed on prosecutors to prove normality, this problem is greatly enhanced. While we would oppose any attempt to restrict the plea of "not guilty by virtue of insanity" to extreme or egregious cases of insanity (e.g., only to be used when a person cannot distinguish between a human being and an inanimate object), we would also oppose any tendency to imply that all criminality must be a product of mental disease.*

The authors of this volume clearly have a position on some of these policy matters. We believe that defining psychiatric illness as limited to gross psychopathology (e.g., psychosis) would be a serious policy error. We reject the concept of normality as equivalent to the absence of gross psychopathology. At the same time, we deplore the opposite tendencies to view mental illness as essentially universal in any population. The fuzziness of this concept and its impracticality need to be widely understood. Unless there is a greater commitment to investigative research on the question of normality, economic forces will lead to irrational arbitrary decisions of national health policy toward mental health.

Normality, Normal Behavior, and Normal Development

We propose the establishment of a new field that will focus on understanding normality, normal behavior, and normal development. This new field will be called *normatology*. It will incorporate the following four perspectives of normality:

1. *Normality as Health.* This area will emphasize studies of high and low risk for mental health.
2. *Normality as Average.* This area will include studies of individuals who function adequately within their social, cultural, and familial settings.
3. *Normality as Utopia.* In this area, the goals of development and questions relating to how an ideal person behaves will be explored.
4. *Normality as Transactional Systems.* Studies in this area will focus on what is expected within each specific stage and how the stages interact throughout personal and historical time.

*For an up-to-date discussion of the complexities of the insanity defense and suggestions for new approaches, see the American Psychiatric Association's position statement on the Insanity Defense (1982).

The purpose of the new field will be to:

1. Encourage more empirical studies of normality, normal behavior, and normal development.
2. Establish criteria regarding normality, normal behavior, and normal development.
3. Utilize the four perspectives of normality in order to distinguish between the theoretical and the empirical.
4. Encourage multidisciplinary studies of normality, normal behavior, and normal development, and create channels for better communication between the different disciplines.
5. Develop an epidemiology of normality, normal behavior, and normal development.
6. Develop new behavioral and psychosocial measurement techniques specifically designed to study normal behavior and normal development.
7. Develop new terminology that will not be bound by or limited to psychopathology.

Just as the concept of disease unifies medicine and psychiatry, normality, normal behavior, and normal development need a new discipline that will help consolidate what is factually known about them. This field will examine systematically the exact nature of transactions by asking such questions as: Given the fact that social and cultural environment seem so similar for some individuals, what, in the idiosyncratic interaction of individual and environment, accounts for some striking individual differences in life outcome? We need to pay more than lip service to adaptation as person-sociocultural interaction. The field will also attempt to understand how matters in a culture come to be defined as relevant to normality. Who decides what the criteria are for normality? If you ask a member of the general culture for an image of normality, how will it differ from the image held by mental health professionals?* Studying the differences might be very revealing. It may be that the differences between the normal within and across class, sex, age, and race are more important than we have appreciated to date. Thus what seems mentally healthy to a seventy-year-old black man may not seem so to a thirty-five-year-old white woman or to a fifty-year-old white male. There may be regional, cohort, and ethnic historical differences in the definition of the normal, at least partly shaped by such variables as available financial resources for mental health care, religious attitudes, and the like. There may also be different interpretations about the meaning of certain biological measurements, based in part on how sophisticated the measurements are in the first place.

*In Offer, Ostrov, and Howard's (1981b) study, it was found that professionals had a significantly different view of the normal adolescent than normal adolescents had of themselves.

Many developmental theorists talk about "the tasks of development." (See chapter 1.) The nature of the task is usually clearly spelled out. However, investigators never address the key question: Who sets these tasks? Is the discovery of these tasks an artifact of theoretical approach; for example, the American culture that tends to cast experience in terms of work-oriented achievement? Or of the stage of life of this group of subjects when interviewed? Or possibly of attitudes common to the cohort from which the subjects were drawn? And so on. Investigators have accepted theories as facts, not concepts to be challenged empirically.

Much data collected in this book is retrospective. It is made up of biographies constructed by the individual and interviewer in light of their need to create a coherent narrative of the person's life story—with a beginning, middle, and end that hang together in a literary sense (see chapter 5). However, it simply is not possible to spawn a valid theory of change in individuals over time without studying individuals as they change over time. The individuals have to be studied together with their familial, social, and cultural environments, a task few researchers in our field have mastered to date. Shortcuts, such as those employed by investigators who study individuals retrospectively, can present fascinating pictures of how people reconstruct memories that serve their need to maintain the sense of personal continuity. Yet they cannot provide the only valid data base for our understanding of what constitutes normal development.

Another problem facing investigators in our field has been cogently summarized by Cumming and Henry (1961). They said that we should be cautious about our conclusions, and question the generalizability of our findings, because:

> It is our impression from interviewing some of the respondents ourselves that there is a survival principle involved and that it is connected with narcissism. In short, those people who like to talk about themselves to outsiders remain, while those who find this distasteful fall out, and this difference may be related to some of our findings. (P. 34)

It has also been an accepted practice for scientists to organize the world around them in bits of information that are measurable and can be reasonably understood by fellow scientists. It is crucial for the ultimate advancement of the behavioral sciences that we recognize that such organization is only for our convenience. It may have very little to do with the real world. Hence when we talk of life cycles or life span and imply that development has an intrinsic order that can be discovered, we may miss much crucial data. Development may have no intrinsic meaning whatsoever.

In our field, we often spend our professional lives justifying our personal experiences. We seem to have a need to make "sense" of our lives. Once we understand ourselves, we often believe that we can better control our future. Hence the tremendous power of anecdotes in our field. It is very threatening for a person to come into contact with someone who had an experience he or she cannot understand. It is then that notions such as stages, crises, norms, cycles, and development seem useful. They help the mental health professional understand almost everything, even if, given our present state of knowledge, it is not truly comprehensible as yet.

How have studies of normality fared in psychology and psychoanalysis? This problem has been discussed in detail in chapters 12 and 13. At this point we only want to stress that *very little* cross-fertilization has taken place between the various behavioral sciences. It seems as if investigators are satisfied dealing only with phenomenon that are directly related to their own professional know-how. Developmental psychologists are not interested in the studies on deviance. And psychiatric or psychoanalytic (and even psychological) clinicians are rarely interested in studying normal development.

We are dissatisfied with several aspects of the way general and developmental psychologists have approached the study of normality. There has not been an effort to integrate findings from psychiatry and other behavioral sciences with psychological data throughout the life cycle. Furthermore, studies of normal populations aimed at clarifying the complexity of the concept of normality have been relatively sparse.

We are not willing to accept psychoanalysis as an exclusive conceptual and theoretical model for the study of normality. Indeed, we have raised a number of questions about how much we can generalize from psychoanalytic investigations to normality, normal behavior, and normal development. We are concerned that psychoanalysis omits, or gives a secondary and lower status to, biological studies and studies of more explicit behavior. In addition, psychoanalysts are clinicians and generally have not studied nonpatients. Even the most recent study of normality in psychoanalysis is based solely on clinical case reports (Joseph 1982).

Psychiatrists, psychoanalysts, and clinical psychologists can make a fundamental contribution to the study of normality for their understanding of psychopathology may help in clarifying numerous borderline problems conceptually related to normality and psychopathology. Furthermore, methodologies developed within psychiatry may be useful in studies on the normal population. The temptation to simply use clinical methods (e.g., case histories) to studying normal samples must be avoided, and new methods must be developed. One subject of great current interest is the attitude of people throughout the life cycle to nuclear energy and the possibility of a nuclear war (see, e.g., Beardslee and Mack 1982). This would be a natural subject for *normatology*, a field that will combine the tools of the social and behavioral scientist with the clinical understanding of the psychiatrist. A new interdisciplinary effort will be necessary in order to move to a more empirical and scientific study of normal populations and indeed in the clarification of what is meant by normality.

One of the problems that behavioral scientists of the future will face is in the organization of data. Material will have to be organized from a systems point of view. Ideally, multidimensional systems of advanced computers could be used to study the many biopsychosocial variables. The analysis would weigh the importance of the variables and accurately predict future behavior *on a group basis*. It is hoped that future technology will also improve our efforts at longitudinal research. Rather than having limited view of the person, he or she would be evaluated through three or more different systems. In the past, behavioral scientists (psychiatrists, psychologists, or social scientists) did well if they evaluated adequately individuals and their self-image, affect, cognition, and all the other personality characteristics, as well as attempting to study individuals' relationship to peers, family, and culture at large, most of the time through each individual's own perception. Obviously behavioral scientists used their own feelings and empathic responses as a barometer to help evaluate the subjects' (or patients') responses. On rare occasions individuals were studied in the context of their family, possibly their peer group, and even, at times, in their habitat—their culture. But it is rare when these things were done together; even if they were done, at no time were the various variables weighed in order to determine how significant each was to the ultimate test—namely, the functioning of the individual.

In addition, it has recently been noted (in studies such as those of Brenner [1979], Easterlin [1980], Holinger and Offer [1982], which were discussed in chapter 12) that the individuals' behavior and peer group respond dramatically to the cohort they were born in. For example, coming from a baby-boom or baby-drop generation made a difference as to how a particular group of cohorts reacted. Therefore, historical contextual analyses are an additional factor that have to be taken into account. We hope behavioral scientists of the future will relate these variables in a meaningful way so that a valence can be assigned to each variable. In this way the scientists will have a much more correct, or at least approximately correct, evaluative procedure.

In closing, we would like to state why we believe that it is important for those working with psychiatric patients to study *normatology*. Mental health professionals, in their daily work, make decisions that affect human beings. They have to know what the socially accepted behavior is, when psychological pain is out of control and needs to be attended to. They are also continuously asked about the biological causes of malfunction. Just like their physician colleagues who have a conceptual bell-shaped curve in mind when working with patients—a person has either too many or too few white blood cells; only the middle range is considered normal—mental health professionals similarly have an idea about the affect, cognition, or behavior of their patients. But the guidelines (i.e., the norms) are not as clear. They are often idiosyncratic, contradictory, and very culture-bound. No criteria for scientifically studying what we have called the four perspectives of normality currently exist.

Mental health professionals bear the final responsibility for their patients' therapy and ultimate recovery (or lack thereof). The professionals are seen by society as the ones who brings, or can bring, their relatives back to a normal state. They also want to help their patients develop more effective coping devices. We believe, with Murphy (1979), that though our understanding is imperfect, it is better than no understanding. We need to continue our attempt to further understand human behavior and development in all their complex variations.

REFERENCES

American Psychiatric Association. 1982. Statement on the Insanity Defense. Washington, D.C.: American Psychiatric Association.

Beardslee, W., and Mack, J. 1982. "The Impact on Children and Adolescents of Nuclear Developments." In *Psychosocial Aspects of Nuclear War*. Washington, D.C.: American Psychiatric Association, Task Force Report 20.

Block, J. 1971. *Lives Through Time*. Berkeley, Calif: Bancroft Books.

Brenner, M. H. 1979. "Mortality and the National Economy: A Review, and the Experience of England and Wales 1936–76." *Lancet* 2:568–73.

Cumming, E., and Henry, W. 1961. *Growing Old*. New York: Basic Books.

Easterlin, R. A. 1980. *Birth and Fortune*. New York: Basic Books.

Elder, G. 1974. *Children of the Great Depression*. Chicago: University of Chicago Press.

Holinger, P. C., and Offer D. 1982. "Prediction of Adolescent Suicide." *American Journal of Psychiatry* 139:302–7.

Joseph, E. D. 1982. "Presidential Address." *International Journal of Psycho-Analysis* 63:3–13.

Kardiner, A. 1939. *The Individual and His Society*. New York: Columbia University Press.

Ludwig, A. M. 1975. "The Psychiatrist As Physician." *Journal of the American Medical Association* 234:603.

MacDonald, M. 1982. *Mystical Bedlam: Madness, Anxiety, and Healing in Seventeenth-Century England*. Cambridge: Cambridge University Press.

McGrath, J. 1981. Statement of the American Psychiatric Association on the Federal Employee Health Benefit Program before the Post Office and Civil Service Subcommittee on Compensation and Employee Benefits.

Murphy, E. A. 1979. "The Epistemology of Normality." *Psychological Medicine* 9:409–15.

Mussen, P., et al. 1980. "Continuity and Change in Women's Characteristics Over Four Decades." *International Journal of Behavioral Development* 3:333–47.

Nelson, G. R. 1981. Statement before the Subcommittee on Compensation and Employee Benefits, Committee on Post Office and Civil Service on the Federal Employees' Health Benefits Program, May 28.

Offer, D.; Ostrov, E.; and Howard, K. I. 1981a. *The Adolescent: A Psychological Self-Portrait.* New York: Basic Books.

———. 1981b. "The Mental Health Professional's Concept of the Normal Adolescent." *Archives of General Psychiatry* 38:149–52.

Schlesinger, H. J., et al. 1983. "Mental Health Treatment and Medical Care Utilization in a Fee-For-Service System: Outpatient Mental Health Treatment Following the Onset of a Chronic Disease." *American Journal of Public Health* 73:422–31.

Sharfstein, S. S. 1978. "Third Party Payers." *American Journal of Psychiatry* 135:1185–88.

Stone, L. 1982. "Madness." *New York Review of Books*, November, 28–36.

Szasz, T. S. 1961. *The Myth of Mental Illness.* New York: Harper & Row.

Vaillant, G. E. 1977. *Adaptation to Life.* Boston: Little, Brown.

Veith, I. 1958. "Glimpses Into the History of Psychotherapy." In *Progress in Psychotherapy*, vol. 3, ed. J. H. Masserman and J. C. Moreno, pp. 1–20. New York: Grune & Stratton.

Veroff, J.; Douvan, E.; and Kulka, R. A. 1981. *The Inner American.* New York: Basic Books.

Werner, E. E., and Smith, R. S. 1982. *Vulnerability and Invincibility.* New York: McGraw-Hill.

NAME INDEX

Arons, Z. A. 114
Abegglen, J. C., 170n
Abend, S. M., 119n, 128
Abraham, K., 152n, 156
Abraham, R., 308
Abrahams, B., 113
Abrams, S., 296, 411
Achenbach, T. M., 67
Ackerman, N. W., 100
Adams, B., 166n
Adams, D. L., 236
Adams, G. R., 120, 128
Adams, J. E., 115, 129
Adams, R. W., 156
Adelman, R. C., 274
Adelson, J., 91, 101n, 126, 136n, 166n
Adler, D. A., 350
Albright, L. A., 44
Aldous, J., 169, 170, 172, 173
Alexandroff, P., 307, 308
Al-Issa, I., 67
Allport, G. W., 128, 129
Amatruda, C., 11
Ames, L. B., 46, 101n
Anders, T. F., 14, 39, 40
Andrews, F., 160
Angres, S., 166n
Antonovsky, A., 207
Apter, D., 84
Arenberg, D., 179, 264
Arendt, H., 169
Arlin, P. K., 114
Arnold, V. I., 306
Arnstein, R. L., 136
Asher, S. R., 59, 61
Astrachan, B. M., 350
Atchley, R. C., 150–51, 211, 212, 215, 216, 218–23, 251
Ausubel, D. P., 128
Avez, A., 306
Axelrad, S., 60
Axelson, L., 167n, 213, 216

Bach, J. S., 371–72
Bach, K. P. E., 372
Back, K., 151n
Bacon, L., 148
Bakan, D., 224
Balazs, R., 44
Bales, R. F., 158
Balswick, J., 177
Baltes, P. B., 97, 114, 147, 181, 237, 262, 267, 375
Barclan, C. R., 47
Bardwick, J., 161n
Barglow, P., 126
Barker, R., 61
Bart, P., 161n
Bates, J. E., 19
Bayley, N., 11, 20, 21, 50, 54
Beardslee, W., 44, 375, 437
Beck, A. T., 388
Beece, D., 305
Begun, M. S., 382
Beintema, D., 13, 14
Bell, R. Q., 12
Bell, S. M., 50
Belsky, J., 158n
Benedek, T., 165, 168, 176, 249
Bengtson, V., 149n, 154n, 166, 217, 234, 245–47, 254, 259
Benjamin, J., 152n
Benjamins, J. A., 44
Bereiter, C., 56
Berger, P., 150
Bergman, A., 60, 121
Bernard, J., 158, 162, 164, 165
Bernstein, B., 67
Bertalanffy, L. von, 5
Bibring, G., 157
Bild, B., 166n
Biller, H. B., 176
Billig, O., 156
Billing, G. D., 309
Bilofsky, H., 305
Binet, A., 10
Biringen, Z., 179
Birkhoff, G. D., 308

Birnbaum, J., 162n
Birren, J. E., 233, 265–68, 271, 277
Blackstone, 116
Blanck, G., 128
Blanck, R., 128
Blasi, A., 57
Bloch, M., 151
Block, J., 91, 133, 147n, 182, 183, 416, 430
Blood, R., 162, 164, 167n
Blos, P., 76, 100, 102, 102n, 113n, 114, 115, 119, 121–23, 125, 125n, 126, 129, 136, 166, 379, 411
Blotcky, M., 125
Blum, J. E., 266
Bogdonoff, M. D., 266
Bogue, D., 155
Bond, D., 127
Bondareff, W., 276
Boocock, S., 149, 154n
Booth, A., 253
Bornstein, B., 59
Bortner, R., 151
Bott, E., 164
Botwinick, J., 234, 236, 239, 261–63, 267
Bourne, E., 120
Bowlby, J., 18
Boyd, J. H., 178
Boyd, R., 247
Boxer, A. M., 151, 165, 397, 398
Brackbill, Y., 36
Bradburn, N., 148, 163
Braine, M. S. D., 51
Bram, S., 160
Brannon, R., 177n
Branson, H. R., 303
Brasel, J., 35
Bray, D. M., 153, 171, 172
Brazelton, B., 8, 16, 24, 396, 411
Brenner, M. H., 375, 437
Breuer, J., 289, 303
Brim, O. G., Jr., 152, 153n, 180

Bringuier, J. C., 88
Britton, J. H., 261
Britton, J. O., 261
Brody, S., 60
Bromberg, W., 368
Bronfenbrenner, U., 23
Bronson, W. C., 67
Brooks, J., 10
Brown, G., 161n, 162n
Brown-Rezanka, L., 155
Bryant, P. J., 308
Bryant, S. V., 308
Bryt, A., 125
Buckholdt, D. R., 150n, 379, 407
Buhler, C., 11, 125, 151n, 389n
Burchfiel, J. H., 39
Burchinal, L., 166n, 245
Burgess, E., 157, 164
Burke, R., 163
Burlingham, D., 18
Bultena, G. L., 177n, 254
Burnet, F. M., 274
Burr, W., 250
Bursk, B. J., 246
Buss, A. H., 19
Busse, E. W., 231, 232
Butler, R., 61, 151n, 168, 244, 250, 269–72
Bynum, T. W., 69
Byrd, G., 230n

Cain, L., 154n, 181
Caldwell, B. M., 24
Campbell, A., 97, 160, 164, 165, 167n, 174
Campbell, E., 166n
Campbell, R. J., 171
Campos, J., 19
Camus, A., 407
Caplan, B., 42, 43
Caplovitz, D., 148
Carey, W. B., 19
Carney, J., 361n
Carp, F. M., 240
Carroll, J. B., 51, 53, 54
Carskadon, M. A., 40
Cath, S. H., 175, 238, 240, 243
Cerella, J., 264
Chandler, M., 17, 22
Charles, D. C., 221, 222
Charlesworth, R., 64
Chesni, Y., 13
Chess, S., 9, 19, 22, 68, 183
Chiriboga, D., 113, 167n, 205, 212–14, 216, 219,

220, 222, 233, 251, 256, 257
Chodorow, N., 126, 158, 161n, 166
Chothia, C., 305
Chudacoff, H. P., 149
Church, J., 102n
Clark, A., 164
Clark, E. T., 266
Clarke, A., 147n
Clarke, R., 42
Clausen, J. A., 149n, 170, 170n
Clayton, P., 334
Coan, R. W., ix
Coelho, G. V., 115, 129
Cohen, F., 153
Cohen, P. J., 44
Cohen, R., 415n
Cohler, B. J., 147n, 151, 157, 161n, 162, 163, 165, 166n, 180, 397, 398, 406–7, 415n
Colarusso, C. A., 112n, 123, 175
Colby, A., 56
Coleman, J. S., 100
Coleman, R., 170n
Collet, P., 302
Collins, J., 167n, 250
Comte, A., 394
Conel, 38
Conger, J. J., 102n
Converse, P., 160, 164, 165, 167n, 174
Cooley, C. H., 183
Cooper, J., 51–53
Corby, N., 175
Corman, H., 21
Corsaro, W. A., 63
Cosati, I., 21
Costa, P., 179
Costello, J., 98
Cottle, T., 151n
Coullet, P., 311n
Cowan, C. P., 158
Cox, R. D., 127, 130, 133, 139
Coyle, P. K., 44
Craik, F. I. M., 263–65
Cratty, B. J., 46
Crick, F. H. C., 303
Crocetti, G., 163
Crockett, D. J., 43
Croughan, 328
Crutchfield, J. B., 309
Csapo, M., 62
Csikszentmihalyi, M., 172
Cumming, E., 237, 259, 435
Cutler, B., 164

Cutler, L., 256
Cutler, N., 154n, 166

Daffner, K. R., 128
Darwin, C., 10–11, 18, 274
Datan, N., 149n, 155, 167, 168, 205–7, 210, 211, 215, 226, 256, 354
Davis, G. C., 175
Day, D., 182, 184, 209
Decarie, T., 21
Degas, E., 371
Dement, W. C., 39, 40
Demos, J., 149, 154n
Deutsch, H., 99, 100, 102, 168, 212
Deutscher, I., 167n, 212, 216
Dilman, V. M., 273
Doehrman, M. J., 126, 136n
Dohrenwend, B., 153n, 330
Donahue, W., 206, 211, 218–22, 237
Dorman, L., x
Dostoyevsky, F., 370n, 407, 415, 423
Douvan, E., 91, 101n, 161n, 166n, 336, 362, 376, 426
Dowd, J. J., 247
Dressler, D. M., 252
Duffy, F. H., 39
Dulit, E., 89
Dunham, H. W., 320
Dusek, J. B., 91, 97
Duvall, E., 157
DuWors, R., 163
Dyer, E., 160n
Dyer, W., 164

Easterlin, R. A., 337, 339, 340, 375, 437
Eaton, W., W., 328
Eckmann, J.-P., 302
Eder, D., 64
Ehrmann, W., 164
Eichorn, D. H., 7, 147n, 181, 182, 184
Eigen, M., 305
Eimas, P. D., 305
Eisdorfer, C., 256, 266
Eisenberg, D., 305
Eissenberg, L., 113
Eissler, K. R., 100, 373n
Elder, G., 147n, 149n, 151, 153–55, 170, 181, 182, 185, 187, 380, 407, 430
Elkin, F., 101n

Elkind, D., *xi*, 89
Emde, R., 4, 8, 9, 14, 25, 351, 396, 397
Endicott, J., 326, 327
England, P., 174
Ensminger, M. A., 176*n*
Epicurus, 368
Erikson, E., 58, 59, 76, 100, 102, 103, 110, 111, 119, 120, 123, 125, 132, 151, 156, 157, 159, 163, 169*n*, 177, 178, 184, 185, 207, 243, 244, 303, 311, 331, 372, 380, 398–402, 405, 411–13
Erlich, I., 127
Escalona, S., 21, 152*n*
Everitt, A. V., 175

Faderman, L., 177
Falek, A., 216*n*, 266
Falk, J., 151*n*
Faris, R. E. L., 320
Farmer, J. D., 306
Farrell, M. P., 179
Faust, M. S., 36
Favazza, A. R., 384
Feigenbaum, M., 311*n*
Fein, G. G., 65, 66
Feld, S., 164, 169*n*
Feldman, H., 160*n*, 250
Feldman, S. S., 113, 179
Ferguson, C. A., 51
Fillenbaum, G. G., 218, 222
Finch, C. E., 276
Firth, R., 158, 161*n*
Fischer, A., 161
Fischer, J. L., 125*n*
Fischer, J. W., 57, 60
Fischer, K., 340
Fischer, S., 161
Fiske, M., 147*n*, 151*n*, 167*n*, 168, 178, 243, 257, 258, 260
Flacks, R., 166*n*
Flaherty, J. F., 91, 97
Flavell, J. H., 267
Flowers, N., 230*n*
Fogarty, M. P., 173
Foner, A., 154*n*
Forge, A., 158, 161*n*
Foucault, M., 382
Fountain, G., 100
Fowler, W., 51
Fozard, J. L., 263
Fraiberg, S., 21
Frank, A. W., 150*n*
Frank, L. E., 151*n*

French, V., 308
Frenkel-Brunswick, E., 207
Freud, A., 18, 32, 76, 99, 100–102, 114, 119, 121, 128, 129, 152, 386, 409, 411
Freud, S., *xii*, 17–18, 58, 88, 89, 103, 111, 126, 127, 132, 152, 176, 204, 224, 289–94, 303, 362, 373*n*, 379, 399, 406, 408, 412
Friedmann, E., 251–53
Friedson, E., 349
Fritz, R. B., 275
Frolkis, V. V., 273
Fromm, E., 387
Furman, E., 59
Furstenberg, F., 149, 162
Furstenberg, F. F., Jr., 108, 110, 118

Gaensbauer, T. J., 9
Gailly, A., 151*n*
Gaines, R., 46, 49
Gaitz, C. M., 174
Galin, D., 42
Gallahue, D. L., 47
Galligan, R., 160
Garai, J., 43
Garfinkle, E. M., 178
Garmezy, N., 416
Garnica, O. K., 51
Garvey, C., 66
Gavish, B., 305
Geertz, C., 377
Geertz, H., 166*n*
Geisel, T., 311*n*
Geleerd, E. R., 100
Gergen, K., 147*n*, 151*n*, 157, 180, 398
Gesell, A., 11, 46, 101*n*
Giambra, L. M., 264
Giele, J. Z., 156
Gilligan, C., 57, 88, 113*n*, 126, 129, 158
Giovacchini, P., 165
Glasmer, F. D., 252
Glazer, J. A., 64
Glenn, N., 167*n*, 214, 216
Glick, P., 155
Glover, E., 127
Glueck, E., 186
Glueck, S., 186
Goethe, J. W. von, 404*n*
Goldfarb, A., 250
Goldman, R. K., 386
Goldsmith, H., 19
Goldstein, J., 116

Gonda, J. N., 264
Goodenough, F. L., 11
Gordon, C., 174
Gorman, B., 151*n*
Gottman, J., 163, 164
Gould, R., 170
Gould, R. E., 209, 213, 216
Gould, R. L., 112*n*, 130, 133, 402
Gove, W., 160, 161*n*, 162, 163
Gover, D., 162*n*
Graham, F. K., 24
Granick, S., 261
Grant, D. L., 171
Grave, G. D., 83*n*
Graves, A. J., 89
Green, L. R., 151
Green, S. K., 254, 266
Greenberg, M., 60
Greenough, W. T., 45
Greenspan, S. I., 58
Griffin, B., 215
Grinker, R. R., Jr., 101*n*
Grinker, R. R., Sr., 101*n*, 146, 389
Grossman, M., 161*n*
Grossmann, S., 310, 311*n*
Gruen, R. K., 35
Grumbach, M. M., 40, 83*n*
Grunebaum, H., 161*n*, 162–64, 166*n*
Grunes, J., 215
Gubrium, J. F., 105*n*, 379, 407
Guntrip, H. A., 109, 125, 167
Gurd, F. R. N., 305
Gurin, G. J., 322
Gurwitt, A. R., 175
Gusseck, D. J., 274
Guthrie, W. K. C., 367
Gutmann, D., 158, 167, 178, 179, 183, 208, 215–16, 224–25, 234–35, 239, 247, 251, 254, 261, 411
Guze, S. B., 326, 327

Haan, N., 129, 147*n*, 152, 153, 182–84, 209
Haddad, A., 245, 246
Hagestad, G. O., 148*n*, 149–51, 378, 379
Hains, A. A., 57
Haith, M. M., 5
Haken, H., 306
Hall, E. H., 266
Hall, G. S., 99, 101, 404*n*

Hallinan, M. T., 64
Hamburg, B., 115
Hamburg, D. A., 115, 129
Hamm, A., 42
Hanson, D., 157
Harker, J. O., 264
Harkins, E. B., 215
Harlow, H. F., 67
Harmon, R. J., 9
Harris, T., 6, 161*n*, 162*n*
Harrison, J. B., 177*n*, 178
Harry, J., 174
Hartley, J. T., 264
Hartmann, H., 110, 119, 123, 124, 127–29, 137, 138, 152, 291, 294, 303, 412
Hartup, W. W., 64
Hauser, S. T., 128
Hausman, C. P., 217
Havighurst, R. J., 110, 156, 169, 207, 215–16, 219, 236, 258–59
Hayflick, L., 274
Heath, C. W., 127, 130, 131
Heath, R., 130, 132, 136*n*, 140
Heilbrun, G., 69
Helzer, 328
Hendricks, J., 110
Henker, F. O., 175
Henry, W. E., 169*n*, 218, 237, 259, 435
Hershberg, T., 108, 110, 118, 149, 162
Hertz, T. W., 12
Hess, B. B., 177
Heston, L. L., 324
Heynemann, S. P., 125
Hicks, M. W., 169, 170, 172, 174
Hill, J. P., 97
Hill, R., 157, 166*n*, 246
Hinckley, J., 432
Hippocrates, 316, 381, 388
Hitler, A., 375
Hobbs, E. D., 89
Hoffman, L., 156, 158*n*, 161, 162*n*
Hoffman, M. L., 56, 57, 388
Hogan, D., 173
Hogarth, P. S., 7
Hollinger, P. C., 340, 375, 437
Holmes, T., 153*n*, 256, 333, 334
Horowitz, F. D., 24
Horowitz, M., 153*n*
Houseknecht, S., 160

Howard, A., 153, 172
Howard, K., 77, 79, 91, 94–95, 101*n*, 362, 375, 380, 386, 405, 429, 434*n*
Howells, J. G., 20
Howes, C., 65
Hoyer, W. J., 264, 265
Hsu, F. L. K., 101*n*
Huang, C. Y., 175
Huberman, B. A., 309
Hubert, J., 158, 161*n*
Hudson, W., 157
Hughes, J. E., 46
Hulbert, A., 77
Hulicka, I. M., 266
Hulme, C., 47
Hultsch, D., 151
Hume, D., 342
Humphrey, M., 160
Hunding, A., 309
Hunt, J. McV., 21
Hurwitz, I., 43
Hunt, S. J., 14

Ilg, F., 101*n*
Illych, I. D., 362
Inhelder, B., 86
Inkeles, A., 154
Ispa, J., 61

Jacklin, C. N., 7, 41, 43
Jacobs, M. A., 129
Jacobson, E., 100
Jaffe, A. J., 170*n*
Jahoda, M., *ix*, 127, 148
James, W., 399
Janet, P., 151
Janowitz, M., 183
Jaques, E., 168
Jarvik, L. F., 361*n*, 262, 266
Jarvis, E., 320
Jeffreys, M., 168
Jenks, J. A., 126
Jennings, M., 166
Jensen, A. R., 110, 134
Johnson, E. S., 246, 294, 300
Johnson, J., 161*n*
Johnson, M., 154*n*
Johnson, V. E., 175
Jones, E., 127
Jones, J., 375
Jones, M. C., 36, 147*n*, 181
Jordan, K., 39
Jordan, W. D., 116
Joseph, E. D., 300, 411, 436

Josselyn, I. M., 100
Jourard, S. M., 177*n*
Jowett, B., 365, 367
Jung, C. G., 109, 111, 151*n*, 167, 237

Kaack, B., 275
Kabat, E. A., 305
Kafka, F., 407
Kafka, J., 164
Kagan, J., 5, 130, 134, 147*n*, 157, 180, 181, 380, 396
Kahana, B., 247–49
Kahana, E., 247–49
Kandel, D., 166
Kandel, E. R., 45
Kanter, R. M., 156, 169*n*, 170
Kaplan, B. H., 148, 153
Kaplan, D., 153
Kardiner, A., 377, 431
Karplus, M., 305
Kasschau, P. L., 149*n*, 219, 222, 234
Kastenbaum, R., 151*n*
Katchadourian, H. A., 11
Katz, J., 110, 131, 136*n*
Kauffman, S. A., 308
Kauzmann, W., 305
Kearsley, R. B., 5
Kellam, S. G., 176*n*
Kelleher, C. H., 221, 222
Keniston, K., 117, 411
Kennedy, J. F., 346
Kennell, J. H., 8
Kernberg, O., 167
Keshet, H. F., 175
Kessen, W., 5
Kett, J. F., 78, 97
Kety, S. S., 324
Kidson, M. C., 171*n*
Kidwell, I., 253
Kierkegaard, S., 407
Kilpatrick, W., 116
Kimmel, D., 109, 125, 129
King, S. H., 116
Kinsbourne, M., 42, 43
Kinsey, A. C., 175
Kivett, V., 236
Klaus, M. H., 8
Klein, 127
Klerman, G., 161, 320, 322, 323, 331, 332
Klineberg, S., 151*n*
Knobloch, H., 46
Koch, S., 303
Kohen, A. I., 171, 172

Kohlberg, L., 56–57, 88, 129, 130, 132, 137, 398
Kohn, M., 163, 169n, 172, 324
Kohut, D., 362, 413, 416
Kohut, H., 119, 121, 124, 136, 224, 240–43
Komarovsky, M., 158, 163, 177n, 179
Korner, A., 152n
Kornhauser, A., 170
Koszykowski, M. L., 305
Kraines, R., 166n
Kramer, M., 326
Kramer, R., 130, 132, 137
Kramer, S., 59
Krantz, D. L., 172
Krapf, E. E., 127
Kris, E., 303, 373n
Kroeber, T. C., 129, 152
Ktsanes, F., 163
Ktsanes, V., 163
Kubie, L. S., 298, 373n
Kuhlen, R. G., 207, 208
Kuhlman, F., 10
Kulka, R. A., 336, 362, 376, 426
Kupfersmid, J. H., 57
Kuypers, J., 147n, 166, 184, 185, 254

Labouvie, G. V., 114
Labouvie-Vief, G., 264
Lachman, J. L., 263
Lachman, R., 263
Lacy, W. B., 110
Laing, R. D., 373n
Lamb, M. E., 158n, 175
Langer, T. S., 322
Larzelere, R., 157, 158
Lasch, C., 167, 335
Laufer, M., 100
Laws, J. L., 164
Layton, B., 264
Lazarus, L. W., 242, 275
Lazarus, R., 153
Lazine, I., 21
Leckman, J. F., 44
Lecours, A. R., 37, 38, 51, 52, 54
Lehr, U., 260, 261
Leites, N., 60
Lefschetz, S., 307
Leighton, D. C., 322
LeMasters, E. E., 160n
Lemkan, P., 320
Lemon, B. W., 259

Lenard, H. G., 14
Lenneberg, E. H., 42, 51
Lens, W., 151n
Lesk, A. M., 305
Lesser, G., 166
Lever, J., 68
Levinson, D. J., 109. 112n, 125n, 126, 130, 134, 147n, 148, 151n, 159, 168, 170n, 176, 179, 208, 209, 213, 237, 244, 331, 350, 420–24, 411
Levinson, S., 154
Levy, D., 18
Lewin, K., 188
Lewis, J. M., 79, 91, 95, 415n
Lewis, M., 44, 45, 51, 58, 244, 250, 269, 272
Lewis, R., 165, 177, 178
Lichtenstein, H., 128
Lidz, T., xi, 125
Lieberman, M. A., 151n, 185, 256, 258–61
Lieberson, J., 394
Liebert, D. E., 87
Liebert, R. M., 87
Lin, T. Y., 323
Ling, E., 308
Linn, P., 24
Lipsitt, L., 42, 147
Lipton, M. A., 276
Litwak, E., 166n
Litz, T., 166
Livson, F., 147n, 183, 184, 236, 252, 259
Livson, N., 130, 179, 182–84, 380
Loeb, M. B., 260
Loevinger, J., 128, 130, 132, 133, 411
Loewald, H. W., 128
Lombrosco, C. T., 39
London, P., 388
Lonner, T., 213
Looney, J., 79, 125
Lopata, H., 150, 162, 225, 251, 256
Lorenz, E. N., 302, 310
Lorenz, K. Z., 4
Lowe, J., 109, 148n, 151, 215
Lowenstein, R. M., 303
Lowenstein, S. F., 159, 160
Lowenthal, M. F., 113, 148, 151n, 167n, 170, 205, 210, 212–14, 216, 219, 220, 222, 233, 251, 256, 257
Lubchenco, L., 14, 16
Luckman, T., 150
Ludwig, A. M., 428

Lundberg, A., 47
Luther, M., 372, 400
Luton, F. H., 320
Lyapounov, 306

Maas, H., 147n, 184, 185
McArthur, C., 147n, 185
Macaulay, T. B., 380
McCall, G., 148n
McCall, R. B., 7, 9
McCandless, B. R., 64
McCarthy, D., 51, 52
Maccoby, E. E., 7, 41, 43
McCollough, P., 211, 212, 216, 217
McCrae, R., 179
MacDonald, M., 429
MacFarlane, J. W., 130, 134, 135
McGeer, D. G., 276
McGrath, J., 427
Mack, J., 375, 437
McKee, P. L., 243
McKhann, G. M., 44
McKinlay, S., 168
MacKinnon, P. C. B., 40
MacMahon, B., 316, 319
McNamara, M. C., 276
MacNeilage, P. F., 43
McNeil, D., 51, 52
McTavish, D. G., 253
Madsen, K. B., 389n
Maddox, G. L., 231
Mahler, G., 372
Mahler, M. S., 18, 60, 121, 409
Mann, T., 371
Mannheim, K., 154, 180
Manin, Y. I., 308
Manion, U. V., 222
Mannis, J., 158n
Maoz, A., 207
Marcia, J. E., 120
Marcus, I. M., 125n
Marcus, R. A., 305
Markin, R. M., 386
Marohn, R. C., 89, 94
Marsden, J. E., 308
Marshall, H. R., 64
Marshall, V. W., 168n
Marshall, W. A., 84, 109, 113
Martin, R., 179
Marx, K., 362
Maslow, A. H., 336, 389n
Mason, E., 153
Massarik, F., 151n

Masters, W. H., 175
Masterson, J. F., Jr., 98, 101*n*
Matarazzo, R. G., 24
Mathey, F. J., 265, 267
Mattessich, P., 157
May, R. M., 310
Mayer, F. E., 83*n*
Mead, M., 112
Mears, C., 67
Mechanic, D., 348
Medley, M. L., 125*n*, 174
Meerloo, J. A. M., 387
Meilman, P. W., 120
Meissner, W. W., 240, 241
Menaghan, E., 167*n*
Mendel, G., 309
Mendelsohn, G. A., 386
Mendelssohn, F., 372
Menninger, K., 127, 353
Metcalf, D. R., 39
Meyer, A., 322
Meyerowitz, J., 160*n*
Meyersburg, H. A., 45, 69
Michels, R., 289, 291–93,
    296, 298, 408–11
Miller, D., 57, 152
Miller, J. B., 126, 129
Miller, S. J., 212, 215, 216,
    219, 220
Milofsky, E., 112*n*, 120,
    147*n*, 179, 186
Minorsky, N., 306
Minuchin, P. P., 62, 67
Minuchin, S., 10
Model, S., 174
Modell, J., 108, 110, 118,
    149, 162
Monge, R. H., 236
Monin, A. S., 310
Monk, A., 220, 222, 223
Montgomery, J., 167*n*, 250
Moodley, M., 51–53
Moore, J., 109, 148*n*, 149*n*,
    151, 215
Moorehead, P. S., 274
Mora, G., 381
Morgan, L. A., 251
Moriarty, A. E., 60, 152*n*
Morin, S. F., 178
Morrison, M. H., 219
Mortimer, J. T., 173
Moskowitz, B. A., 53, 54
Moss, H. A., 130, 134, 147*n*,
    181
Mullan, J., 167*n*
Munnichs, J., 147, 168, 236
Murphey, E. B., 116, 125*n*
Murphy, E. A., 408, 438
Murphy, L. B., 57, 60, 152*n*

Murphy, W., 157
Murstein, B., 163
Musio, J. N., 39
Mussen, P., 407, 430
Mussolini, B., 373
Musto, D. F., 347
Myers, J. K., 330, 332

Nandy, K., 275
Napier, R., 429
Narotzky, R., 276
Nash, S., 113, 179
Nassi, A. J., 166*n*
Nathanson, C., 162*n*
Nawas, M. M., 113*n*
Nelson, G. R., 427
Nelson, K. E., 53, 54
Nemeroff, C. B., 276
Nemi, R. G., 166
Nemiroff, R. A., 112*n*, 123,
    175
Nesselroade, J. R., 97, 181,
    375
Neugarten, B. L., 109, 118,
    125, 136, 137, 147*n*, 148*n*,
    149–52, 155, 157, 166*n*,
    167, 168, 170, 205, 206,
    208–9, 211, 214, 215, 232,
    236–37, 239, 243, 247–49,
    256–57, 261
Nevill, D. D., 36
Newell, F. W., 45
Newell, K. M., 47
Newman, B. M., 102*n*
Newman, P. R., 102*n*
Nichols, I. A., 51
Nichols, P. L., 51
Nicolay, R. C., 236
Nierwetberg, J., 311*n*
Nock, S., 157
Noid, D. W., 305
Norr, K., 162
Notman, M., 168, 217, 225
Nydegger, C. N., 173
Nye, F. I., 156, 161, 162

Oden, M. H., 164
Offer, D., *xii*, 4, 9, 30, 77–79,
    88–91, 94–95, 97, 98,
    101*n*, 109–10, 125, 127,
    130, 146, 147, 152, 315,
    340, 350, 362, 365*n*, 371,
    375, 380, 386, 397, 405,
    415, 416, 429, 434*n*, 437
Offer, J. B., 79, 90, 91, 94,

    98, 101*n*, 109, 125, 130,
    416
Olander, E. B., 245, 246
Olson, D., 164
Olstad, K., 177*n*
Oppenheimer, V., 156, 170
Orbach, H. L., 206, 211,
    218–22, 251–53
Orden, S. R., 163
Ordy, J. M., 275
Orlofsky, J. L., 120
Osherson, S. D., 172
Osmond, M., 169, 170, 172,
    173
Ostrov, E., 77, 79, 88, 89, 91,
    94–95, 101*n*, 362, 375,
    380, 386, 405, 429, 434*n*

Pallie, W., 42
Palmore, E., 236, 270
Parke, R. D., 59
Parker, J., 256
Parmlee, A., 14
Parsons, T., 109, 115, 158,
    160
Parten, M. B., 65
Pasmanick, B., 45
Patel, A. J., 44
Patterson, R. D., 261
Pauling, L., 303
Paykel, E., 153*n*, 334
Pearlin, L., 152, 153*n*, 161*n*,
    165, 334
Pearson, G. H. J., 100
Peck, R. C., 208
Pederson, F. A., 175
Peek, C., 177
Peixoto, M. M., 307
Perls, F., 336
Perris, C., 325
Perry, R., 49, 60
Peskin, H., 130, 179, 182–
    84, 380
Peters, D. L., 58, 59
Petersen, A. C., 81*n*, 362,
    417*n*
Petersen, A. L., 80, 84
Peterson, C., 160, 162, 163
Peterson, P., 147*n*, 151, 152
Peterson, P. G., 236, 252,
    259
Pfeiffer, E., 175, 260, 261*n*
Philoctetes, 373
Piaget, J., 19, 20–21, 48–50,
    55, 56, 59, 65, 86–89, 102,
    129, 130, 132, 398, 411
Pine, F., 60, 121

Pinel, P., 381–82, 388
Pineo, P., 164
Plato, 364–66, 369, 384
Pleck, J., 177n
Plomin, R. A., 19
Plude, D. J., 264, 265
Plutarch, 362, 368
Pollack, O., 206, 211, 218–22
Pollock, G. H., 58
Poon, L. W., 264
Popper, K. A., 394–95
Post, R. M., 45, 69
Powell, A. H., 266
Powell, G. J., 46
Powers, E. A., 177n, 254
Prechtl, H. F. R., 13, 14
Prelinger, E., 115
Preyer, W., 11
Price-Bonham, S., 175
Prosen, H., 179
Prosen, M., 179
Prusoff, B., 153n
Pugatch, D., 129
Pugh, T. F., 316, 319
Pulaski, M. A. S., 48–50

Quirk, D. A., 221, 222

Rabbitt, P., 264–65
Rabichow, H. G., 76, 100
Rabinowicz, T., 38
Radcliffe-Brown, A. E., 160
Radloff, L. S., 161n, 167n
Ragan, P., 149n, 234
Rahe, R., 153n, 256, 333, 334
Rakowski, W., 151n
Rank, O., 373n
Rapoport, R., 157, 159, 162n, 163, 174, 175
Rarick, G. L., 47, 50
Ras, A., 230n
Ratcliffe, 328
Rausch, H., 164
Rebelsky, F. G., x, 51
Rees, J. R., 127
Reese, H. W., 59, 147
Regier, D. A., 330
Reich, W., 152n
Reichard, S., 147n, 236, 252, 259
Reider, N., 300
Reigel, K., 6
Reik, T., 372

Reimanis, G., 266
Reiter, E. O., 40
Rembrandt, 371
Renner, V. J., 233, 271, 277
Rennie, T. A. C., 322
Revere, V., 151n
Reynell, J., 51–53
Rice, R. E., 171
Richmond, J., 332
Rickman, J., 152n
Riegel, K., 147n, 153, 206, 266
Riegel, R. M., 266
Riley, A., 46, 47
Riley, M., 149n, 154n, 181
Ripley, H., 161n
Ritvo, S., 113n, 126, 129
Roazen, P., 401
Roberts, W. L., 238, 250
Robertson, J. F., 247–49
Robins, E., 326, 327
Robins, L. N., 63, 326, 328
Robinson, B., 217
Robinson, D. S., 276
Robinson, J., 4, 8
Rochlin, G., 241
Rockwell, R., 149n, 151, 170
Rodgers, R., 157
Rodgers, W., 160, 164, 165, 167n, 174
Roffwarg, H. P., 39
Rogers, C., 336, 413
Rollins, B., 160, 250
Rosen, G., 315
Rosenberg, M., 91
Rosenberg, S. D., 179
Rosenblatt, D. B., 65, 66
Rosenblith, J. F., 24
Rosenfeld, A. H., 250
Rosenfield, R. L., 84
Rosenthal, D., 324
Rosenthal, K. M., 175
Rosow, I., 221, 244, 254, 255
Ross, J. M., 175, 176
Ross, W. D., 367
Rossi, A., 149n, 150, 153, 157, 160n, 165, 166, 168, 170
Rössler, D. E., 310
Roth, G. S., 274
Roth, W. F., 320
Rothgeb, T. M., 305
Rothstein, S., 168
Rubenstein, J., 65
Rubin, L., 163, 167, 170
Rubin, Z., 64
Rudolph, J., 59
Russell, B., 413n
Russell, C., 160n

Russo, N., 161
Rutter, M., 9, 32, 44, 45, 101n, 125n
Rychlak, J. F., 171
Ryder, N., 181, 182
Ryder, R., 164
Ryff, C., 152, 153n, 237

Sabo, C., 230n
Sabshin, M., xi, 4, 9, 30, 78, 108–10, 127, 146, 147, 152, 315, 340, 350, 365n
Sachs, D. M., 110, 295
Saint-Anne Dargassies, S., 13
Salapatek, P. H., 5
Salk, J., 302, 303, 310, 312
Saltzman, B., 310
Saltzstein, H. D., 57
Sameroff, A. J., 6, 17, 21, 22, 24, 31
Samorajski, R., 276
Sampson, O. C., 54
Sands, J. D., 256
Sarason, S. B., 153, 171, 213
Sarrel, L. J., 130
Sarrel, P. M., 130
Sauer, W., 157, 158
Sawhill, I., 163
Sawyer, J., 177n
Schafer, R., 60, 119n, 125n, 126, 127, 136
Schaie, K. W., 154n, 181, 268
Scheibel, A. B., 276
Scheibel, M. E., 276
Scheinfeld, A., 43
Schiller, J. C. F. von, 404n
Schlesinger, H. J., 427
Schlesinger, I. M., 53
Schmideberg, M., 300
Schmitz-Scherzer, R., 260, 261n
Schneider, A., 230n
Schneider, C. J., 252
Schooler, C., 153n, 172
Schram, R., 160
Schuster, P., 309
Schwab, J., 148
Schwartz, C. C., 324
Schwarz, J. C., 61
Scott, J., 174
Scott, R., 353
Sedgwick, P., 383n
Seidenberg, H., 385
Seltzer, M., 148, 150
Shanan, J., 153

Shanas, E., 166*n*, 234
Shapiro, T., 49, 60
Sharfstein, S. S., 355, 432
Sheldon, E., 163
Sheppard, H. L., 252, 253
Shereshefsky, P., 158*n*
Sherf, M., 62
Shirley, M., 11
Shock, N. W., 273, 274
Shulman, N., 177
Siassi, G., 163
Siefler, R. S., 87
Sigmund, K., 309
Silber, E., 129–31
Silverman, M. A., 50
Simmons, J., 148*n*
Simmons, R. G., 173
Simon, B., 364*n*
Simon, E., 264
Simon, T., 10
Simpson, I. H., 174
Sinclair, D., 36
Siqueland, E. R., 42
Sklansky, M. A., 76, 100
Smilansky, S., 66, 67
Smith, K. F., 217
Smith, M. B., *ix*, 137, 389*n*
Smith, P. K., 67
Smith, R. J., 151
Smith R. S., 430
Smith-Rosenberg, C., 177
Snow, R. B., 177, 179
Socrates, 367–68
Soddy, K., 171*n*
Sofer, C., 171*n*
Solnick, R. L., 175
Sophocles, 373
Sorce, J. F., 351, 396, 397
Spanier, G., 155, 157, 158, 165
Spence, D., 213
Spiegel, J., 125*n*
Spilken, A., 129
Spiro, H., 163
Spitz, R. A., 4, 18, 113*n*
Spitzer, R. L., 326, 327
Srole, L., 148, 161, 322, 340, 376
Stalin, J., 375
Standley, C. C., 323
Stanley, H. E., 307
Stein, S., 146
Sterba, R. F., 372
Sternschein, I., 118
Stillinger, F. H., 305
Stine, D., 371
Stinnet, N., 167*n*, 250
Stone, L., 102*n*, 382, 429
Stouffer, S. A., 321
Stozier, C. B., 399

Strauss, A., 183
Streib, G., 252
Stryker, S., 148*n*, 149
Suchar, C. S., 386
Sullivan, H. S., 59, 125*n*, 128
Sullivan, J. W., 24
Sussman, M., 166*n*, 238, 245, 246
Sutton-Smith, B., 67
Swanson, G., 152
Sweet, J., 162
Symonds, P. M., 110, 134
Szasz, T. S., 362, 387, 388, 428

Tanguay, P. E., 39
Tanner, J. M., 35, 37, 80, 83*n*, 84
Tartakoff, H. H., 127, 300
Taube, C. A., 355
Taylor, B., 80, 81*n*, 84
Taylor, D. C., 42
Terman, L. M., 164
Thom, R., 303, 307, 309
Thomae, H., 147*n*, 232, 236, 237, 239, 253
Thomae, S., 311*n*
Thomas, A., 9, 13, 19, 22, 68, 183
Thomas, J., 354
Thomas, J. A., 89
Thomas, L. E., 166*n*
Thompson, B., 168
Threatt, J., 275
Thurnher, M., 113, 174, 205, 213, 214, 216, 217, 219, 220, 222
Ticho, G. R., 127, 129
Tiger, L., 177
Timberlake, J., 101*n*
Timiras, P. S., 112, 113, 276
Tizard, L., 167
Tobin, S., 151*n*, 168
Tomlinson-Keasey, C., 89
Torrey, E. F., 362
Trapp, B., 275
Treas, J., 245–47, 254
Tressor, J., 311*n*
Trevarthen, C., 37
Trimakas, K. A., 236
Troll, L. E., 151, 164, 212, 215, 216, 219, 247, 248
Troyer, W. G., 266
Tsui, A., 155
Tudor, J., 161*n*
Turner, R. J., 176*n*
Tuttle, R. S., 274

Uhlenberg, P., 162
Uhlenhuth, E., 153*n*
Uzgiris, I. C., 21

Vaillant, G. E., 101*n*, 112*n*, 120, 129, 131, 132, 136*n*, 146, 147*n*, 151*n*, 168, 179, 181, 185, 331, 380, 402, 411, 430
Van Dusen, R., 163
Veevers, J., 159
Veith, I., 369
Vernadakis, A., 276
Veroff, J., 164, 169*n*, 336, 362, 376, 426
Verstraeten, D., 151*n*
Verwoerdt, A., 175
Vico, G., 383
Vihko, R., 84
Virgil, 368
Von Bulow, H., 372

Waber, D. P., 42
Wada, J. A., 42
Waddington, C., 5
Wahler, R. G., 32
Wales, J., 149*n*
Walford, R., 274
Wallach, M. A., 151
Wallerstein, R. S., 110, 116, 136*n*, 410*n*
Wallin, P., 164
Walsh, D. A., 264
Walsh, F., 415*n*
Waring, E., 164
Warner, W. L., 170*n*
Waterman, A. S., 113
Watson, J. D., 303
Weatherly, D., 36
Weber, M., 169
Wechsler, D., 262
Weinberg, J., 234, 238, 247, 277
Weiner, I. B., 102*n*
Weinraub, M., 10
Weinshel, E., 300
Weinstein, K., 247–49
Weir, T., 163
Weitz, L. J., 89
Weiss, P., 308
Weiss, R. S., 175
Weissman, M. M., 161, 178, 320, 322, 330, 332

Weissman, S., 126, 415n
Wenar, C., 31, 61
Wenz, F. V., 178
Werner, E. E., 430
Wessen, A. F., 353
Wessman, A., 151n
Westley, W. A., 101n
Weyer, J., 381, 388
Wheelright, P. E., 368
Whitbourne, S. K., 113
White, N., 42
White, R. W., 110, 152
White, S. H., 49
Whitehead, J. A., 310
Wilder, J., 389n
Wilen, J., 167
Wilensky, H., 170
Wilkie, F., 256
Williams, D. M., 264
Williams, M. V., 265–67
Willis, S. L., 58, 59, 262, 267

Wilner, N., 153n
Wilson, R., 19
Wilson, W. C., 164
Winch, R., 163
Wing, J. K., 326, 327
Winkler-Oswatitsch, R., 305
Witelson, S. F., 42, 43
Withey, S., 160
Wittenberg, R., 125, 135, 137
Wolf, E. S., 124, 241, 243
Wolf, K. M., 4
Wolfe, D., 162, 164, 167n
Wolff, P. H., 14, 35, 43, 152n
Wolff, R. P., 384, 385, 387
Wolman, B. B., xi
Wolpert, L., 308
Wonderly, D. M., 57
Wood, V., 247, 249
Woods, A. M., 265–67
Wright, H., 61

Wright, J. C., 50
Wu, T. T., 305

Yaglom, A. M., 310
Yakovlev, P. I., 37, 38
Yalom, I., 160n
Yankelovich, D., 165, 166n
Yanofsky, C., 305
Young, G. J., 44
Young, H. B., 84
Young, M., 166n

Zarit, S. H., 217
Zeeman, E. C., 309
Zelazo, P. R., 5
Zepelin, H., 179
Zubin, J., 326

SUBJECT INDEX

Abuse, 18, 19
Achievement: in late adulthood, 208; longitudinal studies of, 182
Acting out in adolescence, 93
Activity theory, 259
Adaptation, 119, 123–24, 411–14; in adulthood, 152–53; aging and, 258–60; flexibility in modes of, 298
"Adaptive paranoia" of old age, 261
Adjustment, aging and, 255–61
Adolescence, 76–104; adult expectations and theories of, 103; biological development in, 80–85; cohort effect in, 340; cognitive development in, 86–89, 268; conflict-resolution in, 379; continuous growth in, 417–19; coping ability in, 95–97, 153; correspondence of attributes in adulthood and, 182–84; educational demands and, 115; family during, 94–95; historical perspective on, 97–99; identity crisis in, 399, 400; "identity vs. identity diffusion" in, 119; language development in, 53; late, young adulthood and, 108, 109; medical tasks of psychiatry in, 351; mental health profession and, 386; moral development in, 56; narcissism and, 224, 225; neurobiological development in, 38; neurotransmitters in, 44; normal, definition of, 77–80; of offspring, parenthood and, 165–66, 170; peer relationships in, 62; physical development in, 80–85, 113; physical growth in, 35, 36; predictive value of behavior in, 430; privation in, impact in middle adulthood of, 154; psychoanalytic theory on, 99–102, 121–22, 294–95; psychological tasks of, 114; psychosocial development in, 90–97; relationship with grandparents in, 249; self-image in, 90–97, 375; separation-individuation in, 119; sexuality in, 93–94, 97–98; stability of variables in studies of, 397; study of development in, 415–23, 429; suicide in, 375; surgent growth in, 417–20; tasks of, 125; tumultuous growth in, 420–21; turmoil theory of, 99–102, 404, 405
Adrenal mechanisms, 40

Adulthood: definition of, 112; *see also* Late adulthood; Middle adulthood; Young adulthood
Adultomorphism, 4, 5
Adviser Study, 130
Affectional solidarity, 246
Affective development, 33
Affective disorders: genetic factors in, 324–25, 410; prevalence of, 330
Age, social and chronological, 149–51
Age-grading system, 205
Aggression: in adolescence, 97; longitudinal studies of, 181, 182
Aging, 230–79; adaptation and, 258–60; adaptational model of, 271–72; adjustment and, 255–61; biological aspects of, 269–73; biological theories of, 273–75; as breakdown of regulatory mechanisms, 273–74; cognitive functioning and, 261–69; cultural issues in, 234; diversity in, 231–33; genetic theory of, 274; grandparenthood and, 247–49; immunologic theory of, 274–75; impact of process of, 233–34; as life-stage transition, 233; marriage and, 250; medical tasks of psychiatry and, 352; mental processing capacity and, 264; methodological issues in study of, 234–35; normal, problems in defining, 231–35; parenthood and, 244–47; personality in, 236–44; physiological changes in, 272–73; psychology of self and, 240–43; retirement and, 251–53; sex differences in response to, 168; social change for, 375; social roles and, 244–55; society's view of, 253–54, 270; speed of behavior and, 264–65; stress and, 256–58; survival issues and, 260–61; tasks of, 243–44; widowhood and, 250–51
Aging parents, problems of relations with, 216–17
Alcoholism, 331; expectancy for, 332; in middle-aged males, 178; prevalence of, 330
Aleatoric (autonomous) account of development, 398
Altruism, 132
Alzheimer's disease, 275

American Psychiatric Association, 25, 427; position statement on Insanity Defense of, 433*n*

Anaclitic depression, 18, 19

Anal phase, 58

Anecdotes, 436

Anticipation, 132

Antihypertensive drugs, 271

Antipsychiatry movement, 384*n*

Anxiety: Freud on, 18; in adolescence, 421

Apgar score, 14

Army, U.S., 321

Arteriosclerosis, 270

Artistic connotations of normality, 369–74

Associational solidarity, 246

AT&T managers study, 171

Autoimmune disease, 275

"Autonomy vs. shame and doubt," 58

Average, normality as, *xii–xiii*; in adolescence, 78, 87; artistic connotations of, 371, 374; in childhood, 31; epidemiology and, 341; in infancy, 6–8; rehabilitative tasks and, 353; social policy and, 357; societal-legal tasks and, 356; studies of, 433; in study of adolescence, 417; in young adulthood, 110

"Average expectable environment," 138–39, 297

Babbling, 51–52

Baby boom, 156, 339, 340

Basal ganglia, 37

Bayley Scales of Infant Development, 12, 20

Behavior: normal, research on, 433–38; speed of, 264–65

Behavior therapy, 32

Behavioral disorders, 13

Bereavement, coping with, 334

Berkeley Growth Scale, 54

Berkeley Guidance Study, 130, 133, 134, 407

Berkeley Institute of Human Development study, 181–85

Better Homes and Gardens study, 163

Biological clock, 274, 377

Biological development, 33–46; in adolescence, 80–85; language development and, 51; in late adulthood, 205; maturity and, 113, 115

Biological factors: in aging, 269–75; in etiology of mental illness, 324

Biological psychiatry, 409–10

Biological research, 5–6

Biological state model of development, 401–2

Birth experiences, changes in, 7–8

Birth trauma, 14

Birthweight, 14, 16

Blindness, 21

Blue Cross and Blue Shield Insurance Company, 427

Body image in adolescence, 91

Bonn Longitudinal Study of Aging (BLSA), 267

Brain: age-related changes in, 265, 273, 275–77; development of, *see* Neurobiological development; maturity of, at puberty, 86–87; theories of mechanisms of, 303

Brain Electrical Activity Mapping (BEAM), 39

Brazelton Neonatal Behavioral Assessment Scale (NBAS), 16, 24–25, 396

Buhler Baby Tests, 11

California First Year Mental Scale, 11

California Transitions Study, 170

Cancer, epidemiology of, 316–18

Cardiovascular disease, epidemiology of, 316–18, 334

Careers: marriage and, 164; of men, 169–73; midlife change of, 172–73; motherhood and, 161–63; and voluntary childlessness, 160

Castration anxiety, 59

Cataracts, 45

Catecholamines, 276; psychopharmacology and, 325

Cattell Infant Intelligence Scale, 12

Central nervous system (CNS): aging and, 265, 275–77; *see also* Neurological functioning

Cerebral cortex, 37, 38

Cerebral palsy, 8, 13; assessing infants with, 21

Childhood: cognitive development in, 268; correlation between attributes of adulthood and, 183–86; determinants of occupational choice in, 169; development of self in, 240–41; folk notions about, 396; privation in, impact in middle adulthood of, 154; in psychoanalytic theory, 292–95, 297–99, 409; psychosexual development in, 114; transmission of sex roles in, 158; *see also* Infancy; Middle childhood

Childlessness, voluntary, 160

Chlorpromazine, 325

Chronic mentally ill, 331–32

Chronological age, 149–51; sense of time and, 151

Classification, *see* Diagnosis

Climacteric, male, 175

Climacterium, 168

Clinical approach, 349–50

Cognitive development, 33, 48–51; in adolescence, 86–89; motor development and,

47, 50; neurobiological development and, 38

Cognitive-ecology approach, 22

Cognitive functioning, aging and, 261–69, 276

Cognitive psychology, assessment of handicapped infants and, 20–22

Cognitive theories of infancy, 5

Cohort effects, 339–40; studies of, 437

Combinatorial system, 86

Commerce Bureau, U.S., 159

Community involvement, 159, 207

Community Mental Health Centers (CMHC), 328; development and implementation of, 346–48; preventive programs of, 384

Community surveys, 322, 323

Concept formation, 53

Concrete operations period, 49

Consensual solidarity, 246

Conservation, 49

Continuous growth, 98, 417–19

Conventional morality, 56

Coping mechanisms, 129; in adolescence, 95–97, 418–19; in adulthood, 152–53; aging and, 238–40, 258; epidemiological approach and, 333–35

Crime, equation of mental illness and, 432

Criminal justice system, 355–56, 432–33

Crisis, developmental, 403–6

Cross-cultural studies, 322, 416; of aging, 234

Cross-sex characteristics, 208

Cultural factors in aging, 234

Culture: art and, 372; change in, impact on predictive studies of, 395; as context for development, 400, 402; normality and, 374; values of, 389

Deafness, 21

Death, 205; closeness to, 266, 278–79; of loved one, coping with, 334; preparation for, 168

Death instinct, 413

Decentering, 87

Defenses, 129, 132, 383; in adolescence, 418–21; in adulthood, 152–53

Delinquency: cognitive styles and, 89; equation with mental illness of, 432; sexuality and, 94

Dementias, 275

Demoniacal possession, 381

Denial, 238

Dependency, aging and, 232, 245, 246, 251, 257

Depression: in adolescence, 92, 96, 98, 100, 419, 421; among adult women, 161; aging and, 242, 243, 261, 276; anaclitic, 18, 19;

antihypertensive drugs and, 271; bereavement and, 334; cohort effect and, 340; cross-national differences in diagnosis of, 326; in empty nest period, 215; expectancy for, 332; in middle-aged males, 178; prevalence of, 330, 332; psychopharmacology and, 325; reliability of diagnosis of, 387; in young adults, 135

Deprivation, 18, 19; malnutrition and, 44; permanent effects of, 45

Development, 393–423; adaptation and, 411–14; in adulthood, 111–12; average, 7; biological, see Biological development; cognitive, see Cognitive development; continuity and discontinuity in, 396–99; cultural and historical factors in, 206; dynamic complexity of, 25; epidemiological approach to, 337–39, 342; family and, 414–15; of fathers, 176; of generativity, 207–10; goals of, 5–6; of intellectual functioning, 12, 113–14; language, 51–55; longitudinal studies of, 181–82; meaning of, 393–96; medical tasks of psychiatry and, 351; moral, 55–57; motor, 33, 46–48; multiple pathway theory of, 415–23; neurobiological, 36–38; neurological, 13; peer relationships and, 60–65; physical, 80–85, 113; play and, 65–68; proposals for research on, 433–38; psychoanalytic theory of, 18, 295–96, 408–11; psychological, 57–60, 114–16; psychological time and, 379–81; psychosexual, 57–60; psychosocial, 90–97, 399–403, 406–8; risk concept and, 9; somatic, 34–36; transactional model of, 9; turmoil and crisis and, 403–6; unpredictability of course of, 180

Developmental lines, 121

Deviance: art and, 371, 373–74; high degree of tolerance of clinicians for, 386; societal-legal tasks of psychiatry and, 355–56

Diabetes: late-onset, 275; maternal, 14

Diagnosis: cross-national differences in, 326; in early epidemiological studies, 320; for Epidemiologic Catchment Area program, 329; insurance industry and, 426, 427; psychopharmacology and, 325; rejection of traditional categories of, 322–23; reliability of, 319, 324, 326–27, 387; social norms and, 378; validity of, 319, 324, 327–28

Diagnostic Interview Schedule (DIS), 328–30

Diagnostic and Statistical Manual, Third Edition (DSM-III), 25, 100, 329, 330, 336, 378, 388, 416, 423, 427

Differential psychology, 10–12, 20, 21

Discrimination against elderly, 253

Disengagement theory, 237, 259

Diurnal sleep-wake cycle, 39

Divorce rates, 155, 376

DNA, 274
Down's syndrome, 8
Dreams: Freud on, 18; neurobiological development and, 39
Drive endowment, 297, 298
Drive theory, 58
"Dual career" family, 163
Duke longitudinal study, 260, 270
Dynamical biological systems, 302–12; early simplifying assumptions about, 304; emergent patterns in, 308–9; parabolic manifold and, 310–12; qualitative dimension and transition in, 307–8; stability of, 306; unpredictability in, 305–7

Echolalia, 52
Ecological transitions, 23
Educative-developmental tasks of psychiatry, 353–55
Ego, 60; in adolescence, 98, 99; aging and, 238; changing concepts of, 303; developmental lines and, 131; and mental health, 127–29; in middle adulthood, 152
Ego development, 119, 128–29
Ego ideal, 57, 418
Ego identity, 119, 120, 129
Ego integrity, 243
Ego psychology, 111, 123; adaptation in, 411, 412; preoedipal mother of, 176; values of, 413
Ego transcendence, 208
Elderly, *see* Aging
Electroencephalogram (EEG), 38–40
Embryology, 401–2
Emotional security with peers, 61
Empathy, 57
Empiricism, 394
Employment patterns, 155–56; *see also* Careers
Empty nest, 155, 166–67, 210–18; adjustment to, 206; men and, 178
Endocrine system: aging and, 276; neurological development and, 40–41; stress and, 335; in puberty, 85
Endorphins, 44
Enkephalins, 44
Epidemiologic approach, 315–42; age and development in, 337–39; application to mental illnesses and psychiatry of, 318–19; cohort effects in, 339–40; to coping with stress and life events, 333–35; core population of individuals with mental disorders in, 331–32; current renaissance of, 324; early studies using, 320; to enhancement of personal potential, 335–36; genetics and, 324–25; golden era of, 322–24; integration of life-cycle approach and, 337–40; need for, 427; neurobiology and,

324–25; NIMH Epidemiologic Catchment Area program, 328–30; to normality, 330–31; policy formulation and, 346; psychopathology and, 325–28; psychopharmacology and, 325; to satisfaction and happiness, 337; social policy and, 430; during World War II, 320–21
Epigenetic principle, 207
Erotic relational mode, 224–25
EST, 335
Estrogen, 84, 85
Etiology: biological factors in, 324; concept of, 322–23
Evoked brainstem potential, 39
"Exclusion of stimuli," 238
Existentialism, 407, 408
Expressive language, 52–53
External reality, 297–98

Familial prevalence of psychiatric disorders, 332
Family: during adolescence, 94–95; development and, 414–15; *see also* Marriage; Parenthood
Family environment, changes in, 7
Family life cycle, 155–56; in late adulthood, 210–18; men's happiness patterns and, 174; tasks in, 156–57
Family therapy, transactional model in, 10
Fantasy: adolescent, 135, 418; in infancy, 4; in play, 67; in psychoanalytic theory, 294
Fatherhood, 173–76
Fels Institute Study, 130, 134, 181, 182
Fetal development, 13
Filial maturity, 246
Folk notions, 396
Follicle-stimulating hormone (FSH), 85
Forensic psychiatry, 432–33
Formal operations period, 50, 86–89
Friendship: capacity for, 136; sex differences in patterns of, 177
Fundamental movement, 47

Gender: overt manifestations of, 34; physical growth and, 35–36; *see also* Sex differences
Gender identity, early establishment of, 45
Generativity, 207–10, 243
Genetic theory of aging, 274
Genetics, 324; biological psychiatry and, 410; epidemiology and, 324–25; physical growth and, 35; in psychiatric epidemiology, 318; regulatory phenomena of, 302
Genital development in adolescence, 82, 84
Gesell Developmental Scales, 11
Gestational age, 14, 16

"Good-enough mothering," 297
"Goodness of fit," 22–23, 31, 69
Grandparenthood, 155, 247–49
Grant Study, 130, 131
Gray Panthers, 375
Griffiths' Scale, 12
Growth: maturity and, 113; physical, 34–35; in puberty, 82, 84
Guidance Study, 209

Handicapped infants, 6; assessment of, 20–22; mental movement and, 19
Happiness: Aristotle on, 366–67; epidemiology of, 337
Harvard Grant study, 181, 186
Health, normality as, xii, 417; in adolescence, 78; artistic connotations of, 371, 374; in childhood, 31; educative-developmental tasks and, 354–55; epidemiology and, 315; in infancy, 8–9; medical tasks and, 351; rehabilitative tasks and, 352–53; social policy and 357; societal-legal tasks and, 356; studies in, 433; in young adulthood, 109–10
Health and Human Services, U.S. Department of, 332
Health problems of elderly, cognitive decline and, 266
Health systems perspective, 345–62; clinical approach versus, 349–50; educative-developmental tasks and, 353–55; medical tasks and, 351–52; normality and, 350; policy formulation and, 346–47; program development and, 347–48; rehabilitative tasks in, 353–54; social policy and ideology and, 348–49; societal-legal tasks and, 355–56
Hemispheres of brain, 41–43
Heteronomous morality, 55, 56
High-risk infants, *see* Risk
Historical context, 153–54
History, Whig interpretation of, 380
Homophobia, 178
Homosexuality, 139; concepts of normality and, 430
Hormones in adolescence, 84, 85
Human potential movement, 335–36, 431
Humanistic psychology movement, 389
Humor, 124, 132
Hypothalamic-pituitary-gonadotropin-gonadal system, 40
Hypothalamus, 37; age-related changes in, 273
Hysteria, Freud's early studies of, 289–90

Id, 60; in adolescence, 99; developmental lines and, 121; ego and, 123
Idealization of infancy, 4–5, 23
Identification: of fathers, 176; sex-role, 155
Identity, 119; definitions of, 399–400
Identity crisis, 103–4, 399, 400
Identity Status Scale, 120
"Identity vs. identity diffusion," 119, 120
Ideology: of development, 403, 404; social policy and, 348–49
Immunologic theory of aging, 274–75
Impairment, measures of, 323, 324
Individual variability, 17–18; in neurobiological development, 39
Individuality, 25–26
"Industry vs. inferiority," 59
Infancy, 3–26; behavioral assessment in, 24–25; empathy in, 57; folk notions about, 396; goals of development in, 5–6; handicaps in, 20–22; idealization of, 4–5; instability over time of studies of, 397; intellectual functioning in, 10–12; malnutrition in, 44; medical tasks of psychiatry in, 351; narcissism in, 224; neuroanatomic studies of, 37; neurological functioning in, 13–17; normality as average in, 6–8; normality as health in, 8–9; normality as transactional system in, 9–10; normality as utopia in, 4–6; pathology in, 299; physical growth in, 35, 36; psychiatric syndromes in, 25; psychoanalytic theory of, 17–20; roots of personality development in, 380; social ecology and, 22–23
Infant mental health movement, 19–20
Infectious diseases, 316
Inferiority, 168
"Initiative vs. guilt," 59
Insanity defense, 432–33
"Insecurity of attachment," 18
Institutionalized elderly, 231, 235, 270; grandparenting by, 249; stress in, 256
Instruction by peers, 62
Insurance companies, 426, 427, 429
Integrated functions, 45–46
Intellectual development: maturity and, 113–14; physical growth and, 36; *see also* Cognitive development
Intellectual flexibility, 172
Intellectual functioning in infancy, 10–12
Intelligence, aging and, 262–63
Interpretations, psychoanalytic, 293
Intimacy, 119; capacity for, 163; career consolidation and, 179; in Eriksonian stages, 412; in friendships, 177
"Intimacy vs. isolation," 120
Intrauterine growth, 14
Intuitive stage, 49
IQ in infancy, 10–12, 17
Isle of Wight study, 32

Joint Commission on Mental Health and Mental Illness, 331, 347

K complexes, 39
Kansas City Studies of Adult Life, 239
Kish grid method, 329
Knowledge, specialization of, 171
Kolmogorov-Arnold-Moser theorem, 305

Lagrange-Dirichlet theorem, 306
Language development, 33, 51–55; in pre-operational period, 49
Late adulthood, 204–26; family transitions in, 210–18; intrapersonal dimension of, 207–10; relational modes in, 223–26; retirement and, 218–23
Latency, psychoanalytic concept of, 40, 41, 59
Learning disabilities, 13
Learning theories of infancy, 5
Leisure skills, 219–20
Life cycle, definition of, 111–12
Life-course social science, 146–57; dimensions of time in, 149–51; operational definition of normality in, 147–49
Life events, epidemiological approach and, 333–35
Life review process: empty nest and, 214; generativity and, 210; narcissism and, 224, 225; retirement and, 220
Limbic cortex, 37
Lithium carbonate, 325
Logical positivism, 394, 395
Loneliness in adolescence, 92, 93
Longevity, 260–61
Luteinizing hormone (LH), 85

Male bonding, 177
Malnutrition, 44
Manifestational disorders, 319
Marriage: age of first, 155; aging and, 238, 250; decreasing importance of, 376; empty nest and, 215–16; men and, 174–76; retirement and, 219, 252; women and, 163
Mastery: aging and, 239; through play, 18
Maternal separation, 18
Maturity: definition of, 112–15; interaction of standards of, 115–17
"Me generation," 335
Median zone, 37
Medical tasks of psychiatry, 351–52

Memory: aging and, 263–64; discontinuity of, 397; language development and, 54; reorganization of, 406, 407
Men: careers of, 169–73; family and fatherhood issues for, 173–76; midlife transition of, 176–80; *see also* Sex differences
Menarche, 77, 84
Menopause, 205; assumptions about mental illness during, 430; psychopathology during, 76; self-esteem and, 168
Mental health: concepts of, 127–29; criteria for definition of, 331; positive, 341; psychiatry vs., 428; values and definitions of, 381–83
Mental processing capacity, 264
Mental retardation, 13; assessment of, 21; motor development and, 47; nosological subclasses of, 325
Mental testing movement, 10–12
Mentally handicapped infants, 6
Mentor relationship, 176, 179–80, 209
Metapsychological constructs, 60
Michigan, University of, Survey Research Center, 322, 336
Middle adulthood, 145–88; adaptation, defense and coping in, 152–53; cycles and tasks of, 156–57; family life cycle and, 155–56; historical events and life course in, 153–55; life-course social science and, 146–57; men in, 169–80; mental health during, 397–98; parenthood in, 158–63; place in life course of, 180–86; social and chronological age in, 149–51; subjective perceptions of time in, 151–52; women in, 159–68
Middle childhood, 30–69; biological development in, 33–46; cognitive development in, 48–51; language development in, 51–55; moral development in, 55–57; motor development in, 46–48; neurobiological development in, 36–46; peer relationships in, 60–65; play in, 65–68; psychosocial and psychosexual development in, 57–60; somatic development in, 34–36
Middle class: adolescence in, 79; career building in, 170; family life cycle in, 156; friendship patterns in, 177; responsibility required by jobs in, 172; working women in, 162, 163
Midlife transition: of men, 176–80; of women, 165–68
Midtown Manhattan survey, 148, 322; twenty-year follow-up of, 340
Milbank Memorial Fund, 323
Military service, impact on life course of, 173
Minorities, incidence of psychopathology in, 430
Modeling, 62

Monamine oxidase, 44; aging and, 276
Moral development, 33, 55–57; in adolescence, 93
Motherhood: work and, 161–63; *see also* Parenthood
Motor development, 33, 46–48; cognitive development and, 47, 50; sex differences in, 43
Mourning: coping with, 334; stressors of, 339
Multiple pathway theory of development, 415–23
Myelinization, 37, 38

Narcissism, 224–25; aging and, 238, 241–42; human potential movement and, 335
Narcissistic personality disorders, 124
National Advisory Mental Health Council, 323
National Institute of Mental Health (NIMH), 18, 322; Division of Biometry and Epidemiology of, 328; Epidemiologic Catchment Area Program of, 328–30; Psychopharmacology Research Branch of, 325
National Opinion Research Center (NORC), 159
"Nature vs. nurture," 31
Neglect, 18, 19
Neonates, *see* Infancy
Neurobiological development, 36–46; anatomic studies of, 36–38; endocrine function and, 40–41; environmental factors in, 44–46; physiologic assessment of, 38–40
Neurobiology, 324–25
Neuroleptic drugs, 271
Neurological functioning in infancy, 13–7
Neuropsychology, 41–43
Neurosis: as adaptation, 412; adolescence and, 122; creativity and, 373; goals of psychotherapy for, 431; prevalence of, 332
Neurotransmitters, 44–46; aging and, 276; psychopharmacology and, 325
New York City Community Mental Health Board, 382
New York Longitudinal Study, 19
Newborns, *see* Infancy
Norepinephrine, 44
Norm setting with peers, 62
Normality: ancient roots of, 365–69; artistic connotations of, 369–74; culture and, 374–77; proposals for research on, 433–38; psychoanalytic theory of, 411; *see also* Average, normality as; Health, normality as; Transactional systems, normality as; Utopia, normality as

Normatology, *xi*, *xiii*, 362, 433–38
Northwestern Intelligence Test, 12
Nosology, *see* Diagnosis
"Not guilty by reason of insanity," definition of, 432–33
Nuclear war: attitudes about, 437; threat of, 375

Oakland Growth Study, 130, 133, 209
Object permanence, 21, 48, 50; language development and, 52; self-concept and, 87
Object relations: in adolescence, 418; in late adulthood, 225; in young adulthood, 225
Occupational choice, determinants of, 169
Oedipal period, 58–59, 126, 295
Oedipus complex, 224, 225
Offer Self-Image Questionnaire for Adolescents (OSIQ), 90–91
Office of Personnel Management, 427
Old age, *see* Aging
Ordered change account of development, 398
Organic mental disorders, 275
Organismic states, 14

Parabolic manifold, 310–12
Paramedian zone, 37
Parenthood: and adolescent offspring, 165–66; aging and, 244–47; as cardinal role for adult women, 159–60; developmental tasks of, 157; and empty nest, 166–67, 210–18; morale and, 160–61; process of, 414–15; sex roles and 158–59
Parkinson's disease, 271
Pediatric risk concept, *see* Risk
Peer relationships: in adolescence, 62; in middle childhood, 60–65
People's Temple movement, 375
Perceptual noise, 264
Perceptual theories of infancy, 5
"Personal narrative" theory, 406–8
Personal potential, enhancement of, 335–36
Personality development: infantile roots of, 380; psychoanalytic theory of, 57–60; social norms and, 376–77
Personality disorders, prevalence of, 332
Personality style, aging and, 236–40
Phenothiazines, 325
Phobias: in adolescence, 96, 100; expectancy for, 332; prevalence of, 330
Physical attractiveness in childhood, 34
Physical development: in adolescence, 80–85; maturity and, 113
Physically handicapped infants, 6

Physiological changes in aging, 272–73
Play, 65–68; in games with rules, 68; mastery through, 18; motor development and, 48; psychoanalytic theory and, 59; sociodramatic, 66–68
Policy formulation, 346–47; constructs of normality for, 357
Polycythemia, 16
Postconventional morality, 56
Poverty as disease, 352
Preconceptual stage, 49
Preconventional morality, 56
Predictability, ideal of, 23
Prelogical stage, 49
Premature infants, 8, 14
Preoedipal events, 126
Preoperational period, 48–50
Present State Examination (PSE), 327
President's Commission on Mental Health, 330
Primary memory (PM), 263
Program development and implementation, 347–48
Protestant work ethic, 412
Psychiatric epidemiology, *see* Epidemiologic approach
Psychiatry: biological, 409–10; educative-developmental tasks of, 353–55; forensic, 432–33; medical tasks of, 351–52; vs. mental health, 428; rehabilitative tasks of, 352–53; "remedicalization" of, 388; societal-legal tasks of, 355–56; values in, 384–85, 388
Psychic reality, 292
Psychoanalytic theory, 289–300, 408–11; on adolescence, 99–102, 121–22; on adult development, 123–25, 136; of childhood, 58–60; clinical investigations of, 383; determinants of health in, 298–99; developmental predisposition in, 295–96; developmental tasks in, 156, 157; focus of, 293–95; historical origins of, 289–91; importance of external reality in, 297–98; of infancy, 5, 17–20; latency in, 40; life cycle in, 111–12; on menopause, 168; morality in, 57; normality in, 110, 299–300, 436; Plato and, 365; psychic reality in, 292; psychological determinism of, 379; research and, 129–30; on sex differences in development, 126; stability account of development in, 398; standards of maturity in, 114; turmoil theory and, 406
Psychoanalytic treatment, 385
Psychological development, 57–60; maturity and, 114–16; at midlife, 167–68; in young adulthood, 119–25
Psychological time, 378–81
Psychoneurosis, 292; in military during World War II, 321
Psychopathology: psychoanalytic view of,

409; research on, 324–28; and transitions in life cycle, 338
Psychopharmacology, 324, 325
Psychoses, 331; ancient views of, 368; in military during World War II, 321; prevalence of, 330; reliability of diagnosis of, 387
Psychosexual development, 57–60
Psychosocial development, 399–403, 406–8; in adolescence, 90–97
Psychotherapy: psychoanalytic, 409, 410; social policy and, 431–32; value system in, 383–87
Psychotropic drugs, 325
Puberty, 80–85, 113; maturity of brain at, 86–87; onset of, 77; psychological impact of, 99; stages of, 81

Q-sort technique, 182–84, 209
Quality of American Life survey, 174

Reality: adaptation to, 411, 412; external, 297–98; of observer vs. observed, 405; psychic, 292; role of culture in creation of, 377
Reciprocity, 55
Reflexive movement, 47
Regression in adolescence, 100
Regulatory mechanisms, aging as breakdown of, 273–74
Rehabilitative tasks of psychiatry, 352–53
Relationship patterns: in adolescence, 418, 420, 421; discontinuity of, 397; roots in past of, 423
REM sleep, 39
Remarriage, late-life, 250
Renard Diagnostic Interviews, 328
Research Diagnostic Criteria (RDC), 326–27, 329
Reticular formation, 38
Reticular system, 265
Retirement, 251–53; cultural and historical aspects of, 206; male concern about, 178; preparation for, 218–23; sex differences in response to, 233; stress of, 256
Risk: medical tasks of psychiatry and, 351; neurological functioning and, 13–17; pediatric concept of, 8–9
Role models, occupational choice and, 169
Role strain: fatherhood and, 173; among women, 160–61
Rorschach test, 130, 131
Rudimentary movement, 47

Satisfaction, epidemiology of, 337
Schedule for Affective Disorders and Schizophrenia (SADS), 328
Schizophrenia, 331; cross-national differences in diagnosis of, 326; genetic factors in, 324; prevalence of, 330; psychopharmacology and, 325
Science, philosophy of, 393n, 394
Secondary memory (SM), 263, 264
"Selective inattention," 277
Selective Service System, 321
Self, 119, 128; aging and, 240–43; development of, 124; reorientation of, in middle age, 151
Self-actualization, 413
Self-concept: in adolescence, 87; aging and, 236; retirement and, 253
Self-esteem: in adolescence, 92, 419–20; of adult women, 162; aging and, 242, 243; economic privation and, 154; menopause and, 168; subjective aspects of age and, 150; work and, 172
Self-image: in adolescence, 90–97; changes in, 375; continuity of, 397
Self-regulatory functions, 121; cognitive development and, 48
Sensorimotor deficits, 21
Sensorimotor period, 48
Separation-individuation, 119, 121–23, 295; sex differences in, 126
Serotonin, 44
Sex differences: in adolescent body image, 91–92; in aging process, 232–33; average development and, 7; in coping abilities in adolescence, 96, 97; endocrine function and, 40, 41; in expressivity, 179; in friendship patterns, 177; in impact of childhood privation in adulthood, 154–55; in language development, 54; in life expectancy, 274; in maturing process, 113; in motor development, 46; neuropsychology and, 41–43; in peer relationships, 64; in perceptions of empty nest period, 212–14; in personality stability over time, 184; in play, 67; in puberty, 84–85; in response to aging, 225; in response to widowhood, 233, 251; social change and acknowledgment of, 7; in young adulthood, 125–27, 137–38
Sex roles: changing, 179; development and, 6; empty nest and, 215–16; father-child relationship and, 176; longitudinal studies of, 182, 183; morale and, 161; parenthood and, 158–59; and prototypes for normality, 374; traditional male, 177, 178
Sexuality: adolescent, 93–94, 97–98, 420, 421; aging and, 250, 270; in middle adulthood, 163–65, 174–75
Single parents, 175

Sleep patterns, neurobiological development and, 39–40
Sleep spindle activity, 39
"Small for date" infants, 8
Social age, 149–51
"Social breakdown syndrome" (SBS), 254
Social causation theories, 322
Social change: female development and, 127; notions of normality and, 6; standards of average and, 7; standards of maturity and, 117; subjective definition of age and, 149; transition to adulthood and, 118
Social class differences: in perception of time, 151–52; see also Middle class; Working class
Social development, 38; see also Psychosocial development
Social ecology, 22–23
Social phenomenological approach, 407
Social policy: constructs of normality and, 357; and costs for psychiatric treatment, 426–29; epidemiologic approach and, 430; formulation of, 346–47; ideology and, 348–49; and use of psychotherapy, 431–32
Social relations in adolescence, 92–93
Social role in young adulthood, 135
Societal-legal tasks of psychiatry, 355–56
Sociocultural standard of maturity, 114–16, 118–19
Sociodramatic play, 66–68
Socioeconomic status: language development and, 54; marital solidarity and, 174; neurological risk and, 17
Somatic development, 34–36
Specialization: of knowledge, 171; medical, 271
Speech, see Language development
Speed of behavior, 264–65
Sphincter control, 58
Sports-related movement, 47
Stability account of development, 398
Stanford-Binet Scale, 10
State: assessment process and, 16; definition of, 14
Stationary factor analysis, 407
Stereotypes of elderly, 253–54
Stimuli, exclusion of, 238
Stürm und Drang, 404n
Strabismus, 45
Stress: aging and, 256–58; combat, 321–22; coping with, see Coping mechanisms; in epidemiologic approach, 322–23, 333–35, 338–39
Student Council Studies, 130, 133
Subception, 238
Subjective perceptions of time, 151–52
Sublimation, 132
Sudden infant death syndrome, 8

Suicide: adolescent, 375; cohort effect on, 339–40; of middle-aged males, 178
Superego, 57, 60; aging and, 238; ego and, 123; father as antecedent of, 176; during latency, 59
Suppression, 132
Supralimbic zone, 37
Surgent growth, 98, 419–20
Symbolic interactionist approach, 149–51
Symbolic understanding, 52

Temperament, 19, 22–23; continuity of, 397; impact through life course of, 183
Testosterone, 84, 85
Thalamus, 37
Thalidomide infants, 21
Theoreticomorphism, 4–5
Time: dimensions of, 149–51; psychological, 378–81; subjective perceptions of, 151–52
Toxemia of pregnancy, 14
Transactional system, normality as, *xiii*, 9–10, 20; artistic connotations of, 371; in childhood, 31, 32; neurological functioning and, 17; rehabilitative tasks and, 353; social ecology and, 22; social policy and, 357; societal-legal tasks and, 356; studies in, 433; in young adulthood, 110–11
Transformational system, 86
Traumatic events, 292, 299
Tricyclic antidepressants, 325
Tumultuous growth, 98, 420–21
Turmoil theory of development, 403–6

Unconscious conflicts, 405
Underdeveloped countries, mental health in, 429
United States–United Kingdom (US-UK) study, 326
Unpredictability, 305–6
Utopia, normality as, *xii*, 417; in adolescence, 78, 89; artistic connotations of, 371, 372; in childhood, 31; and costs for psychiatric coverage, 428, 431; in developmental theories, 403; educative-developmental tasks and, 354; epidemiology and, 315, 331, 335, 341; infancy as, 4–6, 23; in psychoanalytic theory, 408; rehabilitative tasks and, 353; social policy and, 357; societal-legal tasks and, 356; studies of, 433; in young adulthood, 110
Uzgiris-Hunt Scales, 21

Values: adaptation and, 412; definitions of

mental health and illness and, 381–83; in developmental theories, 396, 408; in ego psychology, 413; healers and, 387–89; psychotherapy and, 383–87; of researchers, 139; transcendence of, 390
Verbal comprehension, 52
Verbal skills: aging and, 262, 263; *see also* Language development
Visual system, deprivation and, 45
Visuospatial skills, aging and, 262, 263

Weltanschauung, 137
Whig interpretation of history, 380
Widowhood, 155, 250–51; sex differences in response to, 233, 251; sexual deprivation in, 225; stress of, 256
Wisdom, 124, 125
Wish fulfillment, infancy and, 4
Witchcraft, belief in, 381
Women: incidence of psychopathology in, 430; issues of family and work for, 159–60; marriage and, 163–65; midlife transition of, 165–68; motherhood and careers of, 161–63; role strain among, 160–61; *see also* Sex differences
Work, *see* Careers
Work ethic, 412; in adolescence, 92
Working class: adolescents from, 79; family life cycle in, 156; friendship patterns in, 177; occupational movement in, 170; responsibility required for jobs in, 172; role strain of women in, 161; working women in, 162, 163
World Health Organization (WHO), 315, 323, 326, 335, 341, 428
World War II, epidemiology during, 320–22
"Worried well," 427, 429

Yale ECA, 329–30
Young adulthood, 108–40; cognitive development in, 268; cohort effect in, 340; and concepts of mental health, 127–29; conscious choice in, 136; coping ability in, 153; definition of, 108–9; departure from home in, 211; empirical research on, 129–35; friendships in, 136; "intimacy vs. isolation" in, 120; maturity and, 112–17; mental health during, 397; narcissism in, 225; psychodynamic aspects of, 296–97; psychological view of, 119–25; relationship with parents in, 166–67; sex differences in, 125–27; social role in, 135; sociocultural view of, 118–19; tasks of, 125, 135–36; theoretical views of, 117–27; *Weltanschauung* in, 137
Youth, definition of, 109